Digital Visual Fortran Programmer's Guide

Digital Visual Fortran Programmer's Guide

Michael Etzel

Karen Dickinson

Digital
Press

Boston • Oxford • Auckland • Johannesburg • Melbourne • New Delhi • Singapore

Butterworth–Heinemann supports the efforts of American Forests and the Global ReLeaf program in its campaign for the betterment of trees, forests, and our environment.

Library of Congress Cataloging-in-Publication Data

Etzel, Michael.
    Digital Visual Fortran programmer's guide / Michael Etzel, Karen Dickinson.
       p. cm.
    ISBN 1-55558-218-4 (alk. paper)
    1. FORTRAN (Computer program language)   I. Dickinson, Karen.
II. Title.
QA76.73.F25E89   1999
005. 13'3—DC21   98-32422
                                                     CIP

British Library Cataloguing-in-Publication Data

A catalogue record for this book is available from the British Library.

The publisher offers special discounts on bulk orders of this book.
For information, please contact:
Manager of Special Sales
Butterworth–Heinemann
225 Wildwood Avenue
Woburn, MA 01801-2041
Tel: 781-904-2500
Fax: 781-904-2620

For information on all Butterworth–Heinemann publications available, contact our World Wide Web home page at: http://www.bh.com

10 9 8 7 6 5 4 3 2 1

Printed in the United States of America

Contents

Preface

This book is a printed version of the online *Visual Fortran Programmers Guide* provided with the DIGITAL™ Visual Fortran (Digital Visual Fortran or simply Visual Fortran) Version 6 kit.

The "Visual" part of the name "Digital Visual Fortran" comes from its use of the industry-leading visual development environment from Microsoft®. This development environment is also used by the same version of Microsoft Visual C++® and includes an integrated text editor, source debugger, browser, and linker.

Visual Fortran is derived from the highly efficient, optimizing Digital Fortran compiler available on Digital UNIX® and OpenVMS™ Alpha systems. Visual Fortran Version 6 provides full support of the Fortran 95 (and prior) standards and includes numerous Digital Fortran and Microsoft Fortran PowerStation extensions.

Intended Audience

This book assumes you have a working knowledge of the Fortran language. For example, if you see Fortran 90/95 language elements in program examples in this book that you are not familiar with, please consult books about the Fortran 90/95 language to gain a better understanding of such Fortran language elements.

If you will be creating Visual Fortran applications, you should have access to the Visual Fortran documentation provided with your Visual Fortran kit. As needed, you should use this book with the online and printed Visual Fortran documentation, including the printed *DIGITAL Fortran Language Reference Manual* and the *DIGITAL Visual Fortran Getting Started.*

Organization

This book describes the use of Visual Fortran Version 6.0. It contains the following chapters and appendixes that describe:

▶ How to build and debug efficient applications:

Chapter 1: Introducing the Microsoft Visual Development Environment

Chapter 2: Building Programs and Libraries

Chapter 3: Using the Compiler and Linker from the Command Line

Chapter 4: Compiler and Linker Options

Chapter 5: Debugging Fortran Programs

Chapter 6: Performance: Making Programs Run Faster

▶ Special coding and related considerations for certain Visual Fortran project types:

Chapter 7: Using QuickWin

Chapter 8: Creating Fortran DLLs

Chapter 9: Creating Windows Applications

▶ Aspects of Fortran programming with Visual Fortran on Windows NT, Windows 98, and Windows 95 systems:

Chapter 10: Portability and Design Considerations

Chapter 11: Using Dialogs

Chapter 12: Drawing Graphics Elements

Chapter 13: Using Fonts from the Graphics Library

Chapter 14: Using National Language Support Routines

Chapter 15: Portability Library

Chapter 16: Files, Devices, and I/O Hardware

Chapter 17: Using COM and Automation Objects

Chapter 18: Programming with Mixed Languages

Chapter 19: Creating Multithread Applications

▶ Visual Fortran data types and run-time error handling:

Chapter 20: Data Representation

Chapter 21: Handling Run-Time Errors

Chapter 22: The Floating-Point Environment

Chapter 23: Converting Unformatted Numeric Data

▶ The IMSL™ Libraries (Professional Edition) and Visual Fortran tools:

Chapter 24: Using the IMSL Mathematical and Statistical Libraries

Chapter 25: Using Visual Fortran Tools

▶ Numeric conversion tables and compatibility information:

Appendix A: Hexadecimal-Binary-Octal-Decimal Conversions

Appendix B: Compatibility Information

Typographical Conventions

This book uses the following general conventions:

When you see this	*Here is what it means*
DF, LINK, FL32	Uppercase (capital) letters indicate MS®-DOS®-level commands used in the command window.
expression	Words in *italics* indicate placeholders for information that you must supply. A file-name is an example of this kind of information. *Italics* are also used to introduce new terms.
[optional item]	Items inside single square brackets are optional. In some examples, square brackets are used to show arrays.
{choice1 | choice2}	Braces and a vertical bar indicate a choice among two or more items. You must choose one of the items unless all of the items are also enclosed in square brackets.
s[, s] . . .	A horizontal ellipsis (three dots) following an item indicates that the item preceding the ellipsis can be repeated. In code examples, a horizontal ellipsis means that not all of the statements are shown.
! Comment line WRITE (*,*) 'Hello & &World'	This kind of type is used for program examples, program output, and error messages within the text. An exclamation point marks the beginning of a comment in sample programs. Continuation lines are indicated by an ampersand (&) after the code at the end of a line to be continued and before the code on the following line.
AUTOMATIC, INTRINSIC, WRITE	Bold capital letters indicate DIGITAL Fortran statements, functions, subroutines, and keywords. Keywords are a required part of statement syntax, unless enclosed in brackets as explained above. In the sentence, "The following steps occur when a **DO WHILE** statement is executed," the phrase **DO WHILE** is a DIGITAL Fortran keyword.
Fortran, Fortran 90, and Fortran 95	*Fortran* refers to language information that is common to ANSI FORTRAN 77, ANSI/ISO Fortran 90, ANSI/ISO Fortran 95, and DIGITAL Fortran. *Fortran 90* refers to language information that is common to ANSI/ISO Fortran 90 and DIGITAL Fortran. *Fortran 95* refers to language information that is common to ANSI/ISO Fortran 95 and DIGITAL Fortran.

When you see this	*Here is what it means*
integer	This term refers to the INTEGER(KIND=1), INTEGER(KIND=2), INTEGER (INTEGER(KIND=4)), and INTEGER(KIND=8) data types as a group.
real	This term refers to the REAL (REAL(KIND=4)) and DOUBLE PRECISION (REAL(KIND=8)) data types as a group.
complex	This term refers to the COMPLEX (COMPLEX(KIND=4)) and DOUBLE COMPLEX (COMPLEX(KIND=8)) data types as a group.
logical	This term refers to the LOGICAL(KIND=1), LOGICAL(KIND=2), LOGICAL (LOGICAL(KIND=4)), and LOGICAL(KIND=8) data types as a group.

For More Information About Visual Fortran

For up-to-date information about Visual Fortran, please visit the Visual Fortran Web site:

http://www.digital.com/fortran/

Acknowledgments

We thank the many talented software engineers on the DIGITAL Visual Fortran (DVF) team, who helped us learn about Visual Fortran and patiently reviewed this large book for technical accuracy. These talented people help make complex, difficult work seem interesting and fun (especially Stan's meetings). We acknowledge the assistance of Microsoft technical writers, engineers, and others, especially those associated with Microsoft Visual C++ and Microsoft Fortran PowerStation. We extend special thanks to the folks at Butterworth-Heinemann Publishers as well as William Youngs, Ron Stokes, Steve Lionel, and others at Compaq Computer Corporation who supported the creation of this printed book.

Mike: I thank the *many* software engineering giants at the Compaq Nashua (NH) facility and fellow writers like Dick Buttlar, whose informal explanations helped me understand the purpose and uses of various OS and compiler software components. I also thank my wife Kathleen and sons Todd, Danny, Colin, and Kyle for making my life meaningful and sharing our mutual interest in science and nature. Special thanks to my parents and my wife's parents for their many years of love and support.

Karen: Thanks to Digital (now Compaq) for all the experience I've gained here; it's never been boring. I want to thank my parents—my mother for her indomitable spirit, and my late father for his sense of humor. Finally, I want to thank my husband Peter, and Blue and Sheba (my pets), for patiently putting up with my long hours on this project, and looking happy when I finally come home.

Introducing the Microsoft Visual Development Environment

Digital Visual Fortran (Visual Fortran) uses the same Microsoft® visual development environment as the same version of Microsoft Visual C++®. The visual development environment is also known as Microsoft Developer Studio™.

After you install Digital Visual Fortran (Visual Fortran) on your system, you can start the Microsoft visual development environment by performing the following steps:

1. From the Start menu, select Programs.

2. Select Visual Fortran to display the items installed by Setup.

3. Select Developer Studio.

This chapter provides an introduction to the visual development environment. It provides the following sections:

▶ Section 1.1 Visual Development Environment Windows

▶ Section 1.2 Building an Existing Visual Fortran Project (Celsius)

▶ Section 1.3 Editing CELSIUS.FOR

For More Information:

▶ On creating a new project, types of project, defining your project settings, and building your application, see Chapter 2 Building Programs and Libraries.

▶ On debugging a source file, see Chapter 5 Debugging Fortran Programs.

▶ On developing programs from the command line, see Chapter 3 Using the Compiler and Linker from the Command Line.

1.1   Visual Development Environment Windows

Figure 1-1 shows a sample of the visual development environment.

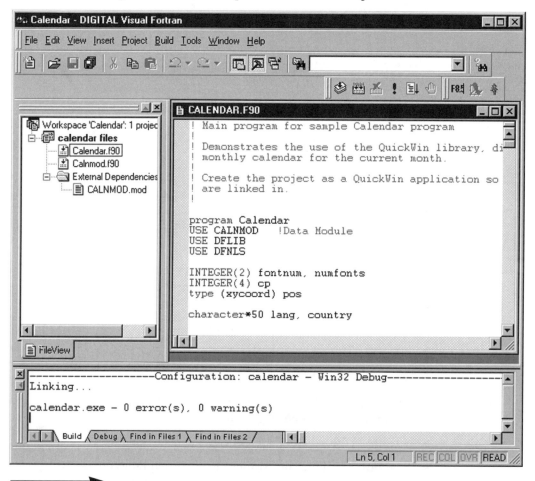

Figure 1–1   *Visual Development Environment Windows*

The left pane contains a FileView tab and may contain a ClassView or ResourceView tab:

▶ FileView-shows each project and their files associated with the Workspace.

▶ ClassView-appears only if Visual C++ is installed. ClassView is not used by Visual Fortran (used by Visual C++ for mixed-language programming).

▶ ResourceView-appears if the Workspace uses Resources (such as dialogs and icons).

After you open a Workspace, the FileView tab shows the files associated with that Workspace. In the FileView pane of Figure 1-1, there are two files: calendar.f90 and calnmod.f90.

In Figure 1-1, calnmod.f90 defines a Fortran 90 module file (a post-compiled binary file with an extension of .mod) that is used by calendar.f90. Because calendar.f90 is dependent on the calnmod.mod file being present, it is listed as under External Dependencies.

In the right pane of Figure 1-1, the file calendar.f90 is shown in the default text editor, which uses different colors to identify source comments (green), Fortran standard language elements (blue), and other language text (black). To edit a file listed on the FileView pane, double-click its file name or use the Open item in the File menu.

The bottom of Figure 1-1 shows the output pane, which shows text displayed from building the project. The output pane has multiple tabs. The output pane Build tab is selected after you open a Workspace and compile one or more project files or build the project. To display the output pane, select Output from the View menu.

A *floating window* can be moved and has a title bar. To move a floating window, drag its title bar.

A *docking window* is docked (attached) along an edge of the visual development environment window and does not have a title bar.

To allow a docking window to float (not be docked) or to allow a floating window to dock along an edge, do one of the following:

▶ Click the appropriate window.

▶ Select the Window menu option Docking View.

To specify which visual development environment windows will be docked windows and which will be floating windows:

1. In the Tools menu, select Options.

2. Click the Workspace tab.

3. In the Docking View list, click the check box for each window to be displayed with a docking view. Unchecked boxes indicate floating windows.

To cycle through your floating windows in the visual development environment, hold down the `Ctrl` key and press `Tab`.

Visual Fortran online documentation is displayed by the Microsoft HTMLHelp Viewer. To use the HTMLHelp Viewer, do one of the following:

► Click the Online Documentation item in the Visual Fortran program folder. (To display the Visual Fortran program folder, click Start, click Programs, and click Visual Fortran.)

► After you start the visual development environment, in the Help menu, click Contents.

► Select a word in a text window and press the `F1` key.

HTMLHelp Viewer appears in a separate window. This comprehensive online help system lets you to display text by using the contents, locate text either by index keyword or full-text search, print sections, and perform other functions (see *Digital Visual Fortran Getting Started*).

1.2   Building an Existing Visual Fortran Project (Celsius)

The visual development environment organizes development into projects. A project consists of the source files required for your application, along with the specifications for building the project.

Projects are contained in a *workspace*. A workspace can contain multiple projects.

To open and execute the sample project workspace file, Celsius.dsw:

1. From the File menu, choose Open Workspace.

The Open Workspace dialog box appears, displaying the default projects directory (for a new installation, the folders within the My Projects folder). The Celsius project workspace is located in the . . . `Common\MSDEV98\ My Projects` folder).

2. In the list of files and directories within the `My Projects` folder, double-click the `Celsius` folder.

The files and directories list now displays the Celsius workspace file.

3. Select the Celsius workspace file, Celsius.dsw.

4. Click the Open button.

The visual development environment displays the contents of the Celsius project in the FileView pane. You can click the plus sign (+) next to the Celsius folder to see the contents of the project. In this case, there is only one file, CELSIUS.FOR.

5. If needed, update dependencies by clicking Update All Dependencies in the Build menu. Select the appropriate configuration for which dependencies need to be updated and click OK. (For projects like CELSIUS.FOR that have no dependencies, this step is not needed.)

For example, if your application uses Fortran modules, the source files that reference modules with a **USE** statement have dependencies on the module (.MOD) files they reference. To update these dependencies means that the source files containing the module definitions (**MODULE** statement) need to be compiled before the source files that reference them, by either clicking Update All Dependencies or build the application twice. The FileView pane shows the files associated with a project, including any dependencies.

6. From the Build menu, choose Build Celsius.exe.

The status of the build is displayed in the Build pane at the bottom of the screen.

7. From the Build menu, choose Execute Celsius.exe to run the program. A console output window appears, displaying the output from the program.

8. If you want to use the Debugger for this project, see Chapter 5 Debugging Fortran Programs.

9. When you are done with this project, select Close Workspace from the File menu.

Visual Fortran includes a number of Samples, most of which include a project workspace file (see Section 2.8 Visual Fortran Samples).

1.3   Editing **CELSIUS.FOR**

The visual development environment text editor and the debugger allow you to edit and debug your projects. The following text assumes you have opened the Celsius Workspace (in the folder . . . `Common \MSDEV98\My Projects`) and have built the Celsius project (see Section 1.2 Building an Existing Visual Fortran Project).

From the Build menu select Set Active Configuration. Select the Debug configuration.

To edit and modify the Celsius source file CELSIUS.FOR:

1. The contents of the Celsius project are displayed in the FileView pane. Click the plus sign (+) next to the Celsius folder to see the contents of the project. In this case, there is only one file, CELSIUS.FOR.

2. Double click on the CELSIUS.FOR file name in the FileView pane. The text editor window appears, displaying the source contents of CELSIUS.FOR.

3. If you want to modify the source code, click on the line to be modified and type the corrections. For example, change the DO loop to have a stride different than 10.

   To Save the modified file, click Save in the File menu.

4. Build the revised program by clicking the Build Celsius.exe menu item in the Build menu.

5. From the Build menu, choose Execute Celsius.exe to run the program. A console output window appears, displaying the output from the program.

6. When you are done with this project, select Close Workspace from the File menu.

The Celsius sample is a Fortran Console application, which is usually a character-cell application. Other Visual Fortran project types include Fortran QuickWin, Fortran Standard Graphics, Fortran Dynamic-Link Library, Fortran Static Library, and Fortran Windows applications. You must select the project type when you create your application.

2

Building Programs and Libraries

Visual Fortran includes the Microsoft visual development environment (also used by the same version of Visual C++) and associated Visual Studio software development tools. This industry-leading environment makes it easy for you to create, debug, and execute your programs. It includes a full-feature text editor, debugger, and interactive help. You can build your source code into several types of programs and libraries, either using the visual development environment or working from the command line. For an introduction to this environment, see *Getting Started*.

This chapter describes how to use the visual development environment to define a project, open and close a project workspace, and build a project:

▶ Section 2.1 Overview of Building Projects

▶ Section 2.2 Types of Projects you can build

▶ Section 2.3 Defining Your Project and selecting project features with the visual development environment

▶ Section 2.4 Errors during the Build Process

▶ Section 2.5 Compiler Limits

▶ Section 2.6 Running Fortran Applications

▶ Section 2.7 Porting Projects between *x*86 and Alpha Platforms

▶ Section 2.8 Visual Fortran Samples

For more information on:

▶ Building programs and libraries at the command line, see Chapter 3 Using the Compiler and Chapter 25 Linker from the Command Line.

▶ Using the Debugger, see Chapter 5 Debugging Fortran Programs.

▶ Details about using the development environment, see the *Visual C++ User's Guide*.

2.1   Overview of Building Projects

The Microsoft Visual C++ Development Environment (also called Developer Studio) organizes development into *projects*. A project consists of the source files required for your application, along with the specifications for building the project. The build process involves defining your project, setting options for it, and building the program or library.

Each project can specify one or more *configurations* to build from its source files. A *configuration* specifies such things as the type of application to build, the platform on which it is to run, and the tool settings to use when building. Having multiple configurations lets you extend the scope of a project but still maintain a consistent source code base from which to work.

When you create a new project, the Microsoft visual development environment automatically creates Debug and Release configurations for you. The default configuration is the Debug configuration. To specify the current configuration, select Set Active Configuration from the Build menu.

Projects are contained in a *workspace*. When you create a new project, you indicate whether the project is created in a new workspace or an existing workspace. To open an existing project, you open its workspace. A workspace can contain multiple projects.

Once you open a workspace, the development environment displays a *FileView* pane, which displays the files contained in the project, and lets you examine visually the relationships among the files in your project. Modules, include files, or special libraries your program uses are automatically listed as *dependencies*. The output window displays information produced by the compiler, linker, Find in Files utility, and the profiler.

You can specify build options in the Project menu Settings dialog box, for one of the following:

▶ The entire project

▶ For certain configurations

▶ For certain files

For example, you can specify certain kinds of compiler optimizations for your project in general, but turn them off for certain configurations or certain files.

Once you have specified the files in your project, the configurations that your project is to build, and the tool settings for those configurations, you can build the project with the commands on the Build menu.

In addition to using the visual development environment, you can also use the command line (DF command). You can also develop the application from the visual development environment and export a makefile for use in command-line processing (NMAKE command). Your choice of development environment determines what you can do at each stage.

Figure 2-1 illustrates the development process for using the visual development environment or command line.

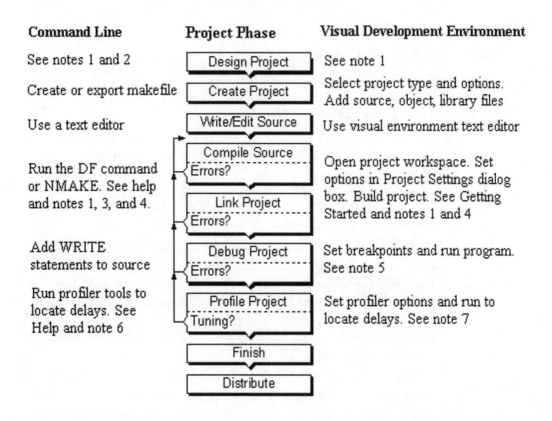

Command Line	**Project Phase**	**Visual Development Environment**
See notes 1 and 2	Design Project	See note 1
Create or export makefile	Create Project	Select project type and options. Add source, object, library files
Use a text editor	Write/Edit Source	Use visual environment text editor
Run the DF command or NMAKE. See help and notes 1, 3, and 4.	Compile Source / Errors? / Link Project / Errors?	Open project workspace. Set options in Project Settings dialog box. Build project. See Getting Started and notes 1 and 4
Add WRITE statements to source	Debug Project / Errors?	Set breakpoints and run program. See note 5
Run profiler tools to locate delays. See Help and note 6	Profile Project / Tuning?	Set profiler options and run to locate delays. See note 7
	Finish	
	Distribute	

Figure 2–1 *Example of Development Process*

Notes in the figure point to places where you can read more about a particular part of the development process:

1. Building Programs and Libraries (the current chapter)

2. Chapter 3, Using the Compiler and Linker from the Command Line

3. Chapter 25, Using Visual Fortran Tools

4. Chapter 22, The Floating-Point Environment and Chapter 21, Handling Run-Time Errors

5. Chapter 5, Debugging Fortran Programs

6. Section 25.12, Profiling Code from the Command Line

7. Section 6.2, Analyze Program Performance

For more overview information about building projects with the visual development environment, see:

▶ Section 2.1.1 How Information Is Displayed

▶ Section 2.1.2 Menu Options

▶ Section 2.1.3 Using the Shortcut Menu

2.1.1   How Information Is Displayed

The Microsoft visual development environment displays information in windows, panes, and folders. One window can contain several panes, and each pane can display one or more folders. A *pane* is a separate and distinct area of a window; a *folder* is a visual representation of files in a project. Folders show the order in which Visual Fortran compiles the files, and the relationship of source files to their dependent files, such as modules.

When you initially create a project, the Project Workspace window contains some default panes, accessible through tabs at the bottom of the window, to display information about the content of the project. You can also open an output window, which has panes that display build output, debug output, Find in Files output, and profiler output. In addition to the default panes, you can create customized panes to organize and display project information in ways most useful to you.

You can access information about components of the project from the panes in the project window. Double-clicking any item in a pane displays that item in an appropriate way: source files in a text editor, dialog boxes in the dialog editor, help topics in the information window, and so on.

Be sure to select the appropriate pane when using the menu commands, in particular the Save and Save As commands. Commands on the File menu affect only the window that currently has the focus.

2.1.2   Menu Options

Menu options that are available to you may look different, depending on which window or pane has current focus. The Debug menu, for example, is only visible when you are debugging.

The visual development environment has the following menu bars and toolbars:

▶ Standard menu bar

▶ Standard toolbar

▶ Build toolbar

▶ Build minibar

▶ Resource toolbar

▶ Edit toolbar

▶ Debug toolbar

▶ Browse toolbar

▶ Fortran toolbar

You can select or deselect the menu bars and toolbars from the Tools menu Customize item, Toolbar tab.

2.1.3   Using the Shortcut Menu

The project window has a shortcut menu that lists commands appropriate for the current selection in the window. This is a quick method to display commands that are also available from the main menu bar.

To display the shortcut menu:

▶ Move the mouse pointer into the project window and click the right mouse button.

You can now select project commands that are appropriate for your current selection in the project window.

2.2   Types of Projects

When you create the project, you must choose a *project type*. You need to create a project for each binary executable file to be created. For example, the main Fortran program and a Fortran dynamic-link library (DLL) would each reside in the same workspace as separate projects.

The project type specifies what to generate and determines some of the options that the visual development environment sets by default for the project. It determines, for instance, the options that the compiler uses to compile the source files, the static libraries that the linker uses to build the project, the default locations for output files, defined constants, and so on.

Table 2-1 shows the six kinds of projects you can build with Visual Fortran. You specify the project type when you create a new project.

Table 2–1 *Project Types*

Project type	Key features
Fortran Console Application (.EXE)	Single window main projects without graphics (resembles character-cell applications). Requires no special programming expertise. For a Visual Fortran Sample of a Console Application, see `\MYPROJECTS\CELSIUS`, as described in Opening an Existing Project in *Getting Started*.
Fortran Standard Graphics Application (.EXE)	Single window main projects with graphics. The programming complexity is simple to moderate, depending on the graphics and user interaction used. Samples of Standard Graphics Applications (QuickWin single window) resemble those for QuickWin Applications (see below).
Fortran QuickWin Application (.EXE)	Multiple window main projects with graphics. The programming complexity is simple to moderate, depending on the graphics and user interaction used. Samples of QuickWin Applications (QuickWin multiple window) are in . . . `\DF98\SAMPLES\ QUICKWIN`, such as QWPIANO and QWPAINT.
Fortran Windows Application (.EXE)	Multiple window main projects with full graphical interface and Win32 API functions. Requires advanced programming expertise and knowledge of the Win32 routines API. Samples of Win32® Applications are in . . . `\DF98\SAMPLES\ ADVANCED\WIN32`, such as PLATFORM or POLYDRAW.
Fortran Static library (.LIB)	Library routines to link into .EXE files.
Fortran Dynamic-Link Library (.DLL)	Library routines to associate during execution.

The first four projects listed in the preceding table are main project types, requiring main programs. The last two are library projects, without main programs. The project types are discussed in detail in:

▶ Section 2.2.1 Fortran Console Application Projects

▶ Section 2.2.2 Fortran Standard Graphics Application Projects

▶ Section 2.2.3 Fortran QuickWin Application Projects

▶ Section 2.2.4 Fortran Windows Application Projects

▶ Section 2.2.5 Fortran Static Library Projects

▶ Section 2.2.6 Fortran Dynamic-Link Library Projects

When migrating legacy applications, choosing a project type that will minimize porting effort depends on what the application does. A character-cell application that does not use any graphics (such as a program ported from a UNIX system) can usually be converted into a Fortran Console Application. When a legacy Windows 3.1 (or older) application uses graphics calls, you can try a Fortran Standard Graphics Application or a Fortran QuickWin Application project type. However, be aware that with such legacy graphics applications:

▶ The routine names of certain legacy graphic routines might need to be changed to the current routine names (and their current argument lists).

▶ The character-oriented method of user interaction can be modernized with menus, mouse clicks, and dialog boxes. If the routine uses the **PEEKCHARQQ** routine, see the PEEKAPP or PEEKAPP3 Visual Fortran Samples in the QuickWin folder.

After you select your project type, you need to define your project (see Section 2.3 Defining Your Project).

If you need to use the command line to build your project, you can:

▶ Initially use the visual development environment and later create a makefile (see The Project Makefile in Section 2.3.1 Files in a Project).

▶ Use the DF command compiler options to specify the project type (see Section 3.5 Specifying Project Types with DF Command Options).

▶ Create the application from the DF command line (see Chapter 3 Using the Compiler and Linker from the Command Line).

2.2.1   Fortran Console Application Projects

A Fortran console application (.EXE) is a character-based Visual Fortran program that does not require screen graphics output. It looks similar to a program running on a UNIX workstation or a terminal connected to a mainframe computer.

Fortran console projects operate in a single window, and let you interact with your program through normal read and write commands. Console applications are better suited to problems that require pure numerical processing rather than graphical output or a graphical user interface. This type of application is also more transportable to other platforms than the other types of application.

Console applications can be faster than standard graphics or QuickWin graphics applications, because of the time required to display graphical output.

Any graphics routine that your program calls will produce no output, but will return error codes. A program will not automatically exit if such an error occurs, so your code should be written to handle this condition.

With a console project, you can use static libraries, DLLs, and dialog boxes, but you cannot use the QuickWin functions. You can select the multi-threaded libraries with this and all of the other project types.

As with all Windows command consoles, you can toggle between viewing the console in a window or in full-screen mode by using the ALT+ENTER key combination.

A sample console project is Celsius (see \MYPROJECTS\CELSIUS), as described in Section 2.3 Defining Your Project, or Opening an Existing Project in *Getting Started*.

2.2.2   Fortran Standard Graphics Application Projects

A Fortran standard graphics application (.EXE) is a Visual Fortran QuickWin program with graphics that runs in a single QuickWin window. A standard graphics (QuickWin single document) application looks similar to an MS-DOS® program when manipulating the graphics hardware directly, without Windows.

A Fortran standard graphics application allows graphics output (such as drawing lines and basic shapes) and other screen functions, such as clearing the screen. Standard Graphics is a subset of QuickWin, sometimes called *QuickWin single window* . You can use all of the QuickWin graphics functions in these projects. You can use dialog boxes with these and all other project types (see Using Dialogs).

You can select displayed text either as a bitmap or as text. Windows provides APIs for loading and unloading bitmap files. Standard graphics applications can be written as either single-threaded or multithreaded applications. (For information about multithreaded programs, see Chapter 19 Creating Multithread Applications.)

Fortran standard graphics (QuickWin single document) applications are normally presented in full-screen mode. The single window can be either full-screen or have window borders and controls available. You can change between these two modes by using ALT+ENTER.

If the resolution selected matches the screen size, the application covers the entire screen; otherwise, it is a resizable window with scroll bars. You cannot open additional windows in a standard graphics application. Standard graphics applications have neither a menu bar at the top of the window, nor a status bar at the bottom.

Fortran standard graphics applications are appropriate for problems that:

▶ Require numerical processing and some graphics

▶ Do not require a sophisticated user interface

When you select the Fortran standard graphics project type, the visual development environment includes the QuickWin library automatically, which lets you use the graphics functions. When building from the command line, you must specify the /libs:qwins option. You cannot use the run-time functions meant for multiple-window projects if you are building a standard graphics project. You cannot make a Standard Graphics application a DLL.

For more information about Standard Graphics (QuickWin single window) applications, see Chapter 7 Using QuickWin.

2.2.3 Fortran QuickWin Application Projects

Fortran QuickWin graphics applications (.EXE) are more versatile than standard graphics (QuickWin single document) applications because you can open multiple windows (usually called multiple-document interface or MDI) while your project is executing. For example, you might want to generate several graphic plots and be able to switch between them while also having a window for controlling the execution of your program. These windows can be full screen or reduced in size and placed in various parts of the screen.

QuickWin library routines lets you build applications with a simplified version of the Windows interface with Visual Fortran. The QuickWin library provides a rich set of Windows features, but it does not include the complete Windows Applications Programming Interface (API). If you need additional capabilities, you must set up a Windows application to call the Win32 API directly rather than using QuickWin to build your program. For more information on QuickWin programming, see Chapter 7 Using QuickWin.

Fortran QuickWin graphics applications (.EXE) have a multiple-document interface. Applications that use a multiple-document interface (MDI) have a menu bar at the top of the window and a status bar at the bottom. The QuickWin library provides a default set of menus and menu items that you can customize with the QuickWin APIs. An application that uses MDI creates many "child" windows within an outer application window. The user area in an MDI application is a child window that appears in the space between the menu bar and status bar of the application window. Your application can have more than one child window open at a time.

Fortran QuickWin applications can also use the DFLOGM.F90 module to access functions to control dialog boxes. These functions allow you to display, initialize, and communicate with special dialog boxes in your application. They are a subset of Win32 API functions, which Windows applications can call directly. For more information on using dialog boxes, see Chapter 11 Using Dialogs.

When you select the QuickWin graphics project type, the visual development environment includes the QuickWin library automatically, which lets you use the graphics functions.

When building from the command line, you must specify the /libs:qwin compiler option to indicate a QuickWin application (or /libs:qwins option to indicate a Fortran standard graphics application). A QuickWin application that uses the compiler option is similar to a standard graphics application in that it has no menu bar or status bar. (In fact, a standard graphics application is a QuickWin application with a set of preset options. It is offered in the program types list for your convenience.) As with a standard graphics application, the application covers the entire screen if the resolution selected matches the screen size; otherwise, it is a resizable window with scroll bars.

You cannot make a QuickWin application a DLL.

For information on how to use QuickWin functions, including how to open and control multiple windows, see Chapter 7 Using QuickWin.

2.2.4   Fortran Windows Application Projects

Fortran Windows applications (.EXE) are main programs selected by choosing the Fortran Windows Application project type. This type of project lets you calls the Windows APIs directly from Visual Fortran. This provides full access to the Win32 APIs, giving you a larger (and different) set of functions to work with than QuickWin.

Although you can call some of the Win32® APIs from the other project types, Fortran Windows applications let you use the full set of Win32 functions and use certain system features not available for the other project types.

The DFWIN.F90 module contains interfaces to the most common Win32 APIs. If you include the **USE DFWIN** statement in your program, nearly all routines are available to you. The DFWIN.F90 module gives you access to a full range of routines including window management, graphic device interface, system services, multimedia, and remote procedure calls.

Window management gives your application the means to create and manage a user interface. You can create windows to display output or prompt for input. Graphics Device Interface (GDI) functions provide ways for you to generate graphical output for displays, printers, and other devices. Win32 system functions allow you to manage and monitor resources such as memory, access to files, directories, and I/O devices. System service functions provide features that your application can use to handle special conditions such as errors, event logging, and exception handling.

Using multimedia functions, your application can create documents and presentations that incorporate music, sound effects, and video clips as well as text and graphics. Multimedia functions provide services for audio, video, file I/O, media control, joystick, and timers.

Remote Procedure Calls (RPC) gives you the means to carry out distributed computing, letting applications tap the resources of computers on a network. A distributed application runs as a process in one address space and makes procedure calls that execute in an address space on another computer. You can create distributed applications using RPC, each consisting of a client that presents information to the user and a server that stores, retrieves, and manipulates data as well as handling computing tasks. Shared databases and remote file servers are examples of distributed applications.

Writing Fortran Windows applications is much more complex than other kinds of Visual Fortran projects. For information on how to create a Fortran Windows application, see Chapter 9 Creating Windows Applications.

You can access the Windows API online documentation help file, Platform SDK, included with Visual Fortran. You can also obtain information through the Microsoft Developer Network. Microsoft offers Developer Network membership, which includes a development library and a quarterly CD containing technical information for Windows programming.

See the online title Platform SDK for information on calling Win32 routines. The full Win32 API set is documented in the *Win32 Application Programming Interface for Windows NT Programmer's Reference*, available from Microsoft Press and also distributed as part of the Windows NT Software Development Kit.

2.2.5   Fortran Static Library Projects

Fortran static libraries (.LIB) are blocks of code compiled and kept separate from the main part of your program. The Fortran static library is one of the Fortran project types.

Static libraries offer important advantages in organizing large programs and in sharing routines between several programs. These libraries contain only subprograms, not main programs. A static library file has a .LIB extension and contains object code.

When you associate a static library with a program, any necessary routines are linked from the library into your executable program when it is built. Static libraries are usually kept in their own directories.

If you use a static library, only those routines actually needed by the program are incorporated into the executable image (.EXE). This means that your executable image will be smaller than if you included all the routines in the library in your executable image. Also, you do not have to worry about exactly which routines you need to include—the Linker takes care of that for you.

Because applications built with a static library all contain the same version of the routines in the library, you can use static libraries to help keep applications current. When you revise the routines in a static library, you can easily update all the applications that use it by relinking the applications.

A static library is a collection of source and object code defined in the File-View pane. The source code is compiled when you build the project. The object code is assembled into a .LIB file without going through a linking process. The name of the project is used as the name of the library file by default.

If you have a library of substantial size, you should maintain it in a dedicated directory. Projects using the library access it during linking.

When you link a project that uses the library, selected object code from the library is linked into that project's executable code to satisfy calls to external procedures. Unnecessary object files are not included.

When compiling a static library from the command line, include the /c compiler option to suppress linking. Without this option, the compiler generates an error because the library does not contain a main program.

To debug a static library, you must use a main program that calls the library routines. Both the main program and the static library should have been compiled using the debug option. After compiling and linking is completed, open the Debug menu and choose Go to reach breakpoints, use Step to Cursor to reach the cursor position, or use the step controls on the Debug toolbar.

Using Static Libraries

You add static libraries to a main project in the visual development environment with the Add to Project, Insert Files option in the Project menu. You can enter the path and library name in the Insert Files into Project dialog box with a .LIB extension on the name. If you are using a foreign makefile, you must add the library by editing the makefile for the main project. If you are building your project from the command line, add the library name with a .LIB extension and include the path specification if necessary.

For an example of a static library project, see the Visual Fortran Samples folder . . . DF98\SAMPLES\ADVANCED\DIALOGM, which creates a static library.

To create a static library from the command line, use the /c compiler option to suppress linking and use the LIB command (see Section 25.8 Managing Libraries with LIB).

To create a static library from the visual development environment, specify the Fortran Static Library project type.

2.2.6 Fortran Dynamic-Link Library Projects

A dynamic-link library (.DLL) is a source-code library that is compiled and linked to a unit independently of the applications that use it. A DLL shares its code and data address space with a calling application. A DLL contains only subprograms, not main programs.

A DLL offers the organizational advantages of a static library, but with the advantage of a smaller executable file at the expense of a slightly more complex interface. Object code from a DLL is not included in your program's executable file, but is associated as needed in a dynamic manner while the program is executing. More than one program can access a DLL at a time.

When routines in a DLL are called, the routines are loaded into memory at run-time, as they are needed. This is most useful when several applications use a common group of routines. By storing these common routines in a DLL, you reduce the size of each application that calls the DLL. In addition, you can update the routines in the DLL without having to rebuild any of the applications that call the DLL.

With Visual Fortran, you can use DLLs in two ways:

▶ You can build a DLL with your own routines. In the visual development environment, select Fortran Dynamic-Link Library as your project type. From the command line, use the /DLL option with the DF command.

▶ You can build applications with the run-time library stored in a separate DLL instead of in the main application file. In the visual development environment, open a workspace then follow these steps:

1. From the Project menu, click Settings to display the project settings dialog box

2. Click the Fortran tab

3. Select the Library category

4. In the Use Fortran Run-Time Libraries box, select DLL.

From the command line, use the /libs:dll compiler option to build applications with the run-time library stored in a separate DLL.

For more information about DLLs, see Chapter 8 Creating Fortran DLLs.

2.3   Defining Your Project

To define your project, you need to:

1. Create the project

2. Populate the project with files

3. Choose a configuration

4. Define build options, including project settings

5. Build (compile and link) the project

To create a new project:

1. Click the File menu and select New. A dialog box opens that has the following tabs:
   ▶ Files
   ▶ Projects
   ▶ Workspaces
   ▶ Other Documents

2. The Projects tab displays various project types. Click the type of Fortran project to be created. (If you have other Visual tools installed, make sure you select a Fortran project type.) You can set the Create New Workspace check box to create a new Workspace.

3. Specify the project name and location.

4. Click OK to create the new project. Depending on the type of project being created, one or more dialog boxes may appear allowing you to only create the project without source files or create a template-like source file.

If a saved Fortran environment exists for the Fortran project type being created, you can also import a Fortran environment to provide default project settings for the new project (see Section 2.3.3.2 Saving and Using the Project Setting Environment for Different Projects).

This action creates a project workspace and one project. It also leaves the project workspace open.

To discontinue using this project workspace, click Close Workspace from the File menu.

To open the project workspace later, in the File menu, click either Open Workspace or Recent Workspaces.

To add files to an existing project:

▶ To add an existing file to the project:

1. If not already open, open the project workspace (use the File menu).

2. In the Project menu, click Add to Project. Select Files... from the submenu.

3. The Insert Files into Project dialog box appears. Use this dialog box to select the Fortran files to be added to the Project. To add more than one file to the project, hold down the `Ctrl` key as you select each file name.

▶ To add a new file to the project:

1. If not already open, open the project workspace (use the File menu).

2. In the Project menu, click Add to Project. Select New... from the submenu.

3. The New dialog box appears. Specify the file name and its location.

4. Click (select) the type of file (Fortran Fixed Format Source or Fortran Free Format Source).

5. Click OK. The editor appears, letting you type in source code. The file name appears in the FileView pane.

▶ To define a project from a set of existing or new source files:

1. On the File menu, click New...

2. Click the Projects tab.

3. Select the type of project.

4. Name the project.

5. Click OK. Depending on the type of project being created, one or more dialog boxes may appear allowing you to only create the project without source files or create template-like source files.

If a saved Fortran environment exists for the project type being created, you can also import a Fortran environment to provide default project settings for the new Fortran project (see Section 2.3.3.2 Saving and Using the Project Setting Environment for Different Projects).

▶ To add an existing file to the project:

1. In the Project menu, select Add to Project. Select Files... from the submenu.

2. The Insert Files into Project dialog box appears. Use this dialog box to select the Fortran files to be added to the Project. To add more than one file to the project, hold down the `Ctrl` key as you select each file name.

▶ To add each new file to the project:

1. In the Project menu, select Add to Project. Select New... from the submenu.

2. The New dialog box appears. Specify the file name and its location.

3. Click the type of file (Fortran Fixed Format Source or Fortran Free Format Source).

4. Click OK. The editor appears allowing you to type in source code. The file name appears in the FileView pane.

▶ You can now select "Build *filename*" from the Build Menu to build your application.

You need to add these kinds of files to your project:

▶ Program files with .FOR, .F or .F90 extension

▶ Resource files with .RC extension

▶ If your project references routines or data in a Fortran dynamic-link library (DLL), you need to add the import library (.LIB file created while building the DLL) as a file to your project (see Section 8.3 Building and Using Dynamic-Link Libraries)

For information on:

▶ How to use icon files, see Chapter 7 Using QuickWin.

▶ Using binary files, see Chapter 16 Files, Devices, and I/O Hardware.

▶ Using the Resource Editor, Dialog Editor, or Graphics Editor, see the *Visual C++ User's Guide.*

For more information on defining and building projects, see:

▶ Section 2.3.1 Files in a Project

▶ Section 2.3.2 Selecting a Configuration

▶ Section 2.3.3 Setting Build Options

▶ Section 2.3.4 Creating the Executable Program

2.3.1   Files in a Project

When you create a project, the Microsoft visual development environment always creates the following files:

▶ A Project workspace file—Has the extension .DSW. It stores project workspace information.

▶ A Project file—Has the extension .DSP. It is used to build a single project or subproject.

▶ A Workspace options file—Has the extension .OPT. It contains environment settings for Visual Fortran, such as window sizes and positions, insertion point locations, state of project breakpoints, contents of the Watch window, and so on.

Directly modifying the .DSW and .DSP files with a text editor is not supported.

For information on creating (exporting) a makefile, see The Project Makefile below.

When you create a project, you also identify a project subdirectory. If the subdirectory does not exist, the visual development environment creates it. Project files that the visual development environment creates are put into this directory.

When you create a project, the visual development environment also specifies subdirectories for intermediate and final output files for the various configurations that you specify. These subdirectories allow you to build configurations without overwriting intermediate and final output files with the same names. The General tab in the Project Settings dialog box lets you modify the subdirectories, if you choose.

If you have existing source code, you should organize it into directories before building a project, although it is easy to move files and edit your project definitions if you should later decide to reorganize your files.

If your program uses modules, you do not need to explicitly add them to your project, they appear as dependencies. The visual development environment scans the file list for modules and compiles them before program units that use them. The visual development environment automatically scans the added project files recursively for modules specified in **USE** statements, as well as any **INCLUDE**s. It scans both source files (.FOR, .F, .F90) and resource files (.RC), and adds all the files it finds to a Dependencies folder. You cannot directly add or delete the files listed in this folder.

The Project Makefile

The visual development environment speeds and simplifies the task of building programs and libraries outside of the visual development environment by allowing you to export a makefile, which is a set of build instructions for each project. Makefiles contain the names of the source, object, and library files needed to build a program or library, plus the compiler and linker options selected in the Project Settings dialog boxes.

The visual development environment updates the build instructions in internal makefiles when you add or remove project files in the project window, and when you make changes to the compiler or linker options in the Project Settings dialog boxes. To get an updated version of a makefile, update project dependencies (use the Build menu) and from the Project menu, select Export Makefile. The makefile is used by the external program maintenance utility, NMAKE.EXE.

You can edit the makefile generated by the visual development environment if you need to perform unusual or exceptional builds. Remember, however, that once you have edited a makefile, exporting the makefile again from the visual development environment will overwrite your changes.

If you use a foreign makefile for a project, the visual development environment calls NMAKE to perform the build. You can run NMAKE from the console command line to perform builds either with makefiles exported by the visual development environment or with foreign makefiles that you have edited. For more about the external program maintenance utility, see Building Projects with NMAKE.

Note: When you use a foreign makefile, the project is considered to be foreign. You cannot use the Project Settings dialog box to make changes to the build options, or use the Add to Project dialog box to add files.

2.3.2   Selecting a Configuration

A configuration defines the final binary output file that you create within a project. A configuration has the following characteristics:

▶ Project type—Specifies the type of Fortran application to build, such as a Fortran Static Library, Fortran Console application, Fortran Quick-Win application, Fortran Windows application, and so on.

▶ Build options—Specifies the build options.

When you create a new project, the visual development environment creates the following configurations:

▶ Debug configuration

By default, the debug configuration sets project options to include the debugging information in the debug configuration. It also turns off optimizations. Before you can debug an application, you must build a debug configuration for the project.

▶ Release configuration

The release configuration does *not* include the debugging information, and it uses any optimizations that you have chosen.

Select the configuration in the Build menu, Set Active Configuration item. Only one configuration can be active at one time.

When you build your project, the currently selected configuration is built:

▶ If you selected the debug configuration, a subfolder called Debug contains the output files created by the build for the debug version of your project.

▶ If you selected the release configuration, a subfolder called Release contains the output files created by the build for the release version of your project.

Although debug and release configurations usually use the same set of source files, the information about project settings usually differs. For example, the default debug configuration supplies full debug information and no optimizations, whereas the default release configuration supplies minimal debug information and full optimizations.

You can also define new configurations within your project. These configurations can use the existing source files in your project, the existing project settings, or other characteristics of existing configurations. A new configuration does not have to share any of the characteristics or content of existing configurations, however.

You could, for instance, create an initial project with debug and release configurations specifying an application for the Win32 environment, and add source files to the project. Later, within the project, you could create debug and release configurations specifying a DLL for the Win32 environment, add an entirely disjoint set of files to this configuration, and make these configurations dependencies of the application configurations.

Platform Types

The platform type specifies the operating environment for a project. The platform type sets options required specifically for a given platform, such as options that the compiler uses for the source files, the static libraries that the linker uses for the platform, the default locations for output files, defined constants, and so on. Visual Fortran supports the Win32 platform type.

For more information:

▶ On viewing and changing the project build options for the current configuration, use the Project settings dialog box (see Section 2.3.3 Setting Build Options).

▶ On errors during the build process, see Section 2.4 Errors during the Build Process.

2.3.3   Setting Build Options

When you create a new configuration, you specify options for file creation and build settings by selecting the Settings item in the Project menu.

For the currently selected configuration of a project, the Project Settings dialog box (see Categories of Compiler Options) allows you to specify the compile and link options, optimization, or browse information.

Configurations have a hierarchical structure of options. The options set at the configuration level apply to all files within the configuration. Setting options at the configuration level is sufficient for most configurations. For instance, if you set default optimizations for the configuration, all files contained within the configuration use default optimizations.

However, you can set different options for files within a configuration, such as specific optimization options—or no optimization at all—for any individual files in the configuration. The options that you set at the file level in the configuration override options set at the configuration level.

The FileView pane shows the files associated with the project configuration and allows you to select certain files.

You can set some types of options, such as linking or requesting browse information, only at the configuration level.

You can set options at the following levels within a configuration:

▶ Configuration level

Any options set for the current configuration apply to every file in the configuration unless overridden at the file level. Options set for the configuration apply to all actions, such as compilation, linking, and requesting browser information.

▶ File level

Any options set for a file apply only to that file and override any options set at the configuration level. Options set for selected files apply to file-level actions, such as compiling.

You can insert both source files (.FOR, .F90, .F, .FI, .FD) and object files (.OBJ) by using the Project menu Add to Project, Files item.

You should always insert all source files used by your application into the project. For example, when you update a source file, the next time you build your application, the visual development environment will create a new object file and link it into your project.

You should also insert the names of any necessary static libraries and DLLs with .LIB extensions to be linked with your project. Use only the library names, not the names of any files within the libraries.

If you have installed the same version of Microsoft Visual C++ and Visual Fortran (in the same directory tree), you can include C/C++ source code files. If the same version of Microsoft Visual C++ is *not* installed, include C/C++ object code instead.

You can set and save project settings as described in the following sections:

▶ Section 2.3.3.1 Compile and Link Options for a Configuration or Certain Files

▶ Section 2.3.3.2 Saving and Using the Project Setting Environment for Different Projects

▶ Section 2.3.3.3 Source Browser Information for a Configuration

2.3.3.1 *Compile and Link Options for a Configuration or Certain Files*

You can set any of the compiler or linker options described in Compiler and Linker Options in the Project menu, Settings dialog box. The Fortran tab of this dialog box presents several categories of options to set. The options are grouped under different categories. Select the category from the Category drop-down list (see Section 4.1.1 Categories of Compiler Options).

The FileView pane shows the files associated with the project configuration and lets you select certain files. The options that you set at the file level in the configuration override options set at the configuration level. Linking options can only be applied at the configuration level (not the file level).

You can choose compiler and linker options through the various dialog boxes. If a compiler option is not available in the dialog boxes, you can enter the option in the lower part of the window just as you would at the command line.

The linker builds an executable program (.EXE), static library (.LIB), or dynamic-link library (.DLL) file from Common Object File Format (COFF) object files and other libraries identified in the linker options. You direct the linker by setting linker options either in the visual development environment, in a build instructions file, or on the console command line. For example, you can use a linker option to specify what kind of debug information to include in the program or library.

For more information on compiler and linker options, see Chapter 4 Compiler and Linker Options.

2.3.3.2 *Saving and Using the Project Setting Environment for Different Projects*

You can set any of the compiler or linker options described in Compiler and Linker Options in the Project menu, Settings dialog box. The Fortran tab of this dialog box presents several categories of options to set.

Visual Fortran provides a facility to save and re-use the Project settings for multiple projects of the same project type. For example, you can save your Project settings environment for a Fortran QuickWin project and use those saved settings as defaults when you create a new Fortran QuickWin project type.

The saved Fortran environment project settings are those associated with the Fortran tab and the diplayed tool tab(s) in the Project Settings dialog box. You can save a Fortran project settings environment for an existing project, use a previously saved project settings environment for a new project, and manage the current set of saved Fortran environment settings.

To save a project settings Fortran environment:

1. Open the appropriate workspace.

2. Modify the Project Settings dialog box as needed. If you specify actual file names for output files, consider changing them to use the default file naming conventions.

3. In the File menu, click Save Fortran Environment or click the green tree on the Fortran toolbar. A window resembling the dialog box appears in Figure 2-2.

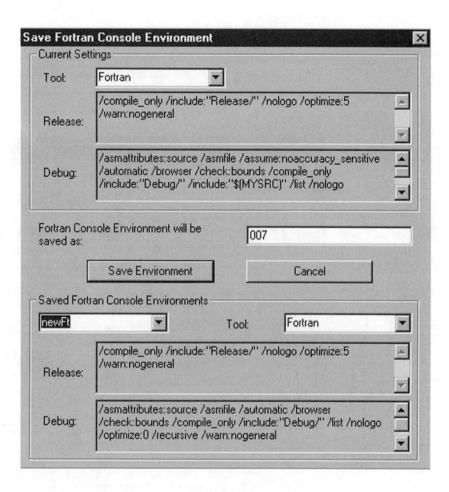

Figure 2–2   *Saving a Project Settings Environment*

4. The Tool Combo box allows you to view the project settings for either the Fortran or the Linker. The Release and Debug configuration values are displayed for the selected tab. Verify that the displayed values are acceptable.

5. The edit box titled Saved Fortran Console Environment allows you to specify the name of the environment to be saved.

6. Click the Save Settings button to save the settings as a project settings environment.

To use an existing Fortran environment when creating a new project:

1. If a Fortran environment exists for the specified new Fortran project type, you will be asked whether you want to apply project settings options from a saved Fortran environment. If you click Yes, a window resembling the dialog box appears in Figure 2-3.

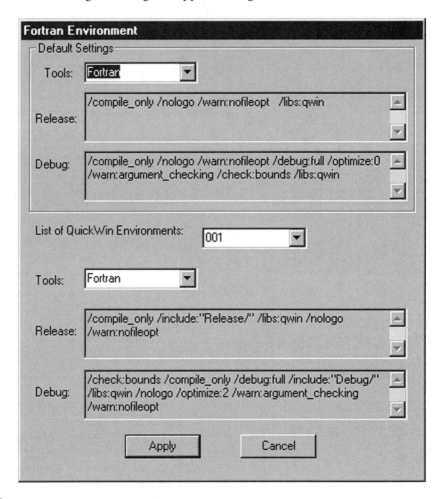

Figure 2–3   *Using an Existing Fortran Project Settings Environment*

2. For the selected Fortran project type, a list of saved Fortran environments appears. Select a Fortran environment. Verify that the selected environment is correct by viewing the Project Settings options.

3. After selecting the appropriate Fortran environment for the Fortran project being created, click the Apply button to use the saved settings for the new project.

4. Complete other tasks associated with creating a new project, such as adding source files, and so on.

To manage saved Fortran environments:

1. In the Tools menu, click Managed Saved Fortran Environment or click the saw on the Fortran toolbar. A dialog box resembling the one shown in appears Figure 2-4.

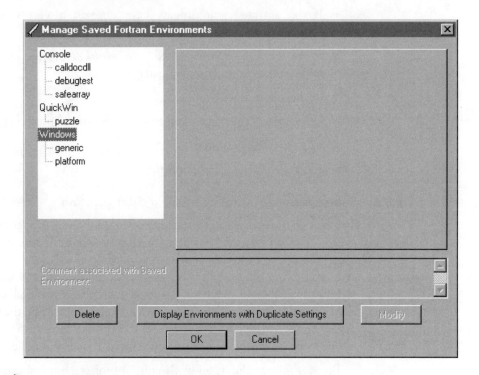

Figure 2–4   *Managing Saved Fortran Project Settings Environments*

2. Initially, this dialog box displays the project types for which there are saved Fortran environments. Double-click on the project type name to view the saved Fortran environments for that project type.

This dialog box allows you to display the Fortran environments associated with each project type. Double-click the name of a project type to display the Fortran environments associated with that project type.

3. To display the project settings for a Fortran environment:

   ▶ Click the name of a Fortran environment.

   ▶ View the project settings for the Fortran tab.

▶ Click the other tool tab (such as Linker) and view that tool's project settings.

▶ If needed, click (select) a different Fortran environment.

4. To determine whether duplicates exist for a Fortran environment:

▶ Click (select) the name of an environment or a project type.

▶ Click the Display Environments with Duplicate Settings button.

▶ If the Fortran environments have *different* project settings, No Duplicates Found is displayed.

▶ If the Fortran environments have *identical* project settings, the duplicate environments are displayed.

5. To delete a Fortran environment:

▶ Click (select) the name of an environment or the project type.

▶ Click the Delete button.

▶ Click OK to the delete confirmation box.

2.3.3.3 *Source Browser Information for a Configuration*

The Source Browser generates a listing of all symbols in your program; information that can be useful when you need to debug it, or simply to maintain large volumes of unwieldy code. It keeps track of locations in your source code where your program declares, defines, and uses names. You can find references to variables or procedures in your main program and all subprograms it calls by selecting one of the files in your project, then using the Go to Definition or Go to Reference button on the Browse toolbar. Source Browser information is available only after you achieve a successful build.

Browser information is off by default for projects, but you can turn it on if you wish. To set the browse option for the current configuration:

▶ From the visual development environment:

1. In the Project menu, click Settings.

2. In the General category of the Fortran tab, set the Generate Source Browse Information check box.

3. Click the BrowseInfo tab and set the Build Browse info check box.

4. Click OK.

5. Build your application.

6. In the Tools menu, click Source Browser.

7. Near the bottom on the Browse window, locate the Case sensitive check box. Since Fortran is a case-insensitive language, make sure the Case sensitive check box is clicked off.

8. When you are done using the Browse window, click OK. The Browse window allows you to view graphs of calling relationships between functions and view the symbols contained within the file, and perform other functions.

▶ From the command line:

1. Specify the /browser option.

2. Use the Browse Information File Maintenance Utility (BSCMAKE) utility to generate a browse information file (.BSC) that can be examined in browse windows in the visual development environment.

When the browse option is on, the compiler creates intermediate .SBR files when it creates the .OBJ files; at link time, all .SBR files in a project are combined into one .BSC file. These files are binary, not readable, but they are used when you access them through the Browser menu.

2.3.4   Creating the Executable Program

Once you are ready to create an executable image of your application, select the Build menu. You can:

▶ Compile a file without linking

▶ Build a project

▶ Rebuild all parts of a project

▶ Batch build several configurations of a project

▶ Clean extra files created by project builds

▶ Execute the program, either in debug mode or not

▶ Update program dependencies

▶ Select the active project and configuration

▶ Edit the project configuration

▶ Define and perform profiling

Once you have completed your project definition, you can build the executable program.

When you select Build *projectname* from the Build menu (or one of the Build toolbars), the visual development environment automatically updates dependencies, compiles and links all files in your project. When you build a project, the visual development environment processes only the files in the project that have changed since the last build.

The Rebuild All mode forces a new compilation of all source files listed for the project.

You either can choose to build a single project, the current project, or you can choose multiple projects (requires batch build) to build in one operation.

You can execute your program from the visual development environment using Ctrl+F5 or Execute from the Build menu (or Build toolbar), or from the command line prompt.

Compiling Files In a Project

You can select and compile individual files in any project in your project workspace. To do this, select the file in the project workspace window (File-View tab). Then, do one of the following:

▶ Press Ctrl+F7.

  -or-

▶ Choose Compile from the Build menu (or Build toolbar).

  -or-

▶ Click the right mouse button to display the pop-up menu and select Compile.

You can also use the Ctrl+F7 or Compile from the Build menu (or Build toolbar) options when the source window is active (input focus).

2.4   Errors during the Build Process

Compiler and linker errors are displayed in the Build pane of the output window. To quickly locate the source line causing the error, follow these steps:

1. Select (click) the error message text in the Build pane of the output window.

2. Press F4.

The editor window appears with a marker in the left margin that identifies the line causing the error.

If you need to set different compiler options for some of your source files, you can highlight the source file name and select the Project menu, Settings item. Options set in this manner are valid only for the file you selected.

If your project has dependencies, such as modules referenced with **USE** statements, choose Update All Dependencies from the Build menu before building your project.

After you have corrected any compiler errors reported during the previous build, choose Build from the Build menu. The build engine recompiles only those files that have changed, or which refer to changed include or module files. If all files in your project compile without errors, the build engine links the object files and libraries to create your program or library.

You can force the build engine to recompile all source files in the project by selecting Rebuild All from the Build menu. This is useful to verify that all of your source code is clean, especially if you are using a foreign makefile, or if you use a new set of compiler options for all of the files in your project.

If your build results in Linker errors, be aware that the project type selected and the project settings in the Libraries category (see Section 4.1.1 Categories of Compiler Options) determine the libraries linked against. Also, you can specify additional user-created libraries.

To view the include file and library directory paths in the visual development environment:

▶ In the Tools menu, click Options.

▶ Click the Directories tab.

▶ In the drop-down list for Show Directories For, select Include files and view the include file paths.

▶ In the drop-down list for Show Directories For, select Library files and view the library paths.

▶ Click OK if you have changed any information.

To view the libraries being passed to the linker in the visual development environment:

▶ If not already open, open your Project Workspace (File menu, Open Workspace).

▶ In the Project menu, click on Settings.

▶ Click on the Link tab to view the list of Object/Library modules (General category).

▶ Click OK if you have changed any information.

With the Professional Edition, if you have trouble linking IMSL libraries, see also Section 24.1 Using the Libraries from Visual Fortran.

To view a description of build and run-time messages, see *Error Messages* in Visual Fortran online Help or, in the visual development environment, highlight the error identifier (such as LNK2001) in the output pane and press F1.

2.5 Compiler Limits

Table 2-2 lists the limits to the size and complexity of a single Digital Visual Fortran program unit and to individual statements contained in it.

The amount of data storage, the size of arrays, and the total size of executable programs are limited only by the amount of process virtual address space available, as determined by system parameters.

Table 2–2 *Visual Fortran Program Unit Limits*

Language Element	Limit
Actual number of arguments per CALL or function reference	255
Arguments in a function reference in a specification expression	255
Array dimensions	7
Array elements per dimension	2,147,483,647 or process limit
Constants; character and Hollerith	2000 characters
Constants; characters read in list-directed I/O	2048 characters
Continuation lines	511
DO and block IF statement nesting (combined)	128
DO loop index variable	2,147,483,647 or process limit
Format group nesting	8
Fortran source line length	132 characters
INCLUDE file nesting	10
Labels in computed or assigned GOTO list	500
Lexical tokens per statement	3000
Named common blocks	250
Parentheses nesting in expressions	40
Structure nesting	20
Symbolic name length	63 characters

2.6   Running Fortran Applications

You can execute programs built with this version of Visual Fortran only on a computer running the Microsoft Windows 98, Windows 95, or Windows NT operating system (see the release notes for the Windows NT version number). You can run the programs from the command console, Start . . . Program ... group, Windows Explorer, and the Microsoft visual development environment.

Each program is treated as a protected user application with a private address space and environment variables. Because of this, your program cannot accidentally damage the address space of any other program running on the computer at the same time.

Environment variables defined for the current user are part of the environment that Windows sets up when you open the command console. You can change these variables and set others within the console session, but they are only valid during the current session.

If you run a program from the console, the operating system searches directories listed in the PATH user environment variable to find the executable file you have requested. You can also run your program by specifying the complete path of the .EXE file. If you are also using DLLs, they must be in the same directory as the .EXE file or in one specified in the path.

You can easily recover from most problems that may arise while executing your program.

If your program is multithreaded, Windows NT starts each thread on whichever processor is available at the time. On a computer with one processor, the threads all run in parallel, but not simultaneously; the single processor switches among them. On a computer with more than one processor, the threads can run simultaneously.

If you specified the /fpscomp:filesfromcmd option (Compatibility category in Project Settings, Fortran tab), the command line that executes the program can also include additional filenames to satisfy **OPEN** statements in your program in which the filename field has been left blank. The first filename on the command line is used for the first such **OPEN** statement executed, the second filename for the second **OPEN** statement, and so on. In the visual development environment, you can provide these filenames in the Project menu Settings item, Debug tab, in the Program Arguments text box.

Each filename on the command line (or in a visual development environment dialog box) must be separated from the names around it by one or more spaces or tab characters. You can enclose each name in double quotation marks ("*filename*"), but this is not required unless the argument contains spaces or tabs. A null argument consists of an empty set of double quotation marks with no filename enclosed (" ").

The following command runs the program MYPROG.EXE from the console:

```
MYPROG " " OUTPUT.DAT
```

Because the first filename argument is null, the first **OPEN** statement with a blank filename field produces the following message:

```
File name missing or blank - please enter file name <R>
UNIT number ?
```

The *number* is the unit number specified in the **OPEN** statement. The filename OUTPUT.DAT is used for the second such **OPEN** statement executed. If additional **OPEN** statements with blank filename fields are executed, you will be prompted for more filenames. Programs built with the QuickWin library prompt for a file to open by presenting a dialog box in which you can browse for the file or type in the name of a new file to be created.

If you use the **GETARG** library routine, to execute the program in the visual development environment, provide the command-line arguments to be passed to the program in the Project menu Settings item, Debug tab, in the Program Arguments text box.

If you use the visual development environment debugger and need to specify a working directory that differs from the directory where the executable program resides, specify the directory in the Project menu Settings item, Debug tab, in the Working Directory text box.

Run-time error messages are displayed in the console or in a dialog box depending upon the type of application you build. If you need to capture these messages, you can redirect *stderr* to a file. For example, to redirect run-time error messages from a program called BUGGY.EXE to a file called BUGLIST.TXT, you would use the following syntax:

```
BUGGY.EXE > BUGLIST.TXT
```

The redirection portion of the syntax must appear last on the command line. You can append the output to an existing file by using two greater-than signs (>>) instead of one. If the file does not exist, one is created. For more information about command-line redirection, see Section 3.6 Redirecting Command-Line Output to Files.

For more information:

▶ On using the debugger with Fortran programs, see Chapter 5 Debugging Fortran Programs.

▶ Locating errors in the debugger, see Section 5.5 Locating Run-Time Errors in the Debugger.

▶ On locating the source of exceptions, see Section 21.3 Locating Run-Time Errors and Section 21.4 Using Traceback Information.

▶ On handling run-time errors with source changes, see Section 21.2 Methods of Handling Errors.

▶ On environment variables recognized during run-time, see Section 21.5 Run-Time Environment Variables.

▶ On each Visual Fortran run-time message, see "Run-Time Errors" in *Error Messages* in Visual Fortran online Help.

2.7   Porting Projects between *x86* and Alpha Platforms

To move an existing Visual Fortran project to another platform:

1. Copy all project files to the new platform

   Keep the folder/directory hierarchy intact by copying the entire project tree to the new computer. For example, if a project resides in the folder \MyProjects\Projapp on one computer, you can copy the contents of that directory, and all subdirectories, to the \MyProjects\Projapp directory on another computer. After copying all of the files, delete any *.opt files. These files are computer specific and should not be copied.

2. Specify new configurations

   After you copy the files, opening the project reveals that the target platform is still set to the original platform. Although this is not obvious, you can tell this is so because the Build, Compile, and Execute options are grayed out in the Build menu. Before you can build the application on the new platform, you must first specify one or more new configurations for the project on the new platform.

   To create Debug and Release targets for this project, you create a new configuration while running Visual Fortran on the new platform. The platform for a new configuration is assumed to be the current platform. For example, if you copy an *x86* project to an Alpha system, and create a new configuration, the target platform can only be Alpha. You cannot specify another platform. This same behavior applies when moving projects between any two platforms.

To create a new project configuration:

a. In the Configurations dialog box, click the Add button. The Add Project Configuration dialog box appears.

b. In the Configuration box, type a new configuration name. The names do not matter, as long as they differ from existing configuration names.

c. Select the configuration from which to copy the settings for this configuration and click OK. Usually, you will want to copy the settings from a similar configuration. For example, if this new configuration is a release configuration, you will usually copy settings from an existing release configuration.

d. The Projects dialog box appears with the new project configuration. Repeat the process as necessary to create as many configurations as you need.

3. Reset project options

Because not all settings are transportable across platforms, you should verify your project settings on the new platform. To verify your project settings:

a. From the Project menu, choose Settings. The Project Settings dialog box appears.

b. Review the tabs and categories to ensure that the project settings you want are selected. Pay special attention to the following items:

▶ General Tab—Review the directories for intermediate and output files.

▶ Custom Build Tab—Review for any custom commands that might change between platforms.

▶ Fortran and Linker tabs—Nonstandard options in the original configurations must be replicated (as applicable) in the new configurations. As listed in Compiler Options, certain options are supported only on x86 or Alpha systems.

▶ Pre-link and Post-build Step tabs—Review for any custom commands that might change between platforms.

2.8   Visual Fortran Samples

On the Visual Fortran media CD-ROM, Samples are located in folders under `INFO\DF\SAMPLES`. After a Custom installation, the Samples are installed by default in folders under . . . `\MICROSOFT VISUAL STUDIO\DF98\SAMPLES`.

You can view and copy the source code samples for use with your own projects. Use a text editor to view the sample programs (Samples); they are not listed as topics in HTMLHelp Viewer.

If you do not install Samples, you can copy appropriate Samples folders or files from the Visual Fortran CD-ROM to your hard disk.

For a description (roadmap) of the Samples, open the file Samples.htm in a Web browser (use File menu, Open). Table 2-3 shows how to find Samples.htm and the Samples on the Visual Fortran CD-ROM (at any time) or on your hard disk (after installation).

Table 2–3   *Locating Samples Files*

To Locate:	*Look:*

Roadmap to the Samples	On the Visual Fortran CD-ROM, open the file:
	`INFO\DF\SAMPLES\Samples.htm`
	On your hard disk (after installation), open the file:
	. . . `MICROSOFT VISUAL STUDIO\DF98\SAMPLES\`
	`Samples.htm`

Samples folders	On the Visual Fortran CD-ROM, locate folders under: `INFO\DF\SAMPLES` On your hard disk (after installation), locate folders under: . . . `MICROSOFT VISUAL STUDIO\DF\98SAMPLES`

For example, after a Custom installation, the . . . `DF98\SAMPLES\` `TUTORIAL` folder contains short example programs. The Tutorial Samples describe (as source comments) how they can be built.

Longer sample programs are also provided in their own subdirectories and include a makefile (for command-line use) as well as the source files. Many samples include a project workspace file, allowing you to open the project workspace in the visual development environment, view the source files in the FileView pane, build the sample, and run it.

Samples for the Digital Array Visualizer (Professional Edition) are located in folders under . . . `\ArrayVisualizer\Samples`.

3

Using the Compiler and Linker from the Command Line

The DF command is used to compile and link your programs. In most cases, you will use a single DF command to invoke the compiler and linker. The DF command invokes a *driver program* that is the actual user interface to the compiler and linker. It accepts a list of command options and file names and directs processing for each file.

If you will be using the DF command from the command line, you can use:

▶ Your own terminal window, in which you have set the appropriate environment variables by executing the DFVARS.BAT file.

▶ The supplied Fortran (Fortran Command Prompt) terminal window in the Visual Fortran program folder, in which the appropriate environment variables are preset.

The driver program does the following:

▶ Calls the Digital Visual Fortran compiler to process Fortran files

▶ Passes the linker options to the linker

▶ Passes object files created by the compiler to the linker

▶ Passes libraries to the linker

▶ Calls the linker or librarian to create the .EXE or library file.

The DF command automatically references the appropriate Visual Fortran Run-Time Libraries when it invokes the linker. Therefore, to link one or more object files created by the Visual Fortran compiler, you should use the DF command instead of the LINK command.

Because the DF driver calls other software components, error messages may be returned by these other components. For instance, the linker may return a message if it cannot resolve a global reference. Using the /watch:cmd option on the DF command line can help clarify which component is generating the error.

This chapter contains the following topics:

▶ Section 3.1 The Format of the DF Command

▶ Section 3.2 Examples of the DF Command Format

▶ Section 3.3 Input and Output Files

▶ Section 3.4 Environment Variables Used with the DF Command

▶ Section 3.5 Specifying Project Types with DF Command Options

▶ Section 3.6 Redirecting Command-Line Output to Files

▶ Section 3.7 Using the DF Command to Compile and Link

▶ Section 3.8 DF Indirect Command File Use

▶ Section 3.9 Compiler and Linker Messages

3.1   The Format of the DF Command

This section describes the format of the DF command. It also provides an alphabetical list of DF command options.

The DF command accepts the following types of options:

▶ Compiler options

▶ Linker options

The command driver requires that the following rules be observed when specifying the DF command:

▶ Except for the linker options, options can be specified in any order.

▶ Linker options must be preceded by the keyword /link and must be specified at the end of the command line, following all other options.

The DF command has the following form:

DF options [/link options]

options

A list of compiler or linker options. These lists of options take the following form:

[/option:[arg]] [filename.ext]...

/option[:arg]

Indicates either special actions to be performed by the compiler or linker, or special properties of input or output files.

The following rules apply to options and their names:

▶ Options begin with a slash (/). You can use a dash (-) instead of a slash.

▶ Visual Fortran options are *not* case-sensitive. Certain options provided for compatibility with Microsoft Fortran PowerStation options *are* case-sensitive, such as /FA and /Fa*file*.

▶ You can abbreviate option names. You need only enter as many characters as are needed to uniquely identify the option.

Certain options accept one or more keyword arguments following the option name. For example, the /warn option accepts several keywords, including argument_checking and declarations.

To specify only a single keyword, specify the keyword after the colon (:). For example, the following specifies the /warn option declarations keyword:

```
DF /warn:declarations test.f90
```

To specify multiple keywords, specify the option name once, and place each keyword in a comma-separated list enclosed within parentheses with no spaces between keywords, as follows:

```
DF /warn:(argument_checking,declarations) test.f90
```

Instead of the colon, you can use an equal sign (=):

```
DF /warn=(argument_checking,declarations) test.f90
```

filename.ext

Specifies the files to be processed. You can use wildcard characters (such as *.f90) to indicate multiple files or you can specify each file name.

The file extension identifies the type of the file. With Fortran source files, certain file extensions indicate whether that source file contains source code in free (such as .f90) or fixed (such as .for) source form. You can also specify compiler options to indicate fixed or free source form (see /[no]free).

The file extension determines whether that file gets passed to the compiler or to the linker. For example, files myfile.for and projfile.f are passed to the compiler and file myobj.obj is passed to the linker.

Table 3-1 lists the DF command options.

Table 3–1   *DF Command Options*

/[no]alignment	/[no]altparam
/architecture	/[no]asmattributes
/[no]asmfile	/assume
/[no]automatic	/bintext
/[no]browser	/[no]check
/[no]comments	/[no]compile_only
/convert	/[no]d_lines
/[no]dbglibs	/[no]debug
/define	/dll
/[no]error_limit	/[no]exe
/[no]extend_source	/extfor
/extfpp	/extlnk
/[no]f66	/[no]f77rtl
/fast	/[no]fixed
/[no]fltconsistency (x86 only)	/[no]fpconstant
/fpe	/fpp
/[no]fpscomp	/[no]free
/granularity (Alpha only)	/help or /?
/iface	/[no]include
/[no]inline	/[no]intconstant
/integer_size	/[no]keep
/[no]libdir	/libs
/[no]link	/[no]list
/[no]logo	/[no]machine_code

Table 3–1   *DF Command Options (Continued)*

/[no]map	/math_library
/[no]module	/names
/[no]object	/[no]optimize
/[no]pad_source	/[no]pdbfile
/[no]pipeline (Alpha only)	/preprocess_only
/real_size	/[no]recursive
/[no]reentrancy	/rounding_mode (Alpha only)
/[no]show	/source
/[no]static	/[no]stand
/[no]synchronous_exceptions (Alpha only)	/[no]syntax_only
/[no]threads	/[no]traceback
/[no]transform_loops	/tune
/undefine	/unroll
/[no]vms	/[no]warn
/[no]watch	/what
/winapp	

For More Information:

▶ On DF command options, see Chapter 4 Compiler and Linker Options.

▶ On DF command examples, see Section 3.2 Examples of the DF Command Format.

▶ On using the FL32 command, see Section 4.3 Microsoft Fortran Power-Station Command-Line Compatibility.

▶ About Fortran PowerStation options (such as /MD) and their DF command equivalents, see Section 4.3.2 Equivalent Visual Fortran Compiler Options.

3.2   Examples of the DF Command Format

The following examples demonstrate valid and invalid DF commands:

Valid DF commands

In the following example, the file to be compiled is test.f90 and the file proj.obj is passed to the linker:

```
DF test.f90 proj.obj
```

In this example, the .f90 file extension indicates test.f90 is a Fortran free-form source file to be compiled. The file extension of obj indicates proj.obj is an object file to be passed to the linker. You can optionally add the /link option before the file proj.obj to indicate it should be passed directly to the linker.

In the following example, the /check:bounds option requests that the Fortran compiler generate additional code to perform run-time checking for out-of-bounds array and substring references for the files myfile.for and test.for (fixed-form source):

```
DF /check:bounds myfile.for test.for
```

In the following example, the /link option indicates that files and options after the /link option are passed directly to the linker:

```
DF myfile.for /link myobject.obj /out:myprog.exe
```

Invalid DF commands

The following DF command is invalid because the /link option indicates that items after the /link option are passed directly to the linker, but the file test.for should be passed to the compiler:

```
DF myfile.for /link test.for /out:myprog.exe
```

The following DF command is invalid because the /link option is missing and the /out linker option is not recognized as a compiler option:

```
DF myfile.for test.for /out:myprog.exe
```

A correct form of this command is:

```
DF myfile.for test.for /link /out:myprog.exe
```

In this case, you can alternatively use one of the DF options (/exe) that specifies information to the linker:

```
DF myfile.for test.for /exe:myprog.exe
```

For More Information:

▶ On environment variables used with the DF command, see Section 3.4.

▶ On specifying project types with DF command options, see Section 3.5.

▶ On redirecting command-line output to files, see Section 3.6.

▶ On using the DF command to compile and link, see Section 3.7.

▶ On DF indirect command file use, see Section 3.8.

▶ On compiler and linker messages, see Section 3.9.

3.3   Input and Output Files

You can use the DF command to process multiple files. These files can be source files, object files, or object libraries.

When a file is not in your path or working directory, specify the directory path before the file name.

The file extension determines whether a file gets passed to the compiler or to the linker. The following types of files are used with the DF command:

▶ Files passed to the compiler: .f90, .for, .f, .fpp, .i, .i90, .inc, .fi, .fd, .f77. Typical Fortran (DF command) source files have a file extension of .f90, .for, and .f.

▶ Files passed to the linker: .lib, .obj, .o, .exe, .res, .rbj, .def, .dll. For example, object files usually have a file extension of .obj. Files with extensions of .lib are usually library files.

The output produced by the DF command includes:

▶ An object file (.OBJ) if you specify the /compile_only, /keep, or /object option on the command line.

▶ An executable file (.EXE) if you do not specify the /compile_only option

▶ A dynamic-link library file (.DLL) if you specify the /dll option and do not specify the /compile_only option

▶ A module file (.MOD) if a source file being compiled defines a Fortran 90 module (**MODULE** statement)

▶ A program database file (.PDB) if you specify the /pdbfile or /debug:full (or equivalent) options

▶ A listing file (.LST) if you specify the /list option

▶ A browser file (.SBR) if you specify the /browser option

You control the production of these files by specifying the appropriate options on the DF command line. Unless you specify the /compile_only option or /keep option, the compiler generates a single temporary object file from one or more source files. The linker is then invoked to link the object file into one executable image file.

If fatal errors are encountered during compilation, or if you specify certain options such as /compile_only, linking does not occur.

When a path or file name includes an embedded space or a special character, enclose the entire file location name in double quotation marks ("). For example:

```
DF "Project xyz\fortmain.f90"
```

For more information about naming input and output files, see:

▶ Section 3.3.1 Naming Output Files

▶ Section 3.3.2 Temporary Files

3.3.1 Naming Output Files

To specify a file name for the executable image file, you can use one of several DF options:

▶ The /exe:*file* or the /out:*file* linker option to name an executable program file.

▶ The /dll:*file* alone or the /dll option with the /out:*file* linker option to name an executable dynamic-link library.

You can also use the /object:*file* option to specify the object file name. If you specify the /compile_only option and omit the /object:*file* option, each source file is compiled into a separate object file. For more information about the output file(s) created by compiling and linking multiple files, see Section 3.7.4 Compiling and Linking Multiple Fortran Source Files.

Many compiler options allow you to specify the name of the *file* being created. If you specify only a filename without an extension, a default extension is added for the file being created, as summarized in Table 3-2.

Table 3–2 *Default File Extensions for Compiler Options*

Option	Default File Extension
/asmfile:*file*	.ASM
/browser:*file*	.SBR

Table 3–2 *Default File Extensions for Compiler Options (Continued)*

Option	Default File Extension
/dll:*file*	.DLL
/exe:*file*	.EXE
/list:*file*	.LST
/map:*file*	.MAP
/pdbfile:*file*	.PDB (default filename is df60.pdb)

3.3.2   Temporary Files

Temporary files created by the compiler or linker reside in the directory used by the operating system to store temporary files. To store temporary files, the operating system first checks for the TMP environment variable.

If the TMP environment variable is defined, the directory that it points to is used for temporary files. If the TMP environment variable is not defined, the operating system checks for the TEMP environment variable. If the TEMP environment variable is not defined, the current working directory is used for temporary files. Temporary files are usually deleted, unless the /keep option was specified. For performance reasons, use a local drive (rather than using a network drive) to contain the temporary files.

To view the file name and directory where each temporary file is created, use the /watch:cmd option. To create object files in your current working directory, use the /compile_only or /keep option. Any object files (.obj files) that you specify on the DF command line are retained.

3.4   Environment Variables Used with the DF Command

Table 3-3 shows the environment variables that affect the DF command.

Table 3–3 *Environment Variables Affecting the DF Command*

Environment Variable	Description
PATH	The PATH environment variable sets the search path.
LIB	The linker uses the LIB environment variable to determine the location of .LIB files. If the LIB environment variable is not set, the linker looks for .LIB files in the current directory.
IMSL_F90	The IMSL_F90 environment variable contains a list of libraries used for linking IMSL libraries (Professional Edition), as listed in Section 24.2 Library Naming Conventions.

Table 3–3 *Environment Variables Affecting the DF Command (Continued)*

Environment Variable	Description
INCLUDE	The make facility (NMAKE) uses the INCLUDE environment variable to locate INCLUDE files and module files. The Digital Fortrtan compiler uses the INCLUDE environment variable to locate files included by an INCLUDE statement or module files referenced by a USE statement. Similarly, the resource compiler uses the INCLUDE environment variable to locate #include and RCINCLUDE files.
DF	The DF environment variable can be used to specify frequently used DF options and files. The options and files specified by the DF environment variable are added to the DF command; they are processed before any options specified on the command line. You can override an option specified in the DF environment variable by specifying an option on the command line. For information about using the DF environment variable to specify frequently-used options, see Section 3.7.2 Using the DF Environment Variable to Specify Options.

You can set these environment variables by using the DFVARS.BAT file or the F90 (Fortran Command Prompt) command-line window (see "Using the Command-Line Interface" in *Getting Started* in Visual Fortran online Help).

For a list of environment variables recognized at run-time, see Section 21.5 Run-Time Environment Variables.

3.5 Specifying Project Types with DF Command Options

This section provides the DF command options that correspond to the visual development environment project types.

When creating an application, you should choose a *project type*. The first four projects are main project types, requiring main programs:

▶ To create a Fortran Console application with the DF command, you do not need to specify any options (if you link separately, specify the link option /subsystem:console). This is the default project type created.

▶ To create a Fortran Standard Graphics application with the DF command, specify the /libs=qwins option (which also sets certain linker options).

▶ To create a Fortran QuickWin application with the DF command, specify the /libs:qwin option (which also sets certain linker options).

▶ To create a Fortran Windows application with the DF command, specify the /winapp option (which also sets certain linker options).

The following types are library projects, without main programs:

▶ To create a Fortran Dynamic-Link library with the DF command, specify the /dll option (sets the /libs:dll option).

▶ To create a Fortran Static library with the DF command:

1. If your application will not call any QuickWin or Standard Graphics routines, specify/libs:static and /compile_only options to create the object files. Use the LIB command to create the library.
2. If your application will call QuickWin routines, specify /libs:qwin and /compile_only options to create the object files. Use the LIB command to create the library.
3. If your application will call Standard Graphics routines, specify /libs:qwins and /compile_only options to create the object files. Use the LIB command to create the library.

For more information:

▶ On DF command options, see Chapter 4 Compiler and Linker Options.

▶ On Visual Fortran project types (such as Fortran Standard Graphics applications), see Section 2.2.

▶ On the LIB command, see Section 25.8 Managing Libraries with LIB.

3.6   Redirecting Command-Line Output to Files

When using the command line, you can redirect standard output and standard error into separate files or into a single file. How you redirect command-line output depends on which operating system you are using:

▶ On Windows NT systems, to place standard output into file one.out and standard error into file two.out, enter the following DF command (with its filenames and options):

```
DF filenames /options 1>one.out 2>two.out
```

You can also use a short-cut form (omit the 1):

```
DF filenames /options >one.out 2>two.out
```

To place standard output and standard error into a single file both.out on a Windows NT system, type the df command as follows:

```
DF filenames /options 1>both.out 2>&1
```

You can also use a short-cut form (omit the 1):

```
DF filenames /options >both.out 2>&1
```

▶ On Windows 95 and Windows 98 systems, use the EC command-line tool to place standard output and standard error into separate files or into a single file. The EC tool is located on the Visual Fortran CD-ROM in the x86\Usupport\Misc\Win95 folder. Copy ec.exe into a folder in your command-line path (PATH environment variable) on your hard disk.

Precede the DF command line with the EC command and place the entire DF command in quotes. For example, to place standard output into the file one.out and standard error into file two.out, enter the following EC and DF command (with its filenames and options):

```
ec "df filenames /options 1>one.out 2>two.out"
```

To place standard output and standard error into a single file both.out on a Windows 95 or Windows 98 system, type the EC and DF commands as follows:

```
ec "df filenames /options 1>both.out 2>&1"
```

3.7   Using the DF Command to Compile and Link

By default, when you use the DF command, your source files are compiled and then linked. To suppress linking, use the /compile_only option. The following topics show how to use the DF command:

▶ Section 3.7.1 Compiling and Linking a Single Source File

▶ Section 3.7.2 Using the DF Environment Variable to Specify Options

▶ Section 3.7.3 Compiling, but Not Linking, a Fortran Source File

▶ Section 3.7.4 Compiling and Linking Multiple Fortran Source Files

▶ Section 3.7.5 Generating a Listing File

▶ Section 3.7.6 Linking against Additional Libraries

▶ Section 3.7.7 Linking Object Files

▶ Section 3.7.8 Compiling and Linking for Debugging

▶ Section 3.7.9 Compiling and Linking for Optimization

▶ Section 3.7.10 Compiling and Linking Mixed-Language Programs

3.7.1   Compiling and Linking a Single Source File

The following command compiles x.for, links, and creates an executable file named x.exe. This command generates a temporary object file, which is deleted after linking:

```
DF x.for
```

To name the executable file, specify the /exe option:

```
DF x.for /exe:myprog.exe
```

Alternatively, you can name the executable file by using linker /out option:

```
DF x.for /link /out:myprog.exe
```

3.7.2   Using the DF Environment Variable to Specify Options

The following command-line sequences show the use of the DF environment variable. In the first command sequence, the SET command sets the DF environment variable. When the DF command is invoked, it uses the options specified by the DF environment variable, in this case, /debug:minimal and /list:

```
set DF=/debug:minimal /list
DF myprog.for
```

You can also specify additional options on the DF command line. In the following command sequence, the SET command sets the DF environment variable. The DF options specified are /debug:minimal and /list.

```
set DF=/debug:minimal /list
DF myprog.for /show:map
```

If the options specified on the command line conflict with the options specified by the DF environment variable, the option specified on the command line takes precedence. In the following command sequence, the /debug:minimal option specified by the DF environment variable is overridden by the /debug:none option specified on the command line:

```
set DF=/debug:minimal /list
DF myprog.for /debug:none
```

3.7.3   Compiling, but Not Linking, a Fortran Source File

The following command compiles x.for and generates the object file x.obj. The /compile_only option prevents linking (it does not link the object file into an executable file):

```
DF x.for /compile_only
```

3.7.4   Compiling and Linking Multiple Fortran Source Files

The following command compiles a.for, b.for, and c.for. It creates a single temporary object file, then links the object file into an executable file named a.exe:

```
DF a.for b.for c.for
```

If the files a.for, b.for, and c.for were the only .for files in the current directory, you could use a wildcard character to similarly compile the three source files:

```
DF *.for
```

If you use the /compile_only option to prevent linking, also use the /object:file option so that multiple sources files are compiled into a single object file, allowing more optimizations to occur:

```
DF /compile_only /object:a.obj a.for b.for c.for
```

When you use modules and compile multiple files, compile the source files that define modules *before* the files that reference the modules (in **USE** statements).

When you use a single DF command, the order in which files are placed on the command line is significant. For example, if the free-form source file moddef.f90 defines the modules referenced by the file projmain.f90, use the following DF command line:

```
DF moddef.f90 projmain.f90
```

3.7.5   Generating a Listing File

To request a listing file, specify the /list option with the DF command. When you request a listing file, a separate listing file is generated for each object file created.

The content of the listing file is affected by the /show option. For more information about this option, see Compiler and Linker Options.

The following command compiles and links a.for, b.for, and c.for. It generates one listing file for the three source files:

```
DF a.for b.for c.for /list
```

The following command compiles a.for, b.for, and c.for. It generates three listing files (and three object files) for the three source files:

```
DF a.for b.for c.for /list /compile_only
```

The following command sequence compiles and links a.for, b.for, and c.for. It generates one named object file (a.obj) and one listing file (a.lst). The second command links the object files into an executable file (a.exe):

```
DF a.for b.for c.for /list /compile_only /object:a.obj
DF a.obj
```

The following command sequence compiles and links a.for, b.for, and c.for. It generates three object files (a.obj, b.obj, and c.obj) and three listing files (a.lst, b.lst, and c.lst). The second command links the object files into an executable file (a.exe).

```
DF a.for b.for c.for /list /compile_only
DF a.obj b.obj c.obj
```

3.7.6 Linking against Additional Libraries

By default, the DF command automatically adds the libraries needed to build a Fortran Console application to the link command that it generates. The /libs:dll option indicates that you want to linkagainst single-threaded DLLs; other /libs options allow you to link against other types of libraries. The /libs:static option (the default) indicates that you want to link against single-threaded static libraries. You can link against additional libraries by listing those libraries on the command line.

For example, the following command links against static libraries. In addition to linking against the default libraries, it links against mylib.lib:

```
DF x.f90 mylib.lib
```

The following command links against single-threaded DLLs:

```
DF x.f90 /libs:dll
```

The following command links against single-threaded DLLs. It links against the default libraries and mylib.lib:

```
DF x.f90 /libs:dll mylib.lib
```

For more information on the types of libraries available to link against, see the following:

▶ Section 4.1.16 /[no]dbglibs

▶ Section 4.1.34 /[no]fpscomp

▶ Section 4.1.45 /libs

▶ Section 4.1.71 /[no]threads

▶ Section 4.1.81 /winapp

To request the creation of a dynamic-link library, see Section 4.1.19 /dll.

For more information about compiling and linking Visual Fortran and Visual C++ programs (and the libraries used), see Section 18.4 Visual Fortran/Visual C++ Mixed-Language Programs.

3.7.7   Linking Object Files

The following command links x.obj into an executable file. This command automatically links with the default Digital Fortran libraries:

```
DF x.obj
```

3.7.8   Compiling and Linking for Debugging

If you use a single DF command to compile and link, specify the /debug option (/debug sets the default optimization level to /optimize:0), as follows:

```
DF x.for /debug
```

By default, the debugger symbol table information is created in a PDB file, which is needed for the debugger integrated within the visual development environment.

If you use separate DF commands to compile and link, you will want to specify the same debugging information level for the compiler and the linker. For example, if you specify /debug:minimal to the compiler, you will also specify /link /debug:minimal. The following command sequence compiles and then links x.for for debugging with the integrated visual development environment debugger:

```
DF x.for /debug:full /optimize:0 /compile_only
DF x.obj /debug:full
```

For more information:

▶ On /[no]debug, see Section 4.1.17.

▶ On preparing your command-line program for debugging, see Section 5.1 Preparing Your Program for Debugging.

3.7.9   Compiling and Linking for Optimization

If you omit both the /compile_only and the /keep options, the specified Fortran source files are compiled together into a single object module and then linked. (The object file is deleted after linking.) Because all the Fortran source files are compiled together into a single object module, full interprocedural optimizations can occur. With the DF command, the default optimization level is /optimize:4 (unless you specify /debug with no keyword).

If you specify the /compile_only or /keep option and you want to allow full interprocedural optimizations to occur, you should also specify the /object option. The combination of the /compile_only and /object:*file* options creates a single object file from multiple Fortran source files, allowing full interprocedural optimizations. The object file can be linked later.

The following command uses both the /compile_only and /object options to allow interprocedural optimization (explicitly requested by the /optimize:4 option):

```
DF /compile_only /object:out.obj /optimize:4 ax.for bx.for
cx.for
```

If you specify the /compile_only or /keep option without specifying the /object option, each source file is compiled into an object file. This is acceptable if you specified no optimization (/optimize:0) or local optimization (/optimize:1). An information message appears when you specify multiple input files and specify an option that creates multiple object files (such as /compile_only without /object) and specify or imply global optimization (/optimize:2 or higher optimization level).

If you specify the /compile_only option, you must link the object file (or files) later by using a separate DF command. You might do this using a makefile processed by the NMAKE command for incremental compilation of a large application.

However, keep in mind that either omitting the /compile_only or /keep option or using the /compile_only option with the /object:*file* option provides the benefit of full interprocedural optimizations for compiling multiple Fortran source files.

Other optimization options are summarized in Section 6.1 Software Environment and Efficient Compilation.

For more information:

▶ On /[no]compile_only, see Section 4.1.13.

▶ On /[no]keep, see Section 4.1.43.

▶ On /[no]object, see Section 4.1.55.

▶ On /[no]optimize, see Section 4.1.56.

3.7.10 Compiling and Linking Mixed-Language Programs

Your application can contain both C and Fortran source files. If your main program is a Fortran source file (myprog.for) that calls a routine written in C (cfunc.c), you could use the following sequence of commands to build your application:

```
cl -c cfunc.c
DF myprog.for cfunc.obj /link /out:myprog.exe
```

The cl command (invokes the C compiler) compiles but does not link cfunc.c. The -c option specifies that the linker is not called. This command creates cfunc.obj. The DF command compiles myprog.for and links cfunc.obj with the object file created from myprog.for to create myprog.exe.

For more information about compiling and linking Visual Fortran and Visual C++ programs, and the libraries used, see Section 18.4 Visual Fortran/ Visual C++ Mixed-Language Programs.

3.8   DF Indirect Command File Use

The DF command allows the use of indirect command files. For example, assume the file text.txt contains the following:

```
/pdbfile:testout.pdb /exe:testout.exe /debug:full
/optimize:0 test.f90 rest.f90
```

The following DF command executes the contents of file text.txt as an indirect command file to create a debugging version of the executable program and its associated PDB file:

```
DF @test.txt
```

Indirect command files do not use continuation characters; all lines are appended together as one command.

3.9   Compiler and Linker Messages

The following sections describe compiler limits and messages:

▶ Section 3.9.1 Compiler Diagnostic Messages and Error Conditions

▶ Section 3.9.2 Linker Diagnostic Messages and Error Conditions

For information on compiler limits, see Section 2.5 Compiler Limits.

3.9.1   Compiler Diagnostic Messages and Error Conditions

The Visual Fortran compiler identifies syntax errors and violations of language rules in the source program. If the compiler finds any errors, it writes messages to the standard error output file and any listing file. If you enter the DF command interactively, the messages are displayed.

Compiler messages have the following format:

```
filename(n) : severity: message-text
         [text-in-error]
--------^
```

The pointer (---^) indicates the exact place on the source program line where the error was found. The following error message shows the format and message text in a listing file when an **END DO** statement was omitted:

```
echar.for(7): Severe: Unclosed DO loop or IF block
         DO I=1,5
--------   ^
```

Diagnostic messages usually provide enough information for you to determine the cause of an error and correct it.

When using the command line, make sure that the appropriate environment variables have been set by executing the DFVARS.BAT file or by using the Fortran Command Window from the Visual Fortran program folder (see "Using the Command-Line Interface" in *Getting Started*). For example, this BAT file sets the environment variables for the include directory paths.

For errors related to **INCLUDE** and module (**USE** statement) file use, see Section 4.1.39 /[no] include.

For a list of environment variables used by the DF command during compilation, see Section 3.4 Environment Variables Used with the DF Command.

To control compiler diagnostic messages (such as warning messages), see Section 4.1.78 /[no]warn.

To view the passes as they execute on the DF command line, specify /watch: cmd or /watch:all (see Section 4.1.79).

3.9.2   Linker Diagnostic Messages and Error Conditions

If the linker detects any errors while linking object modules, it displays messages about their cause and severity. If any errors occur, the linker does not produce an executable file.

Linker messages are descriptive, and you do not normally need additional information to determine the specific error. For a description of each Linker message, see "Linker Messages (LNK*xxxx*)" in *Error Messages* in Visual Fortran online Help.

To view the libraries being passed to the linker on the DF command line, specify /watch:cmd or /watch:all.

On the command line, make sure the DFVARS.BAT file was executed to set the appropriate environment variables (see "Using the Command-Line Interface" in *Getting Started*). For example, this BAT file sets the environment variables for the library directory paths. For a list of environment variables used by the DF command during compilation, see Section 3.4 Environment Variables Used with the DF Command.

You specify the libraries to be linked against using compiler options in the Libraries category (see 4.1.1 Categories of Compiler Options, Libraries category). Also, you can specify libraries (include the path, if needed) on the command line.

With the Professional Edition, if you have trouble linking IMSL libraries, see Section 24.1 Using the Libraries from Visual Fortran.

For information on handling build errors in the visual development environment, see Section 2.4 Errors during the Build Process.

4

Compiler and Linker Options

Most of the compiler and linker options can be specified within the Microsoft visual development environment or on the command line. This section contains a description of the options available to you in building programs.

You can set *compiler options* from:

▶ Within the visual development environment, by using the Fortran tab in the Project menu, Settings dialog box.

▶ The DF command line. Compiler options must precede the /LINK option.

Unless you specify certain options, the DF command line will both compile and link the files you specify. To compile without linking, specify the /compile_only (or equivalent) option.

After the /LINK option on the DF command line, you can specify *linker options*. Linker options and any libraries specified get passed directly to the linker, such as /NODEFAULTLIB. If you choose to use separate compile and link commands, you can also specify linker options on a separate LINK command.

This chapter contains the following topics:

▶ Section 4.1 Compiler Options

▶ Section 4.2 Linker Options and Related information

▶ Section 4.3 Microsoft Fortran PowerStation Command-Line Compatibility

4.1   Compiler Options

This section describes the compiler options and how they are used. It includes the following topics:

▶ Section 4.1.1 Categories of Compiler Options, according to functional grouping.

▶ Section 4.1.2 through Section 4.1.81 are descriptions of each compiler option, listed alphabetically.

4.1.1   Categories of Compiler Options

If you will be using the compiler and linker from the command line, specify the options needed on the DF command line (as described in Chapter 3 Using the Compiler and Linker from the Command Line). You can use the functional categories of options below to locate the options needed for your application.

If you will be using the compiler and linker from the Microsoft visual development environment, select the options needed by using the various tabs in the Project menu Settings item (see Chapter 2 Building Programs and Libraries). Figure 4-1 shows a sample Fortran tab.

The options are grouped under functional categories (the initial Category is General, as shown) to help you locate the options needed for your application. From the Fortran tab, you can select one of the following categories from the Category drop-down list (exception: Miscellaneous Linker Tab and Command-line Only category):

▶ General

▶ Code Generation

▶ Compatibility

▶ Compilation Diagnostics

▶ Debug

▶ External Procedures

▶ Floating Point

▶ Fortran Data

▶ Fortran Language

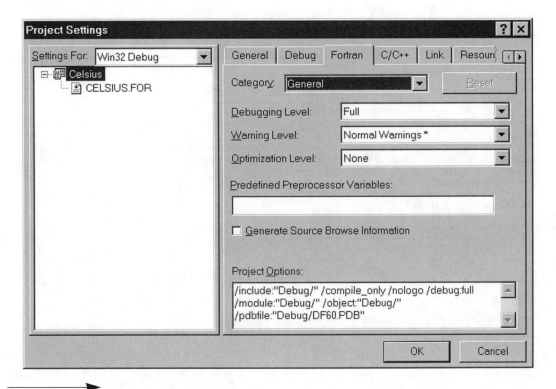

Figure 4–1 *Project Settings, Fortran Tab*

- ▶ Libraries
- ▶ Listing Files
- ▶ Miscellaneous Linker Tab and Command-line Only
- ▶ Optimizations
- ▶ Preprocessor
- ▶ Run time

If a compiler option is not available in the dialog boxes, you can enter the option in the lower part of the Project Settings dialog box just as you would at the command line (under Project Options:).

Table 4-1 lists the Visual Fortran compiler options by category in the Fortran tab.

Table 4–1 *Categories of Compiler Options*

General-Purpose Options	
Debugging Level	/[no]debug
Warning Level	/warn
Optimization Level	/[no]optimize
Predefined Preprocessor Symbols	/define
Generate Source Browse Information	/[no]browser[:*file*]
Code Generation Options	
Generate Most-Optimized Code	/[no]fast
Enable Recursive Routines	/[no]recursive
Object text *string* inserted into object file	/bintext:*string*
Math Library: Checking or Fast Performance	/math_library
Generate Code for *xxx* Chip	/architecture
Compatibility Options	
Unformatted File Conversion(Nonnative Data)	/convert (also see /assume:[no]byterecl)
Enable VMS Compatibility	/[no]vms
Enable F77 Run-Time Compatibility	/[no]f77rtl
Use F77 Integer Constants	/[no]intconstant
Microsoft Fortran PowerStation V4 Compatibility Options	/[no]fpscomp (various keywords listed below)
Microsoft Fortran PowerStation: Filenames from Command Line	/fpscomp:[no]filesfromcmd
Microsoft Fortran PowerStation: I/O Format	/fpscomp:[no]ioformat
Microsoft Fortran PowerStation: Libraries	/fpscomp:[no]libs
Microsoft Fortran PowerStation: Logical Values	/fpscomp:[no]logicals
Microsoft Fortran PowerStation: Other Run-time Behavior	/fpscomp:[no]general
Microsoft Fortran PowerStation: Predefined Preprocessor Symbols	/fpscomp:[no]symbols
See also Fortran Data in this table.	
Compilation Diagnostic Options	
Compilation Error Limit	/[no]error_limit
Warning Levels (Ignore, Normal, Treat Warnings as Errors)	/warn:nogeneral, default settings, or /warn:errors
Fortran Standards Checking (None, Fortran 90, or Fortran 95)	/stand:*keyword*
Treat Fortran Standard Warnings as Errors	/warn:[no]stderrors

Table 4–1 *Categories of Compiler Options (Continued)*

Argument Mismatch	/warn:[no]argument_checking
Data Alignment	/warn:[no]alignments
Inform when Compiling Files Separately (effect on interprocedure optimization)	/warn:[no]fileopt
Truncated Source	/warn:[no]truncated_source
Uncalled Routines	/warn:[no]uncalled
Undeclared Variables/Symbols	/warn:[no]declarations
Uninitialized Variables	/warn:[no]uninitialized
Unused Variables	/warn:[no]unused
Usage (Fortran language)	/warn:[no]usage
Data granularity	/warn:[no]granularity (Alpha only; command line only)

Debug Options

Debugging Level (None, Minimal, Partial, Full)	/[no]debug
Compile Lines with D in Column 1	/[no]d_lines
Use Program Database for Debug Information and File Name	/[no]pdbfile[:*file*]

External Procedures (and Argument Passing) Options

Argument Passing Conventions	/[no]iface:*keyword*
External Names Case Interpretation	/names:keyword
String Length Argument Passing	/[no]iface:mixed_str_len_arg
Append Underscore to External Names	/assume:[no]underscore

Floating-Point Options

Rounding Mode	/rounding_mode (Alpha only)
Floating-Point Exception Handling	/fpe
Enable Synchronous Floating-Point Exceptions	/[no]synchronous_exceptions (Alpha only)
Enable Floating-Point Consistency	/[no]fltconsistency (x86 only)
Extend Precision of Single-Precision Constants	/[no]fpconstant
Enable IEEE Minus Zero Support	/assume:[no]minus0

See also Optimizations in this table.

Table 4–1 *Categories of Compiler Options (Continued)*

Fortran Data Options	
Default REAL and COMPLEX Kind	/real_size:*num*
Default INTEGER and LOGICAL Kind	/integer_size:*num*
Append Underscore to External Names (under Data Options)	/assume:[no]underscore
Enable Dummy Arguments Sharing Memory Locations	/assume:[no]dummy_aliases
Extend Precision of Single-Precision Constants	/[no]fpconstant
Use Bytes as RECL= Unit for Unformatted Files	/assume:[no]byterecl
Variables Default to Automatic or Static Storage	/[no]automatic or /[no]static
Common Element Alignment	/[no]alignment:[no]common
Structure Element Alignment (Derived Type and Record Data)	/alignment:[no]records
Thread Access Granularity	/granularity (Alpha only)
See also Compatibility in this table.	
Fortran Language Options	
Enable FORTRAN 66 Semantics	/[no]f66
Enable Alternate PARAMETER Syntax	/[no]altparam
Name Case Interpretation	/names:*keyword*
Source Form (File Extension, Fixed Form, or Free Form)	/[no]free or /[no]fixed
Fixed-Form Line Length	/[no]extend_source
Pad Fixed-Form Source Records	/[no]pad_source
Library Options	
Use Multi-Threaded Library	/[no]threads
Enable Reentrancy Support	/[no]reentrancy
Use Fortran Run-Time Libraries	/libs:*keyword*
Use Debug C Libraries	/[no]dbglibs
Use Common Windows Libraries	/winapp
Disable Default Library Search Rules	/libdir:noauto
Disable OBJCOMMENT Library Names in Object	/libdir:nouser
See also External Procedures in this table.	
Listing and Assembly File Options	
Source Listing	/[no]list

Table 4–1 *Categories of Compiler Options (Continued)*

Contents of Source Listing File	/show:*keyword*... or /[no]machine_code
Assembly Listing	/[no]asmfile [:*file*] and /[no]asmattributes
Optimization Options	
Optimization Level	/[no]optimize
Variables Default to Automatic Storage	/[no]automatic
Enable Dummy Arguments Sharing Memory Locations	/assume:[no]dummy_aliases
Assume Floating-Point Consistency	/[no]fltconsistency (x86 only)
Transform Loops	/[no]transform_loops
Loop Unrolling	/unroll
Math Library: Checking or Fast Performance	/math_library
Inlining Procedures	/[no]inline
Code Tuning for *x86* or Alpha Chip	/tune
Allow Reordering of Floating-Point Operations	/assume:[no]accuracy_sensitive
Software Instruction Scheduling	/[no]pipeline (Alpha only; command line only)
Preprocessor Options	
Define Preprocessor Symbols	/define
Default INCLUDE and USE Path	/assume:[no]source_include
Module path (to place module files)	/module[:*file*]
INCLUDE and USE Path	/[no]include
Use FPP	/fpp
Predefined Preprocessor Symbols to FPP Only	/nodefine
Run-Time Options	
Generate Traceback Information	/[no]traceback
Array and String Bounds	/check:[no]bounds
Integer Overflow	/check:[no]overflow
Floating-Point Underflow	/check:[no]underflow
Power Operations	/check:[no]power
Edit Descriptor Data Type	/check:[no]format
Flawed Pentium® Chip	/check:[no]flawed_pentium (*x86* only)
Edit Descriptor Data Size	/check:[no]output_conversion

→ **Table 4–1** *Categories of Compiler Options (Continued)*

Enable Synchronous Exceptions	/[no]synchronous_exceptions (Alpha only)
Miscellaneous Linker Tab and Command-Line Options	
Specify Linker Options (after /link)	/link (use Linker tab)
Generate Link Map	/[no]map (use Linker tab)
Compile, Do Not Link	/compile_only or /c (use Compile in Build menu)
Create Dynamic Link Library (DLL project type)	/dll and Section 3.5 Specifying Project Types with DF Command Options
Software Instruction Scheduling	/[no]pipeline (Alpha only; command line only)
Display Help Text File	/help or /? (command line only)
Specify Custom File Extension for Compiler	/source (command line only)
Specify Custom File Extension for Compiler	/extfor (command line only)
Specify Custom File Extension for Linker	/extlnk (command line only)
Create one object file for each input source file	/[no]keep (command line only)
Name of Executable Program or DLL File	/[no]exe[:*file*] (command line only)
Name of Object File	/[no]object[:*file*] (command line only)
Perform Syntax Check Only (No Object File)	/[no]syntax_only (command line only)
Display Copyright and Compiler Version	/nologo and /what (command line only)
Display Compilation Details	/[no]watch (command line only)
Write C-Style Comments for FPP	/comments (command line only; for FPP)
Specify Custom File Extension for Preprocessor	/extfpp (command line only)
Only Preprocess FPP Files	/preprocess_only (command line only)
Undefine Preprocessor Symbols	/undefine (command line only)

For a table of DF command options listed alphabetically, see Section 3.1 The Format of the DF Command.

4.1.2   /[no]alignment

Syntax:

/alignment[:*keyword...*], /noalignment, or /Zp*n*

The /alignment option specifies the alignment of data items in common blocks, record structures, and derived-type structures. The /Zp*n* option specifies the alignment of data items in derived-type or record structures.

The /alignment options are:

▶ /align:[no]commons

The /align:commons option aligns the data items of all **COMMON** data blocks on natural boundaries up to four bytes. The default is /align: nocommons (unless /fast is specified), which does not align data blocks on natural boundaries. In the Microsoft visual development environment, specify the Common Element Alignment as 4 in the Fortran Data Compiler Option Category.

▶ /align:dcommons

The /align:dcommons option aligns the data items of all **COMMON** data blocks on natural boundaries up to eight bytes. The default is /align: nocommons (unless /fast is specified), which does not align data blocks on natural boundaries. In the visual development environment, specify the Common Element Alignment as 8 in the Fortran Data Compiler Option Category.

▶ /align:[no]records

The /align:records option (the default, unless you specify the /vms option) requests that components of derived types and fields of records be aligned on natural boundaries up to 8 bytes. The /align:norecords option (the default if the /vms option is specified) requests that components and fields be aligned on arbitrary byte boundaries, instead of on natural boundaries up to 8 bytes. In the visual development environment, specify the Structure Element Alignment in the Fortran Data Compiler Option Category.

▶ /align:rec$N$byte or /Zpn

The /align:rec$N$byte or /Zpn options request that fields of records and components of derived types be aligned on the smaller of:

• The size byte boundary (N) specified.

• The boundary that will naturally align them.

Specifying /align:rec$N$byte, /Zpn, or /align:[no]records does not affect whether common block fields are naturally aligned or packed. In the visual development environment, specify the Structure Element Alignment in the Fortran Data Compiler Option Category.

Table 4-2 shows equivalent alignment options.

Table 4–2 *Equivalent Options (Alignment)*

Specifying	Is the Same as Specifying
/Zp	/alignment:records or /align:rec8byte
/Zp1	/alignment:norecords or /align:rec1byte
/Zp2	/align:rec2byte
/Zp4	/align:rec4byte
/alignment	/Zp8 with /align:dcommons, /alignment:all, or /alignment:(dcommons,records)
/noalignment	/Zp1, /alignment:none, or /alignment:(nocommons,nodcommons,norecords)
/align:rec1byte	/align:norecords
/align:rec8byte	/align:records

When you omit the /alignment option, records and components of derived types are naturally aligned, but fields in common blocks are packed. This default is equivalent to:

```
/alignment=(nocommons,nodcommons,records)
```

Note that records and record structures are Digital Fortran language extensions.

For more information on the Fortran Data Compiler Option Category, see Section 4.1.1 Categories of Compiler Options.

4.1.3   /[no]altparam

Syntax:

/altparam, /noaltparam, /4Yaltparam, or /4Naltparam

The /altparam option determines how the compiler will treat the alternate syntax for **PARAMETER** statements, which is:

PARAMETER par1=exp1 [, par2=exp2...]

This form does not have parentheses around the assignment of the constant to the parameter name. With this form, the type of the parameter is determined by the type of the expression being assigned to it and not by any implicit typing.

In the visual development environment, specify the Enable Alternate PARAMETER Syntax in the Fortran Language Compiler Option Category (see Section 4.1.1 Categories of Compiler Options).

When the /[no]altparam or equivalent options are not specified, the compiler default will be to allow the alternate syntax for **PARAMETER** statements (/altparam).

To disallow use of this form, specify /noaltparam or /4Naltparam. To allow use of this form, allow the default or specify /altparam or /4Yaltparam.

4.1.4   /architecture

Syntax:

/architecture:*keyword*

The /architecture (/arch) option controls the types of processor-specific instructions generated for this program unit. The /arch:*keyword* option uses the same keywords as the /tune:*keyword* option.

All processors of a certain architecture type (Alpha or *x*86) implement a core set of instructions. Certain (more recent) processor versions include additional instruction extensions.

Whereas the /tune:*keyword* option is primarily used by certain higher-level optimizations for instruction scheduling purposes, the /arch:*keyword* option determines the type of machine-code instructions generated for the program unit being compiled.

In the visual development environment, specify the Generate Code For in the Code Generation Compiler Option Category (see Section 4.1.1 Categories of Compiler Options).

For *x*86 systems, the supported /arch keywords are:

▶ /arch:generic

Generates code (sometimes called blended code) that is appropriate for processor generations for the architecture type in use. This is the default. Programs compiled on an *x*86 system with the generic keyword will run on all *x*86 (486, 586, and 686) systems.

▶ /arch:host

Generates code for the processor generation in use on the system being used for compilation. Depending on the host system used on *x*86 systems, the program may or may not run on other *x*86 systems:

• Programs compiled on a 486 system with the host keyword will run on all *x*86 systems.

• Programs compiled on a 586 (Pentium®) system with the host keyword should *not* be run on 486 systems.

- Programs compiled on a 686 (Pentium Pro™ or Pentium II) system with the host keyword should *not* be run on 486 or 586 systems.

▶ /arch:p5

Generates code for the 586 (Pentium) processor systems. Programs compiled with the p5 keyword will run correctly on 586 and 686 processors, but should *not* be run on 486 processors. /arch:p6

▶ /arch:p6

Generates code for the 686 (Pentium Pro and Pentium II) processor systems only. Programs compiled with the p6 keyword will run correctly on 686 processors, but should *not* be run on 486 or 586 processors.

For Alpha systems, the supported /arch keywords are:

▶ /arch:generic

Generates code that is appropriate for processor generations for the architecture type in use. This is the default. Programs compiled on Alpha systems with the generic keyword will run on all implementations of the Alpha architecture type.

▶ /arch:host

Generates code for the processor generation in use on the system being used for compilation. Depending on the host system used on Alpha systems, the program may or may not run on other Alpha processor generations:

- Programs compiled on an ev4 or ev5 chip Alpha system with the host keyword will run on all Alpha processor generations.

- Programs compiled on an ev56 chip system with the host keyword should *not* be run on ev4 and ev5 processors.

- Programs compiled on a pca56 chip system with the host keyword should *not* be run on ev4, ev5, or ev56 processors.

- Programs compiled on a ev6 chip system with the host keyword should *not* be run on ev4, ev5, ev56, or pca56 processors.

▶ /arch:ev4

Generates code for the 21064, 21064A, 21066, and 21068 implementations of the Alpha architecture. Programs compiled with the ev4 keyword will run on all Alpha processor generations.

▶ /arch:ev5

Generates code for the 21164 chip implementations of the Alpha architecture that use only the base set of Alpha instructions (no extensions).

Programs compiled with the ev5 keyword will run on all Alpha processor generations.

▶ /arch:ev56

Generates code for the 21164 chip implementations that use the byte and word manipulation instruction extensions of the Alpha architecture. Programs compiled with the ev56 keyword will run correctly on ev56 and pca56 processors, but should *not* be run on ev4 and ev5 processors.

▶ /arch:pca56

Generates code for the 21164PC chip implementation that uses the byte and word manipulation instruction extensions and multimedia instruction extensions of the Alpha architecture. Programs compiled with the pca56 keyword will run correctly on pca56 processors, but should *not* be run on ev4, ev5, or ev56 processors.

▶ /arch:ev6

Generates code for the 21264 chip implementation that uses the following instruction extensions of the Alpha architecture: byte and word manipulation, multimedia, square root and floating-point convert, and count extension. Programs compiled with the ev6 keyword will run correctly on ev6 processors, but should *not* be run on ev4, ev5, ev56, or pca56 processors.

For information about timing program execution, see Section 6.2 Analyze Program Performance.

4.1.5   /[no]asmattributes

Syntax:

/asmattributes:*keyword*, /noasmattributes, /FA, /FAs, /FAc, or /FAcs

The /asmattributes option indicates what information, in addition to the assembly code, should be generated in the assembly listing file.

In the visual development environment, specify Assembly Options in the Listing File Compiler Option Category (see Section 4.1.1 Categories of Compiler Options). The /asmattributes options are:

▶ /asmattributes:source or /FAs

Intersperses the source code as comments in the assembly listing file.

▶ /asmattributes:machine or /FAc

Lists the hex machine instructions at the beginning of each line of assembly code.

▶ /asmattributes:all or /FAcs

Intersperses both the source code as comments and lists the hex machine instructions at the beginning of each line of assembly code. This is equivalent to /asmattributes.

▶ /asmattributes:none or /FA

Provides neither interspersed source code comments nor a listing of hex machine instructions. This is equivalent to /noasmattributes.

If you omit the /asmattributes option, /asmattributes:none is used (default).

The /asmattributes option is ignored if the /[no]asmfile[:file] option is *not* specified. The /FA, /FAs, /FAc, or /FAcs options can be used without the /[no]asmfile[:file] option.

4.1.6   /[no]asmfile

Syntax:

/asmfile[:*file*], /noasmfile, /Fa[*file*], /Fc[*file*], /Fl[*file*], or /Fs[*file*]

The /asmfile option or equivalent /F*x* option indicates that an assembly listing file should be generated. If the *file* is not specified, the default filename used will be the name of the source file with an extension of .asm.

In the visual development environment, specify Assembly Listing in the Listing File Compiler Option Category (see Section 4.1.1 Categories of Compiler Options).

When the /asmfile option or equivalent /F*x*[*file*] option is specified and there are multiple source files being compiled, each source file will be compiled separately. Compiling source files separately turns off interprocedural optimization from being performed.

When you specify /noasmfile or the /asmfile option is not specified, the compiler does not generate any assembly files.

To specify the content of the assembly listing file, also specify /[no]asm attributes:*keyword* or specify the /F*x*[*file*] options:

▶ /FA[*file*] provides neither interspersed source code comments nor a listing of hex machine instructions.

▶ /FAs[*file*] provides interspersed source code as comments in the assembly listing file.

▶ /FAc[*file*] provides a list of hex machine instructions at the beginning of each line of assembly code.

▶ /FAcs[*file*] provides interspersed source code as comments and lists hex machine instructions at the beginning of each line of assembly code.

4.1.7   /assume

Syntax:

/assume:*keyword*

The /assume option specifies assumptions made by the Fortran syntax analyzer, optimizer, and code generator.

The /assume options are:

▶ /assume:[no]accuracy_sensitive

Specifying /assume:noaccuracy_sensitive allows the compiler to reorder code based on algebraic identities (inverses, associativity, and distribution) to improve performance. In the visual development environment, specify Allow Reordering of Floating-Point Operations in the Optimizations Compiler Option Category.

The numeric results can be slightly different from the default (/assume: accuracy_sensitive) because of the way intermediate results are rounded.

Numeric results with /assume:noaccuracy_sensitive are not categorically less accurate. They can produce more accurate results for certain floating-point calculations, such as dot product summations. For example, the following expressions are mathematically equivalent but may not compute the same value using finite precision arithmetic:

```
X = (A + B) - C
X = A + (B - C)
```

If you omit /assume:noaccuracy_sensitive and omit /fast, the compiler uses a limited number of rules for calculations, which might prevent some optimizations.

If you specify /assume:noaccuracy_sensitive, or if you specify /fast and omit /assume:accuracy_sensitive, the compiler can reorder code based on algebraic identities to improve performance.

For more information on /assume:noaccuracy_sensitive, see Section 6.8.4 Arithmetic Reordering Optimizations.

▶ /assume:[no]buffered_io

The /assume:buffered_io option controls whether records are written (flushed) to disk as each record is written (default) or accumulated in the buffer.

For disk devices, /assume:buffered_io (or the equivalent **OPEN** statement BUFFERED='YES' specifier) requests that the internal buffer will be filled, possibly by many record output statements (**WRITE**), before it is written to disk by the Fortran run-time system. If a file is opened for direct access, I/O buffering will be ignored.

Using buffered writes usually makes disk I/O more efficient by writing larger blocks of data to the disk less often. However, if you specified /assume:buffered_io or BUFFERED='YES', records not yet written to disk may be lost in the event of a system failure.

The default is BUFFERED='NO' and /assume:nobuffered_io for all I/O, in which case, the Fortran run-time system empties its internal buffer for each **WRITE** (or similar record output statement).

The **OPEN** statement BUFFERED specifier takes precedence over the /assume:[no] buffered_io option.

In the visual development environment, specify the Enable I/O Buffering in the Optimizations Compiler Option Category.

For more information on /assume:buffered_io, see Section 6.5.7 Efficient Use of Record Buffers and Disk I/O.

▶ /assume:[no]byterecl

The /assume:byterecl option applies only to unformatted files. In the visual development environment, specify the Use Bytes as Unit for Unformatted Files in the Fortran Data Compiler Option Category. Specifying the /assume:byterecl option:

- Indicates that the units for an explicit **OPEN** statement RECL specifier value are in bytes.

- Forces the record length value returned by an **INQUIRE** by output list to be in byte units.

Specifying /assume:nobyterecl indicates that the units for RECL values with unformatted files are in four-byte (longword) units. This is the default.

▶ /assume:[no]dummy_aliases

Specifying the /assume:dummy aliases option *requires* that the compiler assume that dummy (formal) arguments to procedures share memory locations with other dummy arguments or with variables shared through use association, host association, or common block use. The default is /assume:nodummy_aliases.

In the visual development environment, specify Enable Dummy Argument Aliasing in the Fortran Data (or Optimizations) Compiler Option Category.

These program semantics do not strictly obey the Fortran 90 Standard and they slow performance. If you omit /assume:dummy_aliases, the compiler does not need to make these assumptions, which results in better run-time performance. However, omitting /assume:dummy_aliases can cause some programs that depend on such aliases to fail or produce wrong answers.

You only need to compile the called subprogram with /assume: dummy_aliases.

If you compile a program that uses dummy aliasing with /assume: nodummy_aliases in effect, the run-time behavior of the program will be unpredictable. In such programs, the results will depend on the exact optimizations that are performed. In some cases, normal results will occur; however, in other cases, results will differ because the values used in computations involving the offending aliases will differ.

For more information, see Section 6.8.5 Dummy Aliasing Assumption.

▶ /assume:[no]minus0

This option controls whether the compiler uses Fortran 95 standard semantics for the IEEE floating-point value of -0.0 (minus zero) in the **SIGN** intrinsic, if the processor is capable of distinguishing the difference between -0.0 and +0.0. The default is /assume:nominus0, which uses Fortran 90 and FORTRAN 77 semantics where the value -0.0 or +0.0 in the **SIGN** function is treated as 0.0.

To request Fortran 95 semantics to allow use of the IEEE value -0.0 in the **SIGN** intrinsic, specify /assume:minus0.

In the visual development environment, specify Enable IEEE Minus Zero Support in the Floating Point Compiler Option Category.

▶ /assume:[no]source_include

This option controls the directory searched for module files specified by a **USE** statement or source files specified by an **INCLUDE** statement:

- Specifying /assume:source_include requests a search for module or include files in the directory where the source file being compiled resides. This is the default.

- Specifying /assume:nosource_include requests a search for module or include files in the current (default) directory.

In the visual development environment, specify the Default INCLUDE and USE Paths in the Preprocessor Compiler Option Category.

▶ /assume:[no]underscore

Specifying /assume:underscore option controls the appending of an underscore character to external user-defined names: the main program name, named **COMMON**, **BLOCK DATA**, and names implicitly or explicitly declared **EXTERNAL**. The name of blank **COMMON** remains _BLNK__, and Fortran intrinsic names are not affected.

In the visual development environment, specify Append Underscore to External Names in the External Procedures (or Fortran Data) Compiler Option Category.

Specifying /assume:nounderscore option does not append an underscore character to external user-defined names. This is the default.

For example, the following command requests the noaccuracy_sensitive and nosource_include keywords and accepts the defaults for the other /assume keywords:

```
df /assume:(noaccuracy_sensitive,nosource_include)
testfile.f90
```

4.1.8   /[no]automatic

Syntax:

/automatic, /noautomatic, /4Ya, or /4Na

The /automatic or /4Ya option requests that local variables be put on the run-time stack. In the visual development environment, specify Variables Default to Automatic in the Fortran Data (or Optimizations) Compiler Option Category.

The /noautomatic or /4Na option is the same as the /static option. The default is /noautomatic or /4Na, which causes all local variables to be statically allocated.

If you specify /recursive, the /automatic (/4Ya) option is set.

For more information on the various compiler option categories in the visual development environment, see Section 4.1.1 Categories of Compiler Options.

4.1.9   /bintext

Syntax:

/bintext:*string* or /V*string*

Specifying /bintext (or /V) places the text *string* specified into the object file (.OBJ) being generated by the compiler. This *string* also gets propagated into the executable file. For example, the string might contain version number or copyright information.

In the visual development environment, specify Object Text in the Code Generation Compiler Option Category.

If the string contains a space or tab, the string must be enclosed by double quotation marks ("). A backslash (\) must precede any double quotation marks contained within the string.

If the command line contains multiple /bintext or /V options, the last (right-most) one is used. You can specify /nobintext to override previous /bintext or /V options on the same command line.

4.1.10 /[no]browser

Syntax:

/browser[:*filename*], /nobrowser, or /FR

The /browser or /FR option controls the generation of source browser information. When the /browser option is not specified, the compiler will not generate browser files (same as /nobrowser).

In the visual development environment, specify Generate Source Browse Information in the General Compiler Option Category. Also, in the BrowseInfo tab, set Build Browse info check box instead of using BCS MAKE.

Browser information includes:

▶ Information about all the symbols in the source file

▶ The source code line in which a symbol is defined

▶ Each source code line where there is a reference to a symbol

▶ The relationships between calling functions and called functions

The default extension for source browser files is .SBR.

The browser output is intended to be used as input to the Browse Information File Maintenance Utility (BSCMAKE), which generates a browse information file (.BSC) that can be examined in browse windows in the Microsoft visual development environment.

Instead of using BCSMAKE, you can use the Project Settings dialog box in the visual development environment:

▶ Click the BrowseInfo tab.

▶ Set the Build browse info file check box.

When the /browser or /FR option is specified and there are multiple source files being compiled, each source file will be compiled separately. Compiling source files separately turns off interprocedural optimizations.

For more information on the various compiler option categories in the visual development environment, see Section 4.1.1 Categories of Compiler Options.

4.1.11 /[no]check

Syntax:

/check:*keyword*, /nocheck, /4Yb, /4Nb

The /check, /4Yb, or /4Nb option controls whether extra code is generated for certain run-time checking. Run-time checks can result in issuing run-time messages for certain conditions.

In the visual development environment, specify the Run-time Error Checking items in the Run-time Compiler Option Category.

The /check keywords and /4Yb, and /4Nb options are:

▶ /check:bounds (Array and String bounds)

Requests a run-time error message if a reference to an array subscript or character substring is outside of the declared bounds. The default for the command line and the release configuration (visual development environment) is /check:nobounds, which does not issue a run-time message for this condition. The default for the debug configuration is /check:bounds, which issues a run-time message for an out-of-bounds array subscript or character substring.

If you specify /check:bounds on an Alpha system, consider specifying either /synchronous_exceptions or a /fpe:*n* value other than /fpe:0 (/fpe:0 is the default for Alpha systems).

▶ /check:flawed_pentium (*x*86 systems)

On *x*86 systems, requests a run-time error message if a flawed Pentium® processor is detected. The default is /check:flawed_pentium, which *does* issue a run-time error message for this condition and stops program execution. To allow program execution to continue when this condition occurs, set the environment variable FOR_RUN_FLAWED_PENTIUM to true and rerun the program (see Section 21.5 Run-Time Environment Variables).

For more information on the Pentium flaw, see Section 22.5 Intel Pentium Floating-Point Flaw. You can also use the **FOR_CHECK_FLAWED_PENTIUM** routine.

▶ /check:format (Edit Descriptor Data Type)

Requests a run-time error message when the data type for an item being formatted for output does not match the FORMAT descriptor. Specifying /check:noformat suppresses the run-time error message for this condition.

▶ /check:output_conversion (Edit Descriptor Data Size)

Requests a run-time message (number 63) when format truncation occurs (when a number is too large to fit in the specified format field length without loss of significant digits). Specifying /check:nooutput_conversion does not display the message when format truncation occurs.

▶ /check:overflow (Integer Overflow)

Requests a continuable run-time message when integer overflow occurs. Specifying /check:nooverflow suppresses the run-time message.

▶ /check:[no]power (Power Operations)

Specifying /check:nopower suppresses the run-time error message for 0.0 ** 0.0 and `negative-value ** integer-value-of-type-real`, so 0.0 ** 0.0 is 1.0 and (-3.0) ** 3.0 is -27.0.

If you *omit* the /math_library:fast and /fast options:

- On *x*86 systems, the default is /check:nopower (suppress the run-time error message). You can specify check:power to allow a run-time error message to be issued for this type of expression.

- On Alpha systems, the default is /check:power, which allows a run-time error message to be issued for this type of expression. You can specify /check:nopower to suppress the run-time error message.

If you *specify* either the /math_library:fast or /fast option:

- On *x*86 systems, /check:nopower is always used (suppresses the run-time error message).

- On Alpha systems, the default is /check:power, which issues a run-time error message for this type of expression. You can specify check:nopower to suppress the run-time error message.

▶ /check:underflow

Requests an informational run-time message when floating-point under-flow occurs. Specifying /check:nounderflow suppresses a run-time message when floating-point underflow occurs.

▶ /4Yb

Sets /check:(overflow,bounds,underflow).

▶ /check:none, /nocheck, or /4Nb

Equivalent to: /check:(nobounds,noformat,nopower,nooutput_conversion, nooverflow,nounderflow).

▶ /check or /check:all

Equivalent to: /check:(bounds,flawed_pentium,format,power,output_ conversion,overflow,underflow).

On *x*86 systems, if you omit these options, the default is:

/check:(nobounds,flawed_pentium,noformat,nopower,nooutput_ conversion,nooverflow,nounderflow).

On Alpha systems, if you omit these options, the default is:

/check:(nobounds,noformat,power,nooutput_conversion,nooverflow, nounderflow).

When using the visual development environment debug configuration, the default for bounds checking changes from /check:nobounds to /check: bounds.

For more information on the various compiler option categories in the visual development environment, see Section 4.1.1 Categories of Compiler Options.

4.1.12 /[no]comments

Syntax:

/comments or /nocomments

The /comments option writes C-style comments to the output file. The /nocomments option does not write C-style comments to the output file. This option applies only to the FPP preprocessor.

For more information, type FPP /? to view FPP options.

4.1.13 /[no]compile_only

Syntax:

/compile_only, /nocompile_only, or /c

The /compile_only or /c option suppresses linking. The default is /nocompile_only (perform linking).

If you specify the /compile_only option at higher levels of optimization and also specify /object:*filename*, the /object:*filename* option causes multiple Fortran input files (if specified) to be compiled into a single object *file*. This allows interprocedural optimizations to occur.

However, if you use multiple source files and the /compile_only option without the /object:*file* option, multiple object files are created and interprocedural optimizations do not occur.

In the visual development environment, to compile (not link) a source file:

1. In the FileView pane, select (highlight) the file to be compiled

2. From the Build menu, select Compile *filename.xxx*

4.1.14 /convert

Syntax:

/convert:*keyword*

The /convert option specifies the format of unformatted files containing numeric data. On *x86* and Alpha systems, the format used in memory is always IEEE® little endian format. If you want to read and write unformatted data in IEEE little endian format, you do not need to convert your unformatted data and can omit this option (or specify /convert:native).

In the visual development environment, specify the Unformatted File Conversion in the Compatibility Compiler Option Category (see Section 4.1.1 Categories of Compiler Options).

The /convert options are:

▶ /convert:big_endian

   Specifies that unformatted files containing numeric data are in IEEE big endian (nonnative) format. The resulting program will read and write unformatted files containing numeric data assuming the following:

   • Big endian integer format (**INTEGER** declarations of the appropriate size).

- Big endian IEEE floating-point formats (**REAL** and **COMPLEX** declarations of the appropriate size).

▶ /convert:cray

Specifies that unformatted files containing numeric data are in CRAY® (nonnative) big endian format. The resulting program will read and write unformatted files containing numeric data assuming the following:

- Big endian integer format (**INTEGER** declarations of the appropriate size).

- Big endian CRAY® proprietary floating-point formats (**REAL** and **COMPLEX** declarations of the appropriate size).

▶ /convert:ibm

Specifies that unformatted files containing numeric data are in IBM® (nonnative) big endian format. The resulting program will read and write unformatted files containing numeric data assuming the following:

- Big endian integer format (**INTEGER** declarations of the appropriate size).

- Big endian IBM proprietary floating-point formats (**REAL** and **COMPLEX** declarations of the appropriate size).

▶ /convert:little_endian

Specifies that numeric data in unformatted files is in native little endian integer format and IEEE little endian floating-point format (same as used in memory), as follows:

- Integer data is in native little endian format.

- **REAL**(KIND=4) and **COMPLEX**(KIND=4) data is in IEEE little endian S_floating format.

- **REAL**(KIND=8) and **COMPLEX** (KIND=8) data is in IEEE little endian T_floating format.

▶ /convert:native

Specifies that numeric data in unformatted files is not converted. This is the default.

▶ /convert:vaxd

Specifies that numeric data in unformatted files is in VAXD little endian format, as follows:

- Integer data is in native little endian format.

- **REAL**(KIND=4) and **COMPLEX**(KIND=4) data is in VAX F_floating format.

- **REAL**(KIND=8) and **COMPLEX** (KIND=8) data is in VAX D_floating format.

▶ /convert:vaxg

Specifies that numeric data in unformatted files is in VAXG little endian format, as follows:

- Integer data is in native little endian format.

- **REAL**(KIND=4) and **COMPLEX**(KIND=4) data is in VAX F_floating format.

- **REAL**(KIND=8) and **COMPLEX**(KIND=8) data is in VAX G_floating format.

REAL(KIND=4) is single-precision real, **REAL**(KIND=8) is double-precision real (also known as the **DOUBLE PRECISION** data type). **COMPLEX**(KIND=8) is double complex (also known as the **DOUBLE COMPLEX** data type, a Digital Fortran language extension).

4.1.15   /[no]d_lines

Syntax:

/d_lines, /nod_lines, /4ccD, or /4ccd

The /d_lines, /4ccD, or /4ccd options indicate that lines in fixed-format files that contain a D in column 1 should be treated as source code. Specifying /nod_lines (the default) indicates that these lines are to be treated as comment lines.

In the visual development environment, specify Compile DEBUG (D) Lines in the Debug Compiler Option Category (see Section 4.1.1 Categories of Compiler Options).

The compiler does not support the use of characters other than a D or d with the /4cc*string* (see the dlines Sample program in . . . Samples\ Advanced\com).

4.1.16   /[no]dbglibs

Syntax:

/dbglibs or /nodbglibs

The /dbglibs option controls whether the debug version or the non-debug version of the C run-time library is linked against. The default is /nodbglibs, which will link against the non-debug version of the C library, even when /debug:full is specified.

If you specify /debug:full for an application that calls C library routines and you need to debug calls into the C library, you should also specify /dbglibs to request that the debug version of the library be linked against.

In the visual development environment, specify the Use Debug C Libraries in the Libraries Compiler Option Category (see Section 4.1.1 Categories of Compiler Options).

When you specify /dbglibs, the C debug library linked against depends on the specified /libs:*keyword* and /[no]threads options, and is one of: libcd.lib, libcmtd.lib, or msvcrtd.lib (see Section 18.4 Visual Fortran/Visual C++ Mixed-Language Programs).

4.1.17 /[no]debug

Syntax:

/debug:*keyword*, /nodebug, /Z7, /Zd, or /Zi

The /debug, /Z7, /Zd, or /Zi options control the level of debugging information associated with the program being compiled.

In the visual development environment, specify the Debugging Level in the General or Debug Compiler Option Category (see Section 4.1.1 Categories of Compiler Options).

The options are:

▶ /debug:none or /nodebug

If you specify /debug:none or /nodebug, the compiler produces no symbol table information needed for debugging or profiling. Only symbol information needed for linking (global symbols) is produced. The size of the resulting object module is the minimum size. If this option is specified, /debug:none is passed to the linker.

▶ /debug:minimal or /Zd

If you specify /debug:minimal or /Zd, the compiler produces minimal debug information, which allows global symbol table information needed for linking, but not local symbol table information needed for debugging. If /debug:minimal is specified, /debug:minimal and /debugtype:cv is passed to the linker.

If you omit the /[no]debug:*keyword*, /Z7, /Zd, and /Zi options, this is the default on the command line and for a release configuration in the visual development environment.

The /Zd option implies /nopdbfile and passes /debug:minimal /pdb: none /debugtype:cv to the linker.

The object module size is somewhat larger than if you specified /debug: none, but is smaller than if you specified /debug:full.

▶ /debug:partial

If you specify /debug:partial, the compiler produces debugging information to allow global symbol table information needed for linking, but not local symbol table information needed for debugging. If /debug:partial is specified, /debug:partial /debugtype:cv /pdb:none is passed to the linker.

The object module size is somewhat larger than if you specified /debug: none, but is smaller than if you specified /debug:full.

▶ /debug:full, /debug, /Zi, or /Z7

If you specify /debug:full, /debug, /Zi, or /Z7, the compiler produces symbol table information needed for full symbolic debugging of unoptimized code and global symbol information needed for linking. This is the default for a debug configuration in the visual development environment.

If you specify /debug:full for an application that make calls to C library routines and you need to debug calls into the C library, you should also specify /dbglibs to request that the appropriate C debug library be linked against.

The /Z7 option implies /nopdbfile and passes /debug:full /debug type:cv /pdb:none to the linker.

The /debug:full, /debug, and /Zi options imply /pdbfile and pass /debug: full and /debugtype:cv to the linker.

If you specify /debug (with no keyword), the default optimization level changes to /optimize:0 (instead of /optimize:4) for the DF command.

To request program counter run-time correlation to source file line numbers (full traceback) for severe run-time errrors, specify the /traceback option.

4.1.18 /define

Syntax:

/define:*symbol*[=*integer*]

The /define option defines the *symbol* specified for use with conditional compilation directives or the Fortran preprocessor, FPP. If a value is specified, it must be an *integer* value (unless you are only using FPP). If a value is not specified, 1 is assigned to *symbol*.

When only using the Fortran preprocessor FPP:

▶ The *integer* value specified by /define can be a character or integer value.

▶ To request that symbol values defined by /define apply only to FPP and are not seen by compiler directives, also specify /nodefine on the DF command line.

In the visual development environment, specify the Predefined Preprocessor Symbols in the General or Preprocessor Compiler Option Category (see Section 4.1.1 Categories of Compiler Options).

You can use the directives to detect symbol definitions, such as the **IF** Directive Construct. Like certain other compiler options, an equivalent directive exists (**DEFINE** directive).

Table 4-3 lists the preprocessor symbols that are predefined by the compiler system and are available to compiler directives and FPP (except _DF_VERSION_):

Table 4–3 *Predefined Preprocessor Symbols*

_DF_VERSION_= 600 (600 for Version 6.0; compiler only)	_WIN32=1 (always defined)
_X86_=1 (on *x*86 systems only)	_ALPHA_=1 (on Alpha systems only)
_WIN95=1 (on Windows 95 systems only)	_WIN98=1 (on Windows 98 systems only)
_MT=1 (only if /threads or /MT is specified)	_DLL=1 (only if /dll or /LD is specified)
MSFORTRAN=401 (only if /fpscomp:symbols is specified or you use the FL32 command)	

4.1.19 /dll

Syntax:

/dll[:*file*], /nodll, or /LD

The /dll or /LD option indicates that the program should be linked as a DLL file. The /dll or /LD option overrides any specification of the run-time routines to be used and activates the /libs:dll option. A warning is generated when the /libs=qwin or /libs=qwins option and /dll option are used together.

In the visual development environment, specify the project type as Fortran Dynamic Link Library (DLL).

If you omit *file*, the /dll or /LD option interacts with the /exe and the /Fe options, as follows:

▶ If neither /exe nor /Fe is specified, the first file name used on the command line is used with an extension of .DLL.

▶ If either /exe:*file* or /Fe*file* is specified with a *file* name, that name is used for the DLL file. If the specified file name does not end with a "." or have an extension, an extension of .DLL is added to it.

To request linking with multithreaded libraries, specify the /threads option.

For information about building DLL files from the visual development environment, see Section 2.2.6 Fortran Dynamic-Link Library Projects and Chapter 8 Creating Fortran DLLs.

For a list of Fortran PowerStation style options (such as /LD and /MDs) and their DF command equivalents, see Section 4.3.2 Equivalent Visual Fortran Compiler Options.

4.1.20   /[no]error_limit

Syntax:

/error_limit[:*count*] or /noerror_limit

The /error_limit option specifies the maximum number of error-level or fatal-level compiler errors allowed for a given file before compilation aborts. If you specify /noerror_limit (command line), there is no limit on the number of errors that are allowed.

In the visual development environment, specify the Compilation Error Limit in the Compilation Diagnostics Compiler Option Category (see Section 4.1.1 Categories of Compiler Options).

The default is /error_limit:30 or a maximum of 30 error-level and fatal-level messages. If the maximum number of errors is reached, a warning message is issued and the next file (if any) on the command line is compiled.

4.1.21   /[no]exe

Syntax:

/exe[:*file*], /noexe, or /Fe*file*

The /exe or /Fe option specifies the name of the executable program (EXE) or dynamic-link library (DLL) *file* being created. To request that a DLL be created instead of an executable program, specify the /dll option.

4.1.22 /[no]extend_source

Syntax:

/extend_source[:*size*], /noextend_source, or /4L*size*

The /extend_source or /4L*size* option controls the column used to end the statement field in fixed-format source files. When a size is specified, that will be the last column parsed as part of the statement field. Any columns after that will be treated as comments.

Specifying /extend_source (or /4L132 or /4L80) sets the /fixed option.

In the visual development environment, specify the Fixed-Form Line Length in the Fortran Language Compiler Option Category (see Section 4.1.1 Categories of Compiler Options). The following options are equivalent:

▶ /noextend_source, /extend_source:72, or /4L72 specify the last column as 72.

▶ /extend_source:80 or /4L80 specify the last column as 80.

▶ /extend_source, /extend_source:132, or /4L132 specify the last column as 132.

4.1.23 /extfor

Syntax:

/extfor:*ext*

The /extfor: option specifies file extensions to be processed (/extfor) by the Digital Fortran compiler. One or more file extensions can be specified. A leading period before each extension is optional (for and .for are equivalent).

4.1.24 /extfpp

Syntax:

/extfpp:*ext*

The /extfpp option specifies file extensions to be processed (/extfpp) by the FPP preprocessor. One or more file extensions can be specified. A leading period before each extension is optional (fpp and .fpp are equivalent).

4.1.25 /extlnk

Syntax:

/extlnk:*ext*

The /extlnk option specifies file extensions to be processed (/extlnk) by the linker. One or more file extensions can be specified. A leading period before each extension is optional (obj and .obj are equivalent).

4.1.26 /[no]f66

Syntax:

/f66 or /nof66

The /f66 option requests that the compiler select FORTRAN-66 interpretations in cases of incompatibility (default is /f66). Difference include the following:

▶ **DO** loops are always executed at least once

▶ FORTRAN-66 **EXTERNAL** statement syntax and semantics are allowed

▶ If the **OPEN** statement STATUS specifier is omitted, the default changes to STATUS='NEW' instead of STATUS='UNKNOWN'

▶ If the **OPEN** statement BLANK specifier is omitted, the default changes to BLANK='ZERO' instead of BLANK='NULL'

In the visual development environment, specify Enable FORTRAN-66 Semantics in the Fortran Language Compiler Option Category (see Section 4.1.1 Categories of Compiler Options).

4.1.27 /[no]f77rtl

Syntax:

/f77rtl or /nof77rtl

The /f77rtl option controls the run-time support that is used when a program is executed. Specifying /f77rtl uses the Digital Fortran 77 run-time behavior. In the visual development environment, specify Enable F77 Run-Time Compatibility in the Compatibility Compiler Option Category (see Section 4.1.1 Categories of Compiler Options).

Specifying /nof77rtl uses the Visual Fortran (Digital Fortran 90) run-time behavior. Unless you specify /f77rtl, /nof77rtl is used.

4.1.28 /fast

Syntax:

/fast

The /fast option sets several options that generate optimized code for fast run-time performance. Specifying this option is equivalent to specifying:

▶ /assume:noaccuracy_sensitive

▶ /math_library:fast (which changes the default of /check:[no]power)

▶ /alignment:(dcommons, records)

In the visual development environment, specify the Generate Most Optimized Code in the Code Generation Compiler Option Category (see Section 4.1.1 Categories of Compiler Options).

If you omit /fast, these performance-related options will not be set.

4.1.29 /[no]fixed

Syntax:

/fixed, /nofixed, /4Nf, or /4Yf

The /fixed or /4Nf option specifies that the source file should be interpreted as being in fixed-source format. Equivalent options are as follows:

▶ The /fixed, /nofree, and /4Nf options request fixed-source form.

▶ The /nofixed, /free, and /4Yf options request free-source form.

In the visual development environment, specify the Source Form in the Fortran Language Compiler Option Category (see Section 4.1.1 Categories of Compiler Options).

If you omit /[no]fixed, /4Nf, and /4Yf:

▶ Files with an extension of .f90 or .F90 are assumed to be free-format source files.

▶ Files with an extension of .f, .for, .FOR, or .i are assumed to be fixed-format files.

4.1.30 /[no]fltconsistency (x86 Only)

Syntax:

/fltconsistency, /nofltconsistency, or /Op

The /fltconsistency or /Op option enables improved floating-point consistency on x86 systems. Floating-point operations are not reordered and the result of each floating-point operation is stored into the target variable rather than being kept in the floating-point processor for use in a subsequent calculation. This option is ignored on Alpha systems.

In the visual development environment, specify Enable Floating-Point Consistency in the Floating Point Compiler Option Category (see Section 4.1.1 Categories of Compiler Options).

The default is /nofltconsistency, which provides better run-time performance at the expense of less consistent floating-point results.

4.1.31 /[no]fpconstant

Syntax:

/fpconstant or /nofpconstant

The /fpconstant option requests that a single-precision constant assigned to a double-precision variable be evaluated in double precision. If you omit /fpconstant (or specify the default /nofpconstant), a single-precision constant assigned to a double-precision variable is evaluated in single precision. The Fortran 90 standard requires that the constant be evaluated in single precision.

In the visual development environment, specify Extended Precision of Single-Precision Constants in the Floating Point (or Fortran Data) Compiler Option Category (see Section 4.1.1 Categories of Compiler Options).

Certain programs created for FORTRAN-77 compilers (including Digital Fortran 77) may show different floating-point results, because they rely on single-precision constants assigned to a double-precision variable to be evaluated in double precision.

In the following example, if you specify /fpconstant, identical values are assigned to D1 and D2. If you omit the /fpconstant option, the compiler will obey the standard and assign a less precise value to D1:

```
REAL (KIND=8) D1, D2
DATA D1 /2.71828182846182/     ! REAL (KIND=4) value expanded
                               ! to double
DATA D2 /2.71828182846182D0/   ! Double value assigned to
                               ! double
```

4.1.32 /fpe

Syntax:

/fpe:*level*

The /fpe:*level* option controls floating-point exception handling at run-time for the main program. This includes whether exceptional floating-point values are allowed and how precisely run-time exceptions are reported.

The /fpe:*level* option specifies how the compiler should handle the following floating-point exceptions:

▶ When floating-point calculations result in a divide by zero, overflow, or invalid data.

▶ When floating-point calculations result in an underflow operation.

▶ When a denormalized number or other exceptional number (positive infinity, negative infinity, or a NaN) is present in an arithmetic expression

For performance reasons:

▶ On *x*86 systems, the default is /fpe:3. Using /fpe:0 will slow run-time performance on *x*86 systems.

▶ On Alpha systems, the default is /fpe:0 (many programs do not need to handle denormalized numbers or other exceptional values). Using /fpe:3 will slow run-time performance on Alpha systems.

On Alpha systems, to associate an exception with the instruction that causes the exception, specify /fpe:3 or specify /synchronous_exceptions.

In the visual development environment, specify the Floating-Point Exception Handling in the Floating Point Compiler Option Category (see Section 4.1.1 Categories of Compiler Options).

Table 4-4 summarizes the /fpe:*level* options.

Table 4-4 *Summary of Floating-Point Exception Command Options*

Option	Handling of Underflow	Handling of Divide by Zero, Overflow, and Invalid Data Operation
/fpe:0 (default on Alpha systems)	Sets any calculated denormalized value (result) to zero and lets the program continue. A message is displayed only if /check:underflow is also specified. Any use of a denormalized number (non-finite data) in an arithmetic expression results in an invalid operation error and the program terminates.	Exceptional values are *not* allowed. The program terminates after displaying a message. The exception location is one or more instructions *after* the instruction that caused the exception, unless (on Alpha systems) /synchronous_exceptions was specified.
/fpe:1 (Alpha systems only)	Sets any calculated denormalized value (result) to zero and lets the program continue. A message is displayed only if /check:underflow is also specified. Use of a denormalized (or exceptional) number in an arithmetic expression results in program continuation, but with slower performance.	The program continues. No message is displayed. A NaN or Infinity (+ or -) will be generated.

Table 4–4 *Summary of Floating-Point Exception Command Options (Continued)*

Option	Handling of Underflow	Handling of Divide by Zero, Overflow, and Invalid Data Operation
/fpe:3 (default on x86 systems)	Leaves any calculated denormalized value as is. The program continues, allowing gradual underflow. Use of a denormalized (or exceptional) number in an arithmetic expression results in program continuation, but with slower performance. A message is displayed only if /check:underflow is also specified.	The program continues. No message is displayed. A NaN or Infinity (+ or -) will be generated.

The exception message reporting specified by the /fpe:*level* option applies only to the main program and cannot be changed during program execution.

When compiling different routines in a program separately, you should use the same /fpe:*level* value.

On *x*86 systems, for programs that flush denormalized values to zero (such as those that allow gradual underflow with /fpe:0), the impact on run-time performance can be significant. On Alpha systems, for programs that use a number of denormalized values (such as those that allow gradual underflow with /fpe:3), the impact on run-time performance can be significant.

On Alpha systems, if you use the /math_library:fast along with an /fpe:*level* option, the /fpe:*level* option is ignored when arithmetic values are evaluated by math library routines.

To help you debug a routine, you can associate an exception with the instruction that caused it by specifying /fpe:3, or, on Alpha systems, by specifying /fpe:0 with /synchronous_exceptions.

Table 4-5 describes how the /fpe option, /check:underflow option, and **MATHERRQQ** routine interact on *x*86 systems.

Table 4–5 *Interaction of Floating-Point Command Options and MATHERRQQ*

Specified /fpe:n Option	Was /check:underflow Specified?	Is a User-Written MATHERRQQ Routine Present?	Underflow Handling by the Visual Fortran Run-Time System on x86 Systems
/fpe:0	No	No	The underflowed result is set to zero (0). The program continues.
/fpe:0	No	Yes	The underflowed result is set to zero (0). The program continues.

Table 4–5 *Interaction of Floating-Point Command Options and MATHERRQQ (Continued)*

Specified /fpe:n Option	Was /check:underflow Specified?	Is a User-Written MATHERRQQ Routine Present?	Underflow Handling by the Visual Fortran Run-Time System on x86 Systems
/fpe:0	Yes	No	The underflowed result is set to zero (0). The program continues. The number of underflowed results are counted and messages are displayed for the first two occurrences.
/fpe:0	Yes	Yes	The underflowed result is set to zero (0). The program continues. The number of underflowed results are counted and messages are displayed for the first two occurrences.
/fpe:3	No	No	Denormalized results are allowed and the program continues. Traps are masked and no handlers are invoked.
/fpe:3	No	Yes	Denormalized results are allowed and the program continues. Traps are masked and no handlers are invoked.
/fpe:3	Yes	No	For Version 6.0, a fatal error results and the program terminates.
/fpe:3	Yes	Yes	Depends on the source causing the underflow: • If the underflow occurs in an intrinsic procedure, the undefined result is left as is. The program continues with the assumption that the user-specified **MATHERRQQ** handler will perform any result fix up needed. • If the underflow does not occur in an intrinsic procedure, for Version 6.0, a fatal error results and the program terminates.

For more information about the floating-point environment and the **MATHERRQQ** routine (*x86* systems), see Chapter 22 The Floating-Point Environment.

For information about routines that can obtain or set the floating-point exception settings used by Visual Fortran at run-time, see **FOR_SET_FPE** and **FOR_GET_FPE** in the A-Z Summary in the *Language Reference* in Visual Fortran online Help.

For more information on IEEE floating-point exception handling, see the *IEEE Standard for Binary Floating-Point Arithmetic* (ANSI/IEEE Standard 754-1985).

4.1.33 /fpp

Syntax:

/fpp[:"*options*"]

The /fpp option activates the FPP preprocessor and optionally passes *options* to FPP as is. The FPP preprocessor can process both free- and fixed-form Fortran source files. Alternatively, you can use compiler directives, such as the **IF** Directive Construct, to detect symbol definitions and perform conditional compilation.

You can run FPP:

▶ On the DF command line, by adding the /fpp option. By default, the specified files are compiled and linked. To retain the intermediate (.i) file, specify the /keep option.

▶ In the visual development environment, by specifying the Use FPP option in the Preprocessor Compiler Option Category (see Section 4.1.1 Categories of Compiler Options). By default, the file is compiled and linked. To retain the intermediate (.i) file, specify the /keep option on the command line or (in the visual development environment, Project Settings dialog box) the Project Options: box.

▶ On the command line, by using the FPP command. In this case, the compiler is not invoked. When using the FPP command line, you need to specify the input file and the output intermediate (.i) file.

FPP is a modified version of the ANSI C preprocessor and supports a similar set of directives (including syntax and semantics). It supports the following directives: #define, #elif, #else, #endif, #if, #ifdef, #ifndef, #include, and #undef.

For example, the following DF command invokes FPP, specifies the /noC option to FPP, uses the /define option to define the symbol testcase, and preprocesses file cond.for before it is compiled and linked:

```
DF /fpp:"/noC" /define:testcase=2 cond.for
```

For a list of predefined preprocessor symbols (such as _X86_), see Section 4.1.18 /define.

For information on FPP options, type FPP /HELP on the command line.

4.1.34 /[no]fpscomp

Syntax:

/fpscomp[:*keyword...*] or /nofpscomp

The /fpscomp option controls whether certain aspects of the run-time system and semantic language features within the compiler are compatible with Visual Fortran or Microsoft Fortran PowerStation.

If you experience problems when porting applications from Fortran PowerStation, specify /fpscomp:*keyword* (or /fpscomp:all). When porting applications from Digital Fortran, use /fpscomp:none or /fpscomp:libs (the default).

In the visual development environment, specify the PowerStation 4.0 Compatibility Options in the Compatibility Compiler Option Category (see Section 4.1.1 Categories of Compiler Options).

The /fpscomp options and their visual development environment names are:

▶ /fpscomp:[no]filesfromcmd (Filenames from Command Line)

Specifying /fpscomp:filesfromcmd for a file where the **OPEN** statement FILE specifier is blank (FILE=' '), requests that the following actions be taken at run-time:

- The program reads a filename from the list of arguments (if any) in the command line that invoked the program. If any of the command-line arguments contain a null string ("), the program asks the user for the corresponding filename. Each additional **OPEN** statement with a nameless FILE specifier reads the next command-line argument.

- If there are more nameless **OPEN** statements than command-line arguments, the program prompts for additional file names.

- In a QuickWin application, a File Select dialog box appears to request file names.

Specifying /fpscomp:nofilesfromcmd disables the run-time system from using the filename specified on the command line when the **OPEN** statement FILE specifier is omitted, allowing the application of default directory, file name, and extensions like Digital Fortran, such as the FORT*n* environment variable and the FORT.*n* file name (where *n* is the unit number).

Specifying /fpscomp:filesfromcmd affects the following Fortran features:

- The **OPEN** statement FILE specifier

For example, assume a program OPENTEST contains the following statements:

```
OPEN(UNIT = 2, FILE = ' ')
OPEN(UNIT = 3, FILE = ' ')
OPEN(UNIT = 4, FILE = ' ')
```

The command line, opentest test.dat " " assigns the file TEST.DAT to Unit 2, prompts the user for a filename to associate with Unit 3, then prompts again for a filename to associate with Unit 4.

- Implicit file open statements such as the **WRITE**, **READ**, and **ENDFILE** statements

Unopened files referred to in **READ** or **WRITE** statements are opened implicitly as if there had been an **OPEN** statement with a name specified as all blanks. The name is read from the command line.

```
WRITE(UNIT = 8, FMT='(2I5)') int1, int2 ! Where "8"
has not been explicitly associated with a file
```

For more information about running Visual Fortran programs with the /fpscomp:filesfromcmd option set, see Section 2.6 Running Fortran Applications.

▶ /fpscomp:[no]general (Other Run-time Behavior)

Controls which run-time behavior is used when a difference exists between Visual Fortran and Microsoft Fortran PowerStation and either semantic must remain available for compatibility reasons. Specify /fpscomp: general to request Fortran PowerStation semantics. Specify /fpscomp: nogeneral to request Visual Fortran semantics. This affects the following Fortran features:

- The **BACKSPACE** statement

  ▶ Allows files opened with ACCESS='APPEND' to be used with the **BACKSPACE** statement.

  ▶ Allows files opened with ACCESS='DIRECT' to be used with the **BACKSPACE** statement.

Note: Allowing files that are not opened with sequential access (such as ACCESS='DIRECT') to be used with the **BACKSPACE** statement violates the Fortran 90 Standard and may be removed in the future. See Section 9.5 of the Standard.

- The **REWIND** statement

Allows files opened with ACCESS='DIRECT' to be used with the **REWIND** statement.

Note: Allowing files that are not opened with sequential access (such as ACCESS='DIRECT') to be used with the **REWIND** statement violates the Fortran 90 Standard and may be removed in the future. See Section 9.5 of the Standard.

- The **READ** statement

  ▶ Formatted: `READ(eunit, format [, advance][, iostat]. . .)`

Reading from a formatted file opened for direct access will read records that have the same record type format as Fortran PowerStation when /fpscomp:general is set. This consists of accounting for the trailing Carriage Return/Line Feed pair (<CR><LF>) which is part of the record.

Allows sequential reads from a formatted file opened for direct access.

Note: Allowing files that are not opened with sequential access (such as ACCESS='DIRECT') to be used with the sequential **READ** statement violates the Fortran 90 Standard and may be removed in the future. See Section 9.2.1.2.2 of the Standard.

  ▶ Allows the last record in a file opened with FORM='FORMAT TED' and a record type of STREAM_LF or STREAM_CR that does not end with a proper record terminator (<line feed> or <carriage return>) to be read without producing an error.

  ▶ Unformatted: `READ(eunit [, iostat]...)`

Allows sequential reads from an unformatted file opened for direct access.

Note: Allowing files that are not opened with sequential access (such as ACCESS='DIRECT') to be read with the sequential **READ** statement violates the Fortran 90 Standard and may be removed in the future. See Section 9.2.1.2.2 of the Standard.

- The **INQUIRE** statement

  ▶ The CARRIAGECONTROL specifier returns the value "UNDEFINED" instead of "UNKNOWN" when the carriage control is not known and when /fpscomp:general is set.

  ▶ The NAME specifier returns the file name "UNKNOWN" instead of space filling the file name when the file name is not known and when /fpscomp:general is set.

  ▶ The SEQUENTIAL specifier returns the value "YES" instead of "NO" for a direct access formatted file when /fpscomp:general is set.

  ▶ The UNFORMATTED specifier returns the value "NO" instead of "UNKNOWN" when it is not known whether unformatted I/O can be performed to the file and when /fpscomp: general is set.

Note: Returning the value "NO" instead of "UNKNOWN" for this specifier violates the Fortran 90 standard and may be removed in the future. See Section 9.6.1.12 of the Standard.

- The **OPEN** statement

  ▶ If a file is opened with an unspecified STATUS value, and is not named (no FILE specifier), the file is opened as a scratch file when /fpscomp:general is set. For example:

```
OPEN (UNIT = 4)
```

In contrast, when /fpscomp:nogeneral is in effect with an unspecified STATUS value with no FILE specifier, the FORT*n* environment variable and the FORT.*n* file name are used (where *n* is the unit number).

  ▶ If the STATUS value was not specified and if the name of the file is "USER", the file is marked for deletion when it is closed when /fpscomp: general is set.

  ▶ Allows a file to be opened with the APPEND and READONLY characteristics when /fpscomp:general is set.

  ▶ If the CARRIAGECONTROL specifier is defaulted, gives "LIST" carriage control to direct access formatted files instead of "NONE" when /fpscomp:general is set.

  ▶ Gives an opened file the additional default of write sharing when /fpscomp:general is set.

▶ Gives the a file a default block size of 1024 when /fpscomp:general is set as compared to 8192 (see Section 6.5.7 Efficient Use of Record Buffers and Disk I/O).

▶ If the MODE and ACTION specifier is defaulted and there was an error opening the file, then try opening the file read only, then write only.

▶ If the CARRIAGECONTROL specifier is defaulted and if the device type is a terminal file the file is given the default carriage control value of "FORTRAN" as opposed to "LIST" when /fpscomp: general is set.

▶ If a file that is being re-opened has a different file type than the current existing file, an error is returned when /fpscomp:general is set.

▶ Gives direct access formatted files the same record type as Fortran PowerStation when /fpscomp:general is set. This means accounting for the trailing Carriage Return/Line Feed pair (<CR><LF>) which is part of the record.

- The **STOP** statement

Writes the Fortran PowerStation output string and/or returns the same exit condition values when /fpscomp:general is set.

- The **WRITE** statement

▶ Formatted: WRITE(eunit, format [, advance][, iostat]. . .)

- Writing to formatted direct files

When writing to a formatted file opened for direct access, records are written in the same record type format as Fortran PowerStation when /fpscomp:general is set. This consists of adding the trailing Carriage Return/Line Feed pair (<CR><LF>) which is part of the record. Ignores the CARRIAGECONTROL specifier setting when writing to a formatted direct access file.

- Interpreting Fortran carriage control characters

When interpreting Fortran carriage control characters during formatted I/O, carriage control sequences are written which are the same as Fortran PowerStation when /fpscomp:general is set. This is true for the "Space, 0, 1 and + " characters.

- Performing non-advancing I/O to the terminal.

When performing non-advancing I/O to the terminal, output is written in the same format as Fortran PowerStation when /fpscomp:general is set.

- Interpreting the backslash (\) and dollar ($) edit descriptors

    When interpreting backslash and dollar edit descriptors during formatted I/O, sequences are written the same as Fortran PowerStation when /fpscomp:general is set.

▶ Unformatted: `WRITE(eunit [, iostat]. . .)`

Allows sequential writes from an unformatted file opened for direct access.

Note: Allowing files that are not opened with sequential access (such as ACCESS='DIRECT') to be read with the sequential **WRITE** statement violates the Fortran 90 Standard and may be removed in the future. See Section 9.2.1.2.2 of the Standard.

▶ /fpscomp:[no]ioformat (I/O Format)

    Controls which run-time behavior is used for the semantic format for list-directed formatted I/O and unformatted I/O. Specify /fpscomp: ioformat to request Microsoft Fortran PowerStation semantic conventions and record formats (see Microsoft Fortran PowerStation Compatible Files in Section 16.1.2 Files). Specify /fpscomp:noioformat to request Digital Fortran semantic conventions. This affects the following Fortran features:

- The **WRITE** statement

    ▶ Formatted List-Directed: `WRITE(eunit, * [, iostat]. . .)`

    ▶ Formatted Internal List-Directed: `WRITE(iunit,   *   [, iostat]. . .)`

    ▶ Formatted Namelist: `WRITE(eunit, nml-group [, iostat]. . .)`

    If /fpscomp:ioformat is set, the output line, field width values, and the list-directed data type semantics are dictated according to the following sample for real constants:

- For $1 <= N < 10^{**}7$, use F15.6 for single precision or F24.15 for double.

- For $10^{**}7 <= N < 1$, use E15.6E2 for single precision or E24.15E3 for double.

    See the Fortran PowerStation documentation for more detailed information about the other data types affected.

    ▶ Unformatted: `WRITE(eunit [, iostat] . . .)`

If /fpscomp:ioformat is set, the unformatted file semantics are dictated according to the Fortran PowerStation documentation. Be aware that the file format differs from that used by Digital Fortran. See the Fortran PowerStation documentation for more detailed information.

Table 4-6 summarizes the default output formats for list-directed output with the intrinsic data types.

Table 4–6 *Default Formats for List-Directed Output*

Data Type	Output Format with /fpscomp: noioformat	Output Format with /fpscomp: ioformat
BYTE	I5	I12
LOGICAL (all)	L2	L2
INTEGER(1)	I5	I12
INTEGER(2)	I7	I12
INTEGER(4)	I12	I12
INTEGER(8) (Alpha only)	I22	I22
REAL(4)	1PG15.7E2	1PG16.6E2
REAL(8)	1PG24.15E3	1PG25.15E3
COMPLEX(4)	'(',1PG14.7E2,',',1PG14.7E2,')'	'(',1PG16.6E2,',',1PG16.6E2,')'
COMPLEX(8)	'(',1PG23.15E3,',',1PG23.15E3,')'	'(',1PG25.15E3,',',1PG25.15E3,')'
CHARACTER	A*w*	A*w*

- The **READ** statement

  ▶ Formatted List-Directed: READ(eunit, * [, iostat]. . . .)

  ▶ Formatted Internal List-Directed: READ(iunit, * [, iostat]. . . .)

  ▶ Formatted Namelist: READ(eunit, nml-group [, iostat]. . . .)

If /fpscomp:ioformat is set, the field width values and the list-directed semantics are dictated according to the following sample for real constants:

For $1 <= N < 10^{**}7$, use F15.6 for single precision or F24.15 for double.

For 10**7 <= N < 1, use E15.6E2 for single precision or E24.15E3 for double.

See the Fortran PowerStation documentation for more detailed information about the other data types affected.

▶ Unformatted: `READ(eunit [, iostat]. . .)`

If /fpscomp:ioformat is set, the unformatted file semantics are dictated according to the Fortran PowerStation documentation. Be aware that the file format to read differs from that used by Digital Fortran. See the Fortran PowerStation documentation for more detailed information.

▶ /fpscomp:[no]libs (Libraries)

Controls whether the library dfport.lib (Portability librray) is passed to the compiler and linker. The default is /fpscomp:libs, which passes this library. Specifying /fpscomp:nolibs does not pass this library.

▶ /fpscomp:[no]logicals (Logical Values)

Controls the value used for logical true. Microsoft Fortran PowerStation and Digital Fortran with the /fpscomp:logical option set uses any non-zero value (default is 1) for true. Digital Fortran with the /fpscomp:nological option set only looks at the low bit of the value, using a -1 for true. Differences can occur when a logical is stored into an integer. Both use 0 (zero) for false.

This affects the results of all logical expressions and affects the return value for following Fortran features:

- The **INQUIRE** statement specifiers OPENED, IOFOCUS, EXISTS, and NAMED.

- The **EOF** intrinsic function.

- The **BTEST** intrinsic function.

- The lexical intrinsic functions **LLT, LLE, LGT,** and **LGE.**

▶ /fpscomp:[no]symbols (Predefined Preprocessor Symbols)

Adds one or more symbols related to Microsoft Fortran PowerStation to preprocessor and compiler invocations. The symbol currently set by specifying /fpscomp:symbols is _MSFORTRAN_=401.

▶ /fpscomp:all and /fpscomp

Enable full Microsoft Fortran PowerStation compatibility or /fpscomp: (filesfromcmd,general,ioformat,libs,logicals,symbols).

▶ /nofpscomp or /fpscomp:none

Enables full Digital Fortran compatibility or /fpscomp:(nofilesfrom cmd,nogeneral,noioformat,nolibs,nologicals,nosymbols).

If you omit /fpscomp, the defaults are /nofpscomp (/fpscomp:libs).

The /fpscomp and /vms options are not allowed in the same command.

4.1.35 /[no]free

Syntax:

/free, /nofree,/4Yf, or /4Nf

The /free or /4Yf option specifies that the source file should be interpreted as being in free source format. Equivalent options are as follows:

▶ /free, /nofixed, or /4Yf request free-source form.

▶ /nofree, /fixed, or /4Nf request fixed-source form.

In the visual development environment, specify the Source Form in the Fortran Language Compiler Option Category (see Section 4.1.1 Categories of Compiler Options).

If you omit /[no]free, /[no]fixed, /4Nf, and /4Yf, the compiler assumes:

▶ Files with an extension of .f90 or .F90 are free-format source files.

▶ Files with an extension of .f, .for, .FOR, or .i are fixed-format files.

4.1.36 /granularity (Alpha Only)

Syntax:

/granularity:*keyword*

On Alpha systems, the /granularity option ensures that data of the specified or larger size can be accessed from different threads sharing data in memory. Such data must be aligned on the natural boundary and declared as **VOLATILE** (so it is not held in registers). This option is ignored on *x*86 processor systems.

In the visual development environment, specify the Thread Access Granularity in the Fortran Data Compiler Option Category (see Section 4.1.1 Categories of Compiler Options).

You do not need to specify this option for local data access by a single process, unless you have requested multithread library use or asynchronous write access from outside the user process might occur.

The /granularity:*keyword* options are:

▶ /granularity:byte

Specifies that all data (one byte or greater) can be accessed from different threads sharing data in memory. This option will slow run-time performance.

▶ /granularity:longword

Specifies that naturally aligned data of four bytes or greater can be accessed safely from different threads sharing access to that data in memory. Accessing data items of three bytes or less and misaligned data may result in data items written from multiple threads being inconsistently updated.

▶ /granularity:quadword

Specifies that naturally aligned data of eight bytes can be accessed safely from different threads sharing data in memory. This is the default. Accessing data items of seven bytes or less and misaligned data may result in data items written from multiple threads being inconsistently updated.

4.1.37   /help

Syntax:

/help or /?

The /help and /? option display information about the DF command. The option can be placed anywhere on the command line.

For a table of DF command options listed alphabetically, see Section 3.1 The Format of the DF Command.

4.1.38   /iface

Syntax: /iface[:*keyword...*]

The /iface option determines the type of argument-passing conventions used by your program for general arguments and for hidden-length character arguments.

In the visual development environment, specify the Default Calling Conventions and the String Length Argument Passing in the External Procedures Compiler Option Category (see Section 4.1.1 Categories of Compiler Options).

The /iface keywords are:

▶ The general argument-passing convention keywords are one of: cref, stdref, and default (stdref and default are equivalent). Table 4-7 describes the functions performed by each keyword.

Table 4–7 *General Argument-Passing Command Options*

	/iface:cref	*/iface:default*	*/iface:stdref*
Arguments are passed	By reference	By reference	By reference
Append @n to names on *x*86 systems?	No	Yes	Yes
Who cleans up stack	Caller	Callee	Callee
Var args support?	Yes	No	No

▶ To specify the convention for passing the hidden-length character arguments, specify /iface:[no]mixed_str_len_arg:

- /iface:mixed_str_len_arg

  Requests that the hidden lengths be placed *immediately after* their corresponding character argument in the argument list, which is the method used by Microsoft Fortran PowerStation.

- /iface:nomixed_str_len_arg

  Requests that the hidden lengths be placed in sequential order at the *end* of the argument list, which is the method used by Digital Fortran on Windows NT Alpha (and Digital UNIX) systems by default. When porting mixed-language programs that pass character arguments, either this option must be specified correctly or the order of hidden length arguments changed in the source code.

  If you omit the /iface option, the following is used:

```
/iface=(default,mixed_str_len_arg)
```

  For more information on argument passing, see Chapter 18 Programming with Mixed Languages.

4.1.39 /[no]include

Syntax:

/include[:*path*...], /noinclude, or /I*path*

The /include or /I option specifies one or more additional directories (*path*) to be searched for module files (**USE** statement) and include files (**INCLUDE** statement).

In the visual development environment, specify Custom INCLUDE and USE Path in the Preprocessor Compiler Option Category (see Section 4.1.1 Categories of Compiler Options).

When module or include file names do not begin with a device or directory name, the directories searched are as follows:

1. The directory containing the first source file or the current directory (depends on whether /assume:source_include was specified).

2. The current default directory where the compilation is taking place.

3. If specified, the directory or directories listed in the /include:*path* or /I*path* option. The order of searching multiple directories occurs within the specified list from left to right.

4. The directories indicated in the environment variable INCLUDE.

To request that the compiler search first in the directory where the source file resides instead of the current directory, specify /assume:source_include.

Specifying /noinclude (or /include or /I without a *path*) prevents searching in the standard directory specified by the INCLUDE environment variable.

4.1.40   /[no]inline

Syntax:

/inline[:*keyword*], /noinline, or /Ob2

The /inline or /Ob2 option allows users to have some control over inlining. Inlining procedures can greatly improve the run-time performance for certain applications.

When requesting procedure inlining (or interprocedural optimizations), compile all source files together into a single object file whenever possible. With very large applications, compile as many related source files together as possible.

If you compile sources without linking (see the /compile_only option), be sure to also specify the /object[:filename] option to create a single object file.

In the visual development environment, specify the Inlining type in the Optimizations Compiler Option Category (see Section 4.1.1 Categories of Compiler Options).

The /inline options are:

▶ /inline:none or /noinline

   Prevents the inlining of procedures, except for statement functions. This type of inlining occurs when you specify /optimize:0 or /Od.

▶ /inline:manual

Prevents the inlining of procedures, except for statement functions. This type of inlining occurs when you specify /optimize:0 or /Od.

▶ /inline:size

Inlines procedures that will improve run-time performance without significantly increasing program size. It includes the types of procedures inlined when you specify /inline:manual. This type of inlining is available with /optimize:1 or higher.

▶ /inline:speed or /Ob2

Inlines procedures that will improve run-time performance with a significant increase in program size. This type of inlining is available with /optimize:1 or higher.

If you omit /[no]inline or /Ob2, /inline:speed occurs automatically if you specify /optimize:4, /optimize:5, /Ox, or /Oxp.

▶ inline:all

Inlines absolutely every call that it is possible to inline while still getting correct code. However, recursive routines will not cause an infinite loop at compile time. This type of inlining is available with /optimize:1 or higher. It includes the types of procedures inlined when you specify other /inline options.

Using /inline:all can significantly increase program size and slow compilation speed.

For more detailed information on this option, see Section 6.8.3 Controlling the Inlining of Procedures.

4.1.41   /[no]intconstant

Syntax:

/intconstant or /nointconstant

The /intconstant option requests that Fortran 77 semantics (type determined by the value) be used to determine the kind of integer constants instead of Fortran 90 default **INTEGER** type. If you do not specify /intconstant, the type is determined by the default **INTEGER** type.

In the visual development environment, specify Use F77 Integer Constants in the Compatibility Compiler Option Category (see Section 4.1.1 Categories of Compiler Options).

4.1.42 /integer_size

Syntax:

/integer_size:*size* or /4I2

The /integer_size or /4I2 option specifies the size (in bits) of integer and logical declarations, constants, functions, and intrinsics. In the visual development environment, specify the Default Integer Kind in the Fortran Data Compiler Option Category (see Section 4.1.1 Categories of Compiler Options).

The /integer_size options are:

▶ /integer_size:16 or /4I2 makes the default integer and logical variables 2 bytes long. **INTEGER** and **LOGICAL** declarations are treated as (KIND=2).

▶ /integer_size:32 makes the default integer and logical variables 4 bytes long (default). **INTEGER** and **LOGICAL** declarations are treated as (KIND=4).

▶ /integer_size:64 (Alpha only) makes the default integer and logical variables 8 bytes long. **INTEGER** and **LOGICAL** declarations are treated as (KIND=8).

4.1.43 /[no]keep

Syntax:

/keep or /nokeep

The /keep option creates one object file for each input source file specified, which may not be desirable when compiling multiple source files. The /keep option does not remove temporary files, which might be created by the FPP preprocessor or the Digital Fortran compiler.

If the /keep option is specified, the FPP output files and object files are created in the current directory and retained. The /keep option also affects the number of files that are created and the file names used for these files.

4.1.44 /[no]libdir

Syntax:

/libdir[:*keyword*], /nolibdir, or /Zl or /Zla

The /libdir, /Zl, or /Zla options control whether library search paths are placed into object files generated by the compiler.

The /libdir options are:

▶ /libdir:all or /libdir

Requests the insertion of linker search path directives for libraries auto-matically determined by the DF command driver and for those specified by the *d*DEC$ OBJCOMMENT LIB source directives. Specifying /libdir:all is equivalent to /libdir:(automatic, user). This is the default.

▶ /libdir:none, /nolibdir, or /Zla

Prevents *all* linker search path directives from being inserted into the object file (neither automatic nor user specified).

▶ /libdir:automatic

Requests the insertion of linker search path directives for libraries auto-matically determined by the DF command driver (default libraries). To prevent the insertion of linker directives for default libraries, specify /libdir:noautomatic or /Zl. In the visual development environment, specify Disable Default Library Search Rules (for /libdir:noautomatic) in the Libraries Compiler Option Category.

▶ /libdir:user

Allows insertion of linker search path directives for any libraries speci-fied by the *d*DEC$ OBJCOMMENT LIB source directives. To prevent the insertion of linker directives for any libraries specified by the OBJCOMMENT directives, specify /libdir:nouser. In the visual develop-ment environment, specify Disable OBJCOMMENT directives (for /libdir:nouser) in the Libraries Compiler Option Category.

For more information on the various compiler option categories in the visual development environment, see Section 4.1.1 Categories of Compiler Options.

4.1.45 /libs

Syntax:

/libs[:*keyword*], /MD, /MDd, /MDs, /ML, /MLd, /MT, /MTd, /MTs, /MW, or /MWs

The /libs option controls the type of libraries your application is linked with. The default is /libs:static (same as /libs). In the visual development envi-ronment, specify the Use Fortran Run-Time Libraries in the Libraries Com-piler Option Category (see Section 4.1.1 Categories of Compiler Options).

The /libs options are:

▶ /libs:dll or /MDs

The /libs:dll or /MDs option causes the linker to search for unresolved references in single threaded, dynamic link reference libraries (DLLs). If the unresolved reference is found in the DLL, it gets resolved when the program is executed (during program loading), reducing executable program size.

Specifying /libs:dll with /threads is equivalent to /MD.

Specifying /libs:dll with /threads and /dbglibs is equivalent to /MDd.

▶ /libs:static or /ML

The /libs:static or /ML option requests that the linker searches only in single threaded, static libraries for unresolved references. This is the default. Specifying /libs:static does *not* request that dynamic link libraries (DLLs), QuickWin, or Standard Graphics libraries be searched. If you use QuickWin or Standard Graphics routines, use /libs:qwin or /libs:qwins. Specifying /libs (with no keyword) is the same as specifying /libs:static.

Specifying /libs:static with /nothreads is equivalent to /ML.

Specifying /libs:static with /nothreads and /dbglibs is equivalent to /MLd.

Specifying /libs:static with /threads is equivalent to /MT.

Specifying /libs:static with /threads and /dbglibs is equivalent to /MTd.

▶ /libs:qwin or /MW

Specifying /libs:qwin or /MW requests linking with libraries required of a Fortran QuickWin multi-doc (QuickWin) application.

▶ /libs:qwins or /MWs

Specifying /libs:qwins or /MWs requests linking with libraries required of a Fortran Standard Graphics (QuickWin single-doc) application.

The following related options request additional libraries to link against:

▶ /dbglibs (see Section 4.1.16)

▶ /fpscomp:libs (see Section 4.1.34)

▶ /threads (see Section 4.1.71)

▶ /winapp (see Section 4.1.81)

To request the creation of a dynamic-link library, see Section 4.1.19 /dll.

For information about compiling and linking Visual Fortran and Visual C++ programs (and the libraries used), see Section 18.4 Visual Fortran/Visual C++ Mixed-Language Programs.

For command-line examples of using the /libs option, see Section 3.7.6 Linking against Additional Libraries.

4.1.46 /[no]link

Syntax:

/link:*options* or /nolink

The /link option (without specifying *options*) precedes options to be passed to the linker as is (see Section 4.2 Linker Options and Related Information). You can also specify the *options* to be passed to the linker as is using the form /link:*options*.

To specify additional libraries to be linked on the command line, specify the library name on the DF command line either before or after the /link option, but the Linker option /nodefaultlib must follow the /link option:

```
DF /compiler-options file.f90 mylib.lib /link /nodefault lib
```

In the visual development environment, you can specify linker options using the Linker tab in the Project menu Settings dialog box. For example, to specify additional libraries to be linked in the visual development environment:

1. In the Project menu, click Settings to display the Project settings dialog box

2. Click the Linker tab

3. Select the General category

4. Type the additional library name to be linked with under Object/Library modules, such as mylib.lib

5. Click OK when done

The /nolink option suppresses linking and forces an object file to be produced even if only one program is compiled. Any options specified after the /nolink option are ignored.

For a list of library names needed to link the IMSL mathematical routines, see Section 24.1 Using the Libraries from Visual Fortran.

4.1.47 /[no]list

Syntax:

/list[:*file*], /nolist, or /Fs*file*

The /list or /Fs option creates a listing of the source file with compile-time information appended. To name the source listing file, specify *file*. If you omit the /list or /Fs options (or specify /nolist), no listing file is created.

In the visual development environment, specify Source Listing in the Listing File Compiler Option Category (see Section 4.1.1 Categories of Compiler Options).

When a diagnostic message is displayed, the listing file contains a column pointer (such as .....1) that points to the specific part of the source line that caused the error.

To specify the content of the listing file, see Section 4.1.65 /[no]show.

To request a listing with Assembly instructions, see Section 4.1.6 /[no] asmfile.

The name of the listing file is the same as the source file (unless specified by *file*), with the extension .LST (unless the extension is specified by *file*).

If multiple object files are created, multiple listing files are usually created. For example, if you specify multiple source files with the /compile_only and /list options without a named object file (/object:*file*), multiple files are created. If you specify multiple source files with the /list, /compile_only, and /object:*file*, a single listing file is created. For command-line examples, see Section 3.7.5 Generating a Listing File.

4.1.48 /[no]logo

Syntax:

/nologo or /logo

The /nologo option suppresses the copyright notice displayed by the compiler and linker. This option can be placed anywhere on the command line.

4.1.49 /[no]machine_code

Syntax:

/machine_code or /nomachine_code

The /machine_code option requests that a machine language representation be included in the listing file. The /machine_code option is a synonym for /show:code. In the visual development environment, specify Source Listing Options, Machine Code in the Listing File Compiler Option Category (see Section 4.1.1 Categories of Compiler Options).

This option is ignored unless you specify /list[:*file*] or /Fs*file*.

4.1.50 /[no]map

Syntax:

/map[:*file*], /nomap, or /Fm*file*

The /map or /Fm option controls whether or not a link map is created. To name the map file, specify *file*.

In the visual development environment, in the Project menu Settings dialog box:

1. Click the Linker tab

2. Select the General category

3. Click the Generate mapfile option check box

If you omit /map or /Fm, a map file is not created.

The link map is a text file (for more information, see Section 4.2.29 Linker option /MAP).

4.1.51 /math_library

Syntax:

/math_library:*keyword*

The /math_library option specifies whether argument checking of math routines is done on *x*86 systems and the type of math library routines used on Alpha systems.

In the visual development environment, specify the Math Library in the Optimizations (or Code Generation) Compiler Option Category (see Section 4.1.1 Categories of Compiler Options).

The /math_library options are:

▶ /math_library:accurate (Alpha only)

On Alpha systems, specifying /math_library:accurate uses the standard math library routines for Fortran intrinsics (for example, **SIN**), that provide highly accurate answers with good performance and error checking. This is the default on Alpha systems (unless the /fast option is specified).

The standard math library routines are designed to obtain very accurate "near correctly rounded" results and provide the robustness needed to check for IEEE exceptional argument values, rather than achieve the fastest possible run-time execution speed. Using /math_library:accurate allows user control of arithmetic exception handling with the /fpe:level option (in addition to the default).

▶ /math_library:fast

On *x*86 systems, /math_library:fast improves performance by not checking the arguments to the math routines. Using /math_library:fast makes tracing the cause of unexpected exceptional values results difficult. On *x*86 systems, /math_library:fast does not change the accuracy of calculated floating-point numbers.

On Alpha systems, /math_library:fast improves performance by using tuned routines in the math library. These routines trade off a small amount of accuracy and less reliable arithmetic exception handling for improved performance. There are tuned routines for such intrinsic procedures as **SQRT** and **EXP**, allowing certain math library functions to get significant performance improvements when the applicable intrinsic procedure is used.

The fast math library routines on Alpha systems do not necessarily check for IEEE exceptional values and should not be used with the /fpe: level option other than fpe:0.

When you use /math_library:fast on Alpha systems, you should carefully check the calculated output from your program to verify that it is not relying on the full fractional accuracy of the floating-point data type to produce correct results and not producing unexpected exceptional values (exception handling is indeterminate).

Programs that do not produce acceptable results on Alpha systems with /math_library:fast and single-precision data might produce acceptable results with /math_library:fast if they are modified (or compiled) to use double-precision data.

▶ /math_library:check

On *x*86 systems, /math_library:check validates the arguments to and results from calls to the Fortran math routines. This provides slower runtime performance than /math_library:fast on *x*86 systems, but with earlier detection of exceptional values. This is the default on *x*86 systems.

On Alpha systems, /math_library:check is equivalent to /math_library: accurate.

4.1.52 /[no]module

Syntax:

/module[:*path*] or /nomodule

The /module option controls where the module files (extension MOD) are placed. If you omit this option (or specify /nomodule), the .MOD files are placed in the directory where the source file being compiled resides.

When /module:*path* is specified, the *path* specifies the directory location where the module files will be placed.

In the visual development environment, specify the Module Path in the Preprocessor Compiler Option Category (see Section 4.1.1 Categories of Compiler Options).

When /module is entered without specifying a path, it is interpreted as a request to place the MOD files in the same location that the object is being created. Should a *path* be specified on the /object option, that location would also be used for the MOD files.

You need to ensure that the module files are created before they are referenced when using the DF command (see Section 6.1.2 Compile with Appropriate Options and Multiple Source Files).

4.1.53 /names

Syntax:

/names:*keyword*, /GNa, /GNl, or /GNu

The /names option specifies how source code identifiers and external names are interpreted and the case convention used for external names. This naming convention applies whether names are being defined or referenced. The default is /names:uppercase (same as /GNu).

In the visual development environment, specify the Name Interpretation in the External Procedures or the Fortran Language Compiler Option Category (see Section 4.1.1 Categories of Compiler Options).

The /names options are:

▶ /names:as_is or /GNa; causes the compiler to:

- Distinguish between uppercase and lowercase letters in source code identifiers (treat uppercase and lowercase letters as different).

- Distinguish between uppercase and lowercase letters in external names.

▶ /names:lowercase or /GNl; causes the compiler to:

- Not distinguish between uppercase and lowercase letters in source code identifiers (treat lowercase and uppercase letters as equivalent).

- Force all letters to be lowercase in external names.

▶ /names:uppercase or /GNu (default) causes the compiler to:

- Not distinguish between uppercase and lowercase letters in source code identifiers (treat lowercase and uppercase letters as equivalent).

- Force all letters to be uppercase in external names.

Instead of using the /names compiler option, consider using the *c*DEC$ ALIAS directive for the specific name needed.

4.1.54 /nodefine

Syntax:

/nodefine

The /nodefine option requests that all *symbols* specified by the accompanying /define:*symbols* option apply only to the Fortran preprocessor, FPP, and are *not* available to conditional compilation directives (such as the IF Directive Construct). For example, the following command defines the symbol release as 1, which is available only to FPP:

```
DF /fpp /define:release /nodefine
```

If you specify /define:*symbols* and omit /nodefine, *symbols* specified by /define:*symbols* are available to both FPP and conditional compilation directives.

In the visual development environment, specify the Predefined Preprocessor Symbols to FPP Only in the Preprocessor Compiler Option Category (see Section 4.1.1 Categories of Compiler Options).

For more information on FPP, see Section 4.1.33 /fpp.

4.1.55 /[no]object

Syntax:

/object[:*filename*], /noobject, or /Fo*filename*

The /object or /Fo option names the object file *filename*. Specify /noobject to prevent creation of an object file. The default is /object, where the file name is the same as the first source file with a file extension of .OBJ.

If you omit /compile_only (or /c) and specify /object:*filename* or /Fo*file name*, the /object option names the object file *filename*.

If you specify /object:*filename* or /Fo*filename* and specify the /compile_only option, the /object or /Fo option causes multiple Fortran input files (if specified) to be compiled into a single object file. This allows interprocedural optimizations to occur at higher optimization levels, which usually improves run-time performance.

For information on where module files are placed, see Section 4.1.52 /[no] module.

4.1.56   /[no]optimize

Syntax:

/optimize[:*level*], /nooptimize, /Od, /Ox, or /Oxp

The /optimize option controls the level of optimization performed by the compiler. To provide efficient run-time performance, Digital Fortran increases compile time in favor of decreasing run-time. If an operation can be performed, eliminated, or simplified at compile time, the compiler does so rather than have it done at run-time. Also, the size of object file usually increases when certain optimizations occur (such as with more loop unrolling and more inlined procedures).

In the visual development environment, specify the Optimization Level in the General or Optimizations Compiler Option Category (see Section 4.1.1 Categories of Compiler Options).

The /optimize options are:

▶ /optimize:0 or /Od

Disables nearly all optimizations. This is the default if you specify /debug (with no keyword). Specifying this option causes certain /warn options to be ignored. Specifying /Od sets the /optimize:0 and /math_library:check options.

▶ /optimize:1

Enables local optimizations within the source program unit, recognition of common subexpressions, and expansion of integer multiplication and division (using shifts).

▶ /optimize:2

Enables global optimization. This includes data-flow analysis, code motion, strength reduction and test replacement, split-lifetime analysis, and instruction scheduling. Specifying /optimize:2 includes the optimizations performed by /optimize:1.

▶ /optimize:3

Enables additional global optimizations that improve speed (at the cost of extra code size). These optimizations include:

- Loop unrolling, including instruction scheduling

- Code replication to eliminate branches

- Padding the size of certain power-of-two arrays to allow more efficient cache use (see Section 6.4 Use Arrays Efficiently)

Specifying /optimize:3 includes the optimizations performed by /optimize:1 and /optimize:2.

▶ /optimize:4, /Ox, and /Oxp

Enables interprocedure analysis and automatic inlining of small procedures (with heuristics limiting the amount of extra code). Specifying /optimize:4 includes the optimizations performed by /optimize:1 /optimize:2, and /optimize:3. For the DF command, /optimize:4 is the default unless you specify /debug (with no keyword).

Specifying /Ox sets: /optimize:4, /math_library:check, and /assume: nodummy_aliases.

Specifying /Oxp sets: /optimize:4, /math_library:check, /assume: nodummy_aliases, and /fpconsistency (x86 systems).

▶ /optimize:5

On x86 systems, activates the loop transformation optimizations (also set by /transform_loops). On Alpha systems, activates the loop transformation optimizations (also set by /transform_loops) and the software pipelining optimization (also set by /pipeline):

- The loop transformation optimizations are a group of optimizations that apply to array references within loops. These optimizations can improve the performance of the memory system and can apply to multiple nested loops.

Loop transformation optimizations include loop blocking, loop distribution, loop fusion, loop interchange, loop scalar replacement, and outer loop unrolling. You can specify loop transformation optimizations without software pipelining (see Section 4.1.73 /[no]transform_loops).

- The software pipelining optimization applies instruction scheduling to certain innermost loops, allowing instructions within a loop to "wrap around" and execute in a different iteration of the loop. This can reduce the impact of long-latency operations, resulting in faster loop execution. Software pipelining also enables the prefetching of data to reduce the impact of cache misses.

You can specify software pipelining without loop transformation optimizations (see Section 4.1.59 /[no]pipeline (Alpha Only)).

In addition to loop transformation and software pipelining on Alpha systems, specifying /optimize:5 activates certain optimizations that are not activated by /transform_loops and /pipeline, including byte-vectorization, and insertion of additional NOP (No Operation) instructions for alignment of multi-issue sequences.

On *x*86 systems, specifying /optimize:5 activates /transform_loops.

To determine whether using /optimize:5 benefits your particular program, you should compare program execution timings for the same program (or subprogram) compiled at levels /optimize:4 and /optimize:5.

Specifying /optimize:5 includes the optimizations performed by /optimize:1 /optimize:2, /optimize:3, and /optimize:4.

For detailed information on these optimizations, see Section 6.7 Optimization Levels: the /optimize Option.

For information about timing your program, see Section 6.2 Analyze Program Performance.

To compile your application for efficient run-time performance, see Section 6.1.2 Compile with Appropriate Options and Multiple Source Files.

4.1.57   /[no]pad_source

Syntax:

/pad_source or /nopad_source

The /pad_source option requests that source records shorter than the statement field width are to be padded with spaces on the right out to the end of the statement field. This affects the interpretation of character and Hollerith literals that are continued across source records.

In the visual development environment, specify the Pad Fixed-Form Source Records in the Fortran Language Compiler Option Category (see Section 4.1.1 Categories of Compiler Options).

The default is /nopad_source, which causes a warning message to be displayed if a character or Hollerith literal that ends before the statement field ends is continued onto the next source record. To suppress this warning message, specify the /warn:nousage option.

Specifying /pad_source can prevent warning messages associated with /warn:usage.

4.1.58 /[no]pdbfile

Syntax:

/pdbfile[:*filename*], /nopdbfile, or /Fd*filename*

The /pdbfile or /Fd option indicates that any debug information generated by the compiler should be to a program database file, *filename*.PDB. If you omit *filename*, the default file name used is df50.pdb.

In the visual development environment, specify Use Program Database for Debug Information (and optionally specify the Program Database .PDB Path) in the Debug Compiler Option Category (see Section 4.1.1 Categories of Compiler Options).

When full debug information is requested (/debug:full, /debug, or equivalent), the debug information is placed in the PDB file (unless /nopdbfile is specified).

The compiler places debug information in the object file if you specify /nopdbfile or omit both /pdbfile and /debug:full (or equivalent).

4.1.59 /[no]pipeline (Alpha Only)

Syntax:

/pipeline or /nopipeline

On Alpha systems, the /pipeline (or /optimize:5) option activates the software pipelining optimization. This optimization applies instruction scheduling to certain innermost loops, allowing instructions within a loop to "wrap around" and execute in a different iteration of the loop. This can reduce the impact of long-latency operations, resulting in faster loop execution.

In the visual development environment, specify the Apply Software Pipelining Optimizations in the Optimizations Compiler Option Category (see Section 4.1.1 Categories of Compiler Options).

For this version of Visual Fortran, loops chosen for software pipelining are always innermost loops and do not contain branches, procedure calls, or **COMPLEX** floating-point data.

Software pipelining can be more effective when you combine /pipeline with the appropriate /tune:keyword keyword option for the target Alpha processor generation.

Software pipelining also enables the prefetching of data to reduce the impact of cache misses.

Software pipelining is a subset of the optimizations activated by /optimize:5. Instead of specifying both /pipeline and /transform_loops, you can specify /optimize:5.

To specify software pipelining without loop transformation optimizations, do one of the following:

▶ Specify /optimize:5 with /notransform_loops (preferred method).

▶ Specify /pipeline with /optimize:4, /optimize:3, or /optimize:2. This optimization is not performed at optimization levels below /optimize:2.

To determine whether using /pipeline benefits your particular program, you should time program execution for the same program (or subprogram) compiled with and without software pipelining (such as with /pipeline and /nonopipeline).

For programs that contain loops that exhaust available registers, longer execution times may result with /optimize:5, requiring use of /unroll:count to limit loop unrolling. The /optimize:5 option applies only to Alpha systems.

For more information, see Section 6.7.6.2 Software Pipelining (Alpha Only).

4.1.60 /preprocess_only

Syntax:

/preprocess_only

The /preprocess_only option runs only the FPP preprocessor and puts the result for each source file in a corresponding .i or .i90 file. The .i or .i90 file does not have line numbers (#) in it.

4.1.61 /real_size

Syntax:

/real_size:*size* or /4R8

The /real_size or /4R8 option controls the *size* (in bits) of **REAL** and **COMPLEX** declarations, constants, functions, and intrinsics. In the visual development environment, specify the Default Real Kind in the Fortran Data Compiler Option Category (see Section 4.1.1 Categories of Compiler Options).

The /real_size options are:

▶ /real_size:32

Defines **REAL** declarations, constants, functions, and intrinsics as **REAL**(KIND=4). It also defines **COMPLEX** declarations, constants, functions, and intrinsics as **COMPLEX**(KIND=4). This is the default.

▶ /real_size:64 or /4R8

Defines REAL declarations, constants, functions, and intrinsics as **REAL**(KIND=8). It also defines **COMPLEX** declarations, constants, functions, and intrinsics as **COMPLEX**(KIND=8).

Specifying /real_size:64 causes intrinsic functions to produce a **REAL**(KIND=8) or **COMPLEX**(KIND=8) result instead of a **REAL**(KIND=4) or **COMPLEX**(KIND=4) result, unless the argument is explicitly typed as **REAL**(KIND=4) or **COMPLEX**(KIND=4), including **CMPLX**, **FLOAT**, **REAL**, **SNGL**, and **AIMAG**.

For example, references to the **CMPLX** intrinsic produce **DCMPLX** results (**COMPLEX**(KIND=8)), unless the argument to **CMPLX** is explicitly typed as **REAL**(KIND=4), REAL*4, **COMPLEX**(KIND=4), or COMPLEX*8. In this case the resulting data type is **COMPLEX** (KIND=4).

REAL(KIND=4) is single-precision real, **REAL**(KIND=8) is double-precision real (also known as the **DOUBLE PRECISION** data type). **COMPLEX**(KIND=8) is double complex (also known as the **DOUBLE COMPLEX** data type, a Digital Fortran language extension).

4.1.62 /[no]recursive

Syntax:

/recursive or /norecursive

The /recursive option compiles all procedures (functions and subroutines) for possible recursive execution. Specifying the /recursive option sets the /automatic option. The default is /norecursive.

In the visual development environment, specify Enable Recursive Routines in the Code Generation Compiler Option Category (see Section 4.1.1 Categories of Compiler Options).

4.1.63 /[no]reentrancy

Syntax:

/reentrancy[:*keyword*] or /noreentrancy

The /reentrancy or /reentrancy:threads option requests that the compiler generate reentrant code that supports a multithreaded application. In the visual development environment, specify the Enable Reentrancy Support or Disable Reentrancy Support in the Libraries Compiler Option Category (see Section 4.1.1 Categories of Compiler Options).

If you omit /reentrancy, /reentrancy:threads, or /threads, /reentrancy:none (same as /noreentrancy) is used.

Specifying /threads sets /reentrancy:threads, since multithreaded code must be reentrant.

4.1.64 /rounding_mode (Alpha Only)

Syntax:

/rounding_mode:*keyword*

On Alpha systems, the /rounding_mode option allows you to control how rounding occurs during floating-point calculations. The rounding mode applies to each program unit being compiled. For information on setting the rounding mode on *x*86 systems, see Section 22.3.2 Floating-Point Control Word (*x*86 only).

In the visual development environment, specify the Rounding Mode in the Floating Point Compiler Option Category (see Section 4.1.1 Categories of Compiler Options).

The /rounding_mode options are:

▶ /rounding_mode:nearest

The normal rounding mode, where results are rounded to the nearest representable value. If you omit other /rounding_mode options, /rounding_mode:nearest is used.

▶ /rounding_mode:chopped

Rounds results toward zero.

▶ /rounding_mode:minus_infinity

Rounds results toward the next smallest representative value.

▶ /rounding_mode:dynamic

Lets you set the rounding mode at run-time. You can modify your program to call the appropriate Windows NT Alpha routine to obtain or set the current rounding mode.

When you call the appropriate Windows NT Alpha routine (such as _controlfp or _control87), you can set the rounding mode to one of the following settings:

- Round toward zero or truncate (same as /rounding_mode:chopped)

- Round toward nearest (same as /rounding_mode:nearest)

- Round toward plus infinity

- Round toward minus infinity (same as /rounding_mode:minus_ infinity)

If you compile with /rounding_mode:dynamic and do not call the appropriate Windows NT routine, the initial rounding mode is round toward nearest /rounding_mode:nearest.

For the fastest run-time performance, avoid using /rounding_ mode:dynamic.

4.1.65 /[no]show

Syntax:

/show:*keyword...* or /noshow

The /show option specifies what information is included in a listing. In the visual development environment, specify the Source Listing Options in the Listing File Compiler Option Category (see Section 4.1.1 Categories of Compiler Options).

The /show keywords are:

▶ /show:code

Includes a machine-language representation of the compiled code in the listing file. The default is /show:nocode. The /show:code and /machine_code options are equivalent.

▶ /show:include

Lists any text file included in the source file (unless that source is included using the **INCLUDE** 'filespec /NOLIST' syntax; see the /vms option). The default is /show:noinclude.

▶ /show:map (default)

Includes a symbol map in the listing file.

▶ /show:nomap

Do not include a symbol map in the listing file.

▶ /show or /show:all

Equivalent to /show:(code,include,map).

▶ /noshow or /show:none

Equivalent to /show:(nocode,noinclude,nomap).

The /show option is ignored unless you specify /list[:*file*] or /Fs*file*.

4.1.66 /source

Syntax:

/source:*file* or /Tf*file*

The /source or /Tf option indicates that the *file* is a Fortran source file with a non-standard file extension (not one of .F, .FOR, or .F90) that needs to be compiled.

The default for any file that does *not* have an extension of .F90 or .f90 is to be a fixed-format Fortran file.

4.1.67 /[no]stand

Syntax:

/stand[:*keyword*], /nostand, or /4Ns

The /stand or /4Ns option issues compile-time messages for language elements that are not standard in the Fortran 90 or Fortran 95 language that can be identified at compile-time. In the visual development environment, specify the Fortran Standards Checking in the Compilation Diagnostics Compiler Option Category (see Section 4.1.1 Categories of Compiler Options).

The /stand options are:

▶ /stand or /stand:f90

Specifies that diagnostic messages be generated with a warning-level severity (allows an object file to be created) for extensions to the Fortran 90 standard.

▶ /stand:f95

Specifies that diagnostic messages be generated with a warning-level severity (allows an object file to be created) for extensions to the Fortran 95 standard.

▶ /stand:none, /nostand, or /4Ns

Specifies that no messages be issued for language elements that are not standard in the Fortran 90 or Fortran 95 language.

The same effect occurs if you omit the /stand, or /stand:*keyword*, /warn: stderrors, or /4Ys options.

Specify /warn:stderrors to request that diagnostic messages be generated with an error-level severity (instead of warning) to prevent an object file from being created.

Specifying /stand issues warning messages for:

▶ Obsolescent and deleted features specified by the Fortran standard.

▶ Syntax extensions to the Fortran 90 standard. Syntax extensions include nonstandard statements and language constructs.

▶ Fortran 90 standard-conforming statements that become nonstandard due to the way in which they are used. Data type information and statement locations are considered when determining semantic extensions.

▶ For fixed-format source files, lines that use tab formatting.

Source statements that do not conform to Fortran 90 language standards are detected by the compiler under the following circumstances:

▶ The statements contain ordinary syntax and semantic errors.

▶ A source program containing nonconforming statements is compiled with the /stand or /check options.

Given these circumstances, the compiler is able to detect *most* instances of nonconforming usage. It does not detect all instances because the /stand option does not produce checks for all nonconforming usage at compile time. In general, the unchecked cases of nonconforming usage arise from the following situations:

▶ The standard violation results from conditions that cannot be checked at compile time.

▶ The compile-time checking is prone to false alarms.

Most of the unchecked cases occur in the interface between calling and called subprograms. However, other cases are not checked, even within a single subprogram.

The following items are known to be unchecked:

▶ Use of a data item prior to defining it

► Use of the **SAVE** statement to ensure that data items or common blocks retain their values when reinvoked

► Association of character data items on the right and left sides of character assignment statements

► Mismatch in order, number, or type in passing actual arguments to subprograms with implicit interfaces

► Association of one or more actual arguments with a data item in a common block when calling a subprogram that assigns a new value to one or more of the arguments

4.1.68   /[no]static

Syntax:

/static or /nostatic

The /static option is the same as the /noautomatic option. The default is /static, which causes all local variables to be statically allocated. The /nostatic option is the same as /automatic. In the visual development environment, specify /nostatic as Variables Default to Automatic in the Fortran Data Compiler Option Category (see Section 4.1.1 Categories of Compiler Options).

If you specify /recursive, the /automatic option is set.

4.1.69   /[no]synchronous_exceptions (Alpha Only)

Syntax:

/synchronous_exceptions or /nosynchronous_exceptions

On Alpha systems, the /synchronous_exceptions option associates an exception with the instruction that causes it. This slows program execution, so only specify it when debugging a specific problem, such as locating the source of an exception.

In the visual development environment, specify Enable Synchronous Floating-Point Exceptions in the Run-Time (or Floating Point) Compiler Option Category (see Section 4.1.1 Categories of Compiler Options).

With /nosynchronous_exceptions, exceptions can be reported one or more instructions *after* the instruction that caused the exception, depending on the /fpe:*level* option used.

On the command line, the default is /nosynchronous_exceptions (if you specify or imply /fpe:0). If you specify a higher /fpe level, the default is /synchronous_exceptions.

In the visual development environment (beginning with Version 6.0.A), the default is /synchronous_exceptions for debug configurations and /nosynchronous_exceptions for release configurations.

4.1.70   /[no]syntax_only

Syntax:

/syntax_only or /nosyntax_only

The /syntax_only option requests that only the syntax of the source file be checked. If the /syntax_only option is specified, code generation is suppressed. The default is /nosyntax_only.

4.1.71   /[no]threads

Syntax:

/threads or /nothreads

The /threads option requests linking with multithreaded libraries, which creates a multithreaded program or DLL. If you specify /threads, this sets the /reentrancy option.

In the visual development environment, specify Use Multithreaded Library in the Libraries Compiler Option Category (see Section 4.1.1 Categories of Compiler Options).

The default is /nothreads, which links with single-threaded libraries to create a single-threaded program or DLL.

Related options that contol the libraries used during linking include:

▶ /fpscomp:libs (see Section 4.1.34)

▶ /libs (see Section 4.1.45)

▶ /winapp (see Section 4.1.81)

4.1.72   /[no]traceback

Syntax:

/traceback or /notraceback or /Zt

The /traceback option requests that the compiler generate extra information in the object file that allows the display of source file traceback information at run-time when a severe error occurs.

Specifying /traceback:

▶ Provides source file, routine name, and line number correlation information in the text that is displayed when a severe error occurs.

▶ Will increase the size of the executable program, but has no impact on run-time execution speeds.

For the DF command line and for release configurations in the visual development environment, the default is /notraceback. For debug configurations in the visual development environment, the default is /traceback.

If traceback is not specified, the displayed call stack hexadecimal addresses (program counter trace) displayed when a severe error occurs do not list the source file name, routine name, and line number. However, advanced users can locate the cause of the error using a .MAP file (linker option /map) and the hexadecimal addresses of the stack displayed when a severe error occurs (see Section 21.4 Using Traceback Information).

In the visual development environment, specify Generate Traceback Information in the Run-Time Compiler Option Category (see Section 4.1.1 Categories of Compiler Options).

The /traceback option functions independently of the /debug option.

If you request traceback, you should also disable incremental linking. For a Debug configuration in the visual development environment for a new project, specifying Traceback turns off incremental linking. When using the command line, specifying /traceback sets /link/incremental:no. You can disable incremental linking either in the Link tab in the Project Settings dialog box or specify DF /link /incremental:no on the command line.

If you omit /traceback (or /Zt), /notraceback is used.

For information about locating run-time errors with traceback information, see Section 21.4 Using Traceback Information.

To disable the stack traceback report for severe errors, set the FOR_DISABLE_STACK_TRACE environment variable (see Section 21.4 Using Traceback Information).

4.1.73 /[no]transform_loops

Syntax:

/transform_loops or /notransform_loops

The /transform_loops (or /optimize:5) option activates a group of loop transformation optimizations that apply to array references within loops. These optimizations can improve the performance of the memory system and usually apply to multiple nested loops. The loops chosen for loop transformation optimizations are always *counted loops* (which include **DO** or **IF** loops, but not uncounted **DO WHILE** loops).

In the visual development environment, specify the Apply Loop Transformation Optimizations in the Optimizations Compiler Option Category (see Section 4.1.1 Categories of Compiler Options).

Conditions that typically prevent the loop transformation optimizations from occurring include subprogram references that are not inlined (such as an external function call), complicated exit conditions, and uncounted loops.

The types of optimizations associated with /transform_loops include the following:

▶ Loop blocking

▶ Loop distribution

▶ Loop fusion

▶ Loop interchange

▶ Loop scalar replacement

▶ Outer loop unrolling

The loop transformation optimizations are a subset of optimizations activated by /optimize:5. On *x*86 systems, instead of specifying /transform_loops, you can specify /optimize:5. On Alpha systems, instead of specifying both /pipeline and /transform_loops, you can specify /optimize:5.

To specify loop transformation optimizations without software pipelining, do one of the following:

▶ Specify /optimize:5 with /nopipeline (preferred method).

▶ Specify /transform_loops with /optimize:4, /optimize:3, or /optimize:2. This optimization is not performed at optimization levels below /optimize:2.

To determine whether using /transform_loops benefits your particular program, you should time program execution for the same program (or subprogram) compiled with and without loop transformation optimizations (such as with /transform_loops and /notransform_loops).

For more information, see Section 6.7.6.1 Loop Transformations.

4.1.74   /tune

Syntax:

/tune:*keyword*

The /tune option specifies the type of processor-specific machine-code instruction tuning for implementations of the processor architecture in use (either *x*86 or Alpha).

Tuning for a specific implementation can improve run-time performance; it is also possible that code tuned for a specific processor may run slower on another processor. Regardless of the /tune:*keyword* option you use, the generated code runs correctly on all implementations of the processor architecture.

If you omit /tune:*keyword*, /tune:generic is used. In the visual development environment, specify the Optimize For in the Optimizations Compiler Option Category (see Section 4.1.1 Categories of Compiler Options).

The /tune keywords have meanings specific to *x*86 systems or Alpha systems.

For *x*86 systems, the /tune keywords are:

▶ /tune:generic

   Generates and schedules code (sometimes called blended code) that will execute well for all *x*86 (486, 586, and 686) systems. This provides generally efficient code for those applications where all *x*86 processor generations are likely to be used. This is the default.

▶ /tune:host

   Generates and schedules code optimized for the processor type in use on the *x*86 system being used for compilation.

▶ /tune:p5 (*x*86 only)

   Generates and schedules code optimized for the 586 (Pentium®) processor systems.

▶ /tune:p6 (*x*86 only)

   Generates and schedules code optimized for 686 (Pentium Pro and Pentium II) processor systems.

For Alpha systems, the /tune keywords are:

▶ /tune:generic

   Generates and schedules code (sometimes called blended code) that will execute well for all generations of Alpha processor chips. This provides generally efficient code for those applications where all processor generations are likely to be used. This is the default.

▶ /tune:host

   Generates and schedules code optimized for the processor generation in use on the Alpha system being used for compilation.

▶ /tune:ev4 (Alpha only)

Generates and schedules code optimized for the 21064, 21064A, 21066, and 21068 implementations of the Alpha chip.

▶ /tune:ev5 (Alpha only)

Generates and schedules code optimized for the 21164 implementations of the Alpha architecture that use only the base set of Alpha instructions (no extensions).

▶ /tune:ev56 (Alpha only)

Generates and schedules code for the 21164 chip implementations that use the byte and word manipulation instruction extensions of the Alpha architecture.

▶ /tune:pca56 (Alpha only)

Generates and schedules code for the 21164PC chip implementation that uses the byte and word manipulation instruction extensions and multimedia instruction extensions of the Alpha architecture.

▶ /tune:ev6 (Alpha only)

Generates and schedules code for the 21264 chip implementation that uses the following instruction extensions of the Alpha architecture: byte and word manipulation, multimedia, square root and floating-point convert, and count extension.

For more information about this option, see Section 6.8.6 Requesting Optimized Code for a Specific Processor Generation.

For information about timing program execution, see Section 6.2 Analyze Program Performance.

To control the processor-specific type of machine-code instructions being generated, see Section 4.1.4 the /architecture:keyword option.

4.1.75 /undefine

Syntax:

/undefine:*symbol*

The /undefine option removes any initial definition of *symbol* for the FPP preprocessor.

4.1.76 /unroll

Syntax:

/unroll:*count*

For higher optimization levels, the /unroll option allows you to specify how many times loops are unrolled. If the /unroll option is not specified, the compiler determines how many times loops are unrolled (4 times for most loops or 2 times for certain loops with large code size or branches outside the loop).

In the visual development environment, specify the Loop Unroll Count in the Optimizations Compiler Option Category (see Section 4.1.1 Categories of Compiler Options).

If the /optimize:3, /optimize:4 (or equivalent), or /optimize:5 options are specified, loop unrolling occurs. The *count* should be an integer in the range 0 to 16. A count value of 0 is used to indicate that the compiler should determine how many times a loop is unrolled (default).

The compiler attempts to unroll certain innermost loops, minimizing the number of branches and grouping more instructions together to allow efficient overlapped instruction execution (instruction pipelining). The best candidates for loop unrolling are innermost loops with limited control flow.

Especially on *x*86 systems, specifying a higher value may improve run-time performance of certain applications. For more information, see Section 6.7.4.1 Loop Unrolling.

4.1.77 /[no]vms

Syntax:

/vms or /novms

The /vms option causes the run-time system to provide functions like Digital Fortran for OpenVMS™ VAX™ Systems (previously called VAX FORTRAN™).

In the visual development environment, specify Enable VMS Compatibility in the Compatibility Compiler Option Category (see Section 4.1.1 Categories of Compiler Options).

The /vms option:

▶ In the absence of other options, sets the following command-line defaults: /align:norecords, /align:nocommons, /check:format, /check:output_conversion, /static, /norecursive, and /names:lowercase.

▶ Allows use of the **DELETE** statement for relative files. When a record in a relative file is deleted, the first byte of that record is set to a known character (currently '@'). Attempts to read that record later result in ATTACCNON errors. The rest of the record (the whole record when /vms is not set) is set to nulls for unformatted files and spaces for formatted files.

▶ When an **ENDFILE** is performed on a sequential unit, an actual 1-byte record containing a Ctrl+D (04 hex) is written to the file. When you omit /vms, an internal **ENDFILE** flag is set and the file is truncated. The /vms option does not affect **ENDFILE** on relative files; the file is truncated.

▶ Changes certain **OPEN** statement BLANK keyword defaults. Changes the default interpretation from BLANK='NULL' to BLANK='ZERO' for an implicit open or internal file **OPEN**. For an explicit **OPEN**, the default is always BLANK='NULL'.

▶ Changes certain **OPEN** statement effects. If the CARRIAGECONTROL is defaulted, the file is formatted, and the unit is connected to a terminal, then the carriage control defaults to FORTRAN. Otherwise, it defaults to LIST. The /vms option affects the record length for relative organization files. The buffer size is increased by 1 to accommodate the deleted record character.

▶ LIST and /NOLIST are recognized at the end of the file specification to the **INCLUDE** statement at compile time. If you specified /vms and if the file specification does not include the directory path, the current working directory is used as the default directory path. If you omitted /vms, the directory path is where the file that contains the **INCLUDE** statement resides.

▶ Changes internal file writes using list-directed I/O. A list-directed write to an internal file results in removal of the first character from the first element; the field length is decremented accordingly.

▶ The run-time direct access **READ** routine checks the first byte of the retrieved record. If this byte is '@' or NULL ('\0'), then ATTACCNON is returned. The run-time sequential access **READ** routine checks to see if the record it just read is 1 byte long and contains a Ctrl+D (04 hex) or a Ctrl+Z (1A hex). If this is true, it returns EOF.

The default is /novms.

4.1.78 /[no]warn

Syntax:

/warn[:*keyword*...]), /nowarn, /4Yd, /4Nd, /4Ys, /W0, /W1, or /WX

The /warn option instructs the compiler to generate diagnostic messages for defined classes of additional checking that can be performed at compile-time. It also can change the severity level of issued compilation messages.

In the visual development environment, specify the Warning Level (/warn: nogeneral, default, or /warn:error) in the General or the Compiler Diagnostic Compiler Option Category. Specify individual Warning Options in the Compiler Diagnostic Compiler Option Category.

The /warn options and their visual development environment names are:

▶ /warn:noalignments (Data Alignment)

Suppresses warning messages for data that is not naturally aligned. The default is /warn:alignments.

▶ /warn:argument_checking (Argument Mismatch)

Enables warnings about argument mismatches between callers and callees, when compiled together. The default is /warn:noargument_checking.

▶ /warn:declarations or /4Yd (Undeclared Variables)

Issues an error message for any undeclared symbols. This option makes the default type of a variable undefined (**IMPLICIT NONE**) rather than using the default Fortran rules. The default is /warn:nodeclarations or /4Nd.

▶ /warn:errors or /WX (Warning Level: Errors)

Changes the severity of all warning diagnostics into error diagnostics. The default is /warn:noerrors. Specifying /warn:errors (or /WX) sets /warn: stderrors.

▶ /warn:nofileopt (Inform when Compiling Files Separately)

Suppresses the display of an informational-level diagnostic message when compiling multiple files separately, which can prevent interproce-dure optimizations. The default is /warn:fileopt (displays the message: Some interprocedural optimizations may be disabled when compiling in this mode).

▶ /warn:nogeneral (Warning Level: Ignore)

Suppresses all informational-level and warning-level diagnostic messages from the compiler. The default is /warn:general or /W1.

▶ /warn:nogranularity (Alpha systems only)

Suppresses the display of a warning message that the compiler cannot generate code for the requested granularity (see /granularity). The default is /warn:granularity.

▶ /warn:stderrors or /4Ys (Treat Fortran Standard Warnings as Errors)

Requests Fortran 90 standards checking (see Section 4.1.67 /[no]stand) with error-level compilation messages instead of warning-level messages. Specifying /warn:stderrors sets /stand:f90 and is equivalent to /4Ys. Specifying /warn:stderrors with /stand:f95 requests error-level messages for extensions to the proposed Fortran 95 standard.

Specifying /warn:errors sets /warn:stderrors. The default is /warn:nostderrrors.

▶ /warn:truncated_source (Truncated Source)

Requests that the compiler issue a warning diagnostic message when it reads a source line with a statement field that exceeds the maximum column width in fixed-format source files. The maximum column width for fixed-format files is column 72 or 132, depending whether the /extend_source option was specified.

This option has no effect on truncation; lines that exceed the maximum column width are always truncated. This option does not apply to free-format source files. The default is /warn:notruncated_source.

▶ /warn:nouncalled (Uncalled Routines)

Suppresses the compiler warning diagnostic message when a statement function is never called. The default is /warn:uncalled.

▶ /warn:nouninitialized (Uninitialized Variables)

Suppresses warning messages for a variable that is used before a value was assigned to it. The default is /warn:uninitialized.

▶ /warn:unused (Unused Variables)

Requests warning messages for a variable that is declared but never used. The default is /warn:nounused.

▶ /warn:nousage (Usage) Suppresses warning messages about questionable programming practices and the use of intrinsic functions that use a two-digit year (year 2000). The questionable programming practices, although allowed, often are the result of programming errors. For example, /warn:usage detects a continued character or Hollerith literal whose first part ends before the statement field ends and appears to end with trailing spaces. The default is /warn:usage. The /pad_source option can prevent warning messages from /warn:usage.

▶ /warn:all or /warn

Requests all possible warning messages, but does not set /warn:errors or /warn:stderrors.

To enable all the additional checking to be performed and force the severity of the diagnostics to be severe enough to not generate an object file, specify /warn:(all,errors) or /warn:(all,stderrors).

▶ /warn:none, /nowarn, or /W0

Suppresses all warning messages.

If you omit /warn, the defaults are:

▶ For the DF command: /warn:(alignments, noargument_checking, nodeclarations, noerrors, fileopts, general, granularity, nostderrors, notruncated_source, uncalled, uninitialized, nounused, usage)

▶ For the FL32 command: /warn:(alignments, argument_checking, nodeclarations, noerrors, nofileopts, general, granularity, nostderrors, notruncated_source, uncalled, uninitialized, nounused, usage)

For example, the following command requests the argument_checking and declarations keywords and accepts the defaults for the other /warn keywords:

```
DF /warn:(argument_checking,declarations) testfile.f90
```

For more information on the various compiler option categories in the visual development environment, see Section 4.1.1 Categories of Compiler Options.

4.1.79 /[no]watch

Syntax:

/watch[:*keyword*] or /nowatch

The /watch option requests the display of processing information to the console terminal. The default is /watch:source. You can request the display of the passes (compiler, linker) with their respective command arguments and/or the input and output files.

The /watch options are:

▶ /watch:cmd

Displays the passes (compiler, linker) with the respective command arguments.

▶ /watch:source

   Displays the names of sources file(s) being processed. Source file names are listed one per line. This is the default.

▶ /watch:all or /watch

   Requests /watch:(cmd, source). This displays both pass information and source file names.

▶ /nowatch or /watch:none

   Requests /watch:(nocmd, nosource).

4.1.80   /what

Syntax:

/what

The /what option displays Visual Fortran version number information.

4.1.81   /winapp

Syntax:

/winapp or /MG

The /winapp or /MG option requests the creation of a graphics or Fortran Windows application and links against the most commonly used libraries. In the visual development environment, specify the Use Common Windows Libraries in the Libraries Compiler Option Category (see Section 4.1.1 Categories of Compiler Options).

The following related options request libraries:

▶ /dbglibs (see Section 4.1.16)

▶ /fpscomp:libs (see Section 4.1.34)

▶ /libs (see Section 4.1.45)

▶ /threads (see Section 4.1.71)

For information on Fortran Windows Applications, including requesting additional link libraries with the FULLAPI.F90 file, see Chapter 9 Creating Windows Applications.

4.2   Linker Options and Related Information

You can set Linker options from:

▶ The DF command line

When using the DF command line, specify linker options *after* the /LINK option. For example:

```
DF file.f90 file.lib /LINK /NODEFAULTLIB
```

▶ The LINK command line

You can specify linker options and libraries with the LINK command. For example:

```
LINK file.obj file.lib /NODEFAULTLIB
```

▶ Within the Microsoft visual development environment, in the Project menu, Settings dialog box

You can specify linker options and libraries by using the Linker tab in the Project menu, Settings dialog box.

Table 4-8 describes the Linker options.

Table 4–8   *Linker Options*

Linker option	Function
/ALIGN	Specifies the alignment of each section within the linear address space of the program.
/BASE	Sets a base address for the program, overriding the default location.
/COMMENT	Inserts a comment string into the header of an executable file or DLL, after the array of section headers.
/DEBUG	Creates debugging information for the executable file or DLL.
/DEBUGTYPE	Generates debugging information in one of three ways: Microsoft format (CV), COFF format, or both.
/DEF	Passes a module-definition (.DEF) file to the linker.
/DEFAULTLIB	Adds one or more *libraries* to the list of libraries that LINK searches when resolving references.
/DELAY	Controls the delayed loading of DDLs.
/DELAYHOLD	Causes delayed loading of DLLs.
/DLL	Builds a DLL as the main output file.
/DRIVER	Used to build a Windows NT kernel mode driver.

Table 4–8 *Linker Options (Continued)*

Linker option	Function
/ENTRY	Sets the starting address for an executable file or DLL.
/EXETYPE	Used when building a virtual device driver (requested by using the /VXD option).
/EXPORT	Exports a function from your program.
/FIXED	Tells the operating system to load the program only at its preferred base address.
/FORCE	Informs the linker to create a valid executable file or DLL even if a symbol is referenced but not defined or is multiply defined.
/GPSIZE	On Alpha systems, controls whether communal variables (uninitialized global data items) are allocated in .sdata or .bss.
/HEAP	Sets the size of the heap in bytes.
/IMPLIB	Sets the name for the import library that LINK creates when it builds a program that contains exports.
/IMPORT	Does not apply to Visual Fortran.
/INCLUDE	Informs the linker to add a specified symbol to the symbol table.
/INCREMENTAL	Controls how the linker handles incremental linking.
/LARGEADDRESS AWARE	Informs the linker that the application can handle addresses larger than 2 gigabytes.
/LIBPATH	Overrides the environment library path.
/LINK50COMPAT	Generates import libraries in the old (Visual C++ version 5.0) format for backward compatibility.
/MACHINE	Specifies the target platform for the program.
/MAP	Informs the linker to generate a mapfile. You can also specify the file name.
/MAPINFO	Informs the linker to include the specified information in a map file (requested by /MAP).
/MERGE	Combines the first section with the second section and names the resulting section.
/NODEFAULTLIB	Informs tells the linker to remove all default libraries from the list of libraries it searches when resolving external references or only the specified library *name*.
/NOENTRY	Prevents LINK from linking a reference to _main into the DLL.
/NOLOGO	Prevents the display of the copyright message and version number. It also suppresses echoing of command files.
/OPT	Controls the optimizations LINK performs during a build.

Table 4–8 *Linker Options (Continued)*

Linker option	Function
/ORDER	Lets you perform optimization by telling LINK to place certain packaged functions into the image in a predetermined order.
/OUT	Overrides the default name and location of the image file that LINK creates.
/PDB	Controls how the linker produces debugging information.
/PDBTYPE	Controls which Program Database (PDB) is used to store the debug type information.
/PROFILE	Creates an output file that can be used with the profiler.
/RELEASE	Sets the checksum in the header of an executable file.
/SECTION	Changes the attributes of a section, overriding the attributes set when the .OBJ file for the section was compiled.
/STACK	Sets the size of the stack in bytes.
/STUB	Attaches an MS-DOS stub program to a Win32 program.
/SUBSYSTEM	Tells the operating system how to run the executable file.
/SWAPRUN	Informs the operating system to first copy the linker output to a swap file, and then run the image from there (Windows NT).
/VERBOSE	Sends information about the progress of the linking session to the Output window.
/VERSION	Informs the linker to put a version number in the header of the executable file or DLL.
/VXD	Creates a virtual device driver (VxD).
/WARN	Determines the output of LINK warnings.
/WS	Adds the WS_AGGRESSIVE attribute to your application's image.

Table 4-9 lists the Linker options and shows equivalent Microsoft visual development environment options, if any exist. Options listed as command-line only can be entered in the "Common Options" text box of the Project ... Settings dialog box. For instructions on how to work with the Microsoft visual development environment, see Chapter 2 Building Programs and Libraries.

Table 4–9 *Equivalent Linker and Development Environment Options*

Linker Option	Microsoft Visual Development Environment Option
/ALIGN	Command-line only
/BASE	Output Category
/DEBUG	Debug Category
/DEBUGTYPE	Debug Category
/DEF	Command-line only
/DEFAULTLIB	Command-line only
/ENTRY	Output Category
/FORCE	Customize Category
/INCLUDE	Input Category
/INCREMENTAL	Customize Category
/LIBPATH	Input Category
/MAP	Debug Category
/NODEFAULTLIB	Input Category
/NOLOGO	Customize Category
/OUT	Customize Category
/PDB	Customize Category
/PDBTYPE	Debug Category
/PROFILE	General Category
/STACK	Output Category
/VERBOSE	Customize Category
/VERSION	Output Category

Besides discussing linker options individually (Sections 4.2.3 through Section 4.2.51), this section also discusses Module-Definition Files (Section 4.2.52) and Linker Reserved Words (Section 4.2.53).

4.2.1   Setting LINK Options in the Visual Development Environment

You can set linker options in the Microsoft visual development environment by using the Link tab in the Build Settings dialog box. Table 4-10 lists the linker options by category in the visual development environment, along with the equivalent command-line options.

Table 4–10   *Categories of Development Environment Linker Options and Equivalents*

Category	Command-Line Equivalent
General	
Output File Name	/OUT:*filename*
Object/Library Modules	*filename* on command line
Generate Debug Info	/DEBUG
Ignore All Default Libraries	/NODEFAULTLIB
Link Incrementally	/INCREMENTAL:{YES|NO}
Generate Mapfile	/MAP
Enable Profiling	/PROFILE
Output	
Base Address	/BASE:*address*
Entry-Point Symbol	/ENTRY:*function*
Stack Allocations	/STACK:*reserve,commit*
Version Information	/VERSION:*major.minor*
Input	
Object/Library Modules	*filename* on command line
Ignore Libraries	/NODEFAULTLIB:*library*
Ignore All Default Libraries	/NODEFAULTLIB
Force Symbol References	/INCLUDE:*symbol*
MS-DOS Stub File Name	/STUB:*filename*
Customize	
Use Program Database	/PDB:*filename*
Link Incrementally	/INCREMENTAL:{YES|NO}

Table 4–10 *Categories of Development Environment Linker Options and Equivalents (Continued)*

Category	Command-Line Equivalent
Program Database Name	/PDB:*filename*
Output File Name	/OUT:*filename*
Force File Output	/FORCE
Print Progress Messages	/VERBOSE
Suppress Startup Banner	/NOLOGO
Debug	
Mapfile Name	/MAP:*filename*
Generate Mapfile	/MAP
Generate Debug Info	/DEBUG
Microsoft Format	/DEBUGTYPE:CV
COFF Format	/DEBUGTYPE:COFF
Both Formats	/DEBUGTYPE:BOTH

4.2.2 Rules for LINK Options

An option consists of an option specifier, either a dash (-) or a forward slash (/), followed by the name of the option. Option names cannot be abbreviated. Some options take an argument, specified after a colon (:). No spaces or tabs are allowed within an option specification, except within a quoted string in the /COMMENT option.

Specify numeric arguments in decimal or C-language notation. (The digits 1-9 specify decimal values, an integer constant preceded by a zero [0] specifies an octal value, and an integer constant preceded by zero and x [0x or 0X] specifies a hexadecimal value.) Option names and their keyword or filename arguments are not case sensitive, but identifiers as arguments are case sensitive.

LINK first processes options specified in the LINK environment variable. Next, LINK processes options in the order specified on the command line and in command files. If an option is repeated with different arguments, the last one processed takes precedence.

Options apply to the entire build. No options can be applied to specific input files.

4.2.3   /ALIGN

Syntax:

/ALIGN:*number*

Specifies the alignment of each section within the linear address space of the program. The *number* argument is in bytes and must be a power of 2. The default is 4K. The linker generates a warning if the alignment produces an invalid image.

4.2.4   /BASE

Syntax:

/BASE:{*address* | @*filename,key*}

Sets a base address for the program, overriding the default location for an executable file (at 0x400000) or a DLL (at 0x10000000). The operating system first attempts to load a program at its specified or default base address. If sufficient space is not available there, the system relocates the program. To prevent relocation, use the /FIXED option.

Specify the preferred base address in the text box (or in the *address* argument on the command line). The linker rounds the specified number up to the nearest multiple of 64K.

Another way to specify the base address is by using a *filename*, preceded by an at sign (@), and a *key* into the file. The *filename* is a text file that contains the locations and sizes of all DLLs your program uses. The linker looks for *filename* in either the specified path or, if no path is specified, in directories named in the LIB environment variable. Each line in *filename* represents one DLL and has the following syntax:

key address size ;*comment*

The *key* is a string of alphanumeric characters and is not case sensitive. It is usually the name of a DLL. The *key* is followed by a base *address* in C-notation hexadecimal or decimal and a maximum *size*. All three arguments are separated by spaces or tabs. The linker issues a warning if the specified *size* is less than the virtual address space required by the program.

Indicate a *comment* by a semicolon (;). Comments can be on the same or a separate line. The linker ignores all text from the semicolon to the end of the line. The following example shows part of such a file:

```
main 0x00010000 0x08000000 ; for PROJECT.EXE
one  0x28000000 0x00100000 ; for DLLONE.DLL
two  0x28100000 0x00300000 ; for DLLTWO.DLL
```

If the file that contains these lines is called DLLS.TXT, the following example command applies this information.

```
link dlltwo.obj /dll /base:dlls.txt,two
```

You can reduce paging and improve performance of your program by assigning base addresses so that DLLs do not overlap in the address space.

An alternate way to set the base address is with the BASE argument in a NAME or LIBRARY module-definition statement. The /BASE and /DLL options together are equivalent to the LIBRARY statement. For information on module-definition statements, see Section 4.2.52 Module-Definition Files.

4.2.5 /COMMENT

Syntax:

/COMMENT:["] *comment* ["]

Inserts a comment string into the header of an executable file or DLL, after the array of section headers. The type of operating system determines whether the string is loaded into memory. This comment string, unlike the comment specified with DESCRIPTION in a .DEF file, is not inserted into the data section. Comments are useful for embedding copyright and version information.

To specify a *comment* that contains spaces or tabs, enclose it in double quotation marks ("). LINK removes the quotation marks before inserting the string. If more than one /COMMENT option is specified, LINK concatenates the strings and places a null byte at the end of each string.

4.2.6 /DEBUG

Syntax:

/DEBUG

Creates debugging information for the executable file or DLL.

The linker puts the debugging information into a program database (PDB). It updates the program database during subsequent builds of the program. For details about PDBs, see Section 4.2.38 /PDB.

An executable file or DLL created for debugging contains the name and path of the corresponding PDB. Visual Fortran reads the embedded name and uses the PDB when you debug the program. The linker uses the base name of the program and the extension .PDB to name the PDB, and embeds the path where it was created. To override this default, use /PDB:*filename*.

The object files must contain debugging information. Use the compiler's /Zi (Program Database), /Zd (Line Numbers Only), or /Z7 (C7 Compatible) option. If an object (whether specified explicitly or supplied from a library) was compiled with Program Database, its debugging information is stored in a PDB for the object file, and the name and location of the .PDB file is embedded in the object. The linker looks for the object's PDB first in the absolute path written in the object file and then in the directory that contains the object file. You cannot specify a PDB's filename or location to the linker.

If you have turned off Use Program Database (or specified /PDB:NONE on the command line), or if you have chosen either /DEBUGTYPE:COFF or /DEBUGTYPE:BOTH, the linker does not create a PDB but instead puts the debugging information into the executable file or DLL.

The /DEBUG option changes the default for the /OPT option from REF to NOREF.

4.2.7   /DEBUGTYPE

Syntax:

/DEBUGTYPE:{CV | COFF | BOTH}

Generates debugging information in one of three ways, Microsoft format (CV), COFF format, or both:

▶ /DEBUGTYPE:CV

Visual Fortran requires new-style Microsoft Symbolic Debugging Information to read a program for debugging. To select this option in the Microsoft visual development environment, choose the Link tab of the Project Settings dialog box. In the Debug category, select the Microsoft Format button, which is only available if you have checked the Generate Debug Info box.

▶ /DEBUGTYPE:COFF

This option generates COFF-style debugging information. Some debuggers require Common Object File Format (COFF) debugging information.

When you set this option, the linker does not create a PDB; in addition, incremental linking is disabled.

To select this option in the visual development environment, choose the Link tab of the Project Settings dialog box. In the Debug category, select the COFF Format button, which is only available if you have checked the Generate Debug Info box.

▶ /DEBUGTYPE:BOTH

This option generates both COFF debugging information and old-style Microsoft debugging information.

When you set this option, the linker does not create a PDB; in addition, incremental linking is disabled. The linker must call the CVPACK.EXE tool to process the old-style Microsoft debugging information. CVPACK must be in the same directory as LINK or in a directory in the PATH environment variable.

In the visual development environment, specify this option with the Both Formats button, which is only available if you have selected Generate Debug Info.

If you do not specify /DEBUG, /DEBUGTYPE is ignored. If you specify /DEBUG but not /DEBUGTYPE, the default type is /DEBUGTYPE:CV.

4.2.8   /DEF

Syntax:

/DEF:*filename*

Passes a module-definition (.DEF) file to the linker. Only one .DEF file can be specified to LINK. For details about .DEF files, see Section 4.2.52 Module-Definition Files.

When a .DEF file is used in a build, whether the main output file is an executable file or a DLL, LINK creates an import library (.LIB) and an exports file (.EXP). These files are created regardless of whether the main output file contains exports.

Do not specify this option in the visual development environment; this option is for use only on the command line. To specify a .DEF file, add it to the project along with other files.

4.2.9   /DEFAULTLIB

Syntax:

/DEFAULTLIB:*libraries*...

Adds one or more *libraries* to the list of libraries that LINK searches when resolving references. A library specified with /DEFAULTLIB is searched after libraries specified on the command line and before default libraries named in object files. To specify multiple libraries, type a comma (,) between library names.

Ignore All Default Libraries (/NODEFAULTLIB) overrides /DEFAULT LIB:*library.* Ignore Libraries (/NODEFAULTLIB:*library*) overrides /DEFAULT LIB:*library* when the same *library* name is specified in both.

4.2.10 /DELAY

Syntax:

/DELAY[:*dllname*]

Controls delayed loading of DDLs:

▶ The unload qualifier tells the delay-load helper function to support explicit unloading of the DLL by resetting the IAT to its original form, invalidating IAT pointers and causing them to be overwritten.

▶ The nobind qualifier tells the linker not to include a bindable IAT in the final image. The resulting image cannot be statically bound. (Images with bindable IATs may be statically bound prior to execution.)

To specify DLLs to delay load, use the /DELAYHOLD option.

4.2.11 /DELAYHOLD

Syntax:

/DELAYHOLD[:*dllname*]

Causes delayed loading of DLLs. The *dllname* specifies a DLL to delay load. You can use this option as many times as necessary to specify as many DLLs as you choose. You must link your program with Delayimp.lib or implement your own delay-load helper function.

4.2.12 /DLL

Syntax:

/DLL

Builds a DLL as the main output file. A DLL usually contains exports that can be used by another program. There are three methods for specifying exports, listed in recommended order of use:

▶ A *c***DEC$ ATTRIBUTES** DLLEXPORT directive in the source code

▶ An /EXPORT specification in a LINK command

▶ An EXPORTS statement in a module definition (.DEF) file

A program can use more than one method.

An alternate way to build a DLL is with the LIBRARY module-definition statement. The /BASE and /DLL options together are equivalent to the LIBRARY statement.

In the visual development environment, you can set this option by choosing Dynamic-Link Library under Project Type in the New Project dialog box.

4.2.13 /DRIVER

Syntax:

/DRIVER[:UPONLY]

Builds a Windows NT kernel mode driver. The linker will perform some special optimizations if this option is selected. The UPONLY keyword causes the linker to add the IMAGE_FILE_UP_SYSTEM_ONLY bit to the characteristics in the output header to specify that it is a uniprocessor (UP) driver. The operating system will refuse to load a UP driver on a multiprocessor (MP) system.

4.2.14 /ENTRY

Syntax:

/ENTRY:*function*

Sets the starting address for an executable file or DLL. Specify a function name that is defined with the *c*DEC$ ATTRIBUTES STDCALL directive. The parameters and return value must be defined as documented in the Win32 API for WinMain (for an .EXE) or DllEntryPoint (for a DLL). It is recommended that you let the linker set the entry point.

By default, the starting address is a function name from the run-time library. The linker selects it according to the attributes of the program, as shown in Table 4-11.

Table 4–11   *Default Starting Addresses for Executables or DLLs*

Function name	Default for
MainCRTStartup	An application using /SUBSYSTEM:CONSOLE; calls main
WinMainCRTStartup	An application using /SUBSYSTEM:WINDOWS; calls WinMain, which must be defined with *c*DEC$ ATTRIBUTES STDCALL
_DllMainCRTStartup	A DLL; calls DllMain (which must be defined with *c*DEC$ ATTRIBUTES STDCALL) if it exists

If the /DLL or /SUBSYSTEM option is not specified, the linker selects a subsystem and entry point depending on whether main or WinMain is defined.

The functions main, WinMain, and DllMain are the three forms of the user-defined entry point.

4.2.15 /EXETYPE

Syntax:

/EXETYPE:DYNAMIC

Used when building a virtual device driver (VxD). A VxD is linked using the /VXD option.

Specify DYNAMIC to create a dynamically-loaded VxD.

4.2.16 /EXPORT

Syntax:

/EXPORT:*entryname*[=*internalname*][, @*ordinal* [, NONAME]] [, DATA]

Lets you export a function from your program to allow other programs to call the function. You can also export data. Exports are usually defined in a DLL.

The *entryname* is the name of the function or data item as it is to be used by the calling program. You can optionally specify the *internalname* as the function known in the defining program; by default, *internalname* is the same as *entryname*. The *ordinal* specifies an index into the exports table in the range 1 - 65535; if you do not specify *ordinal*, LINK assigns one. The NONAME keyword exports the function only as an ordinal, without an *entryname*.

The DATA keyword specifies that the exported item is a data item. The data item in the client program must be declared using *c***DEC$ ATTRIBUTES** DLLIMPORT. (The CONSTANT keyword is supported for compatability but is not recommended.)

There are three methods for exporting a definition, listed in recommended order of usage:

▶ A *c***DEC$ ATTRIBUTES** DLLEXPORT directive in the source code

▶ An /EXPORT specification in a LINK command

▶ An EXPORTS statement in a module definition (.DEF) file

All three methods can be used in the same program. When LINK builds a program that contains exports, it also creates an import library, unless an .EXP file is used in the build.

LINK uses decorated forms of identifiers. A *decorated name* is an internal representation of a procedure name or variable name that contains information about where it is declared; for procedures, the information includes how it is called. Decorated names are mainly of interest in mixed-language programming, when calling Fortran routines from other languages.

The compiler decorates an identifier when it creates the object file. If *entryname* or *internalname* is specified to the linker in its undecorated form as it appears in the source code, LINK attempts to match the name. If it cannot find a unique match, LINK issues an error.

Use the DUMPBIN tool described in Section 25.10 Examining Files with DUMPBIN to get the decorated form of an identifier when you need to specify it to the linker. Do not specify the decorated form of identifiers declared with c**DEC$ ATTRIBUTES** C or STDCALL.

For more information on when and how to use decorated names, see Section 18.1.2 Adjusting Naming Conventions in Mixed-Language Programming.

4.2.17 /FIXED

Syntax:

/FIXED

Tells the operating system to load the program only at its preferred base address. If the preferred base address is unavailable, the operating system does not load the file. For more information on base address, see Section 4.2.4 /BASE.

When you specify /FIXED, LINK does not generate a relocation section in the program. At run-time, if the operating system cannot load the program at that address, it issues an error and does not load the program.

Some Win32 operating systems, especially those that coexist with MS-DOS, frequently must relocate a program. A program created with /FIXED will not run on Win32s operating systems.

Note: Do not use /FIXED when building device drivers.

4.2.18 /FORCE

Syntax:

/FORCE:[{MULTIPLE | UNRESOLVED}]

Tells the linker to create a valid executable file or DLL even if a symbol is referenced but not defined or is multiply defined.

The /FORCE option can take an optional argument:

▶ Use /FORCE:MULTIPLE to create an output file whether or not LINK finds more than one definition for a symbol.

▶ Use /FORCE:UNRESOLVED to create an output file whether or not LINK finds an undefined symbol.

A file created with this option may not run as expected. The linker will not link incrementally with the /FORCE option.

You can select this option in the visual development environment by checking the Force File Output box in the Customize category of the Link tab in the Project Settings dialog box.

4.2.19 /GPSIZE

Syntax:

/GPSIZE:*num*

For Alpha systems, this option controls whether communal variables (uninitialized global data items) are allocated in .sdata or .bss. Communal variables smaller than or equal to the /GPSIZE value are allocated in .sdata. Communal variables larger than this value are allocated in .bss.

4.2.20 /HEAP

Syntax:

/HEAP:*reserve*[, *commit*]

Sets the size of the heap in bytes.

The *reserve* argument specifies the total heap allocation in virtual memory. The default heap size is 1MB. The linker rounds up the specified value to the nearest 4 bytes.

The optional *commit* argument is subject to interpretation by the operating system. In Windows NT, it specifies the amount of physical memory to allocate at a time. Committed virtual memory causes space to be reserved in the paging file. A higher *commit* value saves time when the application needs more heap space but increases the memory requirements and possibly startup time.

Specify the *reserve* and *commit* values in decimal or C-language notation. (Use the digits 1-9 for decimal values, precede octal values with zero [0], and precede hexadecimal values with zero and x [0x or 0X].)

4.2.21 /IMPLIB

Syntax:

/IMPLIB:*filename*

Overrides the default name for the import library that LINK creates when it builds a program that contains exports. The default name is formed from the base name of the main output file and the extension .LIB. A program contains exports if one or more of the following is true:

▶ A *c*DEC$ ATTRIBUTES DLLEXPORT directive in the source code

▶ An /EXPORT specification in a LINK command

▶ An EXPORTS statement in a module definition (.DEF) file

LINK ignores the /IMPLIB option when an import library is not being created. If no exports are specified, LINK does not create an import library. If an export (.EXP) file is used in the build, LINK assumes an import library already exists and does not create one. For information on import libraries and export files, see Section 25.8.5 Import Libraries and Export Files.

4.2.22 /IMPORT

Syntax:

/IMPORT

This option is specific to MACOS and does not apply to Visual Fortran.

4.2.23 /INCLUDE

Syntax:

/INCLUDE:*symbol*

Tells the linker to add a specified symbol to the symbol table.

Specify a *symbol* name in the text box. To specify multiple symbols, specify /INCLUDE:*symbol* once for each symbol.

The linker resolves *symbol* by adding the object that contains the symbol definition to the program. This is useful for including a library object that otherwise would not be linked to the program.

Specifying a symbol in the /INCLUDE option overrides the removal of that symbol by /OPT:REF.

To select this option in the visual development environment, choose the Force Symbol References text box in the Input category of the Link tab of the Project Settings dialog box.

4.2.24 /INCREMENTAL

Syntax:

/INCREMENTAL:{YES | NO}

Controls how the linker handles incremental linking. By default, the linker runs in incremental mode (for exceptions, see Section 4.1.72 /[no]traceback).

To prevent incremental linking, clear the Link Incrementally check box in the Customize category (or specify /INCREMENTAL:NO on the command line).

To link incrementally, set the Link Incrementally check box (or specify /INCREMENTAL:YES on the command line). When you specify this option, the linker issues a warning if it cannot link incrementally and then links the program nonincrementally. Certain options and situations override /INCREMENTAL:YES.

Most programs can be linked incrementally. However, some changes are too great, and some options are incompatible with incremental linking. LINK performs a full link if any of the following options are specified:

▶ Link Incrementally is turned off (/INCREMENTAL:NO)

▶ COFF Format (/DEBUGTYPE:COFF)

▶ Both Formats (/DEBUGTYPE:BOTH)

▶ /OPT:REF

▶ /OPT:ICF is selected.

▶ /ORDER

▶ Use program Database is turned off (/PDB:NONE) when Generate Debug Info (/DEBUG) is specified

Additionally, LINK performs a full link if any of the following occur:

▶ The incremental status (.ILK) file is missing. (LINK creates a new .ILK file in preparation for subsequent incremental linking.)

▶ There is no write permission for the .ILK file. (LINK ignores the .ILK file and links nonincrementally.)

▶ The .EXE or .DLL output file is missing.

▶ The timestamp of the .ILK, .EXE, or .DLL is changed.

▶ A LINK option is changed. Most LINK options, when changed between builds, cause a full link.

▶ An object (.OBJ) file is added or omitted.

▶ An object that was compiled with the /Yu /Z7 option is changed.

To select this option in the visual development environment, select the Link Incrementally check box in the Customize category of the Link tab in the Project Settings dialog box.

4.2.25 /LARGEADDRESSAWARE

Syntax:

/LARGEADDRESSAWARE

Informs the linker that the application can handle addresses larger than 2 gigabytes.

4.2.26 /LIBPATH

Syntax:

/LIBPATH:*dir*

Overrides the environment library path. The linker will first search in the path specified by this option, and then search in the path specified in the LIB environment variable. You can specify only one directory for each /LIBPATH option you enter. If you want to specify more than one directory, you must specify multiple /LIBPATH options. The linker will then search the specified directories in order.

4.2.27 /LINK50COMPAT

Syntax:

/LINK50COMPAT

Generates import libraries in the old (Visual C++ version 5.0) format for backward compatibility.

4.2.28 /MACHINE

Syntax:

/MACHINE:{IX86 | ALPHA}

Specifies the target platform for the program (for Visual Fortran, specify either IX86 or ALPHA).

Usually, you do not need to specify the /MACHINE option. LINK infers the machine type from the .OBJ files. However, in some circumstances LINK cannot determine the machine type and issues linker tools error LNK1113. If such an error occurs, specify /MACHINE.

4.2.29 /MAP

Syntax:

/MAP[:*filename*]

Tells the linker to generate a mapfile. You can optionally specify a map file name to override the default.

The linker names the mapfile with the base name of the program and the extension .MAP. To override the default name, use the *filename* argument.

A map file is a text file that contains the following information about the program being linked:

▶ The module name, which is the base name of the file

▶ The timestamp from the program file header (not from the file system)

▶ A list of groups in the program, with each group's start address (as *section*: *offset*), length, group name, and class

▶ A list of public symbols, with each address (as *section*:*offset*), symbol name, flat address, and object file where the symbol is defined

▶ The entry point (as *section*:*offset*)

▶ A list of fixups

To select this in the visual development environment, select the Generate Mapfile check box in the Debug category of the Link tab in the Project Settings dialog box.

4.2.30 /MAPINFO

Syntax:

/MAPINFO:{EXPORTS | FIXUPS | LINES}

Informs the linker to include the specified information in a map file, which is created if you specify the /MAP option:

▶ EXPORTS tells the linker to include exported functions.

▶ FIXUPS tells the linker to include base-relocation information in the mapfile if relocation information exists in the image. Base relocations will be present in the image if you link with /FIXED:NO.

▶ LINES includes line-number information.

4.2.31 /MERGE

Syntax:

/MERGE:*from=to*

Combines the first section (*from*) with the second section (*to*), naming the resulting section *to*. If the second section does not exist, LINK renames the section *from* as *to*.

The /MERGE option is useful for creating virtual device drivers (VxDs) and overriding the compiler-generated section names.

4.2.32 /NODEFAULTLIB

Syntax:

/NODEFAULTLIB[:*library*]

Tells the linker to remove all default libraries from the list of libraries it searches when resolving external references. If you specify *library*, the linker only ignores the libraries you have named. To specify multiple *libraries*, type a comma (,) between the library names.

The linker resolves references to external definitions by searching first in libraries specified on the command line, then in default libraries specified with the /DEFAULTLIB option, then in default libraries named in object files.

Ignore All Default Libraries (/NODEFAULTLIB) overrides /DE FAULTLIB:*library.* Ignore Libraries (/NODEFAULTLIB:*library*) overrides /DEFAULTLIB:*library* when the same *library* name is specified in both.

To select this in the visual development environment, select the Ignore Libraries or Ignore All Default Libraries check box in the Input category of the Link tab in the Project Settings dialog box.

4.2.33 /NOENTRY

Syntax:

/NOENTRY

This option is required for creating a resource-only DLL.

Use this option to prevent LINK from linking a reference to _main into the DLL.

4.2.34 /NOLOGO

Syntax:

/NOLOGO

Prevents display of the copyright message and version number. This option also suppresses echoing of command files.

By default, this information is sent by the linker to the Output window. On the command line, it is sent to standard output and can be redirected to a file.

To select this option in the visual development environment, select the Suppress Startup Banner check box in the Customize category of the Link tab in the Project Settings dialog box.

4.2.35 /OPT

Syntax:

/OPT:{REF | NOREF}

Controls the optimizations LINK performs during a build. Optimizations generally decrease the image size and increase the program speed, at a cost of increased link time.

By default, LINK removes unreferenced packaged functions (COM-DATs). This optimization is called transitive COMDAT elimination. To override this default and keep unused packaged functions in the program, specify /OPT:NOREF. You can use the /INCLUDE option to override the removal of a specific symbol. It is not possible to create packaged functions with the Visual Fortran compiler. This description is included for mixed-language applications with languages such as Visual C++ that support packaged functions (with the /Gy compiler option).

If you specify the /DEBUG option, the default for /OPT changes from REF to NOREF and all functions are preserved in the image. To override this default and optimize a debugging build, specify /OPT:REF. The /OPT:REF option disables incremental linking.

4.2.36 /ORDER

Syntax:

/ORDER:@*filename*

Lets you perform optimization by telling LINK to place certain packaged functions into the image in a predetermined order. It is not possible to make packaged functions with the Visual Fortran compiler. This description is included for mixed-language applications with languages such as Visual C++ that support packaged functions (with the /Gy compiler option).

LINK places packaged functions in the specified order within each section in the image.

Specify the order in *filename*, which is a text file that lists the packaged functions in the order you want to link them. Each line in *filename* contains the name of one packaged function. Function names are case sensitive. A comment is specified by a semicolon (;) and can be on the same or a separate line. LINK ignores all text from the semicolon to the end of the line.

LINK uses decorated forms of identifiers. A *decorated name* is an internal representation of a procedure name or variable name that contains information about where it is declared; for procedures, the information includes how it is called. Decorated names are mainly of interest in mixed-language programming, when calling Fortran routines from other languages.

The compiler decorates an identifier when it creates the object file. If the name of the packaged function is specified to the linker in its undecorated form as it appears in the source code, LINK attempts to match the name. If it cannot find a unique match, LINK issues an error.

Use the DUMPBIN tool to get the decorated form of an identifier when you need to specify it to the linker. Do not specify the decorated form of identifiers declared with *c***DEC\$ ATTRIBUTES** C or STDCALL. For more information on when and how to use decorated names, see Section 18.1.2 Adjusting Naming Conventions in Mixed-Language Programming.

If more than one /ORDER specification is used, the last one specified takes effect.

Ordering allows you to optimize your program's paging behavior through swap tuning. Group a function with the functions it calls. You can also group frequently called functions together. These techniques increase the probability that a called function is in memory when it is needed and will not have to be paged from disk.

This option disables incremental linking.

4.2.37 /OUT

Syntax:

/OUT:*filename*

Overrides the default name and location of the image file that LINK creates. By default, LINK forms the filename using the base name of the first file specified and the appropriate extension (.EXE or .DLL).

The /OUT option controls the default base name for a mapfile or import library. For details, see Section 4.2.29 /MAP and Section 4.2.21 /IMPLIB.

4.2.38 /PDB

Syntax:

/PDB[:*filename*]

Controls how the linker produces debugging information. The optional *filename*argument overrides the default filename for the program database. The default filename for the PDB has the base name of the program and the extension .PDB.

By default when you specify /DEBUG, the linker creates a program database (PDB), which holds debugging information. If you have not specified /DEBUG, the linker ignores /PDB.

If you specify /PDB:NONE, the linker does not create a PDB, but instead puts old-style debugging information into the executable file or DLL. The linker then calls the CVPACK.EXE tool, which must be in the same directory as LINK.EXE or in a directory in the PATH environment variable.

Debugging information in a program database must be in Microsoft Format (/DEBUGTYPE:CV). If you choose either COFF Format (/DEBUG TYPE:COFF) or Both Formats (/DEBUGTYPE:BOTH), no PDB is created.

Incremental linking is suppressed if you specify /PDB:NONE.

You can select this option in the visual development environment by selecting the Use Program Database check box in the Customize category of the Link tab in the Project Settings dialog box.

4.2.39 /PDBTYPE

Syntax:

/PDBTYPE:{CON[SOLIDATE] | SEPT[YPES]}

Controls which Program Database (PDB) stores the debug type information.

On the command line, the /PDBTYPE option can take one of the following arguments:

► /PDBTYPE:CON[SOLIDATE] tells the linker to place the debug type information in a single .PDB file. This option is the default. This option cannot be used if /PDB:NONE is specified.

► /PDBTYPE:SEPT[YPES] tells the linker to leave the debug type information distributed in the source (compiler) .PDB files. In the Project Settings dialog box, select Separate Types in the Debug category of the Link tab to specify this linker option.

If SEPT[YPES] is specified, linking can be significantly faster. The advantages are:

► The debugger startup time may be slightly faster.

► Less hard disk space is needed to store data.

The disadvantage is more files are needed for the debugger to find the debug information when debugging. Use this option when you plan to debug privately. Do not use this option when the debug build is to be used by multiple users.

4.2.40 /PROFILE

Syntax:

/PROFILE

Creates an output file that can be used with the profiler. This option is found only in the General category on the Link tab.

A profiler-ready program has a map file. If it contains debugging information, the information must be stored in the output file instead of a program database file (.PDB file) and must be in Microsoft old-style format.

In the visual development environment, setting Enable Profiling enables the Generate Mapfile option in the General and Debug categories. If you set the Generate Debug option, be sure to choose Microsoft Format in the Debug category.

On the command line, /PROFILE has the same effect as setting the /MAP option; if the /DEBUG option is specified, then /PROFILE also implies the options /DEBUGTYPE:CV and /PDB:NONE. In either case, /PROFILE implies /INCREMENTAL:NO.

You can select this option in the visual development environment by selecting the Enable Profiling check box in the General category of the Link tab in the Project Settings dialog box.

4.2.41 /RELEASE

Syntax:

/RELEASE

Sets the checksum in the header of an executable file.

The operating system requires the checksum for certain files such as device drivers. To ensure compatibility with future operating systems, set the checksum for release versions of your programs.

This option is set by default when you specify the /SUBSYSTEM: NATIVE option.

4.2.42 /SECTION

Syntax:

/SECTION:*name*,[E][C][I][R][W][S][D][K][L][P][X]

Changes the properties of a section, overriding the properties set when the .OBJ file for the section was compiled.

A section in a portable executable (PE) file is roughly equivalent to a segment or the resources in an NE file. Sections contain either code or data. Unlike segments, sections are blocks of contiguous memory with no size constraints. Some sections contain code or data that your program declared and uses directly, while other data sections are created for you by the linker and librarian, and contain information vital to the operating system.

Specify a colon (:) and a section name. The name is case sensitive.

Specify one or more properties for the section. The property characters, listed below, are not case sensitive. You must specify all properties that you want the section to have; an omitted property character causes that property bit to be turned off. The meanings of the property characters are shown in Table 4-12.

Table 4–12   *Property Characters for Linker option /SECTION*

Character	Property	Meaning
E	Execute	Allows code to be executed
C	Conforming	Marks the section as conforming

Table 4–12   *Property Characters for Linker option /SECTION (Continued)*

Character	Property	Meaning
I	IOPL	Marks the section as IOPL
R	Read	Allows read operations on data
W	Write	Allows write operations on data
S	Shared	Shares the section among all processes that load the image
D	Discardable	Marks the section as discardable
K	Cacheable	Marks the section as not cacheable
L	Preload	VxD only; marks the section as preload
P	Pageable	Marks the section as not pageable
X	Memory-resident	VxD only; marks the section as memory-resident

A section that does not have E, R, or W set is probably invalid.

4.2.43 /STACK

Syntax:

/STACK:*reserve*[,*commit*]

Sets the size of the stack in bytes.

The *reserve* argument specifies the total stack allocation in virtual memory. The default stack size is 1MB. The linker rounds up the specified value to the nearest 4 bytes.

The optional *commit* argument is subject to interpretation by the operating system. In Windows NT, it specifies the amount of physical memory to allocate at a time. Committed virtual memory causes space to be reserved in the paging file. A higher *commit* value saves time when the application needs more stack space but increases the memory requirements and possibly startup time.

Specify the *reserve* and *commit* values in decimal or C-language notation. (Use the digits 1 -9 for decimal values, precede octal values with zero [0], and precede hexadecimal values with zero and x [0x or 0X].

An alternate way to set the stack is with the STACKSIZE statement in a .DEF file (see Section 4.2.52.6). STACKSIZE overrides Stack Allocations (/STACK) if you specify both. You can change the stack after the executable file is built by using the EDITBIN.EXE tool. For more information, see Editing Files with EDITBIN.

To set these options in the visual development environment, type values in the Reserve and Commit boxes in the Output category of the Link tab in the Project Settings dialog box.

4.2.44 /STUB

Syntax:

/STUB:*filename*

Attaches an MS-DOS stub program to a Win32 program.

A stub program is invoked if the file is executed in MS-DOS. Usually, it displays an appropriate message; however, any valid MS-DOS application can be a stub program.

Specify a *filename* for the stub program after a colon (:). The linker checks *filename* to be sure that it is a valid MS-DOS executable file and issues an error if the file is not valid. The program must be an .EXE file; a .COM file is invalid for a stub program.

If you do not specify /STUB, the linker attaches a default stub program that generates the following message:

```
This program cannot be run in MS-DOS mode.
```

You can select this option in the visual development environment by typing the stub file name in the MS-DOS Stub File Name box in the Input category of the Link tab of the Project Settings dialog box.

4.2.45 /SUBSYSTEM

Syntax:

/SUBSYSTEM:{CONSOLE | WINDOWS | NATIVE | POSIX | WINDOWSC}[, *major* [.*minor*]]

Tells the operating system how to run the executable file. The subsystem is specified as follows:

▶ The CONSOLE subsystem is used for Win32 character-mode applications. Console applications are given a console by the operating system. If main or wmain is defined, CONSOLE is the default.

▶ The WINDOWS subsystem is appropriate for an application that does not require a console. It creates its own windows for interaction with the user. If WinMain or wWinMain is defined, WINDOWS is the default.

▶ The NATIVE subsystem is used for device drivers.

▶ The POSIX subsystem creates an application that runs with the POSIX subsystem in Windows NT.

▶ The WINDOWSCE subsystem is not used by Visual Fortran.

The optional *major* and *minor* version numbers specify the minimum required version of the subsystem. The arguments are decimal numbers in the range 0 to 65535. The default is version 3.10 for CONSOLE and WIN-DOWS and 1.0 for NATIVE.

The choice of subsystem affects the default starting address for the program. For more information, see Section 4.2.14 the /ENTRY option.

4.2.46 /SWAPRUN

Syntax:

/SWAPRUN:{NET|CD}

Tells the operating system to first copy the linker output to a swap file, and then run the image from there. This is a Windows NT 4.0 feature.

If NET is specified, the operating system will first copy the binary image from the network to a swap file and load it from there. This option is useful for running applications over the network. When CD is specified, the operating system will copy the image on a removable disk to a page file and then load it.

4.2.47 /VERBOSE

Syntax:

/VERBOSE[:LIB]

The linker sends information about the progress of the linking session to the Output window. If this option is specified on the command line, the information is sent to standard output and can be redirected to a file.

The displayed information includes the library search process and lists each library and object name (with full path), the symbol being resolved from the library, and the list of objects that reference the symbol.

Adding :LIB to the /VERBOSE option restricts progress messages to those indicating the libraries searched.

You can select this option in the Microsoft visual development environment by filling in the Print Progress Messages box in the Customize category of the Link tab of the Project Settings dialog box.

4.2.48 /VERSION

Syntax:

/VERSION:*major* [.*minor*]

Tells the linker to put a version number in the header of the executable file or DLL.

The *major* and *minor* arguments are decimal numbers in the range 0 - 65535. The default is version 0.0.

An alternate way to insert a version number is with the VERSION module-definition statement.

You can select this option in the Microsoft visual development environment by typing version information in the Major and Minor boxes in the Output category of the Link tab of the Project Settings dialog box.

4.2.49 /VXD

Syntax:

/VXD

Creates a virtual device driver (VxD). When this option is specified, the default file name extension changes to .VXD. For details on VxDs, see the Microsoft Windows NT Device Driver Kit.

A .VXD file is not in Common Object File Format, and it cannot be used with DUMPBIN or EDITBIN. It does not contain debugging information. However, you can create a map file when you link a .VXD file.

A .VXD file cannot be incrementally linked.

For related information, see Section 4.2.15 /EXETYPE.

4.2.50 /WARN

Syntax:

/WARN[:*level*]

Lets you determine the output of LINK warnings. The *level*s are described in Table 4-13.

Table 4–13 *Levels in the /WARN Linker Option*

level	Meaning
0	Suppress all warnings.

Table 4–13 *Levels in the /WARN Linker Option (Continued)*

level	Meaning
1	Displays most warnings. Overrides a /WARN:*level* specified earlier on the LINK command line or in the LINK environment variable. Default if /WARN:*level* is not used.
2	Displays additional warnings Default if /WARN is specified without *level*

4.2.51 /WS

Syntax:

/WS:AGGRESSIVE

Adds the WS_AGGRESSIVE property to your application's image. The Windows NT 4.0 loader will recognize this property and aggressively trim the working set of the process when it is not active. Using this option is similar to adding the following call throughout your application:

```
SetProcessWorkingSetSize(hThisProcess, -1, -1)
```

/WS:AGGRESSIVE can be used for applications that must have a low impact on the system's memory pool.

If the speed of your application is important, do not use /WS:AGGRESSIVE without testing the resulting performance implications. Ideal candidates are processes that tend to operate in the background, such as services and screen savers.

4.2.52 Module-Definition Files

A module-definition (.DEF) file is a text file that contains statements that define an executable file or DLL. These files should not be confused with *module program units*, which are described in "Program Units and Procedures" in the *Language Reference* in Visual Fortran online Help.

Because LINK provides equivalent command-line options for most module-definition statements, a typical program for Win32 does not usually require a .DEF file. In contrast, 16-bit programs for Windows almost *always* must be linked using a .DEF file.

Section 4.2.52.1 describes the rules for Module-Definition statements. The following sections describe the statements in a .DEF file:

▶ Section 4.2.52.2 DESCRIPTION

▶ Section 4.2.52.3 EXPORTS

▶ Section 4.2.52.4 LIBRARY

▶ Section 4.2.52.5 NAME

▶ Section 4.2.52.6 STACKSIZE

▶ Section 4.2.52.7 VERSION

You can use one or more of these statements in a .DEF file.

The section describing each module-definition statement gives its command-line equivalent.

4.2.52.1 *Rules for Module-Definition Statements*

The following syntax rules apply to all statements in a .DEF file. Other rules that apply to specific statements are described with each statement.

▶ Statements and attribute keywords *are not* case sensitive. User-specified identifiers *are* case sensitive.

▶ Use one or more spaces, tabs, or newline characters to separate a statement keyword from its arguments and to separate statements from each other. A colon (:) or equal sign (=) that designates an argument is surrounded by zero or more spaces, tabs, or newline characters.

▶ A NAME or LIBRARY statement, if used, must precede all other statements.

▶ Most statements appear only once in the .DEF file and accept one specification of arguments. The arguments follow the statement keyword on the same or subsequent line(s). If the statement is repeated with different arguments later in the file, the latter statement overrides the former.

▶ The EXPORTS statement can appear more than once in the .DEF file. Each statement can take multiple specifications, which must be separated by one or more spaces, tabs, or newline characters. The statement keyword must appear once before the first specification and can be repeated before each additional specification.

▶ Comments in the .DEF file are designated by a semicolon (;) at the beginning of each comment line. A comment cannot share a line with a statement, but it can appear between specifications in a multiline statement. (EXPORTS is a multiline statement.)

▶ Numeric arguments are specified in decimal or in C-language notation.

▶ If a string argument matches a reserved word, it must be enclosed in double quotation (") marks.

Many statements have an equivalent LINK command-line option. For additional details, see Section 4.2 Linker Options and Related Information.

4.2.52.2 DESCRIPTION

Syntax:

DESCRIPTION "*text*"

This statement writes a string into an .rdata section. Enclose the specified *text* in single or double quotation marks (' or "). To use a literal quotation mark (either single or double) in the string, enclose the string with the other type of mark.

This feature differs from the comment specified with the /COMMENT linker option.

4.2.52.3 EXPORTS

Syntax:

EXPORTS

This statement makes one or more definitions available as exports to other programs.

EXPORTS marks the beginning of a list of export *definitions*. Each definition must be on a separate line. The EXPORTS keyword can be on the same line as the first definition or on a preceding line. The .DEF file can contain one or more EXPORTS statements.

The syntax for an export definition is:

entryname[=*internalname*] [@*ordinal* [NONAME]] [DATA]

For information on the *entryname, internalname, ordinal,* NONAME, and DATA arguments, see Section 4.2.16 the /EXPORT option.

There are three methods for exporting a definition, listed in recommended order of use:

▶ A *c***DEC$ATTRIBUTES** DLLEXPORT directive in the source code

▶ An /EXPORT specification in a LINK command

▶ An EXPORTS statement in a .DEF file

All three methods can be used in the same program. When LINK builds a program that contains exports, it also creates an import library, unless the build uses an .EXP file.

4.2.52.4 LIBRARY

Syntax:

LIBRARY [*library*] [BASE=*address*]

This statement tells LINK to create a DLL. LINK creates an import library at the same time, unless you use an .EXP file in the build.

The *library* argument specifies the internal name of the DLL. (Use the Output File Name [/OUT] option to specify the DLL's output name.)

The BASE=*address* argument sets the base address that the operating system uses to load the DLL. This argument overrides the default DLL location of 0x10000000. For details about base addresses, see the description of the Base Address option (Section 4.2.4 /BASE).

You can also use the /DLL linker option to specify a DLL build, and the /BASE option to set the base address.

4.2.52.5 NAME

Syntax:

NAME [*application*] [BASE=*address*]

This statement specifies a name for the main output file. An equivalent way to specify an output filename is with the /OUT option, and an equivalent way to set the base address is with the /BASE option. If both are specified, /OUT overrides NAME. For details about output filenames and base addresses, see Section 4.2.4 /BASE (the Base Address) and Section 4.2.25 Output File Name (/OUT) options.

4.2.52.6 STACKSIZE

Syntax:

STACKSIZE *reserve* [,*commit*]

This statement sets the size of the stack in bytes. An equivalent way to set the stack is with the /STACK option. For details about the *reserve* and *commit* arguments, see Section 4.2.43 /STACK.

4.2.52.7 VERSION

Syntax:

VERSION *major* [.*minor*]

This statement tells LINK to put a number in the header of the executable file or DLL. The *major* and *minor* arguments are decimal numbers in the range 0 - 65535. The default is version 0.0.

An equivalent way to specify a version number is with the Version Information (/VERSION) option.

4.2.53 Linker Reserved Words

Table 4-14 lists the words reserved by the linker. You can use these names as arguments in module-definition statements only if you enclose the name in double quotation marks (").

Table 4–14 *Linker Reserved Words*

APPLOADER	INITINSTANCE	PRELOAD
BASE	IOPL	PROTMODE
CODE	LIBRARY	PURE
CONFORMING	LOADONCALL	READONLY
DATA	LONGNAMES	READWRITE
DESCRIPTION	MOVABLE	REALMODE
DEV386	MOVEABLE	RESIDENT
DISCARDABLE	MULTIPLE	RESIDENTNAME
DYNAMIC	NAME	SEGMENTS
EXECUTE-ONLY	NEWFILES	SHARED
EXECUTEONLY	NODATA	SINGLE
EXECUTEREAD	NOIOPL	STACKSIZE
EXETYPE	NONAME	STUB
EXPORTS	NONCONFORMING	VERSION
FIXED	NONDISCARDABLE	WINDOWAPI
FUNCTIONS	NONE	WINDOWCOMPAT
HEAPSIZE	NONSHARED	WINDOWS
IMPORTS	NOTWINDOWCOMPAT	
IMPURE	OBJECTS	
INCLUDE	OLD	

4.3   Microsoft Fortran PowerStation Command-Line Compatibility

This section provides compatibility information for FL32 command-line users of Microsoft Fortran PowerStation Version 4. It includes the following topics:

▶ Section 4.3.1 Using the DF or FL32 Command Line

▶ Section 4.3.2 Equivalent Visual Fortran Compiler Options

4.3.1   Using the DF or FL32 Command Line

You can use either the DF or FL32 commands to compile (and link) your application. The main difference between the DF and FL32 commands is the defaults set for certain command-line options:

▶ FL32 requests no optimization (/Od on x86 systems, /optimize:0 on Alpha systems). See Section 4.1.56 /[no]optimize.

▶ FL32 requests checking of arguments passed to and results from the math library (/math_library:check or /Od). Math library checking applies to *x*86 systems only. See Section 4.1.51 /[no]math_library.

▶ FL32 provides minimal debug information (/debug:minimal or /Zd). See Section 4.1.17 /[no]debug.

▶ FL32 requests full Microsoft® Fortran PowerStation compatibility (/fpscomp:all). See Section 4.1.34 /[no]fpscomp.

▶ FL32 disallows alternative **PARAMETER** syntax (/noaltparam). See Section 4.1.3 /[no] altparam.

▶ FL32 requests record length units for unformatted files to be in bytes (/assume:byterecl). See Section 4.1.7 /assume.

▶ FL32 requests warnings for mismatched arguments (/warn: argument_checking). See Section 4.1.78 /[no]warn.

▶ FL32 compiles each source unit individually and retains intermediate files that would otherwise be deleted (/keep). This prevents interprocedure optimizations at higher optimization levels. See Section 4.1.43 /[no]keep.

▶ FL32 does not display an informational message related to compiling multiple files individually. See Section 4.1.78 /[no]warn.

▶ FL32 requests no inlining (/inline:none). See Section 4.1.40 /[no] inline.

▶ FL32 places module files in the same directory as the object files. See Section 4.1.52 /[no]module.

The DF and FL32 commands both:

▶ Recognize the *same* set of command-line options. For example, the following commands are supported:

```
DF    /Odx test2.for
FL32  /Odx test2.for
```

Both DF and FL32 command lines allow most Microsoft Fortran PowerStation style options (such as /Ox) and all Visual Fortran options (such as /optimize:4). For a detailed list of equivalent Microsoft Fortran PowerStation style compiler options and Visual Fortran compiler options, see Section 4.3.2 Equivalent Visual Fortran Compiler Options.

▶ Activate the *same* compiler, the Digital Fortran compiler.

For new programs and most existing applications, use the Digital Fortran compiler (default). The Digital Fortran compiler and language used by Visual Fortran provides a superset of the Fortran 90 standard with extensions for compatibility with previous versions of Digital Fortran (DEC Fortran™), VAX FORTRAN™, and Microsoft Fortran PowerStation Version 4.

▶ Pass options specified after /LINK to the LINK command.

The LINK command options after /link are passed directly to the Linker. These options are described in Linker Options.

▶ Allow the use of indirect command files.

For example, assume the file text.txt contains the following:

```
/pdbfile:testout.pdb /exe:testout.exe /debug:full
/opti mize:0 test.f90
```

Either of the following (DF or FL32) commands executes the contents of file text.txt as an indirect command file to create a debugging version of the executable program and its associated PDB file:

```
DF    @test.txt
```

```
FL32  @test.txt
```

To request Microsoft Fortran PowerStation V4 compatibility, specify the /[no]fpscomp option.

For information about using the DF command, see Chapter 3 Using the Compiler and Linker from the Command Line.

4.3.2   Equivalent Visual Fortran Compiler Options

Table 4-15 lists the Microsoft Fortran PowerStation style options and their Visual Fortran equivalents. The Microsoft Fortran PowerStation options (such as /FAc) are *case-sensitive*; other Visual Fortran options (such as /asm file) are not case-sensitive.

Table 4-15 also lists some compiler options that were not supported by Microsoft Fortran PowerStation, but are supported by Visual C++.

Table 4–15   *Equivalent Visual Fortran Compiler Options*

Fortran PowerStation Option (and Category)	Visual Fortran Command-Line Option
Listing Options	
/FA	Assembly listing. Specify /noasmattributes with /asmfile[:*file*]or /FA.
/FAc	Assembly listing with machine code. Specify /asmattributes:machine with /asmfile[:*file*] or /FAc.
/FAs	Assembly listing with source code. Specify /asmattributes:source with /asmfile[:*file*] or /FAs.
/FAcs	Assembly listing with machine instructions and source code. Specify /asmattributes:all with /asmfile[:*file*] or /FAcs.
/Fa[*file*]	Assembly listing to file *file*. Specify /asmfile[:*file*] with /noasmattributes or specify /Fa[*file*].
/Fc[*file*]	Assembly listing with source and machine code to file *file*. Specify /asmfile[:*file*] with /asmattributes:all or specify /Fc[*file*].
/Fl[*file*]	Assembly listing with machine instructions to file *file*. Specify /asmfile[:*file*] with /asmattributes:machine or specify /Fl[*file*].
/Fs[*file*]	Source listing with compiled code. Specify /list[:*file*] with /show:map or specify /Fs[*file*].
Code Generation Options	
/FR[*file*]	Generates extended Source Browser information. Specify /browser [:*file*] or /FR[*file*].
/G4 /G5	Generates code for specific x86 chip architectures. Specify /tune:*keyword*.
/Ob2	Automatic inlining of code, use with /Ox. Specify /inline:speed or /Ob2.
/Od	No code optimization (default for FL32 command). Specify /optimize:0 with /math_library:check, or specify /Od.
/Op	Improved floating-point consistency. Specify /fltconsistency or /Op.

Table 4–15 *Equivalent Visual Fortran Compiler Options (Continued)*

Fortran PowerStation Option (and Category)	Visual Fortran Command-Line Option
/Ox	Full optimization with no error checking. Specify /optimize:4 with /math_library: fast and /assume:nodummy_aliases, or specify /Ox.
/Oxp	Speed optimization and denoted inlining; error checking. Specify /optimize:4 with /assume:nodummy_aliases and /math_library:check with /fltconsistency (*x*86 systems), or specify /Oxp.
/Zp[*n*]	Packs structures on n-byte boundary (*n* is 1, 2, or 4). Specify /alignment[:*keyword*] or /Zp[*n*].
Language Extension Options	
/4L*nn*	Line length for Fortran 90 fixed-form source (*nn* is 72, 80, or 132). Specify /extend_source[:*nn*] or /4L*nn*.
/4Yb or /4Nb	Enable/disable extended error checking. Specify /check[:*keyword*], /4Yb, or /4Nb.
/4Yd or /4Nd	Warnings about undeclared variables. Specify /warn: [no] declarations, /4Yd or /4Nd.
/W0	Suppress warnings. Specify /nowarn or /W0.
/W1	Show warnings (default). Specify /warn:general or /W1.
/WX	Interpret all warnings as errors. Specify /warn:(general,errors) or /WX.
Language Standard, Source Form, and Data Options	
/4Ya or /4Na	Makes all variables **AUTOMATIC**. Specify /[no]automatic, /[no] static, /4Ya, or /4Na.
/4Yaltparam or /4Naltparam	Use the alternate syntax for **PARAMETER** statements. Specify /[no]altparam, /4Yaltparam, or /4Naltparam.
/4Yf or /4Nf	Use free-form source format. Specify /[no]free, /[no]fixed, /4Yf, or /4Nf.
/4I2	Change default KIND for **INTEGER** and **LOGICAL** declarations. Specify /integer_size:*nn* (*nn* is 16 for KIND=2) or /4I2.
/4R8	Change default KIND for **REAL** declarations. Specify /real_size:*nn* (*nn* is 32 for KIND=4) or /4R8.
/4Ys or /4Ns	Strict Fortran 90 syntax. Specify /stand:f90, /warn:stderrors, /4Ys, or /4Ns.
Compiler Directive Options	
/D*symbol*[=*int*]	Define preprocessor symbol. Specify /define:*symbol*[=*int*] or D*symbol*[=*int*].
/4cc*string*	Treat lines with d or D in column 1 as comments. Specify /d_lines or /4ccd or /4ccD (partial support).

Table 4–15 *Equivalent Visual Fortran Compiler Options (Continued)*

Fortran PowerStation Option (and Category)	Visual Fortran Command-Line Option
Build Control Options	
/4Yportlib or /4Nportlib	Specify /4Yportlib or /4Nportlib.
/Fd[*file*]	Controls creation of compiler PDB files. Specify /[no]pdbfile[:*file*] or /Fd[*file*].
/Fe[*file*]	Specifies file name of executable or DLL file. Specify /exe:*file*, /dll:*file*, or /Fe[*file*].
/Fm[*file*]	Controls creation of link map file. Specify /map[:*file*] or /Fm[*file*].
/Fo[*file*]	Controls creation of object file. Specify /object[:*file*] or /Fo[*file*].
/GNa	Keep external names as is and treat source code identifiers as case sensitive. Specify /names:as_is or /GNa.
/GNl	Make external names lowercase and ignore the case of source code identifiers. Specify /names:lowercase or /GNl.
/GNu	Make external names uppercase and ignore the case of source code identifiers. Specify /names:uppercase or /GNu.
/I*path*	Control search path for module or include files. Specify /[no] include[:*path*] or /I*path*.
/LD	Create dynamic-link library. Specify /dll or /LD.
/MD	Link against multithreaded DLL libraries. Specify /libs:dll with /threads or /MD.
/MDd	Link against multithreaded DLL libraries. Specify /libs:dll with /threads and /dbglibs or specify /MDd.
/MDs	Link against single threaded DLL libraries. Specify /libs:dll or /MDs.
/MG	Link against libraries for windows applications. Specify /winapp or /MG.
/ML	Link against single threaded static libraries. Specify /libs:static or /ML.
/MLd	Link against single threaded static libraries. Specify /libs:static with /dbglibs or /MLd.
/MT	Link against multithreaded static libraries. Specify /libs:static with /threads or /MT.
/MTd	Link against multithreaded static libraries. Specify /libs:static with /threads and /dbglibs or specify /MTd.
/MW	Link against quickwin multidoc libraries. Specify /libs:qwin or /MW.
/MWs	Link against quickwin single doc libraries. Specify /libs:qwins or /MWs.
/Tf*file*	Request that *file* be treated as a Fortran source file. Specify /source:*filename* or /Tf*file*.

Table 4–15 *Equivalent Visual Fortran Compiler Options (Continued)*

Fortran PowerStation Option (and Category)	Visual Fortran Command-Line Option
/V"*string*"	Place *string* in object file. Specify /bintext:*string* or /V"*string*".
/Z7	Request full debug information in object file. Specify /debug:full with /nopdbfile or /Z7.
/Zd	Request minimal debug information. Specify /debug:minimal with /pdbfile or /Zd.
/Zi	Request full debug information and create PDB file. Specify /debug:full with /pdbfile or /Zi.
/Zla	Do not insert *any* library names in object file. Specify /nolibdir or /Zla.
/Zl	Do not insert *default* library names in object file. Specify /libdir:noautomatic or /Zl.
/Zs	Perform syntax check only (no object). Specify /syntax_only or /Zs.
/Zt	Requests traceback information (run-time program counter to source file line correlation). Specify /traceback or /Zt.
/link [option]	Begin specifying linker options. Specify /link [option].
Command-Line Specific Options	
/?, /help	Display command help. Specify /? or /help.
/nologo	Prevent display of copyright information. Specify /nologo.

5

Debugging Fortran Programs

Although you can use the command line to develop your programs, Visual Fortran programs are typically debugged in the Microsoft visual development environment integrated debugger.

This chapter discusses how to use the intergrated debugger to debug Visual Fortran programs. The following topics are discussed:

▶ Preparing Your Program for Debugging

▶ Debugging the Squares Example Program

▶ Viewing Fortran Data Types in the Debugger

▶ Using the Array Viewer in the Debugger

▶ Locating Run-Time Errors in the Debugger

5.1   Preparing Your Program for Debugging

This section describes preparing your program for debugging:

▶ When developing your application with the Microsoft visual development environment

▶ When developing your application with the command-line environment

To prepare your program for debugging when using the Microsoft visual development environment:

1. Start the visual development environment (click Development Environment in the Visual Fortran program folder).

2. Open the appropriate Workspace (File menu, either Open Workspaces or Recent Workspaces).

3. Click the FileView pane.

4. To edit the source file to be debugged, double-click on the file name.

5. Click the Project name. The screen might appear as shown in Figure 5-1 (the ClassView tab only appears if Visual C++ is also installed).

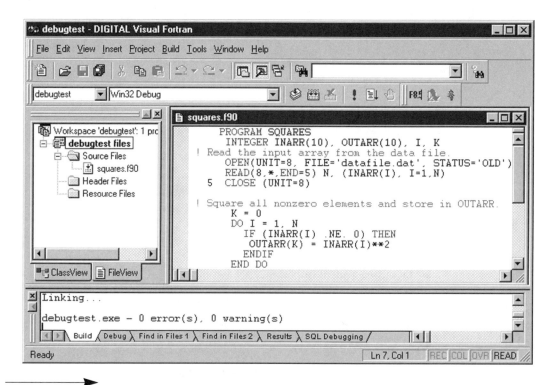

Figure 5–1 *Example Debug Screen 1*

6. In the Build menu, click Set Active Configuration and select the debug configuration.

7. To check your Project Settings, in the Project menu, click Settings, then click the Fortran tab.

8. To compile your program:

   ▶ Click (select) the source file to be compiled

   ▶ In the Build menu, click Compile *filename*

9. Eliminate any compiler diagnostic messages in the text editor and recompile if needed.

10. To build your application, in the Build menu, click Build *file*.EXE.

11. Set breakpoints in the source file and debug the program, as described in Section 5.2 Debugging the Squares Example Program.

To prepare your program for debugging when using the command line (DF command):

1. Correct any compilation and linker errors.

2. In a command window (such as the Fortran command window available from the Visual Fortran program folder), compile and link the program with full debug information and no optimization:

```
DF /debug:full /nooptimize file.f90
```

3. Start the Microsoft visual development environment.

4. In the File menu, click the Open Workspace item. Specify the file name of the executable (.EXE) file to be debugged.

5. In the File menu, click Open. Specify the name of the source file (such as .F90 or .FOR) that corresponds to the file being debugged. The text editor window appears. Your screen might appear as shown in Figure 5-2.

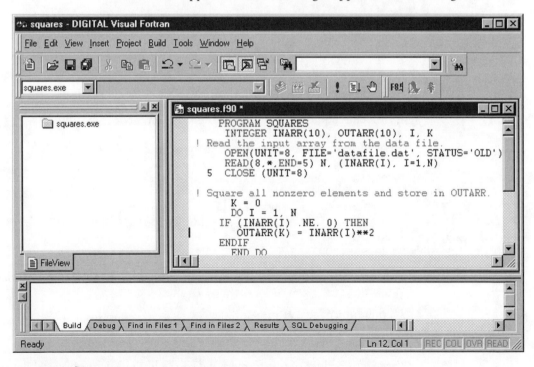

Figure 5–2 *Example Debug Screen 2*

6. Set breakpoints in the source file and debug the program, as described in Section 5.2 Debugging the Squares Example Program.

To add Source Browser Information to your debug configuration, see Section 2.3.3.3 Source Browser Information for a Configuration.

5.2   Debugging the **SQUARES** Example Program

The following program (SQUARES) uses the Fortran Console project type. The SQUARES program reads formatted data from the file datafile.dat and displays the calculated results. With the source code shown below, it does not generate the expected results:

```
PROGRAM SQUARES
   INTEGER INARR(10), OUTARR(10), I, K
! Read the input array from the data file.
   OPEN(UNIT=8, FILE='datafile.dat', STATUS='OLD')
   READ(8,*,END=5) N, (INARR(I), I=1,N)
 5 CLOSE (UNIT=8)

! Square all nonzero elements and store in OUTARR.
   K = 0
   DO I = 1, N
      IF (INARR(I) .NE. 0) THEN
! Is the error in this DO loop?
         OUTARR(K) = INARR(I)**2
      ENDIF
   END DO

! Print the squared output values. Then stop.
   PRINT 20, N
20 FORMAT (' Total number of elements read is',I4)
   PRINT 30, K
30 FORMAT (' Number of nonzero elements is',I4)
   DO, I=1,K
      PRINT 40, I, OUTARR(K)
40    FORMAT(' Element', I4, 'Has value',I6)
   END DO
END PROGRAM SQUARES
```

The formatted file datafile.dat currently contains one record that includes the following:

▶ An INTEGER count of the number of array elements, value 4

▶ The values for each of the four INTEGER array elements

To view the values of this formatted data file in the Microsoft visual development environment, use the Open item in the File menu.

When executed *without* array bounds checking (set by the /check: nobounds option), the output appears as shown in Figure 5-3.

```
Total number of elements read is    4
Number of nonzero elements is    0
Press any key to continue_
```

Figure 5–3 *Example Showing Array Bounds Checking Off*

When the program was executed with array bounds checking on, the output appears as shown in Figure 5-4.

```
forrtl: severe (161): Program Exception - array bounds exceeded
Image              PC         Routine          Line         Source
debugtest.exe      0042F5AF   Unknown          Unknown      Unknown
debugtest.exe      0042E999   Unknown          Unknown      Unknown
debugtest.exe      00425BA4   Unknown          Unknown      Unknown
KERNEL32.dll       77F1B304   Unknown          Unknown      Unknown
Press any key to continue_
```

Figure 5–4 *Example Showing Array Bounds Checking On*

You can either build this program from the command line or within the visual development environment (see Section 5.1 Preparing Your Program for Debugging). This example assumes a project workspace already exists. To debug this program:

1. From the Visual Fortran program folder, start the visual development environment.

2. In the File menu, click Open Workspace.

3. Click the FileView pane in the Workspace window. If the Workspace window is not displayed, click Workspace in the View menu.

4. Edit the file squares.f90: double-click its file name in the FileView pane. The screen appears as shown in Figure 5-5.

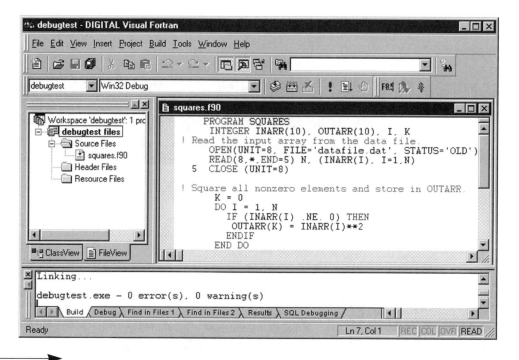

Figure 5–5 *Editing the SQUARES Program*

The following toolbars are shown:

- ▶ Build toolbar

- ▶ Standard toolbar

- ▶ Fortran toolbar

To change the displayed toolbars, select Customize in the Tools menu and click the Toolbars tab. You can move toolbars by dragging the anchor (double vertical line on the left of the toolbar).

5. Click the first executable line to set the cursor position. In this case, click on the beginning of the **OPEN** statement line:

```
OPEN(UNIT=8, FILE='datafile.dat', STATUS='OLD')
```

6. Click on the Set/Remove Breakpoint (open hand symbol) button in the Build toolbar, as shown in Figure 5-6.

The red circle in the left margin of the text editor/debugger window shows where a breakpoint is set.

7. This example assumes you have previously built your application (see Section 5.1 Preparing Your Program for Debugging).

In the Build menu, click the Start Debug, Go item, as shown in Figure 5-7.

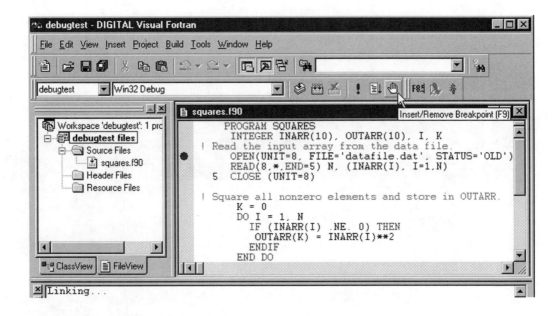

Figure 5–6 *Setting a Breakpoint*

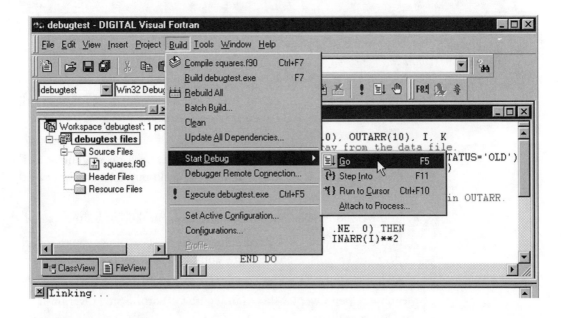

Figure 5–7 *Starting the Debugger*

8. The debugger is now active. The current position is marked by a yellow
arrow at the first executable line (the initial breakpoint) as shown in
Figure 5-8.

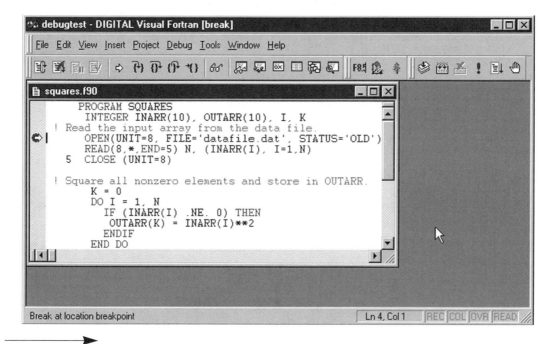

Figure 5–8 *Positioning the Debugger at the First Breakpoint*

The Debug menu appears on the visual development environment title
bar in place of the Build menu. If not displayed previously, the Debug
toolbar appears.

If needed, you can set another breakpoint, position the cursor at the
line where you want to add or remove a breakpoint and do either of the
following:

▶ In the Build toolbar, click the Set/Remove Breakpoint button.

▶ In the Edit menu, click Breakpoints. A dialog box allows you to set or
clear breakpoints, evaluate expressions, and perform other functions.

Step through the lines of source code. You can do this with the Debug
menu item Step Over (as shown in Figure 5-9) or the Step Over button on
the Debug toolbar:

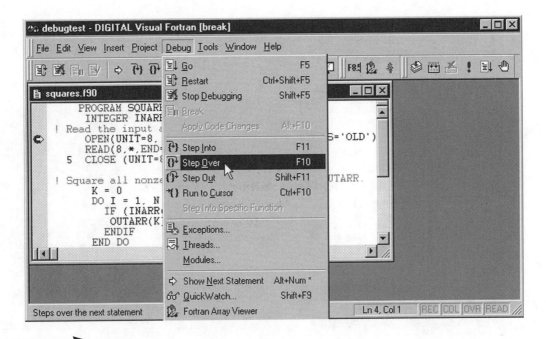

Figure 5–9 *Stepping Over an Item in the Debugger*

9. Repeat the Step Over action and follow program execution into the DO loop. Repeat the Step Over action until you are at the end of the program. Position the cursor over the variable K to view its value (called Data Tips), as shown in Figure 5-10.

The error seems related to the value of variable K!

10. In the text editor, add the line K = K + 1 as follows:

```
! Square all nonzero elements and store in OUTARR.
  K = 0
  DO I = 1, N
    IF (INARR(I) .NE. 0) THEN
    K = K + 1 ! add this line
    OUTARR(K) = INARR(I)**2
    ENDIF
  END DO
```

11. You have modified the source, so you need to rebuild the application:

   ▶ In the Debug menu, click Stop Debugging

   ▶ In the Build menu, click Build Squares.exe

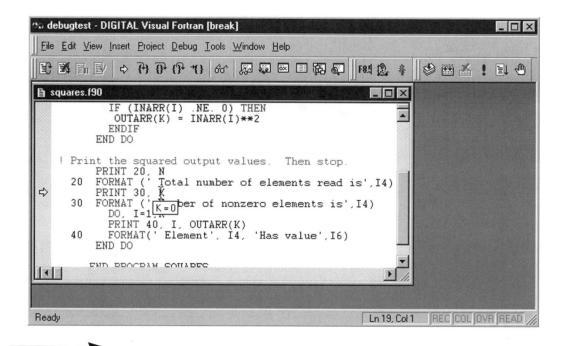

Figure 5–10   *Viewing the Value of a Variable in the Debugger*

▶ In the Build menu, click Execute Squares.exe or click the exclamation point (!) on the Build toolbar.

The output screen appears as shown in Figure 5-11.

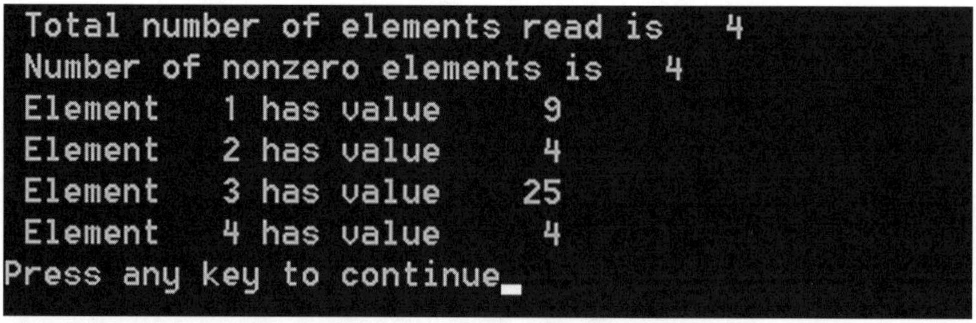

Figure 5–11   *Displaying Output after a Fix in the Debugger*

12. Although the program generates better results, you can examine the values of both the input array INARR (read from the file) and the output array OUTARR that the program calculates. In the text editor window, the previously set breakpoint remains set.

In the Build menu, click the Start Debug, Go item.

13. To view the values of certains variables as the program executes, we need to display the Variables or the Watch window. In the View menu, click the Debug Windows, Variables window item, as shown in Figure 5-12.

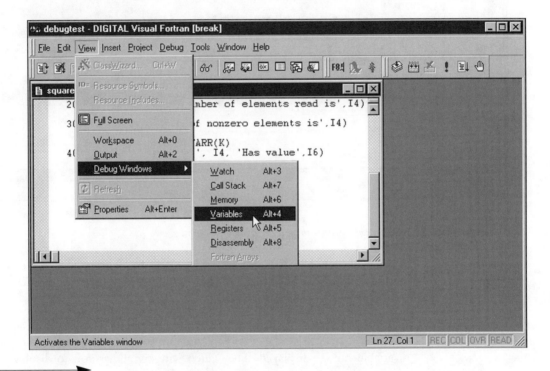

Figure 5–12   *Displaying the Debug Variables Window*

14. In the Variables window, click the Locals tab to display the values of your local variables, as shown in Figure 5-13.

You can view the values of the local variables by using the Locals tab, including the arrays (click on the plus sign).

The Variables window displays a Context menu (after the word Context:). The Context menu can help you debug exceptions.

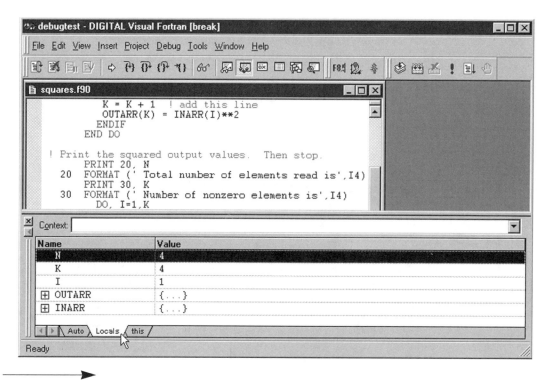

Figure 5–13   *Displaying the Locals Tab in the Variables Window*

The Locals tab does not let you display module variables or other non-local variables. To display non-local variables, display the Watch window, as shown in Figure 5-14.

15. Although this example does not use module variables or non-local variables, you can drag a variable name into the Watch window so the variable can be displayed. The Watch window allows you to display expressions.

In the text editor window, select the variable name INARR (without its subscript syntax), drag it, and drop it into the Watch window, as shown in Figure 5-15.

16. Also drag the OUTARR array name to the Watch window. Click on the Plus sign (+) to the left of the OUTARR variable's name to display the values of its array elements.

17. Execute lines of the program by using the Step Over button on the Debug toolbar. As the program executes, you can view the values of scalar variables with the data tips feature and view the values of arrays (or other variables) in the Watch window.

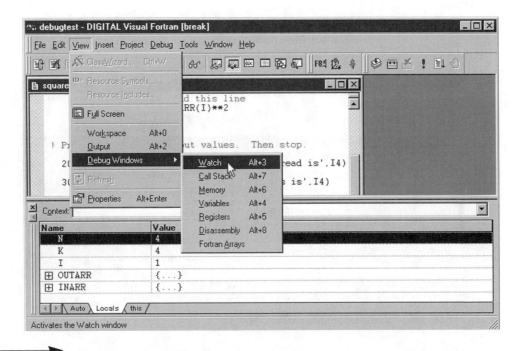

Figure 5–14 *Displaying the Watch Window in the Debugger*

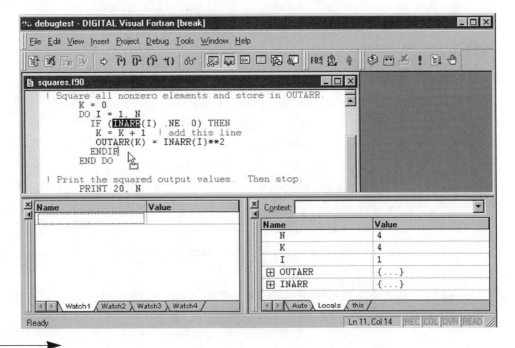

Figure 5–15 *Dragging and Dropping to the Watch Window*

When the program completes execution, the screen appears as shown in Figure 5-16.

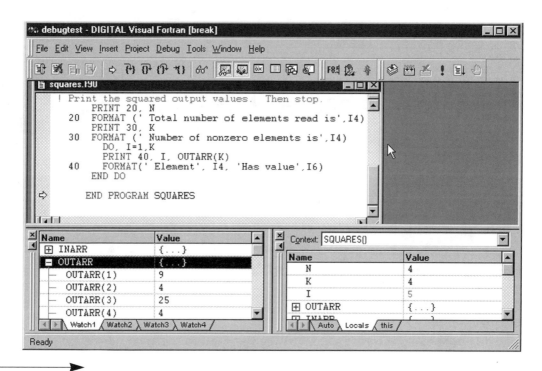

Figure 5–16 *Viewing the Corrected Program in the Watch window*

If you have the Visual Fortran Professional Edition, you can use the Array Viewer to display and graph multidimensional array element values.

For More Information:

▶ On viewing different types of Fortran data, see Section 5.3 Viewing Fortran Data Types in the Debugger.

▶ On displaying array values in the Array Viewer, see Section 5.4 Using the Array Viewer in the Debugger.

▶ On locating errors in your program, see Section 5.5 Locating Run-Time Errors in the Debugger.

▶ On additional debugger capabilities, see the Debugger section of the Visual C++ Users Guide.

5.3   Viewing Fortran Data Types in the Debugger

The following general suggestions apply to different types of Fortran data:

▶ For scalar (nonarray) data, use the data tips (leave pointer on a variable name) feature or use the Local Variables window.

▶ For single-dimension array data, derived-type data, record structure data, and **COMPLEX** data, use the Local Variables window or the Watch window.

▶ For multidimension array data, use the Local Variables window, the Watch window, or (Professional Edition) the Array Viewer.

For information on using Data Tips, the Local Variables window, or a Watch window, see Section 5.2 Debugging the Squares Example Program.

For information on using the Array Viewer in the debugger, see Section 5.4 Using the Array Viewer in the Debugger.

Specifying Array Sections

You can specify array sections in a watch window. For example, consider an array declared as:

```
integer foo(10)
```

You can specify the following statement in a watch window to see the 2nd, 5th, and 8th elements:

```
foo(2:10:3)
```

When working with character arrays, this syntax may be combined with a substring specification. Consider the following array declaration:

```
character*8 chr_arr(10)
```

You can specify the following statement in a watch window to display the substring made up of character 3 through 8 of array elements 2 through 5:

```
chr_arr(2:5)(3:8)
```

This support is available for arrays of any type, including array pointers, assumed-shape, allocatable, and assumed-size arrays.

Any valid integer expression can be used when specifying lower bound, upper bound, or stride. If the lower bound is omitted, the array lower bound is used. If the upper bound is omitted, the array upper bound is used. For example, consider the following declaration:

```
integer foo(10)
```

To display:

▶ Elements 1 through 8, specify `foo(:8)`

▶ Elements 5 through 10, specify `foo(5:)`

▶ All 10 elements, specify `foo(:)`

Specifying Public Module Variables

To view public module variables in the Watch window, specify the module name, followed by "::", followed by the variable name.

For example, to watch variable "bar" of module "foo", specify the following expression:

`foo::bar`

Specifying Format Specifiers

You can use format specifiers in Watch windows to display variables in different data formats.

For example, given a REAL variable 'foo' in a program, it is now possible to see 'foo' in different floating point notation (by typing "foo,f" "foo,g" or "foo,e" in a Watch window) or as an integer ("foo,i" or "foo,d"), a hexadecimal value ("foo,x"), an an octal value ("foo,o"), and so on.

You can change the display format of variables in the Watch window using the formatting symbols in Table 5-1.

Table 5–1 *Formatting Symbols for Display in the Watch Window*

Symbol	Format	Value	Displays
d,i	*signed* decimal integer	0xF000F065	-268373915
o	*unsigned* octal integer	0xF065	0170145
x,X	Hexadecimal integer	61541 (decimal)	#0000F065
f	*signed* floating-point	3./2.	1.5000000
e	*signed* scientific notation	3./2.	0.1500000E+01
g	*signed* floating-point or *signed* scientific notation, whichever is shorter	3./2.	1.500000
c	Single character	0x0065	'e'
s	String	0x0012fde8	"Hello world"

To use a formatting symbol, type the variable name, followed by a comma and the appropriate symbol. For example, if var has a value of 0x0065, and you want to see the value in character form, type var,c in the Name column on the tab of the Watch window. When you press ENTER, the character-format value appears:

```
var,c = 'e'
```

You can use the formatting symbols shown in the Table 5-2 to format the contents of memory locations.

Table 5–2 *Formatting Symbols for the Contents of Memory Locations*

Symbol	Format	Displays
ma	64 ASCII characters	0x0012ffac .4...0...".0W&.......1W&.0.:W..1...."..1.JO&.1.2.."..1...0y....1
m	16 bytes in hexadecimal, followed by 16 ASCII characters	0x0012ffac B3 34 CB 00 84 30 94 80 FF 22 8A 30 57 26 00 00 .4...0...".0W&..
mb	16 bytes in hexadecimal, followed by 16 ASCII characters	0x0012ffac B3 34 CB 00 84 30 94 80 FF 22 8A 30 57 26 00 00 .4...0...".0W&..
mw	8 words	0x0012ffac 34B3 00CB 3084 8094 22FF 308A 2657 0000
md	4 doublewords	0x0012ffac 00CB34B3 80943084 308A22FF 00002657

With the memory location formatting symbols, you can type any value or expression that evaluates to a location.

A formatting character can follow an expression also:

```
rep+1, x
alps[0],mb
xloc,g
count,d
```

Note: You can apply formatting symbols to structures, arrays, pointers, and objects as unexpanded variables only. If you expand the variable, the specified formatting affects all members. You cannot apply formatting symbols to individual members.

5.4   Using the Array Viewer in the Debugger

If you have the Professional Edition, you can use the Array Viewer in the Debugger. Consider the following example program:

```
PROGRAM ARRAY
  INTEGER I1, I2
  REAL VAL(5,5), X

  VAL = 0.0
  X = 1.0
  DO I1 = 1,5
    DO I2 = 1,5
      X = X*1.2
      VAL(I1,I2) = X
    END DO
  END DO

  PRINT *,VAL
END PROGRAM ARRAY
```

1. Start the debugger (see Section 5.2 Debugging the Squares Example Program)

2. Step through the parts of the program that generate the values of the array you want to view, perhaps after stopping program execution at a certain breakpoint.

3. Select (click) the name of the array you want to view in the Array Viewer, as shown in Figure 5-17.

4. In the debug menu, click Fortran Array Viewer or click the Array Viewer button in the Fortran toolbar, as shown in Figure 5-18.

   To display the Fortran toolbar:

   ▶ In the Tools menu, select Customize.

   ▶ Click the Toolbars tab.

   ▶ Set the Fortran toolbar check box.

   The Array Viewer as well as a Fortran Arrays window appears, as shown in Figure 5-19.

   In the upper part (data window), Array Viewer displays the values of the array elements for VAL.

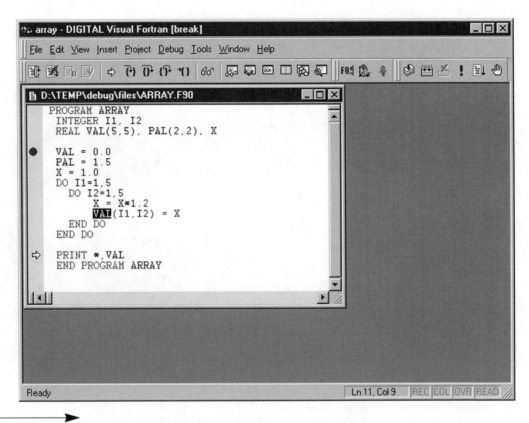

Figure 5–17 *Selecting an Array for Display in Array Viewer*

In the lower part (graph window), the view shown for array VAL is a two-dimensional view. You can also display other types of views, such as a height plot (in the View menu, click Height Plot).

Initially, the Fortran Arrays window shows the current array being displayed and its status.

5. After your program changes the data in the Array being viewed, you can:

▶ Refresh the current Array Viewer data and graph by double-clicking the array name in the Fortran Array window.

▶ Create another instance of Array Viewer with an updated view of the data by clicking the Fortran Arrays button in the Fortran toolbar. The second instance may contain different value limits on the graph.

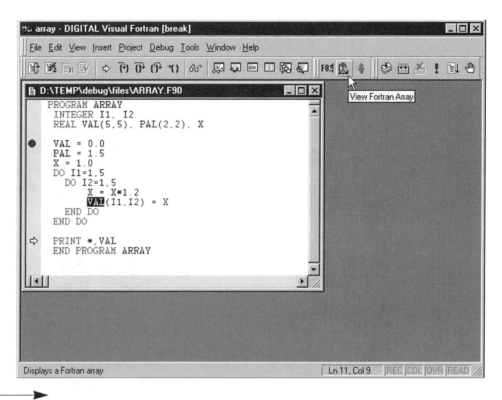

Figure 5–18 *Selecting Array Viewer*

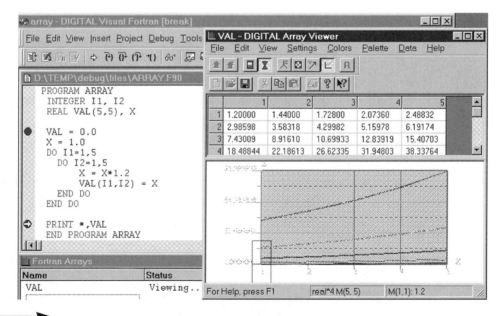

Figure 5–19 *Array Viewer and Fortran Arrays Window*

6. The Fortran Arrays window lets you perform certain functions, as shown in Table 5-3.

Table 5–3 *Functions You Can Perform in the Fortran Arrays Window*

To Do This:	In the Fortran Arrays Window, Do This:
Display a different array in the existing Array Viewer	Click the Name column and type an array name.
Display a different array in a new instance of the Array Viewer	Click in the last row of the Name column, type the array name, and press Enter (Return). A new instance of Array Viewer appears for the specified array.
Update the displayed array's values	Double-click the line for the array.
Discontinue using the Array Viewer (removes the name from the Fortran Arrays window)	Either stop the debugger (Debug menu, Stop Debugging item) or repeatedly select the array name and click the Delete key.
Create a detached instance of Array Viewer (not associated with the debugger)	Click on an array in the Name column and press the Escape (Esc) key. This removes the array name from the Fortran Arrays window and creates a detached instance of the Array Viewer that remains after the debugging session ends.

For more information on using the Array Viewer:

▶ When using the Array Viewer, in the Help menu, click Help Topics

▶ Read the Array Visualizer HTMLHelp documentation

5.5   Locating Run-Time Errors in the Debugger

For many types of errors, using the Debugger can help you isolate the cause of errors:

▶ Be aware that your program must use compiler options that allow the debugger to catch the appropriate error conditions:

- The /check:keyword options generate extra code to catch certain conditions at run-time (see /check or in the visual development environment, specify the Extended Error Checking items in the Run time Compiler Option Category). For example, if you do not specify /check:bounds, the debugger will not catch and stop at array or character string bounds errors.
- If you specify the /fpe:3 compiler option, certain floating-point exceptions will not be caught, since this setting allows IEEE exceptional values and program continuation.

- On Alpha systems, the /synchronous_exceptions option (and certain /fpe:n options) influence the reporting of floating-point arithmetic exceptions at run-time.

  Your program will automatically stop at the point where the exception occurs.

▶ After your program stops at the point where the exception occurs, to display the Call Stack window in the debugger:

  1. In the View menu, click Debug Windows
  2. In the submenu, click Call Stack

▶ A severe unhandled I/O programming error (such as an End-of-File condition) can occur while the program is executing in the debugger. When this occurs, the Fortran run-time system will raise a debug event automatically to stop program execution, allowing display of the Call Stack Display.

  When the severe unhandled I/O error occurs in the debugger:

- An information box is displayed that contains:

```
User breakpoint called from code at 0xnnnnnnnn
```

- A window with your cursor in NTDLL disassembly code

  Click on OK to dismiss the information box.

  Scanning down the Call Stack display, there will be a few frames from NTDLL and the Fortran run-time system displayed, and then the actual Fortran routine with the I/O statement that caused the error. In the Context menu, select the Fortran routine to display the Fortran code. The green arrow points to the I/O statement that caused the error.

  You can view the Context menu to help locate the source code line that executed the I/O statement. The Context menu (after Context:) appears in the top of the Variables window (see Section 5.2 Debugging the Squares Example Program). Use the Context menu to select the viewing context for the routine (use the arrow at the right to display selections).

  This action all occurs after the error message and traceback information has been displayed.

  The error message and traceback information is available in the program output window. To view the program output window, either iconize (minimize) the visual development environment or click on the icon for the output window in the task bar. You should not need the stack dump because you have the Call Stack window in the visual development environment, but the error message with the file name might be useful to see.

► For machine exceptions, you can use the just-in-time debugging feature to debug your programs as they run outside of the visual development environment, if both of the following items have been set:

- In the Tools menu Options item, the Debug tab has the checkbox for Just-In Time debugging set.
- The FOR_IGNORE_EXCEPTIONS environment variable is set to TRUE.

For More Information:

► On locating exceptions and the compiler options needed, see Section 21.3 Locating Run-Time Errors

► On using traceback information, see Section 21.4 Using Traceback Information

6

Performance: Making Programs Run Faster

This chapter discusses the following topics related to improving run-time performance of Digital Visual Fortran programs:

▶ Section 6.1 Software Environment and Efficient Compilation

　　Contains important software environment suggestions that apply to nearly all applications, including using the most recent version of the compiler, related performance tools, and efficient ways to compile using the DF command.

▶ Section 6.2 Analyze Program Performance

　　Contains information on analyzing program performance, including using profiling tools.

▶ Section 6.3 Data Alignment Considerations

　　Contains guidelines related to avoiding unaligned data.

▶ Section 6.4 Use Arrays Efficiently

　　Contains guidelines for efficient array use.

▶ Section 6.5 Improve Overall I/O Performance

　　Contains guidelines related to improving overall I/O performance.

▶ Section 6.6 Additional Source Code Guidelines for Run-Time Efficiency

　　Contains additional performance guidelines related to source code.

▶ Section 6.7 Optimization Levels: the /optimize: *num* Option.

Contains information on the DF /optimize: *num* optimization level options and the types of optimizations performed.

▶ Section 6.8 Other Options Related to Optimization

Contains information on other DF optimization options (besides the /optimize: *num* options).

6.1 Software Environment and Efficient Compilation

Before you attempt to analyze and improve program performance, you should:

▶ Obtain and install the latest version of Visual Fortran, along with performance products that can improve application performance.

▶ Use the DF command and its options in a manner that lets the Digital Visual Fortran compiler perform as many optimizations as possible to improve run-time performance.

▶ Use certain performance capabilities provided by the operating system.

For more information, see:

▶ Section 6.1.1 Install the Latest Version of Visual Fortran and Performance Products

▶ Section 6.1.2 Compile with Appropriate Options and Multiple Source Files

6.1.1 Install the Latest Version of Visual Fortran and Performance Products

To ensure that your software development environment can significantly improve the run-time performance of your applications, obtain and install the following optional software products:

▶ The latest version of Visual Fortran

New releases of the Digital Visual Fortran compiler and its associated run-time libraries may provide new features that improve run-time performance.

For information on more recent Visual Fortran releases, access the Digital Fortran web page at URL http://www.digital.com/fortran.

If you have the appropriate technical support contract, you can also contact the Digital technical support center for information on new releases (see Visual Fortran Technical Support in *Getting Started*).

▶ Performance profiling tools

The visual development environment profiling tools allow function and line profiling. For more information on profiling, see Section 6.2 Analyze Program Performance.

▶ System-wide performance products

Other products are not specific to a particular programming language or application, but can improve system-wide performance, such as minimizing disk device I/O and handling capacity planning.

When running large programs, such as those accessing large arrays, adequate process limits and virtual memory (paging file) space as well as proper system tuning are especially important.

6.1.2　Compile with Appropriate Options and Multiple Source Files

During the earlier stages of program development (such as for the debug configuration in the visual development environment), you can use compilation with minimal optimization. For example:

```
DF /compile_only /optimize:1 sub2.f90
DF /compile_only /optimize:1 sub3.f90
DF /exe:main.exe /debug /optimize:0 main.f90 sub2.obj sub3.obj
```

During the later stages of program development (such as for the release configuration), you should:

▶ Specify multiple source files together and use an optimization level of at least /optimize:4 on the DF command line to allow more interprocedural optimizations to occur. For instance, the following command compiles all three source files together using the default level of optimization (/optimize:4):

```
DF /exe:main.exe main.f90 sub2.f90 sub3.f90
```

▶ Avoid using incremental linking.

▶ Consider building from the command line to allow multiple source files to be compiled together. For information on creating (exporting) makefile for command-line use, see Section 2.3.1 Files in a Project; for information about using NMAKE, see Section 25.6 Building Projects with NMAKE.

Compiling multiple source files lets the compiler examine more code for possible optimizations, which results in:

▶ Inlining more procedures

▶ More complete data flow analysis

▶ Reducing the number of external references to be resolved during linking

When compiling all source files together is not feasible (such as for very large programs), consider compiling related source files together using multiple DF commands rather than compiling source files individually.

If you use the /compile_only option to prevent linking, also use the /object: *file* option so that multiple sources files are compiled into a single object file, allowing more optimizations to occur.

Visual Fortran performs certain optimizations unless you specify the appropriate DF command-line options or corresponding visual development environment options in the Optimization category of the Fortran tab (see Section 4.1.1 Categories of Compiler Options). Additional optimizations can be enabled or disabled using DF command options or in the visual development environment Project Settings dialog box Fortran tab.

Table 6-1 shows DF options that can directly improve run-time performance on both *x*86 and Alpha systems. Most of these options do not affect the accuracy of the results, while others improve run-time performance but can change some numeric results.

Table 6–1   *Options Related to Run-Time Performance*

Option Names	Description	For More Information
/align:*keyword*	Controls whether padding bytes are added between data items within common blocks, derived-type data, and Digital Fortran record structures to make the data items naturally aligned.	See Section 6.3 Data Alignment Considerations.
/architecture:*keyword*	Requests code generation for a specific *x*86 or Alpha chip generation. On *x*86 systems, certain *x*86 chip generations use new instructions that provide improved performance for certain applications, but those instructions are not supported by older *x*86 chips. On Alpha systems, certain Alpha chip generations use new instructions that provide improved performance for certain applications, but those instructions are not supported by older Alpha chips.	See Section 4.1.4 /architecture

Table 6–1 *Options Related to Run-Time Performance (Continued)*

Option Names	Description	For More Information
/fast	Sets the following performance-related options: /align:dcommons, /assume:noaccuracy_sensitive, and /math_library:fast.	See description of each option: Section 4.1.2 /[no]alignment, Section 4.1.7 /assume, and Section 4.1.51 /math_library
/assume: noaccuracy_sensitive	Allows the compiler to reorder code based on algebraic identities to improve performance, enabling certain optimizations. The numeric results can be slightly different from the default (accuracy_sensitive) because of the way intermediate results are rounded. This slight difference in numeric results is acceptable to most programs.	See Section 6.8.4 Arithmetic Reordering Optimizations
/assume:buffered_io	Allows records that are otherwise written (flushed) to disk as each record is written (default) to be accumulated in the buffer and written as a unit. Using buffered writes usually makes disk I/O more efficient by writing larger blocks of data to the disk less often.	See Section 6.5.7 Efficient Use of Record Buffers and Disk I/O
/inline:all	Inlines every call that can possibly be inlined while generating correct code. Certain recursive routines are not inlined to prevent infinite loops.	See Section 6.8.3 Controlling the Inlining of Procedures
/inline:speed	Inlines procedures that will improve run-time performance with a likely significant increase in program size.	See Section 6.8.3 Controlling the Inlining of Procedures
/inline:size	Inlines procedures that will improve run-time performance without a significant increase in program size. This type of inlining occurs with optimization level /optimize:4 or /optimize:5.	See Section 6.8.3 Controlling the Inlining of Procedures
/math_library:fast	On *x*86 systems, requests that arguments to the math library routines are not checked to improve performance. On Alpha systems, requests the use of certain math library routines (used by intrinsic functions) that provide faster speed. Using this option may cause a slight loss of accuracy and provides less reliable arithmetic exception checking to get significant performance improvements in those functions.	See Section 4.1.51 /math_library
/optimize:*level*	Controls the optimization level and thus the types of optimizations performed. The default optimization level is /optimize:4, unless you specify /debug, which changes the default to /optimize:0 (no optimizations). Use /optimize:5 to activate loop transformation optimizations and (on Alpha systems) the software pipelining optimizations.	See Section 6.7 Optimization Levels: the /optimize Option

Table 6–1 *Options Related to Run-Time Performance (Continued)*

Option Names	Description	For More Information
/transform_loops	Activates a group of loop transformation optimizations (a subset of /optimize:5).	See Section 4.1.73 /[no] transform_loops
/tune:*keyword*	Specifies the target processor generation (chip) architecture on which the program will be run, allowing the optimizer to make decisions about instruction tuning optimizations needed to create the most efficient code. Keywords allow specifying one particular processor generation type, multiple processor generation types, or the processor generation type currently in use during compilation. Regardless of the setting of /tune *keyword*, the generated code compiled on *x*86 systems will run correctly on all implementations of the *x*86 architecture; code compiled on Alpha systems will run correctly on all implementations of the Alpha architecture.	See Section 6.8.6 Requesting Optimized Code for a Specific Processor Generation
/unroll:*num*	Specifies the number of times a loop is unrolled (*num*) when specified with optimization level /optimize:3 or higher. If you omit /unroll: *num*, the optimizer determines how many times loops are unrolled. Primarily on *x*86 systems, increasing the default unroll limit may improve run-time performance for certain applications.	See Section 6.7.4.1 Loop Unrolling

Table 6-2 lists the DF options that can directly improve run-time performance on Alpha systems only.

Table 6–2 *Options Related to Run-Time Performance for Alpha Systems Only*

Option Names	Description	For More Information
/math_library:fast	On Alpha systems, requests the use of certain math library routines (used by intrinsic functions) that provide faster speed. Using this option may cause a slight loss of accuracy and provides less reliable arithmetic exception checking to get significant performance improvements in those functions.	See Section 4.1.51 /math_library
/pipeline	Activates the software pipelining optimization (a subset of /optimize:5).	See Section 4.1.59 /[no]pipeline

Table 6-3 lists options that can slow program performance on *x*86 and Alpha systems. Some applications that require floating-point exception handling might need to use a different /fpe:*n* option. Other applications might need to use the /assume: dummy_aliases or /vms options for compatibility reasons. Other options listed in the table are primarily for troubleshooting or debugging purposes.

Table 6–3 *Options that Slow Run-Time Performance*

Option Names	Description	For More Information
/assume: dummy_aliases	Forces the compiler to assume that dummy (formal) arguments to procedures share memory locations with other dummy arguments or with variables shared through use association, host association, or common block use. These program semantics slow performance, so you should specify /assume: dummy_aliases only for the called subprograms that depend on such aliases. The use of dummy aliases violates the FORTRAN 77 and Fortran 90 standards but occurs in some older programs.	See Section 6.8.5 Dummy Aliasing Assumption
/compile_only	If you use /compile_only when compiling multiple source files, also specify /object:*file* to compile many source files together into one object file. Separate compilations prevent certain interprocedural optimizations, the same as using multiple DF commands or using /compile_only *without* the /object:*file* option.	See this section
/check:bounds	Generates extra code for array bounds checking at run time.	See Section 4.1.11 /[no]check
/check:overflow	Generates extra code to check integer calculations for arithmetic overflow at run-time. Once the program is debugged, you may want to omit this option to reduce executable program size and slightly improve run-time performance.	See Section 4.1.11 /[no]check

Table 6–3   *Options that Slow Run-Time Performance (Continued)*

Option Names	Description	For More Information
/fpe:*n* values	On *x*86 systems, /fpe:3 provides the best performance. Using other /fpe values slows program execution. On Alpha systems, using /fpe:0 provides the best performance. Using other /fpe values (or using the **for_set_fpe** routine) to set equivalent exception handling slows program execution. For programs that specify /fpe:3, the impact on run-time performance can be significant.	See Section 4.1.32 /fpe
/rounding_mode: dynamic (Alpha only)	Certain rounding modes and changing the rounding mode can slow program execution slightly.	See Section 4.1.64 /rounding_mode (Alpha Only)
/debug:full, /debug, or equivalent	Generates extra symbol table information in the object file. Specifying /debug also reduces the default level of optimization to /optimize:0.	See Section 4.1.17 /[no]debug
/inline: none /inline: manual	Prevents the inlining of all procedures (except statement functions).	See Section 6.8.3 Controlling the Inlining of Procedures
/optimize:0, /optimize:1, /optimize:2, or /optimize:3	Reduces the optimization level (and types of optimizations). Use during the early stages of program development or when you will use the debugger.	See Section 4.1.56 /[no]optimize and Section 6.7 Optimization Levels: the /optimize Option
/synchronous _exceptions (Alpha only)	Generates extra code to associate an arithmetic exception with the instruction that causes it, slowing instruction execution. Use this option only when troubleshooting, such as when identifying the source of an exception.	See Section 4.1.69 /[no] synchronous_ exceptions (Alpha Only)
/vms	Controls certain VMS-related run-time defaults, including alignment. If you specify the /vms option, you may need to also specify the /align:records option to obtain optimal run-time performance.	See Section 4.1.77 /[no]vms

For more information on compiling multiple files, see Section 3.7.9 Compiling and Linking for Optimization.

6.2   Analyze Program Performance

This section describes how you can analyze program performance using timings and profiling tools.

Before you analyze program performance, make sure any errors you might have encountered during the early stages of program development have been corrected. Only profile code that is stable and has been debugged.

This section covers the following topics:

▶ Section 6.2.1 Timing Your Application

▶ Section 6.2.2 Profiling and Performance Tools

6.2.1 Timing Your Application

The following considerations apply to timing your application:

▶ Run program timings when other users are not active. Your timing results can be affected by one or more CPU-intensive processes also running while doing your timings.

▶ Try to run the program under the same conditions each time to provide the most accurate results, especially when comparing execution times of a previous version of the same program. Use the same system (processor model, amount of memory, version of the operating system, and so on) if possible.

▶ If you do need to change systems, you should measure the time using the same version of the program on both systems, so you know each system's effect on your timings.

▶ For programs that run for less than a few seconds, run several timings to ensure that the results are not misleading. Certain overhead functions like loading DLLs might influence short timings considerably.

▶ If your program displays a lot of text, consider redirecting the output from the program. Redirecting output from the program will change the times reported because of reduced screen I/O.

Methods of Timing Your Application

To perform application timings, use a version of the TIME command in a .BAT file (or the function timing profiling option). You might consider modifying the program to call routines within the program to measure execution time (possibly using conditionally compiled lines). For example:

▶ Digital Fortran intrinsic procedures, such as **CPU_TIME**, **SYSTEM_CLOCK**, **DATE_AND_TIME**, and **TIME**.

▶ Library routines, such as **ETIME** or **TIME**.

Visual Fortran programs created in a Windows 95 or Windows 98 development environment can be run and analyzed on Windows NT *x*86 systems. Whenever possible, perform detailed performance analysis on a system that closely resembles the system (or systems) that will be used for actual application use.

Sample Command Procedure that Uses TIME and Performance Monitor

The following example shows a .BAT command procedure that uses the TIME command and the Performance Monitor (perfmon) tool available on Windows NT systems. The kill command that stops the perfmon tool is included on the Windows NT Resource kit; if the kill tool is not available on your system, manually end the perfmon task (use the task manager).

This .BAT procedure assumes that the program to be timed is myprog.exe.

Before using this batch file, start the performance monitor to setup logging of the statistics that you are interested in:

1. At the DOS prompt type: `Perfmon`

2. In the View menu, select Log

3. In the Edit menu, select Add to Log and select some statistics

4. In the Options menu, select Log. In the dialog box:

   ▶ Name the log file. The following .BAT procedure assumes that you have named the logfile myprog.log.

   ▶ Consider adjusting the Log Interval.

   ▶ As the last step, be sure to select "Start Log."

5. In the File menu, select Save Workspace to save the setup information. The following .BAT procedure assumes you have saved the workspace as my_perfmon_setup.pmw.

The command procedure follows:

```
echo off
rem Sample batch file to record performance statistics for
rem later analysis.
rem This .bat file assumes that you have the utility "kill"
rem available, which is distributed with the NT resource kit.

rem Delete previous logs, then start up Performance
rem Monitor.
rem We use start so that control returns instantly to this
```

```
rem batch file.
del myprog.log
start perfmon my_perfmon_setup.pmw

rem print the time we started
time <nul | findstr current

rem start the program we are interested in, this time using
rem cmd /c so that the batch file waits for the program to
rem finish.
echo on
cmd /c myprog.exe
echo off

rem print the time we stopped
time <nul | findstr current

rem all done logging statistics
kill perfmon
rem if kill is not available, end the perfmon task manually
```

After the run, analyze your data by using Performance Monitor:

1. If it is not currently running, start Performance Monitor.

2. In the View menu, select Chart.

3. In the Options menu, select Data From and specify the name of the logfile.

4. In the Edit menu, select Add To Chart to display the counters.

For more information:

▶ About the optimizations that improve application performance without source code modification, see Section 6.1.2 Compile with Appropriate Options and Multiple Source Files.

▶ About profiling your application, see Section 6.2.2 Profiling and Performance Tools.

6.2.2   Profiling and Performance Tools

To generate profiling information, you use the compiler, linker, and the profiler from either the visual development environment or the command line.

Select those parts of your application that make the most sense to profile. For example, routines that perform user interaction may not be worth profiling. Consider profiling routines that perform a series of complex calculations or call multiple user-written subprograms.

Profiling identifies areas of code where significant program execution time is spent. It can also show areas of code that are not executed. Visual Fortran programs created in a Windows 95, Windows 98, or Windows NT *x*86 development environment can be run and analyzed on a Windows NT *x*86, Windows 95, or Windows 98 system. Whenever possible, perform detailed performance analysis on a system that closely resembles the system(s) that will be used to run the actual application.

For detailed information about profiling from the command line, see Section 25.12 Profiling Code from the Command Line.

There are two main types of profiling: function profiling and line profiling.

Function Profiling

Function profiling helps you locate areas of inefficient code. It can show:

▶ The time spent in functions and the number of times a function was called (function timing).

▶ Only the number of times a function was called (function counting).

▶ A list of functions executed or not executed (function coverage).

▶ Information about the stack when each function is called (function attribution).

Function profiling does not require debug information (it obtains addresses from a .MAP file). Since function profiling (except function attribution) uses the stack, routines that modify the stack cannot be profiled. Exclude object files for routines that modify the stack.

To perform function profiling:

1. In the Project menu, select Settings.

2. Click the Link tab.

3. In the General category, click the Enable profiling checkbox (this turns off incremental linking).

4. In the General category, click the Generate mapfile checkbox.

5. Click OK to accept the current project settings.

6. Build your application.

7. After building your application, profile your project.

Line Profiling

Line profiling collects more information than function profiling. It shows how many times a line is executed and whether certain lines are not executed. Line profiling requires debug information.

To perform line profiling:

1. In the Project menu, select Settings.
2. Click the Link tab.
3. In the General category, click the Enable profiling checkbox (this turns off incremental linking).
4. In the General category, click the Generate debug information checkbox.
5. Click on the Fortran tab.
6. In the category drop-down list, select Debug.
7. In the Debugging level drop-down list, select Full.
8. In the Debugging level drop-down list, click the Use Program Database for Debug Information checkbox.
9. Click OK to accept the current project settings.
10. Build your application
11. After building your application, profile your project.

Performance Tools

Tools that you can use to analyze performance include:

▶ Process Viewer (Pview) lets you view process and thread characteristics.

▶ Spy++ provides a graphical view of system use.

▶ On Windows NT systems, the Windows NT Performance Monitor can help identify performance bottlenecks.

▶ Other performance tools are available in the Microsoft Win32 SDK (see the online *Platform SDK* Tools Guide, Tuning section in HTML-Help Viewer).

You can also purchase separate products to perform performance analysis and profiling.

Efficient Source Code

Once you have determined those sections of code where most of the program execution time is spent, examine these sections for coding efficiency. Suggested guidelines for improving source code efficiency are provided in the following sections:

▶ Section 6.3 Data Alignment Considerations

▶ Section 6.4 Use Arrays Efficiently

▶ Section 6.5 Improve Overall I/O Performance

▶ Section 6.6 Additional Source Code Guidelines for Run-Time Efficiency

For information about timing your application and for an example command procedure that uses the Windows NT Performance Monitor, see Section 6.2.1 Timing Your Application.

6.3   Data Alignment Considerations

For optimal performance with most cases, make sure your data is aligned naturally. If you must use 1- or 2-byte integer or logical data, in some cases specifying 4- or 8-byte alignment provides better performance (see Section 6.3.3 Ordering Data Declarations to Avoid Unaligned Data).

A natural boundary is a memory address that is a multiple of the data item's size (data type sizes are described in Chapter 20 Data Representation). For example, a **REAL**(KIND=8) data item aligned on natural boundaries has an address that is a multiple of 8. An array is aligned on natural boundaries if all of its elements are so aligned.

All data items whose starting address is on a natural boundary are *naturally aligned*. Data not aligned on a natural boundary is called *unaligned data*.

Although the Digital Fortran compiler naturally aligns individual data items when it can, certain Digital Fortran statements (such as **EQUIVALENCE**) can cause data items to become unaligned (see Section 6.3.1 Causes of Unaligned Data and Ensuring Natural Alignment).

Although you can use the DF command /align:*keyword* options to ensure naturally aligned data, you should check and consider reordering data declarations of data items within common blocks and structures. Within each common block, derived type, or record structure, carefully specify the order and sizes of data declarations to ensure naturally aligned data. Start with the largest size numeric items first, followed by smaller size numeric items, and then nonnumeric (character) data.

The following sections discuss data alignment considerations in more detail:

▶ Section 6.3.1 Causes of Unaligned Data and Ensuring Natural Alignment

▶ Section 6.3.2 Checking for Inefficient Unaligned Data

▶ Section 6.3.3 Ordering Data Declarations to Avoid Unaligned Data

▶ Section 6.3.4 Options Controlling Alignment

6.3.1 Causes of Unaligned Data and Ensuring Natural Alignment

Common blocks (**COMMON** statement), derived-type data, and Digital Fortran record structures (**RECORD** statement) usually contain multiple items within the context of the larger structure.

The following declarations can force data to be unaligned:

▶ Common blocks

The order of variables in the **COMMON** statement determines their storage order.

Unless you are sure that the data items in the common block will be naturally aligned, specify either the /align:commons or /align:dcommons option, depending on the largest data size used.

For examples and more information, see Section 6.3.3.1 Arranging Data in Common Blocks.

▶ Derived-type data

Derived-type (user-defined) data members are declared after a **TYPE** statement.

If your data includes derived-type data structures, unless you are sure that the data items in derived-type data structures will be naturally aligned, specify the /align:records option (default unless /vms was specified).

If you omit the **SEQUENCE** statement, the /align:records option ensures all data items are naturally aligned.

If you specify the **SEQUENCE** statement, the /align:records option is prevented from adding necessary padding to avoid unaligned data (data items are packed). When you use **SEQUENCE**, you should specify data declaration order such that all data items are naturally aligned.

For an example and more information, see Section 6.3.3.2 Arranging Data Items in Derived-Type Data.

▶ Digital Fortran record structures

Digital Fortran record structures are language extensions that usually contain multiple data items. The order of variables in the **STRUCTURE** statement determines their storage order. The **RECORD** statement names the record structure.

If your data includes Digital Fortran record structures and you specify the /vms option, you should also specify the /align:records option, unless you are sure that the data items in derived-type data and Digital Fortran record structures will be naturally aligned.

For examples and more information, see Section 6.3.3.3 Arranging Data Items in Digital Fortran Record Structures.

▶ Equivalenced data

EQUIVALENCE statements can force unaligned data or cause data to span natural boundaries.

To avoid unaligned data in a common block, derived-type data, or record structures, use one or both of the following:

▶ For new programs or for programs where the source code declarations can be modified easily, plan the order of data declarations with care. For example, you should order variables in a **COMMON** statement such that numeric data is arranged from largest to smallest, followed by any character data (see the data declaration rules in Section 6.3.3 Ordering Data Declarations to Avoid Unaligned Data).

▶ For existing programs where source code changes are not easily done or for array elements containing derived-type or record structures, you can use command line options to request that the compiler align numeric data by adding padding spaces where needed.

Other possible causes of unaligned data include unaligned actual arguments and arrays that contain a derived-type structure or Digital Fortran record structure.

When actual arguments from outside the program unit are not naturally aligned, unaligned data access will occur. Digital Fortran assumes all passed arguments are naturally aligned and has no information at compile time about data that will be introduced by actual arguments during program execution.

For arrays where each array element contains a derived-type structure or Digital Fortran record structure, the size of the array elements may cause some elements (but not the first) to start on an unaligned boundary.

Even if the data items are naturally aligned within a derived-type structure without the **SEQUENCE** statement or a record structures, the size of an array element might require use of /align options to supply needed padding to avoid some array elements being unaligned.

If you specify /align:norecords or specify /vms without /align:records, no padding bytes are added between array elements. If array elements each contain a derived-type structure with the **SEQUENCE** statement, array elements are packed without padding bytes regardless of the DF command options specified. In this case, some elements will be unaligned.

When /align:records option is in effect, the number of padding bytes added by the compiler for each array element is dependent on the size of the largest data item within the structure. The compiler determines the size of the array elements as an exact multiple of the largest data item in the derived-type structure without the **SEQUENCE** statement or a record structure. The compiler then adds the appropriate number of padding bytes.

For instance, if a structure contains an 8-byte floating-point number followed by a 3-byte character variable, each element contains five bytes of padding (16 is an exact multiple of 8). However, if the structure contains one 4-byte floating-point number, one 4-byte integer, followed by a 3-byte character variable, each element would contain one byte of padding (12 is an exact multiple of 4).

For more information on the /align options, see Section 4.1.2 /[no]align and Section 6.3.4 Options Controlling Alignment.

6.3.2   Checking for Inefficient Unaligned Data

During compilation, the Digital Fortran compiler naturally aligns as much data as possible. Exceptions that can result in unaligned data are described in Section 6.3.1 Causes of Unaligned Data and Ensuring Natural Alignment.

Because unaligned data can slow run-time performance, it is worthwhile to:

▶ Double-check data declarations within common block, derived-type data, or record structures to ensure all data items are naturally aligned (see the data declaration rules in Section 6.3.3 Ordering Data Declarations to Avoid Unaligned Data). Using modules to contain data declarations can ensure consistent alignment and use of such data.

▶ Avoid the **EQUIVALENCE** statement or use it in a way that cannot cause unaligned data or data spanning natural boundaries.

▶ Ensure that passed arguments from outside the program unit are naturally aligned.

▶ Check that the size of array elements containing at least one derived-type data or record structure cause array elements to start on aligned boundaries (see Section 6.3.1 Causes of Unaligned Data and Ensuring Natural Alignment).

During compilation, warning messages are issued for any data items that are known to be unaligned (unless you specify the /warn:noalignments option).

6.3.3 Ordering Data Declarations to Avoid Unaligned Data

For new programs or when the source declarations of an existing program can be easily modified, plan the order of your data declarations carefully to ensure the data items in a common block, derived-type data, record structure, or data items made equivalent by an **EQUIVALENCE** statement will be naturally aligned.

Use the following rules to prevent unaligned data:

▶ Always define the largest size numeric data items first.

▶ If your data includes a mixture of character and numeric data, place the numeric data first.

▶ Add small data items of the correct size (or padding) before otherwise unaligned data to ensure natural alignment for the data that follows.

Using the suggested data declaration guidelines minimizes the need to use the /align options to add padding bytes to ensure naturally aligned data. In cases where the /align options are still needed, using the suggested data declaration guidelines can minimize the number of padding bytes added by the compiler.

The following topics discuss data declaration guidelines:

▶ Section 6.3.3.1 Arranging Data Items in Common Blocks

▶ Section 6.3.3.2 Arranging Data Items in Derived-Type Data

▶ Section 6.3.3.3 Arranging Data Items in Digital Fortran Record Structures

6.3.3.1   *Arranging Data Items in Common Blocks*

The order of data items in a **COMMON** statement determine the order in which the data items are stored. Consider the following declaration of a common block named X:

```
LOGICAL          (KIND=2) FLAG
INTEGER          IARRY_I(3)
CHARACTER(LEN=5) NAME_CH
COMMON /X/ FLAG, IARRY_I(3), NAME_CH
```

As shown in Figure 6-1, if you omit the alignment compiler options, the common block will contain unaligned data items beginning at the first array element of IARRY_I.

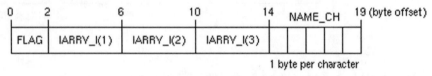

Figure 6–1   *Common Block with Unaligned Data*

As shown in Figure 6-2, if you compile the program units that use the common block with the /align:commons options, data items will be naturally aligned.

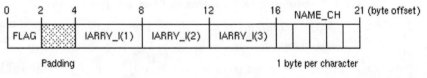

Figure 6–2   *Common Block with Naturally Aligned Data*

Because the common block X contains data items whose size is 32 bits or smaller, specify /align:commons. If the common block contains data items whose size might be larger than 32 bits (such as **REAL**(KIND=8) data), use /align:dcommons.

If you can easily modify the source files that use the common block data, define the numeric variables in the **COMMON** statement in descending order of size and place the character variable last to provide more portability and ensure natural alignment without padding or the DF command options /align:commons or /align:dcommons:

```
LOGICAL (KIND=2)   FLAG
INTEGER            IARRY_I(3)
CHARACTER(LEN=5)   NAME_CH
COMMON /X/ IARRY_I(3), FLAG, NAME_CH
```

As shown in Figure 6-3, if you arrange the order of variables from largest to smallest size and place character data last, the data items will be naturally aligned.

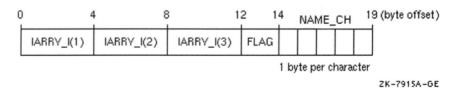

Figure 6–3 *Common Block with Naturally Aligned Reordered Data*

When modifying or creating all source files that use common block data, consider placing the common block data declarations in a module so the declarations are consistent. If the common block is not needed for compatibility (such as file storage or Digital Fortran 77 use), you can place the data declarations in a module without using a common block.

6.3.3.2   *Arranging Data Items in Derived-Type Data*

Like common blocks, derived-type data may contain multiple data items (members).

Data item components within derived-type data will be naturally aligned on up to 64-bit boundaries, with certain exceptions related to the use of the **SEQUENCE** statement and DF options.

Digital Fortran stores a derived data type as a linear sequence of values, as follows:

▶ If you specify the **SEQUENCE** statement, the first data item is in the first storage location and the last data item is in the last storage location. The data items appear in the order in which they are declared. The DF options have no effect on unaligned data, so data declarations must be carefully specified to naturally align data.

▶ If you omit the **SEQUENCE** statement, Digital Fortran adds the padding bytes needed to naturally align data item components, unless you specify the /align:norecords option or the /vms option without /align: records.

Consider the following declaration of array CATALOG_SPRING of derived-type PART_DT:

```
MODULE DATA_DEFS
  TYPE PART_DT
    INTEGER            IDENTIFIER
    REAL               WEIGHT
    CHARACTER(LEN=15)  DESCRIPTION
  END TYPE PART_DT
  TYPE (PART_DT) CATALOG_SPRING(30)
  .
  .
  .
END MODULE DATA_DEFS
```

As shown in Figure 6-4, the largest numeric data items are defined first and the character data type is defined last. There are no padding characters between data items and all items are naturally aligned. The trailing padding byte is needed because CATALOG_SPRING is an array; it is inserted by the compiler when the /align records option is in effect.

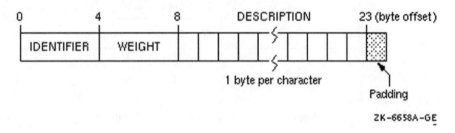

Figure 6–4 *Derived-Type Naturally Aligned Data (in CATALOG_SPRING)*

6.3.3.3 *Arranging Data Items in Digital Fortran Record Structures*

Record structures are a Digital Fortran language extension to the FORTRAN 77 and Fortran 90 Standards. Record structures use the **RECORD** statement and optionally the **STRUCTURE** statement, which are also Digital Fortran language extensions. The order of data items in a **STRUCTURE** statement determine the order in which the data items are stored.

Digital Fortran stores a record in memory as a linear sequence of values, with the record's first element in the first storage location and its last element in the last storage location. Unless you specify the /vms option without the /align:records option or specify /align:norecords, padding bytes are added if needed to ensure data fields are naturally aligned.

The following example contains a structure declaration, a **RECORD** statement, and diagrams of the resulting records as they are stored in memory:

```
STRUCTURE /STRA/
    CHARACTER*1 CHR
    INTEGER*4 INT
END STRUCTURE
    .
    .
    .
RECORD /STRA/ REC
```

Figure 6-5 shows the memory diagram of record REC for naturally aligned records.

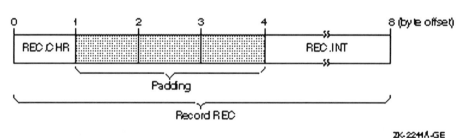

Figure 6–5 *Memory Diagram of REC for Naturally Aligned Records*

6.3.4   Options Controlling Alignment

The following options control whether the Digital Fortran compiler adds padding (when needed) to naturally align multiple data items in common blocks, derived-type data, and Digital Fortran record structures:

▶ The /align:commons option

Requests that data in common blocks be aligned on up to 4-byte boundaries, by adding padding bytes as needed. Unless you specify /fast, the default is /align:nocommons or arbitrary byte alignment of common block data. In this case, unaligned data can occur unless the order of data items specified in the **COMMON** statement places the largest numeric data item first, followed by the next largest numeric data (and so on), followed by any character data.

▶ The /align:dcommons option

Requests that data in common blocks be aligned on up to 8-byte boundaries, by adding padding bytes as needed. Unless you specify /fast, the default is /align:nocommons or arbitrary byte alignment of data items in a common data.

Specify the /align:dcommons option for applications that use common blocks, unless your application has no unaligned data or, if the application might have unaligned data, all data items are four bytes or smaller. For applications that use common blocks where all data items are four bytes or smaller, you can specify /align:commons instead of /align:dcommons.

▶ The /align:norecords option

Requests that multiple data items in derived-type data and record structures (a Digital Fortran extension) be aligned arbitrarily on byte boundaries instead of being naturally aligned. If you omit the /vms option, the default is /align:records. If you specify the /vms option, /align: norecords is used (unless you also specify /align: records).

▶ The /align:records option

Requests that multiple data items in record structures and derived-type data without the **SEQUENCE** statement be naturally aligned, by adding padding bytes as needed. You only need to specify /align records if you specify the /vms option.

▶ The /vms option

Controls certain VMS-related run-time defaults, including alignment (sets /align:norecords) option. If you specify the /vms option, you may need to also specify the /align:records option to ensure that padding bytes are added.

The default behavior is that multiple data items in derived-type data and record structures *will* be naturally aligned; data items in common blocks *will not* be naturally aligned (/align:records) with /align:nocommons. In derived-type data, using the **SEQUENCE** statement prevents /align:records from adding needed padding bytes to naturally align data items.

6.4   Use Arrays Efficiently

The way arrays are accessed and passed as arguments can have a significant impact on run-time performance, especially when using large arrays. This section discusses the following topics:

▶ Section 6.4.1 Accessing Arrays Efficiently

▶ Section 6.4.2 Passing Array Arguments Efficiently

6.4.1   Accessing Arrays Efficiently

On both *x*86 and Alpha systems, many of the array access efficiency techniques described in this section are applied automatically by the Digital Fortran loop transformation optimizations (set at /optimization:5).

Several aspects of array access can improve run-time performance:

▶ The fastest array access occurs when contiguous access to the whole array or most of an array occurs. Perform one or a few array operations that access all of the array or major parts of an array rather than numerous operations on scattered array elements. Rather than use explicit loops for array access, use elemental array operations, such as the following line that increments all elements of array variable A:

```
A = A + 1.
```

When reading or writing an array, use the array name and not a **DO** loop or an implied **DO**-loop that specifies each element number. Fortran 90 array syntax allows you to reference a whole array by using its name in an expression. For example:

```
REAL :: A(100,100)
A = 0.0
A = A + 1.        !  Increment all elements of A by 1
.
.
.
WRITE (8) A       !  Fast whole array use
```

Similarly, you can use derived-type array structure components, such as:

```
TYPE X
 INTEGER A(5)
END TYPE X
.
.
.
TYPE (X) Z
WRITE (8) Z%A !  Fast array structure component use
```

▶ Make sure multidimensional arrays are referenced using proper array syntax and are traversed in the "natural" ascending order *column major* for Fortran. With column-major order, the leftmost subscript varies most rapidly with a stride of one. Whole array access uses column-major order.

Avoid *row-major* order, as is done by C, where the rightmost subscript varies most rapidly.

For example, consider the nested **DO** loops that access a two-dimension array with the J loop as the innermost loop:

```
INTEGER X(3,5), Y(3,5), I, J
Y = 0
DO I=1,3                    ! I outer loop varies slowest
  DO J=1,5                  ! J inner loop varies fastest
    X (I,J) = Y(I,J) + 1 ! Inefficient row-major storage order
  END DO                    ! (rightmost subscript varies fastest)
END DO
.
.
.
END PROGRAM
```

Because J varies the fastest and is the second array subscript in the expression X (I,J), the array is accessed in row-major order.

To make the array accessed in natural column-major order, examine the array algorithm and data being modified.

Using arrays X and Y, the array can be accessed in natural column-major order by changing the nesting order of the **DO** loops so the innermost loop variable corresponds to the leftmost array dimension:

```
INTEGER X(3,5), Y(3,5), I, J
Y = 0
DO J=1,5                    ! J outer loop varies slowest
  DO I=1,3                  ! I inner loop varies fastest
    X (I,J) = Y(I,J) + 1 ! Efficient column-major storage
                            ! order (leftmost subscript varies
 fastest)
    END DO
END DO
.
.
.
END PROGRAM
```

Fortran whole array access (*X= Y + 1*) uses efficient column major order. However, if the application requires that J vary the fastest or if you cannot modify the loop order without changing the results, consider modifying the application program to use a rearranged order of array dimensions. Program modifications include rearranging the order of:

- Dimensions in the declaration of the arrays X(5,3) and Y(5,3)
- The assignment of X(J,I) and Y(J,I) within the DO loops
- All other references to arrays X and Y

In this case, the original **DO** loop nesting is used where J is the innermost loop:

```
INTEGER X(5,3), Y(5,3), I, J
Y = 0
DO I=1,3                ! I outer loop varies slowest
  DO J=1,5              ! J inner loop varies fastest
    X (J,I) = Y(J,I) + 1! Efficient column-major storage order
  END DO                ! order (leftmost subscript varies
                        ! fastest)
END DO
.
.
.
END PROGRAM
```

Code written to access multidimensional arrays in row-major order (like C) or random order can often make inefficient use of the CPU memory cache. For more information on using natural storage order during record I/O operations, see Section 6.5.3 Write Array Data in the Natural Storage Order.

▶ Use the available Fortran 90 array intrinsic procedures rather than creating your own.

Whenever possible, use Fortran 90 array intrinsic procedures instead of creating your own routines to accomplish the same task. Fortran 90 array intrinsic procedures are designed for efficient use with the various Visual Fortran run-time components.

Using the standard-conforming array intrinsics can also make your program more portable.

▶ With multidimensional arrays where access to array elements will be noncontiguous, avoid leftmost array dimensions that are a power of two (such as 256, 512). At higher levels of optimization (/optimize=3 or higher), the compiler pads certain power-of-two array sizes to minimize possible inefficient use of the cache.

Because the *cache sizes* are a power of two, *array dimensions* that are also a power of two may make inefficient use of cache when array access is non-contiguous. On Alpha systems, if the cache size is *an exact multiple* of the leftmost dimension, your program will probably make little use of the cache. This does not apply to contiguous sequential access or whole array access.

One work-around is to increase the dimension to allow some unused elements, making the leftmost dimension larger than actually needed. For example, increasing the leftmost dimension of A from 512 to 520 would make better use of cache:

```
REAL A (512,100)
DO I = 2,511
  DO J = 2,99
    A(I,J)=(A(I+1,J-1) + A(I-1, J+1)) * 0.5
  END DO
END DO
```

In this code, array A has a leftmost dimension of 512, a power of two. The innermost loop accesses the rightmost dimension (row major), causing inefficient access. Increasing the leftmost dimension of A to 520 (REAL A (520,100)) allows the loop to provide better performance, but at the expense of some unused elements.

Because loop index variables I and J are used in the calculation, changing the nesting order of the **DO** loops changes the results.

▶ To minimize data storage and memory cache misses with arrays, use 32-bit data rather than 64-bit data, unless you require the greater range and precision of double precision floating-point numbers or, on Alpha systems, the numeric range of 8-byte integers.

For more information on arrays and their data declaration statements, see "Arrays" in the *Language Reference* in Visual Fortran online help.

6.4.2   Passing Array Arguments Efficiently

In Fortran 90, there are two general types of array arguments:

▶ Explicit-shape arrays were used with FORTRAN 77. These arrays have a fixed rank and extent that is known at compile time. Other dummy argument (receiving) arrays that are not deferred-shape (such as assumed-size arrays) can be grouped with explicit-shape array arguments in the following discussion.

▶ Deferred-shape arrays were introduced with Fortran 90. Types of deferred-shape arrays include array pointers and allocatable arrays. Assumed-shape array arguments generally follow the rules about passing deferred-shape array arguments.

When passing arrays as arguments, either the starting (base) address of the array or the address of an array descriptor is passed:

▶ When using explicit-shape (or assumed-size) arrays to receive an array, the starting address of the array is passed.

▶ When using deferred-shape or assumed-shape arrays to receive an array, the address of the array descriptor is passed (the compiler creates the array descriptor).

Passing an assumed-shape array or array pointer to an explicit-shape array can slow run-time performance, since the compiler needs to create an array temporary for the entire array. The array temporary is created because the passed array may not be contiguous and the receiving (explicit-shape) array requires a contiguous array. When an array temporary is created, the size of the passed array determines whether the impact on slowing run-time performance is slight or severe.

Table 6-4 summarizes what happens with the various combinations of array types. The amount of run-time performance inefficiency depends on the size of the array.

Table 6–4 *Performance Effects of Different Kinds of Arrays*

| **Input Arguments Array Types** | **Output Argument Array Types** | |
	Explicit-Shape Arrays	**Deferred-Shape and Assumed-Shape Arrays**
Explicit-Shape Arrays	Very efficient. Does not use an array temporary. Does not pass an array descriptor. Interface block optional.	Efficient. Only allowed for assumed-shape arrays (not deferred-shape arrays). Does not use an array temporary. Passes an array descriptor. Requires an interface block.
Deferred-Shape and Assumed-Shape Arrays	Depends on whether it's passing an allocatable array: ▶ When passing an allocatable array, very efficient. Does not use an array temporary. Does not pass an array descriptor. Interface block optional. ▶ When not passing an allocatable array, not efficient. Instead use allocatable arrays whenever possible. Uses an array temporary. Does not pass an array descriptor. Interface block optional.	Efficient. Requires an assumed-shape or array pointer as dummy argument. Does not use an array temporary. Passes an array descriptor. Requires an interface block.

6.5 Improve Overall I/O Performance

Improving overall I/O performance can minimize both device I/O and actual CPU time. The techniques listed in this section can greatly improve performance in many applications.

A *bottleneck* limits the maximum speed of execution by being the slowest process in an executing program. In some programs, I/O is the bottleneck that prevents an improvement in run-time performance. The key to relieving I/O bottlenecks is to reduce the actual amount of CPU and I/O device time involved in I/O. Bottlenecks may be caused by one or more of the following:

▶ A dramatic reduction in CPU time without a corresponding improvement in I/O time results in an I/O bottleneck.

▶ By such coding practices as:

- Unnecessary formatting of data and other CPU-intensive processing

- Unnecessary transfers of intermediate results

- Inefficient transfers of small amounts of data

- Application requirements

Improved coding practices can minimize actual device I/O, as well as the actual CPU time.

You can also consider solutions to system-wide problems like minimizing device I/O delays.

The following sections discuss I/O performance considerations in more detail:

▶ Section 6.5.1 Use Unformatted Files Instead of Formatted Files

▶ Section 6.5.2 Write Whole Arrays or Strings

▶ Section 6.5.3 Write Array Data in the Natural Storage Order

▶ Section 6.5.4 Use Memory for Intermediate Results

▶ Section 6.5.5 Enable Implied-DO Loop Collapsing

▶ Section 6.5.6 Use of Variable Format Expressions

▶ Section 6.5.7 Efficient Use of Record Buffers and Disk I/O

▶ Section 6.5.8 Specify RECL

▶ Section 6.5.9 Use the Optimal Record Type

6.5.1   Use Unformatted Files Instead of Formatted Files

Use unformatted files whenever possible. Unformatted I/O of numeric data is more efficient and more precise than formatted I/O. Native unformatted data does not need to be modified when transferred and will take up less space on an external file.

Conversely, when writing data to formatted files, formatted data must be converted to character strings for output, less data can transfer in a single operation, and formatted data may lose precision if read back into binary form.

To write the array A(25,25) in the following statements, S1 is more efficient than S2:

```
S1     WRITE (7) A
S2     WRITE (7,100) A
  100  FORMAT (25(' ',25F5.21))
```

Although formatted data files are more easily ported to other systems, Digital Fortran can convert unformatted data in several formats (see Chapter 23 Converting Unformatted Numeric Data).

6.5.2   Write Whole Arrays or Strings

The general guidelines about array use discussed in Section 6.4 Use Arrays Efficiently also apply to reading or writing an array with an I/O statement.

To eliminate unnecessary overhead, write whole arrays or strings at one time rather than individual elements at multiple times. Each item in an I/O list generates its own calling sequence. This processing overhead becomes most significant in implied-**DO** loops. When accessing whole arrays, use the array name (Fortran 90 array syntax) instead of using implied-**DO** loops.

6.5.3   Write Array Data in the Natural Storage Order

Use the *natural* ascending storage order whenever possible. This is column-major order, with the leftmost subscript varying fastest and striding by 1 (see Section 6.4 Use Arrays Efficiently). If a program must read or write data in any other order, efficient block moves are inhibited.

If the whole array is not being written, natural storage order is the best order possible.

If you must use an *unnatural* storage order, in certain cases it might be more efficient to transfer the data to memory and reorder the data before performing the I/O operation.

6.5.4   Use Memory for Intermediate Results

Performance can improve by storing intermediate results in memory rather than storing them in a file on a peripheral device. One situation that may not benefit from using intermediate storage is when there is a disproportionately large amount of data in relation to physical memory on your system. Excessive page faults can dramatically impede virtual memory performance.

6.5.5   Enable Implied-DO Loop Collapsing

DO loop collapsing reduces a major overhead in I/O processing. Normally, each element in an I/O list generates a separate call to the Digital Fortran RTL. The processing overhead of these calls can be most significant in implied-**DO** loops.

Digital Fortran reduces the number of calls in implied-**DO** loops by replacing up to seven nested implied-**DO** loops with a single call to an optimized run-time library I/O routine. The routine can transmit many I/O elements at once.

Loop collapsing can occur in formatted and unformatted I/O, but only if certain conditions are met:

▶ The control variable must be an integer. The control variable cannot be a dummy argument or contained in an **EQUIVALENCE** or **VOLATILE** statement. Digital Fortran must be able to determine that the control variable does not change unexpectedly at run time.

▶ The format must not contain a variable format expression.

For more information, see:

▶ See the **VOLATILE** attribute and statement in the "A-Z Summary" in the *Language Reference* in Visual Fortran online Help.

▶ On loop optimizations, see Section 6.7 Optimization Levels: the /optimize:num Option.

6.5.6   Use of Variable Format Expressions

Variable format expressions (a Digital Fortran language extension) is a numeric expression enclosed in angle brackets (< >) that can be used in a **FORMAT** statement. Variable format expressions (VFEs) are almost as flexible as run-time formatting, but they are more efficient because the compiler can eliminate run-time parsing of the I/O format. Only a small amount of processing and the actual data transfer are required during run time.

On the other hand, run-time formatting can impair performance significantly. For example, in the following statements, S1 is more efficient than S2 because the formatting is done once at compile time, not at run time:

```
S1      WRITE (6,400) (A(I), I=1,N)
   400  FORMAT (1X,  <N> F5.2)
                      .
                      .
                      .
S2      WRITE (CHFMT,500) '(1X,',N,'F5.2)'
   500  FORMAT (A,I3,A)
        WRITE (6,FMT=CHFMT) (A(I), I=1,N)
```

6.5.7   Efficient Use of Record Buffers and Disk I/O

Records being read or written are transferred between the user's program buffers and one or more disk block I/O buffers, which are established when the file is opened by the Digital Fortran run-time system. Unless very large records are being read or written, multiple logical records can reside in the disk block I/O buffer when it is written to disk or read from disk, minimizing physical disk I/O.

You can specify the size of the disk block I/O buffer by using the **OPEN** statement BLOCKSIZE specifier (see Visual Fortran online Help). If you omit the BLOCKSIZE specifier in the **OPEN** statement, it is set for optimal I/O use with the type of device the file resides on.

The default for BUFFERCOUNT is 1. Any experiments to improve I/O performance should increase the BUFFERCOUNT value and not the BLOCKSIZE value, to increase the amount of data read by each disk I/O.

If the **OPEN** statement includes the BUFFERCOUNT and BLOCKSIZE specifiers, their product is the size in bytes of the internal buffer. If these are not specified, the default size is 1024 bytes if /fpscomp=general (or /fpscomp: all) was specified and 8192 bytes if it was omitted. This internal buffer will grow to hold the largest single record but will never shrink.

For disk writes, the BUFFERED specifier or the /assume:buffered_io option (Version 6.0.A) lets you control whether records written are written (flushed) to disk as each record is written (default) or accumulated in the buffer. The default is BUFFERED='NO' and /assume:nobuffered_io for all I/O, in which case, the Fortran run-time system empties its internal buffer for each **WRITE** (or similar record output statement). If you specify BUFFERED='YES' or /assume:buffered_io and the device is a disk, the internal buffer will be filled, possibly by many record output statements (**WRITE**), before it is written to disk.

Using buffered writes (BUFFERED='YES') usually makes disk I/O more efficient by writing larger blocks of data to the disk less often. However, a system failure when BUFFERED='YES' or /assume:buffered_io was specified can cause records to be lost, since they might *not* yet have been written to disk (such records would have written to disk with BUFFERED='NO' or /assume: nobuffered_io).

6.5.8   Specify RECL

The sum of the record length (RECL specifier in an **OPEN** statement) and its overhead is a multiple or divisor of the blocksize, which is device specific. For example, if the BLOCKSIZE is 8192 then RECL might be 24576 (a multiple of 3) or 1024 (a divisor of 8).

The RECL value should fill blocks as close to capacity as possible (but not over capacity). Such values allow efficient moves, with each operation moving as much data as possible; the least amount of space in the block is wasted. Avoid using values larger than the block capacity, because they create very inefficient moves for the excess data only slightly filling a block (allocating extra memory for the buffer and writing partial blocks are inefficient).

The RECL value unit for formatted files is always 1-byte units. For unformatted files, the RECL unit is 4-byte units, unless you specify the /assume: byterecl option to request 1-byte units.

When porting unformatted data files from non-Digital systems, see Chapter 23 Converting Unformatted Numeric Data.

6.5.9   Use the Optimal Record Type

Unless a certain record type is needed for portability reasons, choose the most efficient type, as follows:

▶ For sequential files of a consistent record size, the fixed-length record type gives the best performance.

▶ For sequential unformatted files when records are not fixed in size, the variable-length record type gives the best performance, particularly for **BACKSPACE** operations.

▶ For sequential formatted files when records are not fixed in size, the Stream_LF record type gives the best performance.

For more information, see:

▶ On **OPEN** statement specifiers and defaults, see the "A-Z Summary" in the *Language Reference* in Visual Fortran online Help.

▶ On Visual Fortran data files, see Section 16.1 Devices and Files.

6.6   Additional Source Code Guidelines for Run-Time Efficiency

In addition to data alignment and the efficient use of arrays and I/O, other source coding guidelines can be implemented to improve run-time performance.

The amount of improvement in run-time performance is related to the number of times a statement is executed. For example, improving an arithmetic expression executed within a loop many times has the potential to improve performance, more than improving a similar expression executed once outside a loop.

Suggested guidelines for improving source code efficiency are provided in the following sections:

▶ Section 6.6.1 Avoid Small Integer and Small Logical Data Items (Alpha Only)

▶ Section 6.6.2 Avoid Mixed Data Type Arithmetic Expressions

▶ Section 6.6.3 Use Efficient Data Types

▶ Section 6.6.4 Avoid Using Slow Arithmetic Operators

▶ Section 6.6.5 Avoid EQUIVALENCE Statement Use

▶ Section 6.6.6 Use Statement Functions and Internal Subprograms

▶ Section 6.6.7 Code DO Loops for Efficiency

6.6.1   Avoid Small Integer and Small Logical Data Items (Alpha Only)

To minimize data storage and memory cache misses with arrays, use 32-bit data rather than 64-bit data, unless you require the greater range and precision of double precision floating-point numbers or, on Alpha systems, the numeric range of 8-byte integers.

On Alpha systems, avoid using integer or logical data less than 32 bits (KIND=4). Accessing a 16-bit (KIND=2) or 8-bit (KIND=1) data type can result in a sequence of machine instructions to access the data, rather than a single, efficient machine instruction for a 32-bit data item.

6.6.2   Avoid Mixed Data Type Arithmetic Expressions

Avoid mixing integer and floating-point (**REAL**) data in the same computation. Expressing all numbers in a floating-point arithmetic expression (assignment statement) as floating-point values eliminates the need to convert data between fixed and floating-point formats. Expressing all numbers in an integer arithmetic expression as integer values also achieves this. This improves run-time performance.

For example, assuming that I and J are both **INTEGER** variables, expressing a constant number (2.) as an integer value (2) eliminates the need to convert the data:

```
Original Code:     INTEGER I, J
                   I= J / 2.
Efficient Code:    INTEGER I, J
                   I= J / 2
```

For applications with numerous floating-point operations, consider using the /assume: accuracy_sensitive option (see Section 6.8.4 Arithmetic Reordering Optimizations) if a small difference in the result is acceptable.

You can use different *sizes* of the same general data type in an expression with minimal or no effect on run-time performance. For example, using **REAL**, **DOUBLE PRECISION**, and **COMPLEX** floating-point numbers in the same floating-point arithmetic expression has minimal or no effect on run-time performance.

6.6.3   Use Efficient Data Types

In cases where more than one data type can be used for a variable, consider selecting the data types based on the following hierarchy, listed from most to least efficient:

▶ On *x*86 systems:

- Integer

- Double-precision real, expressed explicitly as **DOUBLE PRECISION**, **REAL** (KIND=8), or **REAL**(8)

- Single-precision real, expressed explicitly as **REAL**, **REAL**(KIND=4), or **REAL** (4)

▶ On Alpha systems:

- Integer (also see Section 6.6.1 Avoid Small Integer and Small Logical Data Items (Alpha Only))

- Single-precision real, expressed explicitly as **REAL**, **REAL**(KIND=4), or **REAL** (4)

- Double-precision real, expressed explicitly as **DOUBLE PRECISION**, **REAL** (KIND=8), or **REAL**(8)

However, keep in mind that in an arithmetic expression, you should avoid mixing integer and floating-point (**REAL**) data (see Section 6.6.2 Avoid Mixed Data Type Arithmetic Expressions).

6.6.4   Avoid Using Slow Arithmetic Operators

Before you modify source code to avoid slow arithmetic operators, be aware that optimizations convert many slow arithmetic operators to faster arithmetic operators. For example, the compiler optimizes the expression H=J**2 to be H=J*J.

Consider also whether replacing a slow arithmetic operator with a faster arithmetic operator will change the accuracy of the results or impact the maintainability (readability) of the source code.

Replacing slow arithmetic operators with faster ones should be reserved for critical code areas. The following hierarchy lists the Digital Fortran arithmetic operators, from fastest to slowest:

▶ Addition (+), subtraction (-), and floating-point multiplication (*)

▶ Integer multiplication (*)

▶ Division (/)

▶ Exponentiation (**)

6.6.5   Avoid EQUIVALENCE Statement Use

Avoid using **EQUIVALENCE** statements; they can:

▶ Force unaligned data or cause data to span natural boundaries.

▶ Prevent certain optimizations, including:

• Global data analysis under certain conditions (see Section 6.7.3 Global Optimizations)

• Implied-**DO** loop collapsing when the control variable is contained in an **EQUIVALENCE** statement

6.6.6   Use Statement Functions and Internal Subprograms

Whenever the Digital Visual Fortran compiler has access to the use and definition of a subprogram during compilation, it may choose to inline the subprogram. Using statement functions and internal subprograms maximizes the number of subprogram references that will be inlined, especially when multiple source files are compiled together at optimization level /optimize:4 or / optimize:5 (or an appropriate /inline keyword was specified).

For more information, see Section 6.1.2 Compile with Appropriate Options and Multiple Source Files.

6.6.7   Code DO Loops for Efficiency

Minimize the arithmetic operations and other operations in a **DO** loop whenever possible. Moving unnecessary operations outside the loop will improve performance (for example, when the intermediate nonvarying values within the loop are not needed).

For more information, see:

▶ On loop optimizations, see Section 6.7.6.1 Loop Transformations, Section 6.8.2 Controlling Loop Unrolling, and Section 6.7.6.2 Software Pipelining (Alpha Only).

▶ On the **DO** statement, see the "A-Z Summary" in the *Language Reference* in Visual Fortran online Help.

6.7   Optimization Levels: the /optimize Option

Visual Fortran performs many optimizations by default. You do not have to recode your program to use them. However, understanding how optimizations work helps you remove any inhibitors to their successful function.

If an operation can be performed, eliminated, or simplified at compile time, Visual Fortran does so, rather than have it done at run time. The time required to compile the program usually increases as more optimizations occur.

The program will likely execute faster when compiled at /optimize:4, but will require more compilation time than if you compile the program at a lower level of optimization.

The size of object files varies with the optimizations requested. Factors that can increase object file size include an increase of loop unrolling or procedure inlining.

Table 6-5 lists the levels of Digital Fortran optimization with different /optimize:num options (for example, /optimize:0 specifies no selectable optimizations); some optimizations always occur. All levels of optimizations available on the architecture can be specified using /optimize:5. On *x*86 systems, /optimize:5 includes loop transformations; on Alpha systems, /optimize:5 includes loop transformation and software pipelining.

Table 6–5 *Levels of Optimization with Different /optimize:num Options*

	Option					
Optimization Type	**/optimize: 0**	**/optimize: 1**	**/optimize: 2**	**/optimize: 3**	**/optimize: 4**	**/optimize: 5**
Software pipelining						**x** (Alpha only)
Loop transformation						x
Automatic inlining					x	x
Additional global optimizations				x	x	x
Global optimizations			x	x	x	x
Local (minimal) optimizations	x	x	x	x	x

The default is /optimize:4. However, when /debug is specified, the default is /optimize:0 (no optimizations).

In Table 6-5, the following terms are used to describe the levels of optimization (described in detail in the following sections:

▶ *Local (minimal) optimizations* (/optimize:1) or higher occur within the source program unit and include recognition of common subexpressions and the expansion of multiplication and division.

▶ *Global optimizations* (/optimize:2) or higher include such optimizations as data-flow analysis, code motion, strength reduction, split-lifetime analysis, and instruction scheduling.

▶ *Additional global optimizations* (/optimize:3) or higher improve speed at the cost of extra code size. These optimizations include loop unrolling, code replication to eliminate branches, and padding certain power-of-two array sizes for more efficient cache use.

▶ *Automatic inlining* (/optimize:4) or higher applies interprocedure analysis and inline expansion of small procedures, usually by using heuristics that limit extra code size.

▶ *Loop transformation and software pipelining* (/optimize:5), include a group of loop transformation optimizations and, on Alpha systems, also include the software pipelining optimization. The loop transformation optimizations apply to array references within loops and can apply to multiple nested loops. Loop transformation optimizations can improve the performance of the memory system.

On Alpha systems, software pipelining applies instruction scheduling to certain innermost loops, allowing instructions within a loop to "wrap around" and execute in a different iteration of the loop. This can reduce the impact of long-latency operations, resulting in faster loop execution. Software pipelining also enables the prefetching of data to reduce the impact of cache misses.

The following sections discuss I/O performance considerations in more detail:

▶ Section 6.7.1 Optimizations Performed at All Optimization Levels

▶ Section 6.7.2 Local (Minimal) Optimizations

▶ Section 6.7.3 Global Optimizations

▶ Section 6.7.4 Additional Global Optimizations

▶ Section 6.7.5 Automatic Inlining

▶ Section 6.7.6 Loop Transformation and Software Pipelining

6.7.1 Optimizations Performed at All Optimization Levels

The following optimizations occur at any optimization level (/optimize:0 through /optimize:5):

▶ Space optimizations

Space optimizations decrease the size of the object or executing program by eliminating unnecessary use of memory, thereby improving speed of execution and system throughput. Visual Fortran space optimizations are as follows:

• Constant Pooling

Only one copy of a given constant value is ever allocated memory space. If that constant value is used in several places in the program, all references point to that value.

• Dead Code Elimination

If operations will never execute or if data items will never be used, Visual Fortran eliminates them. Dead code includes unreachable code and code that becomes unused as a result of other optimizations, such as value propagation.

▶ Inlining arithmetic statement functions and intrinsic procedures

Regardless of the optimization level, Visual Fortran inserts arithmetic statement functions directly into a program instead of calling them as functions. This permits other optimizations of the inlined code and eliminates several operations, such as calls and returns or stores and fetches of the actual arguments. For example:

```
SUM(A,B) = A+B
  .
  .
  .
Y = 3.14
X = SUM(Y,3.0)     ! With value propagation, becomes: X = 6.14
```

Many intrinsic procedures are automatically inlined.

Inlining of other subprograms, such as contained subprograms, occurs at optimization level /optimize:4 or /optimize:5 (or when you specify appropriate /inline keywords at /optimize:1 or higher).

▶ Implied-**DO** loop collapsing

DO loop collapsing reduces a major overhead in I/O processing. Normally, each element in an I/O list generates a separate call to the Visual Fortran RTL. The processing overhead of these calls can be most significant in implied-**DO** loops.

If Visual Fortran can determine that the format will not change during program execution, it replaces the series of calls in up to seven nested implied-DO loops with a single call to an optimized RTL routine (see Section 6.5.5 Enable Implied-Do Loop Collapsing). The optimized RTL routine can transfer many elements in one operation.

Visual Fortran collapses implied-DO loops in formatted and unformatted I/O operations, but it is more important with unformatted I/O, where the cost of transmitting the elements is a higher fraction of the total cost.

▶ Array temporary elimination and **FORALL** statements

Certain array store operations are optimized. For example, to minimize the creation of array temporaries, Visual Fortran can detect when no overlap occurs between the two sides of an array assignment. This type of optimization occurs for some assignment statements in **FORALL** constructs.

Certain array operations are also candidates for loop unrolling optimizations (see Section 6.7.4.1 Loop Unrolling).

6.7.2   Local (Minimal) Optimizations

To enable local optimizations, use /optimize:1 or a higher optimization level /optimize:2, /optimize:3, /optimize:4, or /optimize:5.

To prevent local optimizations, specify the /optimize:0 option.

The following sections discuss the local optimizations:

▶ Section 6.7.2.1 Common Subexpression Elimination

▶ Section 6.7.2.2 Integer Multiplication and Division Expansion

▶ Section 6.7.2.3 Compile-Time Operations

▶ Section 6.7.2.4 Value Propagation

▶ Section 6.7.2.5 Dead Store Elimination

▶ Section 6.7.2.6 Register Usage

▶ Section 6.7.2.7 Mixed Real/Complex Operations

6.7.2.1   Common Subexpression Elimination

If the same subexpressions appear in more than one computation and the values do not change between computations, Visual Fortran computes the result once and replaces the subexpressions with the result itself:

```
DIMENSION A(25,25), B(25,25)
A(I,J) = B(I,J)
```

Without optimization, these statements can be coded as follows:

```
t1 = ((J-1)*25+(I-1))*4
t2 = ((J-1)*25+(I-1))*4
A(t1) = B(t2)
```

Variables t1 and t2 represent equivalent expressions. Visual Fortran eliminates this redundancy by producing the following:

```
t = ((J-1)*25+(I-1)*4
A(t) = B(t)
```

6.7.2.2   Integer Multiplication and Division Expansion

Expansion of multiplication and division refers to bit shifts that allow faster multiplication and division while producing the same result. For example, the integer expression (I*17) can be calculated as I with a 4-bit shift plus the original value of I. This can be expressed using the Digital Fortran **ISHFT** intrinsic function:

```
J1 = I*17
J2 = ISHFT(I,4) + I       ! equivalent expression for I*17
```

The optimizer uses machine code that, like the **ISHFT** intrinsic function, shifts bits to expand multiplication and division by literals.

6.7.2.3   *Compile-Time Operations*

Visual Fortran does as many operations as possible at compile time rather than having them done at run time.

Constant Operations

Visual Fortran can perform many operations on constants (including **PARAMETER** constants):

▶ Constants preceded by a unary minus sign are negated.

▶ Expressions involving +, -, *, or / operators are evaluated; for example:

```
PARAMETER (NN=27)
I = 2*NN+J                     ! Becomes: I = 54 + J
```

Evaluation of some constant functions and operators is performed at compile time. This includes certain functions of constants, concatenation of string constants, and logical and relational operations involving constants.

▶ Lower-ranked constants are converted to the data type of the higher-ranked operand:

```
REAL X, Y
X = 10 * Y                     ! Becomes: X = 10.0 * Y
```

▶ Array address calculations involving constant subscripts are simplified at compile time whenever possible:

```
INTEGER I(10,10)
I(1,2) = I(4,5)                ! Compiled as a direct load and store
```

Algebraic Reassociation Optimizations

Visual Fortran delays operations to see whether they have no effect or can be transformed to have no effect. If they have no effect, these operations are removed. A typical example involves unary minus and .NOT. operations:

```
X = -Y * -Z                    ! Becomes: Y * Z
```

6.7.2.4   *Value Propagation*

Visual Fortran tracks the values assigned to variables and constants, including those from **DATA** statements, and traces them to every place they are used. Visual Fortran uses the value itself when it is more efficient to do so.

When compiling subprograms, Visual Fortran analyzes the program to ensure that propagation is safe if the subroutine is called more than once.

Value propagation frequently leads to more value propagation. Visual Fortran can eliminate run-time operations, comparisons and branches, and whole statements.

In the following example, constants are propagated, eliminating multiple operations from run time:

```
Original Code              Optimized Code


 PI = 3.14                  .
 .                          .
 .                          .
 .                          PIOVER2 = 1.57
 PIOVER2 = PI/2             .
 .                          .
 .                          .
 .                          I = 100
 I = 100                    .
 .                          .
 .                          .
 .                          10 A(100) = 3.0*Q
 IF (I.GT.1) GOTO 10

10 A(I) = 3.0*Q
```

6.7.2.5 Dead Store Elimination

If a variable is assigned but never used, Visual Fortran eliminates the entire assignment statement:

```
X = Y*Z
   .
   .
   .         ! If X is not used in between, X=Y*Z is eliminated.
X = A(I,J)* PI
```

Some programs used for performance analysis often contain such unnecessary operations. When you try to measure the performance of such programs compiled with Visual Fortran, these programs may show unrealistically good performance results. Realistic results are possible only with program units using their results in output statements.

6.7.2.6 Register Usage

A large program usually has more data that would benefit from being held in registers than there are registers to hold the data. In such cases, Visual Fortran typically tries to use the registers according to the following descending priority list:

1. For temporary operation results, including array indexes

2. For variables

3. For addresses of arrays (base address)

4. All other usages

Visual Fortran uses heuristic algorithms and a modest amount of computation to attempt to determine an effective usage for the registers.

Holding Variables in Registers

Because operations using registers are much faster than using memory, Visual Fortran generates code that uses the integer and floating-point registers instead of memory locations. Knowing when Visual Fortran uses registers may be helpful when doing certain forms of debugging.

Visual Fortran uses registers to hold the values of variables whenever the Fortran language does not require them to be held in memory, such as holding the values of temporary results of subexpressions, even if /optimize:0 (no optimization) was specified.

Visual Fortran may hold the same variable in different registers at different points in the program:

```
V = 3.0*Q
     .
     .
     .
X = SIN(Y)*V
     .
     .
     .
V = PI*X
     .
     .
     .
Y = COS(Y)*V
```

Visual Fortran may choose one register to hold the first use of V and another register to hold the second. Both registers can be used for other purposes at points in between. There may be times when the value of the variable does not exist anywhere in the registers. If the value of V is never needed in memory, it might not ever be assigned.

Visual Fortran uses registers to hold the values of I, J, and K (so long as there are no other optimization effects, such as loops involving the variables):

```
A(I) = B(J) + C(K)
```

More typically, an expression uses the same index variable:

```
A(K) = B(K) + C(K)
```

In this case, K is loaded into only one register, which is used to index all three arrays at the same time.

6.7.2.7 *Mixed Real/Complex Operations*

In mixed **REAL** and **COMPLEX** operations, Visual Fortran avoids the conversion and performs a simplified operation on:

▶ Add (+), subtract (-), and multiply (*) operations if either operand is **REAL**

▶ Divide (/) operations if the divisor is **REAL**

For example, if variable R is **REAL** and A and B are **COMPLEX**, no conversion occurs with the following:

```
COMPLEX A, B
     .
     .
     .
B = A + R
```

6.7.3 Global Optimizations

To enable global optimizations, use /optimize:2 or a higher optimization level. Using /optimize:2 or higher also enables local optimizations (/optimize:1).

Global optimizations include:

▶ Data-flow analysis

▶ Split lifetime analysis

▶ Strength reduction (replaces a CPU-intensive calculation with one that uses fewer CPU cycles)

▶ Code motion (also called code hoisting)

▶ Instruction scheduling

Data-flow and split lifetime analysis (global data analysis) traces the values of variables and whole arrays as they are created and used in different parts of a program unit. During this analysis, Visual Fortran assumes that any pair of array references to a given array might access the same memory location, unless constant subscripts are used in both cases.

To eliminate unnecessary recomputations of invariant expressions in loops, Visual Fortran hoists them out of the loops so they execute only once.

Global data analysis includes which data items are selected for analysis. Some data items are analyzed as a group and some are analyzed individually. Visual Fortran limits or may disqualify data items that participate in the following constructs, generally because it cannot fully trace their values.

Data items in the following declarations can make global optimizations less effective:

▶ **VOLATILE** declarations

   VOLATILE declarations are needed to use certain run-time features of the operating system. Declare a variable as **VOLATILE** if the variable can be accessed using rules in addition to those provided by the Fortran 90/95 language. Examples include:

   • **COMMON** data items or entire common blocks that can change value by means other than direct assignment or during a routine call. For such applications, you must declare the variable or the **COM-MON** block to which it belongs as volatile.

   • An address not saved by the **%LOC** built-in function.

   • Variables read or written by a signal handler, including those in a common block or module.

   As requested by the **VOLATILE** statement, Visual Fortran disqualifies any volatile variables from global data analysis.

▶ Subroutine calls or external function references

   Visual Fortran cannot trace data flow in a called routine that is not part of the program unit being compiled, unless the same DF command compiled multiple program units (see Section 6.1.2 Compile with Appropriate Options and Multiple Source Files). Arguments passed to a called routine that are used again in a calling program are assumed to be modified, unless the proper **INTENT** is specified in an interface block (the compiler must assume they are referenced by the called routine).

▶ Common blocks

Visual Fortran limits optimizations on data items in common blocks. If common block data items are referenced inside called routines, their values might be altered. In the following example, variable I might be altered by FOO, so Visual Fortran cannot predict its value in subsequent references:

```
COMMON /X/ I


DO J=1,N
I = J
  CALL FOO
  A(I) = I
ENDDO
```

▶ Variables in Fortran 90 modules

Visual Fortran limits optimizations on variables in Fortran 90 modules. Like common blocks, if the variables in Fortran 90 modules are referenced inside called routines, their values might be altered.

▶ Variables referenced by a **%LOC** built-in function or variables with the **TARGET** attribute

Visual Fortran limits optimizations on variables indirectly referenced by a **%LOC** function or on variables with the **TARGET** attribute, because the called routine may dereference a pointer to such a variable.

▶ Equivalence groups

An *equivalence group* is formed explicitly with the **EQUIVALENCE** statement or implicitly by the **COMMON** statement. A program section is a particular common block or local data area for a particular routine. Visual Fortran combines equivalence groups within the same program section and in the same program unit.

The equivalence groups in separate program sections are analyzed separately, but the data items within each group are not, so some optimizations are limited to the data within each group.

6.7.4   **Additional Global Optimizations**

To enable additional global optimizations, use /optimize:3 or a higher optimization level. Using /optimize:3 or higher also enables local optimizations (/optimize:1) and global optimizations (/optimize:2).

Additional global optimizations improve speed at the cost of longer compile times and possibly extra code size. These optimizations include:

▶ Loop unrolling, including instruction scheduling (see Section 6.7.4.1 Loop Unrolling)

▶ Code replication to eliminate branches (see Section 6.7.4.2 Code Replication to Eliminate Branches)

▶ Padding the size of certain power-of-two arrays to allow more efficient cache use (see Section 6.4 Use Arrays Efficiently)

6.7.4.1 *Loop Unrolling*

At optimization level /optimize:3 or above, Visual Fortran attempts to unroll certain innermost loops, minimizing the number of branches and grouping more instructions together to allow efficient overlapped instruction execution (instruction pipelining). The best candidates for loop unrolling are innermost loops with limited control flow.

As more loops are unrolled, the average size of basic blocks increases. Loop unrolling generates multiple copies of the code for the loop body (loop code iterations) in a manner that allows efficient instruction pipelining.

The loop body is replicated some number of times, substituting index expressions. An initialization loop might be created to align the first reference with the main series of loops. A remainder loop might be created for leftover work.

The number of times a loop is unrolled can be determined either by the optimizer or by using the /unroll option, which can specify the limit for loop unrolling. Unless the user specifies a value, the optimizer unrolls a loop four times for most loops or two times for certain loops (large estimated code size or branches out of the loop).

Array operations are often represented as a nested series of loops when expanded into instructions. The innermost loop for the array operation is the best candidate for loop unrolling (like **DO** loops). For example, the following array operation (once optimized) is represented by nested loops, where the innermost loop is a candidate for loop unrolling:

```
A(1:100,2:30) = B(1:100,1:29) * 2.0
```

6.7.4.2 *Code Replication to Eliminate Branches*

In addition to loop unrolling and other optimizations, the number of branches are reduced by replicating code that will eliminate branches. Code replication decreases the number of basic blocks (a stream of instructions entered only at the beginning and exited only at the end) and increases instruction-scheduling opportunities.

Code replication normally occurs when a branch is at the end of a flow of control, such as a routine with multiple, short exit sequences. The code at the exit sequence gets replicated at the various places where a branch to it might occur.

For example, consider the following unoptimized routine and its optimized equivalent that uses code replication, where R0 (EAX on *x*86 systems) is register 0:

```
Unoptimized Instructions  Optimized (Replicated) Instructions
        .                           .
        .                           .
        .                           .
        branch to exit1             move 1 into R0
        .                           return
        .                           .
        .                           .
        branch to exit1             .
        .                           move 1 into R0
        .                           return
        .                           .
exit1:  move 1 into R0              .
        return                      .
                                    move 1 into R0
                                    return
```

Similarly, code replication can also occur within a loop that contains a small amount of shared code at the bottom of a loop and a case-type dispatch within the loop. The loop-end test-and-branch code might be replicated at the end of each case to create efficient instruction pipelining within the code for each case.

6.7.5 Automatic Inlining

To enable optimizations that perform automatic inlining, use /optimize:4 (or /optimize:5). Using /optimize:4 also enables local optimizations (/optimize:1), global optimizations (/optimize:2), and additional global optimizations (/optimize:3).

To request inlining at lower optimization levels (/optimize:1, /optimize:2, or /optimize:3), use the /inline option.

The default is /optimize:4 (unless /debug is specified).

This section also discusses the following topics:

▶ 6.7.5.1 Interprocedure Analysis

▶ 6.7.5.2 Inlining Procedures

6.7.5.1 *Interprocedure Analysis*

Compiling multiple source files at optimization level /optimize:4 or higher lets the compiler examine more code for possible optimizations, including multiple program units. This results in:

▶ Inlining more procedures

▶ More complete global data analysis

▶ Reducing the number of external references to be resolved during linking

As more procedures are inlined, the size of the executable program and compile times may increase, but execution time should decrease.

6.7.5.2 *Inlining Procedures*

Inlining refers to replacing a subprogram reference (such as a **CALL** statement or function invocation) with the replicated code of the subprogram. As more procedures are inlined, global optimizations often become more effective.

The optimizer inlines small procedures, limiting inlining candidates based on such criteria as:

▶ Estimated size of code

▶ Number of call sites

▶ Use of constant arguments

You can specify:

▶ One of the /optimize options to control the optimization level. For example, specifying /optimize:4 or /optimize:5 enables interprocedure optimizations.

   Different /optimize options set different /inline:*keyword* options. For example, /optimize:4 sets /inline:speed.

▶ One of the /inline options to directly control the inlining of procedures (see Section 6.8.3 Controlling the Inlining of Procedures). For example, /inline:speed inlines more procedures than /inline:size. Certain /inline keywords require /optimize:1 or higher.

6.7.6 Loop Transformation and Software Pipelining

A group of optimizations known as loop transformation optimizations and software pipelining with its associated additional software dependence analysis are enabled by using the /optimize:5 option. In certain cases, this improves run-time performance.

The loop transformation optimizations apply to array references within loops and can apply to multiple nested loops. These optimizations can improve the performance of the memory system.

On Alpha systems, software pipelining applies instruction scheduling to certain innermost loops, allowing instructions within a loop to "wrap around" and execute in a different iteration of the loop. This can reduce the impact of long-latency operations, resulting in faster loop execution.

Software pipelining also enables the prefetching of data to reduce the impact of cache misses.

This section also discusses the following topics:

▶ 6.7.6.1 Loop Transformations

▶ 6.7.6.2 Software Pipelining (Alpha Only)

6.7.6.1   *Loop Transformations*

The loop transformation optimizations are enabled by using the /transform_ loops option or the /optimize:5 option. Loop transformation attempts to improve performance by rewriting loops to make better use of the memory system. By rewriting loops, the loop transformation optimizations can increase the number of instructions executed, which can degrade the run-time performance of some programs.

To request loop transformation optimizations without software pipelining, do one of the following:

▶ Specify /optimize:5 with /nopipeline (preferred method)

▶ Specify /transform_loops with /optimize:4, /optimize:3, or /opti-mize:2. This optimization is not performed at optimization levels below /optimize:2.

The loop transformation optimizations apply to array references within loops. These optimizations can improve the performance of the memory system and usually apply to multiple nested loops. The loops chosen for loop transformation optimizations are always *counted loops*. Counted loops are those loops that use a variable to count iterations in a manner that the number of iterations can be determined before entering the loop. For example, most DO loops are counted loops.

Conditions that typically prevent the loop transformation optimizations from occurring include subprogram references that are not inlined (such as an external function call), complicated exit conditions, and uncounted loops.

The types of optimizations associated with /transform_loops include the following:

▶ Loop blocking

Can minimize memory system use with multidimensional array elements by completing as many operations as possible on array elements currently in the cache. Also known as loop tiling.

▶ Loop distribution

Moves instructions from one loop into separate, new loops. This can reduce the amount of memory used during one loop so that the remaining memory may fit in the cache. It can also create improved opportunities for loop blocking.

▶ Loop fusion

Combines instructions from two or more adjacent loops that use some of the same memory locations into a single loop. This can avoid the need to load those memory locations into the cache multiple times and improves opportunities for instruction scheduling.

▶ Loop interchange

Changes the nesting order of some or all loops. This can minimize the stride of array element access during loop execution and reduce the number of memory accesses needed. Also known as loop permutation.

▶ Scalar replacement

Replaces the use of an array element with a scalar variable under certain conditions.

▶ Outer loop unrolling

Unrolls the outer loop inside the inner loop under certain conditions to minimize the number of instructions and memory accesses needed. This also improves opportunities for instruction scheduling and scalar replacement.

For more information on the interaction of compiler options and timing programs compiled with the loop transformation optimizations, see Section 4.1.73 /[no]transform_loops.

6.7.6.2 *Software Pipelining (Alpha Only)*

Software pipelining and additional software dependence analysis are enabled by using the /pipeline option or by the /optimize:5 option. Software pipelining in certain cases improves run-time performance.

The software pipelining optimization applies instruction scheduling to certain innermost loops, allowing instructions within a loop to "wrap around" and execute in a different iteration of the loop. This can reduce the impact of long-latency operations, resulting in faster loop execution.

Loop unrolling (enabled at /optimize:3 or above) *cannot* schedule across iterations of a loop. Because software pipelining *can* schedule across loop iterations, it can perform more efficient scheduling to eliminate instruction stalls within loops.

For instance, if software dependence analysis of data flow reveals that certain calculations can be done before or after that iteration of the loop, software pipelining reschedules those instructions ahead of or behind that loop iteration, at places where their execution can prevent instruction stalls or otherwise improve performance.

Software pipelining also enables the prefetching of data to reduce the impact of cache misses.

Software pipelining can be more effective when you combine /pipeline (or /optimize:5) with the appropriate /tune *keyword* for the target Alpha processor generation (see Section 6.8.6 Requesting Optimized Code for a Specific Processor Generation).

To specify software pipelining without loop transformation optimizations, do one of the following:

▶ Specify /optimize:5 with /notransform_loops (preferred method).

▶ Specify /pipeline with /optimize:4, /optimize:3, or /optimize:2. This optimization is not performed at optimization levels below /optimize:2.

For this version of Visual Fortran, loops chosen for software pipelining:

▶ Are always innermost loops (those executed the most).

▶ Do not contain branches or procedure calls.

▶ Do not use **COMPLEX** floating-point data.

By modifying the unrolled loop and inserting instructions as needed before and/or after the unrolled loop, software pipelining generally improves run-time performance, except where the loops contain a large number of instructions with many existing overlapped operations. In this case, software pipelining may not have enough registers available to effectively improve execution performance. Run-time performance using /optimize:5 (or /pipeline) may not improve performance, as compared to using /optimize:4.

For programs that contain loops that exhaust available registers, longer execution times may result with /optimize:5 or /pipeline. In cases where performance does not improve, consider compiling with the /unroll 1 option along with /optimize:5 or /pipeline, to possibly improve the effects of software pipelining.

For more information on the interaction of command-line options and timing programs compiled with software pipelining, see Section 4.1.59 /[no] pipeline (Alpha Only).

6.8   Other Options Related to Optimization

In addition to the /optimize options (discussed in Section 6.7 Optimization Levels: the /optimize Option), several other compiler options can prevent or facilitate improved optimizations, as discussed in the following sections:

▶ Section 6.8.1 Options Set by the /fast Option

▶ Section 6.8.2 Controlling Loop Unrolling

▶ Section 6.8.3 Controlling the Inlining of Procedures

▶ Section 6.8.4 Arithmetic Reordering Optimizations

▶ Section 6.8.5 Dummy Aliasing Assumption

▶ Section 6.8.6 Requesting Optimized Code for a Specific Processor Generation

▶ Section 6.8.7 Requesting Code Generation for a Specific Processor Generation

▶ Section 6.7.6.1 Loop Transformation

▶ Section 6.7.6.2 Software Pipelining (Alpha Only)

6.8.1   Options Set by the /fast Option

Specifying the /fast option sets the following options:

▶ /align:(dcommons,records) (see Section 6.3 Data Alignment Considerations)

▶ /assume:noaccuracy_sensitive (see Section 6.8.4 Arithmetic Reordering Optimizations)

▶ /math_library: fast (see Section 4.1.51 /math_library)

6.8.2 Controlling Loop Unrolling

You can specify the number of times a loop is unrolled by using the /unroll option.

Although unrolling loops usually improves run-time performance, the size of the executable program may increase.

On Alpha systems, the /unroll: *num* option can also influence the run-time results of software pipelining optimizations performed when you specify /optimize:5 or /pipeline.

For more information on loop unrolling, see Section 6.7.4.1 Loop Unrolling.

6.8.3 Controlling the Inlining of Procedures

To specify the types of procedures to be inlined, use the /inline options. Also, compile multiple source files together and specify an adequate optimization level, such as /optimize:4.

If you omit /noinline and the /inline options, the optimization level /optimize option used determines the types of procedures that are inlined.

The /inline options are as follows:

▶ /inline:none (same as /noinline)

Inlines statement functions but not other procedures. This type of inlining occurs if you specify /optimize:0 or /optimize:1 and omit /inline options.

▶ /inline:manual

Inlines statement functions but not other procedures. This type of inlining occurs if you omit /inline options.

▶ /inline:size

In addition to inlining statement functions, inlines any procedures that the Digital Fortran optimizer expects will improve run-time performance with no likely significant increase in program size.

▶ /inline:speed

In addition to inlining statement functions, inlines any procedures that the Digital Fortran optimizer expects will improve run-time performance with a likely significant increase in program size. This type of inlining occurs if you specify /optimize:4 (or /optimize:5) and omit /inline options.

▶ /inline:all

Inlines every call that can possibly be inlined while generating correct code, including the following:

- Statement functions (always inlined)

- Any procedures that Digital Fortran expects will improve run-time performance with a likely significant increase in program size.

- Any other procedures that can possibly be inlined and generate correct code. Certain recursive routines are not inlined to prevent infinite expansion.

For information on the inlining of other procedures (inlined at optimization level /optimize:4 or higher), see Section 6.7.5.2 Inlining Procedures.

Maximizing the types of procedures that are inlined usually improves run-time performance, but compile-time memory usage and the size of the executable program may increase.

To determine whether using /inline all benefits your particular program, time program execution for the same program compiled with and without /inline:all.

6.8.4   Arithmetic Reordering Optimizations

If you use the /assume:noaccuracy_sensitive option, Digital Fortran may reorder code (based on algebraic identities) to improve performance. For example, the following expressions are mathematically equivalent but may not compute the same value using finite precision arithmetic:

```
X = (A + B) + C

X = A + (B + C)
```

The results can be slightly different from the default /assume: accuracy_sensitive because of the way intermediate results are rounded. However, the /assume:noaccuracy_sensitive results are not categorically less accurate than those gained by the default. In fact, dot product summations using /assume:noaccuracy_sensitive can produce more accurate results than those using /assume:accuracy_sensitive.

The effect of /assume:noaccuracy_sensitive is important when Digital Fortran hoists divide operations out of a loop. If /assume:noaccuracy_sensitive is in effect, the unoptimized loop becomes the optimized loop:

```
Unoptimized Code      Optimized Code
DO I=1,N              T= 1/V
```

```
    .                         DO I=1,N
    .                           .
    .                           .
                                .
B(I)= A(I)/V                    .
END DO                        B(I)= A(I)*T
                              END DO
```

The transformation in the optimized loop increases performance significantly, and loses little or no accuracy. However, it does have the potential for raising overflow or underflow arithmetic exceptions.

6.8.5 Dummy Aliasing Assumption

Some programs compiled with Visual Fortran (or Digital FORTRAN 77) may have results that differ from the results of other Fortran compilers. Such programs may be aliasing dummy arguments to each other or to a variable in a common block or shared through use association, and at least one variable access is a store.

This program behavior is prohibited in programs conforming to the Fortran 90 standard, but not by Visual Fortran. Other versions of Fortran allow dummy aliases and check for them to ensure correct results. However, Visual Fortran assumes that no dummy aliasing will occur, and it can ignore potential data dependencies from this source in favor of faster execution.

The Visual Fortran default is safe for programs conforming to the Fortran 90 standard. It will improve performance of these programs because the standard prohibits such programs from passing overlapped variables or arrays as actual arguments if either is assigned in the execution of the program unit.

The /assume:dummy_aliases option allows dummy aliasing. It ensures correct results by assuming the exact order of the references to dummy and common variables is required. Program units taking advantage of this behavior can produce inaccurate results if compiled with /assume:nodummy_aliases.

The following example is taken from the DAXPY routine in the FORTRAN 77 version of the Basic Linear Algebra Subroutines (BLAS). It demonstrates how to use the /assume:dummy_aliases option:

```
    SUBROUTINE DAXPY(N,DA,DX,INCX,DY,INCY)
C Constant times a vector plus a vector.
C uses unrolled loops for increments equal to 1.

    DOUBLE PRECISION DX(1), DY(1), DA
    INTEGER I,INCX,INCY,IX,IY,M,MP1,N
C
```

```
      IF (N.LE.0) RETURN
      IF (DA.EQ.0.0) RETURN
      IF (INCX.EQ.1.AND.INCY.EQ.1) GOTO 20

C  Code for unequal increments or equal increments
C  not equal to 1.
      .
      .
      .
      RETURN
C  Code for both increments equal to 1.
C  Clean-up loop

20 M = MOD(N,4)
      IF (M.EQ.0) GOTO 40
      DO I=1,M
          DY(I) = DY(I) + DA*DX(I)
      END DO

      IF (N.LT.4) RETURN
40 MP1 = M + 1
      DO I = MP1, N, 4
          DY(I) = DY(I) + DA*DX(I)
          DY(I + 1) = DY(I + 1) + DA*DX(I + 1)
          DY(I + 2) = DY(I + 2) + DA*DX(I + 2)
          DY(I + 3) = DY(I + 3) + DA*DX(I + 3)
      END DO

      RETURN
      END SUBROUTINE
```

The second **DO** loop contains assignments to DY. If DY is overlapped with DA, any of the assignments to DY might give DA a new value, and this overlap would affect the results. If this overlap is desired, then DA must be fetched from memory each time it is referenced. The repetitious fetching of DA degrades performance.

Linking Routines with Opposite Settings

You can link routines compiled with the /assume:dummy_aliases option to routines compiled with /assume:nodummy_aliases. For example, if only one routine is called with dummy aliases, you can use /assume:dummy_aliases when compiling that routine, and compile all the other routines with /assume: nodummy_aliases to gain the performance value of that option.

Programs calling DAXPY with DA overlapping DY do not conform to the FORTRAN 77 and Fortran 90 standards. However, they are accommodated if /assume:dummy_aliases was used to compile the DAXPY routine.

6.8.6 Requesting Optimized Code for a Specific Processor Generation

You can specify the types of optimized code to be generated by using the /tune option. Tuning for a specific implementation can improve run-time performance; it is also possible that code tuned for a specific target may run slower on another target.

On *x*86 systems, regardless of the specified *keyword* for /tune, the generated code will run correctly on all implementations of the *x*86 architecture. Specifying the correct keyword for /tune for the target *x*86 processor generation type usually slightly improves run-time performance.

On Alpha systems, regardless of the specified *keyword*, the generated code will run correctly on all implementations of the Alpha architecture. Specifying the correct keyword for /tune for the target Alpha processor generation type usually slightly improves run-time performance.

On Alpha systems, unless you request software pipelining, the run-time performance difference for using the wrong keyword for /tune (such as using /tune ev4 for an ev5 processor) is usually less than 5%. When using software pipelining (such as using /optimize:5) with /tune, the difference can be more than 5%.

The /tune keywords are described in Section 4.1.74 /tune.

The combination of the specified keyword for /tune and the type of processor generation used has no effect on producing the expected correct program results. To request a specific set of instructions for an *x*86 or Alpha architecture generation, see Section 4.1.4 /architecture.

6.8.7 Requesting Code Generation for a Specific Processor Generation

The /architecture (/arch) option determines the type of code that will be generated for this program.

On an *x*86 system, you can specify whether the code to be generated can be run:

▶ On Pentium Pro and Pentium II (686) processor systems only, using the 686 set of instructions.

▶ On Pentium (586) and 686 systems only, using the 586 set of instructions.

▶ On all *x*86 (486, 586, and 686) systems, using the 486 set of instructions only.

▶ On all *x*86 systems, using a generic blend of instructions that runs with moderate efficiency on all *x*86 systems.

On an Alpha system, you can specify whether the code to be generated can be run:

▶ On 21264 chip processor systems only, using the following instruction extensions of the Alpha architecture: byte and word manipulation, multimedia, square root and floating-point convert, and count extension.

▶ On 21164PC chip processor systems only, using byte and word manipulation instruction extensions and multimedia instruction extensions of the Alpha architecture.

▶ On some 21164 and 21164PC chip processor systems only, using the byte and word manipulation instruction extensions of the Alpha architecture.

▶ On all Alpha chip processor systems, using the base set of Alpha instructions (no extensions).

▶ On all Alpha processor systems only, using a generic blend of instructions that runs with moderate efficiency on all Alpha systems.

The /arch:*keyword* option uses the same keywords as the /tune:*keyword* option.

For more information, see Section 4.1.4 /architecture.

7

Using QuickWin

This chapter introduces the major categories of QuickWin library routines. It gives an overview of QuickWin features and their use in creating and displaying graphics, and customizing your QuickWin applications with custom menus and mouse routines. Chapter 12 Drawing Graphics Elements, and Chapter 13 Using Fonts from the Graphics Library cover graphics and fonts in more detail.

The Visual Fortran QuickWin run-time library helps you turn graphics programs into simple Windows applications. Though the full capability of Windows is not available through QuickWin, QuickWin is simpler to learn and to use. QuickWin applications do support pixel-based graphics, real-coordinate graphics, text windows, character foi   user-defined menus, mouse events, and editing (select/copy/paste) of text   iphics, or both.

In Visual Fortran, graphics programs must be either Fortran QuickWin, Fortran Standard Graphics, Fortran Windows, or use OpenGL routines. Fortran Standard Graphics Applications are a subset of QuickWin that support only one window.

You can choose the Fortran QuickWin or Standard Graphics application type from the drop-down list of available project types when you create a new project in the visual development environment. Or you can use the /libs:qwin compiler option for Fortran QuickWin or the /libs:qwins compiler option for Fortran Standard Graphics.

Note that Fortran QuickWin and Standard Graphics applications cannot be DLLs, and QuickWin and Standard Graphics cannot be linked with run-time routines that are in DLLs. This means that the /libs=qwin option and the /libs=dll with /threads options cannot be used together.

You can access the QuickWin routines library from Visual Fortran as well as other languages that support the Fortran calling conventions. The graphics package supports all video modes supported by Windows NT, Windows 98, and Windows 95.

A program using the QuickWin routines must explicitly access the Quick-Win graphics library routines with the statement **USE DFLIB** (see Section 7.6 USE Statement Needed for QuickWin Applications).

This section includes the following topics:

▶ Section 7.1 Capabilities of QuickWin

▶ Section 7.2 Comparing QuickWin with Windows-Based Applications

▶ Section 7.3 Using Win32 with QuickWin

▶ Section 7.4 Types of QuickWin Programs

▶ Section 7.5 The QuickWin User Interface

▶ Section 7.6 USE Statement Needed for QuickWin Applications

▶ Section 7.7 Creating QuickWin Windows

▶ Section 7.8 Using Graphics and Character-Font Routines

▶ Section 7.9 Defining Graphics Characteristics

▶ Section 7.10 Displaying Graphics Output

▶ Section 7.11 Working with Screen Images

▶ Section 7.12 Enhancing QuickWin Applications

▶ Section 7.13 Customizing QuickWin Applications

▶ Section 7.14 QuickWin Programming Precautions

▶ Section 7.15 Simulating Nonblocking I/O

7.1   Capabilities of QuickWin

You can use the QuickWin library to do the following:

▶ Compile console programs into simple applications for Windows.

▶ Minimize and maximize QuickWin applications like any Windows-based application.

▶ Call graphics routines.

▶ Load and save bitmaps.

▶ Select, copy, and paste text, graphics, or a mix of both.

▶ Detect and respond to mouse clicks.

▶ Display graphics output.

▶ Alter the default application menus or add programmable menus.

▶ Create custom icons.

▶ Open multiple child windows.

7.2 Comparing QuickWin with Windows-Based Applications

QuickWin does not provide the total capability of Windows. Although you can call many Win32 APIs (Application Programming Interface) from QuickWin and console programs, many other Win32 APIs (such as GDI functions) should be called only from a full Windows application. You need to use Windows-based applications, not QuickWin, if any of the following applies:

▶ Your application has an OLE (Object Linking and Embedding) container.

▶ You want direct access to GDI (Graphical Data Interface) functions.

▶ You want to add your own customized Help information to QuickWin Help.

▶ You want to create something other than a standard SDI (Single Document Interface) or MDI (Multiple Document Interface) application. (For example, if you want your application to have a dialog such as Windows' Calculator in the client area.)

7.3 Using Win32 with QuickWin

You can convert the unit numbers of QuickWin windows to Win32 handles with the **GETHWNDQQ** QuickWin function. You should not use Windows GDI to draw on QuickWin windows because QuickWin keeps a window buffer and the altered window would be destroyed on redraw. You can use Windows subclassing to intercept graphics messages bound for QuickWin before QuickWin receives them.

See the sample program POKER in the Visual Fortran Samples . . . `DF98\SAMPLES\QUICKWIN\POKER` folder for a demonstration of this technique.

7.4   Types of QuickWin Programs

You can create a Fortran Standard Graphics application or a Fortran Quick-Win application, depending on the project type you choose. Fortran Standard Graphics (QuickWin single document) applications support only one window and do not support programmable menus. Fortran QuickWin applications support multiple windows and user-defined menus. Any Fortran program, whether it contains graphics or not, can be compiled as a Quick-Win application. You can use the Microsoft visual development environment to create, debug, and execute Fortran Standard Graphics programs and Fortran QuickWin programs.

To build a Fortran QuickWin application in the visual development environment, select Fortran Standard Graphics or QuickWin Application from the list of available project types you see when you create a new project. In the dialog box, specify a Fortran QuickWin multiple-window project.

To build a Fortran Standard Graphics application in the visual development environment, select Fortran Standard Graphics or QuickWin Application from the list of available project types. In the dialog box, specify a Fortran Standard Graphics single-window project.

To build a Fortran QuickWin application from the command line, use the /libs:qwin option. For example:

```
DF /libs=qwin qw_app.f90
```

To build a Fortran Standard Graphics application from the command line, use the /libs:qwins option. For example:

```
DF /libs=qwins stdg_app.f90
```

For information about building projects in the visual development environment, see Chapter 2 Building Programs and Libraries.

Some of the QuickWin project Visual Fortran Samples are in folders in `. . . DF98\SAMPLES\QUICKWIN`.

The following sections discuss the two types of QuickWin applications:

▶ Section 7.4.1 Fortran Standard Graphics Applications

▶ Section 7.4.2 Fortran QuickWin Graphic Applications

7.4.1   Fortran Standard Graphics Applications

A Fortran standard graphics application has a single maximized application window covering the entire screen area, whose appearance resembles a MS-

DOS screen without scrolls bars or menus. The Esc key can be used to exit a program that does otherwise terminate. When the Esc key is pressed, the frame window appears with a border, title bar, scroll bars, and a menu item in the upper-left corner that allows you to close the application.

Programmable menus and multiple child windows cannot be created in this mode.

Figure 7-1 shows a typical Fortran Standard Graphics application, which resembles an MS-DOS application running in a window.

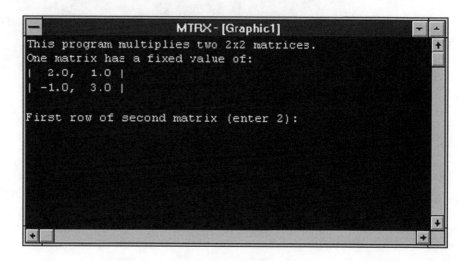

Figure 7–1   *MTRX.F90 Compiled as a Fortran Standard Graphics Application*

7.4.2   Fortran QuickWin Graphics Applications

Figure 7-2 shows a typical Fortran QuickWin application. The frame window has a border, title bar, scroll bars, and default menu bar. You can modify, add, or delete the default menu items, respond to mouse events, and create multiple child windows within the frame window using QuickWin enhanced features. Routines to create enhanced features are listed in Section 7.12 Enhancing QuickWin Applications. Using these routines to customize your QuickWin application is described in Section 7.13 Customizing QuickWin Applications.

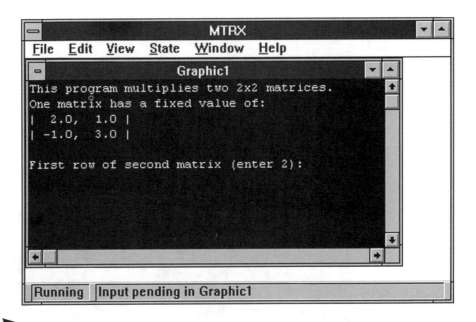

Figure 7–2 *MTRX.FOR Compiled as a QuickWin Application*

Some of the Fortran QuickWin applications provided as Samples include PLATFORM and POLYDRAW (see the respective folders in . . . `DF98\SAMPLES\ADVANCED\WIN32`).

7.5   The QuickWin User Interface

All QuickWin applications create an application or frame window; child windows are optional. Fortran Standard Graphics applications and Fortran QuickWin applications have these general characteristics:

▶ Window contents can be copied as bitmaps or text to the Clipboard for printing or pasting to other applications. In Fortran QuickWin applications, any portion of the window can be selected and copied.

▶ Vertical and horizontal scroll bars appear automatically, if needed.

▶ The base name of the application's .EXE file appears in the window's title bar.

▶ Closing the application window terminates the program.

In addition, the Fortran QuickWin application has a status bar and menu bar. The status bar at the bottom of the window reports the current status of the window program (for example, running or input pending).

See also Section 7.5.1 Default QuickWin Menus.

7.5.1   Default QuickWin Menus

The default MDI (Multiple Document Interface) menu bar has six menus: File, Edit, View, State, Window, and Help.

Figure 7–3   *File Menu*

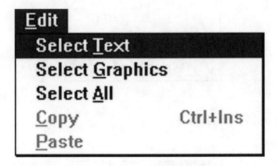

Figure 7–4   *Edit Menu*

For instructions on using the Edit options within QuickWin see Section 7.11.3 Editing Text and Graphics from the QuickWin Edit Menu.

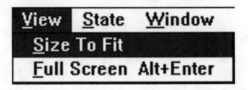

Figure 7–5   *View Menu*

The resulting graphics might appear somewhat distorted whenever the logical graphics screen is enlarged or reduced with the Size to Fit and Full Screen commands. While in Full Screen or Size To Fit mode, cursors are not scaled.

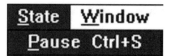

Figure 7–6   *State Menu*

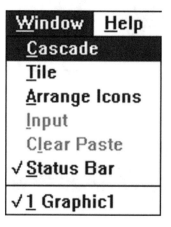

Figure 7–7   *Window Menu*

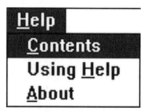

Figure 7–8   *Help Menu*

For instructions on replacing the About default information within the Help menu with your own text message, see Section 7.13.4 Defining an About Box.

For instructions on how to create custom QuickWin menus, see Section 7.13 Customizing QuickWin Applications.

7.6   USE Statement Needed for QuickWin Applications

A program using the Fortran QuickWin or Standard Graphics features must explicitly access the QuickWin graphics library routines with the statement **USE DFLIB**.

Any program using the QuickWin features must include the statement **USE DFLIB** to access the QuickWin graphics library. The DFLIB.MOD module file contains subroutine and function declarations in **INTERFACE** statements, derived-type declarations, and symbolic constant declarations for each QuickWin routine.

Because **INTERFACE** statements must appear before the body of a program, the **USE DFLIB** statement must appear before the body of a program unit. This usually means putting **USE DFLIB** before any other statement (such as **IMPLICIT NONE** or **INTEGER**).

Depending on the type of routines used by your application, other **USE** statements that include other Visual Fortran modules may be needed in addition to **USE DFLIB**. The description of each Visual Fortran routine in the "A-Z Summary" in the *Language Reference* in Visual Fortran online Help indicates the module that needs to be included for external routines (such as **USE DFLIB** or **USE DFPORT**).

7.7   Creating QuickWin Windows

The QuickWin library contains many routines to create and control your QuickWin windows. These routines are discussed in the following topics:

▶ Section 7.7.1 Accessing Window Properties

▶ Section 7.7.2 Creating Child Windows

▶ Section 7.7.3 Giving a Window Focus and Setting the Active Window

▶ Section 7.7.4 Keeping Child Windows Open

▶ Section 7.7.5 Controlling Size and Position of Windows

7.7.1   Accessing Window Properties

SETWINDOWCONFIG and **GETWINDOWCONFIG** set and get the current *virtual window* properties. Virtual window properties set by **SETWINDOWCONFIG** contain the maximum amount of text and graphics for that unit. The **SETWSIZEQQ** routine sets the properties of the *visible window*, which is generally smaller than a virtual window. All the text and graphics in a virtual window can be displayed by using scroll bars.

These virtual window properties are stored in the windowconfig derived type defined in DFLIB.MOD, which contains the following parameters:

```
TYPE windowconfig
  INTEGER(2) numxpixels          ! Number of pixels on x-axis.
  INTEGER(2) numypixels          ! Number of pixels on y-axis.
  INTEGER(2) numtextcols         ! Number of text columns available.
  INTEGER(2) numtextrows         ! Number of scrollable text lines available.
  INTEGER(2) numcolors           ! Number of color indexes.
  INTEGER(4) fontsize            ! Size of default font. Set to
                                 ! QWIN$EXTENDFONT when using multibyte
                                 ! characters, in which case
                                 ! extendfontsize sets the font size.
  CHARACTER(80) title            ! Window title, where title is a C string.
  INTEGER(2) bitsperpixel        ! Number of bits per pixel. This value
                                 ! is calculated by the system and is an
                                 ! output-only parameter.
                                 ! The next three parameters support multibyte
                                 ! character sets (such as Japanese)
  CHARACTER(32) extendfontname   ! Any non-proportionally spaced font
                                 ! available on the system.
  INTEGER(4) extendfontsize      ! Takes same values as fontsize, but
                                 ! used for multiple-byte character sets
                                 ! when fontsize set to QWIN$EXTENDFONT.
  INTEGER(4) extendfontattributes ! Font attributes such as bold and
                                 ! italic for multibyte character sets.
END TYPE windowconfig
```

If you use **SETWINDOWCONFIG** to set the variables in windowconfig to -1, the highest resolution will be set for your system, given the other fields you specify, if any. You can set the actual size of the window by specifying parameters that influence the window size—the number of x and y pixels, the number of rows and columns, and the font size. If you do not call **SETWIN-DOWCONFIG**, the window defaults to the best possible resolution and a font size of 8 by 16. The number of colors depends on the video driver used. In the following example, the number of *x* and *y* pixels is specified and the system calculates the number of rows and columns for the window:

```
      USE DFLIB
      TYPE (windowconfig) wc
      LOGICAL status
!Set the x & y pixels to 800X600 and font size to 8x12.
      wc.numxpixels    = 800
      wc.numypixels    = 600
      wc.numtextcols   = -1
      wc.numtextrows   = 302
      wc.numcolors     = -1
      wc.title         = " "C
      wc.fontsize      = #0008000C
      status           = SETWINDOWCONFIG(wc)
```

In this example, the variable wc.numtextrows is set to 302 to allow 300 lines of scollable text (n-2 is used).

If the requested configuration cannot be set, **SETWINDOWCONFIG** returns .FALSE. and calculates parameter values that will work and best fit the requested configuration. Another call to **SETWINDOWCONFIG** establishes these values:

```
IF(.NOT.status) status = SETWINDOWCONFIG(wc)
```

7.7.2   Creating Child Windows

The FILE='USER' option in the **OPEN** statement opens a unit that Visual Fortran treats like any other unit. However, Windows NT, Windows 98, and Windows 95 treat the unit as a child window. The child window defaults to a scrollable text window, 30 rows by 80 columns. You can open up to 40 child windows.

Running a QuickWin application displays the frame window, but not the child window. You must call **SETWINDOWCONFIG** or execute an I/O statement or a graphics statement to display the child window. The window receives output by its unit number, as in:

```
OPEN (UNIT= 12, FILE= 'USER', TITLE= 'Product Matrix')
WRITE (12, *) 'Enter matrix type: '
```

Child windows opened with FILE='USER' must be opened as sequential-access formatted files (the default). Other file specifications (direct-access, binary, or unformatted) result in run-time errors.

7.7.3   Giving a Window Focus and Setting the Active Window

When a window is made *active*, it receives graphics output (from **ARC**, **LINETO**, and **OUTGTEXT**, for example) but is not brought to the foreground, so it does not have the *focus*. When a window acquires focus, either by a mouse click, I/O to it, or by a **FOCUSQQ** call, it also becomes the *active* window. When a window gains focus, the window that previously had focus will lose focus.

If a window needs to be brought to the foreground, it must be given *focus*. The window that has the focus is always on top, and all other windows have their title bars grayed out. A window can have the focus and yet not be active and not have graphics output directed to it. Graphical output is independent of focus.

Under most circumstances, *focus* and *active* should apply to the same window. This is the default behavior of QuickWin and a programmer must consciously override this default.

Certain QuickWin routines (such as **GETCHARQQ**, **PASSDIRKEY-SQQ**, and **SETWINDOWCONFIG**) that do not take a unit number as an input argument usually effect the *active* window whether or not it is in *focus*.

If another window is made *active* but is not in *focus*, these routines effect the window *active* at the time of the routine call. This may appear unusual to the user since a **GETCHARQQ** under these circumstances will expect input from a grayed, background window. The user would then have to click on that window before input could be typed to it.

To use these routines (that effect the *active* window), either do I/O to the unit number of the window you wish to put in *focus* (and also make *active*), or call **FOCUSQQ** (with a unit number specified). If only one window is open then that window is the one effected. If several windows are opened, then the last one opened is the one effected since that window will get *focus* and *active* as a side effect of being opened.

The **OPEN** (IOFOCUS) parameter also can determine whether a window receives the focus when a I/O statement is executed on that unit. For example:

```
OPEN (UNIT = 10, FILE = 'USER', IOFOCUS = .TRUE.)
```

With an explicit **OPEN** with the FILE='USER', IOFOCUS defaults to .TRUE. For child windows opened implicitly (no **OPEN** statement before the **READ**, **WRITE**, or **PRINT**) as unit 0, 5, or 6, IOFOCUS defaults to .FALSE. If IOFOCUS=.TRUE., the child window receives focus prior to each **READ**, **WRITE**, or **PRINT**. Calls to **OUTTEXT** or graphics functions (for example, **OUTGTEXT**, **LINETO**, and **ELLIPSE**) do not cause the focus to shift. If you use IOFOCUS with any unit other than a QuickWin child window, a run-time error occurs.

The focus shifts to a window when it is given the focus with **FOCUSQQ**, when it is selected by a mouse click, or when an I/O operation other than a graphics operation is performed on it, unless the window was opened with IOFOCUS=.FALSE.. **INQFOCUSQQ** determines which unit has the focus. For example:

```
    USE DFLIB
    INTEGER(4) status, focusunit
    OPEN(UNIT = 10, FILE = 'USER', TITLE = 'Child Window 1')
    OPEN(UNIT = 11, FILE = 'USER', TITLE = 'Child Window 2')
! Give focus to Child Window 2 by writing to it:
    WRITE (11, *) 'Giving focus to Child 2.'
! Give focus to Child Window 1 with the FOCUSQQ function:
    status = FOCUSQQ(10)
    ...
! Find out the unit number of the child window that currently
    status = INQFOCUSQQ(focusunit) ! has focus:
```

SETACTIVEQQ makes a child window active without bringing it to the foreground. **GETACTIVEQQ** returns the unit number of the currently active child window. **GETHWNDQQ** converts the unit number into a Windows handle for functions that require it.

7.7.4 Keeping Child Windows Open

A child window remains open as long as its unit is open. The STATUS parameter in the **CLOSE** statement determines whether the child window remains open after the unit has been closed. If you set STATUS='KEEP', the associated window remains open but no further input or output is permitted. Also, the Close command is added to the child window's menu and the word Closed is appended to the window title. The default is STATUS='DELETE', which closes the window.

A window that remains open when you use STATUS='KEEP' counts as one of the 40 child windows available for the QuickWin application.

7.7.5 Controlling Size and Position of Windows

SETWSIZEQQ and **GETWSIZEQQ** set and get the size and position of the visible representation of a window. The positions and dimensions of visible child windows are expressed in units of character height and width. The position and dimensions of the frame window are expressed in screen pixels. The position and dimensions are returned in the derived type qwinfo defined in DFLIB.MOD as follows:

```
TYPE QWINFO
  INTEGER(2) TYPE ! Type of action performed by SETWSIZEQQ.
  INTEGER(2) X    ! x-coordinate for upper left corner.
  INTEGER(2) Y    ! y-coordinate for upper left corner.
  INTEGER(2) H    ! Window height.
  INTEGER(2) W    ! Window width.
END TYPE QWINFO
```

The options for the qwinfo type are listed under **SETWSIZEQQ** in the "A-Z Summary" in the *Language Reference* in Visual Fortran online Help.

GETWSIZEQQ returns the position and the current or maximum window size of the current frame or child window. To access information about a child window, specify the unit number associated with it. Unit numbers 0, 5, and 6 refer to the default startup window if you have not explicitly opened them with the **OPEN** statement. To access information about the frame window, specify the unit number as the symbolic constant QWIN$FRAMEWINDOW. For example:

```
USE DFLIB
INTEGER(4) status
TYPE (QWINFO) winfo
OPEN (4, FILE='USER')
...
! Get current size of child window associated with unit 4.
status = GETWSIZEQQ(4, QWIN$SIZECURR, winfo)
WRITE (*,*) "Child window size is ", winfo.H, " by ", &
  & winfo.W
! Get maximum size of frame window.
status = GETWSIZEQQ(QWIN$FRAMEWINDOW, QWIN$SIZEMAX, winfo)
WRITE (*,*) "Max frame window size is ", winfo.H, " by ", &
  & winfo.W
```

SETWSIZEQQ is used to set the visible window position and size. For example:

```
USE DFLIB
INTEGER(4) status
TYPE (QWINFO) winfo
OPEN (4, FILE='USER')
winfo.H = 30
winfo.W = 80
winfo.TYPE = QWIN$SET
status = SETWSIZEQQ(4, winfo)
```

7.8 Using Graphics and Character-Font Routines

Graphics routines are functions and subroutines that draw lines, rectangles, ellipses, and similar elements on the screen. Font routines create text in a variety of sizes and styles. The QuickWin graphics library provides routines that:

▶ Change the window's dimensions.

▶ Set coordinates.

▶ Set color palettes.

▶ Set line styles, fill masks, and other figure attributes.

▶ Draw graphics elements.

▶ Display text in several character styles.

▶ Display text in fonts compatible with Microsoft Windows.

▶ Store and retrieve screen images.

7.9 Defining Graphics Characteristics

The following topics discuss groups of routines that define the way text and graphics are displayed:

▶ Section 7.9.1 Selecting Display Options

▶ Section 7.9.2 Setting Graphics Coordinates

▶ Section 7.9.3 Using Color

▶ Section 7.9.4 Setting Figure Properties

7.9.1 Selecting Display Options

The QuickWin run-time library provides a number of routines that you can use to define text and graphics displays. These routines determine the graphics environment characteristics and control the cursor.

SETWINDOWCONFIG is the command you use to configure window properties. You can use **DISPLAYCURSOR** to control whether the cursor will be displayed. The cursor becomes invisible after a call to **SETWINDOWCONFIG**. To display the cursor you must explicitly turn on cursor visibility with **DISPLAYCURSOR**($GCURSORON).

SETGTEXTROTATION sets the current orientation for font text output, and **GETGTEXTROTATION** returns the current setting. The current orientation is used in calls to **OUTGTEXT**.

For more information on these routines, see the "A-Z Summary" in the *Language Reference* in Visual Fortran online Help.

7.9.2 Setting Graphics Coordinates

The coordinate-setting routines control where graphics can appear on the screen. Visual Fortran graphics routines recognize the following sets of coordinates:

▶ Fixed *physical coordinates*, which are determined by the hardware and the video mode used

▶ *Viewport coordinates*, which you can define in the application

▶ *Window coordinates*, which you can define to simplify scaling of floating-point data values

Unless you change it, the viewport-coordinate system is identical to the physical-coordinate system. The physical origin (0, 0) is always in the upper-left corner of the *display*. For QuickWin, *display* means a child window's client area, not the actual monitor screen (unless you go to Full Screen mode). The x-axis extends in the positive direction left to right, while the y-axis extends in the positive direction top to bottom. The default viewport has the dimensions of the selected mode. In a QuickWin application, you can draw outside of the child window's current client area. If you then make the child window bigger, you will see what was previously outside the frame.

You can also use coordinate routines to convert between physical-, viewport-, and window-coordinate systems. (For more detailed information on coordinate systems, see Chapter 12 Drawing Graphics Elements.)

You can set the pixel dimensions of the x- and y-axes with **SETWINDOWCONFIG**. You can access these values through the wc.numxpixels and wc.numypixels values returned by **GETWINDOWCONFIG**. Similarly, **GETWINDOWCONFIG** also returns the range of colors available in the current mode through the wc.numcolors value.

You can also define the graphics area with **SETCLIPRGN** and **SETVIEWPORT**. Both of these functions define a subset of the available window area for graphics output. **SETCLIPRGN** does not change the viewport coordinates, but merely masks part of the screen. **SETVIEWPORT** resets the viewport bounds to the limits you give it and sets the origin to the upper-left corner of this region.

The origin of the viewport-coordinate system can be moved to a new position relative to the physical origin with **SETVIEWORG**. Regardless of the viewport coordinates, however, you can always locate the currrent graphics output position with **GETCURRENTPOSITION** and **GETCURRENTPOSITION_W**. (For more detailed information on viewports and clipping regions, see Chapter 12 Drawing Graphics Elements.)

Using the window-coordinate system, you can easily scale any set of data to fit on the screen. You define any range of coordinates (such as 0 to 5000) that works well for your data as the range for the window-coordinate axes. By telling the program that you want the window-coordinate system to fit in a particular area on the screen (map to a particular set of viewport coordinates), you can scale a chart or drawing to any size you want. **SETWINDOW** defines a window-coordinate system bounded by the specified values. See the Visual Fortran Sample SINE.F90 in the . . . `DF98\SAMPLES\TUTORIAL` directory for an example of this technique.

GETPHYSCOORD converts viewport coordinates to physical coordinates, and **GETVIEWCOORD** translates from physical coordinates to viewport coordinates. Similarly, **GETVIEWCOORD_W** converts window coordinates to viewport coordinates, and **GETWINDOWCOORD** converts viewport coordinates to window coordinates.

For more information on these routines, see the A-Z Summary in the *Language Reference* in Visual Fortran online Help.

7.9.3　Using Color

If you have a VGA machine, you are restricted to displaying at most 256 colors at a time. These 256 colors are held in a palette. You can choose the palette colors from a range of 262,144 colors (256K), but only 256 at a time. The palette routines **REMAPPALETTERGB** and **REMAPALLPALETTERGB** assign Red-Green-Blue (RGB) colors to palette indexes.

Functions and subroutines that use color indexes create graphic outputs that depend on the mapping between palette indexes and RGB colors. **REMAPPALETTERGB** remaps one color index to an RGB color, and **REMAPALLPALETTERGB** remaps the entire palette, up to 236 colors, (20 colors are reserved by the system). You cannot remap the palette on machines capable of displaying 20 colors or fewer.

SVGA and true color video adapters are capable of displaying 262,144 (256K) colors and 16.7 million colors respectively. If you use a palette, you are restricted to the colors available in the palette.

To access the entire set of available colors, not just the 256 or fewer colors in the palette, you should use functions that specify a color value directly. These functions end in RGB and use Red-Green-Blue color values, not indexes to a palette. For example, **SETCOLORRGB**, **SETTEXTCOLOR-RGB**, and **SETPIXELRGB** specify a direct color value, while **SETCOLOR**, **SETTEXTCOLOR**, and **SETPIXEL** each specify a palette color index. If you are displaying more than 256 colors simultaneously, you need to use the RGB direct color value functions exclusively.

To set the physical display properties of your monitor, open the Control Panel and click the Display icon.

QuickWin only supports a 256-color palette, regardless of the number of colors set for the monitor.

For more information on setting colors, see Section 12.2 Adding Color in Chapter 12 Drawing Graphics Elements.

7.9.4   Setting Figure Properties

The output routines that draw arcs, ellipses, and other primitive figures do not specify color or line-style information. Instead, they rely on properties set independently by other routines.

GETCOLORRGB (or **GETCOLOR**) and **SETCOLORRGB** (or **SET-COLOR**) obtain or set the current color value (or color index), which **FLOODFILLRGB** (or **FLOODFILL**), **OUTGTEXT**, and the shape-drawing routines all use. Similarly, **GETBKCOLORRGB** (or **GETBKCOLOR**) and **SETBKCOLORRGB** (or **SETBKCOLOR**) retrieve or set the current background color.

GETFILLMASK and **SETFILLMASK** return or set the current fill mask. The mask is an 8-by-8-bit array with each bit representing a pixel. If a bit is 0, the pixel in memory is left untouched: the mask is transparent to that pixel. If a bit is 1, the pixel is assigned the current color value. The array acts as a template that repeats over the entire fill area. It "masks" the background with a pattern of pixels drawn in the current color, creating a large number of fill patterns. These routines are particularly useful for shading.

GETWRITEMODE and **SETWRITEMODE** return or set the current *logical write mode* used when drawing lines. The logical write mode, which can be set to $GAND, $GOR, $GPRESET, $GPSET, or $GXOR, determines the interaction between the new drawing and the existing screen and current graphics color. The logical write mode affects the **LINETO**, **RECTANGLE**, and **POLYGON** routines.

GETLINESTYLE and **SETLINESTYLE** retrieve and set the current line style. The line style is determined by a 16-bit-long mask that determines which of the five available styles is chosen. You can use these two routines to create a wide variety of dashed lines that affect the **LINETO**, **RECTANGLE**, and **POLYGON** routines.

For more information on these routines, see the "A-Z Summary" in the *Language Reference* in Visual Fortran online Help.

7.10 Displaying Graphics Output

The run-time graphics library routines can draw geometric features, display text, display font-based characters, and transfer images between memory and the screen. These capabilities are discussed in the following topics:

▶ Section 7.10.1 Drawing Graphics

▶ Section 7.10.2 Displaying Character-Based Text

▶ Section 7.10.3 Displaying Font-Based Characters

7.10.1 Drawing Graphics

If you want anything other than the default line style (solid), mask (no mask), background color (black), or foreground color (white), you must call the appropriate routine before calling the drawing routine. Subsequent output routines employ the same attributes until you change them or open a new child window.

Table 7-1 lists routines that ask about the current graphics settings, set new graphics settings, and draw graphics.

Table 7–1 *Routines for Graphics*

Routine	*Description*
ARC, ARC_W	Draws an arc
CLEARSCREEN	Clears the screen, viewport, or text window
ELLIPSE, ELLIPSE_W	Draws an ellipse or circle
FLOODFILL, FLOODFILL_W	Fills an enclosed area of the screen with the current color index using the current fill mask
FLOODFILLRGB, FLOODFILLRGB_W	Fills an enclosed area of the screen with the current RGB color using the current fill mask
GETARCINFO	Determines the endpoints of the most recently drawn arc or pie
GETCURRENTPOSITION, GETCURRENTPOSITION_W	Returns the coordinates of the current graphics-output position

Table 7–1   *Routines for Graphics (Continued)*

Routine	Description
GETPIXEL, GETPIXEL_W	Returns a pixel's color index
GETPIXELRGB, GETPIXELRGB_W	Returns a pixel's Red-Green-Blue color value
GETPIXELS	Gets the color indices of multiple pixels
GETPIXELSRGB	Gets the Red-Green-Blue color values of multiple pixels
GRSTATUS	Returns the status (success or failure) of the most recently called graphics routine
INTEGERTORGB	Convert a true color value into its red, green, and blue components
LINETO, LINETO_W	Draws a line from the current graphics-output position to a specified point
LINETOARR, LINETOAREX	Draws lines from arrays at x,y coordinate points
MOVETO, MOVETO_W	Moves the current graphics-output position to a specified point
PIE, PIE_W	Draws a pie-slice-shaped figure
POLYGON, POLYGON_W	Draws a polygon
RECTANGLE, RECTANGLE_W	Draws a rectangle
RGBTOINTEGER	Convert a trio of red, green, and blue values to a true color value for use with RGB functions and subroutines
SETPIXEL, SETPIXEL_W	Sets a pixel at a specified location to a color index
SETPIXELRGB, SETPIXELRGB_W	Sets a pixel at a specified location to a Red-Green-Blue color value
SETPIXELS	Set the color indices of multiple pixels
SETPIXELSRGB	Set the Red-Green-Blue color value of multiple pixels

All routines are fully described in the "A-Z Summary" in the *Language Reference* in Visual Fortran online Help.

Most of these routines have multiple forms. Routine names that end with _W use the window-coordinate system and **REAL**(8) argument values. Routines without this suffix use the viewport-coordinate system and **INTEGER**(2) argument values.

Curved figures, such as arcs and ellipses, are centered within a *bounding rectangle*, which is specified by the upper-left and lower-right corners of the rectangle. The center of the rectangle becomes the center for the figure, and the rectangle's borders determine the size of the figure. In Figure 7-9, the points $(x1, y1)$ and $(x2, y2)$ define the bounding rectangle.

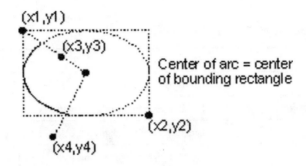

Figure 7–9 *Bounding Rectangle*

7.10.2 Displaying Character-Based Text

The routines in the following table ask about screen attributes that affect text display, prepare the screen for text and send text to the screen. To print text in specialized fonts, see Section 7.10.3 Displaying Font-Based Characters and Chapter 13 Using Fonts from the Graphics Library.

In addition to these general text routines, you can customize the text in your menus with **MODIFYMENUSTRINGQQ**. You can also customize any other string that QuickWin produces, including status bar messages, the state message (for example, "Paused" or "Running"), and dialog box messages, with **SETMESSAGEQQ**.

Table 7-2 lists routines that recognize text-window boundaries.

Table 7–2 *Routines for Text Display*

Routine	Description
CLEARSCREEN	Clears the screen, viewport, or text window
DISPLAYCURSOR	Sets the cursor on or off
GETBKCOLOR	Returns the current background color index
GETBKCOLORRGB	Returns the current background Red-Green-Blue color value
GETTEXTCOLOR	Returns the current text color index
GETTEXTCOLORRGB	Returns the current text Red-Green-Blue color value
GETTEXTPOSITION	Returns the current text-output position
GETTEXTWINDOW	Returns the boundaries of the current text window

Table 7–2 *Routines for Text Display (Continued)*

Routine	Description
OUTTEXT	Sends text to the screen at the current position
SCROLLTEXTWINDOW	Scrolls the contents of a text window
SETBKCOLOR	Sets the current background color index
SETBKCOLORRGB	Sets the current background Red-Green-Blue color value
SETTEXTCOLOR	Sets the current text color to a new color index
SETTEXTCOLORRGB	Sets the current text color to a new Red-Green-Blue color value
SETTEXTPOSITION	Changes the current text position
SETTEXTWINDOW	Sets the current text-display window
WRAPON	Turns line wrapping on or off

All routines are fully described in the "A-Z Summary" in the *Language Reference* in Visual Fortran online Help. Use of these customization routines is described in Section 7.13 Customizing QuickWin Applications.

These routines do not provide text-formatting capabilities. If you want to print integer or floating-point values, you must convert the values into a string (using an internal **WRITE** statement) before calling these routines. The text routines specify all screen positions in character-row and column coordinates.

SETTEXTWINDOW is the text equivalent of the **SETVIEWPORT** graphics routine, except that it restricts only the display area for text printed with **OUTTEXT**, **PRINT**, and **WRITE**. **GETTEXTWINDOW** returns the boundaries of the current text window set by **SETTEXTWINDOW**. **SCROLLTEXTWINDOW** scrolls the contents of a text window. **OUTTEXT**, **PRINT**, and **WRITE** display text strings written to the current text window.

Warning: The **WRITE** statement sends its carriage return (CR) and line feed (LF) to the screen at the beginning of the first I/O statement following the **WRITE** statement. This can cause unpredictable text positioning if you mix the graphics routines **SETTEXTPOSITION** and **OUTTEXT** with the **WRITE** statement. To minimize this effect, use the backslash (\) or dollar sign ($) format descriptor (to suppress CR-LF) in the associated **FORMAT** statement.

7.10.3 Displaying Font-Based Characters

Because the Visual Fortran Graphics Library provides a variety of fonts, you must indicate which font to use when displaying font-based characters. After you select a font, you can make inquiries about the width of a string printed in that font or about font characteristics.

Table 7-3 lists routines that control the display of font-based characters.

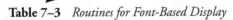

Table 7–3   *Routines for Font-Based Display*

Routine	Description
GETFONTINFO	Returns the current font characteristics
GETGTEXTEXTENT	Determines the width of specified text in the current font
GETGTEXTROTATION	Gets the current orientation for font text output in 0.1° increments
INITIALIZEFONTS	Initializes the font library
OUTGTEXT	Sends text in the current font to the screen at the current graphics output position
SETFONT	Finds a single font that matches a specified set of characteristics and makes it the current font used by **OUTGTEXT**
SETGTEXTROTATION	Sets the current orientation for font text output in 0.1° increments

All routines are fully described in the "A-Z Summary" in the *Language Reference* in Visual Fortran online Help.

Characters may be drawn ("mapped") in one of two ways: as bitmapped letters (a "picture" of the letter) or as TrueType characters. For detailed explanations and examples of how to use the font routines from the QuickWin Library, see Chapter 13 Using Fonts from the Graphics Library.

7.11   Working with Screen Images

The routines described in the following sections offer the following ways to store and retrieve images:

▶ Section 7.11.1 Transferring Images in Memory

Transferring images from memory buffers is a quick and flexible way to move things around the screen. Memory images can interact with the current screen image; for example, you can perform a logical **AND** of a memory image and the current screen or superimpose a negative of the memory image on the screen.

▶ Section 7.11.2 Loading and Saving Images to Files

   Transferring images from screen and Windows bitmap files gives access to images created by other programs, and saves graphs and images for later use. However, images loaded from bitmap files overwrite the portion of the screen they are pasted into and retain the attributes they were created with, such as the color palette, rather than accepting current attributes.

▶ Section 7.11.3 Editing Text and Graphics from the QuickWin Edit Menu

   Editing screen images from the QuickWin Edit menu is a quick and easy way to move and modify images interactively on the screen, retaining the current screen attributes, and also provides temporary storage (the Clipboard) for transferring images among applications.

   These routines let you cut, paste, and move images around the screen.

7.11.1 Transferring Images in Memory

The **GETIMAGE** and **PUTIMAGE** routines transfer images between memory and the screen and give you options that control the way the image and screen interact. When you hold an image in memory, the application allocates a memory buffer for the image. The **IMAGESIZE** routines calculate the size of the buffer needed to store a given image.

   Table 7-4 lists the routines that transfer images in memory. Routines that end with _W use window coordinates; the other functions use viewport coordinates.

Table 7–4 *Routines that Transfer Images in Memory*

Routine	*Description*
GETIMAGE, GETIMAGE_W	Stores a screen image in memory
IMAGESIZE, IMAGESIZE_W	Returns image size in bytes
PUTIMAGE, PUTIMAGE_W	Retrieves an image from memory and displays it

   All routines are fully described in the "A-Z Summary" in the *Language Reference* in Visual Fortran online Help.

7.11.2 Loading and Saving Images to Files

Table 7-5 lists the routines that transfer images between the screen and Windows bitmap files.

Table 7–5 *Routines that Load and Save Images to Files*

Routine	Description
LOADIMAGE, LOADIMAGE_W	Reads a Windows bitmap file (.BMP) from disk and displays it as specified coordinates
SAVEIMAGE, SAVEIMAGE_W	Captures a screen image from the specified portion of the screen and saves it as a Windows bitmap file

All routines are fully described in the "A-Z Summary" in the *Language Reference* in Visual Fortran online Help.

You can use a Windows format bitmap file created with a graphics program as a backdrop for graphics that you draw with the Visual Fortran graphics functions and subroutines.

7.11.3 Editing Text and Graphics from the QuickWin Edit Menu

From the QuickWin Edit menu you can choose the Select Text, Select Graphics, or Select All options. You can then outline your selection with the mouse or the keyboard arrow keys. When you use the Select Text option, your selection is highlighted. When you use the Select Graphics or Select All option, your selection is marked with a box whose dimensions you control.

Once you have selected a portion of the screen, you can copy it onto the Clipboard by using the Edit/Copy option or by using the `Ctrl+INS` key combination. If the screen area you have selected contains only text, it is copied onto the Clipboard as text. If the selected screen area contains graphics, or a mix of text and graphics, it is copied onto the Clipboard as a bitmap.

The Edit menu's Paste option will only paste text. Bitmaps can be pasted into other Windows applications from the Clipboard (with the `Ctrl+V` or `Shift+INS` key combinations).

Remember the following when selecting portions of the screen:

▶ If you have chosen the Select All option from the Edit menu, the whole screen is selected and you cannot then select a portion of the screen.

▶ Text selections are not bounded by the current text window set with **SETTEXTWINDOW**.

▶ When text is copied to the Clipboard, trailing blanks in a line are removed.

▶ Text that is written to a window can be overdrawn by graphics. In this case, the text is still present in the screen text buffer, though not visible on the screen. When you select a portion of the screen to copy, you can select text that is actually present but not visible, and that text will be copied onto the Clipboard.

▶ When you chose Select Text or Select Graphics from the Edit menu, the application is paused, a caret (^) appears at the top left corner of the currently active window, all user-defined callbacks are disabled, and the window title changes to "Mark Text—*windownam*" or "Mark Graphics—*windowname*," where *windowname* is the name of the currently active window.

As soon as you begin selection (by pressing an arrow key or a mouse button), the Window title changes to "Select Text—*windowname*" or "Select Graphics—*windowname*" and selection begins at that point. If you do not want selection to begin in the upper-left corner, your first action when "Mark Text" or "Mark Graphics" appears in the title is to use the mouse to place the cursor at the position where selection is to be begin.

7.12 Enhancing QuickWin Applications

In addition to the basic QuickWin features, you can optionally customize and enhance your QuickWin applications using the routines listed in Table 7-6.

Table 7–6 *Routines to Enhance QuickWin Applications*

Category	QuickWin Function	Description
Initial settings	**INITIALSETTINGS**	Controls initial menu settings and/or initial frame window
Display/add box	**MESSAGEBOXQQ**	Displays a message box
	ABOUTBOXQQ	Adds an About Box with customized text
Menu items	**CLICKMENUQQ**	Simulates the effect of clicking or selecting a menu item
	APPENDMENUQQ	Appends a menu item
	DELETEMENUQQ	Deletes a menu item
	INSERTMENUQQ	Inserts a menu item
	MODIFYMENUFLAGSQQ	Modifies a menu item's state
	MODIFYMENUROUTINEQQ	Modifies a menu item's callback routine
	MODIFYMENUSTRINGQQ	Changes a menu item's text string
	SETWINDOWMENUQQ	Sets the menu to which a list of current child window names are appended

Table 7–6   *Routines to Enhance QuickWin Applications (Continued)*

Category	QuickWin Function	Description
Directional	**PASSDIRKEYSQQ**	Enables (or disables) use of the arrow keys directional keys and page keys as input (see sample DIRKEYS.F90 in the . . . `DF98\SAMPLES\ADVANCED\DIRKEYS` folder)
QuickWin messages	**SETMESSAGEQQ**	Changes any QuickWin message, including status bar messages, state messages and dialog box messages
Mouse actions	**REGISTERMOUSEEVENT**	Registers the application defined routines to be called on mouse events
	UNREGISTERMOUSEEVENT	Removes the routine registered by **REGISTERMOUSEEVENT**
	WAITONMOUSEEVENT	Blocks return until a mouse event occurs

All routines are fully described in the "A-Z Summary" in the *Language Reference* in Visual Fortran online Help. The use of these features to create customized menus, respond to mouse events, and add custom icons is described in Section 7.13 Customizing QuickWin Applications.

7.13   Customizing QuickWin Applications

The QuickWin library is a set of routines you can use to create graphics programs or simple applications for Windows. For a general overview of Quick-Win and a description of how to create and size child windows, see the beginning of this section. For information on how to compile and link QuickWin applications, see Chapter 2 Building Programs and Libraries.

The following topics describe how to customize and fine-tune your Quick-Win applications:

▶ Section 7.13.1 Program Control of Menus

▶ Section 7.13.2 Changing Status Bar and State Messages

▶ Section 7.13.3 Displaying Message Boxes

▶ Section 7.13.4 Defining an About Box

▶ Section 7.13.5 Using Custom Icons

▶ Section 7.13.6 Using a Mouse

7.13.1 Program Control of Menus

You do not have to use the default QuickWin menus. You can eliminate and alter menus, menu item lists, menu titles or item titles:

▶ Controlling the Initial Menu and Frame Window

You can change the initial appearance of an application's default frame window and menus by defining an **INITIALSETTINGS** function. If no user-defined **INITIALSETTINGS** function is supplied, QuickWin calls a predefined **INITIALSETTINGS** routine to control the default frame window and menu appearance. Your application does not need to call **INITIALSETTINGS**. If you supply the function in your project, QuickWin calls it automatically.

If you supply it, **INITIALSETTINGS** can call QuickWin functions that set the initial menus and the size and position of the frame window. Besides the menu functions, **SETWSIZEQQ** can be called from your **INITIALSETTINGS** function to adjust the frame window size and position before the window is first drawn.

The following is a sample of **INITIALSETTINGS**:

```
      LOGICAL(4) FUNCTION INITIALSETTINGS( )
         USE DFLIB
         LOGICAL(4) result
         TYPE (qwinfo) qwi
! Set window frame size.
         qwi.x = 0
         qwi.y = 0
         qwi.w = 400
         qwi.h = 400
         qwi.type = QWIN$SET
         i = SetWSizeQQ( QWIN$FRAMEWINDOW, qwi )
! Create first menu called Games.
         result = APPENDMENUQQ(1, $MENUENABLED, '&Games'C, NUL )
! Add item called TicTacToe.
         result = APPENDMENUQQ(1, $MENUENABLED, '&TicTacToe'C, WINPRINT)
! Draw a separator bar.
         result = APPENDMENUQQ(1, $MENUSEPARATOR, ''C, NUL )
! Add item called Exit.
         result = APPENDMENUQQ(1, $MENUENABLED, 'E&xit'C, WINEXIT )
! Add second menu called Help.
         result = APPENDMENUQQ(2, $MENUENABLED, '&Help'C, NUL )
         result = APPENDMENUQQ(2, $MENUENABLED, '&QuickWin Help'C, WININDEX)
         INITIALSETTINGS= .true.
      END FUNCTION INITIALSETTINGS
```

This is an example of the interface for **INITIALSETTINGS**:

```
PROGRAM MENUS
  USE DFLIB
  LOGICAL(4) res
  INTERFACE
    LOGICAL(4) FUNCTION INITIALSETTINGS
    END FUNCTION
  END INTERFACE
OPEN (10, FILE="User")
WRITE(10, *) "Hello, child window"
END
```

QuickWin executes your **INITIALSETTINGS** function during initialization, before creating the frame window. When your function is done, control returns to QuickWin and it does the remaining initialization. The control then passes to the Visual Fortran application.

Your function should return .TRUE. if it succeeds, and .FALSE. otherwise. The QuickWin default function returns a value of .TRUE. only.

Default menus are created after **INITIALSETTINGS** has been called, and only if you do not create your own menus. Therefore, using **DELETEMENUQQ**, **INSERTMENUQQ**, **APPENDMENUQQ**, and the other menu configuration QuickWin functions while in **INITIALSETTINGS** affects your custom menus, not the default QuickWin menus.

▶ Deleting, Inserting, and Appending Menu Items

Menus are defined from left to right, starting with 1 at the far left. Menu items are defined from top to bottom, starting with 0 at the top (the menu title itself). Within **INITIALSETTINGS**, if you supply it, you can delete, insert, and append menu items in custom menus. Outside **INITIALSETTINGS**, you can alter the default QuickWin menus as well as custom menus at any point in your application. (Default QuickWin menus are not created until after **INITIALSETTINGS** has run and only if you do not create custom menus.)

To delete a menu item, specify the menu number and item number in **DELETEMENUQQ**. To delete an entire menu, delete item 0 of that menu. For example:

```
USE DFLIB
LOGICAL status
status = DELETEMENUQQ(1, 2)  ! Delete the second menu item
                             ! from menu 1 (the default FILE
                             ! menu).
```

```
status = DELETEMENUQQ(5, 0)  ! Delete menu 5 (the default
                             ! Windows menu).
```

INSERTMENUQQ inserts a menu item or menu and registers its callback routine. QuickWin supplies several standard callback routines such as WINEXIT to terminate a program, WININDEX to list QuickWin Help, and WINCOPY which copies the contents of the current window to the Clipboard. For a list of callbacks, see **APPENDMENUQQ** or **INSERTMENUQQ** in the "A-Z Summary" in the *Language Reference* in Visual Fortran online Help.

Often, you will supply your own callback routines to perform a particular action when a user selects something from one of your menus.

In general, you should not assign the same callback routine to more than one menu item because a menu item's state might not be properly updated when you change it (put a check mark next to it, gray it out, or disable, or enable it). You cannot insert a menu item or menu beyond the existing number; for example, inserting item 7 when 5 and 6 have not been defined yet. To insert an entire menu, specify menu item 0. The new menu can take any position among or immediately after existing menus.

If you specify a menu position occupied by an existing menu, the existing menu and any menus to the right of the one you add are shifted right and their menu numbers are incremented.

For example, the following code inserts a fifth menu item called Position into menu 5 (the default Windows menu):

```
USE DFLIB
LOGICAL(4) status
status = INSERTMENUQQ (5, 5, $MENUCHECKED, 'Position'C, &
& WINPRINT)
```

The next code inserts a new menu called My List into menu position 3. The menu currently in position 3 and any menus to the right (the default menus View, State, Windows, and Help) are shifted right one position:

```
USE DFLIB
LOGICAL(4) status
status = INSERTMENUQQ(3,0, $MENUENABLED, 'My List'C, &
& WINSTATE)
```

You can append a menu item with **APPENDMENUQQ**. The item is added to the bottom of the menu list. If there is no item yet for the menu, your appended item is treated as the top-level menu item, and the string you assign to it appears on the menu bar. The following code appends the menu item called Cascade Windows to the first menu (the default File menu):

```
USE DFLIB
LOGICAL(4) status
status = APPENDMENUQQ(1, $MENUCHECKED, 'Cascade Windows'C, &
& WINCASCADE)
```

The $MENUCHECKED flag in the example puts a check mark next to the menu item. To remove the check mark, you can set the flag to $MENUUNCHECKED in the **MODIFYMENUFLAGSQQ** function. Some predefined routines (such as WINSTATUS) take care of updating their own check marks. However, if the routine is registered to more than one menu item, the check marks might not be properly updated. For the list of callback routines and other flags, see **APPENDMENUQQ** or **INSERTMENUQQ** in the "A-Z Summary" in the *Language Reference* in Visual Fortran online Help.

▶ Modifying Menu Items

MODIFYMENUSTRINGQQ can modify the string identifier of a menu item, **MODIFYMENUROUTINEQQ** can modify the callback routine called when the item is selected, and **MODIFYMENUFLAG-SQQ** can modify a menu item's state (such as enabled, grayed out, checked, and so on).

The following example code uses **MODIFYMENUSTRINGQQ** to modify the menu string for the fourth item in the first menu (the File menu by default) to Tile Windows, it uses **MODIFYMENUROU-TINEQQ** to change the callback routine called if the item is selected to WINTILE, and uses **MODIFYMENUFLAGSQQ** to put a check mark next to the menu item:

```
status = MODIFYMENUSTRINGQQ( 1, 4, 'Tile Windows'C)
status = MODIFYMENUROUTINEQQ( 1, 4, WINTILE)
status = MODIFYMENUFLAGSQQ( 1, 4, $MENUCHECKED)
```

▶ Creating a Menu List of Available Child Windows

By default, the Windows menu contains a list of all open child windows in your QuickWin applications. **SETWINDOWMENUQQ** changes the menu which lists the currently open child windows to the menu you specify. The list of child window names is appended to the end of the menu you choose and deleted from any other menu that previously contained it. For example:

```
USE DFLIB
LOGICAL(4) status
```

```
   ...
! Append list of open child windows to menu 1 (the default
! File menu)
   status = SETWINDOWMENUQQ(1)
```

▶ Simulating Menu Selections   ·

CLICKMENUQQ simulates the effect of clicking or selecting a menu command from the Window menu. The QuickWin application behaves as though the user had clicked or selected the command. The following code fragment simulates the effect of selecting the Tile item from the Window menu:

```
USE DFLIB
INTEGER(4) status
status = CLICKMENUQQ(QWIN$TILE)
```

Only items from the Window menu can be specified in **CLICK-MENUQQ**.

7.13.2 Changing Status Bar and State Messages

Any string QuickWin produces can be changed by calling **SETMES-SAGEQQ** with the appropriate message ID. Unlike other QuickWin message functions, **SETMESSAGEQQ** uses regular Fortran strings, not null-terminated C strings. For example, to change the PAUSED state message to "I am waiting":

```
USE DFLIB
CALL SETMESSAGEQQ('I am waiting', QWIN$MSG_PAUSED)
```

This function is useful for localizing your QuickWin applications for countries with different native languages. A list of message IDs is given in **SETMESSAGEQQ** in the "A-Z Summary" in the *Language Reference* in Visual Fortran online Help.

7.13.3 Displaying Message Boxes

MESSAGEBOXQQ causes your program to display a message box. You can specify the message the box displays and the caption that appears in the title bar. Both strings must be null-terminated C strings. You can also specify the type of message box. Box types are symbolic constants defined in DFLIB.MOD, and can be combined by means of the **IOR** intrinsic function or the .OR. operator. For example:

```
USE DFLIB
INTEGER(4) response
```

```
response = MESSAGEBOXQQ('Retry or Cancel?'C, 'Smith Chart &
& Simulator'C, MB$RETRYCANCELQWIN .OR. MB$DEFBUTTON2)
```

The available box types are listed under **MESSAGEBOXQQ** in the "A-Z Summary" in the *Language Reference* in Visual Fortran online Help.

7.13.4 Defining an About Box

The **ABOUTBOXQQ** function specifies the message displayed in the message box that appears when the user selects the About command from a QuickWin application's Help menu. (If your program does not call **ABOUTBOXQQ**, the QuickWin run-time library supplies a default string.) The message string must be a null-terminated C string. For example:

```
USE DFLIB
INTEGER(4) status
status = ABOUTBOXQQ ('Sound Speed Profile Tables Version &
& 1.0'C)
```

ABOUTBOXQQ is fully described in the "A-Z Summary" in the *Language Reference* in Visual Fortran online Help.

7.13.5 Using Custom Icons

The QuickWin run-time library provides default icons that appear when the user minimizes the application's frame window or its child windows. You can add custom-made icons to your executable files, and Windows will display them instead of the default icons.

To add a custom child window icon to your QuickWin program:

1. Select Resource from the Insert menu in the visual development environment. Select Icon from the list that appears. The screen will become an icon drawing tool.

2. Draw the icon. (For more information about using the Graphics Editor in the visual development environment, see "Resource Editors, Graphics Editor" in the *Visual C++ User's Guide*.)

-or-

If your icon already exists (for example, as a bitmap) and you want to import it, not draw it, select Resource from the Insert menu, then select Import from the buttons in the Resource dialog. You will be prompted for the file containing your icon.

3. Name the icon. The frame window's icon must have the name "frameicon," and the child window's icon must have the name "childicon."

These names must be entered as strings into the Icon Properties dialog box.

To display the Icon Properties dialog box, double-click in the icon editor area outside the icon's grid or press ALT+ENTER.

In the ID field on the General tab of Icon Properties dialog box, type over the default icon name with "frameicon" or "childicon." You must add the quotation marks to the text you type in order to make the name be interpreted as a string.

Your icon will be saved in a file with the extension .ICO.

4. Create a script file to hold your icons. Select File/Save As. You will be prompted for the name of the script file that will contain your icons. Name the script file. It must end with the extension .RC; for example, myicons.rc. Using this method, the icons and their string values will be automatically saved in the script file. (Alternatively, you can create a script file with any editor and add the icon names and their string values by hand.)

5. Add the script file to the project that contains your QuickWin application. Select Build and the script file will be built into the application's executable. (The compiled script file will have the extension .RES.)

When you run your application, the icon you created will take the place of the default child or frame icon. Your custom icon appears in the upper-left corner of the window frame. When you minimize the window, the icon appears on the left of the minimized window bar.

7.13.6 Using a Mouse

Your applications can detect and respond to mouse events, such as left mouse button down, right mouse button down, or double-click. Mouse events can be used as an alternative to keyboard input or for manipulating what is shown on the screen.

The mouse is an asynchronous device, so the user can click the mouse anytime while the application is running (mouse input does not have to be synchronized to anything). When a mouse-click occurs, Windows sends a message to the application, which takes the appropriate action. Mouse support in applications is most often event-based, that is, a mouse-click occurs and the application does something.

However, an application can use blocking functions to wait for a mouse-click. This allows an application to execute in a particular sequential order and yet provide mouse support. QuickWin performs default processing based on mouse events.

QuickWin provides two types of mouse functions:

▶ Event-Based Functions

The QuickWin function **REGISTERMOUSEEVENT** registers the routine to be called when a particular mouse event occurs (left mouse button, right mouse button, double-click, and so on). You define what events you want it to handle and the routines to be called if those events occur. **UNREGISTERMOUSEEVENT** unregisters the routines so that Quick-Win doesn't call them but uses default handling for the particular event.

By default, QuickWin typically ignores events except when mouse-clicks occur on menus or dialog controls. Note that no events are received on a minimized window. A window must be restored or maximized in order for mouse events to happen within it.

For example:

```
USE DFLIB
INTEGER(4) result
OPEN (4, FILE= 'USER')
...
result = REGISTERMOUSEEVENT (4, MOUSE$LBUTTONDBLCLK, &
& CALCULATE)
```

This registers the routine CALCULATE, to be called when the user double-clicks the left mouse button while the mouse cursor is in the child window opened as unit 4. Table 7-7 lists the symbolic constants available to identify mouse events.

Table 7–7   *Symbolic Constants that Identify Mouse Events*

Mouse Event	*Description*
MOUSE$LBUTTONDOWN	Left mouse button down
MOUSE$LBUTTONUP	Left mouse button up
MOUSE$LBUTTONDBLCLK	Left mouse button double-click
MOUSE$RBUTTONDOWN	Right mouse button down
MOUSE$RBUTTONUP	Right mouse button up
MOUSE$RBUTTONDBLCLK	Right mouse button double-click
MOUSE$MOVE	Mouse moved

For every BUTTONDOWN and BUTTONDBLCLK event there is an associated BUTTONUP event. When the user double-clicks, four events happen: BUTTONDOWN and BUTTONUP for the first click, and BUTTONDBLCLK and BUTTONUP for the second click. The difference between getting BUTTONDBLCLK and BUTTONDOWN for the second click depends on whether the second click occurs in the double-click interval, set in the system's CONTROL PANEL/MOUSE.

To unregister the routine in the preceding example, use the following code:

```
result = UNREGISTERMOUSEEVENT (4, MOUSE$LBUTTONDBLCLK)
```

If **REGISTERMOUSEEVENT** is called again without unregistering a previous call, it overrides the first call. A new callback routine is then called on the specified event.

The callback routine you create to be called when a mouse event occurs should have the following prototype:

```
INTERFACE
    SUBROUTINE MouseCallBackRoutine (unit, mouseevent, &
      & keystate, MouseXpos,MouseYpos)
        INTEGER unit
        INTEGER mouseevent
        INTEGER keystate
        INTEGER MouseXpos
        INTEGER MouseYpos
    END SUBROUTINE
END INTERFACE
```

The unit parameter is the unit number associated with the child window where events are to be detected, and the mouseevent parameter is one of those listed in the preceding table. The MouseXpos and the MouseYpos parameters specify the x and y positions of the mouse during the event.

The keystate parameter indicates the state of the shift and control keys at the time of the mouse event, and can be any **OR**ed combination of the constants listed in Table 7-8.

Table 7–8 *State of Shift and Control Keys during Mouse Events*

Keystate Parameter	Description
MOUSE$KS_LBUTTON	Left mouse button down during event
MOUSE$KS_RBUTTON	Right mouse button down during event
MOUSE$KS_SHIFT	Shift key held down during event
MOUSE$KS_CONTROL	Control key held down during event

QuickWin callback routines for mouse events should do a minimum of processing and then return. While processing a callback, the program will appear to be non-responsive because messages are not being serviced, so it is important to return quickly. If more processing time is needed in a callback, another thread should be started to perform this work; threads can be created by calling the Win32 API **CreateThread**. (For more information on creating and using threads, see Chapter 19 Creating Multithread Applications.) If a callback routine does not start a new thread, the callback will not be reentered until it is done processing.

Note: In event-based functions, there is no buffering of events. Therefore, issues such as multithreading and synchronizing access to shared resources must be addressed. To avoid multithreading problems, use blocking functions rather than event-based functions. Blocking functions work well in applications that proceed sequentially. Applications where there is little seqential flow and the user jumps around the application are probably better implemented as event-based functions.

▶ Blocking (Sequential) Functions

The QuickWin blocking function **WAITONMOUSEEVENT** blocks execution until a specific mouse input is received. This function is similar to **INCHARQQ**, except that it waits for a mouse event instead of a keystroke.

For example:

```
USE DFLIB
INTEGER(4) mouseevent, keystate, x, y, result
...
  mouseevent = MOUSE$RBUTTONDOWN .OR. MOUSE$LBUTTONDOWN
  result = WAITONMOUSEEVENT (mouseevent, keystate, x , y)
! Wait until right or left mouse button clicked, then check
```

```
! the keystate with the following:
 if ((MOUSE$KS_SHIFT .AND. keystate) == MOUSE$KS_SHIFT) &
& then write (*,*) 'Shift key was down'
 if ((MOUSE$KS_CONTROL .AND. keystate) == MOUSE$KS_CONTROL)&
& then write (*,*) 'Ctrl key was down'
```

Your application passes a mouse event parameter, which can be any **OR**ed combination of mouse events, to **WAITONMOUSEEVENT**. The function then waits and blocks execution until one of the specified events occurs. It returns the state of the Shift and Ctrl keys at the time of the event in the parameter keystate, and returns the position of the mouse when the event occurred in the parameters x and y.

A mouse event must happen in the window that had focus when **WAITONMOUSEEVENT** was initially called. Mouse events in other windows will not end the wait. Mouse events in other windows cause callbacks to be called for the other windows, if callbacks were previously registered for those windows.

All routines are fully described in the "A-Z Summary" in the *Language Reference* in Visual Fortran online Help.

Default QuickWin Processing

QuickWin performs some actions based on mouse events. It uses mouse events to return from the FullScreen mode and to select text and/or graphics to copy to the Clipboard. Servicing the mouse event functions takes precedence over return from FullScreen mode. Servicing mouse event functions does not take precedence over Cut/Paste selection modes. Once selection mode is over, processing of mouse event functions resumes.

7.14   QuickWin Programming Precautions

Two features of QuickWin programming need to applied thoughtfully to avoid non-responsive programs that halt an application while waiting for a process to execute or input to be entered in a child window. The two features are described in the topics:

▶ Section 7.14.1 Blocking Procedures

▶ Section 7.14.2 Callback Routines

7.14.1   Blocking Procedures

Procedures that wait for an event before allowing the program to proceed, such as **READ** or **WAITONMOUSEEVENT**, both of which wait for user input, are called *blocking procedures* because they block execution of the program until the awaited event occurs. QuickWin child processes can contain multiple callback routines; for example, a different routine to be called for each menu selection and each kind of mouse-click (left button, right button, double-click, and so on).

Problems can arise when a process and its callback routine, or two callback routines within the same process, both contain blocking procedures. This is because each QuickWin child process supports a primary and secondary thread.

As a result of selecting a menu item, a menu procedure may call a blocking procedure, while the main thread of the process has also called a blocking procedure. For example, say you have created a file menu, which contains an option to LOAD a file. Selecting the LOAD menu option calls a blocking function that prompts for a filename and waits for the user to enter the name. However, a blocking call such as **WAITONMOUSEEVENT** can be pending in the main process thread when the user selects the LOAD menu option, so two blocking functions are initiated.

When QuickWin has two blocking calls pending, it displays a message in the status bar that corresponds to the blocking call first encountered. If there are further callbacks with other blocking procedures in the two threads, the status bar may not correspond to the actual input pending, execution can appear to be taking place in one thread when it is really blocked in another, and the application can be confusing and misleading to the user.

To avoid this confusion, you should try not to use blocking procedures in your callback routines. QuickWin will not accept more than one **READ** or **INCHARQQ** request through user callbacks from the same child window at one time. If one **READ** or **INCHARQQ** request is pending, subsequent **READ** or **INCHARQQ** requests will be ignored and -1 will be returned to the caller.

If you have a child window that in some user scenario might call multiple callback routines containing **READ** or **INCHARQQ** requests, you need to check the return value to make sure the request has been successful, and if not, take appropriate action, for example, request again.

This protective QuickWin behavior does not guard against multiple blocking calls through mouse selection of menu input options. As a general rule, using blocking procedures in callback routines is not advised, since the results can lead to program flow that is unexpected and difficult to interpret.

7.14.2 Callback Routines

All callback routines run in a separate thread from the main program. So, all multithread issues are in full force. In particular, sharing data, drawing to windows, and doing I/O must be properly coordinated and controlled. The Visual Fortran Sample POKER.F90 (in the . . . DF98\SAMPLES\QUICKWIN\ POKER folder) is a good example of how to control access to shared resources.

QuickWin callback routines, both for menu callbacks and mouse callbacks, should do a minimum of processing and then return. While processing a callback, the program will appear to be non-responsive because messages are not being serviced. This is why it is important to return quickly.

If more processing time is needed in a callback, another thread should be started to perform this work; threads can be created by calling the Win32 API CreateThread. (For more information on creating and using threads, see Chapter 19 Creating Multithread Applications.) If a callback routine does not start a new thread, the callback will not be reentered until it is done processing.

7.15   Simulating Nonblocking I/O

QuickWin does not accept unsolicited input. You get beeps if you type into an active window if no **READ** or **GETCHARQQ** has been done. Because of this, it is necessary to do a **READ** or **GETCHARQQ** in order for a character to be accepted. But this type of blocking I/O puts the program to sleep until a character has been typed.

In Fortran Console applications, **PEEKCHARQQ** can be used to see if a character has already been typed. However, **PEEKCHARQQ** does not work under Fortran QuickWin applications, since QuickWin has no console buffer to accept unsolicited input. Because of this limitation, **PEEKCHARQQ** cannot be used as it is with Fortran Console applications to see whether a character has already been typed.

One way to simulate **PEEKCHARQQ** with QuickWin applications is to use a multithread application. One thread does a **READ** or **GETCHARQQ** and is blocked until a character is typed. The other thread is in a loop doing useful work and checking in the loop to see if the other thread has received input.

For more information, see the Visual Fortran Samples PEEKAPP and PEEKAPP3 in the . . . DF98\SAMPLES\QUICKWIN folder.

8

Creating Fortran DLLs

A dynamic-link library (DLL) contains one or more subprogram procedures (functions or subroutines) that are compiled, linked, and stored separately from the applications using them. Because the functions or subroutines are separate from the applications using them, they can be shared or replaced easily.

Like a static library, a DLL is an executable file. Unlike a static library where routines are included in the base executable image during linking, the routines in a DLL are loaded when an application that references that DLL is loaded (run time). A DLL can also be used as a place to share data across processes.

The advantages of DLLs include:

▶ You can change the functions in a DLL without recompiling or relinking the applications that use them, as long as the functions' arguments and return types do not change.

This allows you to upgrade your applications easily. For example, a display driver DLL can be modified to support a display that was not available when your application was created.

▶ When general functions are placed in DLLs, the applications that share the DLLs can have very small executables.

▶ Multiple applications can access the same DLL.

This reduces the overall amount of memory needed in the system, which results in fewer memory swaps to disk and improves performance.

▶ Common blocks or module data placed in a DLL can be shared across multiple processes.

To build a DLL in the visual development environment, specify the Fortran Dynamic-Link Library project type. On the command line, specify the /dll option.

You cannot make a QuickWin application into a DLL (see Chapter 7 Using QuickWin) and QuickWin applications cannot be used with Fortran run-time routines in a DLL.

This chapter describes the following aspects of creating Fortran DLLs:

▶ Section 8.1 Coding Requirements for Sharing Procedures in DLLs

▶ Section 8.2 Coding Requirements for Sharing Data in DLLs

▶ Section 8.3 Building and Using Dynamic-Link Libraries

8.1   Coding Requirements for Sharing Procedures in DLLs

A dynamic-link library (DLL) contains one or more subprograms that are compiled, linked, and stored separately from the applications using them.

Coding requirements include using *c***DEC$ ATTRIBUTES** DLLIMPORT and DLLEXPORT compiler directives. Variables and routines declared in the main program and in the DLL are not visable to each another unless you use DLLIMPORT and DLLEXPORT.

This section discusses aspects of sharing subprogram procedures (functions and subroutines) in a Fortran DLL. To export and import each DLL subprogram:

1. Within your Fortran DLL, export each subprogram that will be used outside the DLL. Add a *c***DEC$ ATTRIBUTES** DLLEXPORT directive to declare that a function, subroutine, or data is being exported outside the DLL. For example:

```
SUBROUTINE ARRAYTEST(arr)
!DEC$ ATTRIBUTES DLLEXPORT :: ARRAYTEST
  REAL(4) arr(3, 7)
  INTEGER i, j
  DO i = 1, 3
    DO j = 1, 7
      arr (i, j) = 11.0 * i + j
    END DO
  END DO
END SUBROUTINE
```

2. Within your Fortran application, import each DLL subprogram. Add a c**DEC$ ATTRIBUTES** DLLIMPORT directive to declare that a function, subroutine, or data is being imported from outside the current image. For example:

```
INTERFACE
  SUBROUTINE ARRAYTEST (rarray)
  !DEC$ ATTRIBUTES DLLIMPORT :: ARRAYTEST
    REAL rarray(3, 7)
  END SUBROUTINE ARRAYTEST
END INTERFACE
```

The DLLEXPORT and DLLIMPORT options (for the c**DEC$ ATTRIBUTES** directive) define a DLL's interface.

The DLLEXPORT property declares that functions or data are being exported to other images or DLLs, usually eliminating the need for a Linker module definition (.DEF) file to export symbols for the functions or subroutines declared with DLLEXPORT. When you declare a function, subroutine, or data with the DLLEXPORT property, it must be defined in the same module of the same program.

A program that uses symbols defined in another image (such as a DLL) must import them. The DLL user needs to link with the import LIB file from the other image and use the DLLIMPORT property inside the application that imports the symbol. The DLLIMPORT option is used in a declaration, not a definition, because you do not define the symbol you are importing.

3. Build the DLL and then build the main program, as described in Section 8.3 Building and Using Dynamic-Link Libraries.

Fortran and C applications can call Fortran and C DLLs provided the calling conventions are consistent (see Chapter 18 Programming with Mixed Languages, especially Section 18.4 Visual Fortran/Visual C++ Mixed-Language Programs).

Visual Basic applications can also call Fortran functions and subroutines in the form of DLLs (see Chapter 18 Programming with Mixed Languages, especially Section 18.5.1 Calling Visual Fortran from Visual Basic).

For more information, see:

▶ About building DLLs, see Section 8.3 Building and Using Dynamic-Link Libraries.

▶ On sharing either common block or module data in a DLL, see Section 8.2 Coding Requirements for Sharing Data in DLLs.

▶ About importing and exporting subprograms using a Sample program, see the Visual Fortran Sample TLS in folder . . . `DF98\SAMPLES\ADVANCED\WIN32`.

8.2   Coding Requirements for Sharing Data in DLLs

A dynamic-link library (DLL) is an executable file that can be used as a place to share data across processes.

Coding requirements include using c**DEC$ ATTRIBUTES** DLLIMPORT and DLLEXPORT directives. Variables and routines declared in the program and in the DLL are not visible to each another unless you use DLLIMPORT and DLLEXPORT.

When sharing data among multiple threads or processes, do the following:

▶ Declare the order, size, and data types of shared data consistently in the DLL and in all procedures importing the DLL exported data.

▶ If more than one thread or process can write to the common block simultaneously, use the appropriate features of the Windows operating system to control access to the shared data. Such features on Windows NT systems include critical sections (for single process, multiple thread synchronization) and mutex objects (for multi-process synchronization).

Exporting and Importing Common Block Data

Data and code in a dynamic-link library is loaded into the same address space as the data and code of the program that calls it. However, variables and routines declared in the program and in the DLL are not visible to one another unless you use the c**DEC$ ATTRIBUTES** DLLIMPORT and DLLEXPORT compiler directives. These directives enable the compiler and linker to map to the correct portions of the address space so that the data and routines can be shared, allowing use of common block data across multiple images.

You can use DLLEXPORT to declare that a common block in a DLL is being exported to a program or another DLL. Similarly, you can use DLLIMPORT within a calling routine to tell the compiler that a common block is being imported from the DLL that defines it.

To export and import common block data:

1. Create a common block in the subprogram that will be built into a Fortran DLL. Export that common block with a c**DEC$ ATTRIBUTES** DLLEXPORT directive, followed by the **COMMON** statement, associated data declarations, and any procedure declarations to be exported. For example:

```
!DEC$ ATTRIBUTES DLLEXPORT :: /X/
   COMMON /X/ C, B, A
   REAL C, B, A
   END
      ...
```

If the Fortran DLL procedure contains only a common block declaration, you can use the **BLOCK DATA** statement:

```
   BLOCK DATA T
!DEC$ ATTRIBUTES DLLEXPORT :: /X/
   COMMON /X/ C, B, A
   REAL C, B, A
   END
```

The Fortran procedure to be linked into a DLL can contain a procedure, such as the following:

```
   SUBROUTINE SETA(I)
!DEC$ ATTRIBUTES DLLEXPORT :: SETA, /X/
     COMMON /X/ C, B, A
     REAL C, B, A
     INTEGER I
     A = A + 1.
     I = I + 1
     WRITE (6,*) 'In SETA subroutine, values of A and I:&
      & ' A, I
     RETURN
   END SUBROUTINE
```

2. Refer to the common block in the main image with a *d***DEC$ ATTRIBUTES** DLLIMPORT directive, followed by the local data declarations and any procedure declarations defined in the exported DLL. For example:

```
PROGRAM COMMONX
   INTERFACE
     SUBROUTINE SETA(I)
!DEC$ ATTRIBUTES DLLIMPORT:: SETA, /X/
       COMMON /X/ C, B, A
       REAL C, B, A, Q
       EQUIVALENCE (A,Q)
     END SUBROUTINE SETA
   END INTERFACE

  A = 0.
  I = 0
```

```
WRITE (6,*) 'In Main program before calling SETA...'
WRITE (6,*) 'values of A and I:' , A, I

CALL SETA(I)
WRITE (6,*) 'In Main program after calling SETA...'
WRITE (6,*) 'values of A and I:' , Q, I

A = A + 1.
I = I + 1
WRITE (6,*) 'In Main program after incrementing values'
END PROGRAM COMMONX
```

3. Build the DLL and then build the main program, as described in Section 8.3 Building and Using Dynamic-Link Libraries.

Exporting and Importing Data Objects in Modules

You can give data objects in a module the DLLEXPORT property, in which case the object is exported from a DLL.

When a module is used in other program units, through the **USE** statement, any objects in the module with the DLLEXPORT property are treated in the program using the module as if they were declared with the DLLIMPORT property. So, a main program that uses a module contained in a DLL has the correct import attributes for all objects exported from the DLL.

You can also give some objects in a module the DLLIMPORT property. Only procedure declarations in **INTERFACE** blocks and objects declared **EXTERNAL** or with c**DEC$ ATTRIBUTES** EXTERN can have the DLLIMPORT property. In this case, the objects are imported by any program unit using the module.

If you use a module that is part of a DLL and you use an object from that module that does not have the DLLEXPORT or DLLIMPORT property, the results are undefined.

For more information, see:

▶ On building a DLL, see Section 8.3 Building and Using Dynamic-Link Libraries.

▶ On multithread programming, see Chapter 19 Creating Multithread Applications.

8.3   Building and Using Dynamic-Link Libraries

A dynamic-link library is a collection of source and object code in the same manner as a static library. The differences between the two libraries are:

▶ The DLL requires an interface specification.

▶ The DLL is associated with a main project during execution, not during linking.

For more information, see:

▶ Section 8.3.1 Building Dynamic-Link Libraries

▶ Section 8.3.2 The DLL Build Output

▶ Section 8.3.3 Checking the DLL Symbol Export Table

▶ Section 8.3.4 Building Executables that Use DLLs

▶ Section 8.3.5 DLL Sample Programs

8.3.1   Building Dynamic-Link Libraries

When you first create a DLL, you follow the general steps described in Section 2.3 Defining Your Project. Select Fortran Dynamic-Link Library as the project type when you create a new project in the Microsoft visual development environment.

To debug a DLL, you must use a main program that calls the library routines (or references the data). From the Project Settings menu, choose the Debug tab. A dialog box is available for you to specify the executable for a debug session.

To build the DLL from the Microsoft visual development environment:

1. A Fortran DLL project is created like any other project, but you must specify Fortran Dynamic-Link Library as the project type (see Section 2.3 Defining Your Project).

2. Add files to your Fortran DLL project (see Section 2.3 Defining Your Project). Include the DLL Fortran source that exports procedures or data as a file in your project.

3. If your DLL exports data, for both the DLL and any image that references the DLL's exported data, consistently use the following project settings options in the Fortran Data category:

   ▶ Consistently specify whether padding is needed to ensure that exported data items are naturally aligned. In the Fortran Data compiler option category, specify the appropriate values for Common Element Alignment (common block data) and Structure Element Alignment (structures in a module). This sets the /alignment option.

▶ On Alpha systems, consistently specify the size of data that can be safely accessed from different threads. In the Fortran Data compiler option category, specify the appropriate value for Thread Access Granularity. This sets the /granularity option.

For example, in the case of a common block containing four-byte variables, in the Project Setting dialog box you might specify:

- Open the appropriate workspace
- From the Project menu, click Settings
- Click the Fortran tab
- Select the Fortran Data category
- In the Common Element Alignment box, specify 4.

4. Use the Project Settings dialog box (Settings in the Project menu) to check the settings in the Fortran tab for the Libraries category. In particular, the Use Multithreaded Library, Reentrancy Support and Use Fortran Run-Time Libraries settings must match the equivalent settings used by the executable program or other DLL that will call the Fortran DLL being built. If the calling program or DLL is written in Visual C++ in the Project Settings dialog box, click the C/C++ tab and check the category Code Generation for the item Use run-time libraries.

5. If you need to specify linker options, use the Linker tab of the Project Settings dialog box.

6. Build your Fortran DLL project.

The Microsoft visual development environment automatically selects the correct linker instructions for loading the proper run-time library routines (located in a DLL themselves). Your DLL is created as a multithread-enabled library. An import library (.LIB) is created for use when you link images that reference the DLL.

To build the DLL from the command line:

1. If you build a DLL from the command line or use an exported make-file, you must specify the /dll option. For example, if the Fortran DLL source code is in the file f90arr.f90, use the following command line:

```
DF /dll f90arr.f90
```

This command creates:

▶ A DLL named f90arr.dll.

▶ An import library, f90arr.lib, that you must link with applications that call your DLL.

If you also specify /exe:*file* or /link /out:*file*, you name a .DLL rather than an .EXE file (the default file extension becomes *projectname*.DLL instead of *projectname*.EXE)

The /dll option selects as the default the DLL run-time libraries to support multithreaded operation.

2. If your DLL will export data, the procedures must be compiled and linked consistently. Consistently use the following DF command options (or equivalent visual development environment options in the Fortran Data Compiler Option Category) for the DLL export procedure and the application that references (imports) it:

▶ Use the /alignment option consistently to specify whether padding is needed to ensure that common block data items are naturally aligned.

▶ On Alpha systems, use the /granularity option consistently to specify the size of data that can be safely accessed from different threads.

3. The /threaded, /reentrancy and /libs options must match the equivalent settings used by the executable program or other DLL that will call the Fortran DLL being built.

4. If you need to specify linker options, place them after the /link option on the DF command line.

5. Build the application.

For example, if your DLL exports a common block containing four-byte variables, you might use the following command line (specify the /dll option):

```
DF /align:commons /dll dllfile.for
```

The /dll option automatically selects the correct linker instructions for loading the proper run-time library routines (located in a DLL themselves). Your DLL is created as a multithread-enabled library.

8.3.2   The DLL Build Output

When a DLL is built, two library files are created:

▶ An import library (.LIB), which the linker uses to associate a main program with the DLL.

▶ The .DLL file containing the library's executable code.

Both files have the same basename as the library project by default.

Your library routines are contained in the file *projectname*.DLL located in the default directory for your project, unless you specified another name and location. Your import library file is *projectname*.LIB, located in the default directory for your project.

8.3.3 Checking the DLL Symbol Export Table

To make sure that everything that you want to be visible shows up in the export table, look at the export information of an existing DLL *file* by using QuickView in the Windows Explorer File menu or the following DUMPBIN command:

```
DUMPBIN /exports file.dll
```

8.3.4 Building Executables that Use DLLs

When you build the executable that imports the procedures or data defined in the DLL, you must link using the import library, check certain project settings or command-line options, copy the import library so the Linker can locate it, and then build the executable.

To use the DLL from another image:

1. Add the import .LIB file with its path and library name to the other image.

In the visual development environment, add the .LIB import library file to your project. In the Project menu, click Add to project, then Files.

On the command line, specify the .LIB file on the command line.

The import .LIB file contains information that your program needs to work with the DLL.

2. If your DLL exports data, consistently use the same project settings options in the Fortran Data category (the /alignment option) as was used to create the DLL:

► Consistently specify whether padding is needed to ensure that imported data items are naturally aligned. In the Fortran Data compiler option category, specify the appropriate values for Common Element Alignment (common block data) and Structure Element Alignment (structures in a module). This sets the /alignment option.

► On Alpha systems, consistently specify the size of data that can be safely accessed from different threads. In the Fortran Data compiler option category, specify the appropriate value for Thread Access Granularity. This sets the /granularity option.

3. Make sure the type of library specified is consistent with that specified for the Fortran DLL. In the visual development environment, check the Project Settings dialog box, Fortran tab, Libraries category. From the command-line, check the /threaded, /reentrancy and /libs options.

4. If you need to specify linker options:

   ▶ In the visual development environment, specify linker options in the Linker tab of the Project Settings dialog box.

   ▶ On the DF command line, place linker options after the /link option.

5. Copy the DLL into your path.

   For an application to access your DLL, it must be located in a directory on the search path or in the same directory as the main project. If you have more than one program accessing your DLL, you can keep it in a convenient directory identified in the environment path. If you have several DLLs, you can place them all in the same directory to avoid adding numerous directories to the path specification.

   When changing your path specification in Windows 95 or Windows 98, you must restart the operating system for the change to take effect. In the Windows NT system, you should log out and back in after modifying the system path.

6. Build the image that references the DLL.

   When using the visual development environment:

   ▶ Make sure you have added the import library (created when you built the DLL file) to the project (click the FileView tab).

   ▶ Like building other projects in the visual development environment, use the Build menu items to create the executable (see Section 2.3 Defining Your Project).

   When using the command line:

   ▶ Specify the import library at the end of the command line.

   ▶ If your DLL exports data that will be used by the application being built, specify the same /alignment options that were used to build the DLL.

   ▶ If you are building a main application, omit the /dll option.

   ▶ When building a Fortran DLL that references another DLL, specify the /dll option.

For example, to build the main application from the command line that references 4-byte items in a common block defined in dllfile.dll:

```
DF /align:commons mainapp.f90 dllfile.lib
```

8.3.5 DLL Sample Programs

Visual Fortran provides Sample programs that are installed in . . . `DF98\SAMPLES\` when you request the Samples with a custom installation. You can copy the Samples folders from the . . . `DF\SAMPLES\` folder on the Visual Fortran CD-ROM to your hard disk.

For an example of a DLL, see the Samples folder . . . `DF98\SAMPLES\ADVANCED\WIN32\TLS`, which creates a DLL as a subproject. The subproject DLL is used in a second project.

Other Samples that use DLLs are folders in . . . `DF98\SAMPLES\DLL\`. For example, the files associated with Sample DLLEXP2 are in the folder . . . `DF98\SAMPLES\DLL\DLLEXP2\`. To build DLLEXP2, use the makefile.

For a description of all Samples, in a Web browser:

▶ If Samples were installed, open the file Samples.htm in . . . `DF98\SAMPLES\` on your disk

▶ Open the file Samples.htm in . . . `DF\SAMPLES\` on the Visual Fortran CD-ROM

9

Creating Windows Applications

With Visual Fortran, you can build Fortran applications that are also fully-featured Windows applications. You can create full Windows applications that use the familiar Windows interface, complete with tool bars, pull-down menus, dialog boxes, and other features. You can include data entry and mouse control, and interaction with programs written in other languages or commercial programs such as Microsoft Excel.

With full Windows programming you can:

▶ Deliver Fortran applications with a Windows Graphical User Interface (GUI). GUI applications typically use at least the GDI and USER32 Win32 routines.

▶ Access all available Windows Graphic Device Interface (GDI) calls with your Fortran applications. GDI functions use a 32-bit coordinate system, allowing coordinates in the +/-2 GB range, and performs skewing, reflection, rotation, and shearing.

The Win32 Application Programming Interface (API) routines provide sophisticated window management, memory management, graphics support, threading, security, and networking (these routines are described in the Platform SDK online document).

You can access many Win32 APIs from any Fortran application, including Fortran Console and Fortran QuickWin applications. Only the Fortran Windows project type provides access to the full set of Win32 routines needed to create GUI applications. Windows projects are much more complex than other kinds of Visual Fortran projects. Before attempting to use the full capabilities of Windows programming, you should be comfortable with writing C applications and should familiarize yourself with the Win32 Software Development Kit (SDK).

Fortran Console projects usually use limited graphics. Fortran QuickWin projects let you build Windows style applications easily, but access only a small subset of the available Win32 API features. For differences between Fortran QuickWin and Fortran Windows projects, see Section 7.2 Comparing QuickWin with Windows-Based Applications.

To build your application as a Fortran Windows application in the visual development environment, choose Fortran Windows Application from the list of Project types when you open a new project.

When using the command line, specify the /winapp option to search the commonly used link libraries.

Fortran Windows applications must use the DFWIN module or subset of DFWIN (see Section 9.1 Coding Requirements for Fortran Windows Applications). If you specify **USE DFWIN** and unresolved references occur when linking your Fortran Windows application in the visual development environment or when using the command-line option /winapp, consider adding the . . . DF98\INCLUDE\FULLAPI.F90 file to your project.

The following Fortran Windows application topics are discussed in this chapter:

▶ Section 9.1 Coding Requirements for Fortran Windows Applications

▶ Section 9.2 The Visual Fortran Windows Module

▶ Section 9.3 Sample Fortran Windows Applications

▶ Section 9.4 Getting Help with Windows Programming

9.1   Coding Requirements for Fortran Windows Applications

Coding requirements for Fortran Windows applications include (in the following order):

1. WinMain function declaration and interface

The WinMain function declaration and interface are required for Windows Graphical User Interface (GUI) applications (typically use at least the GDI and USER32 Win32 routines). An interface block for the function declaration can be provided. On *x86* systems, the following function must be defined by the user:

```
      INTEGER(4) function WinMain ( hInstance, hPrevInstance, &
            & lpszCmdLine, nCmdShow )
!DEC$ ATTRIBUTES STDCALL, ALIAS:'_WinMain@16' :: WinMain
      INTEGER(4), INTENT(IN) :: hInstance, hPrevInstance
      INTEGER(4), INTENT(IN) :: lpszCmdLine
      INTEGER(4), INTENT(IN) :: nCmdShow
```

In a program that includes a WinMain function, no program unit can be identified as the main program with the **PROGRAM** statement.

2. The statement **USE DFWIN**

The **USE DFWIN** statement makes all parameters and interfaces for most Windows routines available to your Visual Fortran program. Any program or subprogram that uses the Windows features must include the statement **USE DFWIN**, which must appear in each subprogram that makes graphics calls, before any declaration statements (such as **IMPLICIT NONE** or **INTEGER**) or any other modules containing declaration statements.

If you use **USE DFWIN** and unresolved references occur when linking your Fortran Windows application in the visual development environment or when using the command-line option /winapp, consider adding the . . . DF98\INCLUDE\FULLAPI.F90 file to your project. This file contains search directives for almost all of the libraries needed.

If you want to limit the type of parameters and interfaces for Windows applications, you can instead include only the subsets of the Win32 API needed in multiple **USE** statements, instead of **USE WIN32**, which includes all parameters and interfaces for Windows applications (see the file . . . DF98\INCLUDED\FWIN.F90).

3. Data declarations for the WinMain function arguments.

4. Application-dependent code (other **USE** statements, variable declarations, and then executable code).

For example, the first lines of the Visual Fortran Sample named Generic uses the following free-form source code and conditional x86 and Alpha code:

```
integer function WinMain( hInstance, hPrevInstance, &
& lpszCmdLine, nCmdShow )
!DEC$ IF DEFINED(_X86_)
!DEC$ ATTRIBUTES STDCALL, ALIAS : '_WinMain@16' :: WinMain
!DEC$ ELSE
!DEC$ ATTRIBUTES STDCALL, ALIAS : 'WinMain' :: WinMain
!DEC$ ENDIF
use dfwin
```

```
integer hInstance
integer hPrevInstance
integer nCmdShow
integer lpszCmdLine
   .
   .
   .
```

This Sample uses the **IF** Directive Construct and a predefined preprocessor symbol (see the /define compiler option) to generate portable conditional code.

DFWIN.F90 is a Fortran version (a subset) of the Win32 WINDOWS.H header file (see Section 9.2 The Visual Fortran Windows Module).

9.2   The Visual Fortran Windows Module

DFWIN.F90 is a Fortran version (a subset) of the Win32 WINDOWS.H header file. The correspondence of data types is given in Table 9-1.

Table 9–1   *Win32 and Equivalent Fortran Data Types*

Win32 Data Type	*Equivalent Fortran Data Type*
BOOL, BOOLEAN	LOGICAL(4)
BYTE	BYTE
CHAR, CCHAR, UCHAR	CHARACTER
COLORREF	INTEGER(4)
DWORD, INT, LONG, ULONG	INTEGER(4)
SHORT, USHORT, WORD	INTEGER(2)
FLOAT	REAL(4)
All Handles	INTEGER(4)
All Pointers (LP*, P*)	INTEGER(4) (Integer Pointers)

The structures in WINDOWS.H have been converted to derived types in DFWIN.F90. Unions in structures are converted to union/maps within the derived type. Names of components are unchanged. Bit fields are converted to Fortran's **INTEGER**(4) data type. Functions accessing bit fields are contained in the DFWIN.F90 module with names of the form:

structurename$bitfieldname

These functions take an integer argument and return an integer. All bit fields are unsigned integers. The following is an example of the translation from Win32 structures to Fortran derived types.

WINDOWS.H Definition

```
typedef struct _LDT_ENTRY {
  WORD LimitLow;
  WORD BaseLow;
  union {
    struct {
      BYTE BaseMid;
      BYTE Flags1;
      BYTE Flags2;
      BYTE BaseHi;
      } Bytes;
    struct {
      DWORD BaseMid : 8;
      DWORD Type : 5;
      DWORD Opl : 2;
      DWORD Pres : 1;
      DWORD LimitHi : 4;
      DWORD Sys : 1;
      DWORD Reserved_0 : 1;
      DWORD Default_Big : 1;
      DWORD Granularity : 1;
      DWORD BaseHi : 8;
    } Bits;
  } HighWord;
} LDT_ENTRY, *PLDT_ENTRY;
```

Fortran Definition

```
type LDT_ENTRY$HIGHWORD_BYTES
    BYTE BaseMid
    BYTE Flags1
    BYTE Flags2
    BYTE BaseHi
end type

type LDT_ENTRY$HIGHWORD
    union
      map
          type( LDT_ENTRY$HIGHWORD_BYTES) Bytes
      end map
      map
          INTEGER(4) Bits
      end map
    end union
end type

type LDT_ENTRY
    INTEGER(2) LimitLow
    INTEGER(2) BaseLow
    type(LDT_ENTRY$HIGHWORD) HighWord
end type

INTEGER(4) function LDT_ENTRY$BaseMid( Bits )
INTEGER(4) Bits
LDT_ENTRY$BaseMid = IAND( Bits, #ff )
end
INTEGER(4) function LDT_ENTRY$Type( Bits )
INTEGER(4) Bits
LDT_ENTRY$Type = IAND( ISHFT( Bits, -8 ), #1f )
end
...
```

Note that _LDT_ENTRY and PLDT_ENTRY do not exist in the Fortran definition. Also note that Bits.xxx is not the same as the C version. In the Fortran case, the bit field functions must be used. For example, the C variable:

`yyy.HighWord.Bits.BaseHi`

is replaced with the Fortran variable:

`LDT_ENTRY$BaseHi( yyy.HighWord.Bits )`

All macros in the WINDOWS.H file are converted to functions in the DFWIN.F90 module. The object modules that this conversion creates are in DFWIN.LIB in the LIB directory.

9.3   Sample Fortran Windows Applications

The Visual Fortran Samples . . . `DF98\SAMPLES\ADVANCED` folder contains many Fortran Windows applications that demonstrate Windows functionality or a particular Win32 function. Each sample application is in separate folder.

Users unfamiliar with full Windows applications should start by looking at the sample programs in . . . `DF98\SAMPLES\ADVANCED\WIN32`, such as PLATFORM or POLYDRAW.

9.4   Getting Help with Windows Programming

In HTMLHelp Viewer, you can access the folder "Platform SDK Documentation."

The full Win32 API set is documented in the *Win32 Application Programming Interface for Windows NT Programmer's Reference*, available from Microsoft Press® and also distributed as part of the Windows NT Software Development Kit.

10

Portability and Design Considerations

Before you can start to write new programs or port existing ones to Visual Fortran, you must decide what to build and how to build it. This chapter covers the following topics:

▶ Section 10.1 Portability considerations

▶ Section 10.2 Choosing Your Development Environment with Visual Fortran

▶ Section 10.3 Selecting a Program Type that you can build

▶ Section 10.4 Structuring Your Program

▶ Section 10.5 Special Design Considerations

▶ Section 10.6 Using the Special Features of Microsoft Windows with your programs

10.1   Portability

This section presents topics to help you understand how language standards, operating system differences, and computing hardware influence your use of Visual Fortran and the portability of your programs.

Your program is portable if you can implement it on one hardware-software platform and then move it to additional systems with a minimum of changes to the source code. Correct results on the first system should be correct on the additional systems. The number of changes you might have to make when moving your program varies significantly. You might have no changes at all (strictly portable), or so many (non-portable customization) that it is more efficient to design or implement a new program. Most programs in their lifetime will need to be ported from one system to another, and this section can help you write code that makes this easy.

For information on special library routines to help port your program from one system to another, see Chapter 15 Portability Library.

For more information, see:

▶ Section 10.1.1 Standard Fortran Language

▶ Section 10.1.2 Operating System

▶ Section 10.1.3 Storage and Representation of Data

10.1.1   Standard Fortran Language

A language standard specifies the form and establishes the interpretation of programs expressed in the language. Its primary purpose is to promote, among vendors and users, portability of programs across a variety of systems.

The vendor-user community has adopted four major Fortran language standards. ANSI (American National Standards Institute) and ISO (International Standards Organization) are the primary organizations that develop and publish the standards.

The major Fortran language standards are:

▶ FORTRAN IV

American National Standard Programming Language FORTRAN, ANSI X3.9-1966. This was the first attempt to standardize the languages called FORTRAN by many vendors.

▶ FORTRAN 77

American National Standard Programming Language FORTRAN, ANSI X3.9-1978. This standard added new features based on vendor extensions to FORTRAN IV and addressed problems associated with large-scale projects, such as improved control structures.

▶ Fortran 90

American National Standard Programming Language Fortran, ANSI X3.198-1992 and International Standards Organization, ISO/IEC 1539: 1991, Information technology—Programming languages—Fortran. This standard emphasizes modernization of the language by introducing new developments. For information about differences between Fortran 90 and

FORTRAN 77, see "Features of Fortran 90" in the *Language Reference* in Visual Fortran online Help or the printed *Digital Fortran Language Reference Manual*.

▶ Fortran 95

American National Standard Programming Language Fortran and International Standards Organization, ISO/IEC 1539: 1995, Information technology—Programming languages—Fortran. This recent standard introduces certain language elements and corrections into Fortran 90. Fortran 95 includes Fortran 90 and most features of FORTRAN 77. For information about differences between Fortran 95 and Fortran 90, see "Features of Fortran 95" in the *Language Reference* in Visual Fortran online Help or the printed *Digital Fortran Language Reference Manual*.

Although a language standard seeks to define the form and the interpretation uniquely, a standard might not cover all areas of interpretation. It might also include some ambiguities. You need to carefully craft your program in these cases so that you get the answers that you want when producing a portable program.

For more information, see:

▶ Section 10.1.1.1 Standard vs. Extensions

▶ Section 10.1.1.2 Compiler Optimizations

10.1.1.1 *Standard vs. Extensions*

Use standard features to achieve the greatest degree of portability for your Visual Fortran programs. You can design a robust implementation to improve the portability of your program, or you can choose to use extensions to the standard to increase the readability, functionality, and efficiency of your programs. You can ensure your program enforces the Fortran standard by using the /stand:f90 or /stand:f95 compiler option to flag extensions.

Not all extensions will cause problems in porting to other platforms. Many extensions are supported on a wide range of platforms, and if a system you are porting a program to supports an extension, there is no reason to avoid using it. There is no guarantee, however, that the same feature on another system will be implemented in the same way as it is in Visual Fortran. Only the Fortran standard is guaranteed to coexist uniformly on all platforms.

Digital Fortran supports many language extensions on multiple platforms, including Digital Alpha systems. For information on compatibility with Digital Fortran on Alpha systems, see Section B.2 Compatibility with Digital Fortran on Other Platforms. Also, the printed *Digital Fortran Language Reference Manual* identifies whether each language element is supported on other Digital Fortran platforms.

It is a good programming practice to declare any external procedures either in an **EXTERNAL** statement or in a procedure interface block, for the following reasons:

▶ The Fortran 90 standard added many new intrinsic procedures to the language. Programs that conformed to the FORTRAN 77 standard may include nonintrinsic functions or subroutines having the same name as new Fortran 90 procedures.

▶ Some processors include nonstandard intrinsic procedures that might conflict with procedure names in your program.

If you do not explicitly declare the external procedures and the name duplicates an intrinsic procedure, the processor calls the intrinsic procedure, not your external routine. For more information on how the Fortran compiler resolves name definitions, see "Resolving Procedure References" in the *Language Reference* in Visual Fortran online Help.

10.1.1.2 *Compiler Optimizations*

Many Fortran compilers perform code-generation optimizations to increase the speed of execution or to decrease the required amount of memory for the generated code. Although the behaviors of both the optimized and nonoptimized programs fall within the language standard specification, different behaviors can occur in areas not covered by the language standard. Compiler optimization especially can influence floating-point numeric results.

The Digital Visual Fortran compiler can perform optimizations to increase execution speed and to improve floating-point numerical consistency. For a summary of optimization levels, see Section 6.7 Optimization Levels: the /optimize Option.

Floating-point consistency refers to obtaining results consistent with the IEEE binary floating-point standards (see Section 4.1.30 /[no]fltconsistency option, (*x*86 Only)).

Unless you properly design your code, you might encounter numerical difficulties when you optimize for fastest execution. The /nofltconsistency option uses the floating-point registers, which have a higher precision than stored variables, whenever possible. This tends to produce results that are inconsistent with the precision of stored variables. The /fltconsistency option (also set by /Oxp) can improve the consistency of generated code by rounding results of statement evaluations to the precision of the standard data types, but it does produce slower execution times.

10.1.2 Operating System

The operating system envelops your program and influences it both externally and internally. To achieve portability, you need to minimize the amount of operating-system-specific information required by your program. The Fortran language standards do not specify this information.

Operating-system-specific information consists of nonintrinsic extensions to the language, compiler and linker options, and possibly the graphical user interface of Windows. Input and output operations use devices that may be system-specific, and may involve a file system with system-specific record and file structures.

The operating system also governs resource management and error handling. You can depend on default resource management and error handling mechanisms or provide mechanisms of your own. For information on special library routines to help port your program from one system to another, see Chapter 15 Portability Library.

The minimal interaction with the operating system is for input/output operations and usually consists of knowing the standard units preconnected for input and output. You can use default file units with the asterisk (*) unit specifier.

To increase the portability of your programs across operating systems, consider the following:

▶ Do not assume the use of a particular type of file system.

▶ Do not embed filenames or paths in the body of your program. Define them as constants at the beginning of the program or read them from input data.

▶ Do not assume a particular type of standard I/O device or the "size" of that device (number of rows and columns).

▶ Do not assume display attributes for the standard I/O device. Some environments do not support attributes such as color, underlined text, blinking text, highlighted text, inverse text, protected text, or dim text.

10.1.3 Storage and Representation of Data

The Fortran language standard specifies little about the storage of data types. This loose specification of storage for data types results from a great diversity of computing hardware. This diversity poses problems in representing data and especially in transporting stored data among a multitude of systems.

The size (as measured by the number of bits) of a storage unit (a word, usually several bytes) varies from machine to machine. In addition, the ordering of bits within bytes and bytes within words varies from one machine to another. Furthermore, binary representations of negative integers and floating-point representations of real and complex numbers take several different forms.

If you are careful, you can avoid most of the problems involving data storage. The simplest and most reliable means of transferring data between dissimilar systems is in character and not binary form. Simple programming practices ensure that your data as well as your program is portable.

For more information, see:

▶ Section 10.1.3.1 Size of Basic Types

▶ Section 10.1.3.2 Bit, Byte, and Word Characteristics

▶ Section 10.1.3.3 Transportability of Data

10.1.3.1 Size of Basic Types

Table 10-1 shows the sizes for the intrinsic data types: **INTEGER**, **REAL**, **LOGICAL**, **COMPLEX**, and **CHARACTER**.

Table 10–1 *Data Types and Storage Sizes*

Types	*Number of Bytes*
INTEGER(1), LOGICAL (1), CHARACTER	1
INTEGER(2), LOGICAL(2)	2
INTEGER, LOGICAL, REAL	Depending on default integer size (set by the /integer_size compiler option or equivalent directive) , INTEGER and LOGICAL can have 2, 4, or (on Alpha systems only) 8 bytes; default allocation is 4 bytes. Depending on default real size (set by the /real_size compiler option or equivalent directive), REAL can have 4 or 8 bytes; default allocation is 4 bytes.
INTEGER(4), REAL(4), LOGICAL(4)	4
INTEGER(8), LOGICAL (8) (Alpha only)	8

Table 10–1 *Data Types and Storage Sizes (Continued)*

Types	Number of Bytes
COMPLEX	Depending on default real, COMPLEX can have 8 or 16 bytes; default allocation is 8 bytes.
DOUBLE PRECISION, REAL(8), COMPLEX(8)	8
DOUBLE COMPLEX, COMPLEX(16)	16
CHARACTER(n)	n
Structures	Size of derived type (can be affected by *c*DEC$ PACK directive)
RECORD	Size of record structure (can be affected by *c*DEC$ PACK directive)

Structures and the **RECORD** statement are Digital Fortran language extensions.

10.1.3.2 Bit, Byte, and Word Characteristics

In a 32-bit word environment such as that of Visual Fortran, it might seem as though there should be no problems with data storage, since all data types are consecutive subcomponents (bytes) of a word or are consecutive, multiple words. However, when transporting binary data among disparate systems—either by intermediate storage medium (disk, tape) or by direct connection (serial port, network)—problems arise from different definitions of serial bit and serial byte order.

For simplicity, the following discussion considers only byte order within a word, since that is the usual case of difficulty. (For more information, refer to "On Holy Wars and a Plea for Peace" by Danny Cohen, *IEEE Computer*, vol. 14, pp. 48-54, 1981.)

Big End or Little End Ordering

Computer memory is a linear sequence of bits organized into a hierarchical structure of bytes and words. One system is the "Big End," where bits and bytes are numbered starting at the most significant bit (MSB, "left," or high end). Another system is the "Little End," where bits and bytes start at the least significant bit (LSB, "right," or low end). Figure 10-1 illustrates the difference between the two conventions for the case of addressing bytes within words.

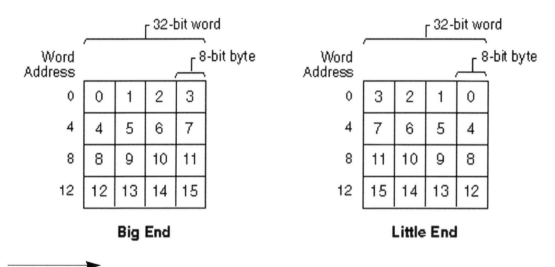

Figure 10–1 *Byte Order within Words: (left) Big End, (right) Little End*

Data types stored as subcomponents (bytes stored in words) end up in different locations within corresponding words of the two conventions. Figure 10-2 illustrates the difference between the representation of several data types in the two conventions. Letters represent 8-bit character data, while numbers represent the 8-bit partial contribution to 32-bit integer data.

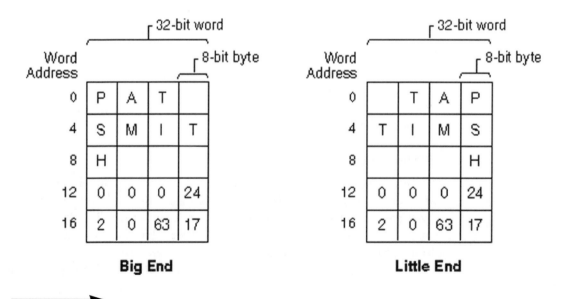

Figure 10–2 *Character and Integer Data in Words: (left) Big End, (right) Little End*

If you serially transfer bytes now from the Big End words to the Little End words (BE byte 0 to LE byte 0, BE byte 1 to LE byte 1, . . .), the left half of the figure shows how the data ends up in the Little End words. Note that data of size one byte (characters in this case) is ordered correctly, but that integer data no longer correctly represents the original binary values. The right half of the figure shows that you need to swap bytes around the middle of the word to reconstitute the correct 32-bit integer values. After swapping bytes, the two preceding figures are identical, as shown in Figure 10-3.

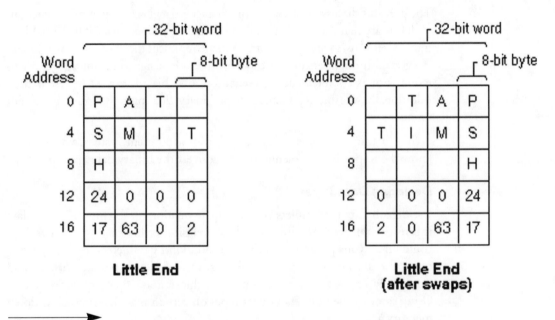

Figure 10–3   *Data Sent from Big to Little: (left) After Transfer, (right) After Byte Swaps*

You can generalize the previous example to include floating-point data types and to include multiple-word data types. Table 10-2 summarizes the ordering nature of several common processors.

Table 10–2   *Ordering Nature of Processors*

Processor	Byte Order	Bit Order
Intel® 80486, Pentium®, Series Pro	Little	Little
Digital Alpha and VAX™	Little	Little
Motorola® 680XX	Big	Little
IBM® Mainframes	Big	Big

The important result is that portable, serial transport of 8-bit character data between most systems is possible with little or no knowledge about the ordering nature of each system.

For more information on big and little endian data and Visual Fortran unformatted data conversion capabilities, see Chapter 23 Converting Unformatted Numeric Data.

Binary Representations

The previous discussion stresses 8-bit character data because you might encounter hardware that uses a different representation of binary data. The Visual Fortran system uses the two's-complement representation of negative binary integers. You might encounter a system that uses a signed magnitude representation, a one's complement representation, or a biased (excess) representation. Additionally, the bit representation of binary floating-point numbers is not unique.

If you transport binary data to or from a different system, you need to know the respective representations to convert the binary data appropriately.

Declaring Data Types

Use default data types unless you anticipate memory problems, or if your data is sensitive to overflow limits. If data precision errors or numeric overflow could affect your program, specify type and kind parameters for the intrinsic types as well as for declared data objects. Default data types are portable and are usually aligned by the compiler to achieve good memory access speed. Using some of the nondefault data types on certain machines may slow down memory access.

10.1.3.3 Transportability of Data

You can achieve the highest transportability of your data by formatting it as 8-bit character data. Use a standard character set such as the ASCII standard for encoding your character data. Although this practice is less efficient than using binary data, it will save you from shuffling and converting your data.

If you are transporting your data by means of a record-structured medium, it is best to use the Fortran sequential formatted (as character data) form. You can also use the direct formatted form, but you need to know the record length of your data. Remember also that some systems use a carriage return-linefeed pair as an end-of-record indicator, while other systems use linefeed only. If you use either the direct unformatted or the sequential unformatted form, there might be system-dependent values embedded within your data that complicate its transport.

Implementing a strictly portable solution requires a careful effort. Maximizing portability may also mean making compromises to the efficiency and functionality of your solution. If portability is not your highest priority, you can use some of the techniques that appear in later sections to ease your task of customizing a solution.

For more information on big and little endian data and unformatted data conversion, see Chapter 23 Converting Unformatted Numeric Data.

10.2 Choosing Your Development Environment

With Visual Fortran, you can build programs either from a console-line window (which allows you to enter text commands directly into a command prompt) or from the Microsoft visual development environment.

For information on using the Microsoft visual development environment, see Chapter 2 Building Programs and Libraries. For information on using the command-line environment, see Chapter 3 Using the Compiler and Linker from the Command Line.

The visual development environment offers a number of ways to simplify the task of compiling and linking programs. For example, a dialog box presents compiler and linker options in logical groupings, with descriptive names and simple mouse or keyboard selection methods. (If you need assistance using this or any other dialog box, choose the Help button in the dialog box.)

The visual development environment also provides a default text editor, which is integrated with Help, the debugger, and error tracking features. The default visual development environment text editor can be customized for keyboard compatibility with certain editors (in the Tools menu, select Customize and click the Compatibilty tab) and you can customize keyboard bindings (in the Tools menu, select Customize and click the Keyboard tab). You can also use your favorite ASCII text editor outside the visual development environment. If you do, however, you may not be able to use the integrated Help, debugger, and error tracking features.

Because software development is an iterative process, it is important to be able to move quickly and efficiently to various locations in your source code. If you use the visual development environment to compile and link your programs, you can call up both the description of the error message and the relevant source code directly from the error messages in the output window.

You also use the visual development environment text editor to view and control execution of your program with the integrated source level debugger. Finally, when you use the project browser to locate routines, data elements, and references to them, the visual development environment uses its editor to go directly to the source code.

When you build programs from the console, you are in complete control of the build tools. If you choose to, you can customize how your program is built by your selection of compiler and linker options. Compiler and linker options are described in Chapter 4 Compiler and Linker Options.

Even if you choose to edit and build your program from the command line, you can still use the visual development environment debugger and browser after your program has compiled and linked cleanly (see Section 5.1 Preparing Your Program for Debugging). Finally, you can run the profiler to produce a text report of your program's execution statistics either from the command console or from the visual development environment.

10.3   Selecting a Program Type

When you create a new project, you need to select the appropriate Fortran project type. You can build four basic kinds of executable programs:

▶ Fortran Console applications

▶ Fortran Standard graphics applications

▶ Fortran QuickWin graphics applications

▶ Fortran Windows applications

In addition, you can create library projects that contains subprograms (functions or subroutines) called from your main application:

▶ Static libraries

▶ Dynamic-Link Libraries (DLLs)

Code that works in one application may not work in others. For example, graphics calls are not appropriate in a Fortran console application.

Fortran console applications are the most portable to other systems because they are text-only and do not support graphics.

With Fortran standard graphics (QuickWin single document) applications, you can add graphics to your text without the additional overhead of menus and other interface features of typical programs for Windows. Fortran QuickWin (QuickWin multiple document) graphics applications provide a simple way to use some features of Windows in a Visual Fortran program with graphics.

Fortran Windows applications give users full access to the Win32 Application Programming Interface (API), giving you a larger set of functions than QuickWin offers. With Windows applications, you can access low-level system services directly, or access higher level system services such as OpenGL.

None of the graphics functions in Visual Fortran, except for those in the OpenGL library, are directly portable to operating systems offered by other vendors. A graphical interface does, however, offer certain advantages to the application designer and to the person who will use the program. The choice of what kind of program to build is a trade-off between performance, portability, ease of coding, and ease of use. The advantages and disadvantages of each type of application are summarized in the following sections.

All four kinds of main applications can be maximized, minimized, resized, and moved around the screen when displayed in a window. If the drawing area of a window in your application is larger than the window in which it is displayed, scroll bars are automatically added to the bottom and right edges of the window.

You can write any of the applications with one section of the program beginning execution before another has completed. These threads of execution run either concurrently on a computer with one processor or simultaneously on a computer with multiple processors. (See Chapter 19 Creating Multithread Applications.)

For more information on the Visual Fortran application project types, see Section 2.2 Types of Projects.

10.4   Structuring Your Program

There are several ways to organize your projects and the applications that you build with Visual Fortran. This section introduces several of these options and offers suggestions for when you might want to use them.

For more information, see:

▶ Section 10.4.1 Creating Fortran Executables

▶ Section 10.4.2 Advantages of Modules

▶ Section 10.4.3 Advantages of Internal Procedures

▶ Section 10.4.4 Storing Object Code in Static Libraries

▶ Section 10.4.5 Storing Routines in Dynamic-Link Libraries

10.4.1 Creating Fortran Executables

The simplest way to build an application is to compile all of your Visual Fortran source files (.FOR) and then link the resulting object files (.OBJ) into a single executable file (.EXE). You can build single-file executables either with the visual development environment or by using the DF (or FL32) command from the console command line.

The executable file you build with this method contains all of the code needed to execute the program, including the run-time library. Because the program resides in a single file, it is easy to copy or install. However, the project contains all of the source and object files for the routines that you used to build the application. If you need to use some of these routines in other projects, you must link all of them again.

10.4.2 Advantages of Modules

One way to reduce potential confusion when you use the same source code in several projects is to organize the routines into modules. There are two main uses for modules in Visual Fortran:

▶ Internal encapsulation—A single complex program can be made up of many modules. Each module can be a self-contained entity, incorporating all the procedures and data required for one of your program's tasks. When a task is encapsulated, it is easy to share the code between two different projects.

  In this case, all the modules should be included in the main project directory. If many projects all share the same module, the module should reside in only one directory. All projects that use it should specify the /I compiler option to indicate the location of the module.

▶ External modules—If you use a module provided from an outside source, you need only the .MOD file at compile time, and the .OBJ file at link time. Use the /[no]include[*path*] (or /I*path*) command line option (or the INCLUDE environment variable) to specify the location of these files, which will probably not be the same as your project directory.

During the building of a project, the compiler scans the project files for dependencies. If you specify the /[no]include[*path*] (or /I*path*) command line option or the INCLUDE environment variable, the compiler is able to find the external modules.

Store precompiled module files, with the extension .MOD, in a directory included in the path. When the compiler sees the **USE** statement in a program, it finds the module based on the name given in the **USE** statement, so there is no need to maintain several copies of the same source or object code.

Modules are excellent ways to organize programs. You can set up separate modules for:

▶ Commonly used routines

▶ Data definitions specific to certain operating systems

▶ System-dependent language extensions

10.4.3 Advantages of Internal Procedures

Functions or subroutines that are used in only one program can be organized as internal procedures, following the **CONTAINS** statement of a program or module.

Internal procedures have the advantage of host association, that is, variables declared and used in the main program are also available to any internal procedure it may contain. For more information on procedures and host association, see "Program Units and Procedures" in the *Language Reference* in Visual Fortran online Help.

Internal procedures, like modules, provide a means of encapsulation. Where modules can be used to store routines commonly used by many programs, internal procedures separate functions and subroutines whose use is limited or temporary.

10.4.4 Storing Object Code in Static Libraries

Another way to organize source code used by several projects is to build a static library (.LIB) containing the object files for the reused procedures. You can create a static library:

▶ From the visual development environment, build a Fortran Static Library project type.

▶ From the command line, use the LIB command.

After you have created a static library, you can use it to build any of the other types of Visual Fortran projects.

For more information, see Section 2.2.5 Fortran Static Library Projects.

10.4.5 Storing Routines in Dynamic-Link Libraries

Another method of organizing the code in your application involves storing the executable code for certain routines in a separate file called a Dynamic-Link Library (DLL) and building your applications so that they call these routines from the DLL.

When routines in a DLL are called, the routines are loaded into memory at run-time as they are needed. This is most useful when several applications use a common group of routines. By storing these common routines in a DLL, you reduce the size of each application that calls the DLL. In addition, you can update the routines in the DLL without having to rebuild any of the applications that call the DLL.

For more information on compiler and linker options and how to build a project, see Section 2.2.6 Fortran Dynamic-Link Library Projects.

10.5   Special Design Considerations

You can write your code any way you want if you plan to run it on a single computer, use only one variation of one programming language, and never hand your code to anyone else. If any of these assumptions changes, there are several other issues to consider when you design your program.

For more information, see:

▶ Section 10.5.1 Porting Fortran Source between Systems

▶ Section 10.5.2 Mixed-Language Issues

▶ Section 10.5.3 Porting Data between Systems

10.5.1   Porting Fortran Source Code between Systems

In general, Visual Fortran is a portable language. One of the main advantages of the language is the availability of large and well-tested libraries of Fortran code. You also might have existing code addressing your problem that you want to reuse. Math and scientific code libraries from most vendors should port to Visual Fortran with virtually no problems.

You might also want to use Visual Fortran as a development platform for code that can later be ported to another system, such as mainframe-class Alpha systems running the Digital UNIX or the OpenVMS operating system.

Whether you are bringing code from another system or planning to export it to another system, you will need to do the following:

▶ Isolate system-dependent code into separate modules. Maintain distinct modules with similar functionality for each separate platform.

▶ In your main program, use only language extensions that will compile on both platforms, putting system-dependent code into modules.

▶ Place language extension subsets into modules.

▶ If you use Microsoft compiler directives, replace the older **$**_directive_ format with the **!DEC$** _directive_ format, because this will be ignored by other systems.

▶ Specify data precision, for integers and logicals as well as for floating-point numbers when the size matters. If you do not explicitly specify KIND for variables, this could be the source of problems if one system uses a default of (KIND=2) for integers, while your program assumes (KIND=4).

▶ Conversely, if the size of a variable is not significant, avoid specifying data precision. Code that does specify precision will run slower on systems that do not use the same default integer and real sizes.

▶ Avoid using algorithms that exhibit floating-point instability. For information on handling floating-point numbers, see Chapter 22 The Floating-Point Environment.

▶ Specify equivalent floating-point precision on each platform.

▶ Specify the appropriate attributes when defining routines and data that will be interacting with code written in Microsoft Visual C/C++ or assembly language.

For more information on porting code between systems, see Section 10.1 Portability.

Choosing a Language Extension Subset

The Visual Fortran compiler supports extensions used on a variety of platforms, plus some that are specific to Visual Fortran. Because there are Fortran compilers for many different computers, you might need to move your source code from one to another. If the trip is one-way and it is permanent, you can simply change the code to work on the second platform. But if you need to make sure you can move the code wherever needed, you must be aware of the extensions to Fortran that are supported on each platform.

You can use some of the Visual Fortran compiler options to help you write portable code. For example, by specifying ANSI/ISO syntax adherence in the Project Settings (Fortran tab) dialog box or on the command line, you can have the compiler enforce Fortran 90 or 95 syntax. Code that compiles cleanly with this option set is very likely to compile cleanly on any other computer with a Fortran compiler that obeys strict Fortran syntax.

If you choose to use platform-specific extensions, you need to note whether there are any differences in how those extensions are implemented on each computer, and use only those features that are identical on both. (For more information, see Section 10.1 Portability.) The default is to compile with the full set of extensions available.

Because Visual Fortran compiler directives look like standard Fortran comments (**!DEC$** *directive*), programs that use directives can compile on other systems. They will, however, lose their function as compiler directives.

Floating-Point Issues

Floating-point answers can differ from system to system, because different systems have different precisions and treat rounding errors in different ways.

One programming practice that can be a serious source of floating-point instability is performing an **IF** test (either obvious or implied) that takes some action if and only if a floating-point number exactly equals a particular value. If your program contains code like this, rewrite the code to a version that is stable in the presence of rounding error. For more details, see Chapter 22 The Floating-Point Environment and Section 10.1 Portability.

Another source of floating-point instability is the use of mathematical algorithms that tend to diminish precision. Incorrect answers can result when the code is moved to a system with less precision. For more information, see Chapter 22 The Floating-Point Environment.

One way of making all **REAL** variables on one system **DOUBLE PRECISION** on another is to use modules to declare explicit data types for each system. Specify a different KIND parameter in each module. Another way is to add an include file that declares explicit data types on each system in all source files.

10.5.2 Mixed-Language Issues

You can combine object modules generated by Visual Fortran with object files from compilers for 32-bit Windows that compile other languages (such as Microsoft Visual C++, or Microsoft MASM), so long as the compilers use the COFF object module format used by Microsoft.

You need to respect certain calling, naming, and argument-passing conventions when combining object modules from different languages. These conventions are discussed in Chapter 18 Programming with Mixed Languages.

10.5.3 Porting Data between Systems

The easiest way to port data to or from the Visual Fortran environment is as a formatted, sequential, 8-bit ASCII character file that can be read using Fortran formatted input statements; if you do this, you should have no trouble.

If you try to transfer unformatted binary data between systems, you need to be aware of the different orders (low-order byte first or high-order byte first) in which different systems store bytes within words. If you need to transfer unformatted binary data, review Section 10.1 Portability and Chapter 23 Converting Unformatted Numeric Data. You can avoid these problems by using a formatted ASCII file.

10.6   Using the Special Features of Microsoft Windows

One of the greatest advantages to building applications for Windows is the power and security provided by the operating system. By simply recompiling your old source code and building a (text-only) Fortran Console application, you can run your program in a protected address space where it cannot damage other applications, hang the processor, or cause the computer to crash.

If you choose to take advantage of the power of Windows NT, Windows 98, or Windows 95, your programs can run more efficiently on single-processor computers. Window NT also supports multi-processor computers.

For more information, see:

▶ Section 10.6.1 Built-in Benefits of Windows

▶ Section 10.6.2 Single or Multithread Program Execution

▶ Section 10.6.3 Dialog Boxes

▶ Section 10.6.4 QuickWin and Windows Programs

10.6.1   Built-in Benefits of Windows

Windows executes your application in a secure environment that includes the support services your application needs to execute efficiently and with a minimum of problems. This environment is a flat virtual address space that can be as large as 2 gigabytes, providing you have enough available disk space. While executing, your program is protected by Windows from damaging other applications and from being damaged by other applications.

The operating system uses *preemptive multitasking* to control how much processor time each application uses. Instead of waiting for an application to voluntarily yield control of the computer back to the operating system, Windows allocates a period of processor time to the application and regains control when that period has expired. This prevents a program with an infinite loop from hanging the computer. If your program hangs, you can easily and safely stop it by using the Windows task manager. (For information about using this or any other feature of Windows, see the manuals that came with the operating system.)

Because you can use one application while another continues to execute, you can make better use of your own time. For example, you can use the visual development environment to edit the source for one project while another project is building, or use Microsoft Excel to prepare a graph for data that your program is busy producing. And if your computer has multiple processors and you are using Windows NT, the computation-intensive program producing your data might be executing on an otherwise idle processor, making it less likely that your other work will slow it down.

10.6.2   Single or Multithread Program Execution

You can take further advantage of preemptive multitasking by designing your program so that portions of it, called *threads*, can be executed in parallel. For example, one thread can perform a lengthy input/output operation while another thread processes data. All of the threads in your application share the same virtual address space.

Windows 98, Windows 95, and Windows NT support multithreading. On a Windows NT system with multiple processors sharing memory, threads can execute in parallel (symmetric multiprocessing).

Multithreaded code must be written so that the threads do not interfere with each other and overwrite each other's data, as described in Chapter 19 Creating Multithread Applications.

10.6.3   Dialog Boxes

Visual Fortran gives you an easy way to create simple dialog boxes that can be used for data entry and application control. Dialogs are a user-friendly way to get and process input. As your application executes, you can make a dialog box appear on the screen and the user can click on a button or scroll bar to enter data or choose what happens next. You can add dialog boxes to any Fortran application, including Windows, QuickWin, and console applications.

You design your dialog with the Resource Editor, and drive them with a combination of the dialog functions, such as **DLGSET**, and your own subroutines. A complete discussion of how to design and use dialog boxes is given in Chapter 11 Using Dialogs.

10.6.4   QuickWin and Windows Programs

One decision you must make when designing a program is how it will be used. If the person using your program must interact with it, the method of interaction can be important. For example, anytime the user must supply data, that data must be validated or it could cause errors. One way to minimize data errors is to change how the data is provided. In this example, if the data is one of several values that are known when the program is executed, the user can select a menu item instead of typing on the keyboard.

When you design programs to be interactive, you use a different structure than if you design them to be run in unattended batches. Interactive applications behave more like state machines than numerical algorithms, because they perform the actions you request when you request them. You may also find that once you can change what your program is doing while it runs, you will be more likely to experiment with it.

The QuickWin library lets you build simple Windows applications. Because QuickWin is a wrapper around a subset of the Windows API, there are limitations to what you can do, but it can fulfill the requirement of most users. If you need additional capabilities, you can call the Windows API directly rather than using QuickWin to build your program. (For more information, see Chapter 7 Using QuickWin). You can also build a graphic user interface in either Microsoft Visual C++ or Visual Basic® that calls your Fortran code.

11

Using Dialogs

Dialogs are a user-friendly way to solicit application control. As your application executes, you can make a dialog box appear on the screen and the user can click on a dialog box control to enter data or choose what happens next.

With the dialog functions provided with Visual Fortran, you can add dialog boxes to your application. These functions define dialog boxes and their controls (scroll bars, buttons, and so on), and call your subroutines to respond to user selections.

There are two types of dialog boxes:

▶ *Modal* dialog boxes, which you can use with any Fortran project type, including Fortran Windows, Fortran QuickWin (multiple doc.), Fortran Standard Graphics (QuickWin single doc.), Fortran Console, Fortran DLL, and Fortran Static library project types.

▶ *Modeless* dialog boxes, which you can use only with the Fortran Windows project type.

When your program displays a modal dialog box (any project type), the user must explicitly enter data and close the dialog box before your application resumes execution.

When your program displays a modeless dialog box (Fortran Windows project type), your application continues executing. The user can switch between the modeless dialog box and the other windows in the application.

There are two steps to making a dialog:

1. Specify the appearance of the dialog box and the names and properties of the controls it contains.

2. Write an application that activates those controls by recognizing and responding to user selections.

This chapter covers the following topics:

▶ Section 11.1 Using the Resource Editor to Design aDialog

▶ Section 11.2 Writing a Dialog Application

▶ Section 11.3 Dialog Functions

▶ Section 11.4 Dialog Controls

▶ Section 11.5 Using Dialog Controls

11.1   Using the Resource Editor to Design a Dialog

You design the appearance of the dialog box, choose and name the dialog controls within it, and set other control properties with the Resource Editor. This section goes through the design of a dialog box, and uses as an example a dialog that converts temperatures between Celsius and Fahrenheit.

To open the dialog editor:

1. From the Insert menu, choose Resource.

2. From the list of possible resources, choose Dialog.

3. Click the New button. The dialog editor appears on the screen as shown in Figure 11-1.

A blank dialog box appears at the left and a toolbar of available controls appears on the right. If you place the cursor over a control on the toolbar, the name of the control appears.

To add controls to the dialog box:

1. Point at one of the available controls on the toolbar, hold down the left mouse button and drag the control to the dialog box.

2. Place the dialog control where you want it to be on the dialog box and release the mouse button. You can delete controls by selecting them with the mouse, then pressing the DEL key.

Figure 11-2 shows a Horizontal Scroll bar, two Edit boxes, two Static text lines, and a Group box added to the dialog box. The OK and CAN-CEL buttons were added for you by the Resource Editor, but they are not in any way special and can be deleted, moved, resized, or renamed.

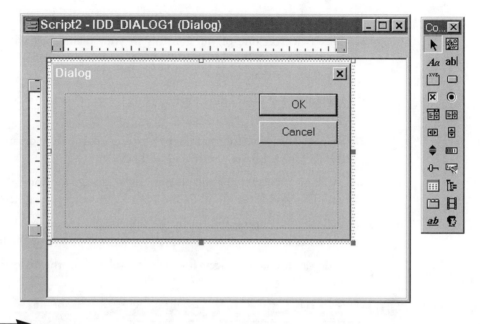

Figure 11–1   *Dialog Editor Sample 1*

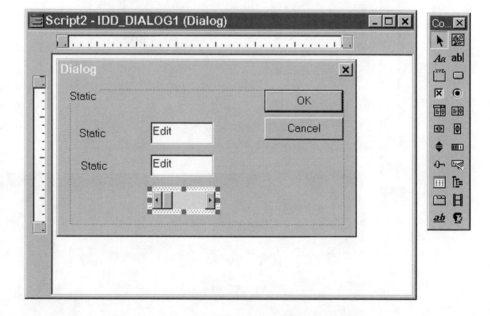

Figure 11–2   *Dialog Editor Sample 2*

To specify the names and properties of the added controls:

1. Click twice on one of the controls in your dialog box with the left mouse button. A Properties box appears showing the default name and properties for that control.

   Figure 11-3 shows the Properties box for the Horizontal Scroll bar with the default values.

2. Change the control name by typing over the default name (IDC_SCROLLBAR1 in the Figure 11-3).

3. Check or uncheck the available options to change the control's properties. (The Visible option in Figure 11-3 is checked by default.)

4. Click the left mouse button in the upper-right corner of the window Properties box to save the control's properties and to close the box.

   Repeat the same process for each control and for the dialog box itself.

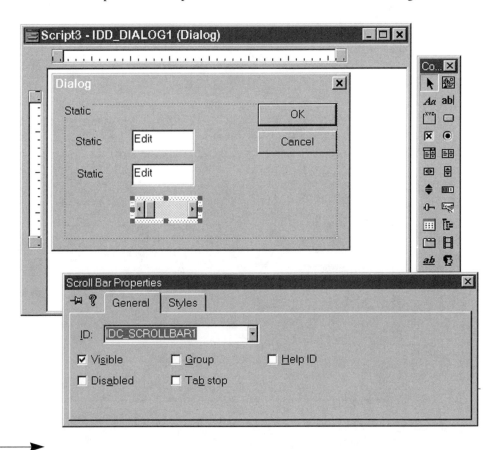

Figure 11–3 *Dialog Editor Sample 3*

To use the controls from within a program, you need symbolic names for each of them. In this example, the Horizontal Scroll bar symbolic name is changed in the Properties box to IDC_SCROLLBAR_TEMPERATURE. This is how the control will be referred to in your program; for example, when you get the slide position:

```
INTEGER slide_position
retlog = DLGGET (dlg, IDC_SCROLLBAR_TEMPERATURE, &
                 slide_position, DLG_POSITION)
```

The top Edit box is named IDC_EDIT_CELSIUS. The Static text next to it is named IDC_TEXT_CELSIUS and set to the left-aligned text "Celsius." The lower Edit box is named IDC_EDIT_FAHRENHEIT, and the Static text next to it is named IDC_TEXT_FAHRENHEIT and set to the left-aligned text "Fahrenheit."

The Group box is named IDC_BOX_TEMPERATURE, and its caption is set to &Temperature (the ampersand [&] underlines the letter "T" and makes it a Windows hotkey, activated with ALT+T). The dialog itself is named IDD_TEMP and its caption is set to Temperature Conversion. All other control properties are left at the default values. The resulting dialog box is shown in Figure 11-4.

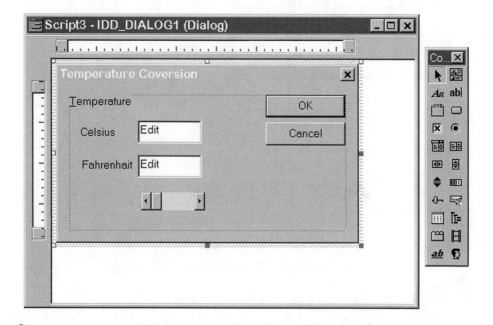

Figure 11–4   *Dialog Editor Sample 4*

To save the dialog box as a resource file:

1. From the File menu, choose Save As.

2. Enter a resource filename for your file.

In this example, the resource file is given the name TEMP.RC. The visual development environment saves the resource file and creates an include file with the name RESOURCE.FD.

At this point the appearance of the dialog box is finished and the controls are named, but the box cannot function on its own. An application must be created to run it.

Not all the controls on the Resource Editor control toolbar bar are supported by Visual Fortran dialog functions. The supported dialog controls are:

▶ Button (see Section 11.5.5)

▶ Check box (see Section 11.5.4)

▶ Combo box; such as a drop-down list box (see Section 11.5.6)

▶ Edit box (see Section 11.5.2)

▶ Group box (see Section 11.5.3)

▶ List box (see Section 11.5.6)

▶ Picture (see Section 11.5.8)

▶ Progress bar (see Section 11.5.9)

▶ Radio button (see Section 11.5.4)

▶ Scroll bar; Horizontal and Vertical (see Section 11.5.7)

▶ Slider (see Section 11.5.11)

▶ Spin control (see Section 11.5.10)

▶ Static text (see Section 11.5.1)

▶ Tab control (see Section 11.5.12)

This section covers the following topics:

• Section 11.1.1 Setting Control Properties

• Section 11.1.2 The Include (.FD) File

11.1.1 Setting Control Properties

Help is available within the Resource Editor to explain the options for each of the dialog controls.

Some of the controls have multiple Properties sets. Click the mouse on the name of the Properties set you want to view or modify. You can change the dialog box itself by double-clicking the left mouse button in any clear area in the box. The Properties box opens for the dialog.

To change where your dialog appears on the screen, change the *x* and *y* values in the Properties box. These specify the screen pixel position of the dialog box's upper-left corner. You can change the size of the dialog box by holding down the left mouse button as you drag the right or lower perimeter of the box.

You can use the scroll bars to move the view region if you have sized your dialog window to be larger than the edit window. If you want to edit the appearance of the dialog box later, you can open the resource file (.RC) from the File menu, and click on the dialog icon. Alternatively, you can select the Resource View pane. The Resource Editor is automatically invoked and the dialog box can be opened.

11.1.2 The Include (.FD) File

Each control in a dialog box has a unique integer identifier. When the Resource Editor creates the include file (.FD), it assigns the PARAMETER attribute to each control and to the dialog box itself, so they become named constants. It also assigns each control and the dialog box an integer value. You can read the list of names and values in your dialog boxes include file (for example, TEMP.FD).

When your application uses a control, it can refer to the control or dialog box by its name (for example, IDC_SCROLLBAR_TEMPERATURE or IDD_TEMP), or by its integer value. If you want to rename a control or make some other change to your dialog box, you should make the change through the Resource Editor in the visual development environment. Do not use a text editor to alter your .FD include file because the dialog resource will not be able to access the changes.

11.2 Writing a Dialog Application

When creating a dialog box with the Resource Editor, you specify the types of controls that are to be included in the box. You then must provide procedures to make the dialog box active. These procedures use both dialog functions and your subroutines to control your program's response to the user's dialog box input.

You give your application access to your dialog resource file by adding the .RC file to your project, giving your application access to the dialog include file, and associating the dialog properties in these files with the dialog type (see Section 11.2.1 Initializing and Activating the Dialog Box).

Your application must include the statement **USE DFLOGM** to access the dialog functions, and it must include the .FD file the Resource Editor created for your dialog. For example:

```
PROGRAM TEMPERATURE
USE DFLOGM
IMPLICIT NONE
INCLUDE 'TEMP.FD'
CALL DoDialog( )
END PROGRAM
```

The following sections describe how to code a dialog application:

▶ Section 11.2.1 Initializing and Activating the Dialog Box

▶ Section 11.2.2 Dialog Callback Routines

▶ Section 11.2.3 Using a Modeless Dialog Box

11.2.1   Initializing and Activating the Dialog Box

Each dialog box has an associated variable of the derived type dialog. The dialog derived type is defined in the DFLOGM.F90 module; you access it with **USE DFLOGM**. When you write your dialog application, refer to your dialog box as a variable of type dialog. For example:

```
USE DFLOGM
INCLUDE 'TEMP.FD'
TYPE (dialog) dlg
LOGICAL return
return DLGINIT( IDD_TEMP, dlg )
```

This code associates the dialog type with the dialog (IDD_TEMP in this example) defined in your resource and include files (TEMP.RC and TEMP.FD in this example).

You give your application access to your dialog resource file by adding the .RC file to your project. You give your application access to the dialog include file by including the .FD file in each subprogram. You associate the dialog properties in these files with the dialog type by calling **DLGINIT** with your dialog name.

An application that controls a dialog box should perform the following actions:

1. Call **DLGINIT** or **DLGINITWITHRESOURCEHANDLE** to initialize the dialog type and associate your dialog and its properties with the type.

2. Initialize the controls with the dialog set functions, such as **DLGSET**.

3. Set the callback routines to be executed when a user manipulates a control in the dialog box with **DLGSETSUB**.

4. Depending on whether you want a modal or modeless dialog type:

   ▶ To use a modal dialog, run the dialog with **DLGMODAL**.

   ▶ To use a modeless dialog, call **DLGMODELESS** and use **DLGISDLGMESSAGE** in your message loop.

5. Retrieve control information with the dialog get functions, such as **DLGGET**.

6. Free resources from the dialog with **DLGUNINIT**.

As an example of activating a dialog box and controls, the following code initializes the temperature dialog box and controls created in the previous example. It also sets the callback routine as UpdateTemp, displays the dialog box, and releases the dialog resources when done:

```
SUBROUTINE DoDialog( )
USE DFLOGM
IMPLICIT NONE
INCLUDE 'TEMP.FD'

INTEGER retint
LOGICAL retlog
TYPE (dialog) dlg
EXTERNAL UpdateTemp
! Initialize.
 IF ( .not. DlgInit( idd_temp, dlg ) ) THEN
    WRITE (*,*) "Error: dialog not found"
 ELSE
! Set up temperature controls.
    retlog = DlgSet( dlg, IDC_SCROLLBAR_TEMPERATURE, 200, DLG_RANGEMAX)
    retlog = DlgSet( dlg, IDC_EDIT_CELSIUS, "100" )
    CALL UpdateTemp( dlg, IDC_EDIT_CELSIUS, DLG_CHANGE)
    retlog = DlgSetSub( dlg, IDC_EDIT_CELSIUS, UpdateTemp )
    retlog = DlgSetSub( dlg, IDC_EDIT_FAHRENHEIT, UpdateTemp )
    retlog = DlgSetSub( dlg, IDC_SCROLLBAR_TEMPERATURE, UpdateTemp )
```

```
! Activate the modal dialog.
              retint = DlgModal( dlg )
! Release dialog resources.
              CALL DlgUninit( dlg )
  END IF
  END SUBROUTINE DoDialog
```

The dialog functions, such as **DLGSET** and **DLGSETSUB**, refer to the dialog controls by the names you assigned to them in the Properties box while creating the dialog box in the Resource Editor. For example:

```
retlog = DlgSet( dlg, IDC_SCROLLBAR_TEMPERATURE, 200, &
& DLG_RANGEMAX)
```

In this statement, the dialog function **DLGSET** assigns the control named IDC_SCROLLBAR_TEMPERATURE a value of 200. The index DLG_RANGEMAX specifies that this value is a scroll bar maximum range. Consider the following:

```
retlog = DlgSet( dlg, IDC_EDIT_CELSIUS, "100" )
CALL UpdateTemp( dlg, IDC_EDIT_CELSIUS, DLG_CHANGE)
```

The preceding statements set the dialog's top Edit box, named IDC_EDIT_CELSIUS in the Resource Editor, to an initial value of 100, and calls the routine UpdateTemp to inform the application that the value has changed. Consider the following:

```
retlog = DlgSetSub( dlg, IDC_EDIT_CELSIUS, UpdateTemp )
retlog = DlgSetSub( dlg, IDC_EDIT_FAHRENHEIT, UpdateTemp )
retlog = DlgSetSub( dlg, IDC_SCROLLBAR_TEMPERATURE,UpdateTemp )
```

The preceding statements associate the callback routine UpdateTemp with the three controls.

Routines are assigned to the controls with the function **DLGSETSUB**. Its first argument is the dialog variable, the second is the control name, the third is the name of the routine you have written for the control, and the optional fourth argument is an index to select between multiple routines. You can set the callback routines for your dialog controls anywhere in your application: before opening your dialog with either **DLGMODAL** or **DLGMODELESS**, or from within another callback routine.

All routines are described in the "A-Z Summary" in the *Language Reference* in Visual Fortran online Help.

11.2.2 Dialog Callback Routines

All callback routines should have the following interface:

SUBROUTINE callback (*dlg, control_name, callbacktype*)

dlg

Refers to the dialog box and allows the callback to change values of the dialog controls.

control_name

Is the name of the control that caused the callback.

callbacktype

Indicates what callback is occuring (for example, DLG_CLICKED, DLG_CHANGE, DLG_DBLCLICK).

The last two parameters let you write a single subroutine that can be used with multiple callbacks from more than one control. Typically, you do this for controls comprising a logical group. For example, all the controls in the temperature dialog in the previous example are associated with the same callback routine, UpdateTemp. You can also associate more than one callback routine with the same control, but you must then provide an index parameter to indicate which callback is to be used.

The following is an example of a callback routine:

```
SUBROUTINE UpdateTemp( dlg, control_name, callbacktype )
USE DFLOGM
IMPLICIT NONE
TYPE (dialog) dlg
INTEGER control_name
INTEGER callbacktype
INCLUDE 'TEMP.FD'
CHARACTER(256) text
INTEGER cel, far, retint
LOGICAL retlog
! Suppress compiler warnings for unreferenced arguments.
INTEGER local_callbacktype
local_callbacktype = callbacktype

SELECT CASE (control_name)
  CASE (IDC_EDIT_CELSIUS)
  ! Celsius value was modified by the user so
  ! update both Fahrenheit and Scroll bar values.
    retlog = DlgGet( dlg, IDC_EDIT_CELSIUS, text )
    READ (text, *, iostat=retint) cel
    IF ( retint .eq. 0 ) THEN
```

```
          far = (cel-0.0)*((212.0-32.0)/100.0)+32.0
          WRITE (text,*) far
          retlog = DlgSet( dlg, IDC_EDIT_FAHRENHEIT, &
&            TRIM(ADJUSTL(text)) )
          retlog = DlgSet( dlg, IDC_SCROLLBAR_TEMPERATURE, cel, &
&            DLG_POSITION )
     END IF
CASE (IDC_EDIT_FAHRENHEIT)
! Fahrenheit value was modified by the user so
! update both celsius and Scroll bar values.
     retlog = DlgGet( dlg, IDC_EDIT_FAHRENHEIT, text )
     READ (text, *, iostat=retint) far
     IF ( retint .eq. 0 ) THEN
        cel = (far-32.0)*(100.0/(212.0-32.0))+0.0
        WRITE (text,*) cel
        retlog = DlgSet( dlg, IDC_EDIT_CELSIUS, TRIM(ADJUSTL(text)) )
        retlog = DlgSet( dlg, IDC_SCROLLBAR_TEMPERATURE, cel, &
&            DLG_POSITION )
     END IF
CASE (IDC_SCROLLBAR_TEMPERATURE)
! Scroll bar value was modified by the user so
! update both Celsius and Fahrenheit values.
     retlog = DlgGet( dlg, IDC_SCROLLBAR_TEMPERATURE, cel, &
&            DLG_POSITION )
     far = (cel-0.0)*((212.0-32.0)/100.0)+32.0
     WRITE (text,*) far
     retlog = DlgSet( dlg, IDC_EDIT_FAHRENHEIT, TRIM(ADJUSTL(text)) )
     WRITE (text,*) cel
     retlog = DlgSet( dlg, IDC_EDIT_CELSIUS, TRIM(ADJUSTL(text)) )
   END SELECT
END SUBROUTINE UpdateTemp
```

Each control in a dialog box, except a pushbutton, has a default callback that performs no action. The default callback for a pushbutton's click event sets the return value of the dialog to the pushbutton's name and then exits the dialog. This makes all pushbuttons exit the dialog by default, and gives the OK and CANCEL buttons good default behavior. A routine that calls **DLGMODAL** can then test to see which pushbutton caused the modal dialog to exit.

Callbacks for a particular control are called after the value of the control has been changed by the user's action. Calling **DLGSET** does not cause a callback to be called for the changing value of a control. In particular, when inside a callback, performing a **DLGSET** on a control will not cause the associated callback for that control to be called.

Calling **DLGSET** before or after **DLGMODAL** or **DLGMODELESS** has been called also does not cause the callback to be called. If the callback needs to be called, it can be called manually using **CALL** after the **DLGSET** is performed.

11.2.3   Using a Modeless Dialog Box

To display a modeless dialog box, call the **DLGMODELESS** function. A modeless dialog box remains displayed until the **DLGEXIT** routine is called, either explicitly or by a default button callback. The application must provide a message loop to process Windows messages and must call the **DLGISDLG-MESSAGE** function at the beginning of the message loop.

The variable of type **DIALOG** passed to **DLGMODELESS** must remain in memory for the duration of the dialog box (from the **DLGINIT** call through the **DLGUNINIT** call). The variable can be declared as global data in a Fortran module, as a variable with the **STATIC** attribute (or statement), or in a calling procedure that is active for the duration on the dialog box. For more information, see the Syntax for **DLGMODELESS**.

Modeless dialog boxes can only be used in a Fortran Windows project.

As an example of using a modeless dialog box, the following code is the WinMain function of an application that displays a modeless dialog box as its main window.

```
integer*4 function WinMain(hInstance, hPrevInstance, lpszCmdLine, nCmdShow)
!DEC$ IF DEFINED(_X86_)
!DEC$ ATTRIBUTES STDCALL, ALIAS : '_WinMain@16' :: WinMain
!DEC$ ELSE
!DEC$ ATTRIBUTES STDCALL, ALIAS : 'WinMain' :: WinMain
!DEC$ ENDIF

    use dfwin
    use dflogm

    integer(4) hInstance
    integer(4) hPrevInstance
    integer(4) lpszCmdLine
    integer(4) nCmdShow

    ! Include the constants provided by the Resource Editor
    include 'resource.fd'

    ! A dialog box callback
    external ThermometerSub
```

```
! Variables
type (dialog) dlg
type (T_MSG) mesg
integer(4)        ret
logical(4)        lret

! Create the thermometer dialog box and set up the controls and callbacks
lret = DlgInit(IDD_THERMOMETER, dlg_thermometer)
lret = DlgSetSub(dlg_thermometer, IDD_THERMOMETER, ThermometerSub)
lret = DlgSet(dlg_thermometer, IDC_PROGRESS1, 32, DLG_RANGEMIN)
lret = DlgSet(dlg_thermometer, IDC_PROGRESS1, 212, DLG_RANGEMAX)
lret = DlgSet(dlg_thermometer, IDC_PROGRESS1, 32)
lret = DlgModeless(dlg_thermometer, nCmdShow)

! Read and process messages until GetMessage returns 0 because
! PostQuitMessage has been called
do while( GetMessage (mesg, NULL, 0, 0) )
  ! Note that DlgIsDlgMessage must be called in order to give
  ! the dialog box first chance at the message.
  if ( DlgIsDlgMessage(mesg) .EQV. .FALSE. ) then
    lret = TranslateMessage( mesg )
    ret = DispatchMessage( mesg )
  end if
end do

! Cleanup dialog box memory
call DlgUninit(dlg)

! The return value is the wParam of the Quit message
WinMain = mesg.wParam
return
end
```

11.3   Dialog Functions

You can use dialog functions as you would any intrinsic or run-time function.

As described in the introduction to this chapter, Visual Fortran supports two types of dialog boxes: modal and modeless. You can use a modal dialog box with any Fortran project type. You can use a modeless dialog box only with the Fortran Windows project types.

The dialog functions can:

▶ Initialize and close the dialog box

▶ Retrieve user input from a dialog box

▶ Display data in the dialog box

▶ Modify the dialog box controls

The include file (.FD) of the dialog box contains the names of the dialog controls that you specified in the Properties box of the Resource Editor when you created the dialog box. The module DFLOGM.MOD contains predefined variable names and type definitions. These control names, variables, and type definitions are used in the dialog function argument lists to manage your dialog box.

Table 11-1 lists the dialog functions.

Table 11–1 *Dialog Functions*

Dialog Function	*Description*
DLGEXIT	Closes an open dialog
DLGGET	Gets the value of a control variable
DLGGETCHAR	Gets the value of a character control variable
DLGGETINT	Gets the value of an integer control variable
DLGGETLOG	Gets the value of a logical control variable
DLGINIT	Initializes the dialog
DLGINITWITHRESOURCEHANDLE	Initializes the dialog (alternative to **DLGINIT**)
DLGISDLGMESSAGE	Determines whether a message is intended for a modeless dialog box
DLGMODAL	Displays a modal dialog box
DLGMODELESS	Displays a modeless dialog box
DLGSENDCTRLMESSAGE	Sends a message to a control
DLGSET	Assigns a value to a control variable
DLGSETCHAR	Assigns a value to a character control variable
DLGSETINT	Assigns a value to an integer control variable
DLGSETLOG	Assigns a value to a logical control variable

Table 11–1 *Dialog Functions (Continued)*

Dialog Function	Description
DLGSETRETURN	Sets the return value for **DLGMODAL**
DLGSETSUB	Assigns a defined callback routine to a control
DLGUNINIT	Deallocates memory for an initialized dialog

These functions are described in the the "A-Z Summary" in the *Language Reference* in Visual Fortran online Help.

11.4 Dialog Controls

Each dialog control in a dialog box has a unique integer identifier and name. You specify the name in the Properties box for each control within the Resource Editor, and the Resource Editor assigns the **PARAMETER** attribute and an integer value to each control name. You can refer to a control by its name, for example IDC_SCROLLBAR_TEMPERATURE, or by its integer value, which you can read from the include (.FD) file.

Each dialog control has one or more variables associated with it, called *control indexes*. These indexes can be integer, logical, character, or external. For example, a plain Button has three associated variables: one is a logical value associated with its current enabled state, one is a character variable that determines its title, and the third is an external variable that indicates the subroutine to be called if a mouse click occurs.

Dialog controls can have multiple variables of the same type. For example, the scroll bar control has four integer variables associated with it:

▶ Scroll bar position

▶ Scroll bar minimum range

▶ Scroll bar maximum range

▶ Position change if the user clicks on the scroll bar space next to the slide (big step)

Dialog controls and their indexes are discussed in:

▶ Section 11.4.1 Control Indexes

▶ Section 11.4.2 Available Indexes for Each Dialog Control

▶ Section 11.4.3 Specifying Control Indexes

11.4.1   Control Indexes

The value of a dialog control's index is set with the **DLGSET** functions: **DLGSET, DLGSETINT, DLGSETLOG, DLGSETCHAR**, and **DLGSET-SUB**. The control name and control index name are arguments to the **DLG-SET** functions and specify the particular control index being set. For example:

```
retlog = DlgSet( dlg, IDC_SCROLLBAR_TEMPERATURE, 45, &
& DLG_POSITION )
```

The index DLG_POSITION specifies the scroll bar position is set to 45. Consider the following:

```
retlog = DlgSet( dlg, IDC_SCROLLBAR_TEMPERATURE, 200, &
& DLG_RANGEMAX)
```

In this statement, the index DLG_RANGEMAX specifies the scroll bar maximum range is set to 200. The **DLGSET** functions have the following syntax:

result = **DLGSET** (*dlg, control_name, value, control_index_name*)

The *control_index_name* determines what the *value* in the **DLGSET** function means.

The control index names are declared in the module DFLOGM.MOD and should not be declared in your routines. Table 11-2 lists the available control indexes and how they specify the interpretation of the *value* argument.

Table 11–2   *Control Indexes*

Control Index	How the Value Is Interpreted
DLG_ADDSTRING	Used with **DLGSETCHAR** to add an entry to a List box or Combo box
DLG_BIGSTEP	The amount of change that occurs in a Scroll bar's or Slider's position when the user clicks beside the Scroll bar's or slider's slide (default = 10)
DLG_CHANGE	A subroutine called after the user has modified a control and the control has been updated on the screen
DLG_CLICKED	A subroutine called when the control receives a mouse-click
DLG_DBLCLICK	A subroutine called when a control is double-clicked
DLG_DEFAULT	Same as not specifying a control index
DLG_ENABLE	The enable state of the control (*value* = .TRUE. means enabled, *value* = .FALSE. means disabled)
DLG_GAINFOCUS	A subroutine called when an Edit Box receives input focus

Table 11–2   *Control Indexes (Continued)*

Control Index	How the Value Is Interpreted
DLG_LOSEFOCUS	A subroutine called when an Edit Box loses input focus
DLG_NUMITEMS	The total number of items in a List box, Combo box, or Tab control
DLG_POSITION	The current position of the Scroll bar, Spin, Slider, or Progress bar
DLG_RANGEMIN	The minimum value of a Scroll bar's, Spin's, Slider's, or Progress' position (default = 1 for scroll bar, 0 for other controls)
DLG_RANGEMAX	The maximum value of a Scroll bar's, Spin's, Slider's, or Progress' position (default = 100)
DLG_SELCHANGE	A subroutine called when the selection in a List Box or Combo Box changes
DLG_SELCHANGING	A subroutine called when the selected Tab control is about to be changed. In this subroutine, calling **DLGGETINT** with the index DLG_STATE refers to the Tab that was active before the change.
DLG_SMALLSTEP	The amount of change that occurs in a Slider's position when the user presses the keyboard arrow keys (default = 1)
DLG_STATE	The user changeable state of a control
DLG_TICKFREQ	The interval frequency for tick marks in a Slider (default = 1)
DLG_TITLE	The title text associated with a control
DLG_UPDATE	A subroutine called after the user has modified the control state but before the control has been updated on the screen

The index names associated with dialog controls do not need to be used unless there is more than one variable of the same type for the control and you do not want the default variable. For example:

```
retlog = DlgSet(dlg, IDC_SCROLLBAR_TEMPERATURE, 45, &
&       DLG_POSITION)
retlog = DlgSet(dlg, IDC_SCROLLBAR_TEMPERATURE, 45)
```

These statements both set the Scroll bar position to 45, because DLG_POSITION is the default control index for the scroll bar.

Dialog Indexes

The control identifier specified in **DLGSETSUB** can also be the identifier of the dialog box. In this case, the index must be the value listed in Table 11-3.

Table 11–3 *Dialog Indexes*

Dialog Index	How the Value Is Interpreted
DLG_INIT	A subroutine called after the dialog box is created but before it is displayed (with callback-type=DLG_INIT) and immediately before the dialog box is destroyed (with callback-type=DLG_DESTROY)

For more information on dialog controls, see Section 11.4.2 Available Indexes for Each Dialog Control.

11.4.2 Available Indexes for Each Dialog Control

Table 11-4 lists the available indexes and defaults for each of the controls.

Table 11–4 *Dialog Controls and Their Indexes*

Control Type	Integer Index Name	Logical Index Name	Character Index Name	Subroutine Index Name
Button		DLG_ENABLE	DLG_TITLE	DLG_CLICKED
Check box		DLG_STATE (default) DLG_ENABLE	DLG_TITLE	DLG_CLICKED
Combo box	DLG_NUMITEMS sets or returns the total number of items in a list	DLG_ENABLE	Use DLG_STATE, DLG_ADDSTRING, or an index: DLG_STATE by default, sets or returns the text of the selected item or first item in the list DLG_ADDSTRING Used with **DLGSETCHAR** to add a new item. It automatically increments DLG_NUMITEMS. An index, 1 to *n* Sets or returns the text of a particular item	DLG_SELCHANGE (default) DLG_DBLCLICK DLG_CHANGE DLG_UPDATE

Table 11–4 *Dialog Controls and Their Indexes (Continued)*

Control Type	Integer Index Name	Logical Index Name	Character Index Name	Subroutine Index Name
Drop-down list box	Use DLG_NUMITEMS or DLG_STATE: DLG_NUMITEMS (default) sets or returns the total number of items in a list DLG_STATE sets or returns the index of the selected item	DLG_ENABLE	Use DLG_STATE, DLG_ADDSTRING, or an index: DLG_STATE by default, sets or returns the text of the selected item or first item in the list, or you can include an index, 1 to *n*, to set or return indicates the text of a particular item DLG_ADDSTRING used with **DLGSET-CHAR** to add a new item. It automatically increments DLG_NUMITEMS.	DLG_SELCHANGE (default) DLG_DBLCLICK
Edit box		DLG_ENABLE	DLG_STATE	DLG_CHANGE (default) DLG_UPDATE DLG_GAINFOCUS DLG_LOSEFOCUS
Group box		DLG_ENABLE	DLG_TITLE	
List box	Use DLG_NUMITEMS or an index: DLG_NUMITEMS sets or returns he total number of items in a list An index, 1 to *n* determines which list items have been selected and their order	DLG_ENABLE	Use DLG_STATE, DLG_ADDSTRING, or an index: DLG_STATE by default, returns the text of the first selected item DLG_ADDSTRING Used with **DLGSET-CHAR** to add a new item. It automatically increments DLG_NUMITEMS. An index, 1 to *n* sets or returns the text of a particular item	DLG_SELCHANGE (default) DLG_DBLCLICK

Table 11–4 *Dialog Controls and Their Indexes (Continued)*

Control Type	*Integer Index Name*	*Logical Index Name*	*Character Index Name*	*Subroutine Index Name*
Picture		DLG_ENABLE		
Progress bar	DLG_POSITION (default) DLG_RANGEMIN DLG_RANGEMAX	DLG_ENABLE		
Radio button		DLG_STATE (default) DLG_ENABLE	DLG_TITLE	DLG_CLICKED
Scroll bar	DLG_POSITION (default) DLG_RANGEMIN DLG_RANGEMAX DLG_BIGSTEP	DLG_ENABLE		DLG_CHANGE
Slider	DLG_POSITION (default) DLG_RANGEMIN DLG_RANGEMAX DLG_SMALLSTEP DLG_BIGSTEP DLG_TICKFREQ	DLG_ENABLE		DLG_CHANGE
Spin controls	DLG_POSITION (default) DLG_RANGEMIN DLG_RANGEMAX	DLG_ENABLE		DLG_CHANGE
Static text		DLG_ENABLE	DLG_TITLE	
Tab control	Use DLG_NUMITEMS (default), DLG_STATE, or an index: DLG_NUMITEMS sets or returns the total number of tabs DLG_STATE sets or returns the currently selected tab An index, 1 to *n* sets or returns the dialog name of the dialog box associated with a particular tab	DLG_ENABLE	Use DLG_STATE or an index: DLG_STATE by default, sets or returns the currently selected tab An index, 1 to *n* sets or returns the text of a particular Tab	DLG_SELCHANGE (default) DLG_ SELCHANGING

For an overview on control indexes, see Section 11.4.1 Control Indexes.

11.4.3 Specifying Control Indexes

Where there is only one possibility for a particular dialog control's index type
(integer, logical, character, or subroutine), you do not need to specify the control index name in an argument list. For example, you can set the Static text
control IDC_TEXT_CELSIUS to a new value with either of the following
statements:

```
  retlog = DLGSETCHAR (dlg, IDC_TEXT_CELSIUS, "New Celsius &
&                     Title", DLG_TITLE)
retlog = DLGSET (dlg, IDC_TEXT_CELSIUS, "New Celsius Title")
```

You do not need the control index DLG_TITLE because there is only one
character index for a Static text control. The generic function **DLGSET**
chooses the control index to change based on the argument type, in this case
CHARACTER.

For each type of index, you can use the generic **DLGSET** function or the
specific **DLGSET** function for that type: **DLGSETINT**, **DLGSETLOG**, or
DLGSETCHAR. For example, you can disable the Static text control
IDC_TEXT_CELSIUS by setting its logical value to .FALSE. with either
DLGSET or **DLGSETLOG**:

```
retlog = DLGSETLOG (dlg, IDC_TEXT_CELSIUS, .FALSE., &
&                   DLG_ENABLE)
retlog = DLGSET (dlg, IDC_TEXT_CELSIUS, .FALSE., DLG_ENABLE)
```

In both these cases, the control index DLG_ENABLE can be omitted
because there is only one logical control index for Static text controls.

You can query the value of a particular control index with the **DLGGET**
functions, **DLGGET**, **DLGGETINT**, **DLGGETLOG**, and **DLGGET-
CHAR**. For example:

```
INTEGER current_val
LOGICAL are_you_enabled
    retlog = DLGGET (dlg, IDC_SCROLLBAR_TEMPERATURE, &
&                   current_val, DLG_RANGEMAX)
    retlog = DLGGET (dlg, IDC_SCROLLBAR_TEMPERATURE, &
&                   are_you_enabled, DLG_ENABLE)
```

This code returns the maximum range and the enable state of the scroll
bar. The arguments you declare (current_val and are_you_enabled in the preceding example) to hold the queried values must be of the same type as the
values retrieved. If you use specific **DLGGET** functions such as **DLGGET-
INT** or **DLGGETCHAR**, the control index value retrieved must be the

appropriate type. For example, you cannot use **DLGGETCHAR** to retrieve an integer or logical value. The **DLGGET** functions return .FALSE. for illegal type combinations. You cannot query for the name of an external callback routine.

In general, it is better to use the generic functions **DLGSET** and **DLGGET** rather than their type-specific variations because then you do not have to worry about matching the function to type of value set or retrieved. **DLGSET** and **DLGGET** perform the correct operation automatically, based on the type of argument you pass to them.

More information on these routines is available in the "A-Z Summary" in the *Language Reference* in Visual Fortran online Help.

11.5   Using Dialog Controls

The dialog controls provided in the Resource Editor are versatile and flexible and when used together can provide a sophisticated user-friendly interface for your application. This section discusses the available dialog controls.

Any control can be disabled by your application at any time, so that it no longer changes or responds to the user. This is done by setting the control index DLG_ENABLE to .FALSE. with **DLGSET** or **DLGSETLOG**. For example:

```
LOGICAL retlog
retlog = DLGSET (dlg, IDC_CHECKBOX1, .FALSE., DLG_ENABLE)
```

This example disables the control named IDC_CHECKBOX1.

When you create your dialog box in the Resource Editor, the dialog controls are given a tab order. When the user hits the Tab key, the dialog box focus shifts to the next control in the tab order. By default, the tab order of the controls follows the order in which they were created. This may not be the order you want.

You can change the order by opening the Layout menu and choosing Tab Order (or by pressing the key combination CTRL+D) in the Resource Editor. A tab number will appear next to each control. Click the mouse on the control you want to be first, then on the control you want to be second in the tab order and so on. Tab order also determines which control gets the focus if the user presses the Group box hotkey. (See Section 11.5.3 Using Group Boxes.)

For information on Visual Fortran Samples that use the Dialog functions, see the . . . DF98\SAMPLES\DIALOG folder.

The following sections describe the function and use of the dialog controls:

- ▶ Section 11.5.1 Using Static Text
- ▶ Section 11.5.2 Using Edit Boxes
- ▶ Section 11.5.3 Using Group Boxes
- ▶ Section 11.5.4 Using Check Boxes and Radio Buttons
- ▶ Section 11.5.5 Using Buttons
- ▶ Section 11.5.6 Using List Boxes and Combo Boxes
- ▶ Section 11.5.7 Using Scroll Bars
- ▶ Section 11.5.8 Using Pictures
- ▶ Section 11.5.9 Using Progress Bars
- ▶ Section 11.5.10 Using Spin Controls
- ▶ Section 11.5.11 Using Sliders
- ▶ Section 11.5.12 Using Tab Controls
- ▶ Section 11.5.13 Setting Return Values and Exiting

11.5.1 Using Static Text

Static text is an area in the dialog that your application writes text to. The user cannot change it. Your application can modify the Static text at any time, for instance to display a current user selection, but the user cannot modify the text. Static text is typically used to label other controls or display messages to the user.

11.5.2 Using Edit Boxes

An Edit box is an area that your application can write text to at anytime. However, unlike Static Text, the user can write to an Edit box by clicking the mouse in the box and typing. The following statements write to an Edit box:

```
CHARACTER(20) text /"Send text"/
retlog = DLGSET (dlg, IDC_EDITBOX1, text)
```

The next statement reads the character string in an Edit box:

```
retlog = DLGGET (dlg, IDC_EDITBOX1, text)
```

The values a user enters into the Edit box are always retrieved as character strings, and your application needs to interpret these strings as the data they represent. For example, numbers entered by the user are interpreted by your application as character strings. Likewise, numbers you write to the Edit box are sent as character strings. You can convert between numbers and strings by using internal read and write statements to make type conversions.

To read a number in the Edit box, retrieve it as a character string with **DLGGET** or **DLGGETCHAR**, and then execute an internal read using a variable of the numeric type you want (such as integer or real). For example:

```
REAL x
LOGICAL retlog
CHARACTER(256) text
retlog = DLGGET (dlg, IDC_EDITBOX1, text)
READ (text, *) x
```

In this example, the real variable x is assigned the value that was entered into the Edit box, including any decimal fraction.

Complex and double complex values are read the same way, except that your application must separate the Edit box character string into the real part and imaginary part. You can do this with two separate Edit boxes, one for the real and one for the imaginary part, or by requiring the user to enter a separator between the two parts and parsing the string for the separator before converting. If the separator is a comma (,) you can read the string with two real edit descriptors without having to parse the string.

To write numbers to an Edit box, do an internal write to a string, then send the string to the Edit box with **DLGSET**. For example:

```
INTEGER j
LOGICAL retlog
CHARACTER(256) text
WRITE (text,'(I4)') j
retlog = DLGSET (dlg, IDC_EDITBOX1, text)
```

Visual Fortran dialog functions do not support multi-line Edit boxes. The maximum number of characters in an Edit box is 256.

11.5.3 Using Group Boxes

A Group box visually organizes a collection of controls as a group. When you select Group box in Resource Editor, you create an expanding (or shrinking) box around the controls you want to group and give the group a title. You can add a hotkey to your group title with an ampersand (&). For example, consider the following group title:

```
&Temperature
```

This causes the "T" to be underlined in the title and makes it a hotkey. When the user presses the key combination ALT+T, the focus of the dialog box shifts to the next control after the Group box in the tab order. This control should be a control in the group. (You can view and change the tab order from the Layout/Tab Order menu option in the Resource Editor.)

Disabling the Group box disables the hotkey, but does not disable any of the controls within the group. As a matter of style, you should generally disable the controls in a group when you disable the Group box.

11.5.4 Using Check Boxes and Radio Buttons

Check boxes and Radio buttons present the user with an either-or choice. A Radio button is pushed or not, and a Check box is checked or not. You use **DLGGET** or **DLGGETLOG** to check the state of these controls. Their state is a logical value that is .TRUE. if they are pushed or checked, and .FALSE. if they are not. For example:

```
LOGICAL pushed_state, checked_state, retlog
retlog = DLGGET (dlg, IDC_RADIOBUTTON1, pushed_state)
retlog = DLGGET (dlg, IDC_CHECKBOX1, checked_state)
```

If you need to change the state of the button, for initialization or in response to other user input, you use **DLGSET** or **DLGSETLOG**. For example:

```
LOGICAL retlog
retlog = DLGSET (dlg, IDC_RADIOBUTTON1, .FALSE.)
retlog = DLGSET (dlg, IDC_CHECKBOX1, .TRUE.)
```

11.5.5 Using Buttons

Unlike Check Boxes and Radio Buttons, Buttons do not have a state. They do not hold the value of being pushed or not pushed. When the user clicks on a Button with the mouse, the Button's callback routine is called. Thus, the purpose of a Button is to initiate an action. The external procedure you assign as a callback determines the action initiated. For example:

```
LOGICAL retlog
EXTERNAL DisplayTime
retlog = DlgSetSub( dlg, IDC_BUTTON_TIME, DisplayTime)
```

Visual Fortran dialog functions do not support user-drawn Buttons.

11.5.6 Using List Boxes and Combo Boxes

List boxes and Combo boxes are used when the user needs to select a value from a set of many values. They are similar to a set of Radio buttons except that List boxes and Combo boxes are scrollable and can contain more items than a set of Radio buttons which are limited by the screen display area. Also, unlike Radio buttons, the number of entries in a List box or Combo box can change at run-time.

The difference between a List box and a Combo box is that a List box is simply a list of items, while a Combo box is a combination of a List box and an Edit box. A List box allows the user to choose multiple selections from the list at one time, while a Combo box allows only a single selection, but a Combo box allows the user to edit the selected value while a List box only allows the user to choose from the given list.

A Drop-down list box looks like a Combo box since it has a drop-down arrow to display the list. Like a Combo box, only one selection can be made at a time in a Drop-down list box, but, like a List box, the selected value cannot be edited. A Drop-down list box serves the same function as a List box except for the disadvantage that the user can choose only a single selection, and the advantage that it takes up less dialog screen space.

Visual Fortran dialog functions do not support user-drawn List boxes or user-drawn Combo boxes. You must create List boxes and Combo boxes with the Resource Editor.

Using List Boxes

For both List boxes and Combo boxes, the control index DLG _NUMITEMS determines how many items are in the box. Once this value is set, you set the text of List box items by specifying a character string for each item index. Indexes run from 1 to the total number of list items set with DLG_NUMITEMS. For example:

```
LOGICAL retlog
retlog = DlgSet ( dlg, IDC_LISTBOX1, 3, DLG_NUMITEMS )
retlog = DlgSet ( dlg, IDC_LISTBOX1, "Moe", 1 )
retlog = DlgSet ( dlg, IDC_LISTBOX1, "Larry", 2 )
retlog = DlgSet ( dlg, IDC_LISTBOX1, "Curly", 3 )
```

These statements put three items in the List box. The initial value of each List box entry is a blank string and the value becomes nonblank after it has been set.

You can change the list length and item values at any time, including from within callback routines. If the list is shortened, the set of entries is truncated. If the list is lengthened, blank entries are added. In the preceding example, you could extend the list length and define the new item with the following:

```
retlog = DLGSET ( dlg, IDC_LISTBOX1, 4)
retlog = DLGSET ( dlg, IDC_LISTBOX1, "Shemp", 4)
```

Since List boxes allow selection of multiple entries, you need a way to determine which entries are selected. When the user selects a List box item, it is assigned an integer index equal to the order in which the item was selected. You can test which list items are selected by reading the selection indexes in order until a zero value is read. For example, if in the previous List box the user selected Moe and then Curly, the List box selection indexes would have the following values:

```
Selection index        Value
1                      1 (for Moe)
2                      3 (for Curly)
3                      0 (no more selections)
```

If Larry alone had been selected, the List box selection index values would be:

```
Selection index        Value
1                      2 (for Larry)
2                      0 (no more selections)
```

To determine the items selected, the List box values can be read with **DLGGET** until a zero is encountered. For example:

```
INTEGER j, num, test
INTEGER, ALLOCATABLE :: values(:)
LOGICAL retlog

retlog = DLGGET (dlg, IDC_LISTBOX1, num, DLG_NUMITEMS)
ALLOCATE (values(num))
j = 1
test = -1
DO WHILE (test .NE. 0)
  retlog = DLGGET (dlg, IDC_LISTBOX1, values(j), j)
  test = values(j)
  j = j + 1
END DO
```

In this example, j is the selection index and values(j) holds the list numbers, in order, of the items selected by the user, if any.

To read a single selection, or the first selected item in a set, you can use DLG_STATE, since for a List Box DLG_STATE holds the character string of the first selected item (if any). For example:

```
! Get the string for the first selected item.
retlog = DLGGET (dlg, IDC_LISTBOX1, str, DLG_STATE)
```

Alternatively, you can first retrieve the list number of the selected item, and then get the string associated with that item:

```
INTEGER value
CHARACTER(256) str
! Get the list number of the first selected item.
retlog = DLGGET (dlg, IDC_LISTBOX1, value, 1)
! Get the string for that item.
retlog = DLGGET (dlg, IDC_LISTBOX1, str, value)
```

In these examples, if no selection has been made by the user, str will be a blank string.

In the Properties/Styles box in the Resource Editor, List boxes can be specified as sorted or unsorted. The default is sorted, which causes List box items to be sorted alphabetically starting with A. If a List box is specified as sorted, the items in the list are sorted whenever they are updated on the screen. This occurs when the dialog box is first displayed and when the items are changed in a callback.

The alphabetical sorting follows the ASCII collating sequence, and uppercase letters come before lowercase letters. For example, if the List box in the example above with the list "Moe," "Larry," "Curly," and "Shemp" were sorted, before a callback or after **DLGMODAL** returned, index 1 would refer to "Curly," index 2 to "Larry," index 3 to "Moe," and index 4 to "Shemp." For this reason, when using sorted List boxes, indexes should not be counted on to be the same once the dialog is displayed and any change is made to the list. ns.

 u can also call **DLGSETCHAR** with the DLG_ADDSTRING index to add items to a List box or Combo box. For example:

```
retlog = DlgSet(dlgtab, IDC_LIST, "Item 1", DLG_ADDSTRING)
```

When you use DLG_ADDSTRING, the DLG_NUMITEMS control index of the List or Combo box is automatically incremented.

When adding items to a sorted list or Combo box, using DLG_ADDSTRING can be much easier than the alternative (setting DLG_NUMITEMS and then setting items using an index value), because you need not worry about the list being sorted and the index values changing between calls.

Using Combo Boxes

A Combo box is a combination of a List box and an Edit box. The user can make a selection from the list that is then displayed in the Edit box part of the control, or enter text directly into the Edit box.

All dialog values a user enters are character strings, and your application must interpret these strings as the data they represent. For example, numbers entered by the user are returned to your application as character strings.

Because user input can be given in two ways, selection from the List box portion or typing into the Edit box portion directly, you need to register two callback types with **DLGSETSUB** for a Combo box. These callback types are dlg_selchange to handle a new list selection by the user, and dlg_update to handle text entered by the user directly into the Edit box portion. For example:

```
retlog = DlgSetSub(dlg, IDC_COMBO1, UpdateCombo, &
&                   dlg_selchange)
retlog = DlgSetSub(dlg, IDC_COMBO1, UpdateCombo, dlg_update)
```

A Combo box list is created the same way a List box list is created, as described in the previous section, but the user can select only one item from a Combo box at a time. When the user selects an item from the list, Windows automatically puts the item into the Edit box portion of the Combo box. Thus, there is no need, and no mechanism, to retrieve the item list number of a selected item.

If the user is typing an entry directly into the Edit box part of the Combo box, again Windows automatically displays it and you do not need to. You can retrieve the character string of the selected item or Edit box entry with the following statement:

```
! Returns the character string of the selected item or Edit
! box entry as str.
retlog = DLGGET (dlg, IDC_COMBO1, str)
```

Like List boxes, Combo boxes can be specified as sorted or unsorted. The notes about sorted List boxes also apply to sorted Combo boxes.

You have three choices for Combo box Type in the Styles tab of Combo box Properties:

▶ Simple

▶ Drop list

▶ Drop-down

Simple and Drop-down are the same, except that a simple Combo box always displays the Combo box choices in a list, while a Drop-down list Combo box has a Drop-down button and displays the choices in a Drop-down list, conserving screen space. The Drop list type is halfway between a Combo box and a List box and is described below.

Using Drop-Down List Boxes

To create a Drop-down list box, choose a Combo box from the control tool-bar and place it in your dialog. Double-click the left mouse button on the Combo box to open the Properties box. On the Styles Tab, choose Drop List as the control type.

A Drop-down list box has a drop-down arrow to display the list. Like a Combo box, only one selection can be made at a time in the list, but like a List Box, the selected value cannot be edited. A Drop-down list box serves the same function as a List box except for the disadvantage that the user can choose only a single selection, and the advantage that it takes up less dialog screen space.

A Drop-down list box has the same control indexes as a Combo box with the addition of another **INTEGER** index to set or return the list number of the item selected in the list. For example:

```
INTEGER num
  ! Returns index of the selected item.
  retlog = DLGGET (dlg, IDC_DROPDOWN1, num, DLG_STATE)
```

11.5.7   Using Scroll Bars

With a Scroll bar, the user determines input by manipulating the slide up and down or right and left. Your application sets the range for the Scroll bar, and thus can interpret a position of the slide as a number If you want to display this number to the user you need to send the number (as a character string) to a Static text or Edit Box control.

You set the lower and upper limits of the Scroll bar range by setting the control index DLG_RANGEMIN and DLG_RANGEMAX with **DLGSET** or **DLGSETINT**. The default values are 1 and 100. For example:

```
LOGICAL retlog
retlog = DLGSET (dlg, IDC_SCROLLBAR1, 212, DLG_RANGEMAX)
```

You get the slide position by retrieving the control index DLG_POSITION with **DLGGET** or **DLGGETINT**. For example:

```
INTEGER slide_position
retlog = DLGGET (dlg, IDC_SCROLLBAR1, slide_position, &
&              DLG_POSITION)
```

You can also set the increment taken when the user clicks in the blank area above or below the slide in a vertical Scroll bar, or to the left or right of the slide in a horizontal Scroll bar, by setting the control index DLG_BIGSTEP. For example:

```
retlog = DLGSET (dlg, IDC_SCROLLBAR1, 20, DLG_BIGSTEP)
```

When the user clicks on the arrow buttons of the Scroll bar, the position is always incremented or decremented by 1.

11.5.8 Using Pictures

The Picture control is an area of your dialog box in which your application displays a picture.

The user cannot change it, since it is an output-only window. It does not respond to user input and therefore does not support any callbacks.

The picture displayed can be set using the Properties dialog box in the Resource Editor. The options that can be fully defined using the Resource Editor include an icon, a bitmap, a frame, and a rectangle.

11.5.9 Using Progress Bars

The Progress bar is a window that can be used to indicate the progress of a lengthy operation. It consists of a rectangle that is gradually filled as an operation progresses.

Your application sets the range of the Progress bar, using DLG_RANGEMIN and DLG_RANGEMAX, and the current position, using DLG_POSITION. Both the minimum and maximum range values must be between 0 and 65535.

A Progress bar is an output-only window. It does not respond to user input and therefore does not support any callbacks.

11.5.10 Using Spin Controls

The Spin control contains up and down arrows that allow the user to step through values. Your application sets or gets the range of the Spin control's values, using DLG_RANGEMIN and DLG_RANGEMAX, and the current value, using DLG_POSITION.

The Spin control is usually associated with a companion control that is called a "buddy window." To the user, the Spin control and its buddy window often look like a single control. You can specify that the Spin control automatically position itself next to its buddy window and that it automatically set the title of its buddy window to its current value. This is accomplished by setting the "Auto buddy" and "Set buddy integer" styles on the Spin control.

The buddy window is usually an Edit Box or Static Text control. When the "Auto buddy" style is set, the Spin control automatically uses the previous control in the dialog box tab order as its buddy window.

The Spin Control calls the DLG_CHANGE callback whenever the user changes the current value of the control.

The Spin control is named the "Up-down" control in Windows programming documentation.

11.5.11 Using Sliders

The Slider Control is a window that contains a slider and optional tick marks. Your application sets or gets the range of the Slider control's values, using DLG_RANGEMIN and DLG_RANGEMAX, and the current value, using DLG_POSITION. Your application can also set:

▶ The number of logical positions the slider moves in response to keyboard input from the arrow keys using DLG_SMALLSTEP.

▶ The number of logical positions the slider moves in response to keyboard input, such as the PAGE UP or PAGE DOWN keys, or mouse input, such as clicks in the slider's channel, using DLG_BIGSTEP.

▶ The interval frequency for tick marks on the slider using DLG_TICKFREQ.

The Slider Control calls the DLG_CHANGE callback whenever the user changes the current value of the control.

The Slider control is named the "Trackbar" control in Windows programming documentation.

11.5.12 Using Tab Controls

The Tab control is like the dividers in a notebook or the labels on a file cabinet. By using a Tab control, an application can define multiple pages for the same area of a dialog box. Each page is associated with a particular Tab and only one page is displayed at a time.

The control index DLG_NUMITEMS determines how many Tabs are contained in the Tab control. For each Tab, you specify the label of the Tab using **DLGSETCHAR** and an index value from 1 to the number of Tabs set with DLG_NUMITEMS. Each Tab has an associated dialog box which is displayed when the Tab is selected. You specify the dialog box using **DLG-SETINT** with the dialog name and an index value corresponding to the the Tab. For example, the code below defines three Tabs in a Tab control. The Tab with the label "Family" is associated with the dialog box named IDD_TAB_DIALOG1, and so on.

```
! Set initial Tabs
lret = DlgSet(gdlg, IDC_TAB, 3)
lret = DlgSet(gdlg, IDC_TAB, "Family", 1)
lret = DlgSet(gdlg, IDC_TAB, "Style", 2)
lret = DlgSet(gdlg, IDC_TAB, "Size", 3)
lret = DlgSet(gdlg, IDC_TAB, IDD_TAB_DIALOG1, 1)
lret = DlgSet(gdlg, IDC_TAB, IDD_TAB_DIALOG2, 2)
lret = DlgSet(gdlg, IDC_TAB, IDD_TAB_DIALOG3, 3)
```

You define each of the Tab dialogs using the resource editor as you do for the dialog box that contains the Tab control. In the Dialog Properties, you must make the following style settings for each Tab dialog:

1. Set the "Style" to "Child"

2. Set "Border" to "None"

3. Uncheck "Title Bar"

Before displaying the dialog box that contains the Tab control (using **DLGMODAL** or **DLGMODELESS**):

1. Call **DLGSETSUB** to define a DLG_INIT callback for the dialog box

2. Call **DLGINIT** for each Tab dialog

In the DLG_INIT callback of the dialog box that contains the Tab control, if the callbacktype is DLG_INIT, call **DLGMODELESS** for each of the Tab dialog boxes. Specify SW_HIDE as the second parameter, and the window handle of the Tab control as the third parameter. After calling **DLG-MODELESS**, call **DLGSET** with the DLG_STATE index to set the initial Tab. For example:

```
! When the Main dialog box is first displayed, call
! DlgModeless to display the Tab dialog boxes. Note the use
! of SW_HIDE. The Dialog Functions will "show" the proper Tab
! dialog box.
if (callbacktype == dlg_init) then
        hwnd = GetDlgItem(dlg % hwnd, IDC_TAB)
        lret = DlgModeless(gdlg_tab1, SW_HIDE, hwnd)
        lret = DlgModeless(gdlg_tab2, SW_HIDE, hwnd)
        lret = DlgModeless(gdlg_tab3, SW_HIDE, hwnd)

        ! Note that we must set the default Tab after the calls
        ! to DlgModeless. Otherwise, no Tab dialog box will be
        ! displayed initially.
        lret = DlgSet(dlg, IDC_TAB, 1, dlg_state)
```

Call **DLGUNINIT** for each Tab dialog when you are done with it.

For a complete example of using a Tab control, see the Visual Fortran Sample ShowFont in the . . . DF98\SAMPLES\DIALOG folder.

11.5.13 Setting Return Values and Exiting

When the user selects the dialog's OK or CANCEL button, your dialog procedure is exited and the dialog box is closed. **DLGMODAL** returns the control name (associated with an integer identifier in your include (.FD) file) of the control that caused it to exit; for example, IDOK or IDCANCEL. If you want to exit your dialog box on a condition other than the user selecting the OK or CANCEL button, you need to include a call to the dialog subroutine **DLGEXIT** from within your callback routine. For example:

```
SUBROUTINE EXITSUB (dlg, exit_button_id, callbacktype)
USE DFLOGM
TYPE (DIALOG) dlg
INTEGER exit_button_id, callbacktype
...
  CALL DLGEXIT (dlg)
```

The only argument for **DLGEXIT** is the dialog derived type. The dialog box is exited after **DLGEXIT** returns control back to the dialog manager, not immediately after calling **DLGEXIT**. That is, if there are other statements following **DLGEXIT** within the callback routine that contains it, those statements are executed and the callback routine returns before the dialog box is exited.

If you want **DLGMODAL** to return with a value other than the control name of the control that caused the exit, (or -1 if **DLGMODAL** fails to open the dialog box), you can specify your own return value with the subroutine **DLGSETRETURN**. For example:

```
TYPE (DIALOG) dlg
INTEGER altreturn
...
altreturn = 485
CALL DLGSETRETURN (dlg, altreturn)
CALL DLGEXIT(dlg)
```

To avoid confusion with the default failure condition, use return values other than -1.

It is not possible to return a value when a modeless dialog box exits. However, you can call **DLGSETSUB** to set the DLG_INIT callback routine to have a procedure called immediately before the dialog box is destroyed.

If you want the user to be able to close the dialog from the system menu or by pressing the ESC key, you need a control that has the ID of IDCANCEL. When a system escape or close is performed, it simulates pressing the dialog button with the ID IDCANCEL. If no control in the dialog has the ID IDCANCEL, then the close command will be ignored (and the dialog can not be closed in this way).

If you want to enable system close or ESC to close a dialog, but don't want a cancel button, you can add a button with the ID IDCANCEL to your dialog and then remove the visible property in the button's Properties box. Pressing ESC will then activate the default click callback of the cancel button and close the dialog.

12

Drawing Graphics Elements

The graphics routines provided with Visual Fortran set points, draw lines, draw text, change colors, and draw shapes such as circles, rectangles, and arcs. This section assumes you have read the overview in Chapter 7 Using QuickWin.

This chapter uses the following terms:

► The *origin* (point 0, 0) is the upper-left corner of the screen or the client area (defined user area) of the child window being written to. The x-axis and y-axis start at the origin. You can change the origin in some coordinate systems.

► The horizontal direction is represented by the *x-axis*, increasing to the right.

► The vertical direction is represented by the *y-axis*, increasing down.

► Some graphics adapters offer a *color palette* that can be changed.

► Some graphics adapters (VGA and SVGA) let you change the color that a color index refers to by providing a *color value* that describes a new color. The color value indicates the mix of red, green, and blue in a screen color. A color value is always an **INTEGER**(4) number.

The sections on drawing graphics are organized as follows:

► Section 12.1 Working with Graphics Modes

► Section 12.2 Adding Color

► Section 12.3 Understanding Coordinate Systems

This chapter also includes information for advanced graphics programmers about using OpenGL graphics:

▶ Section 12.4 Advanced Graphics Using OpenGL

12.1 Working with Graphics Modes

To display graphics, you need to set the desired graphics mode using **SET-WINDOWCONFIG**, and then call the routines needed to create the graphics.

These sections explain each step:

▶ Section 12.1.1 Checking the Current Graphics Mode

▶ Section 12.1.2 Setting the Graphics Mode

▶ Section 12.1.3 Writing a Graphics Program

12.1.1 Checking the Current Graphics Mode

Call **GETWINDOWCONFIG** to get the child window settings. The DFLIB.F90 module in the . . . \DF98\INCLUDE subdirectory defines a derived type, windowconfig, that **GETWINDOWCONFIG** uses as a parameter:

```
TYPE windowconfig
  INTEGER(2) numxpixels    ! Number of pixels on x-axis
  INTEGER(2) numypixels    ! Number of pixels on y-axis
  INTEGER(2) numtextcols   ! Number of text columns available
  INTEGER(2) numtextrows   ! Number of text rows available
  INTEGER(2) numcolors     ! Number of color indexes
  INTEGER(4) fontsize      ! Size of default font
  CHARACTER(80) title      ! window title
  INTEGER(2) bitsperpixel  ! Number of bits per pixel
END TYPE windowconfig
```

By default, a QuickWin child window is a scrollable text window 640x480 pixels, has 30 lines and 80 columns, and a font size of 8x16. Also by default, a Standard Graphics window is Full Screen. You can change the values of window properties at any time with **SETWINDOWCONFIG**, and retrieve the current values at any time with **GETWINDOWCONFIG**.

12.1.2 Setting the Graphics Mode

Use **SETWINDOWCONFIG** to configure the window for the properties you want. To set the highest possible resolution available with your graphics driver, assign a -1 value for numxpixels, numypixels, numtextcols, and numtextrows in the windowconfig derived type. This causes Fortran Standard Graphics applications to start in Full Screen mode.

If you specify less than the largest graphics area, the application starts in a window. You can use ALT+ENTER to toggle between Full Screen and windowed views. If your application is a QuickWin application and you do not call **SETWINDOWCONFIG**, the child window defaults to a scrollable text window with the dimensions of 640x480 pixels, 30 lines, 80 columns, and a font size of 8x16. The number of colors depends on the video driver used.

If **SETWINDOWCONFIG** returns .FALSE., the video driver does not support the options specified. The function then adjusts the values in the windowconfig derived type to ones that will work and are as close as possible to the requested configuration. You can then call **SETWINDOWCONFIG** again with the adjusted values, which will succeed. For example:

```
LOGICAL statusmode
TYPE (windowconfig) wc
wc.numxpixels   = 1000
wc.numypixels   = 300
wc.numtextcols  = -1
wc.numtextrows  = -1
wc.numcolors    = -1
wc.title = "Opening Title"C
wc.fontsize = #000A000C ! 10 X 12
statusmode = SETWINDOWCONFIG(wc)
IF (.NOT. statusmode) THEN statusmode = SETWINDOWCONFIG(wc)
```

If you use **SETWINDOWCONFIG**, you should specify a value for each field (-1 or your own number for numeric fields, and a C string for the title). Calling **SETWINDOWCONFIG** with only some of the fields specified can result in useless values for the other fields.

12.1.3 Writing a Graphics Program

Like many programs, graphics programs work well when written in small units. Using discrete routines aids debugging by isolating the functional components of the program. The following example program and its associated subroutines show the steps involved in initializing, drawing, and closing a graphics program.

The SINE program draws a sine wave. Its procedures call many of the common graphics routines. The main program calls five subroutines that carry out the actual graphics commands (also located in the SINE.F90 file):

```
!   SINE.F90 - Illustrates basic graphics commands.
!
    USE DFLIB
    CALL graphicsmode( )
    CALL drawlines( )
    CALL sinewave( )
    CALL drawshapes( )
    END
    .
    .
    .
```

For information on the subroutines used in the SINE program, see:

▶ Section 12.1.3.1 Activating a Graphics Mode (subroutine graphics-mode)

▶ Section 12.1.3.2 Drawing Lines on the Screen (subroutine drawlines)

▶ Section 12.1.3.3 Drawing a Sine Curve (subroutine sinewave)

▶ Section 12.1.3.4 Adding Shapes (subroutine drawshapes)

The SINE program's output appears in Figure 12-1. The SINE routines are in the Visual Fortran . . . \DF98\SAMPLES\TUTORIAL folder. The project is built as a Fortran Standard Graphics application.

12.1.3.1 *Activating a Graphics Mode*

If you call a graphics routine without setting a graphics mode with **SETWIN-DOWCONFIG**, QuickWin automatically sets the graphics mode with default values.

The SINE program (see Section 12.1.3) selects and sets the graphics mode in the subroutine graphicsmode, which selects the highest possible resolution for the current video driver:

```
SUBROUTINE graphicsmode( )
  USE DFLIB
  LOGICAL              modestatus
  INTEGER(2)           maxx, maxy
  TYPE (windowconfig)  myscreen
  COMMON               maxx, maxy

! Set highest resolution graphics mode.

  myscreen.numxpixels=-1
  myscreen.numypixels=-1
  myscreen.numtextcols=-1
  myscreen.numtextrows=-1
  myscreen.numcolors=-1
```

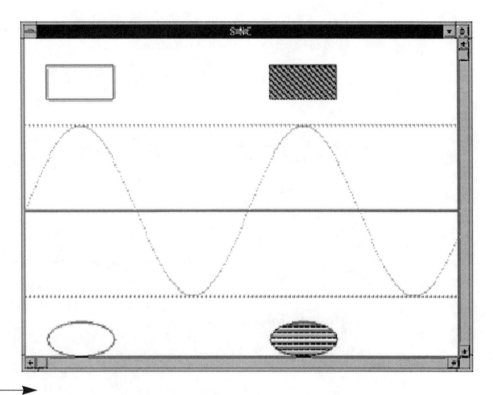

Figure 12–1 *Sine Program Output*

```
myscreen.fontsize=-1
myscreen.title = " "C ! blank

modestatus=SETWINDOWCONFIG(myscreen)

! Determine the maximum dimensions.

modestatus=GETWINDOWCONFIG(myscreen)
maxx=myscreen.numxpixels - 1
maxy=myscreen.numypixels - 1
END
```

Pixel coordinates start at zero, so, for example, a screen with a resolution of 640 horizontal pixels has a maximum x-coordinate of 639. Thus, maxx (the highest available x-pixel coordinate) must be 1 less than the total number of pixels. The same applies to maxy.

To remain independent of the video mode set by graphicsmode, two short functions convert an arbitrary screen size of 1000x1000 pixels to whatever video mode is in effect. From now on, the program assumes it has 1000 pixels in each direction. To draw the points on the screen, newx and newy map each point to their physical (pixel) coordinates:

```fortran
! NEWX - This function finds new x-coordinates.

  INTEGER(2) FUNCTION newx( xcoord )

  INTEGER(2) xcoord, maxx, maxy
  REAL(4) tempx
  COMMON maxx, maxy

  tempx = maxx / 1000.0
  tempx = xcoord * tempx + 0.5
  newx = tempx
  END

! NEWY - This function finds new y-coordinates.
!
  INTEGER(2) FUNCTION newy( ycoord )

  INTEGER(2) ycoord, maxx, maxy
  REAL(4) tempy
  COMMON maxx, maxy

  tempy = maxy / 1000.0
  tempy = ycoord * tempy + 0.5
  newy = tempy
  END
```

You can set up a similar independent coordinate system with *window coordinates*, described in Section 12.3 Understanding Coordinate Systems.

12.1.3.2 *Drawing Lines on the Screen*

The SINE program (see Section 12.1.3) next calls the subroutine drawlines, which draws a rectangle around the outer edges of the screen and three horizontal lines that divide the screen into quarters. (See Figure 12-1.)

```fortran
! DRAWLINES - This subroutine draws a box and
! several lines.

  SUBROUTINE drawlines( )

  USE DFLIB

  EXTERNAL              newx, newy
  INTEGER(2)            status, newx, newy, maxx, maxy
  TYPE (xycoord)        xy
  COMMON                maxx, maxy
```

```
!
! Draw the box.

  status = RECTANGLE($GBORDER, INT2(0), INT2(0), maxx, maxy )
  CALL SETVIEWORG( INT2(0), newy( INT2( 500 ) ), xy ) ! This
!          sets the new origin to 0 for x and 500 for y.
!          See comment after subroutine

! Draw the lines.

  CALL MOVETO( INT2(0), INT2(0), xy )
  status = LINETO( newx( INT2( 1000 )), INT2(0))
  CALL SETLINESTYLE( INT2( #AA3C ))
  CALL MOVETO( INT2(0), newy( INT2( -250 )), xy )
  status = LINETO(newx( INT2( 1000 )),newy( INT2( -250 )))
  CALL SETLINESTYLE( INT2( #8888 ))
  CALL MOVETO(INT2(0), newy( INT2( 250 )), xy )
  status = LINETO( newx( INT2( 1000 )),newy( INT2( 250 ) ) )
  END
```

The first argument to **RECTANGLE** is the *fill flag*, which can be either $GBORDER or $GFILLINTERIOR. Choose $GBORDER if you want a rectangle of four lines (a border only, in the current line style), or $GFILL-INTERIOR if you want a solid rectangle (filled in with the current color and fill pattern). Choosing the color and fill pattern is discussed in Section 12.2 Adding Color and Section 12.1.3.4 Adding Shapes.

The second and third **RECTANGLE** arguments are the x- and y-coordinates of the upper-left corner of the rectangle. The fourth and fifth arguments are the coordinates for the lower-right corner. Because the coordinates for the two corners are (0, 0) and (maxx, maxy), the call to **RECTANGLE** frames the entire screen.

The program calls **SETVIEWORG** to change the location of the viewport origin. By resetting the origin to (0, 500) in a 1000x1000 viewport, you effectively make the viewport run from (0, -500) at the top left of the screen to (1000, 500) at the bottom right of the screen:

```
CALL SETVIEWORG( INT2(0), newy( INT2( 500 ) ), xy )
```

Changing the coordinates illustrates the ability to alter the viewport coordinates to whatever dimensions you prefer. (Viewports and the **SET-VIEWORG** routine are explained in more detail in Section 12.3 Understanding Coordinate Systems.)

The call to **SETLINESTYLE** changes the line style from a solid line to a dashed line. A series of 16 bits tells the routine which pattern to follow. A "1" indicates a solid pixel and "0" an empty pixel. Therefore, 1111 1111 1111 1111 represents a solid line. A dashed line might look like 1111 1111 0000 0000 (long dashes) or 1111 0000 1111 0000 (short dashes). You can choose any combination of ones and zeros. Any INTEGER(2) number in any base is an acceptable input, but binary and hexadecimal numbers are easier to envision as line-style patterns.

In the example, the hexadecimal constant #AA3C equals the binary value 1010 1010 0011 1100. You can use the decimal value 43580 just as effectively.

When drawing lines, first set an appropriate line style. Then, move to where you want the line to begin and call **LINETO**, passing to it the point where you want the line to end. The drawlines subroutine uses the following code:

```
CALL SETLINESTYLE(INT2( #AA3C ) )
CALL MOVETO( INT2(0), newy( INT2( -250 ) ), xy )
dummy = LINETO( newx( INT2( 1000 )), newy( INT2( -250 )))
```

MOVETO positions an imaginary pixel cursor at a point on the screen (nothing appears on the screen), and **LINETO** draws a line. When the program called **SETVIEWORG**, it changed the viewport origin, and the initial y-axis range of 0 to 1000 now corresponds to a range of -500 to +500. Therefore, the negative value -250 is used as the y-coordinate of **LINETO** to draw a horizontal line across the center of the top half of the screen, and the value of 250 is used as the y-coordinate to draw a horizontal line across the center of the bottom half of the screen.

12.1.3.3 *Drawing a Sine Curve*

With the axes and frame in place, the SINE program (see Section 12.1.3) is ready to draw the sine curve. The sinewave routine calculates the x and y positions for two cycles and plots them on the screen:

```
! SINEWAVE - This subroutine calculates and plots a sine
!            wave.
!
    SUBROUTINE sinewave( )
    USE DFLIB

    INTEGER(2)          dummy, newx, newy, locx, locy, i
    INTEGER(4)          color
    REAL                rad
    EXTERNAL            newx, newy
```

```
        PARAMETER          ( PI = 3.14159 )
!
!       Calculate each position and display it on the screen.
        color = #0000FF ! red
!
        DO i = 0, 999, 3
           rad = -SIN( PI * i / 250.0 )
           locx = newx( i )
           locy = newy( INT2( rad * 250.0 ) )
           dummy = SETPIXELRGB( locx, locy, color )
        END DO
        END
```

SETPIXELRGB takes the two location parameters, locx and locy, and sets the pixel at that position with the specified color value (red).

12.1.3.4 *Adding Shapes*

After drawing the sine curve, the SINE program (see Section 12.1.3) calls drawshapes to put two rectangles and two ellipses on the screen. The fill flag alternates between $GBORDER and $GFILLINTERIOR:

```
! DRAWSHAPES - Draws two boxes and two ellipses.
!
  SUBROUTINE drawshapes( )

  USE DFLIB

  EXTERNAL newx, newy
  INTEGER(2) dummy, newx, newy
!
! Create a masking (fill) pattern.
!
  INTEGER(1) diagmask(8), horzmask(8)
  DATA diagmask / #93, #C9, #64, #B2, #59, #2C, #96, #4B /
  DATA horzmask / #FF, #00, #7F, #FE, #00, #00, #00, #CC /
!
! Draw the rectangles.
!
  CALL SETLINESTYLE( INT2(#FFFF ))
  CALL SETFILLMASK( diagmask )
  dummy = RECTANGLE( $GBORDER,newx(INT2(50)),&
  & newy(INT2(-325)), newx(INT2(200)),newy(INT2(-425)))
  dummy = RECTANGLE( $GFILLINTERIOR,newx(INT2(550)), &
  & newy(INT2(-325)),newx(INT2(700)),newy(INT2(-425)))
!
! Draw the ellipses.
!
```

```
CALL SETFILLMASK( horzmask )
dummy = ELLIPSE( $GBORDER,newx(INT2(50)),newy(INT2(325)), &
& newx(INT2(200)),newy(INT2(425)))
dummy = ELLIPSE( $GFILLINTERIOR,newx(INT2(550)), &
& znewy(INT2(325)),newx(INT2(700)),newy(INT2(425)))
END
```

The call to **SETLINESTYLE** resets the line pattern to a solid line. Omitting this routine causes the first rectangle to appear with a dashed border, because the drawlines subroutine called earlier changed the line style to a dashed line.

ELLIPSE draws an ellipse using parameters similar to those for **RECTANGLE**. It, too, requires a fill flag and two corners of a bounding rectangle. The following figure shows how an ellipse uses a bounding rectangle:

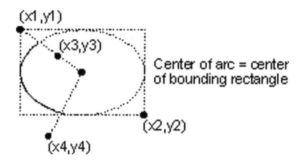

Figure 12–2 *Bounding Rectangle*

The $GFILLINTERIOR constant fills the shape with the current fill pattern. To create a pattern, pass the address of an 8-byte array to **SETFILLMASK**. In drawshapes, the diagmask array is initialized with the following fill pattern:

Bit pattern									Value in diagmask
Bit No. 7	6	5	4	3	2	1	0		
x	o	o	x	o	o	x	x		diagmask(1) = #93
x	x	o	o	x	o	o	x		diagmask(2) = #C9
o	x	x	o	o	x	o	o		diagmask(3) = #64
x	o	x	x	o	o	x	o		diagmask(4) = #B2
o	x	o	x	x	o	o	x		diagmask(5) = #59
o	o	x	o	x	x	o	o		diagmask(6) = #2C
x	o	o	x	o	x	x	o		diagmask(7) = #96
o	x	o	o	x	o	x	x		diagmask(8) = #4B

12.2   Adding Color

The Visual Fortran QuickWin Library supports color graphics. The number of total available colors depends on the current video driver and video adapter you are using. The number of available colors you use depends on the graphics functions you choose. The different color modes and color functions are discussed and demonstrated in the following sections:

▶ Section 12.2.1 Color Mixing

▶ Section 12.2.2 VGA Color Palette

▶ Section 12.2.3 Using Text Colors

12.2.1   Color Mixing

If you have a VGA machine, you are restricted to displaying at most 256 colors at a time. These 256 colors are held in a palette. You can choose the palette colors from a range of 262,144 colors (256K), but only 256 at a time. Some display adapters (most SVGAs) are capable of displaying all of the 256K colors and some (true color display adapters) are capable of displaying 256 * 256 * 256 = 16.7 million colors.

If you use a palette, you are restricted to the colors available in the palette. In order to access all colors available on your system, you need to specify an explicit Red-Green-Blue (RGB) value, not a palette index.

When you select a color index, you specify one of the colors in the system's predefined palette. **SETCOLOR, SETBKCOLOR,** and **SETTEXTCOLOR** set the current color, background color, and text color to a palette index.

SETCOLORRGB, SETBKCOLORRGB, and **SETTEXTCOLORRGB** set the colors to a color value chosen from the entire available range. When you select a color value, you specify a level of intensity with a range of 0-255 for each of the red, green, and blue color values. The long integer that defines a color value consists of 3 bytes (24 bits) as follows:

```
MSB                         LSB
BBBBBBBB GGGGGGGG RRRRRRRR
```

where R, G, and B represent the bit values for red, green, and blue intensities. To mix a light red (pink), turn red all the way up and mix in some green and blue:

```
10000000 10000000 11111111
```

In hexadecimal notation, this number equals #8080FF. You can use the function:

```
i = SETCOLORRGB (#8080FF)
```

to set the current color to this value.

You can also pass decimal values to this function. Keep in mind that 1 (binary 00000001, hex 01) represents a low color intensity and that 255 (binary 11111111, hex FF) equals full color intensity. To create pure yellow (100-percent red plus 100-percent green) use this line:

```
i = SETCOLORRGB( #00FFFF )
```

For white, turn all of the colors on:

```
i = SETCOLORRGB( #FFFFFF)
```

For black, set all of the colors to 0:

```
i = SETCOLORRGB( #000000)
```

Table 12-1 lists the RGB values for example colors.

Table 12–1   *RGB Color Values*

Color	RGB Value	Color	RGB Value
Black	#000000	Bright White	#FFFFFF
Dull Red	#000080	Bright Red	#0000FF
Dull Green	#008000	Bright Green	#00FF00
Dull Yellow	#008080	Bright Yellow	#00FFFF
Dull Blue	#800000	Bright Blue	#FF0000
Dull Magenta	#800080	Bright Magenta	#FF00FF
Dull Turquoise	#808000	Bright Turquoise	#FFFF00
Dark Gray	#808080	Light Gray	#C0C0C0

If you have a 64K-color machine and you set an RGB color value that is not equal to one of the 64K preset RGB color values, the system approximates the requested RGB color to the closest available RGB value. The same thing happens on a VGA machine when you set an RGB color that is not in the palette. (You can remap your VGA color palette to different RGB values. See Section 12.2.2 VGA Color Palette.)

However, although your graphics are drawn with an approximated color, if you retrieve the color with **GETCOLORRGB**, **GETBKCOLORRGB**, or **GETTEXTCOLORRGB**, the color you specified is returned, not the actual color used. This is because the **SETCOLORRGB** functions do not execute any graphics, they simply set the color and the approximation is made when the drawing is made (by **ELLIPSE** or **ARC**, for example). **GETPIXELRGB** and **GETPIXELSRGB** do return the approximated color actually used, because **SETPIXELRGB** and **SETPIXELSRGB** actually set a pixel to a color on the screen and the approximation, if any, is made at the time they are called.

12.2.2 VGA Color Palette

A VGA machine is capable of displaying at most 256 colors at a time. Quick-Win provides support for VGA monitors and more advanced monitors that are set at 256 colors. Only a 256-color palette (or less) is supported internally regardless of the current number of colors set for the display (in the Control Panel). The number of colors you select for your VGA palette depends on your application, and is set by setting the wc.numcolors variable in the windowconfig derived type to 2, 16, or 256 with **SETWINDOWCONFIG**.

An RGB color value must be in the palette to be accessible to your VGA graphic displays. You can change the default colors and customize your color palette by using **REMAPPALETTERGB** to change a palette color index to any RGB color value. The following example remaps the color index 1 (default blue color) to the pure red color value given by the RGB value #0000FF. After this is executed, whatever was displayed as blue will appear as red:

```
USE DFLIB
INTEGER(4) status
status = REMAPPALETTERGB( 1, #0000FF ) ! Reassign color index
                                       ! 1 to RGB red
```

REMAPALLPALETTERGB remaps one or more color indexes simultaneously. Its argument is an array of RGB color values that are mapped into the palette. The first color number in the array becomes the new color associated with color index 0, the second with color index 1, and so on. At most 236 indexes can be mapped, because 20 indexes are reserved for system use.

If you request an RGB color that is not in the palette, the color selected from the palette is the closest approximation to the RGB color requested. If the RGB color was previously placed in the palette with **REMAPPALETTERGB** or **REMAPALLPALETTERGB**, then that exact RGB color is available.

Remapping the palette has no effect on 64K-color machines, SVGA, or true-color machines, unless you limit yourself to a palette by using color index functions such as **SETCOLOR**. On a VGA machine, if you remap all the colors in your palette and display that palette in graphics, you cannot then remap and simultaneously display a second palette.

For instance, in VGA 256-color mode, if you remap all 256 palette colors and display graphics in one child window, then open another child window, remap the palette and display graphics in the second child window, you are attempting to display more than 256 colors at one time. The machine cannot do this, so whichever child window has the focus will appear correct, while the one without the focus will change color.

Note: Machines that support more than 256 colors will not be able to do animation by remapping the palette. Windows operating systems create a logical palette that maps to the video hardware palette. On video hardware that supports a palette of 256 colors or less, remapping the palette maps over the current palette and redraws the screen in the new colors.

On large hardware palettes that support more than 256 colors, remapping is done into the unused portion of the palette. It does not map over the current colors nor redraw the screen. So, on machines with large palettes (more than 256 colors), the technique of changing the screen through remapping, called palette animation, cannot be used. For more information, see the *Win32 SDK Manual.*

Symbolic constants (names) for the default color numbers are supplied in the graphics modules. The names are self-descriptive; for example, the color numbers for black, yellow, and red are represented by the symbolic constants $BLACK, $YELLOW, and $RED.

12.2.3   Using Text Colors

SETTEXTCOLORRGB (or **SETTEXTCOLOR**) and **SETBKCOLOR-RGB** (or **SETBKCOLOR**) set the foreground and background colors for text output. All use a single argument specifying the color value (or color index) for text displayed with **OUTTEXT** and **WRITE**. For the color index functions, colors are represented by the range 0-31. Index values in the range of 16-31 access the same colors as those in the range of 0-15.

You can retrieve the current foreground and background color values with **GETTEXTCOLORRGB** and **GETBKCOLORRGB** or the color indexes with **GETTEXTCOLOR** and **GETBKCOLOR**. Use **SETTEXTPOSI-**

TION to move the cursor to a particular row and column. **OUTTEXT** and **WRITE** print the text at the current cursor location.

For more information on these routines, see the "A-Z Summary" in the *Language Reference* in Visual Fortran online Help.

12.3 Understanding Coordinate Systems

Several different coordinate systems are supported by the Visual Fortran QuickWin Library. Text coordinates work in rows and columns; physical coordinates serve as an absolute reference and as a starting place for creating custom window and viewport coordinates. Conversion routines make it simple to convert between different coordinate systems.

The coordinate systems are demonstrated and discussed in the following sections:

▶ Section 12.3.1 Text Coordinates

▶ Section 12.3.2 Graphics Coordinates

▶ Section 12.3.3 Real Coordinates Sample Program

12.3.1 Text Coordinates

The text modes use a coordinate system that divides the screen into rows and columns as shown in Figure 12-3.

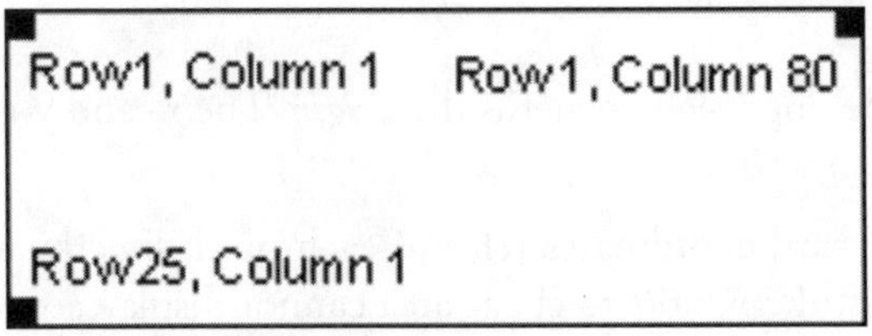

Figure 12–3 *Text Screen Coordinates*

Text coordinates use the following conventions:

▶ Numbering starts at 1. An 80-column screen contains columns 1-80.

▶ The row is always listed before the column.

If the screen displays 25 rows and 80 columns (as shown in the above Figure), the rows are numbered 1-25 and the columns are numbered 1-80. The text-positioning routines, such as **SETTEXTPOSITION** and **SCROLL-TEXTWINDOW**, use row and column coordinates.

12.3.2   Graphics Coordinates

Three coordinate systems describe the location of pixels on the screen: physical coordinates, viewport coordinates, and window coordinates. In all three coordinate systems, the x-coordinate is listed before the y-coordinate.

Physical Coordinates

Physical coordinates are integers that refer to pixels in a window's client area. By default, numbering starts at 0, not 1. If there are 640 pixels, they are numbered 0-639.

Suppose your program calls **SETWINDOWCONFIG** to set up a client area containing 640 horizontal pixels and 480 vertical pixels. Each individual pixel is referred to by its location relative to the x-axis and y-axis, as shown in Figure 12-4.

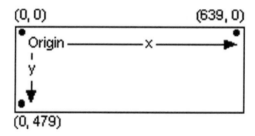

Figure 12–4 *Physical Coordinates*

The upper-left corner is the *origin*. The x- and y-coordinates for the origin are always (0, 0).

Physical coordinates refer to each pixel directly and are therefore integers (that is, the window's client area cannot display a fractional pixel). If you use variables to refer to pixel locations, declare them as integers or use type-conversion routines when passing them to graphics functions. For example:

```
ISTATUS = LINETO( INT2(REAL_x), INT2(REAL_y))
```

If a program uses the default dimension of a window, the *viewport* (drawing area) is equal to 640x480. **SETVIEWORG** changes the location of the viewport's origin. You pass it two integers, which represent the x and y physical screen coordinates for the new origin. You also pass it an xycoord type that the routine fills with the physical coordinates of the previous origin. For example, the following line moves the viewport origin to the physical screen location (50, 100):

```
TYPE (xycoord) origin
CALL SETVIEWORG(INT2(50), INT2(100), origin)
```

The effect on the screen is illustrated in Figure 12-5.

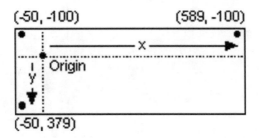

Figure 12–5 *Origin Coordinates Changed by SETVIEWORG*

The number of pixels hasn't changed, but the coordinates used to refer to the points have changed. The x-axis now ranges from -50 to +589 instead of 0 to 639. The y-axis now covers the values -100 to +379.

All graphics routines that use viewport coordinates are affected by the new origin, including **MOVETO**, **LINETO**, **RECTANGLE**, **ELLIPSE**, **POLYGON**, **ARC**, and **PIE**. For example, if you call **RECTANGLE** after relocating the viewport origin and pass it the values (0, 0) and (40, 40), the upper-left corner of the rectangle would appear 50 pixels from the left edge of the screen and 100 pixels from the top. It would not appear in the upper-left corner of the screen.

SETCLIPRGN creates an invisible rectangular area on the screen called a *clipping region*. You can draw inside the clipping region, but attempts to draw outside the region fail (nothing appears outside the clipping region).

The default clipping region occupies the entire screen. The QuickWin Library ignores any attempts to draw outside the screen.

You can change the clipping region by calling **SETCLIPRGN**. For example, suppose you entered a screen resolution of 320x200 pixels. If you draw a diagonal line from (0, 0) to (319, 199), the upper-left to the lower-right corner, the screen looks like Figure 12-6.

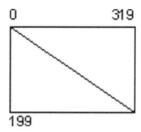

Figure 12–6 *Line Drawn on a Full Screen*

You could create a clipping region by entering:

```
CALL SETCLIPRGN(INT2(10), INT2(10), INT2(309), INT2(189))
```

With the clipping region in effect, the same **LINETO** command would put the line shown in Figure 12-7 on the screen.

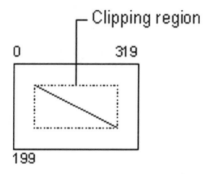

Figure 12–7 *Line Drawn within a Clipping Region*

The dashed lines indicate the outer bounds of the clipping region and do not actually print on the screen.

Viewport Coordinates

The viewport is the area of the screen displayed, which may be only a portion of the window's client area. Viewport coordinates represent the pixels within the current viewport. **SETVIEWPORT** establishes a new viewport within the boundaries of the physical client area. A standard viewport has two distinguishing features:

▶ The origin of a viewport is in the upper-left corner.

▶ The default clipping region matches the outer boundaries of the viewport.

SETVIEWPORT has the same effect as SETVIEWORG and SETCLIP-RGN combined. It specifies a limited area of the screen in the same manner as SETCLIPRGN, then sets the viewport origin to the upper-left corner of the area.

Window Coordinates

Functions that refer to coordinates on the client-area screen and within the viewport require integer values. However, many applications need floating-point values—for frequency, viscosity, mass, and so on. SETWINDOW lets you scale the screen to almost any size. In addition, window-related functions accept double-precision values.

Window coordinates use the current viewport as their boundaries. A window overlays the current viewport. Graphics drawn at window coordinates beyond the boundaries of the window—the same as being outside the viewport—are clipped.

For example, to graph 12 months of average temperatures on the planet Venus that range from -50 to +450, add the following line to your program:

```
status = SETWINDOW(.TRUE., 1.0D0, -50.0D0, 12.0D0, 450.0D0)
```

The first argument is the invert flag, which puts the lowest y value in the lower-left corner. The minimum and maximum x- and y-coordinates follow; the decimal point marks them as floating-point values. The new organization of the screen is shown in Figure 12-8.

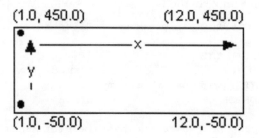

Figure 12–8 *Window Coordinates*

January and December plot on the left and right edges of the screen. In an application like this, numbering the x-axis from 0.0 to 13.0 provides some padding space on the sides and would improve appearance.

If you next plot a point with SETPIXEL_W or draw a line with LINETO_W, the values are automatically scaled to the established window.

To use window coordinates with floating-point values:

1. Set a graphics mode with **SETWINDOWCONFIG**.

2. Use **SETVIEWPORT** to create a viewport area. This step is not necessary if you plan to use the entire screen.

3. Create a real-coordinate window with **SETWINDOW**, passing a **LOGICAL** invert flag and four **DOUBLE PRECISION** x- and y-coordinates for the minimum and maximum values.

4. Draw graphics shapes with **RECTANGLE_W** and similar routines. Do not confuse **RECTANGLE** (the viewport routine) with **RECTANGLE_W** (the window routine for drawing rectangles). All window function names end with an underscore and the letter W (_W).

Real-coordinate graphics give you flexibility and device independence. For example, you can fit an axis into a small range (such as 151.25 to 151.45) or into a large range (-50000.0 to +80000.0), depending on the type of data you graph. In addition, by changing the window coordinates, you can create the effects of zooming in or panning across a figure. The window coordinates also make your drawings independent of the computer's hardware. Output to the viewport is independent of the actual screen resolution.

12.3.3 Real Coordinates Sample Program

The program REALG.F90 shows how to create multiple window-coordinate sets, each in a separate viewport, on a single screen. REALG.F90 is a Visual Fortran Sample in the . . . \DF98\SAMPLES\TUTORIAL folder.

```
! REALG.F90 (main program) - Illustrates coordinate graphics.
!
    USE DFLIB
    LOGICAL                statusmode
    TYPE (windowconfig)    myscreen
    COMMON                 myscreen
!
! Set the screen to the best resolution and maximum number of
! available colors.
  myscreen.numxpixels    = -1
  myscreen.numypixels    = -1
  myscreen.numtextcols   = -1
  myscreen.numtextrows   = -1
  myscreen.numcolors     = -1
  myscreen.fontsize      = -1
  myscreen.title         = " "C
  statusmode = SETWINDOWCONFIG(myscreen)
  IF(.NOT. statusmode) statusmode = SETWINDOWCONFIG(myscreen)
```

```
statusmode = GETWINDOWCONFIG( myscreen )
CALL threegraphs( )
END
```
.
.
.

The main body of the program is very short. It sets the window to the best resolution of the graphics driver (by setting the first four fields to -1) and the maximum number of colors (by setting numcolors to -1). The program then calls the threegraphs subroutine that draws three graphs (see below in Drawing the Graphs). The program output is shown in Figure 12-9.

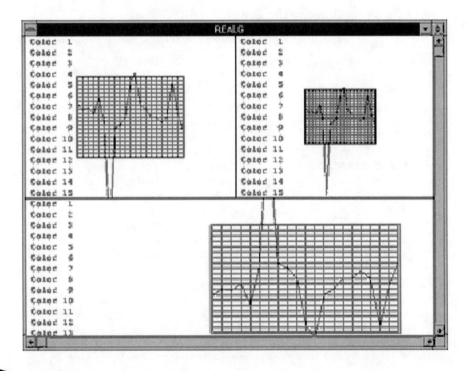

Figure 12–9 *REALG Program Output*

The gridshape subroutine, which draws the graphs, uses the same data in each case (see below in Drawing the Graphs). However, the program uses three different coordinate windows. The two viewports in the top half are the same size in physical coordinates, but have different window sizes. Each window uses different maximum and minimum values.

In all three cases, the graph area is two units wide. The window in the upper-left corner has a range in the x-axis of four units (4 units wide); the window in the upper-right corner has a range in the x-axis of six units, which makes the graph on the right appear smaller.

In two of the three graphs, one of the lines goes off the edge, outside the clipping region. The lines do not intrude into the other viewports, because defining a viewport creates a clipping region.

Finally, the graph on the bottom inverts the data with respect to the two graphs above it.

The next section describes and discusses the subroutine invoked by REALG.F90.

Drawing the Graphs

The main program calls threegraphs, which prints the three graphs.

```
SUBROUTINE threegraphs()
USE DFLIB
INTEGER(2)              status, halfx, halfy
INTEGER(2)              xwidth, yheight, cols, rows
TYPE (windowconfig)     myscreen
COMMON                  myscreen

CALL CLEARSCREEN( $GCLEARSCREEN )
xwidth              = myscreen.numxpixels
yheight             = myscreen.numypixels
cols                = myscreen.numtextcols
rows                = myscreen.numtextrows
halfx               = xwidth / 2
halfy               = (yheight / rows) * ( rows / 2 )
!
! First window
!
    CALL SETVIEWPORT( INT2(0), INT2(0), halfx - 1, halfy - 1 )
    CALL SETTEXTWINDOW( INT2(1), INT2(1), rows / 2, cols / 2 )
    status = SETWINDOW( .FALSE., -2.0_8, -2.0_8, 2.0_8, 2.0_8)
! The 2.0_8 notation makes these constants REAL(8)

    CALL gridshape( rows / 2 )
    status = RECTANGLE( $GBORDER,INT2(0),INT2(0),halfx-1,halfy-1)


!
! Second window
!
```

```
    CALL SETVIEWPORT( halfx, INT2(0), xwidth - 1, halfy - 1 )
    CALL SETTEXTWINDOW( INT2(1), (cols/2) + 1, rows/2, cols)
    status = SETWINDOW( .FALSE., -3.0D0, -3.0D0, 3.0D0, 3.0D0)
! The 3.0D0 notation makes these constants REAL(8)

    CALL gridshape( rows / 2 )
    status = RECTANGLE_W( $GBORDER, -3.0_8,-3.0_8,3.0_8, 3.0_8)


!
! Third window
!
    CALL SETVIEWPORT( 0, halfy, xwidth - 1, yheight - 1 )
    CALL SETTEXTWINDOW( (rows / 2 ) + 1, 1_2, rows, cols )
    status = SETWINDOW( .TRUE., -3.0_8, -1.5_8, 1.5_8, 1.5_8)
    CALL gridshape( INT2( (rows / 2) + MOD( rows, INT2(2))))
    status = RECTANGLE_W( $GBORDER, -3.0_8, -1.5_8, 1.5_8, 1.5_8)
    END
```

Although the screen is initially clear, threegraphs makes sure by calling the **CLEARSCREEN** routine to clear the window:

```
CALL CLEARSCREEN( $GCLEARSCREEN )
```

The $GCLEARSCREEN constant clears the entire window. Other options include $GVIEWPORT and $GWINDOW, which clear the current viewport and the current text window, respectively.

After assigning values to some variables, threegraphs creates the first window:

```
CALL SETVIEWPORT( INT2(0), INT2(0), halfx - 1, halfy - 1)
CALL SETTEXTWINDOW( INT2(1), INT2(1), rows / 2, cols / 2)
status = SETWINDOW( .FALSE., -2.0_8, -2.0_8, 2.0_8, 2.0_8)
```

The first instruction defines a viewport that covers the upper-left quarter of the screen. The next instruction defines a text window within the boundaries of that border. Finally, the third instruction creates a window with both x and y values ranging from -2.0 to 2.0. The .FALSE. constant causes the y-axis to increase from top to bottom, which is the default. The _8 notation identifies the constants as **REAL**(8).

Next, the function gridshape inserts the grid and plots the data, and a border is added to the window:

```
CALL gridshape( rows / 2 )
status = RECTANGLE( $GBORDER,INT2(0),INT2(0),halfx-1,halfy-1)
```

This is the standard **RECTANGLE** routine, which takes coordinates relative to the viewport, not the window.

The gridshape subroutine plots the data on the screen.

```
! GRIDSHAPE - This subroutine plots data for REALG.F90
!
    SUBROUTINE gridshape( numc )
!
    USE DFLIB
    INTEGER(2)            numc, i, status
    INTEGER(4)            rgbcolor, oldcolor
    CHARACTER(8)          str
    REAL(8)               bananas(21), x
    TYPE (windowconfig)   myscreen
    TYPE (wxycoord)       wxy
    TYPE (rccoord)        curpos
    COMMON                myscreen
!
!   Data for the graph:
!
    DATA bananas / -0.3, -0.2, -0.224, -0.1, -0.5, 0.21, 2.9, &
  & 0.3, 0.2, 0.0, -0.885, -1.1, -0.3, -0.2, &
  & 0.001, 0.005, 0.14, 0.0, -0.9, -0.13, 0.31 /
!
! Print colored words on the screen.
!
    IF(myscreen.numcolors .LT. numc) numc = myscreen.numcolors-1
    DO i = 1, numc
       CALL SETTEXTPOSITION( i, INT2(2), curpos )
       rgbcolor = 12**i -1
       rgbcolor = MODULO(rgbcolor, #FFFFFF)
       oldcolor = SETTEXTCOLORRGB( rgbcolor )
       WRITE ( str, '(I8)' ) rgbcolor
       CALL OUTTEXT( 'Color ' // str )
    END DO
!
!   Draw a double rectangle around the graph.
!
    oldcolor = SETCOLORRGB( #0000FF ) ! full red
    status = RECTANGLE_W( $GBORDER, -1.00_8, -1.00_8, 1.00_8,1.00_8)
! constants made REAL(8) by appending _8
    status = RECTANGLE_W( $GBORDER, -1.02_8, -1.02_8, 1.02_8, 1.02_8)
!
!   Plot the points.
!
    x = -0.90
```

```
DO i = 1, 19
  oldcolor = SETCOLORRGB( #00FF00 ) ! full green
  CALL MOVETO_W( x, -1.0_8, wxy )
  status = LINETO_W( x, 1.0_8 )
  CALL MOVETO_W( -1.0_8, x, wxy )
  status = LINETO_W( 1.0_8, x )
  oldcolor = SETCOLORRGB( #FF0000 ) ! full blue
  CALL MOVETO_W( x - 0.1_8, bananas( i ), wxy )
  status = LINETO_W( x, bananas( i + 1 ) )
  x = x + 0.1
END DO

CALL MOVETO_W( 0.9_8, bananas( i ), wxy )
status = LINETO_W( 1.0_8, bananas( i + 1 ) )
oldcolor = SETCOLORRGB( #00FFFF ) ! yellow
END
```

The routine names that end with _W work in the same way as their viewport equivalents, except that you pass double-precision floating-point values instead of integers. For example, you pass **INTEGER**(2) to **LINETO**, but **REAL**(8) values to **LINETO_W**.

The two other windows are similar to the first. All three call the gridshape function, which draws a grid from location (-1.0, -1.0) to (1.0, 1.0). The grid appears in different sizes because the coordinates in the windows vary. The second window ranges from (-3.0, -3.0) to (3.0, 3.0), and the third from (-3.0, -1.5) to (1.5, 1.5), so the sizes change accordingly.

The third window also contains a .TRUE. inversion argument. This causes the y-axis to increase from bottom to top, instead of top to bottom. As a result, this graph appears upside down with respect to the other two.

After calling gridshape, the program frames each window, using a statement such as the following:

```
status = RECTANGLE_W( $GBORDER, -3.0_8, -1.5_8, 1.5_8, 1.5_8)
```

The first argument is a fill flag indicating whether to fill the rectangle's interior or just to draw its outline. The remaining arguments are the x and y coordinates for the upper-left corner followed by the x and y coordinates for the lower-right corner. **RECTANGLE** takes integer arguments that refer to the viewport coordinates. **RECTANGLE_W** takes four double-precision floating-point values referring to window coordinates.

After you create various graphics elements, you can use the font-oriented routines to polish the appearance of titles, headings, comments, or labels. Chapter 13 Using Fonts from the Graphics Library describes in more detail how to print text in various fonts with font routines.

12.4   Advanced Graphics Using OpenGL

OpenGL® is a library of graphic functions that create sophisticated graphic displays such as 3-D images and animation. OpenGL is commonly available on workstations. Writing to this standard allows your program to be ported easily to other platforms.

OpenGL windows are used independently of, and in addition to, any console, QuickWin, and regular Windows windows your application uses. Every window in OpenGL uses a pixel format, and the pixels carry, among other things, RGB values, opacity values, and depth values so that pixels with a small depth (shallow) overwrite deeper pixels. The basic steps in creating OpenGL applications are:

▶ Specify the pixel format

▶ Specify how the pixels will be rendered on the video device

▶ Call OpenGL commands

OpenGL programming is straightforward, but requires a particular initialization and order, like other software tools. References to get you started are:

▶ *The OpenGL Reference Manual,* Addison-Wesley, ISBN 0-201-46140-4.

▶ *The OpenGL Programming Guide,* Addison-Wesley, ISBN 0-201-46138-2.

▶ *OpenGL SuperBible: The Complete Guide to OpenGL Programming on Windows NT and Windows 95,* Richard Wright and Michael Sweet, Waite Group Press (Division of Sams Publishing), 1996, ISBN 1-57169-073-5.

▶ OpenGL documentation in the Windows NT, Windows 98, and Windows 95 Platform SDK in HTML Help Viewer.

▶ The OpenGL description from the Microsoft Visual C++ manuals.

Visual Fortran provides an OpenGL module, DFOPNGL.MOD, invoked with the **USE DFOPNGL** statement line.

When you use this module, all constants and interfaces that bind Fortran to the OpenGL routines become available. Any link libraries required to link with an OpenGL program are automatically searched if **USE DFOPNGL** is present in your Fortran program.

An OpenGL window can be opened from a console, Windows, or QuickWin application. The OpenGL window uses OpenGL calls exclusively, not normal Graphic Device Interface (GDI) calls. Likewise, OpenGL calls cannot be made within an ordinary Windows window or QuickWin child window, because special initialization is required for OpenGL calls.

The Fortran OpenGL identifiers are the same as the C identifiers, except that the gl prefix is changed to fgl, and the GL prefix is changed to FGL. The data types in the OpenGL C binding are translated to Fortran types as shown in Table 12-2.

Table 12–2 *OpenGL/C and Equivalent Fortran Data Types*

OpenGL/C Type	Fortran Data Type
GLbyte	INTEGER(1)
GLshort	INTEGER(2)
GLint, GLsizei	INTEGER(4)
GLfloat, GLclampf	REAL(4)
GLdouble, GLclampd	REAL(8)
GLubyte	INTEGER(1)
GLboolean	LOGICAL
GLushort	INTEGER(2)
GLuint, GLenum, GLbitfield	INTEGER(4)
GLvoid	not needed
pointers	INTEGER

Visual Fortran Samples that use OpenGL are available in separate folders in . . . \DF98\SAMPLES\ADVANCED\OPENGL. For example, OLYMPIC is a Fortran QuickWin project and CUBE5 is a Fortran Windows project.

13

Using Fonts from the Graphics Library

The Visual Fortran Graphics Library includes routines that print text in various sizes and type styles. These routines provide control over the appearance of your text and add visual interest to your screen displays.

This section assumes you have read Chapter 12 Drawing Graphics Elements and that you understand the general terminology it introduces. You should also be familiar with the basic properties of both the **SETWINDOW-CONFIG** and **MOVETO** routines. Also, remember that graphics programs containing graphics routines must be built as Fortran QuickWin or Fortran Standard Graphics applications.

The project type is set in the visual development environment when you select New from the File menu, then click on the Projects tab, and select Fortran QuickWin or Standard Graphics Application from the application types listed. Graphics applications can also be built with the /libs:qwin or /libs: qwins compiler option.

Font types and the use of fonts are described in the following sections:

▶ Section 13.1 Available Typefaces

▶ Section 13.2 Using Fonts

▶ Section 13.3 SHOWFONT.F90 Example

13.1   Available Typefaces

A *font* is a set of text characters of a particular size and style. A *typeface* (or *type style*) refers to the style of the displayed text—Arial, for example, or Times New Roman.

Type size measures the screen area occupied by individual characters. The term comes from the printer's lexicon, but uses screen pixels as the unit of measure rather than the traditional points. For example, "Courier 12 9" denotes the Courier typeface, with each character occupying a screen area of 12 vertical pixels by 9 horizontal pixels. The word "font," therefore implies both a typeface and a type size.

The QuickWin Library's font routines use all Windows operating system installed fonts. The first type of font used is a *bitmap* (or *raster-map*) font. Bitmap fonts have each character in a binary data map. Each bit in the map corresponds to a screen pixel. If the bit equals 1, its associated pixel is set to the current screen color. Bit values of 0 appear in the current background color.

The second type of font is called a TrueType font. Some screen fonts look different on a printer, but TrueType fonts print exactly as they appear on the screen. TrueType fonts may be bitmaps or soft fonts (fonts that are downloaded to your printer before printing), depending on the capabilities of your printer. TrueType fonts are scalable and can be sized to any height. It is recommended that you use TrueType fonts in your graphics programs.

Each type of font has advantages and disadvantages. Bitmapped characters appear smoother on the screen because of the predetermined pixel mapping. However, they cannot be scaled. You can scale TrueType text to any size, but the characters sometimes don't look quite as solid as the bitmapped characters on the screen. Usually this screen effect is hardly noticeable, and when printed, TrueType fonts are as smooth or smoother than bitmapped fonts.

The bitmapped typefaces come in preset sizes measured in pixels. The exact size of any font depends on screen resolution and display type.

13.2   Using Fonts

QuickWin's font routines can use all the Windows operating system installed fonts. To use fonts in your program, you must:

1. Initialize the fonts (see Section 13.2.1).

2. Select a current font from the initialized fonts (see Section 13.2.2).

3. Display font text with **OUTGTEXT** (see Section 13.2.2).

13.2.1 Initializing Fonts

A program that uses fonts must first organize the fonts into a list in memory, a process called initializing. The list gives the computer information about the available fonts.

Initialize the fonts by calling the **INITIALIZEFONTS** routine:

```
USE DFLIB
INTEGER(2) numfonts
numfonts = INITIALIZEFONTS( )
```

If the computer successfully initializes one or more fonts, **INITIALIZE-FONTS** returns the number of fonts initialized. If the function fails, it returns a negative error code.

13.2.2 Setting the Font and Displaying Text

Before a program can display text in a particular font, it must know which of the initialized fonts to use. **SETFONT** makes one of the initialized fonts the current (or "active") font. **SETFONT** has the following syntax:

SETFONT(*options*)

The function's argument consists of letter codes that describe the desired font: typeface, character height and width in pixels, fixed or proportional, and attributes such as bold or italic. For more information on the options, see **SETFONT** in the "A-Z Summary" in the *Language Reference* in Visual Fortran online Help. For example:

```
USE DFLIB
INTEGER(2) index, numfonts
numfonts = INITIALIZEFONTS ( )
index = SETFONT('t''Cottage''h18w10')
```

This sets the typeface to Cottage, the character height to 18 pixels and the width to 10 pixels.

The following example sets the typeface to Arial, the character height to 14, with proportional spacing and italics (the pi codes):

```
index = SETFONT('t''Arial''h14pi')
```

If **SETFONT** successfully sets the font, it returns the font's index number. If the function fails, it returns a negative integer. Call **GRSTATUS** to find the source of the problem; its return value indicates why the function failed. If you call **SETFONT** before initializing fonts, a run-time error occurs.

SETFONT updates the font information when it is used to select a font. **GETFONTINFO** can be used to obtain information about the currently selected font. **SETFONT** sets the user fields in the fontinfo type (a derived type defined in DFLIB.MOD), and **GETFONTINFO** returns the user-selected values. The following user fields are contained in fontinfo:

```
TYPE fontinfo
  INTEGER(2) type ! 1 = truetype, 0 = bit map
  INTEGER(2) ascent ! Pixel distance from top to baseline
  INTEGER(2) pixwidth ! Character width in pixels, 0=prop
  INTEGER(2) pixheight ! Character height in pixels
  INTEGER(2) avgwidth ! Average character width in pixels
  CHARACTER(32) facename ! Font name
END TYPE fontinfo
```

To find the parameters of the current font, call **GETFONTINFO**. For example:

```
USE DFLIB
TYPE (fontinfo) font
INTEGER(2) i, numfonts
numfonts = INITIALIZEFONTS()
i = SETFONT ( ' t ' 'Arial ' )
i = GETFONTINFO(font)
WRITE (*,*) font.avgwidth, font.pixheight, font.pixwidth
```

After you initialize the fonts and make one the active font, you can display the text on the screen. To display text on the screen after selecting a font:

1. Select a starting position for the text with **MOVETO**.

2. Optionally, set a text display angle with **SETGTEXTROTATION**.

3. Send the text to the screen (in the current font) with **OUTGTEXT**.

MOVETO moves the current graphics point to the pixel coordinates passed to it when it is invoked. This becomes the starting position of the upper-left corner of the first character in the text. **SETGTEXTROTATION** can set the text's orientation in one-degree increments.

13.3   SHOWFONT.F90 Example

The Visual Fortran Sample program SHOWFONT.F90 in the . . . \DF98\ SAMPLES\TUTORIAL folder displays text in the fonts available on your system. (Once the screen fills with text, press Enter to display the next screen.) An abbreviated version follows. SHOWFONT calls **SETFONT** to specify the typeface. **MOVETO** then establishes the starting point for each text string. The program sends a message of sample text to the screen for each font initialized:

```fortran
! Abbreviated version of SHOWFONT.F90.
    USE DFLIB

    INTEGER(2) grstat, numfonts,indx, curr_height
    TYPE (xycoord) xyt
    TYPE (fontinfo) f
    CHARACTER(6) str ! 5 chars for font num
                                    ! (max. is 32767), 1 for 'n'


! Initialization.
    numfonts=INITIALIZEFONTS( )
    IF (numfonts.LE.0) PRINT *,"INITIALIZEFONTS error"
    IF (GRSTATUS().NE.$GROK) PRINT *,'INITIALIZEFONTS GRSTATUS error.'
    CALL MOVETO (0,0,xyt)
    grstat=SETCOLORRGB(#FF0000)
    grstat=FLOODFILLRGB(0, 0, #00FF00)
    grstat=SETCOLORRGB(0)
! Get default font height for comparison later.
    grstat = SETFONT('n1')
    grstat = GETFONTINFO(f)
    curr_height = f.pixheight
! Done initializing, start displaying fonts.
    DO indx=1,numfonts
       WRITE(str,10)indx
       grstat=SETFONT(str)
       IF (grstat.LT.1) THEN
          CALL OUTGTEXT('SetFont error.')
       ELSE
          grstat=GETFONTINFO(f)
          grstat=SETFONT('n1')
          CALL OUTGTEXT(f.facename(:len_trim(f.facename)))
          CALL OUTGTEXT(' ')
! Display font.
          grstat=SETFONT(str)
          CALL OUTGTEXT('ABCDEFGabcdefg12345!@#$%')
       END IF
! Go to next line.
       IF (f.pixheight .GT. curr_height) curr_height=f.pixheight
       CALL GETCURRENTPOSITION(xyt)
       CALL MOVETO(0,INT2(xyt.ycoord+curr_height),xyt)
    END DO
10    FORMAT ('n',I5.5)
    END
```

14

Using National Language Support Routines

Visual Fortran provides a complete National Language Support (NLS) library of language-localization routines and multibyte-character routines. You can use these routines to write applications in many different languages. In many languages, the standard ASCII character set is not enough because it lacks common symbols and punctuation (such as the British pound sign), or because the language uses a non-ASCII script (such as Cyrillic for Russian) or because the language consists of too many characters for each to be represented by a single byte (such as Chinese).

In the case of many non-ASCII languages, such as Arabic and Russian, an extended single-byte character set is sufficient. You need only change the language locale and codepage, which can be done at a system level or within your program. However, Eastern languages such as Japanese and Chinese use thousands of separate characters that cannot be encoded as single-byte characters. Multibyte characters are needed to represent them.

Character sets are stored in tables called code sets. There are three components of a code set: the locale, which is a language and country (since, for instance, the language Spanish may vary among countries), the codepage, which is a table of characters to make up the computer's alphabet, and the font used to represent the characters on the screen. These three components can be set independently.

Each computer running Windows NT or Windows 95 comes with many code sets built into the system, such as English, Arabic, and Spanish. Multibyte code sets, such as Chinese and Japanese, are not standard but come with special versions of the operating system (for instance, Windows NT-J comes with the Japanese code set).

The default code set is obtained from the operating system when a program starts up. When you install your operating system, you should install the system supplied code sets. Thereafter, they are always available. You can switch among them by:

▶ Open the Control Panel (available from Settings)

▶ Click the Regional Settings icon

▶ Choose from the dropdown list of available locales (languages and countries)

When you select a new locale, it becomes the default system locale, and will remain the default locale until you change it. Each locale has a default codepage associated with it, and a default currency, number, and date format.

Note: The default codepage does not change when you select a new locale until you reboot your computer.

You can change the currency, number, and date format in the International dialog box or the Regional Setting dialog box independently of the locale.

The locale determines the character set available to the user. The locale you select becomes the default for the NLS routines described in this section, but the NLS routines allow you to change locales and their parameters from within your programs. These routines are useful for creating original foreign-language programs or different versions of the same program for various international markets. Changes you make to the locale from within a program affect only the program. They do not change the system default settings.

The codepage you select, which can be set independently, controls the multibyte (MB routines) character routines described in this section. Only users with special multibyte-character code sets installed on their computers need to use MB routines. The standard code sets all use single-byte character code sets.

Note that in Visual Fortran source code, multibyte characters can be used only in character strings and source comments. They cannot be used within variable names or statements. Like program changes to the locale, program changes to codepages affect only the program, not the system defaults.

The NLS and MB routines are contained in the library DFNLS.LIB which consists of DFNLS.MOD and DFNLS.F90. To access the routines, the statement **USE DFNLS** should be present in any program unit that uses NLS or MB routines.

This section includes a discussion of character sets and the NLS library routines:

▶ Section 14.1 Single and Multibyte Character Sets

▶ Section 14.2 National Language Support Library Routines

14.1   Single and Multibyte Character Sets

The ASCII character set defines the characters from 0 to 127 and an extended set from 128 to 255. Several alternative single-byte character sets, primarily European, define the characters from 0 to 127 identically to ASCII, but define the characters from 128 to 255 differently. With this extension, 8-bit representation is sufficient for defining the needed characters in most European-derived languages. However, some languages, such as Japanese Kanji, include many more characters than can be represented with a single byte. These languages require multibyte coding.

A multibyte character set consists of both one-byte and two-byte characters. A multibyte-character string can contain a mix of single and double-byte characters. A two-byte character has a lead byte and a trail byte. In a particular multibyte character set, the lead and trail byte values can overlap, and it is then necessary to use the byte's context to determine whether it is a lead or trail byte.

14.2   National Language Support Library Routines

The library routines for handling extended and multibyte character sets are divided into three categories:

▶ Locale Setting and Inquiry Routines to set locales (local code sets) and inquire about their current settings (see Section 14.2.1)

▶ NLS Formatting Routines to format dates, currency, and numbers (see Section 14.2.2)

▶ Multibyte character routines (see Section 14.2.3)

All of these routines are described in detail in the "A-Z Summary" in the *Language Reference* in Visual Fortran online Help.

In the descriptions that follow, function and parameter names are given with a mixture of upper- and lowercase letters. This is to make the names easier to understand. You can use any case for these names when writing your applications.

14.2.1 Locale Setting and Inquiry Routines

At program startup, the current language and country setting is retrieved from the operating system. The user can change this setting through the Control Panel Regional Settings icon. The current codepage is also retrieved from the system. There is a system default console codepage and a system default Windows codepage. Console programs retrieve the system console codepage, while Windows programs (including QuickWin applications) retrieve the system Windows codepage.

The NLS Library provides routines to determine the current locale (local code set), to return parameters of the current locale, to provide a list of all the system supported locales, and to set the locale to another language, country and/or codepage. These routines are summarized in Table 14-1.

The locales and codepages set with these routines affect only the program or console that calls the routine. They do not change the system defaults or affect other programs or consoles.

Table 14–1 *Routines to Set and Inquire about the Locales*

Name	Procedure Type	Description
NLSSetLocale	Function	Sets the language, country, and codepage
NLSGetLocale	Subroutine	Retrieves the current language, country, and codepage
NLSGetLocaleInfo	Function	Retrieves requested information about the current local code set
NLSEnumLocales	Function	Returns all the languages and country combinations supported by the system
NLSEnumCodepages	Function	Returns all the supported codepages on the system
NLSSetEnvironment Codepage	Function	Changes the codepage for the current console
NLSGetEnvironment Codepage	Function	Returns the codepage number for the system (Window) codepage or the console codepage

As an example:

```
USE DFNLS
INTEGER(4) strlen, status
CHARACTER(40) str

strlen = NLSGetLocaleInfo(NLS$LI_SDAYNAME1, str)
print *, str ! prints Monday
strlen = NLSGetLocaleInfo(NLS$LI_SDAYNAME2, str)
print *, str ! prints Tuesday
strlen = NLSGetLocaleInfo(NLS$LI_SDAYNAME3, str)
print *, str ! prints Wednesday
! Change locale to Spanish, Mexico
status = NLSSetLocale("Spanish", "Mexico")
strlen = NLSGetLocaleInfo(NLS$LI_SDAYNAME1, str)
print *, str ! prints lunes
strlen = NLSGetLocaleInfo(NLS$LI_SDAYNAME2, str)
print *, str ! prints martes
strlen = NLSGetLocaleInfo(NLS$LI_SDAYNAME3, str)
print *, str ! prints miércoles
END
```

14.2.2 NLS Formatting Routines

You can set time, date, currency, and number formats from the Control Panel, by clicking on the Regional Settings icon. The NLS Library also provides formatting routines for the current locale. These routines are summarized in Table 14-2. These routines return strings in the current codepage, set by default at program start or by **NLSSetLocale**.

All the formatting routines return the number of bytes in the formatted string (not the number of characters, which can vary if multibyte characters are included). If the output string is longer than the formatted string, the output string is blank padded. If the output string is shorter than the formatted string, an error occurs, NLS$ErrorInsufficientBuffer is returned, and nothing is written to the output string.

Table 14–2 *Formatting Routines*

Name	Procedure Type	Description
NLSFormatCurrency	Function	Formats a number string and returns the correct currency string for the current locale
NLSFormatDate	Function	Returns a correctly formatted string containing the date for the current locale

Table 14–2 *Formatting Routines (Continued)*

Name	Procedure Type	Description
NLSFormatNumber	Function	Formats a number string and returns the correct number string for the current locale
NLSFormatTime	Function	Returns a correctly formatted string containing the time for the current locale

As an example:

```
USE DFNLS
INTEGER(4) strlen, status
CHARACTER(40) str
strlen = NLSFormatTime(str)
print *, str ! prints 11:42:24 AM
strlen = NLSFormatDate(str, flags= NLS$LongDate)
print *, str ! prints Friday, July 14, 1995
status = NLSSetLocale ("Spanish", "Mexico")
strlen = NLSFormatTime(str)
print *, str ! prints 11:42:24
print *, str ! prints viernes 14 de julio de 1995
```

14.2.3 Multibyte Character Routines

All of the routines in this section are intended for use with Multibyte Character Sets (MBCS). Examples of such characters sets are Japanese, Korean, and Chinese. The routines in this section work from the current codepage, set with **NLSSetLocale** and read back with **NLSGetLocale**. String comparison routines, such as **MBLLT**, are based on the current language and country settings.

Routines discussed in this section are:

▶ Section 14.2.3.1 MBCS Inquiry Routines

▶ Section 14.2.3.2 MBCS Conversion Routines

▶ Section 14.2.3.3 MBCS Fortran Equivalent Routines

▶ Section 14.2.3.4 Standard Fortran 90 Routines That Handle MBCS Characters

14.2.3.1 MBCS Inquiry Routines

The MBCS inquiry routines provide information on the maximum length of multibyte characters, the length, number and position of multibyte characters in strings, and whether a multibyte character is a leading or trailing byte. These routines are summarized in Table 14-3.

The NLS library provides a parameter, MBLenMax, defined in the NLS module to be the longest length (in bytes) of any character, in any codepage. This parameter can be useful in comparisons and tests. To determine the maximum character length of the current codepage, use the **MBCurMax** function.

Table 14–3 *MBCS Inquiry Routines*

Name	*Procedure Type*	*Description*
MBCharLen	Function	Returns the length of the first multibyte character in a string
MBCurMax	Function	Returns the longest possible mutlibyte character for the current codepage
MBLead	Function	Determines whether a given character is the first byte of a multibyte character
MBLen	Function	Returns the number of multibyte characters in a string, including trailing spaces
MBLen_Trim	Function	Returns the number of multibyte characters in a string, not including trailing spaces
MBNext	Function	Returns the string position of the first byte of the multibyte character immediately after the given string position
MBPrev	Function	Returns the string position of the first byte of the multibyte character immediately before the given string position
MBStrLead	Function	Performs a context sensitive test to determine whether a given byte in a character string is a lead byte

As an example:

```
USE DFNLS
CHARACTER(4) str
INTEGER status
status = NLSSetLocale ("Japan")
str = " ·, " ¿"
PRINT '(1X,''String by char = '',\)'
DO i = 1, len(str)
PRINT '(A2,\)',str(i:i)
END DO
PRINT '(/,1X,''MBLead = '',\)'
DO i = 1, len(str)
   PRINT '(L2,\)',mblead(str(i:i))
END DO
```

```
PRINT '(/,1X,''String as whole = '',A,\)',str
PRINT '(/,1X,''MBStrLead = '',\)'
DO i = 1, len(str)
  PRINT '(L1,\)',MBStrLead(str,i)
END DO
END
```

Figure 14-1 shows the output produced by the preceding code for str = · , " ¿

```
String by char  =   · · ·ソ
MBLead          =  T T T F
String as whole = 高徳
MBStrLead       = TFTF
```

Figure 14–1 *MBCS Inquiry Example*

14.2.3.2 MBCS Conversion Routines

There are four MBCS conversion routines: two convert Japan Industry Standard characters to Microsoft Kanji characters or vice versa, and the other two convert between a codepage mutlibyte character string and a Unicode string. These routines are summarized in Table 14-4.

Table 14–4 *MBCS Conversion Routines*

Name	Procedure Type	Description
MBConvertMBToUnicode	Function	Converts a character string from a multibyte codepage to a Unicode string
MBConvertUnicodeToMB	Function	Converts a Unicode string to a multibyte character string of the current codepage
MBJISToJMS	Function	Converts a Japan Industry Standard (JIS) character to a Microsoft Kanji (Shift JIS or JMS) character
MBJMSToJIS	Function	Converts a Microsoft Kanji (Shift JIS or JMS) character to a Japan Industry Standard (JIS) character

14.2.3.3 MBCS Fortran 90 Equivalent Routines

The NLS Library provides several functions that are the exact equivalents of Fortran 90 functions except that the MBCS equivalents allow character strings to contain multibyte characters. These routines are summarized in Table 14-5.

Table 14–5 *MBCS Fortran 90 Equivalent Routines*

Name	Procedure Type	Description
MBINCHARQQ	Function	Same as **INCHARQQ** but can read a single multibyte character at once and returns the number of bytes read
MBINDEX	Function	Same as **INDEX** except that multibyte characters can be included in its arguments
MBLGE, MBLGT, MBLLE, MBLLT, MBLEQ, MBLNE	Functions	Same as **LGE**, **LGT**, **LLE**, **LLT** and the operators .EQ. and .NE. except that multibyte characters can be included in their arguments
MBSCAN	Function	Same as **SCAN** except that multibyte characters can be included in its arguments
MBVERIFY	Function	Same as **VERIFY** except that multibyte characters can be included in its arguments

The following example is included in Visual Fortran Samples in the . . . \DF98\SAMPLES\TUTORIAL folder as MBCOMP.FOR:

```
USE DFNLS

INTEGER(4) i, len(7), infotype(7)
CHARACTER(10) str(7)
LOGICAL(4) log4

data infotype / NLS$LI_SDAYNAME1, NLS$LI_SDAYNAME2, &
&     NLS$LI_SDAYNAME3, NLS$LI_SDAYNAME4, &
&     NLS$LI_SDAYNAME5, NLS$LI_SDAYNAME6, &
&     NLS$LI_SDAYNAME7 /
WRITE(*,*) 'NLSGetLocaleInfo'
WRITE(*,*) '----------------'
WRITE(*,*) ' '
WRITE(*,*) 'Getting the names of the days of the week...'

DO i = 1, 7
  len(i) = NLSGetLocaleInfo(infotype(i), str(i))
   WRITE(*, 11) 'len/str/hex = ', len(i), str(i), str(i)
END DO
11 FORMAT (1X, A, I2, 2X, A10, 2X, '[', Z20, ']')

WRITE(*,*) ' '
WRITE(*,*) 'Lexically comparing the names of the days...'

DO i = 1, 6
  log4 = MBLGE(str(i), str(i+1), NLS$IgnoreCase)
   WRITE(*, 12) 'Is day ', i, ' GT day ', i+1, '? Answer = &
```

```
&     ', log4
      END DO
12    FORMAT (1X, A, I1, A, I1, A, L1)

      WRITE(*,*) ' '
      WRITE(*,*) 'Done.'
      END
```

Figure 14-2 shows the output produced by the preceding code when the locale is Japan:

```
NLSGetLocaleInfo
----------------

Getting the names of the days of the week...
len/str/hex =  6  月曜日      [8C8E976A93FA20202020]
len/str/hex =  6  火曜日      [89CE976A93FA20202020]
len/str/hex =  6  水曜日      [9085976A93FA20202020]
len/str/hex =  6  木曜日      [96D8976A93FA20202020]
len/str/hex =  6  金曜日      [8BE0976A93FA20202020]
len/str/hex =  6  土曜日      [9379976A93FA20202020]
len/str/hex =  6  日曜日      [93FA976A93FA20202020]

Lexically comparing the names of the days...
Is day 1 GT day 2?  Answer = T
Is day 2 GT day 3?  Answer = F
Is day 3 GT day 4?  Answer = F
Is day 4 GT day 5?  Answer = T
Is day 5 GT day 6?  Answer = F
Is day 6 GT day 7?  Answer = F

Done.
```

Figure 14–2   *MBCS Equivalents Example*

14.2.3.4 Standard Fortran Routines That Handle MBCS Characters

This section describes Fortran routines that work as usual even if MBCS characters are included in strings.

Because a space can never be a lead or tail byte, many routines that deal with spaces work as expected on strings containing MBCS characters. Such functions include:

ADJUSTL(*string*), **ADJUSTR**(*string*), **TRIM** (*string*)

Some routines work with the computer collating sequence to return a character in a certain position in the sequence or the position in the sequence of a certain character. These functions are not dependent on a particular collating sequence. (You should note, however, that elsewhere in this manual the ASCII collating sequence is mentioned in reference to these functions.) Such functions use position and c values between 0 and 255 (inclusive) and include:

ACHAR(*position*), **CHAR**(*position* [, *kind*]), **IACHAR**(*c*), **ICHAR**(*c*)

Because Fortran uses character lengths instead of NULLs to indicate the length of a string, some functions work solely from the length of the string, and not with the contents of the string. These functions work as usual on strings containing MBCS characters, and include:

REPEAT (*string, ncopies*)

15

Portability Library

Visual Fortran includes functions and subroutines that ease porting of code from a different platform to a PC, or allow you to write code on a PC that is compatible with other platforms. Frequently used routines are included in a module called DFPORT.

This chapter describes how to use the portability module, and describes routines available in the following categories:

▶ Section 15.1 Using the Portability Library

▶ Section 15.2 Routines for Information Retrieval

▶ Section 15.3 Process Control Routines

▶ Section 15.4 Numeric Routines

▶ Section 15.5 Input and Output with Portability Routines

▶ Section 15.6 Date and Time Routines

▶ Section 15.7 Error Handling Routines

▶ Section 15.8 Miscellaneous String and Sorting Routines

▶ Section 15.9 Other Compatibility Routines

Fortran 90 contains intrinsic procedures for many of these routines. New code should use standard Fortran 90 procedures whenever possible.

15.1 Using the Portability Library

You can use the portability library (DFPORT) in one of two ways:

▶ Add the statement **USE DFPORT** to your program. This includes the DFPORT module.

▶ Call portability routines using the correct parameters and return value.

The portability library DFPORT.LIB library is passed to the linker by default during linking. To prevent DFPORT.LIB library from being passed to the linker, specify the /fpscomp:nolibs option.

Using the DFPORT module provides interface blocks and parameter definitions for the routines, as well as compiler verification of calls.

Some routines in this library can be called with different sets of arguments, and sometimes even as a function instead of a subroutine. In these cases, the arguments and calling mechanism determine the meaning of the routine. The DFPORT module contains generic interface blocks that give procedure definitions for these routines.

15.2 Routines for Information Retrieval

Table 15-1 lists the routines classified as information retrieval routines. These routines return information about system commands, command-line arguments, environment variables, and process or user information. All routines are fully described in the "A-Z Summary" in the *Language Reference* in Visual Fortran online Help.

All portability routines that take path names also accept long file names or UNC (Universal Naming Convention) file names. A forward slash in a path name is treated as a backslash. All path names can contain drive specifications as well as MBCS (multiple-byte character set) characters. For information on MBCS characters, see Chapter 14 Using National Language Support Routines.

Table 15–1   *Information Retrieval Routines for Portability*

Portability Routine	Description
IARGC	Returns the index of the last command-line argument
GETENV	Searches the environment for a given string, and returns its value if found
GETGID	Returns the group ID of the user
GETLOG	Get user's login name
GETPID	Returns the process ID of the process

Table 15–1   *Information Retrieval Routines for Portability (Continued)*

Portability Routine	Description
GETUID	Returns the user ID of the user of the process
HOSTNAM	Returns the name of the user's host

Group, user, and process ID are **INTEGER**(4) variables. Login name and host name are character variables. The routines **GETGID** and **GETUID** are provided for portability, but always return 1.

IARGC is best used with **GETARG**. **GETARG**, which returns command line arguments, and is available in the standard Visual Fortran library; you do not have to specify **USE DFPORT** in your program unit.

For more information, see Section 15.2.1 Device and Directory Information Routines.

15.2.1   Device and Directory Information Routines

You can retrieve information about devices, directories, and files with the routines listed in Table 15-2. File names can be long file names or UNC file names. A forward slash in a path name is treated as a backslash. All path names can contain drive specifications. All routines are fully described in the "A-Z Summary" in the *Language Reference* in Visual Fortran online Help.

Table 15–2   *Device and Directory Information Routines for Portability*

Portability Routine	Description
CHDIR	Changes the current working directory
FSTAT	Returns information about a logical file unit
GETCWD	Returns the current working directory path name
RENAME	Renames a file
STAT, LSTAT	Returns information about a named file
UNLINK	Removes a directory entry from the path

Standard Fortran 90 provides the **INQUIRE** statement, which returns detailed file information either by file name or unit number (see the "A-Z Summary" in the *Language Reference* in Visual Fortran online Help). Use **INQUIRE** as an equivalent to **FSTAT**, **LSTAT** or **STAT**. **LSTAT** and **STAT** return the same information; **STAT** is the preferred routine.

15.3   Process Control Routines

Table 15-3 lists the process control routines. These routines control the operation of a process or subprocess. You can wait for a subprocess to complete with either **SLEEP** or **ALARM**, monitor its progress and send signals via **KILL**, and stop its execution with **ABORT**.

In spite of its name, **KILL** does not necessarily stop execution of a program. Rather, the routine signaled could include a handler routine that examines the signal and takes appropriate action depending on the code passed. The routines are described fully in the "A-Z Summary" in the *Language Reference* in Visual Fortran online Help.

Table 15–3   *Process Control Routines for Portability*

Portability Routine	Description
ABORT	Stops execution of the current process, clears I/O buffers, and writes a string to external unit 0
ALARM	Executes an external subroutine after waiting a specified number of seconds
KILL	Sends a signal code to a process ID
SIGNAL	Changes the action for a signal
SLEEP	Suspends program execution for a specified number of seconds
SYSTEM	Executes a command in a separate shell

Note that when you use **SYSTEM**, commands are run in a separate shell. Defaults set with the **SYSTEM** routine, such as current working directory or environment variables, do not affect the environment the calling program runs in.

The portability library does not include the **FORK** routine. On U*X systems, **FORK** creates a duplicate image of the parent process. Child and parent processes each have their own copies of resources, and become independent from one another. In Windows NT, Windows 98, or Windows 95, you can create a child process (called a thread), but both parent and child processes share the same address space and share system resources. If you need to create another process, use the CreateProcess call through the Win32 API.

For information on how to implement threading, see Chapter 19 Creating Multithread Applications.

15.4 Numeric Routines

Table 15-4 lists the numeric routines available for calculating Bessel routines, data type conversion, and generating random numbers. All routines are fully described in the "A-Z Summary" in the *Language Reference* in Visual Fortran online Help.

Table 15–4 *Numeric Routines for Portability*

Portability Routine	Description
BESJ0, BESJ1, BESJN, BESY0, BESY1, BESYN	Computes the single precision values of Bessel functions of the first and second kind of orders 1, 2, and *n*, respectively
DBESJ0, DBESJ1, DBESJN, DBESY0, DBESY1, DBESYN	Computes the double- precision values of Bessel functions of the first and second kind of orders 1, 2, and *n*, respectively
LONG	Converts an INTEGER(2) variable to an INTEGER(4) type
SHORT	Converts an INTEGER(4) variable to an INTEGER(2) type
IRAND, IRANDM	Returns a positive integer in the range 0 through (2**31)-1, or (2**15)-1 if called without an argument
RAN	Returns random values in the range 0 through 1.0
RAND, DRAND	Returns random values in the range 0 through 1.0
DRANDM, RANDOM	Returns random values in the range 0 through 1.0
SRAND	Seeds the random number generator used with **IRAND** and **RAND**.
BIC, BIS, BIT	Perform bit level clear, set, and test for integers

Some of these routines have equivalents in standard Fortran 90. Object conversion can be accomplished by using the **INT** intrinsic function instead of **LONG** or **SHORT**. The intrinsic subroutines **RANDOM_NUMBER** and **RANDOM_SEED** perform the same routines as the random number routines listed in the previous table.

Other bit manipulation routines such as **AND**, **XOR**, **OR**, **LSHIFT**, and **RSHIFT** are intrinsic routines. You do not need the DFPORT module to access them. Standard Fortran 90 includes many bit operation procedures; these are listed in the Bit Operation Procedures table in the "A-Z Summary" in the *Language Reference* in Visual Fortran online Help.

15.5   Input and Output with Portability Routines

The portability library contains routines that change file properties, read and write characters and buffers, and change the offset position in a file. These input and output routines can be used with standard Fortran input or output statements such as **READ** or **WRITE** on the same files, provided that you take into account the following:

▶ When used with direct files, after an **FSEEK**, **GETC**, or **PUTC** operation, the record number is the number of the next whole record. Any subsequent normal Fortran I/O to that unit occurs at the next whole record. For example, if you seek to absolute location 1 of a file whose record length is 10, the NEXTREC returned by an inquire would be 2. If you seek to absolute location 10, NEXTREC would still return 2.

▶ On units with CARRIAGECONTROL='FORTRAN' (the default), **PUTC** and **FPUTC** characters are treated as carriage control characters if they appear in column 1.

▶ On sequentially formatted units, the C string "\n"c, which represents the carriage return/line feed escape sequence, is written as **CHAR**(13) (carriage return) and **CHAR**(10) (line feed), instead of just line feed, or **CHAR**(10). On input, the sequence 13 followed by 10 is returned as just 10. (The length of character string "\n"c is 1 character, whose ASCII value, indicated by **ICHAR**('\n'c), is 10.)

▶ Reading and writing is in a raw form for direct files. Separators between records can be read and overwritten. Therefore, be careful if you continue using the file as a direct file.

I/O errors arising from the use of these routines result in a Visual Fortran run-time error.

Table 15-5 lists the input and output routines. All routines are described fully in the "A-Z Summary" in the *Language Reference* in Visual Fortran online Help.

Table 15–5   *Input and Output Routines for Portability*

Portability Routine	Description
ACCESS	Checks a file for accessibility according to mode
CHMOD	Changes file attributes
FGETC	Reads a character from an external unit
FLUSH	Flushes the buffer for an external unit to its associated file

Table 15–5 *Input and Output Routines for Portability (Continued)*

Portability Routine	Description
FPUTC	Writes a character to an external unit
FSEEK	Repositions a file on an external unit
FTELL	Returns the offset, in bytes, from the beginning of the file
GETC	Reads a character from unit 5
PUTC	Writes a character to unit 6

All path names can include drive specifications, forward slashes, or back-slashes.

Some portability file I/O routines have equivalents in standard Fortran 90. The **ACCESS** function checks a file specified by name for accessibility according to mode. It tests a file for read, write, or execute permission, as well as checking to see if the file exists. It works on the file attributes as they exist on disk, not as a program's **OPEN** statement specifies them. You can use the **INQUIRE** statement, with the ACTION parameter, to arrive at the same information. (The **ACCESS** function always returns 0 for read permission on FAT files, meaning that all files have read permission.)

15.6   Date and Time Routines

Table 15-6 lists the date and time routines. These routines determine system time, or convert it to local time, Greenwich Mean Time, arrays of date and time elements, or an ASCII character string.

The sample output column in Table 15-6 assumes the current date to be 2/24/97 7:11 PM Pacific Daylight Time. The third column shows what each routine returns, either when reporting the current time or when that date and time is passed to it in an appropriate argument.

All routines are described fully in the "A-Z Summary" in the *Language Reference* in Visual Fortran online Help.

Table 15–6 *Date and Time Routines for Portability*

Portability Routine	Description	Sample Output
CLOCK	Current time in "hh:mm:ss" format using a 24-hour clock	19:11:00

Table 15–6 *Date and Time Routines for Portability (Continued)*

Portability Routine	Description	Sample Output
CTIME	Converts a system time to a 24-character ASCII string	"Wed Feb 24 19:11:00 1997"
DATE	A string representation of the current date	As a subroutine: "24-Feb-97" As a function: "02/24/97"
DTIME	Elapsed CPU time since later of (1) start of program, or (2) most recent call to DTIME	(/0.0, 0.0/) (Actual results depend on the program and the system)
ETIME	Elapsed CPU time since the start of program execution	(/0.0, 0.0/) (Actual results depend on the program and the system)
FDATE	The current date and time as an ASCII string	"Wed Feb 24 19:11:00 1997"
GMTIME	Greenwich Mean Time as a 9-element integer array	(/0,12,03,24,2,97,3,55,0/)
IDATE	Current date either as one 3-element array or three scalar parameters (month, day, year)	(1) (/24,2,1997/) (2) month=2, day=24, year=97
ITIME	Current time as a 3-element array (hour, minute, second)	(/7,11,00/)
JDATE	Current date as an 8-character string with the Julian date	"97055 "
LTIME	Local time as a 9-element integer array	(/0,11,7,24,2,97,3,55,0/)
RTC	Number of seconds since 00:00:00 GMT, Jan 1, 1970	762145860
SECNDS	The number of seconds since midnight, less the value of its argument	0.00
TIME	As a subroutine, returns the time formatted as hh:mm:ss As a function, returns the time in seconds since midnight GMT Jan 1, 1970	Subroutine: "07:11:00" Function: 762145860
TIMEF	The number of seconds since the first time this routine was called (or zero)	0.0

TIME and **DATE** are available as either a function or subroutine. Because of the name duplication, if your programs do not include the **USE DFPORT** statement, each separately compiled program unit can use only one of these versions. For example, if a program calls the subroutine **TIME** once, it cannot also use **TIME** as a function.

Standard Fortran 90 includes new date and time intrinsic subroutines. For more information, see **DATE_AND_TIME** in the "A-Z Summary" in the *Language Reference* in Visual Fortran online Help.

15.7   Error Handling Routines

Table 15-7 lists the routines available for detecting and reporting errors. All routines are described fully in the "A-Z Summary" in the *Language Reference* in Visual Fortran online Help.

Table 15–7   *Error Handling Routines for Portability*

Portability Routine	Description
IERRNO	Returns the last error code
GERROR	Returns the **IERRNO** error code as a string variable
PERROR	Sends an error message, preceded by a string, for the last error detected

IERRNO error codes are analogous to *errno* on U*X systems. The DFPORT module provides parameter definitions for many of U*X's *errno* names, found typically in errno.h on U*X systems.

IERRNO is updated only when an error occurs. For example, if a call to the **GETC** routine results in an error, but two subsequent calls to **PUTC** succeed, a call to **IERRNO** returns the error for the **GETC** call. Examine **IERRNO** immediately after returning from one of the portability library routines. Other standard Fortran 90 routines might also change the value to an undefined value.

If your application uses multithreading, remember that **IERRNO** is set on a per-thread basis.

15.8   Miscellaneous String and Sorting Routines

Table 15-8 lists the routines that perform miscellaneous string and sorting operations. All routines are described fully in the "A-Z Summary" in the *Language Reference* in Visual Fortran online Help.

Table 15–8 *Miscellaneous String and Sorting Routines for Portability*

Portability Routine	Description
LNBLNK	Returns the index of the last non-blank character in a string.
QSORT	Sorts a one-dimensional array of a specified number of elements of a named size.
RINDEX	Returns the index of the last occurrence of a substring in a string.

15.9   Other Compatibility Routines

If you need to call a routine not listed in the portability library, you may find it in the standard Visual Fortran library.

Table 15-9 lists routines implemented as intrinsic or in the DFLIB module. All routines are described fully in the "A-Z Summary" in the *Language Reference* in Visual Fortran online Help.

Table 15–9 *Compatibility Routines for Portability*

Procedure	Description
AND	Bitwise **AND**
OR	Bitwise **OR**
XOR	Bitwise **XOR**
FREE	Frees dynamic memory
GETARG	Returns command line arguments
MALLOC	Allocates dynamic memory
LSHIFT	Left bitwise shift
RSHIFT	Right bitwise shift
EXIT	Exits program with a return code

Table 15-10 lists unsupported portability routines and provides the names of supported routines and techniques that provide similar functionality.

➤ **Table 15–10** *Equivalent Portability Routines*

Routine	Description	Similar Visual Fortran Functionality
CMVGM, CMVGN, CMVGP, CMVGT, CMVGZ	Conditional merge	**MERGE** intrinsic routine
FORK	Creates an identical process	CreateProcess, System
LINK	Creates a hard link between two files	none
SYMLNK	Creates a symbolic link between two files	none

CreateProcess is a Win32 API call described in Chapter 19 Creating Multithread Applications.

Replace conditional merge routines with the standard Fortran 90 intrinsic **MERGE** routine, using the arguments shown in Table 15-11.

➤ **Table 15–11** *Arguments to Substitute for Conditional Merge Routines*

Routine	Fortran 90 Replacement
CVMGP(*tsrc* , *fsrc* , *mask*)	**MERGE**(*tsrc* , *fsrc* , *mask* >= 0)
CVMGM(*tsrc* , *fsrc* , *mask*)	**MERGE**(*tsrc* , *fsrc* , *mask* < 0)
CVMGZ(*tsrc* , *fsrc* , *mask*)	**MERGE**(*tsrc* , *fsrc* , *mask* = 0)
CVMGN(*tsrc* , *fsrc* , *mask*)	**MERGE**(*tsrc* , *fsrc* , *mask* /= 0)
CVMGT(*tsrc* , *fsrc* , *mask*)	**MERGE**(*tsrc* , *fsrc* , *mask* = .TRUE.)

There is no analogy to U*X file system links or soft links under Windows.

There is also no analogy to the U*X FORK routine, since FORK creates a duplicate image of the parent process which is independent from the parent process. In Windows NT, Windows 98, and Windows 95, both parent and child processes share the same address space and share system resources. For more information on creating child processes, see Chapter 19 Creating Multithread Applications.

16

Files, Devices, and I/O Hardware

This chapter discusses Visual Fortran files and devices, and using your input/output (I/O) hardware. Together with the sections on I/O statements and I/O editing, these sections explain where and how Fortran data is input and output. Files and devices are where data is stored and retrieved, I/O editing determines how the data is organized when it is read or written, and I/O statements determine what input/output operations are performed on the data. This section is organized as follows:

▶ Section 16.1 Devices and Files

▶ Section 16.2 I/O Hardware

16.1   Devices and Files

In Fortran's I/O system, data is stored and transferred among files. All I/O data sources and destinations are considered files. Devices such as the screen, keyboard, and printer are external files, as are data files stored on a device such as a disk.

Variables in memory can also act as a file on a disk, and are typically used to convert ASCII representations of numbers to binary form. When variables are used in this way, they are called internal files.

The discussion of I/O files is divided into two sections:

▶ Section 16.1.1 Logical Devices

▶ Section 16.1.2 Files

16.1.1 Logical Devices

Every file, internal or external, is associated with a logical device. You identify the logical device associated with a file by a *unit specifier* (UNIT). The unit specifier for an internal file is the name of the character variable associated with it. The unit specifier for an external file is either a number you assign with the **OPEN** statement, a number preconnected as a unit specifier to a device, or an asterisk (*).

External unit specifiers that are preconnected to certain devices do not have to be opened. External units that you connect are disconnected when program execution terminates or when the unit is closed by a **CLOSE** statement.

A unit must not be connected to more than one file at a time, and a file must not be connected to more than one unit at a time. You can **OPEN** an already opened file but only to change some of the I/O options for the connection, not to connect an already opened file or unit to a different unit or file.

You must use a unit specifier for all I/O statements, except in the following three cases:

▶ **ACCEPT**, which always reads from standard input, unless the FOR_ACCEPT environment variable is defined. The **ACCEPT** statement is a Digital Fortran language extension.

▶ **INQUIRE** by file, which specifies the filename, rather than the unit with which the file is associated

▶ **PRINT**, which always writes to standard output, unless the FOR_PRINT environment variable is defined.

▶ **READ** statements that contain only an I/O list and format specifier, which read from standard input (UNIT=5), unless the FOR_READ environment variable is defined.

▶ **WRITE** statements that contain only an I/O list and format specifier, which write to standard output, unless the FOR_PRINT environment variable is defined.

▶ **TYPE**, which always writes to standard output, unless the FOR_TYPE environment variable is defined. The **TYPE** statement is a Digital Fortran language extension.

External Files

A unit specifier associated with an external file must be either an integer expression or an asterisk (*). The integer expression must be in the range 0 (zero) to a maximum value of 2,147,483,640. The following example connects the external file UNDAMP.DAT to unit 10 and writes to it:

```
OPEN (UNIT = 10, FILE = 'undamp.dat')
WRITE (10, '(A18,\)') ' Undamped Motion:'
```

The asterisk (*) unit specifier specifies the keyboard when reading and the screen when writing. The following example uses the asterisk specifier to write to the screen:

```
WRITE (*, '(1X, A30,\)') ' Write this to the screen.'
```

Visual Fortran has four units preconnected to external files (devices), as shown in Table 16-1.

Table 16–1 *Preconnected Units*

External Unit Specifier	Description
Asterisk (*)	Always represents the keyboard and screen (unless the appropriate environment variable is defined, such as FOR_READ)
0	Initially represents the screen (unless FORT0 is defined)
5	Initially represents the keyboard (unless FORT5 is defined)
6	Initially represents the screen (unless FORT6 is defined)

The asterisk (*) specifier is the only unit specifier that cannot be reconnected to another file, and attempting to close this unit causes a compile-time error. Units 0, 5, and 6, however, can be connected to any file with the **OPEN** statement. If you close unit 0, 5, or 6, it is automatically reconnected to its respective device the next time an I/O statement attempts to use that unit.

When you omit the file name in the **OPEN** statement or use an implicit **OPEN**, you can define the environment variable FORTn to specify the file name for a particular unit number (n) (except when the compiler option /fpscomp: filesfromcmd is *not* specified). For example, if you want unit 6 to write to a file instead of standard output, set the environment variable FORT6 to the path and filename to be used before you run the program.

The following example writes to the preconnected unit 6 (the screen), then reconnects unit 6 to an external file and writes to it, and finally reconnects unit 6 to the screen and writes to it:

```
        REAL a, b
!  Write to the screen (preconnected unit 6).
        WRITE(6, '('' This is unit 6'')')
!  Use the OPEN statement to connect unit 6
!  to an external file named 'COSINES'.
        OPEN (UNIT = 6, FILE = 'COSINES', STATUS = 'NEW')
        DO a = 0.1, 6.3, 0.1
           b = COS (a)
!  Write to the file 'COSINES'.
           WRITE (6, 100) a, b
100        FORMAT (F3.1, F5.2)
        END DO
!  Close it.
        CLOSE (6)
!  Reconnect unit 6 to the screen, by writing to it.
        WRITE(6,' ('' Cosines completed'')')
        END
```

Internal Files

The unit specifier associated with an internal file is a character string or character array. There are two types of internal files:

▶ An internal file that is a character variable, character array element, or noncharacter array element that has exactly one record, which is the same length as the variable, array element, or noncharacter array element.

▶ An internal file that is a character array, a character derived type, or a noncharacter array that is a sequence of elements, each of which is a record. The order of records is the same as the order of array elements or type elements, and the record length is the length of one array element or the length of the derived-type element.

Follow these rules when using internal files:

▶ Use only formatted I/O, including I/O formatted with a format specification and list-directed I/O. (List-directed I/O is treated as sequential formatted I/O.) Namelist formatting is not allowed.

▶ If the character variable is an allocatable array or array part of an allocatable array, the array must be allocated before use as an internal file. If the character variable is a pointer, it must be associated with a target.

▶ Use only **READ** and **WRITE** statements. You cannot use file connection (**OPEN, CLOSE**), file positioning (**REWIND, BACKSPACE**) or file inquiry (**INQUIRE**) statements with internal files.

You can read and write internal files with **FORMAT** I/O statements or list-directed I/O statements exactly as you can external files. Before an I/O statement is executed, internal files are positioned at the beginning, before the first record.

With internal files, you can use the formatting capabilities of the I/O system to convert values between external character representations and Fortran internal memory representations. That is, reading from an internal file converts the ASCII representations into numeric, logical, or character representations, and writing to an internal file converts these representations into their ASCII representations.

This feature makes it possible to read a string of characters without knowing its exact format, examine the string, and interpret its contents. It also makes it possible, as in dialog boxes, for the user to enter a string and for your application to interpret it as a number.

If less than an entire record is written to an internal file, the rest of the record is filled with blanks.

In the following example, str and fname specify internal files:

```
      CHARACTER(10) str
      INTEGER n1, n2, n3
      CHARACTER(14) fname
      INTEGER i

      str = " 1 2 3"
!   List-directed READ sets n1 = 1, n2 = 2, n3 = 3.
      READ(str, *) n1, n2, n3
      i = 4
!   Formatted WRITE sets fname = 'FM004.DAT'.
      WRITE (fname, 200) i
200   FORMAT ('FM', I3.3, '.DAT')
```

16.1.2 Files

File organization refers to the way records are physically arranged on a storage device.

Record type refers to whether records in a file are all the same length, are of varying length, or use other conventions to define where one record ends and another begins.

Record access refers to the method used to read records from or write records to a file, regardless of its organization. The way a file is organized does not necessarily imply the way in which the records within that file will be accessed.

Fortran supports two kinds of file organizations: sequential and relative. The organization of a file is specified by means of the ORGANIZATION specifier in the **OPEN** statement. Relative files must be stored on disk. However, sequential files can be stored on either magnetic tape or disk. Other peripheral devices, such as terminals, pipes, card readers, and line printers, are treated as sequential files.

A sequentially organized file consists of records arranged in the sequence in which they are written to the file (the first record written is the first record in the file, the second record written is the second record in the file, and so on). As a result, records can be added only at the end of the file. Attempting to add records at someplace other than the end of the file will result in the file begin truncated at the end of the record just written.

Within a relative file are numbered positions, called cells. These cells are of fixed equal length and are consecutively numbered from 1 to *n*, where 1 is the first cell, and *n* is the last available cell in the file. Each cell either contains a single record or is empty. Records in a relative file are accessed according to cell number. A cell number is a record's relative record number; its location relative to the beginning of the file. By specifying relative record numbers, you can directly retrieve, add, or delete records regardless of their locations. (Detecting deleted records is only available if you specified the /vms option when the program was compiled. For information, see the /vms option.)

Digital Fortran supports two methods of file access (sequential and direct) and three kinds of file structure (formatted, unformatted, and binary). Sequential-access and direct-access files can have any of the three file structures. The following kinds of files are possible:

▶ Formatted Sequential

▶ Formatted Direct

▶ Unformatted Sequential

▶ Unformatted Direct

▶ Binary Sequential

▶ Binary Direct

Each kind of file has advantages and the best choice depends on the application you are developing:

▶ Formatted Files

You create a formatted file by opening it with the FORM='FORMAT-TED' option, or by omitting the FORM parameter when creating a sequential file. The records of a formatted file are stored as ASCII characters; numbers that would otherwise be stored in binary form are converted to ASCII format. Each record ends with the ASCII carriage return (CR) and line feed (LF) characters.

If you need to view a data file's contents, use a formatted file. You can load a formatted file into a text editor and read its contents directly, that is, the numbers would look like numbers and the strings like character strings, whereas an unformatted or binary file looks like a set of hexadecimal characters.

▶ Unformatted Files

You create an unformatted file by opening it with the FORM='UNFORMATTED' option, or by omitting the FORM parameter when creating a direct-access file. An unformatted file is a series of records composed of physical blocks. Each record contains a sequence of values stored in a representation that is close to that used in program memory. Little conversion is required during input/output.

The lack of formatting makes these files quicker to access and more compact than files that store the same information in a formatted form. However, if the files contain numbers, you will not be able to read them with a text editor.

▶ Binary Files

You create a binary file by specifying FORM='BINARY'. Binary files are the most compact, and good for storing large amounts of data. Binary files are a Digital Fortran language extension.

▶ Sequential-Access Files

Data in sequential files must be accessed in order, one record after the other (unless you change your position in the file with the **REWIND** or **BACKSPACE** statements). Some methods of I/O are possible only with sequential files, including nonadvancing I/O, list-directed I/O, and namelist I/O. Internal files also must be sequential files. You must use sequential access for files associated with sequential devices.

A sequential device is a physical storage device that does not allow explicit motion (other than reading or writing). The keyboard, screen, and printer are all sequential devices.

▶ Direct-Access Files

Data in direct-access files can be read or written to in any order. Records are numbered sequentially, starting with record number 1. All records have the length indicated by the RECL specifier in the **OPEN** statement. Data in direct files is accessed by specifying the record you want within the file. If you need random access I/O, use direct-access files. A common example of a random-access application is a database.

All files are composed of records. Each record is one entry in the file. It can be a line from a terminal or a logical record on a magnetic tape or disk file. All records within one file are of the same type.

In Fortran, the number of bytes written to a record must be less than or equal to the record length. One record is written for each unformatted **READ** or **WRITE** statement. A formatted **READ** or **WRITE** statement can transfer more than one record using the slash (/) edit descriptor.

For binary files, a single **READ** or **WRITE** statement reads or writes as many records as needed to accommodate the number of bytes being transferred. On output, incomplete formatted records are padded with spaces. Incomplete unformatted and binary records are padded with undefined bytes (zeros).

For more information, see:

▶ Section 16.1.2.1 Record Types

▶ Section 16.1.2.2 Microsoft Fortran PowerStation Compatible Files (when /fpscomp:ioformat is specified during compilation)

16.1.2.1 Record Types

An I/O record is a collection of data items, called fields, that are logically related and are processed as a unit. The record type refers to the convention for storing fields in records.

The record type of the data within a file is not maintained as an attribute of the file. The results of using a record type other than the one used to create the file are indeterminate.

If you omit /fpscomp:ioformat during compilation, the following six record types are available:

▶ Fixed-length

You can use fixed-length records with the relative or sequential file organizations.

▶ Variable-length

The variable-length record type is generally the most portable record type across multi-vendor platforms. It can be used only with the sequential file organization.

▶ Segmented

The segmented record type can only be used with sequential file organization and only for unformatted sequential access. The segmented record type is unique to Digital Fortran and should not be used for portability with programs written in languages other than Fortran or for places where Digital Fortran is not used. However, because the segmented record type is unique to Digital Fortran products, formatted data in segmented files can be ported across Digital Fortran platforms.

▶ Stream (uses no record delimiters)

The stream record type can be used only with the sequential file organization.

▶ Stream_CR (uses CR as record delimiters)

The stream_CR record type can be used only with the sequential file organization.

▶ Stream_LF (uses CR and LF as a record delimiter)

The stream_LF record type can be used only with the sequential file organization.

Fixed-Length Records

When you specify fixed-length records, you are specifying that all records in the file contain the same number of bytes. When you open a file that is to contain fixed-length records, you must specify the record size using the RECL keyword. A sequentially organized opened file for direct access must contain fixed-length records, to allow the record position in the file to be computed correctly.

For relative files, the layout and overhead of fixed-length records depends on whether the program accessing the file was compiled using the /vms option or whether the /vms option was omitted:

▶ For relative files where the /vms option was omitted (the default), each record has no control information.

▶ For relative files where the /vms option was specified, each record has one byte of control information at the beginning of the record.

Figure 16-1 shows the layout of fixed-length records.

For all sequential and relative files where the /vms option was omitted:

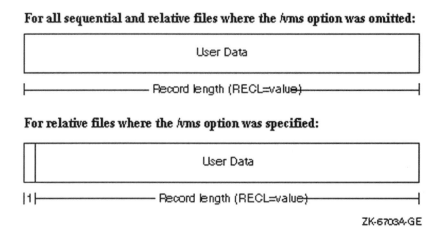

For relative files where the /vms option was specified:

Figure 16–1   *Record Layout of Fixed-Length Records*

Variable-Length Records

Variable-length records can contain any number of bytes, up to a specified maximum record length, and only apply to sequential files. These records are generally prefixed and suffixed by four bytes of control information containing count fields. The 4-byte integer value stored in each count field indicates the number of data bytes (excluding overhead bytes) in that particular variable-length record.

Figure 16-2 shows the layout of variable-length records.

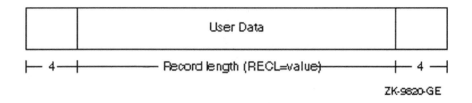

Figure 16–2   *Record Layout of Variable-Length Records*

The count field of a variable-length record is available when you read the record by issuing a **READ** statement with a **Q** format descriptor. You can then use the count field information to determine how many bytes should be in the associated I/O list.

Files written with variable-length records by Digital Fortran programs usually cannot be accessed as text files. Instead, use the Stream_LF record format for text files with records of varying length.

Segmented Records

A segmented record is a single logical record consisting of one or more variable-length, unformatted records in a sequentially organized disk file. Unformatted data written to sequentially organized files using sequential access is stored as segmented records by default.

Segmented records are useful when you want to write exceptionally long records but cannot or do not wish to define one long variable-length record, perhaps because virtual memory limitations can prevent program execution. By using smaller, segmented records, you reduce the chance of problems caused by virtual memory limitations on systems on which the program may execute.

For disk files, the segmented record is a single logical record that consists of one or more segments. Each segment is a physical record. A segmented (logical) record can exceed the absolute maximum record length (2.14 billion bytes), but each segment (physical record) individually cannot exceed the maximum record length.

To access an unformatted sequential file that contains segmented records, specify FORM='UNFORMATTED' and RECORDTYPE='SEGMENTED' when you open the file. Otherwise, the file may be processed erroneously.

As shown in Figure 16-3, the layout of segmented records consists of 4 bytes of control information followed by the user data.

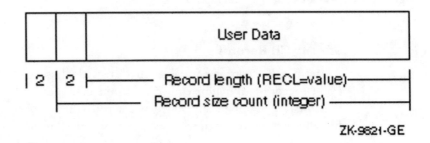

ZK-9821-GE

Figure 16–3 *Record Layout of Segmented Records*

The control information consists of a 2-byte integer record length count (includes the 2 bytes used by the segment identifier), followed by a 2-byte integer segment identifier that identifies this segment as one of the following:

▶ The first segment (equals 1)

▶ The last segment (equals 2)

▶ The only segment (equals 3)

▶ One of the segments between the first and last segments (equals 0)

If the specified record length is an odd number, the user data will be padded with a single blank (1 byte), but this extra byte is not added to the 2-byte integer record length count.

Stream File Data

A stream file is not grouped into records and contains no control information. Stream files are used with CARRIAGECONTROL='NONE' and contain character or binary data that is read or written only to the extent of the variables specified on the input or output statement.

Figure 16-4 shows the layout of a stream file.

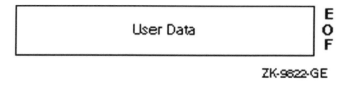

ZK-9822-GE

Figure 16–4   *Record Layout of Stream Records*

Stream_CR Records

A stream_CR record is a variable-length record whose length is indicated by explicit record terminators embedded in the data, not by a count. These terminators are automatically added when you write records to a stream-type file, and they are removed when you read records. Stream_CR files use only a carriage-return as the terminator, so Stream_CR files must not contain embedded carriage-return characters.

Figure 16-5 shows the layout of stream_CR records.

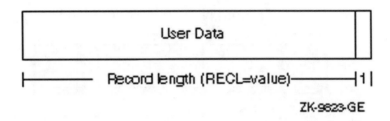

ZK-9823-GE

Figure 16–5 *Record Layout of Stream_CR Records*

Stream_LF Records

A stream_LF record is a variable-length record whose length is indicated by explicit record terminators embedded in the data, not by a count. These terminators are automatically added when you write records to a stream-type file, and they are removed when you read records. Stream_LF files use a carriage return followed by line-feed (new line) as the terminator, so Stream_LF files must not contain embedded line-feed (new line) characters. This is the usual operating system text file record type.

Figure 16-6 shows the layout of stream_LF records.

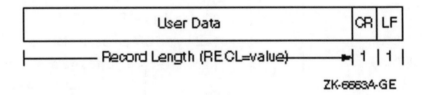

ZK-68634-GE

Figure 16–6 *Record Layout of Stream_LF Records*

16.1.2.2 Microsoft Fortran PowerStation Compatible Files

When using the /fpscomp:ioformat option for Microsoft Fortran PowerStation compatibility, the following types of files are possible:

▶ Formatted Sequential Files

A formatted sequential file is a series of formatted records written sequentially and read in the order in which they appear in the file. Records can vary in length and can be empty. They are separated by carriage return (0D) and line feed (0A) characters as shown in Figure 16-7.

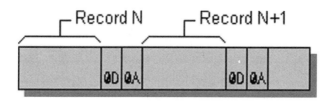

Figure 16–7 *Formatted Records in a Formatted Sequential File*

An example of a program writing three records to a formatted sequential file is given below. The resulting file is shown in Figure 16-8.

```
       OPEN (3, FILE='FSEQ')
!          FSEQ is a formatted sequential file by default.
       WRITE (3, '(A, I3)') 'RECORD', 1
       WRITE (3, '()')
       WRITE (3, '(A11)') 'The 3rd One'
       CLOSE (3)
       END
```

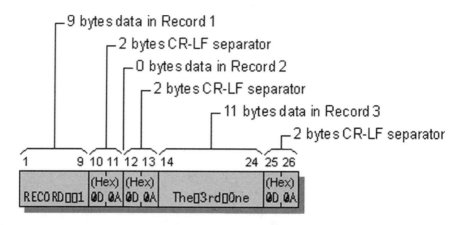

Figure 16–8 *Formatted Sequential File*

▶ Formatted Direct Files

In a formatted direct file, all of the records are the same length and can be written or read in any order. The record size is specified with the RECL option in an **OPEN** statement and should be equal to or greater than the number of bytes in the longest record.

The carriage return (CR) and line feed (LF) characters are record separators and are not included in the RECL value. Once a direct-access record has been written, you cannot delete it, but you can rewrite it.

During output to a formatted direct file, if data does not completely fill a record, the compiler pads the remaining portion of the record with blank spaces. The blanks ensure that the file contains only completely filled records, all of the same length. During input, the compiler by default also pads the input if the input list and format require more data than the record contains.

You can override the default blank padding on input by setting PAD='NO' in the **OPEN** statement for the file. If PAD='NO', the input record must contain the amount of data indicated by the input list and format specification. Otherwise, an error occurs. PAD='NO' has no effect on output.

An example of a program writing two records, record one and record three, to a formatted direct file is given below. The result is shown in Figure 16-9.

```
OPEN (3,FILE='FDIR', FORM='FORMATTED',
ACCESS='DIRECT',RECL=10)
WRITE (3, '(A10)', REC=1) 'RECORD ONE'
WRITE (3, '(I5)', REC=3) 30303
CLOSE (3)
END
```

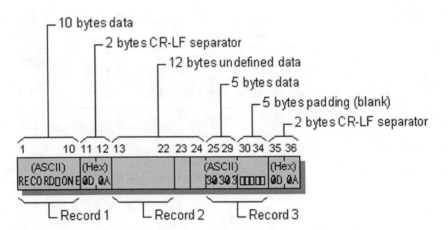

Figure 16–9 *Formatted Sequential File*

► Unformatted Sequential Files

Unformatted sequential files are organized slightly differently on different platforms. This section describes unformatted sequential files created by Visual Fortran when the /fpscomp:ioformat option was specified. If you are accessing files from another platform that organizes them differently, see Chapter 23 Converting Unformatted Numeric Data or you can use the conversion utility in the . . . \DF98\SAMPLES\TUTORIAL folder called UNFSEQ.F90.

The records in an unformatted sequential file can vary in length. Unformatted sequential files are organized in chunks of 130 bytes or less called *physical blocks* . Each physical block consists of the data you send to the file (up to 128 bytes) plus two 1-byte length bytes inserted by the compiler. The length bytes indicate where each record begins and ends.

A *logical record* refers to an unformatted record that contains one or more physical blocks. (See the following figure.) Logical records can be as big as you want; the compiler will use as many physical blocks as necessary.

When you create a logical record consisting of more than one physical block, the compiler sets the length byte to 129 to indicate that the data in the current physical block continues on into the next physical block. For example, if you write 140 bytes of data, the logical record has the structure shown in Figure 16-10.

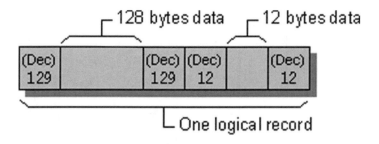

Figure 16–10 *Logical Record in Unformatted Sequential File*

The first and last bytes in an unformatted sequential file are reserved; the first contains a value of 75, and the last holds a value of 130. Fortran uses these bytes for error checking and end-of-file references.

The following program creates the unformatted sequential file shown in Figure 16-11.

```
!          Note: The file is sequential by default
!              -1 is FF FF FF FF hexadecimal.
!
           CHARACTER xyz(3)
           INTEGER(4) idata(35)
           DATA        idata /35 * -1/, xyz /'x', 'y', 'z'/
!
!      Open the file and write out a 140-byte record:
!      128 bytes (block) + 12 bytes = 140 for IDATA, then 3
       bytes for XYZ.
           OPEN (3, FILE='UFSEQ',FORM='UNFORMATTED')
           WRITE (3) idata
           WRITE (3) xyz
           CLOSE (3)
           END
```

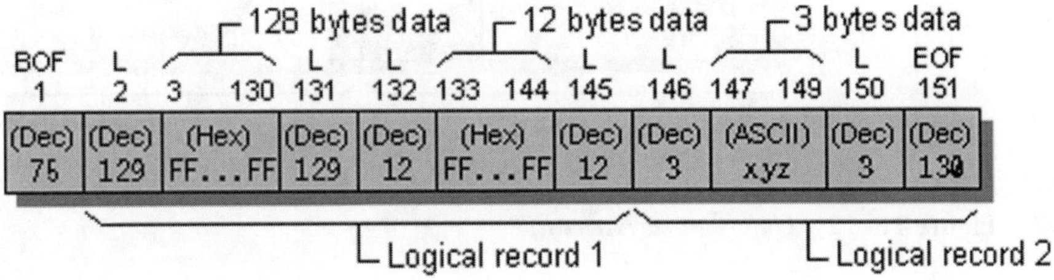

BOF   Beginning-of-file byte (75 decimal)
L   Physical-block-length byte (0 <= L <= 129)
EOF   End-of-file byte (130 decimal)

Figure 16–11   *Unformatted Sequential File*

▶ Unformatted Direct Files

An unformatted direct file is a series of unformatted records. You can write or read the records in any order you choose. All records have the same length, given by the RECL specifier in an **OPEN** statement. No delimiting bytes separate records or otherwise indicate record structure.

You can write a partial record to an unformatted direct file. Visual Fortran pads these records to the fixed record length with ASCII NULL characters. Unwritten records in the file contain undefined data.

The following program creates the sample unformatted direct file shown in Figure 16-12.

```
OPEN (3, FILE='UFDIR', RECL=10,&
  & FORM = 'UNFORMATTED', ACCESS = 'DIRECT')
WRITE (3, REC=3) .TRUE., 'abcdef'
WRITE (3, REC=1) 2049
CLOSE (3)
END
```

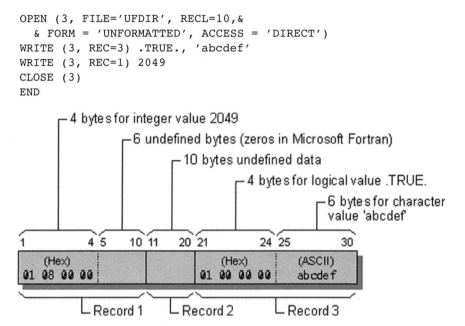

Figure 16–12 *Unformatted Direct File*

▶ Binary Sequential Files

A binary sequential file is a series of values written and read in the same order and stored as binary numbers. No record boundaries exist, and no special bytes indicate file structure. Data is read and written without changes in form or length. For any I/O data item, the sequence of bytes in memory is the sequence of bytes in the file.

The next program creates the binary sequential file shown in Figure 16-13.

```
!   NOTE: 07 is the bell character
!        Sequential is assumed by default.
!
    INTEGER(1) bells(4)
    CHARACTER(4) wys(3)
    CHARACTER(4) cvar
    DATA bells /4*7/
    DATA cvar /' is '/,wys /'What',' you',' see'/

    OPEN (3, FILE='BSEQ',FORM='BINARY')
    WRITE (3) wys, cvar
    WRITE (3) 'what ', 'you get!'
    WRITE (3) bells
    CLOSE (3)
    END
```

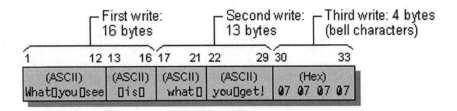

Figure 16–13 *Binary Sequential File*

▶ Binary Direct Files

A binary direct file stores records as a series of binary numbers, accessible in any order. Each record in the file has the same length, as specified by the RECL argument to the **OPEN** statement. You can write partial records to binary direct files; any unused portion of the record will contain undefined data.

A single read or write operation can transfer more data than a record contains by continuing the operation into the next records of the file. Performing such an operation on an unformatted direct file would cause an error. Valid I/O operations for unformatted direct files produce identical results when they are performed on binary direct files, provided the operations do not depend on zero padding in partial records.

The following program creates the binary direct file shown in Figure 16-14.

```
OPEN (3, FILE='BDIR',RECL=10,FORM='BINARY',ACCESS='DIRECT')
WRITE (3, REC=1) 'abcdefghijklmno'
WRITE (3) 4,5
WRITE (3, REC=4) 'pq'
CLOSE (3)
END
```

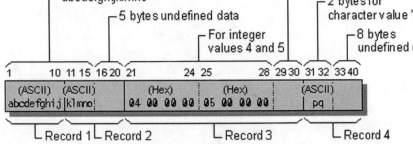

Figure 16–14 *Binary Direct File*

16.2   I/O Hardware

Most of your hardware configuration and setup is done through your computer's operating system. To connect and communicate with your printer, for example, you should read your system and printer manuals. This section describes how Visual Fortran refers to physical devices and shortcuts for printing text and graphics from the Microsoft visual development environment.

For more information, see:

▶ Section 16.2.1 Printing

▶ Section 16.2.2 Physical Devices

16.2.1   Printing

The simplest way to print a file while you are in the visual development environment is to choose File/Print from the file menu. You are prompted for the file name and the file is printed on the printer connected to your computer.

You can also print files with the extension .F90, .FOR, .FD, .FI, or .RC by dragging the file from Windows Explorer and dropping it on the Print Manager icon.

If you have drawn graphics on the screen and want to print the screen, the simplest way is to press the key combination ALT+PRINT SCREEN. This copies the active window (the one with graphical focus) onto the Clipboard. (If you only press PRINT SCREEN, it prints your entire screen including any background applications.)

Once you have copied your screen onto the Clipboard, open Paintbrush and select Edit/Paste to paste the image from the Clipboard into Paintbrush, then select File/Print to print it to the printer connected to your computer. You can also save the image as a bitmap (.BMP) file.

16.2.2   Physical Devices

I/O statements that do not refer to a specific file or I/O device read from standard input and write to standard output. Standard input is the keyboard, and standard output is the screen (console). To perform input and output on a physical device other than the keyboard or screen, you specify the device name as the filename to be read from or written to.

Some physical device names are determined by the host operating system; others are recognized by Visual Fortran. Extensions on most device names are ignored.

Table 16-2 lists the filenames for device input and output.

Table 16–2   *Filenames for Device I/O*

Device	Description
CON	Console (standard output)
PRN	Printer
COM1	Serial port #1
COM2	Serial port #2
COM3	Serial port #3
COM4	Serial port #4
LPT1	Parallel Port #1
LPT2	Parallel Port #2
LPT3	Parallel Port #3
LPT4	Parallel Port #4
NUL	NULL device. Discards all output; contains no input
AUX	Serial port #1
LINE	Serial port #1; if you use this name with an extension—for example, LINE.TXT—Fortran will write to a file rather than to the device
USER	Standard output; if you use this name with an extension—for example, USER.TXT—Fortran will write to a file rather than to the device
ERR	Standard error; if you use this name with an extension—for example, ERR.TXT—Fortran will write to a file rather than to the device
CONOUT$	Standard output
CONIN$	Standard input

Examples of opening physical devices as units are:

```
OPEN (UNIT = 4, FILE = 'PRN')
OPEN (UNIT = 7, FILE = 'LPT2', ERR = 100)
```

17

Using COM and Automation Objects

Visual Fortran provides a wizard to simplify the use of Component Object Model (COM) and Automation (formerly called OLE Automation) objects. The Visual Fortran Module Wizard generates Fortran 90 modules that simplify calling COM and Automation services from Fortran programs. This Fortran code lets you invoke routines in a dynamic link library, methods of an Automation object, and member functions of a Component Object Model (COM) object.

The following sections describe the use of COM and Automation objects with Visual Fortran:

▶ Section 17.1 The Role of the Module Wizard

▶ Section 17.2 Using the Module Wizard to Generate Code

▶ Section 17.3 Calling the Routines Generated by the Module Wizard

▶ Section 17.4 Additional Information about COM and Automation Objects

17.1   The Role of the Module Wizard

To use COM and Automation objects from a Fortran program, the following steps need to occur:

1. Find or install the object on the system. COM and Automation objects can be registered:

   ▶ By other programs you install.

▶ By creating the object yourself, for example, by using Visual C++ or Visual Basic.

For example, the Microsoft visual development environment registers certain objects during installation (see the documentation on the Developer Studio object model).

Creating an object involves deciding what type of object and what type of interfaces or methods should be available. The object's server must be designed, coded, and tested like any other application. For general information about object creation and related information, see Section 17.4 Additional Information about COM and Automation Objects.

2. Determine:

▶ Whether the object has a COM interface, Automation interface, or both.

▶ Where the object's type information is located.

You should be able to obtain this information from the object's documentation. You can use the OLE-COM Object Viewer tool (provided in the Visual Fortran program folder) to determine the characteristics of an object on your system.

3. Use the Visual Fortran module wizard to generate code.

The Visual Fortran module wizard is a application that interactively asks certain questions about the object, including its name, type, and other information. The information collected by the module wizard is used in the generated code. To learn about using the Visual Fortran module wizard, see Section 17.2 Using the Module Wizard to Generate Code.

4. Write a Fortran 90 program to invoke the code generated by the Visual Fortran module wizard.

To understand more about calling the interfaces and jacket routines created by the module wizard, see Section 17.4 Additional Information about COM and Automation Objects.

17.2   Using the Module Wizard to Generate Code

To run the Visual Fortran Module Wizard, choose the Tools menu item Fortran Module Wizard. The module wizard asks a series of questions, including the name and type of the object as well as certain characteristics. If you have not already obtained the object's characteristics, see Section 17.1 The Role of the Module Wizard.

The Visual Fortran Module Wizard presents a series of dialog boxes that allow you to select the type of information needed.

An object's type information contains programming language independent descriptions of the object's interfaces. Depending on the implementation of the object, type information can be obtained from the running object (see Automation Object below) or from a type library.

A type library is a collection of type information for any number of object classes, interfaces, and so on. A type library can also be used to describe the routines in a DLL. You can store a type library in a file of its own (usually with an extension of .TLB) or it can be part of another file. For example, the type library that describes a DLL can be stored in the DLL itself.

After you start the Module Wizard (Tools menu, Fortran Module Wizard), a dialog box requests the source of the type information that describes the object you need to use. You need to determine what type of object it is (or DLL) and how it makes its type information available. The choices are:

▶ Automation Object

▶ Type Library containing Automation information

▶ Type Library containing COM interface information

▶ Type Library containing DLL information

▶ DLL containing type information

Figure 17-1 shows the initial screen that appears after you select the Visual Fortran Module Wizard.

After you select one of the five choices, one of two different screens will appear depending on the selection made. The Module Name in the initial Module Wizard screen is used as the name of the Fortran module being generated. It is also used as the default file name of the generated source file.

If You Select Automation Object

If you select Automation Object, the screen in Figure 17-2 appears.

Microsoft recommends that object servers provide a type library. However some applications do not, but do provide type information dynamically when running. Use this option for such an application. Enter the name of the application, name of the object, and version number. The version number is optional. If you do not specify it, you will get the latest version of the object. Note that this method only works for objects that provide a programmatic

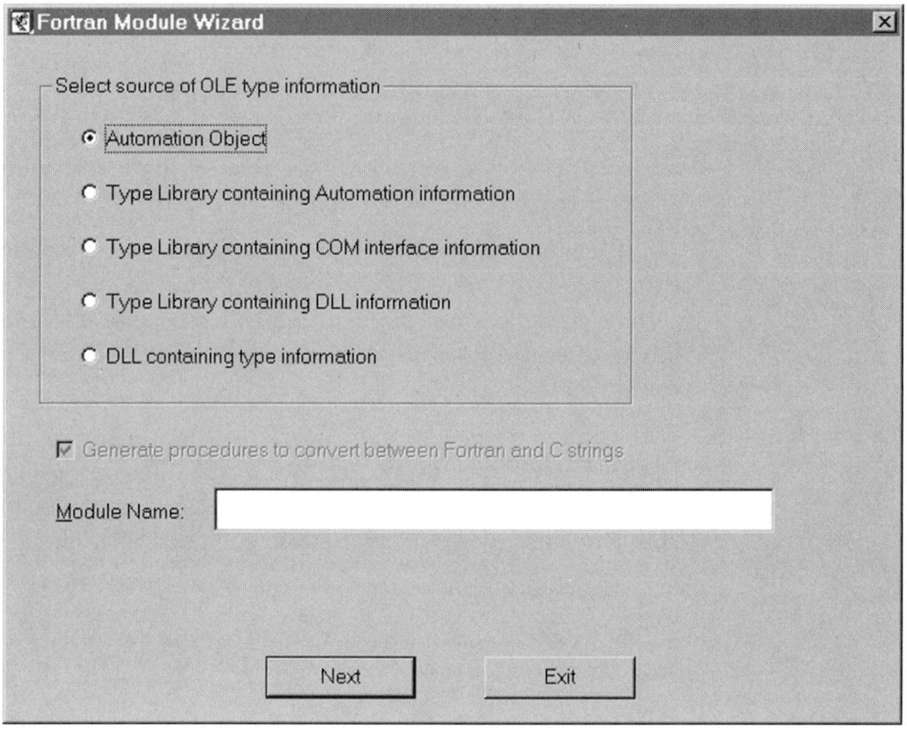

Figure 17–1 *Initial Module Wizard Screen*

identifier (ProgID). ProgIDs are entered into the system registry and identify, among other things, the executable program that is the object's server.

After entering the information and pressing the "Generate" button, the Fortran Module Wizard asks you for the name of the source file to be generated. It then asks COM to create an instance of the object identified by the ProgID that the wizard constructs using the supplied information. COM starts the object's server if it needs to do so. The wizard then asks the object for its type information and generates a file containing Fortran modules.

If You Select Other Options

After selecting any of the remaining options in the initial screen and press the "Next" button, the Module Wizard displays the screen in Figure 17-3.

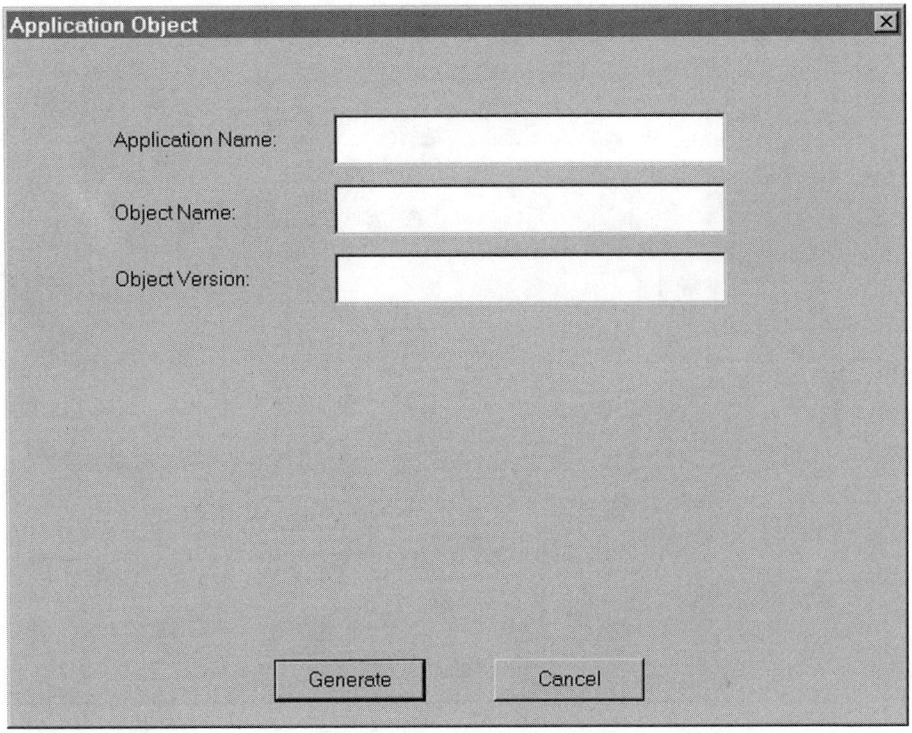

Figure 17–2 *Application Object Screen*

Choose the type library (or file containing the type library), and optionally specific components of the type library.

At the top of the dialog box is a combo box that lists all of the type libraries that have been registered with the system. You will notice a number of different file extensions, for example, .OLB (object libraries) and .OCX (ActiveX® controls). Select a type library from the list or press "Browse" to find the file using the standard "Open" dialog box. Once you have selected a type library press the "Show" button to list the components you can select from the type library. By default, the Fortran Module Wizard will use all of the components. Optionally, you can select the ones desired from the list.

After entering the information and pressing the "Generate" button, the Fortran Module Wizard asks you for the name of the source file to be generated. It then asks COM to open the type library and generates a file containing Fortran modules.

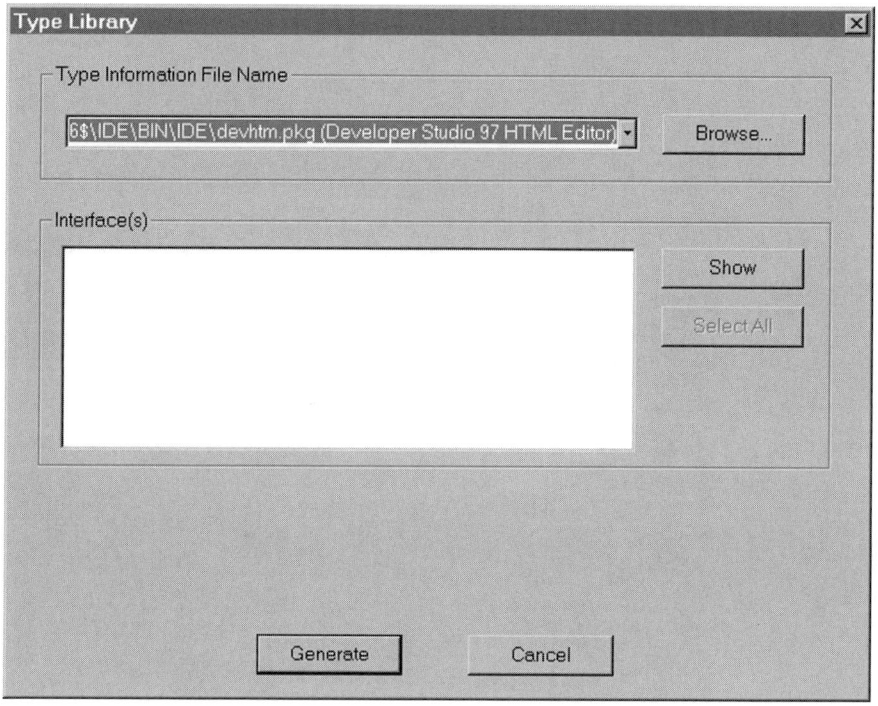

Figure 17–3 *Type Library Screen*

17.3   Calling the Routines Generated by the Module Wizard

Although Fortran 90 does not support objects, it does provide Fortran 90 *modules*. A *module* is a set of declarations that are grouped together under a global name, and are made available to other program units by using the **USE** statement.

The Fortran Module Wizard generates a source file containing one or more modules. The types of information placed in the modules include:

▶ *Derived-type definitions* are Fortran equivalents of data structures that are found in the type information.

▶ *Constant definitions* are Fortran **PARAMETER** declarations that include identifiers and enumerations found in the type information.

▶ *Procedure interface definitions* are Fortran interface blocks that describe the procedures found in the type information.

▶ *Procedure definitions* are Fortran functions and subroutines that are jacket routines for the procedures found in the type information.

The jacket routines make the external procedures easier to call from Fortran by handling data conversion and low-level invocation details.

The use of modules allows the Visual Fortran Module Wizard to encapsulate the data structures and procedures exposed by an object or DLL in a single place. You can then share these definitions in multiple Fortran programs.

The appropriate **USE** statement needs to be added in your program, as well as function invocations or subroutine calls.

The routines generated by the Visual Fortran Module Wizard are designed to be called from Fortran. These routines in turn call the appropriate system routines (not designed to be called from Fortran), thereby simplifying the coding needed to use COM and Automation objects.

Visual Fortran provides a set of run-time routines that present to the Fortran programmer a higher level abstraction of the COM and Automation functionality. The Fortran interfaces that the Wizard generates hide most of the differences between Automation objects and COM objects.

Depending on the options specified, the routines in Table 17-1 can be present in the generated code, allowing you to call them to use COM or Automation objects. All routines are fully described in the "A-Z Summary" in the *Language Reference* in Visual Fortran online Help.

Table 17–1   *COM and Automation Routines*

DFCOM Routines (COMxxxxx)	
COMAddObject Reference	Adds a reference to an object's interface.
COMCLSIDFromProgID	Passes a programmatic identifier and returns the corresponding class identifier.
COMCLSIDFromString	Passes a class identifier string and returns the corresponding class identifier.
COMCreateObjectByGUID	Passes a class identifier and creates an instance of an object. It returns a pointer to the object's interface.
COMCreateObjectByProgID	Passes a programmatic identifier and creates an instance of an object. It returns a pointer to the object's IDispatch interface.
COMGetActiveObjectByGUID	Pass a class identifier and returns a pointer to the interface of a currently active object.
COMGetActiveObjectByProgID	Passes a programmatic identifier and returns a pointer to the IDispatch interface of a currently active object.
COMInitialize	Initializes the COM library. You must initialize the library before calling any other COM or AUTO routine.

Table 17–1 *COM and Automation Routines (Continued)*

DFCOM Routines (COMxxxxx)	
COMGetFileObject	Passes a file name and returns a pointer to the IDispatch interface of an Automation object that can manipulate the file.
COMQueryInterface	Passes an interface identifier and it returns a pointer to an object's interface.
COMReleaseObject	Indicates that the program is done with a reference to an object's interface.
COMUninitialize	Uninitializes the COM library. This must be the last COM routine that you call.
DFAUTO Automation Routines (AUTOxxxxx)	
AUTOAddArg	Passes an argument name and value and adds the argument to the argument list data structure.
AUTOAllocateInvokeArgs	Allocates an argument list data structure that holds the arguments that you will pass to AUTOInvoke.
AUTODeallocateInvokeArgs	Deallocates an argument list data structure.
AUTOGetExceptInfo	Retrieves the exception information when a method has returned an exception status.
AUTOGetProperty	Passes the name or identifier of the property and gets the value of the Automation object's property.
AUTOGetPropertyByID	Passes the member ID of the property and gets the value of the Automation object's property into the argument list's first argument.
AUTOGetPropertyInvokeArgs	Passes an argument list data structure and gets the value of the Automation object's property specified in the argument list's first argument.
AUTOInvoke	Passes the name or identifier of an object's method and an argument list data structure. It invokes the method with the passed arguments.
AUTOSetProperty	Passes the name or identifier of the property and a value. It sets the value of the Automation object's property.
AUTOSetPropertyByID	Passes the member ID of the property and sets the value of the Automation object's property using the argument list's first argument.
AUTOSetPropertyInvokeArgs	Passes an argument list data structure and sets the value of the Automation object's property specified in the argument list's first argument.

Visual Fortran Samples include several projects in the . . . `\DF98\ SAMPLES\ADVANCED\COM` folder that demonstrate the use of the Fortran Module Wizard. For example:

▶ AUTODICE uses Automation to drive the Microsoft Excel® 97 to create a chart from Fortran data.

- ▶ DSBUILD uses Automation to drive the visual development environment to rebuild a project configuration.

- ▶ DSLINES uses COM to drive the Microsoft visual development environment to edit a Fortran source file and convert Debug lines (column 1) to IFDEF directives.

- ▶ IWEB uses COM interfaces to start a Web browser and direct the browser to open a specified URL.

Example of Generated Code Used by the DSLINES Sample

The DLINES Sample contains the code that invokes this and other Microsoft visual development environment functionality using COM interfaces.

The following code shows an annotated version of the code generated by the Fortran Module Wizard from the COM type information in . . . \COMMON\MSDEV98\BIN\devshl.dll. This COM type information describes the top-level objects in the Microsoft visual development environment object model.

```
INTERFACE
!    Saves the document to disk.                                  1

INTEGER*4 FUNCTION IGenericDocument_Save($OBJECT, &
&                       vFilename, vBoolPrompt, pSaved)          2

USE DFCOMTY
INTEGER*4, INTENT(IN) :: $OBJECT      ! Object Pointer

!DEC$ ATTRIBUTES VALUE :: $OBJECT                                 3

TYPE (VARIANT), INTENT(IN)  :: vFilename ! (Optional Arg)    4
!DEC$ ATTRIBUTES VALUE      :: vFilename
TYPE (VARIANT), INTENT(IN)  :: vBoolPrompt ! (Optional Arg)
!DEC$ ATTRIBUTES VALUE      :: vBoolPrompt

INTEGER*4, INTENT(OUT)      :: pSaved ! Void               5
!DEC$ ATTRIBUTES REFERENCE  :: pSaved
!DEC$ ATTRIBUTES STDCALL    :: IGenericDocument_Save
END FUNCTION IGenericDocument_Save
END INTERFACE

POINTER(IGenericDocument_Save_PTR, IGenericDocument_Save)  6
! routine pointer
```

Notes for this example:

1. If the type information provides a comment that describes the member function, then the comment is placed before the beginning of the procedure.

2. The first argument to the procedure is always $OBJECT. It is a pointer to the object's interface. The remaining argument names are determined from the type information.

3. This is an example of an **ATTRIBUTE** directive statement used to specify the calling convention of an argument.

4. A VARIANT is a data structure that can contain any type of Automation data. It contains a field that identifies the type of data and a union that holds the data value. The use of a VARIANT argument allows the caller to use any data type that can be converted into the data type expected by the member function.

5. Nearly every COM member function returns a status of type HRESULT. Because of this, if a COM member function produces output it uses output arguments to return the values. In this example, the "pSaved" argument returns a routine specific status value.

6. The interface of a COM member function looks very similar to the interface for a dynamic link library function with one major exception. Unlike a DLL function, the address of a COM member function is never known at program link time. You must get a pointer to an object's interface at run-time, and the address of a particular member function is computed from that.

The following code shows an annotated version of the wrapper generated by the Fortran Module Wizard for the "Save" function. The name of a wrapper is the same as the name of the corresponding member function, prefixed with a "$" character.

```
! Saves the document to disk.
INTEGER*4 FUNCTION $IGenericDocument_Save($OBJECT, &        I
& vFilename, vBoolPrompt, pSaved)
!DEC$ ATTRIBUTES DLLEXPORT :: $IGenericDocument_Save
IMPLICIT NONE

INTEGER*4, INTENT(IN)          :: $OBJECT ! Object Pointer
!DEC$ ATTRIBUTES VALUE         :: $OBJECT
TYPE (VARIANT), INTENT(IN), OPTIONAL :: vFilename
!DEC$ ATTRIBUTES REFERENCE     :: vFilename
TYPE (VARIANT), INTENT(IN), OPTIONAL :: vBoolPrompt
```

```
!DEC$ ATTRIBUTES REFERENCE      :: vBoolPrompt
  INTEGER*4, INTENT(OUT)        :: pSaved ! Void
  !DEC$ ATTRIBUTES REFERENCE    :: pSaved

  INTEGER*4 $RETURN
  INTEGER*4 $VTBL               ! Interface Function Table    2
POINTER($VPTR, $VTBL)
TYPE (VARIANT) :: $VAR_vFilename
TYPE (VARIANT) :: $VAR_vBoolPrompt
  IF (PRESENT(vFilename)) THEN                                 3
    $VAR_vFilename = vFilename
  ELSE
    $VAR_vFilename = OPTIONAL_VARIANT
  END IF
  IF (PRESENT(vBoolPrompt)) THEN
    $VAR_vBoolPrompt = vBoolPrompt
  ELSE
    $VAR_vBoolPrompt = OPTIONAL_VARIANT
  END IF
$VPTR = $OBJECT               ! Interface Function Table    4
$VPTR = $VTBL + 84            ! Add routine table offset
IGenericDocument_Save_PTR = $VTBL
$RETURN = IGenericDocument_Save($OBJECT, $VAR_vFilename, &
$   VAR_vBoolPrompt, pSaved)
$IGenericDocument_Save = $RETURN
END FUNCTION $IGenericDocument_Save
```

Notes for this example:

1. The wrapper takes the same argument names as the member function interface.

2. The wrapper computes the address of the member function from the interface pointer and an offset found in the interface's type information. In implementation terms, an interface pointer is a pointer to a pointer to an array of function pointers called an "Interface Function Table."

3. Arguments to a COM or Automation routine can be optional. The wrapper handles the invocation details for specifying an optional argument that is not present in the call.

4. The offset of the "Save" member function is 84. The code assigns the computed address to the function pointer IGenericDocument_Save_PTR, which was declared in the previous example, and then calls the function.

The DLINES Sample contains the code that invokes this and other Microsoft visual development environment functionality using COM interfaces.

Example of Generated Code Used by the DSBUILD Sample

The DSBUILD example contains the code that invokes this and other Microsoft visual development environment functionality using Automation interfaces.

The following code shows an annotated version of the code generated by the Fortran Module Wizard from the Automation type information in . . . `\COMMON\MSDEV98\BIN\devshl.dll`.

```
! Rebuilds all files in a specified configuration.
SUBROUTINE IApplication_RebuildAll($OBJECT, &               1
& Configura tion, $STATUS)
!DEC$ ATTRIBUTES DLLEXPORT :: IApplication_RebuildAll
IMPLICIT NONE

INTEGER*4, INTENT(IN)      :: $OBJECT       ! Object Pointer
!DEC$ ATTRIBUTES VALUE     :: $OBJECT
TYPE (VARIANT), INTENT(IN), OPTIONAL :: Configuration
!DEC$ ATTRIBUTES REFERENCE        :: Configuration
INTEGER*4, INTENT(OUT), OPTIONAL :: $STATUS ! Method status
!DEC$ ATTRIBUTES REFERENCE        :: $STATUS
INTEGER*4 $$STATUS
INTEGER*4 invokeargs
invokeargs = AUTOALLOCATEINVOKEARGS()                       2
IF (PRESENT(Configuration)) '$ARG1', CALL &
& AUTOADDARG(invokeargs, Configuration, .FALSE.)
$$STATUS = AUTOINVOKE($OBJECT, 28, invokeargs)             3
IF (PRESENT($STATUS)) $STATUS = $$STATUS                    4
CALL AUTODEALLOCATEINVOKEARGS (invokeargs)                  5
END SUBROUTINE IApplication_RebuildAll
```

Notes for this example:

1. The first argument to the procedure is always $OBJECT. It is a pointer to an Automation object's IDispatch interface. The last argument to the procedure is always $STATUS. It is an optional argument that you can specify if you wish to examine the return status of the method. The IDispatch Invoke member function returns a status of type HRESULT. An HRESULT is a 32-bit value. It has the same structure as a Win32 error code. In between the $OBJECT and $STATUS arguments are the method arguments' names determined from the type information. Sometimes, the type information does not provide a name for an argument. The Fortran Module Wizard creates a "$ARGn" name in this case.

2. **AUTOAllocateInvokeArgs** allocates a data structure that is used to collect the arguments that you will pass to the method. **AUTOAddArg** adds an argument to this data structure.

3. **AUTOInvoke** invokes the named method passing the argument list. This returns a status result.

4. If the caller supplied a status argument, the code copies the status result to it.

5. **AUTODeallocateInvokeArgs** deallocates the memory used by the argument list data structure.

The DSBUILD Sample in the . . . `\DF98\SAMPLES\ADVANCED\COM` folder contains the code that invokes this and other Microsoft visual development environment functionality using Automation interfaces.

17.4 Additional Information about COM and Automation Objects

This section provides some information about COM and Automation objects.

COM Objects

The Component Object Model (COM) provides mechanisms for creating reusable software components. COM is an object-based programming model designed to promote software interoperability; that is, to allow two or more applications or "components" to easily cooperate with one another, even if they were written by different vendors at different times, in different programming languages, or if they are running on different machines running different operating systems.

With COM, components interact with each other and with the system through collections of function calls, also known as methods or member functions or requests, called *interfaces*. An interface is a semantically related set of member functions. The interface as a whole represents a features of an object. The member functions of an interface represent the operations that make up the feature. In general, an object can support multiple interfaces and you can use the **COMQueryInterface** routine to get a pointer to any of them.

The Visual Fortran COM routines provide a Fortran interface to basic COM functions.

Automation Objects

The capabilities of an *Automation object* resemble those of a COM object. An Automation object is in fact a COM object. An Automation object exposes:

▶ *Methods*, which are functions that perform an action on an object. These are very similar to the member functions of COM objects.

▶ *Properties*, which hold information about the state of an object. A property can be represented by a pair of methods; one for getting the property's current value, and one for setting the property's value.

The Visual Fortran AUTO routines provide a Fortran interface to invoking an automation object's methods and setting and getting its properties.

Object Identification

Object identification enables the use of COM objects created by disparate groups of developers. To provide a method of uniquely identifying an object class regardless of where it came from, COM uses *globally unique identifiers* (GUIDs). A GUID is a 16-byte integer value that is guaranteed (for all practical purposes) to be unique across space and time. COM uses GUIDs to identify object classes, interfaces, and other things that require unique identification.

To create an instance of an object, you need to tell COM what the GUID of the object is. While using 16-byte integers for identification is fine for computers, it poses a challenge for the typical developer. So, COM also supports the use of a less precise, textual name called a *programmatic identifier* (ProgID). A ProgID takes the form:

```
application_name.object_name.object_version
```

Additional Resources

There are a number of published books and articles about COM and Automation. Digital lists some of these publications as additional resources to assist customers who want to learn more about the subject matter. This list does not comment—either negatively or positively—on any documents listed or not yet listed. Books and related resources include:

▶ *How OLE and COM Solve the Problems of Component Software Design* by K. Brockschmidt. Microsoft Systems Journal, vol. 11, no. 5 (May 1996): 63-80

▶ *Inside OLE, Second Edition* by K. Brockschmidt. Published by Microsoft Press (Redmond, Washington) 1995

▶ *Visual C++ User's Guide* (HTMLHelp Viewer, provided with Visual Fortran)

▶ *OLE 2 Programmer's Reference, Volume Two*. Published by Microsoft Press (Redmond, Washington) 1994

▶ *Understanding ActiveX and OLE* by David Chappell. Published by Microsoft Press (Redmond, Washington) 1996

▶ *Win 32 SDK, OLE Programmer's Reference* online version

▶ *Win 32 SDK, Automation* online version

Microsoft Press can be reached at the URL `http://mspress.microsoft.com/`.

18

Programming with Mixed Languages

Mixed-language programming is the process of building programs in which the source code is written in two or more languages. It lets you:

▶ Call existing code that is written in another language

▶ Use procedures that may be difficult to implement in a particular language

▶ Gain advantages in processing speeds

Mixed-language programming is possible among the 32-bit languages Visual Fortran, Visual C/C++, Visual Basic, and MASM. Mixed-language programming in Win32 is different from that in 16-bit environments, and in many respects it is easier.

To properly create mixed-language programs, rules must be established for naming variables and procedures, for stack use, and for argument passing among routines written in different languages. These rules, as a whole, are the calling convention.

A calling convention includes:

▶ Stack considerations

- Does a routine receive a varying or fixed number of arguments?
- Which routine clears the stack after a call?

▶ Naming conventions

- Is lowercase or uppercase significant or not significant?
- Are names decorated (as in Visual C++)?

▶ Argument passing protocol

- Are arguments passed by value or by reference?
- What are the equivalent data types and data structures among languages?

This chapter provides information on the calling conventions available when writing routines written in Fortran, C, Visual C++, Visual Basic, and *x*86 assembly language. It is organized into the following topics:

▶ Section 18.1 Overview of Mixed-Language Issues

▶ Section 18.2 Exchanging and Accessing Data in Mixed-Language Programming

▶ Section 18.3 Handling Data Types in Mixed-Language Programming

▶ Section 18.4 Visual Fortran/Visual C++ Mixed-Language Programs

▶ Section 18.5 Fortran/Visual Basic Mixed-Language Programs

▶ Section 18.6 Fortran/MASM Mixed-Language Programs

18.1   Overview of Mixed-Language Issues

Mixed-language programming involves a call from a routine written in one language to a function, procedure, or subroutine written in another language. For example, a Fortran main program may need to execute a specific task that you want to program separately in an assembly-language procedure, or you may need to call an existing DLL or system procedure.

Mixed-language programming is possible with Visual Fortran, Visual C/C++, Visual Basic, and assembly language (MASM) because each language implements functions, subroutines, and procedures in approximately the same way. Table 18-1 shows how different kinds of routines from each language correspond to each other. For example, a C main program could call an external void function, which is actually implemented as a Fortran subroutine.

Table 18–1   *Language Equivalents for Calls to Routines*

Language	Call with Return Value	Call with No Return Value
Fortran	FUNCTION	SUBROUTINE
C and Visual C++	Function	(void) Function
Visual Basic	Function	Sub
Assembly language	Procedure	Procedure

There are some important differences in the way languages implement routines. Argument passing, naming conventions and other interface issues must be thoughtfully and consistently reconciled between any two languages to prevent program failure and indeterminate results. However, the advantages of mixed-language programming often make the extra effort worthwhile.

A summary of a few mixed-language advantages and restrictions follows:

► Fortran/Assembly Language

Assembly-language routines are small and execute very quickly because they don't require initialization as do high-level languages like Fortran and C. Also, they allow access to hardware instructions unavailable to the high-level language user. In a Fortran/assembly-language program, compiling the main routine in Fortran gives the assembly code access to high-level procedures and library functions, yet allows freedom to tune the assembly-language routines for maximum speed and efficiency. The main program can also be an assembly-language program.

► Fortran/Visual Basic

A mix of Fortran and Visual Basic 4.0 or higher (32-bit) allows you to use the easy-to-implement user-interface features of Visual Basic, yet do all your computation, especially floating-point math, in Fortran routines. In a Fortran/Visual Basic program, the main routine must be Visual Basic. It is not possible to call Basic routines from Fortran.

► Fortran/C (or C++)

Generally, Fortran/C programs are mixed to allow one to use existing code written in the other language. Either Fortran or C can call the other, so the main routine can be in either language.

To use the same Microsoft visual development environment for multiple languages, you must have the same version of the visual development environment for your languages (see Mixed-Language Development Support in *Getting Started*).

This section provides an explanation of the keywords, attributes, and techniques you can use to reconcile differences between Fortran and other languages. Adjusting calling conventions, adjusting naming conventions and writing interface procedures are discussed in the next sections:

► Section 18.1.1 Adjusting Calling Conventions in Mixed-Language Programming

► Section 18.1.2 Adjusting Naming Conventions in Mixed-Language Programming

▶ Section 18.1.3 Prototyping a Procedure in Fortran

After establishing a consistent interface between mixed-language procedures, you then need to reconcile any differences in the treatment of individual data types (strings, arrays, and so on). This is discussed in Section 18.2
Exchanging and Accessing Data in Mixed-Language Programming.

Note: This section uses the term "routine" in a generic way, to refer to functions, subroutines, and procedures from different languages.

18.1.1 Adjusting Calling Conventions in Mixed-Language Programming

The calling convention determines how a program makes a call to a routine,
how the arguments are passed, and how the routines are named (discussed in
Section 18.1.2 Adjusting Naming Conventions in Mixed-Language Programming). In a single-language program, calling conventions are nearly always
correct, because there is one default for all routines and because header files or
Fortran module files with interface blocks enforce consistency between the
caller and the called routine.

In a mixed-language program, different languages cannot share the same
header files. If, as a result, you link Fortran and C routines that use different
calling conventions, the error isn't apparent until the bad call is made at run-
time. During execution, the bad call causes indeterminate results and/or a
fatal error, often somewhere in the program that has no apparent relation to
the actual cause: memory/stack corruption due to calling errors. Therefore,
you should check carefully the calling conventions for each mixed-language
call.

The discussion of calling conventions between languages applies only to
external procedures. You cannot call internal procedures from outside the
program unit that contains them.

A calling convention affects programming in five ways:

1. The caller routine uses a calling convention to determine the order in
   which to pass arguments to another routine; the called routine uses a
   calling convention to determine the order in which to receive the arguments passed to it. In Fortran, you can specify these conventions in a
   mixed-language interface with the **INTERFACE** statement or in a data
   or function declaration. 32-bit Visual C/C++ and Fortran both pass
   arguments in order from left to right.

2. The caller routine and the called routine use a calling convention to determine which of them is responsible for adjusting the stack in order to remove arguments when the execution of the called routine is complete. You can specify these conventions with **ATTRIBUTES** (*c*DEC$ **ATTRIBUTES** compiler directive) options such as C or STDCALL.

3. The caller routine and the called routine use a calling convention to select the option of passing a variable number of arguments.

4. The caller routine and the called routine use a calling convention to pass arguments by value (values passed) or by reference (addresses passed). Individual Fortran arguments can also be designated with **ATTRIBUTES** option VALUE or REFERENCE.

5. The caller routine and the called routine use a calling convention to establish naming conventions for procedure names. You can establish any procedure name you want, regardless of its Fortran name, with the **ALIAS** directive (or **ATTRIBUTES** option ALIAS). This is useful because C is case sensitive, while Fortran is not.

Specific calling-convention issues are discussed in the following sections:

▶ Section 18.1.1.1 ATTRIBUTES Properties and Calling Conventions

▶ Section 18.1.1.2 Stack Considerations in Calling Conventions

▶ Section 18.1.1.3 Fortran/C Calling Conventions

▶ Section 18.1.1.4 Fortran/Visual Basic Calling Conventions

▶ Section 18.1.1.5 Fortran/MASM Calling Conventions

18.1.1.1 *ATTRIBUTES Properties and Calling Conventions*

The **ATTRIBUTES** properties (or options) C, STDCALL, REFERENCE, VALUE, and VARYING all affect the calling convention of routines. You can specify these properties to individual arguments or to an entire routine. The **ATTRIBUTES** directive (*c*DEC$ **ATTRIBUTES**) is a Digital Fortran language extension.

By default, Fortran passes all data by reference (except the hidden length argument of strings, which is passed by value). If the C or STDCALL option is used, the default changes to passing almost all data except arrays by value. However, in addition to the calling-convention options C and STDCALL, you can specify argument options, VALUE and REFERENCE, to pass arguments by value or by reference, regardless of the calling convention option. Arrays can only be passed by reference.

Different Fortran calling conventions can be specified by declaring the Fortran procedure to have certain attributes. For example, on *x86* systems:

```
INTERFACE
  SUBROUTINE MY_SUB (I)
    !DEC$ ATTRIBUTES C, ALIAS:'_My_Sub' :: MY_SUB ! x86 systems
    INTEGER I
  END SUBROUTINE MY_SUB
END INTERFACE
```

This code (on *x86* systems) declares a subroutine named MY_SUB with the C property and the external name _My_Sub set with the ALIAS property.

On Alpha systems, there is no leading underscore for external names like MY_SUB, so the correct **ATTRIBUTES** line is:

```
!DEC$ ATTRIBUTES C, ALIAS:'My_Sub' :: MY_SUB ! Alpha systems
```

To write code for both *x86* and Alpha platforms, use the conditional compilation features of the **IF** Directive Construct, perhaps using the predefined preprocessor macros _X86_ and _ALPHA_ (listed under the /define option).

Table 18-2 summarizes the effect of the most common Fortran calling-convention directives.

Table 18–2 *Calling Conventions for ATTRIBUTES Options*

	Default	*C*	*STDCALL*	*C, REFERENCE*	*STDCALL, REFERENCE*
Argument					
Scalar	Reference	Value	Value	Reference	Reference
Scalar [value]	Value	Value	Value	Value	Value
Scalar [reference]	Reference	Reference	Reference	Reference	Reference
String	Reference, either Len: Mixed or Len:End	String(1:1)	String(1:1)	Reference, either Len: Mixed or Len:End	Reference, either Len: Mixed or Len:End
String [value]	Error	String(1:1)	String(1:1)	String(1:1)	String(1:1)
String [reference]	Reference, either Len: Mixed or No Len	Reference, No Len	Reference, No Len	Reference, No Len	Reference, No Len
Array	Reference	Reference	Reference	Reference	Reference

Table 18–2 *Calling Conventions for ATTRIBUTES Options (Continued)*

	Default	C	STDCALL	C, REFERENCE	STDCALL, REFERENCE
Array [value]	Error	Error	Error	Error	Error
Array [reference]	Reference	Reference	Reference	Reference	Reference
Derived Type	Reference	Value, size dependent	Value, size dependent	Reference	Reference
Derived Type [value]	Value, size dependent	Value, size dependent	Value, size dependent	Value, size dependent	Value, size dependent
Derived Type [reference]	Reference	Reference	Reference	Reference	Reference
F90 Pointer	Descriptor	Descriptor	Descriptor	Descriptor	Descriptor
F90 Pointer [value]	Error	Error	Error	Error	Error
F90 Pointer [reference]	Descriptor	Descriptor	Descriptor	Descriptor	Descriptor
Procedure Name					
Suffix	@*n* (*x*86 systems)	none	@*n* (*x*86 systems)	none	@*n* (*x*86 systems)
Case	Upper Case	Lower Case	Lower Case	Lower Case	Lower Case
Stack Cleanup	Callee	Caller	Callee	Caller	Callee

The terms in the Table 18-2 mean the following:

[value]	Argument Assigned the VALUE attribute.
[reference]	Argument assigned the REFERENCE attribute.
Value	The argument value is pushed on the stack. All values are padded to the next 4-byte boundary.
Reference	The 4-byte argument address is pushed on the stack.
Len: Mixed or Len: End	For certain string arguments:

- Len: Mixed applies when /iface:mixed_str_len_arg is set. The length of the string is pushed (by value) on the stack immediately after the address of the beginning of the string.

	• Len: End applies when /iface:nomixed_str_len_arg is set. The length of the string is pushed (by value) on the stack after all of the other arguments.
Len: Mixed or No Len	For certain string arguments:
	• Len: Mixed applies when /iface:mixed_str_len_arg is set. The length of the string is pushed (by value) on the stack immediately after the address of the beginning of the string.
	• No Len applies when /iface:nomixed_str_len_arg is set. The length of the string is not available to the called procedure.
No Len	For string arguments, the length of the string is not available to the called procedure.
String(1:1)	For string arguments, the first character is converted to **INTEGER**(4) as in **ICHAR**(string(1:1)) and pushed on the stack by value.
Error	Produces a compiler error.
Descriptor	4-byte address of the array descriptor.
@n	On x86 systems, the at sign (@) followed by the number of bytes (in decimal) required for the argument list.
Size dependent	Derived-type arguments specified by value are passed as follows:
	• Arguments from 1 to 4 bytes are passed by value.
	• Arguments from 5 to 8 bytes are in two registers (two arguments).
	• Arguments more than 8 bytes provide value semantics by passing a temporary storage address by reference.
Upper Case	Procedure name in all uppercase.
Lower Case	Procedure name in all lowercase.
Callee	The procedure being called is responsible for removing arguments from the stack before returning to the caller.
Caller	The procedure doing the call is responsible for removing arguments from the stack after the call is over.

Table 18-3 shows which Digital Fortran **ATTRIBUTES** options match other language calling conventions.

Table 18–3 *Matching Calling Conventions*

Other Language Calling Convention	Matching ATTRIBUTES Option
Visual C/C++ cdecl (default)	C
Visual C/C++ __stdcall	STDCALL
Visual Basic	none
Visual Basic CDECL keyword	C
MASM C (in PROTO and PROC declarations)	C
MASM STDCALL (in PROTO and PROC declarations)	STDCALL

The ALIAS option can be used with any other Fortran calling-convention option to preserve mixed-case names.

Note: When interfacing to the Windows graphical user interface or making API calls, you will typically use STDCALL. See Chapter 9 Creating Windows Applications for more information on Windows programming.

18.1.1.2 *Stack Considerations in Calling Conventions*

In the C calling convention, the calling routine always adjusts the stack immediately after the called routine returns control. This produces slightly larger object code because the code that restores the stack must exist at every point a procedure is called. In the STDCALL calling convention, the called procedure controls the stack. The code to restore the stack resides in the called procedure, so the code needs to appear only once.

However, the C calling convention makes calling with a variable number of arguments possible. Since in the C calling convention the caller cleans up the stack, it is possible to write a routine with a variable number of arguments. Therefore, it has the same address relative to the frame pointer, regardless of how many arguments are actually passed. Because of this, when the calling routine controls the stack, it knows how many arguments it passed, how big they are and where they reside in the stack. It can thus skip passing an argument and still keep track.

You can call routines with a variable number of arguments by including the **ATTRIBUTES** C and VARYING options in your interface to a routine. The VARYING option prevents Fortran from enforcing a matching number of arguments in routines. The VARYING option is not necessary with intrinsic Fortran 90 routines with optional arguments, where argument order and/or keywords determine which arguments are present and which are absent.

In MASM, stack control is also set by the C or STDCALL convention declared for the procedure, but you can write MASM code to control the stack within the procedure any way you wish. In addition, you can specify the USES option in the PROC directive to save and restore certain registers automatically.

18.1.1.3 *Fortran/C Calling Conventions*

In C and Visual C++ modules, you can specify the STDCALL calling convention by using the __stdcall keyword in a function prototype or definition. The __stdcall convention is also used by window procedures and API functions. As an example, the following C language prototype sets up a function call to a subroutine using the STDCALL calling convention:

```
extern void __stdcall FORTRAN_ROUTINE (int n);
```

Alternatively, instead of changing the calling convention of the C code, you can adjust the Fortran source code by using the C option. This is set with the **ATTRIBUTES** directive. For example, the following declaration assumes the subroutine is called with the C calling convention:

```
SUBROUTINE CALLED_FROM_C (A)
   !DEC$ ATTRIBUTES C :: CALLED_FROM_C
   INTEGER A
```

18.1.1.4 *Fortran/Visual Basic Calling Conventions*

You establish Fortran subroutines and functions in Visual Basic forms and the Fortran routines are then invoked from a Basic module. A Fortran routine has to be a DLL (dynamic-link library) to be called from Basic. For more information on DLLs, see Section 2.2.6 Fortran Dynamic-Link Library Projects and Chapter 8 Creating Fortran DLLs.

The calling-convention **ALIAS** directive (or **ATTRIBUTES** option ALIAS) is needed if mixed-case names are to be preserved (by default Fortran translates names to all uppercase). However, two special cases require different treatment:

▶ If a varying number of arguments are to be passed, the C and VARYING options are needed in the Fortran procedure definition and the

CDECL keyword needed in the Basic DECLARE statement in order to establish the C calling and naming convention.

▶ When passing character arguments, the Fortran routine must not pass the hidden length of character arguments, such as by using the **ATTRIBUTES** option STDCALL. Since STDCALL also lowercases Fortran names, the Fortran subprogram name should be referenced in lowercase from the Visual Basic program.

The following Fortran and Visual Basic statements establish an example Fortran function to be called from Basic:

```
! Fortran Subprogram establishing Fortran function.
   INTERFACE
      DOUBLE PRECISION FUNCTION GetFVal (r1)
         !DEC$ ATTRIBUTES ALIAS:'GetFVal' :: GetFVal
         !DEC$ ATTRIBUTES VALUE :: r1
         REAL r1
      END FUNCTION
   END INTERFACE
'FORM.FRM Basic Form to establish Fortran function
Declare Function GetFVal Lib "C:\f90\FVAL.DLL" _
(ByVal r1 As Single) As Double
```

18.1.1.5 Fortran/MASM Calling Conventions

You specify the calling convention for a MASM procedure in the PROTO and PROC directives. The STDCALL option in the PROTO and PROC directives tells the procedure to use the STDCALL calling convention. The C option in the PROTO and PROC directives tells the procedure to use the C calling convention. The USES option in the PROC directive specifies which registers to save and restore in the called MASM routine. The VARARG option to the PROTO and PROC directives specifies that the procedure allows a variable number of arguments.

As an example, the following Fortran and MASM statements set up a MASM function that can be called from Visual Fortran, using the STDCALL calling convention:

```
!Fortran STDCALL prototype.
   INTERFACE
      INTEGER FUNCTION forfunc(I1, I2)
      !DEC$ ATTRIBUTES STDCALL :: forfunc
      INTEGER I1
      INTEGER(2) I2
   END INTERFACE
   WRITE (*,*) forfunc(I1,I2)

;MASM STDCALL Prototype
```

```
        .MODEL FLAT, STDCALL
forfunc PROTO STDCALL, forint: SDWORD, shorti: ptr SWORD
        .CODE
forfunc PROC STDCALL, forint: SDWORD, shorti: ptr SWORD
        ...
forfunc ENDP END
```

The following Fortran and MASM statements set up a Fortran-callable MASM function using the C calling convention:

```
!Fortran C prototype
    INTERFACE
        INTEGER FUNCTION Forfunc (I1, I2)
        !DEC$ ATTRIBUTES C, ALIAS:'Forfunc' :: Forfunc
        INTEGER I1
        INTEGER(2) I2
    END INTERFACE
    WRITE(*,*) Forfunc (I1, I2)
    END

;MASM C PROTOTYPE
        .MODEL FLAT, C
Forfunc PROTO C, forint:SDWORD, shorti: ptr SWORD
        .CODE
Forfunc PROC C, forint:SDWORD, shorti: ptr SWORD
        ...
Forfunc ENDP END
```

18.1.2 Adjusting Naming Conventions in Mixed-Language Programming

The **ATTRIBUTES** options C and STDCALL determine naming conventions as well as calling conventions. Calling conventions specify how arguments are moved and stored; naming conventions specify how symbol names are altered when placed in an .OBJ file. Names are an issue for external data symbols shared among parts of the same program as well as among external routines. Symbol names (such as the name of a subroutine) identify a memory location that must be consistent among all calling routines.

Parameter names (names given in a procedure definition to variables that are passed to it) are never affected.

Names are altered because of case sensitivity (in C, Visual Basic, and MASM), lack of case sensitivity (in Fortran), name decoration (in Visual C++), or other issues. If naming conventions are not reconciled, the program cannot successfully link and you will receive an "unresolved external" error.

This section discusses:

▶ Section 18.1.2.1 Visual C/C++ and Visual Basic Naming Conventions

18.1.2.1 *Visual C/C++ and Visual Basic Naming Conventions*

Visual C/C++ and Visual Basic preserve case sensitivity in their symbol tables while Fortran by default does not, a difference that requires attention. Fortunately, you can use the Fortran directive **ATTRIBUTES** ALIAS option to resolve discrepancies between names, to preserve mixed-case names, or to override the automatic conversion of names to all uppercase by the Fortran default naming, or the automatic conversion to all lowercase by Fortran's STDCALL and C naming convention.

Visual C++ uses the same calling convention and argument-passing techniques as C, but naming conventions are different because of Visual C++ decoration of external symbols. When the C++ code resides in a .cpp file (created when you select C/C++ file from the visual development environment), C++ name decoration semantics are applied to external names, often resulting in linker errors. The extern "C" syntax makes it possible for a Visual C++ module to share data and routines with other languages by causing Visual C++ to drop name decoration.

The following example declares prn as an external function using the C naming convention. This declaration appears in Visual C++ source code:

```
extern "C" { void prn(); }
```

To call functions written in Fortran, declare the function as you would in C and use a "C" linkage specification. For example, to call the Fortran function FACT from Visual C++, declare it as follows:

```
extern "C" { int __stdcall FACT( int n ); }
```

The extern "C" syntax can be used to adjust a call from Visual C++ to other languages, or to change the naming convention of Visual C++ routines called from other languages. However, extern "C" can only be used from within Visual C++. If the Visual C++ code does not use extern "C" and cannot be changed, you can call Visual C++ routines only by determining the name decoration and generating it from the other language. Such an approach should only be used as a last resort, because the decoration scheme is not guaranteed to remain the same between versions.

Use of extern "C" has some restrictions:

▶ You cannot declare a member function with extern "C".

▶ You can specify extern "C" for only one instance of an overloaded function; all other instances of an overloaded function have Visual C++ linkage.

For more information on the extern "C" linkage specification, see the *Microsoft Visual C++ Language Reference.*

18.1.2.2 MASM Naming Conventions

In MASM (Microsoft Assembler, for *x*86 systems), specifying the C or STDCALL naming convention in PROC and PROTO statements preserves case sensitivity if no CASEMAP option exists. The MASM OPTION CASEMAP directive (and the command line option /C) also sets case sensitivity and overrides naming conventions specified within PROTO and PROC statements.

CASEMAP: NONE (equivalent to /Cx) preserves the case of identifiers in PUBLIC, COMM, EXTERNDEF, EXTERN, PROTO, and PROC declarations. CASEMAP: NOTPUBLIC (equivalent to /Cp) preserves the case of all user identifiers; this is the default. CASEMAP: ALL (equivalent to /Cu) translates all identifiers to uppercase.

18.1.2.3 Naming Conventions for Fortran, C, Visual C++, Visual Basic, and MASM

Table 18-4 summarizes how Fortran, Visual C/C++, Visual Basic, and MASM handle procedure names. Note that for MASM, the table does not apply if the CASEMAP: ALL option is used.

Table 18–4   *Naming Conventions in Fortran, C, Visual C++, Visual Basic, and MASM*

Language	Attributes	Name Translated As	Case of Name in .OBJ File
Fortran	**cDEC$ ATTRIBUTES** C	*_name*	All lowercase
	cDEC$ ATTRIBUTES STDCALL	*_name@n*	All lowercase
	default	*_name@n*	All uppercase
C	cdecl (default)	*_name*	Mixed case preserved
	__stdcall	*_name@n*	Mixed case preserved
Visual C++	Default	*_name@@decoration*	Mixed case preserved

Table 18–4 *Naming Conventions in Fortran, C, Visual C++, Visual Basic, and MASM (Continued)*

Language	Attributes	Name Translated As	Case of Name in .OBJ File
Visual Basic	Default	_name@n	Mixed case preserved
MASM	C (in PROTO and PROC declarations)	_name	Mixed case preserved
	STDCALL (in PROTO and PROC declarations)	_name@n	Mixed case preserved

In Table 18-4:

▶ The leading underscore (such as *_name*) is used on *x*86 systems only (not on Alpha systems).

▶ *@n* represents the stack space, in decimal notation, occupied by parameters on *x*86 systems only (not on Alpha systems).

For example, assume a function is declared in C as:

```
extern int __stdcall Sum_Up( int a, int b, int c );
```

Each integer occupies 4 bytes, so the symbol name placed in the .OBJ file on *x*86 systems is:

```
_Sum_Up@12
```

On Alpha systems, the symbol name placed in the .OBJ file is:

```
Sum_Up
```

18.1.2.4 Reconciling the Case of Names

The following summarizes how to reconcile names between languages:

▶ All-Uppercase Names

If you call a Fortran routine that uses Fortran defaults and cannot recompile the Fortran code, then in C and Visual Basic you must use an all-uppercase name to make the call. In MASM you must either use an all-uppercase name or set the OPTION CASEMAP directive to ALL, which translates all identifiers to uppercase. Use of the __stdcall convention in C code or STDCALL in MASM PROTO and PROC declarations is not enough, because __stdcall and STDCALL always preserve case in these languages. Fortran generates all-uppercase names by default and the C or MASM code must match it.

For example, these prototypes establish the Fortran function FFARCTAN(angle) where the argument angle has the **ATTRIBUTES** VALUE property:

- In C:

  ```
  extern float __stdcall FFARCTAN( float angle );
  ```

- In Visual Basic:

  ```
  Declare Function FFARCTAN Lib "C:f90psFBAS.DLL"
  (ByVal angle As Single
  ```

- In MASM:

  ```
  .MODEL FLAT, STDCALL
  FFARCTAN PROTO STDCALL, angle: REAL4
  ...
  FFARCTAN PROC STDCALL, angle: REAL4
  ```

▶ All-Lowercase Names

If the name of the routine appears as all lowercase in C or MASM, then naming conventions are automatically correct when the C or STDCALL option is used in the Fortran declaration. Any case may be used in the Fortran source code, including mixed case since the C and STDCALL options change the name to all lowercase. You cannot call a Visual Basic routine from Fortran directly (see Section 18.5 Fortran/Visual Basic Mixed-Language Programs), so Basic routine names are never translated.

▶ Mixed-case Names

If the name of a routine appears as mixed-case in C or MASM and you cannot change the name, then you can resolve this naming conflict by using the Fortran **ATTRIBUTES** ALIAS option. ALIAS is required in this situation because otherwise Fortran will not preserve the mixed-case name.

To use the ALIAS option, place the name in quotation marks exactly as it is to appear in the .OBJ file. The following is an example on *x86* systems for referring to the C function My_Proc:

```
!DEC$ ATTRIBUTES ALIAS:'_My_Proc' :: My_Proc
```

On Alpha systems, this would be coded without the leading underscore as:

```
!DEC$ ATTRIBUTES ALIAS:'My_Proc' :: My_Proc
```

18.1.2.5 *Fortran Module Names and ATTRIBUTES*

Fortran module entities (data and procedures) have external names that differ from other external entities. Module names use the convention:

_MODULENAME_mp_ENTITY [@stacksize]

MODULENAME is the name of the module and is all uppercase by default. *ENTITY* is the name of the module procedure or module data contained within *MODULENAME*. *ENTITY* is also uppercase by default. *_mp_* is the separator between the module and entity names and is always lowercase.

For example:

```
MODULE mymod
   INTEGER a
CONTAINS
   SUBROUTINE b (j)
      INTEGER j
   END SUBROUTINE
END MODULE
```

results in the following symbols being defined in the compiled .OBJ file on *x*86 systems:

```
_MYMOD_mp_A
_MYMOD_mp_B@4
```

Or, on Alpha systems:

```
MYMOD_mp_A
MYMOD_mp_B
```

Compiler options can affect the naming of module data and procedures.

Note: Except for ALIAS, **ATTRIBUTES** options do not affect the module name, which remains uppercase.

Table 18-5 shows how each **ATTRIBUTES** option affects the subroutine in the previous example module.

Table 18–5 *Effect of ATTRIBUTES options on Fortran Module Names*

ATTRIBUTES Option Given to Routine 'b'	Procedure Name in .OBJ File on x86 Systems	Procedure Name in .OBJ File on Alpha Systems
None	_MYMOD_mp_B@4	MYMOD_mp_B
C	_MYMOD_mp_b	MYMOD_mp_b
STDCALL	_MYMOD_mp_b@4	MYMOD_mp_b
ALIAS	Overrides all others, name as given in the alias	Overrides all others, name as given in the alias
VARYING	No effect on name	No effect on name

You can write code to call Fortran modules or access module data from other languages. As with other naming and calling conventions, the module name must match between the two languages. Generally, this means using the C or STDCALL convention in Fortran, and if defining a module in another language, using the ALIAS option to match the name within Fortran. Examples are given in the section Section 18.2.2 Using Modules in Mixed-Language Programming.

18.1.3   Prototyping a Procedure in Fortran

You define a prototype (interface block) in your Fortran source code to tell the Fortran compiler which language conventions you want to use for an external reference. The interface block is introduced by the **INTERFACE** statement. For a more detailed description of the **INTERFACE** statement, see "Program Units and Procedures" in the *Language Reference* in Visual Fortran online Help.

The general form for the **INTERFACE** statement is:

INTERFACE
routine statement
[*routine **ATTRIBUTE** options*]
[*argument **ATTRIBUTE** options*]
formal argument declarations
END *routine name*
END INTERFACE

The *routine statement* defines either a **FUNCTION** or a **SUBROUTINE**, where the choice depends on whether a value is returned or not, respectively. The optional *routine **ATTRIBUTE*** options (such as C and STDCALL) determine the calling, naming, and argument-passing conventions for the routine in the prototype statement. The optional *argument **ATTRIBUTE*** options (such as VALUE and REFERENCE) are properties attached to individual arguments. The *formal argument declarations* are Fortran data type declarations. The same **INTERFACE** block can specify more than one procedure.

For example, suppose you are calling a C function that has the following prototype:

```
extern void My_Proc (int i);
```

The Fortran call to this function should be declared with the following **INTERFACE** block on *x86* systems:

```
INTERFACE
  SUBROUTINE my_Proc (I)
    !DEC$ ATTRIBUTES C, ALIAS:'_My_Proc' :: my_Proc
    INTEGER I
  END SUBROUTINE my_Proc
END INTERFACE
```

Note that:

▶ On Alpha systems, the leading underscore in _My_Proc should be omitted. The **ATTRIBUTES** line on Alpha systems contains:

!DEC$ ATTRIBUTES C, ALIAS:'My_Proc' :: my_Proc

▶ Except in the ALIAS string, the case of My_Proc in the Fortran program doesn't matter.

18.2 Exchanging and Accessing Data in Mixed-Language Programming

You can use several approaches to sharing data between mixed-language routines, which can be used within the individual languages as well. These approaches are:

▶ Passing Arguments in Mixed-Language Programming (see Section 18.2.1)

▶ Using Modules in Mixed-Language Programming (see Section 18.2.2)

▶ Using Common External Data in Mixed-Language Programming (see Section 18.2.2)

Generally, if you have a large number of parameters to work with or you have a large variety of parameter types, you should consider using modules or external data declarations. This is true when using any given language, and to an even greater extent when using mixed languages.

18.2.1 Passing Arguments in Mixed-Language Programming

You can pass data between Fortran and C, Visual C++, Visual Basic and MASM through calling argument lists just as you can within each language (for example, the argument list a, b, and c in CALL MYSUB(a,b,c)). There are two ways to pass individual arguments:

▶ *By value*, which passes the argument's value.

▶ *By reference*, which passes the address of the argument. (In Fortran, Visual Basic, C, and Visual C++, all addresses are 4 bytes on *x*86 and Alpha systems.)

You need to make sure that for every call, the calling program and the called routine agree on how each argument is passed. Otherwise, the called routine receives bad data.

The Fortran technique for passing arguments changes depending on the calling convention specified. By default, Fortran passes all data by reference (except the hidden length argument of strings, which is passed by value).

If the **ATTRIBUTES** C or STDCALL option is used, the default changes to passing all data by value except arrays. If the procedure has the REFERENCE option as well as the C or STDCALL option, all arguments by default are passed by reference.

In Fortran, in addition to establishing argument passing with the calling-convention options C and STDCALL, you can specify argument options, VALUE and REFERENCE, to pass arguments by value or by reference. In mixed-language programming, it is a good idea to specify the passing technique explicitly rather than relying on defaults.

Note: In addition to **ATTRIBUTES**, the compiler option /iface also establishes some default argument passing conventions (such as for hidden length of strings).

Examples of passing by reference and value for C, Visual Basic, and MASM follow. All are interfaces to the example Fortran subroutine TESTPROC below. The definition of TESTPROC declares how each argument is passed. The REFERENCE option is not strictly necessary in this example, but using it makes the argument's passing convention conspicuous.

```
SUBROUTINE TESTPROC( VALPARM, REFPARM )
    !DEC$ ATTRIBUTES VALUE :: VALPARM
    !DEC$ ATTRIBUTES REFERENCE :: REFPARM
    INTEGER VALPARM
    INTEGER REFPARM
END
```

▶ Fortran/C example of arguments passed by value and reference

In C and Visual C++ all arguments are passed by value, except arrays, which are passed by reference to the address of the first member of the array. Unlike Fortran, C and Visual C++ do not have calling-convention directives to affect the way individual arguments are passed. To pass non-array C data by reference, you must pass a pointer to it. To pass a C array by value, you must declare it as a member of a structure and pass the structure. The following C declaration sets up a call to the example Fortran TESTPROC subroutine:

```
extern void __stdcall TESTPROC( int ValParm, int *RefParm );
```

► Fortran/Visual Basic example of arguments passed by value and reference

In Visual Basic, arguments are passed by reference by default. To pass arguments by value, you use the keyword BYVAL in front of the argument in the DECLARE statement. For example:

```
Declare Sub TESTPROC Lib "C:\f90_TESTPROC.DLL"
    (ByVal Valparm As Long, Refparm As Long)
```

Strings are a special case. See the discussion on character strings in Section 18.3.5 Handling Character Strings.

► Fortran/MASM example of arguments passed by value and reference

In MASM, arguments are passed by value by default. Arguments to be passed by reference are designated with PTR in the PROTO and PROC directives. For example:

```
TESTPROC PROTO STDCALL, valparm: SDWORD, refparm: PTR SDWORD
```

To use an argument passed by value, use the value of the variable. For example:

```
mov eax, valparm ; Load value of argument
```

This statement places the value of valparm into the EAX register.

To use an argument passed by reference, use the address of the variable. For example:

```
mov ecx, refparm   ; Load address of argument
mov eax, [ecx]     ; Load value of argument
```

These statements place the value of refparm into the EAX register.

Table 18-6 summarizes how to pass arguments by reference and value. An array name in C is equated to its starting address because arrays are normally passed by reference. You can assign the REFERENCE property to a procedure, as well as to individual arguments.

Table 18-6 does not describe argument passing of strings and Fortran 90 pointer arguments in Visual Fortran, which are constructed differently than other arguments. By default, Fortran passes strings by reference along with the string length. String length placement depends on whether the compiler

Table 18–6 *Passing Arguments by Reference and Value*

Language	ATTRIBUTE	Argument Type	To Pass by Reference	To Pass by Value
Fortran	Default	Scalars and derived types	Default	VALUE option
	C or STDCALL option	Scalars and derived types	REFERENCE option	Default
	Default	Arrays	Default	Cannot pass by value
	C or STDCALL option	Arrays	Default	Cannot pass by value
Visual C/C++		Non-arrays	Pointer argument_name	Default
		Arrays	Default	Struct {type} array_name
Visual Basic		All types	Default	ByVal
Assembler (x86) MASM		All types	PTR	Default

option /iface:mixed_str_len_arg (immediately after the address of the beginning of the string) or /iface:nomixed_str_len_arg (after all arguments) is set.

Fortran 90 array pointers and assumed-shape arrays are passed by passing the address of the array descriptor.

For a discussion of the effect of attributes on passing Fortran 90 pointers and strings, see Section 18.3.2 Handling Fortran 90 Pointers and Allocatable Arrays and Section 18.3.5 Handling Character Strings.

18.2.2 Using Modules in Mixed-Language Programming

Modules are the simplest way to exchange large groups of variables with C, because Visual Fortran modules are directly accessible from Visual C/C++. The following example declares a module in Fortran, then accesses its data from C. The Fortran code:

```
! F90 Module definition
    MODULE EXAMP
        REAL A(3)
        INTEGER I1, I2
        CHARACTER(80) LINE
        TYPE MYDATA
        SEQUENCE
        INTEGER N
```

```
      CHARACTER(30) INFO
   END TYPE MYDATA
END MODULE EXAMP
```

The C code:

```
\* C code accessing module data *\
extern float EXAMP_mp_A[3];
extern int EXAMP_mp_I1, EXAMP_mp_I2;
extern char EXAMP_mp_LINE[80];
extern struct {
      int N;
      char INFO[30];
} EXAMP_mp_MYDATA;
```

When the C++ code resides in a .cpp file (created when you select C/C++ file from the visual development environment), C++ semantics are applied to external names, often resulting in linker errors. In this case, use the extern "C" syntax (see Section 18.1.2.1 Visual C/C++ and Visual Basic Naming Conventions):

```
\* C code accessing module data in .cpp file*\
extern "C" float EXAMP_mp_A[3];
extern "C" int EXAMP_mp_I1, EXAMP_mp_I2;
extern "C" char EXAMP_mp_LINE[80];
extern "C" struct {
      int N;
      char INFO[30];
} EXAMP_mp_MYDATA;
```

You can also define a module procedure in C and make that routine part of a Fortran module by using the **ALIAS** directive. The C code:

```
// C procedure
void pythagoras (float a, float b, float *c)
{
      *c = (float) sqrt(a*a + b*b);
}
```

Using the same example when the C++ code resides in a .cpp file, use the extern "C" syntax (see Section 18.1.2.1 Visual C/C++ and Visual Basic Naming Conventions):

```
// C procedure
extern "C" void pythagoras (float a, float b, float *c)
{
      *c = (float) sqrt(a*a + b*b);
}
```

The Fortran code to define the module CPROC:

```
! Fortran 90 Module including procedure
   MODULE CPROC
      INTERFACE
      SUBROUTINE PYTHAGORAS (a, b, res)
         !DEC$ ATTRIBUTES C :: PYTHAGORAS
         !DEC$ ATTRIBUTES REFERENCE :: res
! res is passed by REFERENCE because its individual attribute
! overrides the subroutine's C attribute
         REAL a, b, res
! a and b have the VALUE attribute by default because
! the subroutine has the C attribute
      END SUBROUTINE
   END INTERFACE
   END MODULE
```

The Fortran code to call this routine using the module CPROC:

```
! Fortran 90 Module including procedure
   USE CPROC
      CALL PYTHAGORAS (3.0, 4.0, X)
      TYPE *,X
   END
```

18.2.3   Using Common External Data in Mixed-Language Programming

Common external data structures include Fortran common blocks, and C structures and variables that have been declared global or external. All of these data specifications create external variables, which are variables available to routines outside the routine that defines them.

This section applies only to Fortran/C and Fortran/MASM mixed-language programs because there is no way to share common data with Visual Basic. You must pass all data between Visual Basic and Fortran as arguments. This process can be streamlined by passing user-defined types between them, described in Section 18.3.6 Handling User-Defined Types.

External variables are case sensitive, so the cases must be matched between different languages, as discussed in the section on naming conventions. Common external data exchange is described in the following sections.

Using Global Variables in Mixed-Language Programming

A variable can be shared between Fortran and C or MASM by declaring it as global (or **COMMON**) in one language and accessing it as an external variable in the other language. Visual Basic cannot access another language's global data or share its own. In Fortran/Basic programs, variables must be passed as arguments.

In Fortran, a variable can access a global parameter by using the EXTERN option for **ATTRIBUTES**. For example:

```
!DEC$ ATTRIBUTES C, EXTERN :: idata
INTEGER idata (20)
```

EXTERN tells the compiler that the variable is actually defined and declared global in another source file. If Fortran declares a variable external with EXTERN, the language it shares the variable with must declare the variable global.

In C, a variable is declared global with the statement:

```
int idata[20]; // declared as global (outside of any function)
```

MASM declares a parameter global (PUBLIC) with the syntax:

PUBLIC [*langtype*] *name*

where *name* is the name of the global variable to be referenced, and the optional *langtype* is STDCALL or C. The option *langtype*, if present, overrides the calling convention specified in the .MODEL directive.

Conversely, Fortran can declare the variable global (**COMMON**) and other languages can reference it as external:

```
!Fortran declaring PI global
 REAL PI
 COMMON /PI/ PI ! Common Block and variable have the same
name
```

In C, the variable is referenced as an external with the statement:

```
//C code with external reference to PI
extern float PI;
```

Note that the global name C references is the name of the Fortran common block, not the name of a variable within a common block. Thus, you cannot use blank common to make data accessible between C and Fortran. In the preceding example, the common block and the variable have the same name, which helps keep track of the variable between the two languages. Obviously, if a common block contains more than one variable they cannot all have the common block name. (See Using Fortran Common Blocks and C Structures below.)

MASM can also access Fortran global (**COMMON**) parameters with the EXTERN directive. The syntax is:

EXTERN [*langtype*] *name*

where *name* is the name of the global variable to be referenced, and the optional *langtype* is STDCALL or C.

Using Fortran Common Blocks and C Structures

To reference C structures from Fortran common blocks and vice versa, you must take into account the way the common blocks and structures differ in their methods of storing member variables in memory. Fortran places common block variables into memory in order as close together as possible, with the following rules:

▶ A single **BYTE**, **INTEGER**(1), **LOGICAL**(1), or **CHARACTER** variable in common block list begins immediately following the previous variable or array in memory.

▶ All other types of single variables begin at the next even address immediately following the previous variable or array in memory.

▶ All arrays of variables begin on the next even address immediately following the previous variable or array in memory, except for **CHARACTER** arrays which always follow immediately after the previous variable or array.

▶ All common blocks begin on a four-byte aligned address.

Because of these padding rules, you must consider the alignment of C structure elements with Fortran common block elements and assure matching either by making all variables exactly equivalent types and kinds in both languages (using only 4-byte and 8-byte data types in both languages simplifies this) or by using the C pack pragmas in the C code around the C structure to make C data packing like Fortran's. For example:

```
#pragma pack(2)
struct {
        int N;
        char INFO[30];
} examp;
#pragma pack()
```

To restore the original packing, you must add #pragma pack( ) at the end of the structure. (Remember: Fortran module data can be shared directly with C structures with appropriate naming.)

Once you have dealt with alignment and padding, you can give C access to an entire common block or set of common blocks. Alternatively, you can pass individual members of a Fortran common block in an argument list, just as you can any other data item. Use of common blocks for mixed-language data exchange is discussed in the following sections.

Accessing Common Blocks and C Structures Directly

You can access Fortran common blocks directly from C by defining an external C structure with the appropriate fields, and making sure that alignment and padding between Fortran and C are compatible. The **ATTRIBUTES** options C and ALIAS can be used with a common block to allow mixed-case names.

As an example, suppose your Fortran code has a common block named Really, as shown:

```
!DEC$ ATTRIBUTES ALIAS:'Really' :: Really
REAL(4) x, y, z(6)
REAL(8) ydbl
COMMON / Really / x, y, z(6), ydbl
```

You can access this data structure from your C code with the following external data structure:

```
#pragma pack(2)
extern struct {
    float x, y, z[6];
    double ydbl;
} Really;
#pragma pack()
```

You can also access C structures from Fortran by creating common blocks that correspond to those structures. This is the reverse case from that just described. However, the implementation is the same because after common blocks and structures have been defined and given a common address (name), and assuming the alignment in memory has been dealt with, both languages share the same memory locations for the variables.

Passing the Address of a Common Block

To pass the address of a common block, simply pass the address of the first variable in the block, that is, pass the first variable by reference. The receiving C or Visual C++ module should expect to receive a structure by reference.

In the following example, the C function initcb receives the address of a common block with the first variable named n, which it considers to be a pointer to a structure with three fields:

Fortran source code:

```
!
  INTERFACE
    SUBROUTINE initcb (BLOCK)
      !DEC$ ATTRIBUTES C :: initcb
```

```
        !DEC$ ATTRIBUTES REFERENCE :: BLOCK
        INTEGER BLOCK
      END SUBROUTINE
    END INTERFACE
!
    INTEGER n
    REAL(8) x, y
    COMMON /CBLOCK/n, x, y
    . . .
    CALL initcb( n )
```

C source code:

```
//
#pragma pack(2)
struct block_type
{
  int n;
  double x;
  double y;
};
#pragma pack()
//
void initcb( struct block_type *block_hed )
{
  block_>hed-n = 1;
  block_>hed-x = 10.0;
  block_>hed-y = 20.0;
}
```

18.3   Handling Data Types in Mixed-Language Programming

Even when you have reconciled calling conventions, naming conventions, and methods of data exchange, you must still be concerned with data types, because each language handles them differently. Table 18-7 lists the equivalent data types among Fortran, C, Visual Basic, and MASM:

Table 18–7   *Equivalent Data Types*

Fortran Data Type	C Data Type	Visual Basic Data Type	MASM Data Type
INTEGER(1)	char	---	SBYTE
INTEGER(2)	short	Integer	SWORD
INTEGER(4)	int, long	Long	SDWORD

Table 18–7 *Equivalent Data Types (Continued)*

Fortran Data Type	C Data Type	Visual Basic Data Type	MASM Data Type
REAL(4)	float	Single	REAL4
REAL(8)	double	Double	REAL8
CHARACTER(1)	unsigned char	—	BYTE
CHARACTER*(*)	See Section 18.3.5 Handling Character Strings		
COMPLEX(4)	struct complex4 {float real, imag;};	—	COMPLEX4 STRUCT 4 real REAL4 0 imag REAL4 0 COMPLEX4 ENDS
COMPLEX(8)	struct complex8 {double real, imag;};	—	COMPLEX8 STRUCT 8 real REAL8 0 imag REAL8 0 COMPLEX8 ENDS
All LOGICAL types	Use integer types for C, MASM, and Visual Basic		

The following sections describe how to reconcile data types between the different languages:

▶ Section 18.3.1 Handling Numeric, Complex, and Logical Data Types

▶ Section 18.3.2 Handling Fortran 90 Array Pointers and Allocatable Arrays

▶ Section 18.3.3 Handling Digital Fortran Pointers

▶ Section 18.3.4 Handling Arrays and Visual Fortran Array Descriptors

▶ Section 18.3.5 Handling Character Strings

▶ Section 18.3.6 Handling User-Defined Types

18.3.1 Handling Numeric, Complex, and Logical Data Types

Normally, passing numeric data does not present a problem. If a C program passes an unsigned data type to a Fortran routine, the routine can accept the argument as the equivalent signed data type, but you should be careful that the range of the signed type is not exceeded.

Table 18-7 (included in Section 18.3 Handling Data Types in Mixed-Language Programming) summarizes equivalent numeric data types for Fortran, MASM, and Visual Visual C/C++.

C, Visual C++, and MASM do not directly implement the Fortran types **COMPLEX**(4) and **COMPLEX**(8). However, you can write structures that are equivalent. The type **COMPLEX**(4) has two fields, both of which are 4-byte floating-point numbers; the first contains the real-number component, and the second contains the imaginary-number component. The type **COMPLEX** is equivalent to the type **COMPLEX**(4). The type **COMPLEX**(8) is similar except that each field contains an 8-byte floating-point number.

Note: Fortran functions of type **COMPLEX** place a hidden **COMPLEX** argument at the beginning of the argument list. C functions that implement such a call from Fortran must declare this hidden argument explicitly, and use it to return a value. The C return type should be void.

Following are the Visual C/C++ structure definitions for the Fortran **COMPLEX** types:

```
struct complex4 {
    float real, imag;
};
struct complex8 {
    double real, imag;
};
```

Following are the MASM structure definitions for the Fortran **COMPLEX** types:

```
COMPLEX4 STRUCT 4
  real REAL4 0
  imag REAL4 0
COMPLEX4 ENDS
COMPLEX8 STRUCT 8
  real REAL8 0
  imag REAL8 0
COMPLEX8 ENDS
```

A Fortran **LOGICAL**(2) value is stored as a 2-byte indicator value (0=false, and the /fpscomp:[no] logicals compiler option determines how true values are handled). A Fortran **LOGICAL**(4) value is stored as a 4-byte indicator value, and **LOGICAL**(1) is stored as a single byte. The type **LOGICAL** is the same as **LOGICAL**(4), which is equivalent to type int in C.

You can use a variable of type **LOGICAL** in an argument list, module, common block, or global variable in Fortran and type int in C for the same argument. Type **LOGICAL**(4) is recommended instead of the shorter variants for use in common blocks.

The Visual C++ class type has the same layout as the corresponding C struct type, unless the class defines virtual functions or has base classes. Classes that lack those features can be passed in the same way as C structures.

18.3.2   Handling Fortran 90 Array Pointers and Allocatable Arrays

How Fortran 90 array pointers and arrays are passed is affected by the **ATTRIBUTES** options in effect, and by the **INTERFACE**, if any, of the procedure they are passed to. If the **INTERFACE** declares the array pointer or array with deferred shape (for example, ARRAY(:)), its descriptor is passed. This is true for array pointers and all arrays, not just allocatable arrays. If the **INTERFACE** declares the array pointer or array with fixed shape, or if there is no interface, the array pointer or array is passed by base address, which is like passing the first element of an array.

When a Fortran 90 array pointer or array is passed to another language, either its descriptor or its base address can be passed.

The following shows how allocatable arrays and Fortran 90 array pointers are passed with different attributes in effect:

▶ If the property of the array pointer or array is none, it is passed by descriptor, regardless of the property of the passing procedure (None; C; STDCALL; C, REFERENCE; or STDCALL, REFERENCE).

▶ If the property of the array pointer or array is VALUE, an error is returned, regardless of the property of the passing procedure.

▶ If the property of the array pointer or array is REFERENCE, it is passed by descriptor, regardless of the property of the passing procedure.

Note that the VALUE option cannot be used with descriptor-based arrays.

When you pass a Fortran array pointer or an array by descriptor to a non-Fortran routine, that routine needs to know how to interpret the descriptor. Part of the descriptor is a pointer to address space, as a C pointer, and part of it is a description of the pointer or array properties, such as its rank, stride, and bounds.

For information about the Visual Fortran array descriptor format, see Section 18.3.4 Handling Arrays and Visual Fortran Array Descriptors.

Fortran 90 pointers that point to scalar data contain the address of the data and are not passed by descriptor.

For information about performance implications of passing different types of array arguments, see Section 6.4 Use Arrays Efficiently.

18.3.3 Handling Digital Fortran Pointers

Digital Fortran (integer) pointers are not the same as Fortran 90 pointers, but are instead like C pointers. Digital Fortran pointers are 4-byte **INTEGER** quantities.

When passing a Digital Fortran pointer to a routine written in another language:

▶ The argument should be declared in the non-Fortran routine as a pointer of the appropriate data type.

▶ The argument passed from the Fortran routine should be the Digital Fortran pointer name, not the pointer-based variable name.

For example, on *x*86 systems:

```
! Fortran main program.
   INTERFACE
     SUBROUTINE Ptr_Sub (p)
     !DEC$ ATTRIBUTES C, ALIAS:'_Ptr_Sub' :: Ptr_Sub
       INTEGER p
     END SUBROUTINE Ptr_Sub
   END INTERFACE
   REAL A(10), VAR(10)
   POINTER (p, VAR) ! VAR is the pointer-based
                    ! variable, p is the int.
   p = LOC(A)

   CALL Ptr_Sub (p)
   WRITE(*,*) 'A(4) = ', A(4)
   END
!

//C subprogram
   void Ptr_Sub (float *p)
   {
      p[3] = 23.5;
   }
```

On Alpha systems, the alias name for Ptr_Sub should not have a leading underscore, as follows:

```
!DEC$ ATTRIBUTES C, ALIAS:'Ptr_Sub' :: Ptr_Sub
```

When the main Fortran program and C function are built and executed, the following output appears:

```
A(4) = 23.50000
```

When receiving a pointer from a routine written in another language:

▶ The argument should be declared in the non-Fortran routine as a pointer of the appropriate data type and passed as usual.

▶ The argument received by the Fortran routine should be declared as a Digital Fortran pointer name, then the **POINTER** statement should associate it with a pointer-based variable of the appropriate data type (matching the data type of the passing routine). When inside the Fortran routine, use the pointer-based variable to set and access what the pointer points to.

For example, on *x86* systems:

```
! Fortran subroutine.
   SUBROUTINE Iptr_Sub (p)
   !DEC$ ATTRIBUTES C, ALIAS:'_Iptr_Sub' :: Iptr_Sub
     integer VAR(10)
     POINTER (p, VAR)
     OPEN (8, FILE='STAT.DAT')
     READ (8, *) VAR(4) ! Read from file and store the
                        ! fourth element of VAR
   END SUBROUTINE Iptr_Sub
!

//C main program
extern void Iptr_Sub(int *p);

main ( void )
{
  int a[10];
  Iptr_Sub (&a[0]);
  printf("a[3] = %i\n", a[3]);
}
```

On Alpha systems, the alias name for Iptr_Sub should not have a leading underscore, as follows:

```
!DEC$ ATTRIBUTES C, ALIAS:'Iptr_Sub' :: Iptr_Sub
```

When the main C program and Fortran subroutine are built and executed, the following output appears if the STAT.DAT file contains "4":

```
a[3] = 4
```

18.3.4 Handling Arrays and Visual Fortran Array Descriptors

Fortran 90 allows arrays to be passed as array elements, as array subsections, or as whole arrays referenced by array name. Within Fortran 90, array elements are ordered in column-major order, meaning the subscripts of the lowest dimensions vary first.

When using arrays between Fortran and another language, differences in element indexing and ordering must be taken into account. You must reference the array elements individually and keep track of them. Fortran, Visual Basic, MASM, and C vary in the way that array elements are indexed. Array indexing is a source-level consideration and involves no difference in the underlying data.

Visual Basic stores arrays and character strings as descriptors: data structures that contain array size and location. This storage difference is transparent to the user, however.

To pass an array from Visual Basic to Fortran, pass the first element of the array. By default, Visual Basic passes variables by reference, so passing the first element of the array will give Fortran the starting location of the array, just as Fortran expects. Visual Basic indexes the first array element as 0 by default, while Fortran by default indexes it as 1. Visual Basic indexing can be set to start with 1 using the statement:

```
Option Base 1
```

Alternatively, in the array declaration in either language you can set the array lower bound to any integer in the range -32,768 to 32,767. For example:

```
' In Basic
Declare Sub FORTARRAY Lib "fortarr.dll" (Barray as Single)
DIM barray (1 to 3, 1 to 7) As Single
Call FORTARRAY(barray (1,1))

! In Fortran
Subroutine FORTARRAY(arr)
  REAL arr(3,7)
```

In MASM, arrays are one-dimensional and array elements must be referenced byte-by-byte. The assembler stores elements of the array consecutively in memory, with the first address referenced by the array name. You then access each element relative to the first, skipping the total number of bytes of the previous elements. For example:

```
xarray     REAL4    1.1, 2.2, 3.3, 4.4 ; initializes
                              ; a four element array with
                              ; each element 4 bytes
```

Referencing xarray in MASM refers to the first element, the element containing 1.1. To refer to the second element, you must refer to the element 4 bytes beyond the first with xarray[4] or xarray+4. Similarly:

```
yarray    BYTE      256 DUP      ; establishes a
                 ; 256 byte buffer, no initialization
zarray    SWORD     100 DUP(0)   ; establishes 100
                 ; two-byte elements, initialized to 0
```

Fortran and C arrays differ in two ways:

▶ The value of the lower array bound is different. By default, Fortran indexes the first element of an array as 1. C and Visual C++ index it as 0. Fortran subscripts should therefore be one higher. (Fortran also provides the option of specifying another integer lower bound.)

▶ In arrays of more than one dimension, Fortran varies the left-most index the fastest, while C varies the right-most index the fastest. These are sometimes called column-major order and row-major order, respectively.

In C, the first four elements of an array declared as X[3][3] are:

```
X[0][0] X[0][1] X[0][2] X[1][0]
```

In Fortran, the first four elements are:

```
X(1,1) X(2,1) X(3,1) X(1,2)
```

The order of indexing extends to any number of dimensions you declare. For example, consider the C declaration:

```
int arr1[2][10][15][20];
```

This is equivalent to the Fortran declaration:

```
INTEGER arr1( 20, 15, 10, 2 )
```

The constants used in a C array declaration represent extents, not upper bounds as they do in other languages. Therefore, the last element in the C array declared as int arr[5][5] is arr[4][4], not arr[5] [5].

Table 18-8 shows equivalencies for array declarations.

Table 18–8 *Equivalent Array Declarations for Different Languages*

Language	Array Declaration	Array Reference from Fortran
Fortran	**DIMENSION** x(i, k) -or- *type* x(i, k)	x(i, k)

Table 18–8 *Equivalent Array Declarations for Different Languages (Continued)*

Language	Array Declaration	Array Reference from Fortran
Visual Basic	DIM x(i, k) As *type*	x(i -1, k -1)
Visual C/C++	*type* x[k] [i]	x(i -1, k -1)
MASM	Declare and reference arrays as elements in consecutive storage	

Visual Fortran Array Descriptor Format

For cases where Fortran 90 needs to keep track of more than a pointer memory address, the Digital Visual Fortran compiler uses an *array descriptor*, which stores the details of how an array is organized.

When using an explicit interface (by association or procedure interface block), Visual Fortran will generate a descriptor for the following types of array arguments:

▶ Pointers to arrays (array pointers)

▶ Assumed-shape arrays

Certain data structure arguments do not use a descriptor, even when an appropriate explicit interface is provided. For example, explicit-shape and assumed-size arrays do not use a descriptor. In contrast, array pointers and allocatable arrays use descriptors regardless of whether they are used as arguments.

When calling between Visual Fortran and a non-Fortran language (such as C), using an *implicit* interface allows the array argument to be passed *without* a Visual Fortran descriptor (see Section 6.4.2 Passing Array Arguments Efficiently). However, for cases where the called routine needs the information in the Visual Fortran descriptor, declare the routine with an *explicit* interface and specify the dummy array as either an assumed-shape array or with the pointer attribute.

You can associate a Fortran 90 pointer with any piece of memory, organized in any way desired (so long as it is "rectangular" in terms of array bounds). You can also pass Fortran 90 pointers to other languages, such as C, and have the other language correctly interpret the descriptor to obtain the information it needs.

However, using array descriptors can increase the opportunity for errors and is not portable:

▶ If the descriptor is not defined correctly, the program might access the wrong memory address, possibly causing a General Protection Fault.

▶ Array descriptor formats are specific to each Fortran compiler. Code that uses array descriptors is *not* portable to other compilers or platforms. For example, the Visual Fortran array descriptor format (for Win32 systems) differs from the array descriptor format for Digital Fortran on Digital UNIX and OpenVMS systems. The Visual Fortran array descriptor format is the same format used by Microsoft Fortran PowerStation.

▶ The array descriptor format might change in the future.

The components of the current Visual Fortran array descriptor follow:

▶ The first longword (bytes 0 to 3) contains the base address. The base address plus the offset defines the first memory location (start) of the array.

▶ The second longword (bytes 4 to 7) contains the size of a single element of the array.

▶ The third longword (bytes 8 to 11) contains the offset. The offset is added to the base address to define the start of the array.

▶ The fourth longword (bytes 12 to 15) contains the low-order bit set if the array has been defined (storage allocated).

▶ The fifth longword (bytes 16 to 19) contains the number of dimensions (rank) of the array.

▶ The remaining longwords (bytes 20 up to 103) contain information about each dimension (up to seven). Each dimension is described by three additional longwords:

 • The number of elements (extent)
 • The distance between the starting address of two successive elements, in bytes.
 • The lower bound

An array of rank one would require three additional longwords for a total of in eight longwords (5 + 3*1) and end at byte 31. An array of rank seven would be described in a total of 26 longwords (5 + 3*7) and end at byte 103.

For example, consider the following declaration:

```
integer,target :: a(10,10)
integer,pointer :: p(:,:)
p => a(9:1:-2,1:9:3)
call f(p)
  .
  .
  .
```

The descriptor for actual argument p would contain the following values:

▶ The first longword (bytes 0 to 3) contain the base address (assigned at run-time).

▶ The second longword (bytes 4 to 7) is set to 4 (size of a single element).

▶ The third longword (bytes 8 to 11) contain the offset (assigned at run-time).

▶ The fourth longword (bytes 12 to 15) contains 1 (low bit is set).

▶ The fifth longword (bytes 16 to 19) contains 2 (rank).

▶ The sixth, seventh, and eighth longwords (bytes 20 to 31) contain information for the first dimension, as follows:

- 5 (extent)
- -8 (distance between elements)
- 1 (the lower bound)

▶ For the second dimension, the ninth, tenth, and eleventh longwords (bytes 32 to 43) contain

- 3 (extent)
- 120 (distance between elements)
- 1 (the lower bound)

▶ Byte 43 is the last byte for this example.

For information about performance implications of passing different types of array arguments, see Section 6.4.2 Passing Array Arguments Efficiently.

18.3.5 Handling Character Strings

By default, Visual Fortran passes a hidden length argument for strings. The hidden length argument consists of an unsigned 4-byte integer, always passed by value, immediately following the address of the character string. You can alter the default way strings are passed by using attributes. Table 18-9 shows the effect of various attributes on passed strings.

The important things to note in Table 18-9 are:

▶ Character strings without the VALUE or REFERENCE attribute that are passed to C or STDCALL routines are not passed by reference. Instead, only the first character is passed and it is passed by value.

▶ Character strings with the VALUE option passed to C or STDCALL routines are not passed by reference. Instead, only the value of the first character is passed.

Table 18–9 *Effect of ATTRIBUTES Options on Character Strings Passed as Arguments*

Argument	Default	C	STDCALL	C, REFERENCE	STDCALL, REFERENCE
String	Passed by reference, along with length	First Character converted to INTEGER (4) and passed by value	First Character converted to INTEGER(4) and passed by value	Passed by reference, along with length	Passed by reference, along with length
String with VALUE option	Error	First character converted to INTEGER (4) and passed by value	First character converted to INTEGER(4) and passed by value	First character converted to INTEGER(4) and passed by value	First character converted to INTEGER(4) and passed by value
String with REFERENCE option	Passed by reference, possibly along with length	Passed by reference, no length	Passed by reference, no length	Passed by reference, no length	Passed by reference, no length

▶ For string arguments with default **ATTRIBUTES**, **ATTRIBUTES** C, REFERENCE, or **ATTRIBUTES** STDCALL, REFERENCE:

- When /iface:mixed_str_len_arg is set, the length of the string is pushed (by value) on the stack immediately after the address of the beginning of the string.
- When /iface:nomixed_str_len_arg is set, the length of the string is pushed (by value) on the stack after all of the other arguments.

▶ For string arguments passed by reference with default **ATTRIBUTES**:

- When /iface:mixed_str_len_arg is set, the length of the string is pushed (by value) on the stack immediately after the address of the beginning of the string.
- When /iface:nomixed_str_len_arg is set, the length of the string is not available to the called procedure.

Since all strings in C are pointers, C expects strings to be passed by reference, without a string length. In addition, C strings are null-terminated while Fortran strings are not. There are two basic ways to pass strings between Fortran and C: convert Fortran strings to C strings, or write C routines to accept Fortran strings.

To convert a Fortran string to C, choose a combination of attributes that passes the string by reference without length, and null terminate your strings. For example, on *x86* systems:

```
INTERFACE
  SUBROUTINE Pass_Str (string)
    !DEC$ ATTRIBUTES C, ALIAS:'_Pass_Str' :: Pass_Str
    CHARACTER*(*) string
    !DEC$ ATTRIBUTES REFERENCE :: string
  END SUBROUTINE
END INTERFACE
CHARACTER(40) forstring
DATA forstring /'This is a null-terminated string.'C/
```

On Alpha systems, the first **ATTRIBUTES** line would omit the leading underscore and be as follows:

```
!DEC$ ATTRIBUTES C, ALIAS:'Pass_Str' :: Pass_Str
```

This example shows the extension of using the null-terminator for the string in the Fortran **DATA** statement (see "C Strings" in the *Language Reference* in Visual Fortran online Help):

```
DATA forstring /'This is a null-terminated string.'C/
```

The C interface is:

```
void Pass_Str (char *string)
```

To get your C routines to accept Fortran strings, C must account for the length argument passed along with the string address. For example:

```
! Fortran code
INTERFACE
SUBROUTINE Pass_Str (string)
CHARACTER*(*) string
END INTERFACE
```

The C routine must expect two arguments:

```
void __stdcall PASS_STR (char *string, unsigned int length_arg )
```

This interface handles the hidden-length argument, but you must still reconcile C strings that are null-terminated and Fortran strings that are not. In addition, if the data assigned to the Fortran string is less than the declared length, the Fortran string will be blank padded.

Rather than trying to handle these string differences in your C routines, the best approach in Fortran/C mixed programming is to adopt C string behavior whenever possible. Another good reason for using C strings is that Win32 APIs and most C library functions expect null-terminated strings.

Fortran functions that return a character string using the syntax CHAR-ACTER*(*) place a hidden string argument and the address of the string at the beginning of the argument list.

C functions that implement such a Fortran function call must declare this hidden string argument explicitly and use it to return a value. The C return type should be void. However, you are more likely to avoid errors by not using character-string return functions. Use subroutines or place the strings into modules or global variables whenever possible.

Visual Basic strings must be passed by value to Fortran. Visual Basic strings are actually stored as structures containing length and location information. Passing by value dereferences the structure and passes just the string location, as Fortran expects. For example:

```
! In Basic
  Declare Sub forstr Lib "forstr.dll" (ByVal Bstring as
String)
  DIM bstring As String * 40 Fixed-length string
  CALL forstr(bstring)

! In Fortran
  SUBROUTINE forstr(s)
  !DEC$ ATTRIBUTES STDCALL :: forstr
  !DEC$ ATTRIBUTES REFERENCE :: s
  CHARACTER(40) s
  s = 'Hello, Visual Basic!'
  END
```

The Fortran directive **!DEC$ ATTRIBUTES** STDCALL informs Fortran not to expect the hidden length arguments to be passed from the Visual Basic calling program. The name in the Visual Basic program is specified as lower-case since STDCALL makes the Fortran name lowercase.

MASM does not add either a string length or a null character to strings by default. To append the string length, use the syntax:

lenstring BYTE "String with length", LENGTHOF lenstring

To add a null character, append it by hand to the string:

```
nullstring BYTE "Null-terminated string", 0
```

18.3.6   Handling User-Defined Types

Fortran 90 supports user-defined types (data structures similar to C structures). User-defined types can be passed in modules and common blocks just as other data types, but the other language must know the type's structure. For example:

```
! Fortran CODE
   TYPE LOTTA_DATA
      SEQUENCE
      REAL A
      INTEGER B
      CHARACTER(30) INFO
      COMPLEX CX
      CHARACTER(80) MOREINFO
   END TYPE LOTTA_DATA
   TYPE (LOTTA_DATA) D1, D2
   COMMON /T_BLOCK/ D1, D2

/* C code accessing D1 and D2 */
extern struct {
   struct {
      float a;
      int b;
      char info[30];
      struct {
      float real, imag;
      } cx;
      char moreinfo[80];
   } d1, d2;
} T_BLOCK;
```

18.4   Visual Fortran/Visual C++ Mixed-Language Programs

When you understand and reconcile the calling, naming and argument passing conventions between Fortran and C, you are ready to build an application.

If you are using Visual C/C++ you can edit, compile, and debug your code within the Microsoft visual development environment. If you are using another C compiler, you can edit your code within the visual development environment by selecting File/New and choosing Visual C/C++ source in the File tab or, after activating the editor, by selecting the View menu Properties item and selecting from the drop-down list.

However, if you are not using Visual C/C++, you must compile your code outside the Microsoft visual development environment and either build the Fortran/C program on the command line or add the compiled C .OBJ file to your Fortran project in the Microsoft visual development environment.

As an example of building from the command line, if you have a main C program CMAIN.C that calls Fortran subroutines contained in FOR-

SUBS.F90, you can create the CMAIN application with the following commands:

```
cl /c cmain.c
DF cmain.obj forsubs.f90
```

The Fortran (DF) compiler accepts an object file for the main program written in C and compiled by the C compiler. The DF compiler compiles the .F90 file and then has the linker create an executable file under the name CMAIN.EXE using the two object files.

Either compiler can do the linking, regardless of which language the main program is written in; however, if you use the DF compiler first, you must include DFOR.LIB with the C compiler, and you might experience some difficulty with the version of LIBC.LIB used by the C compiler. For these reasons, you may prefer to use the C compiler first or get your project settings for both Fortran and C to agree on the default C library to link against.

You need to link your application against one and only one copy of the C library.

When using the visual development environment to build your application, Fortran uses default libraries depending on the information specified in the Fortran tab in the Project menu, Settings item (Project Settings dialog box). You can also specify linker settings with the Linker tab in the Project Settings dialog box.

In the Fortran tab, within the Libraries category, the following options determine the default libraries selected:

▶ Use Fortran Run-time Libraries (see Section 2.2 Types of Projects)

▶ Use Multithreaded Libraries (see Section 4.1.71 /[no]threads)

▶ Use C Debug Libraries (see Section 4.1.16 /[no]dbglibs)

The combinations of these options use the libraries shown in Table 18-10.

Table 18–10 *Determining Visual Fortran Default Libraries*

Static or DLL Project?	*Use Multi-Theaded Libraries?*	*Use C Debug Libraries?*	*Fortran Link Library Used*	*C Link Library Used*
Static	No	No	dfor.lib	libc.lib
Static	No	Yes	dfor.lib	libcd.lib
Static	Yes	No	dformt.lib	libcmt.lib

Table 18–10 *Determining Visual Fortran Default Libraries (Continued)*

Static or DLL Project?	Use Multi-Theaded Libraries?	Use C Debug Libraries?	Fortran Link Library Used	C Link Library Used
Static	Yes	Yes	dformt.lib	libcmtd.lib
DLL	No	No	dfordll.lib (dforrt.dll)	msvcrt.lib (msvcrt.dll)
DLL	No	Yes	dfordll.lib (dforrt.dll)	msvcrtd.lib (msvcrtd.dll)
DLL	Yes	No	dformd.lib (dformd.dll)	msvcrt.lib (msvcrt.dll)
DLL	Yes	Yes	dformd.lib (dformd.dll)	msvcrtd.lib (msvcrtd.dll)

The way Visual C++ chooses libraries is also based upon the Project menu Settings item, but within the C/C++ tab. In the Code Generation category, the "Use run-time library" item lists the C libraries shown in Table 18-11.

Table 18–11 *Determining Visual C++ Default Libraries*

Menu Item Selected	CL Option or Project Type Enabled	Default Library Specified in Object File
Single-threaded	/ML	libc.lib
Multithreaded	/MT	libcmt.lib
Multithreaded DLL	/MD	msvcrt.lib (msvcrt.dll)
Debug Single-threaded	/MLd	libcd.lib
Debug Multithreaded	/MTd	libcmtd.lib
Debug Multithreaded DLL	/MDd	msvcrtd.lib (msvcrt.dll)

If you are using Microsoft Visual C/C++, the Microsoft visual development environment can create mixed Fortran/C applications transparently, with no special directives or steps on your part. You can edit and browse your C and Fortran programs with appropriate syntax coloring for the language. You can add C source files to your Fortran project or Fortran source files to a C project, and they will be compiled and linked automatically.

When you debug a mixed Visual C/Fortran application, the debugger will adjust to the code type as it steps through: the C or Fortran expression evaluator will be selected automatically based on the code being debugged, and the stack window will show Fortran data types for Fortran procedures and C data types for C procedures.

When printing from Visual C++ programs while calling Fortran subprograms that also print, the output may not appear in the order you expect. In Visual C++, the output buffer contents are not written immediately, but written when the buffer is full, the I/O stream is closed or the program terminates normally. The buffer is said to be "flushed" when this occurs.

To make sure interleaving Visual C++ and Fortran program units print in the order expected, you can explicitly flush the Visual C++ buffers after an output command with the flushall, fflush, fclose, setbuf, or setvbuf Visual C++ library calls.

Multithreaded applications should have full multithread support, so if you use DFORMT.LIB, be sure LIBCMT.LIB is specified as a default library.

18.5   Fortran/Visual Basic Mixed-Language Programs

Visual Fortran and Visual Basic mixed-language programs typically use:

▶ Visual Basic for the user-interface features

▶ Visual Fortran for computation

In Fortran/Visual Basic programs, the Visual Basic must be 32-bit (at least Version 5.0). You can also use the Visual Basic for Applications (VBA) included with Microsoft Excel to call Fortran subprograms.

The Visual Basic development environment is separate from the Visual Fortran Version 6 development environment. However, the two languages can coexist in the same final application.

The usual case is to call Fortran subprograms from Visual Basic. Because Visual Basic subprograms are interpreted and not compiled, they cannot be called directly from compiled language programs like Fortran. Instead, Visual Basic creates OLE objects that export properties and routines.

When calling a Fortran subprogram from Visual Basic, you need to:

1. Create the Visual Fortran subprogram as a Fortran DLL project.

2. Reference the DLL from Visual Basic with a Declare Sub or Declare Func statement.

It is also possible for Visual Basic to pass the address of its procedures to a Fortran program, to be called later by that Fortran program. For an example of Visual Fortran calling Visual Basic callback routines, see the Sample in the `. . . \DF98\SAMPLES\MIXLANG\VB\CALLBACK` folder.

The following sections discuss Visual Basic calling a Fortran DLL subprogram:

▶ Section 18.5.1 Calling Visual Fortran from Visual Basic

▶ Section 18.5.2 Visual Basic Debugging Considerations

▶ Section 18.5.3 Examples of Fortran/Visual Basic Programs

18.5.1 Calling Visual Fortran from Visual Basic

When calling a Visual Fortran DLL from Visual Basic, important argument passing and data type considerations are:

▶ Visual Basic uses the STDCALL standard of argument passing with one exception: it does not append the "@n" count to the name on *x*86 systems.

▶ Within Visual Basic, you declare the name of the routine that will be called and the arguments to be passed to it. Scalar numeric arguments can be directly passed from Basic and directly used by Fortran, but strings, arrays, and types require some extra handling.

Declaring the Fortran Routine in Visual Basic

When you declare a Fortran routine in Basic the routine name is exported in exactly the same case as you declared it. Optionally, you can specify a directory path to the Fortran DLL in the declaration.

The following Visual Basic example declares a Fortran subroutine named FortranCall that takes two single-precision arguments:

```
Declare Sub FortranCall Lib "d:\MyProjects\FCall.dll" _
                        (A1 as Single, A2 as Single)
```

The following example declares a Fortran function named FortranFunc that takes two integer (32-bit) arguments and returns a single precision value:

```
Declare Function FortranFunc Lib "d:\MyProject\FFun.dll" _
                        (A1 as Long, A2 as Long) _
                        As Single
```

Exporting the Routine from the Fortran DLL

When you create the Fortran DLL, you need to add two additional attributes to the function or subroutine declaration so that it can be accessed from outside the DLL.

The Fortran routine name must be exported from the DLL, and it must be aliased to match exactly the name expected by Basic. The **ATTRIBUTES** (*d***DEC$ ATTRIBUTES** compiler directive) and ALIAS declarations export the name and alias, as shown below for a Fortran subroutine:

```
    SUBROUTINE FortranCall
!DEC$ ATTRIBUTES DLLEXPORT :: FortranCall ! exports the name
!DEC$ ATTRIBUTES ALIAS : "FortranCall" :: FortranCall
!This sets it
```

This is also true for Fortran functions, must be exported and aliased to match exactly the name expected by Basic:

```
    REAL Function FortranFunc
!DEC$ ATTRIBUTES DLLEXPORT :: FortranFunc
!DEC$ ATTRIBUTES ALIAS : "FortranFunc" :: FortranFunc
```

Data Type Considerations

When you pass data between Visual Basic and Visual Fortran, you need to keep in mind the calling standard used by the two languages, the size of the data, and the on-disk format of the data.

Table 18-12 summaries the calling considerations for the data types:

Table 18–12 *Calling Considerations for Data in Visual Basic and Visual Fortran*

Data Type	Calling Considerations
Integer	By default, both Visual Basic and Visual Fortran pass integers by reference. The default integer size in Basic is 2 bytes, equivalent to INTEGER(2) in Fortran. No extra action is required by either language to access integer arguments.
Floating point	By default, both Visual Basic and Visual Fortran pass single- and double-precision floating point numbers by reference. The size of a single-precision floating point number is 4 bytes in both languages. The size of a double-precision floating point number is 8 bytes in both languages. No extra action is required by either language to access floating point arguments.
Logical	By default, both Basic and Fortran pass logical data by reference. The default logical size in Basic is two bytes, equivalent to LOGICAL(2) in Fortran. No extra action is required by either language to access logical arguments.

Table 18–12 *Calling Considerations for Data in Visual Basic and Visual Fortran (Continued)*

Data Type	Calling Considerations
Strings	By default, Basic passes strings in a structure called a BSTR. By default, Fortran passes strings in two arguments: the string's address and a hidden argument containing the string's length. These defaults can be easily overridden by making changes in the Basic declaration, and sometimes in the Fortran declaration too. Whenever you pass a string from Basic to Fortran, the passing mechanism should be declared as ByVal. See the String Passing Examples below.
Arrays	By default, Basic arrays are 0-based. Fortran arrays are 1-based by default. When you declare a Basic array to be of size "*n*", *n*+1 elements are allocated, including the 0th element. This can be overridden, as show in the Array Passing Examples below. To pass arrays of numbers from Basic to Fortran, whether they are integer or floating-point numbers, pass the first element. In the Fortran code declare the argument to be an array. Usually the Basic code will pass the number of elements in the array. To pass arrays of strings or types from Basic to Fortran requires the use of COM utilities to read the structures created by Basic. The arrays are passed as is from Basic, and then extracted in the Fortran code using SafeArray*xx* utilities. For more detail, please refer to the Visual Fortran Samples found in the . . . \DF98\SAMPLES\MIXLANG\VB\ARRAYS and . . . \DF98\ SAMPLES\MIXLANG\VB\TYPEARRAYS folders.
Types	Basic-declared types can be passed from Basic to Fortran. The Basic-declared type will also have to be declared in Fortran; care should be taken to keep the two structures the same. In Fortran, the TYPE should be declared to be packed, usually PACK:2. You should be aware of the default sizes of the TYPE elements in the two languages, and adjust the defaults accordingly. Note that strings in Basic-declared types are stored as Unicode, which can be declared in Fortran as an array of Integer*2. To access these strings from Fortran, use the Natural Language System (NLS) API calls. For information, see Chapter 14 Using National Language Support Routines and the Visual Fortran Samples found in the . . . \DF98\SAMPLES\MIXLANG\VB\ TYPEARRAYS folder.

String Passing Examples

The following example shows passing strings using the usual case, where the string will have varying length, and the length must also be passed to Fortran ByVal:

Visual Basic code:

```
Declare Sub FortString1 Lib "forttest" (ByVal S1 as String, _
                                         ByVal L1 as Long)
Dim S1 as String * 12
Call FortString1(S1, Len(S1))
```

Visual Fortran code:

```
Subroutine FortString1 (mystring)
!DEC$ ATTRIBUTES DLLEXPORT, ALIAS : "FortString1" :: &
  FortString1
CHARACTER*(*) mystring
```

The following example shows passing strings where the length of the string will be constant and known by both the Basic and Fortran code, so you do not need to pass the length to Fortran, but you need to tell Fortran not to expect its length:

Visual Basic code:

```
Declare Sub FortString2 Lib "forttest" (ByVal S2 as String)
Dim S2 as String * 25
```

Visual Fortran code:

```
Subroutine FortString2 (mystring)
!DEC$ ATTRIBUTES DLLEXPORT, ALIAS : "FortString2" :: &
  FortString2
!DEC$ ATTRIBUTES REFERENCE :: mystring
CHARACTER*25 mystring
```

Array Passing Examples

The following example shows shows passing arrays:

Visual Basic code:

```
Basic declaration:
    Declare Sub FortArray1 Lib "forttest" (A1 as Long, _
NumElem as long)
    Dim A1(1:3) as Long
    Call FortArray1(A1(1), 3)
```

Visual Fortran code:

```
Subroutine FortArray1 (Array1, N)
    !DEC$ ATTRIBUTES DLLEXPORT, ALIAS : "FortArray1" :: &
& FortArray1
    Integer array1(N)
```

18.5.2 Visual Basic Debugging Considerations

This section describes how to debug the Fortran code in the DLL being called by Visual Basic. It is not intended to describe how to debug the Visual Basic code itself.

Debugging the Fortran DLL

In Visual Basic, create an executable of your project. Use the pulldown menu item File-Make myproject.exe. Note where the executable was created.

In the Visual Fortran development environment:

1. In the Project menu, click Settings

2. Click the Debug tab

3. In the box labelled "Executable for debug session," enter the full path and filename of the executable you created above.

You can now use the full power of the visual development environment debugger to debug your DLL.

If you are using VBA within Microsoft Excel, the steps are similar for debugging your DLL. Enter the full path and filename for Excel into the box labelled "Executable for debug session." Optionally, you can enter the name of the worksheet into the box labeled "Program arguments:". You can now use the visual development environment to debug your DLL.

For a sample Fortran debugging session, see Section 5.2 Debugging the Squares Example Program.

Visual Basic Error 53: File not found: yy.dll

If you get the error message "File not found: yy.dll" when you run the Visual Basic application, check the following:

▶ If you built the DLL on one system and copied it to another, did you also copy the Fortran run-time DLLs?

These files are DFORRT.DLL, DFORMD.DLL, and MSVCRT.DLL on the Visual Fortran CD-ROM. They can be freely distributed with your application (see *Visual Fortran Getting Started*).

▶ Is the correct path to *yy.dll* specified in the Basic declaration?

Carefully check the path and file name in the Visual Basic Declare statement.

Visual Basic Error 453: Can't find DLL entry point xx in yy.dll

If you get the error message "Can't find DLL entry point xx in *yy.dll*," check the following:

▶ Make sure the Fortran code has specified the **ATTRIBUTES** DLLEX-PORT for the routine name (see the *c***DEC$ ATTRIBUTES** compiler directive).

► Make sure the Fortran code has specified an **ATTRIBUTES** ALIAS name that exactly matches the name declared by the Basic code (see the *cDEC$ ALIAS* directive, which can also be used as an **ATTRIBUTES** option ALIAS).

► Make sure you are referencing the correct *yy.dll*.

For an example of calling a Fortran DLL from Visual Basic, see Section 18.5.3 Examples of Fortran/Visual Basic Programs.

18.5.3   Examples of Fortran/Visual Basic Programs

The following brief code demonstrates the interface for a Fortran subroutine and function (free-form Fortran source):

1. In the visual development environment, create a new project of type Fortran Dynamic-Link Library. Name the project FCALL.

2. Create a new free-form source file (Project menu, Add to Project, New) for the project named FCALL.F90 with the following code:

```
! Fortran Code establishing subroutine
! Computes the MOD of R1 and 256.0 and stores the
! result in the argument NUM

SUBROUTINE FortranCall (r1, num)

! Specify that the routine name is to be made available to
! callers of the DLL and that the external name should not
! have any prefix or suffix

!DEC$ ATTRIBUTES DLLEXPORT :: FortranCall
!DEC$ ATTRIBUTES ALIAS:'FortranCall' :: FortranCall

REAL,INTENT(IN) :: r1 ! Input argument
REAL,INTENT(OUT) :: num

num = MOD (r1, 256.0)

END SUBROUTINE
```

3. Build the Fortran DLL as described in Section 8.3 Building and Using Dynamic-Link Libraries.

4. Start Visual Basic and create a new project Standard EXE:

► On the control toolbar, click on the CommandButton icon and then, with the cursor over the form, draw out a button.

▶ In the button's Properties box, double-click on Caption and change the caption to "Do it!".

▶ Click on the TextBox icon and, in the same fashion, draw a text box on the form. In its Properties box, find the Text property and change it to an empty string.

5. Double-click on the Command button on the form—a code window will appear. Fill in the code so that it looks like this:

```
Private Sub Command1_Click()
r1 = 456.78
Call FortranCall(r1, Num)
Text1.Text = Str$(Num)
End Sub
```

6. Select Project..Add Module and click on Open to create a new module. Add the following code to the module:

```
Declare Sub FortranCall Lib"c:\MyProjects\Fcall\Debug\
Fcall.dll _"
            (r1 As Single, Num As Single)
```

Replace the filename with the location of the Fortran DLL, if it is different.

7. Run the Basic program by pressing F5. Click on the *Do it!* button. The Fortran routine will be called to compute the modulus, returning the result to the Basic code. The Basic code will then convert the result to a string and display it in the text box.

Visual Basic, like Fortran, passes numeric values (such as integers and reals) by reference, so it is not necessary to change the passing mechanism on either side. The ALIAS attribute is required because Visual Basic, even though it uses the STDCALL calling mechanism, does not "decorate" routine names with the @n suffix. If the Fortran routine were also to be called by other Fortran code, it would be appropriate to use the Alias option on the Basic side to name it with the proper suffix.

18.6   Fortran/MASM Mixed-Language Programs

With Microsoft Macro Assembler (MASM), you can combine the unique strengths of assembly-language programming with Visual Fortran. If you structure your assembly-language procedures appropriately, you can call them from Visual Fortran programs and subprograms. MASM works with Visual Fortran, C, and Visual C++. These high-level languages can call MASM procedures, and each of the languages can be called from MASM programs.

Details of the MASM interfaces with the other languages can be found in the *Microsoft MASM Programmer's Guide*.

Compile your Fortran source module with Visual Fortran, and assemble your assembly-language procedure with the MASM assembler. Then, link the two object files. The following example shows how to call a MASM assembler-language program from Fortran.

The Fortran code:

```
INTERFACE
  INTEGER (4) FUNCTION POWER2 (V,E)
  !DEC$ ATTRIBUTES STDCALL :: Power2
  INTEGER V, E
  END FUNCTION
END INTERFACE
```

The MASM code:

```
POWER2 PROTO STDCALL, v, e
...
POWER2 PROC STDCALL, v, e
...
POWER2 ENDP
END
```

In the example, the Fortran call to MASM is power2(v,e), which is identical to a Fortran function call.

There are two differences between this mixed-language call and a call between two Fortran modules:

▶ The subprogram power2(v,e) is implemented in MASM using standard MASM syntax. The PROTO declaration in MASM specifies that the procedure use the STDCALL calling convention.

▶ The **INTERFACE** statement in the Fortran module specifies the STDCALL calling convention, so the Fortran program uses same convention that the MASM procedure specifies.

This section covers the following topics:

▶ Section 18.6.1 Creating a MASM Procedure

▶ Section 18.6.2 Fortran/MASM Alignment and Return Value Considerations

▶ Section 18.6.3 Examples of Fortran/MASM Programming

18.6.1 Creating a MASM Procedure

Normally you follow these steps in creating a MASM procedure:

1. Set up the procedure, defining compatible segments and declaring the procedure.

2. Enter the procedure and set up an appropriate stack frame.

3. Preserve register values by pushing any registers on the stack that you modify later.

4. Reserve space on the stack for any local data (optional).

5. Access arguments in the main body of your procedure.

6. Deallocate any local data by returning space from the stack.

7. Restore register values by popping any preserved registers from the stack.

8. If you called the procedure as a function, return a value (optional).

9. Set up the caller routine by restoring the caller stack frame.

10. Exit the procedure and return to the caller program.

18.6.2 Fortran/MASM Alignment and Return Value Considerations

Visual Fortran lets you specify alignment for all data objects. Requesting alignment specifies that bytes may be added as padding, so that the object and its data start on a natural boundary (see Section 6.3 Data Alignment Considerations). The MASM default is byte-alignment, so you should specify an alignment of 4 for MASM structures or use the Fortran compiler option /alignment:*keyword* (or /Zp*n*).

Your MASM procedure can return a value to your Fortran routine if you prototype it as a function. All return values of 4 bytes or less (except for floating-point values) are returned in the EAX register.

Procedures that return floating-point values return their results on the floating-point processor stack. This is possible because there is always a coprocessor or emulator available for 32-bit compilers.

To return **REAL** and **COMPLEX** floating-point values, records, arrays, and values larger than 4 bytes and return user-defined types larger than 8 bytes from assembly language to Fortran, you must use a special convention. Fortran creates space in the stack segment to hold the actual return value and passes an extra parameter as the last parameter pushed onto the stack. This extra parameter contains the address of the stack space that contains the return value. For user-defined types, values of 4 bytes or less are returned in EAX and values of 5 to 8 bytes are returned in EAX:EDX.

In the assembly procedure, put the data for the return value at the location pointed to by the return value offset. Then copy the return-value offset (located at EBP+8 if you've created a stack frame in your assembly code) to EAX. This is necessary because the calling module expects EAX to point to the return value.

Table 18-13 summarizes ways to return values.

Table 18–13 *Ways to Return Values for Fortran/MASM Alignment*

Type of Value to Return	*Method of Returning Value*
Integer, logical variable, or user-defined type of size 4 bytes or less	Return value in EAX register
Floating-point variable	Return value on the FPU stack
Variable of size more than 4 bytes (strings, complex values) or user-defined types more than 8 bytes	Return value on stack, address of value in EAX register
User-defined structures between 5 and 8 bytes	Return value in EAX:EDX registers.

18.6.3   Examples of Fortran/MASM Programming

Several sample programs have been provided which illustrate Visual Fortran routines that call MASM procedures (see the . . . \DF98\SAMPLES\ MIXLANG folder).

19

Creating Multithread Applications

Visual Fortran provides support for creating multithread applications. You should consider using more than one thread if your application needs to manage multiple activities, such as simultaneous keyboard input and calculations. One thread can process keyboard input while a second thread performs data transformation calculations. A third thread can update the display screen based on data from the keyboard thread. At the same time, other threads can access disk files, or get data from a communications port.

When using Windows NT on a multiprocessor machine (sometimes called an "SMP machine") you can achieve a substantial speedup on numerically intensive problems by dividing the work among different threads; the operating system will assign the different threads to different processors (symmetric multiprocessing or parallel execution). Even if you have a single-processor machine, multiple-window applications might benefit from multithreading because threads can be associated with different windows; one thread can be calculating while another is waiting for input.

While you might gain execution speed by having a program executed in multiple threads, there is overhead involved in managing the threads. You need to evaluate the requirements of your project to determine whether you should run it with more than one thread.

If your multithreaded code calls functions from the run-time library or does input/output, you must also link your code to the multithreaded version of the run-time libraries instead of the regular single-threaded ones. This is described in Section 19.3 Compiling and Linking Multithread Programs and Chapter 2 Building Programs and Libraries.

For additional resources about threads, processes, and multithreading, see Section 19.4 Other Sources of Information.

For more information, see:

▶ Section 19.1 Basic Concepts of Multithreading

▶ Section 19.2 Writing a Multithread Program

▶ Section 19.3 Compiling and Linking Multithread Programs

▶ Section 19.4 Other Sources of Information

19.1   Basic Concepts of Multithreading

A *thread* is a path of execution through a program. It is an executable entity that belongs to one and only one process. Each process has at least one thread of execution, automatically created when the process is created. Your main program runs in the first thread. A Win32 thread consists of a stack, the state of the CPU registers, a security context, and an entry in the execution list of the system scheduler. Each thread shares all of the process's resources.

A *process* consists of one or more threads and the code, data, and other resources of a program in memory. Typical program resources are open files, semaphores (a method of interthread communication), and dynamically allocated memory. A program executes when the system scheduler gives one of its threads execution control. The scheduler determines which threads should run and when they should run. Threads of lower priority might need to wait while higher priority threads complete their tasks. On multiprocessor machines, the scheduler can move individual threads to different processors to balance the CPU load.

Because threads require less system overhead and are easier to create than an entire process, they are useful for time- or resource-intensive operations that can be performed concurrently with other tasks. Threads can be used for operations such as background printing, monitoring a device for input, or backing up data while it is being edited.

When threads, processes, files, and communications devices are opened, the function that creates them returns a *handle*. Each handle has an associated Access Control List (ACL) that is used to check the security credentials of the process. Processes and threads can inherit a handle or give one away using functions described in this section. Objects and handles regulate access to system resources. For more information on handles and security, see the Win32

Application Programming Interface reference (such as the *Platform SDK* online title).

All threads in a process execute independently of one another. Unless you take special steps to make them communicate with each other, each thread operates while completely unaware of the existence of other threads in a process. Threads sharing common resources must coordinate their work by using semaphores or another method of interthread communication. For more information on interthread communication, see Section 19.2.4 Sharing Resources.

19.2 Writing a Multithread Program

Multiple threads are best used for:

▶ Background tasks such as data calculations, database queries, and input gathering, which do not directly involve window management or user interface.

▶ Operations that are independent from one another that can benefit from concurrent processing.

▶ Asynchronous tasks such as polling on a serial port.

If your application contains tasks that require a private address space and private resources, you can protect them from the activities of other threads by creating multiple processes rather than multiple threads. See Section 19.2.8 Working with Multiple Processes.

The sections that follow discuss the steps you need to consider in creating a multithread application:

▶ Section 19.2.1 Modules for Multithread Programs

▶ Section 19.2.2 Starting and Stopping Threads

▶ Section 19.2.3 Thread Routine Format

▶ Section 19.2.4 Sharing Resources

▶ Section 19.2.5 Thread Local Storage (TLS)

▶ Section 19.2.6 Synchronizing Threads

▶ Section 19.2.7 Handling Errors in Multithread Programs

▶ Section 19.2.8 Working with Multiple Processes

▶ Section 19.2.9 Table of Multithread Routines

19.2.1   Modules for Multithread Programs

A module called DFMT.MOD is supplied with Visual Fortran. It contains
interface statements to the underlying Win32 API routines as well as parameter and structure definitions used by the routines. You need to include a **USE
DFMT** statement in the declarations section of every Fortran program unit
(program, subroutine, function, or module) that uses multithread APIs.

The source code for the DFMT module (file name DFMT.F90) contains
type definitions and external function declarations. You can use it as an added
reference for the calling syntax, number, and type of arguments for a multithread procedure.

Other Windows APIs that support multithreading tasks (such as window
management functions) are included in the DFWIN.F90 module, available
to your programs with the **USE DFWIN** statement. For information about
creating a Fortran Windows application, see Chapter 9 Creating Windows
Applications.

19.2.2   Starting and Stopping Threads

When you add threads to a process, you need to consider the costs to your
process. Create only the number of threads that help your application
respond and perform better. You can save time by multitasking, but remember that additional CPU time is needed to keep track of multiple threads.
When you are deciding how many threads to create, you also need to consider
what data can be process-specific, and what data is thread-specific. Section
19.2.4 Sharing Resources discusses synchronizing access to variables and data.

One single call to the CreateThread function creates a thread, specifies
security attributes and memory stack size, and names the routine for the
thread to run. Windows allocates memory for the thread stack in the virtual
address space of the application that contains the thread. Once a thread has
finished processing, the CloseHandle routine frees the resources used by the
thread.

Starting Threads

The function CreateThread creates a new thread. Its return value is an **INTE-
GER**(4) thread handle, used in communicating to the thread and when closing it. The syntax for this function is:

CreateThread (*security, stack, thread_func, argument, flags, thread_id*)

security

INTEGER(4). Is the SECURITY_ATTRIBUTES type, defined in DFMT.F90. If *security* is zero, the thread has the default security attributes of the parent process. For more information about setting security attributes for processes and threads, see the Platform SDK online reference.

stack

INTEGER(4). Defines the stack size of the new thread. All of an application's default stack space is allocated to the first thread of execution. As a result, you must specify how much memory to allocate for a separate stack for each additional thread your program needs. The CreateThread call allows you to specify the value for the stack size on each thread you create. A value of zero indicates the stack has the same size as the application's primary thread. The size of the stack is increased dynamically, if necessary, up to a limit of 1 MB.

thread_func

Is the starting address for the thread function. Minimum requirements for *thread_func* are discussed in Section 19.2.3 Thread Routine Format.

argument

INTEGER(4). Is an optional argument for *thread_func*. Your program defines this parameter and how it is used.

flags

INTEGER(4). Creates a thread and determines when it begins processing. It can take either of two values: 0, or CREATE_SUSPENDED. If you specify 0, the thread is created and runs immediately after creation. If you specify CREATE_SUSPENDED, the thread is created, but does not run until you call the ResumeThread function.

thread_id

INTEGER(4). Is returned by CreateThread. It is a unique identifier for the thread, which you can use when calling other multithread routines. While the thread is running, no other thread has the same identifier. However, the operating system may use the identifier again for other threads once this one has completed.

A thread can be referred to by its handle as well as its unique thread identifier. Synchronization functions such as WaitForSingleObject and WaitForMultipleObjects take the thread handle as an argument.

Stopping Threads

The ExitThread routine allows a thread to stop its own execution. The syntax is:

CALL EXITTHREAD ([*Termination Status*])

Termination status may be queried by another thread. A termination status of 0 indicates normal termination. You can assign other termination status values and their meaning in your program.

When the called thread is no longer needed, the calling thread needs to close the handle for the thread. Use the CloseHandle routine to free memory used by the thread. A thread object is not deleted until the last thread handle is closed.

It is possible for more than one handle to be open to a thread: for example, if a program creates two threads, one of which waits for information from the other. In this case, two handles are open to the first thread: one from the thread requesting information, the other from the thread that created it. All handles are closed implicitly when the enclosing process terminates.

The TerminateThread routine allows one thread to terminate another, if the security attributes are set appropriately for both threads. DLLs attached to the thread are not notified that the thread is terminating, and its initial stack is not deallocated. Use Terminate Thread for emergencies only.

Other Thread Support Functions

Scheduling thread priorities is supported through the functions GetThreadPriority and SetThreadPriority. Use the priority class of a thread to differentiate between applications that are time critical and those that have normal or below normal scheduling requirements. If you need to manipulate priorities, be very careful not to give a thread too high a priority, or it can consume all of the available CPU time. A thread with a base priority level above 11 interferes with the normal operation of the operating system. Using REALTIME_PRIORITY_CLASS may cause disk caches to not flush, hang the mouse, and so on.

When communicating with other threads, a thread uses a *pseudohandle* to refer to itself. A pseudohandle is a special constant that is interpreted as the current thread handle. Pseudohandles are only valid for the calling thread; they cannot be inherited by other threads. The GetCurrentThread function returns a pseudohandle for the current thread. The calling thread can use this handle to specify itself whenever a thread handle is required. Pseudohandles are not inherited.

To get the thread's identifier, use the GetCurrentThreadId function. The identifier uniquely identifies the thread in the system until it terminates. You can use the identifier to specify the thread itself whenever an identifier is required.

Use GetExitCodeThread to find out if a thread is still active, or if it is not, to find its exit status. Call GetLastError for more detailed information on the exit status. If one routine depends on a task being performed by a different thread, use the wait functions described in Section 19.2.6 Synchronizing Threads instead of GetExitCodeThread.

19.2.3 Thread Routine Format

A function or subroutine that runs in a separate thread from the main program can take an argument. The code below shows a skeleton for a function and a subroutine:

```
      INTEGER(4) FUNCTION thrdfnc(arg)
      USE DFMT
      integer(4) arg
!DEC$ ATTRIBUTES VALUE :: arg
      arg = arg + 1        ! Sample only; real work goes here.
      thrdfnc = 0          ! Sets exit code to 0.
      END FUNCTION

      SUBROUTINE thrdfnc2 (arg2)
      USE DFMT
      integer(4) arg2
!DEC$ ATTRIBUTES VALUE :: arg2
              ! Subroutine work goes here.
      Call exitthread(0)   ! Exit code is 0.
      END SUBROUTINE
```

The arguments arg or arg2 are passed to the function or subroutine when the main program calls CreateThread, as the fourth argument. The arguments arg or arg2 are passed by value.

Threads automatically terminate when the function or subroutine terminates.

19.2.4 Sharing Resources

Each thread has its own stack and its own copy of the CPU registers. Other resources, such as files, units, static data, and heap memory, are shared by all threads in the process. Threads using these common resources must coordinate their work. There are several ways to synchronize resources:

▶ Critical section

A critical section is a block of code that accesses a non-shareable resource. Critical sections are typically used to restrict access to data or code that can only be used by one thread at a time within a process (for example, modification of shared data in a common block).

Before you can synchronize threads with a critical section, you must initialize it by calling InitializeCriticalSection, passing to it the address of a global variable or **COMMON** block that different threads have access to. Call EnterCriticalSection when beginning to process the global variable, and LeaveCriticalSection when the application is finished with it. Both Enter-CriticalSection and LeaveCriticalSection can be called several times within an application. For a Multithreaded Visual Fortran Sample that uses Critical Sections, see PEEKAPP.F90 in the . . . \DF98\SAMPLES\QUICKWIN folder.

▶ MUTual EXclusion object (Mutex)

A mutex is a mechanism that allows only one thread at a time to access a resource. Mutexes are typically used to restrict access to a system resource that can only be used by one thread at a time (for example, a printer), or when sharing might produce unpredictable results.

CreateMutex creates a mutex object. It returns an error if the mutex already exists (one by the same name was created by another process or thread). Call GetLastError after calling CreateMutex to look for the error status ERROR_ALREADY_EXISTS. You can also use the OpenMutex function to determine whether or not a named mutex object exists. When called, OpenMutex returns the object's handle if it exists, or null if a mutex with the specified name is not found. Using OpenMutex does not change a mutex object to a signaled state; this is accomplished by one of the wait routines described in Section 19.2.6 Synchronizing Threads.

ReleaseMutex changes a mutex from the not-signaled state to the signaled state. This function only has an effect if the thread calling it also owns the mutex. When the mutex is in a signaled state, any thread waiting for it can acquire it and begin executing.

▶ Semaphore

A semaphore is a counter that regulates the number of threads that can use a resource. Semaphores are typically used to control access to a specified number of identical resources.

Functions for handling semaphores are nearly identical to functions that manage mutexes. CreateSemaphore creates a semaphore, specifying an initial as well as a maximum count for the number of threads that can access the resource. OpenSemaphore, like OpenMutex, returns the handle of the named semaphore object, if it exists. The handle can then be used in any function that requires it (such as one of the wait functions described in Section 19.2.6 Synchronizing Threads). Calling OpenSemaphore does not reduce a resource's available count; this is accomplished by the function waiting for the resource.

Use ReleaseSemaphore to increase the available count for a resource by a specified amount. You can call this function when the thread is finished with the resource. Another possible use is to call CreateSemaphore, specifying an initial count of zero to protect the resource from access during an initialization process. When the application has finished its initialization, call ReleaseSemaphore to increase the resource's count to its maximum.

▶ Event

An event is an object that announces an event has happened to one or more threads.

Event objects can trigger execution of other threads. You can use events if one thread provides data to several other threads. An event object is created by the CreateEvent function. The creating thread specifies the initial state of the object and whether it is a manual-reset or auto-reset event. A manual-reset event is one whose state remains signaled until it is explicitly reset by a call to ResetEvent. An auto-reset event is automatically reset by the system when a single waiting thread is released.

Use either SetEvent or PulseEvent to set an event object's state to signaled. OpenEvent returns a handle to the event, which can be used in other function calls. ReleaseEvent releases ownership of the event.

The state of each of these objects is either signaled or not-signaled. A signaled state indicates a resource is available for a process or thread to use it. A not-signaled state indicates the resource is in use. The routines described in the following sections manage the creation, initialization, and termination of resource sharing mechanisms. Some of them change the state to signaled from not-signaled. The routines WaitForSingleObject and WaitForMultipleObjects also change the signal status of an object. For information on these functions, see Section 19.2.6 Synchronizing Threads.

For resources about coordinating and synchronizing Win32 threads, see Section 19.4 Other Sources of Information.

Memory Use and Thread Stacks

Because each thread has its own stack, you can avoid potential collisions over data items by using as little static data as possible. Design your program to use automatic stack variables for all data that can be private to a thread. All the variables declared in a multithread routine are by default static and shared among the threads. If you do not want one thread to overwrite a variable used by another, you can do one of the following:

▶ Declare the variable as **AUTOMATIC**.

▶ Create a vector of variable values, one for each thread, so that the variable values for different threads are in different storage locations. (You can use the single integer parameter passed by CREATETHREAD as an index to identify the thread.)

▶ Use Thread Local Storage (TLS) (see Section 19.2.5).

Variables declared as automatic are placed on the stack, which is part of the thread context saved with the thread. Automatic variables within procedures are discarded when the procedure completes execution.

I/O Operations

Although files and units are shared between threads, you may not need to coordinate the use of these shared resources by threads. Fortran treats each input/output statement as an atomic operation. If two separate threads try to write to the same unit and one thread's output operation has started, the operation will complete before the other thread's output operation can begin.

The operating system does not impose an ordering on threads' access to units or files. For example, the non-determinate nature of multithread applications can cause records in a sequential file to be written in a different order on each execution of the application as each thread writes to the file. Direct access files might be a better choice than sequential files in such a case. If you cannot use direct access files, use mutexes to impose an ordering constraint on input or output of sequential files.

Certain restrictions apply to blocking functions for input procedures in QuickWin programs. For details on these restrictions, see Chapter 7 Using QuickWin.

19.2.5 Thread Local Storage

Thread Local Storage (TLS) calls allow you to store per-thread data. TLS is the method by which each thread in a multithreaded process can allocate locations in which to store thread-specific data.

Dynamically bound (run-time) thread-specific data is supported by routines such as TlsAlloc (allocates an index to store data), TlsGetValue (retrieves values from an index), TlsSetValue (stores values into an index), and TlsFree (frees the dynamic storage). Threads allocate dynamic storage and use Tls-SetValue to associate the index with a pointer to that storage. When a thread needs to access the storage, it calls TlsGetValue, specifying the index.

When all threads have finished using the index, TlsFree frees the dynamic storage.

19.2.6 Synchronizing Threads

The routines WAITFORSINGLEOBJECT and WAITFORMULTIPLEOB-JECTS enable threads to wait for a variety of different occurrences, such as thread completion or signals from other threads. They enable threads and processes to wait efficiently, consuming no CPU resources, either indefinitely or until a specified timeout interval has elapsed.

WAITFORSINGLEOBJECT takes an object handle as the first parameter and does not return until the object referenced by the handle either reaches a signaled state or until a specified timeout value elapses. The syntax is:

WaitResult = WAITFORSINGLEOBJECT (*ObjectHandle*, [*Timeout*])

If you are using a timeout, specify the value in milliseconds as the second parameter. The value WAIT_INFINITE represents an infinite timeout, in which case the function waits until *ObjectHandle* completes.

WAITFORMULTIPLEOBJECTS is similar, except that its second parameter is an array of Windows object handles. Specify the number of handles to wait for in the first parameter. This can be less than the total number of threads created, and its maximum is 64. The function can either wait until all events have completed, or resume as soon as any one of the objects completes.

Deadlocks occur when a thread waits for objects that never become available. Use the timeout parameter when there is a chance that the thread you are waiting for may never terminate. See "Detecting Deadlocks in Multi-threaded Win32 Applications," by Ruediger Asche, in the *Microsoft Systems Journal*, vol. 8, for a discussion of how to find and avoid potential resource collisions.

Suspending and Resuming Threads

You can use SuspendThread to stop a thread from executing. SuspendThread is not particularly useful for synchronization because it does not control the point in the code at which the thread's execution is suspended. However, you could suspend a thread if you need to confirm a user's input that would terminate the work of the thread. If confirmed, the thread is terminated; otherwise, it resumes.

If a thread is created in a suspended state, it does not begin to run until Resume Thread is called with a handle to the suspended thread. This can be useful for initializing the thread's state before it begins to run. Suspending a thread at creation can be useful for one-time synchronization, because ResumeThread ensures that the suspended thread will resume running at the starting point of its code.

19.2.7 Handling Errors in Multithread Programs

Use the GetLastError function to obtain error information if any of the multithreading routines returns an error code. Remember that it returns the error code of the last error, not necessarily the error status of the last call.

Error codes are 32-bit values. Bit 29 is reserved for application-defined error codes. You can set this bit and use SetLastError if you are creating your own dynamic-link library, to emulate Win32 API behavior. Win32 functions only call SetLastError when they fail, not when they succeed.

The last error code value is kept in Thread Local Storage, so that multiple threads do not overwrite each other's values.

19.2.8 Working with Multiple Processes

The multithread libraries provide a number of routines for working with multiple processes. An application can use multiple processes for functions that require a private address space and private resources, to protect them from the activities of other threads. It is usually more efficient to implement multitasking by creating several threads in one process, rather than by creating multiple processes, for these reasons:

▶ The system can create and execute threads more quickly than it can create processes, since the code for threads has already been mapped into the address space of the process, while the code for a new process must be loaded.

▶ All threads of a process share the same address space and can access the process's global variables, which can simplify communications between threads.

▶ All threads of a process can use open handles to resources such as files and pipes.

If you want to create an independent process that runs concurrently with the current one, use CreateProcess. CreateProcess returns a 32-bit process identifier that is valid until the process terminates. ExitProcess stops the process and notifies all DLLs the process is terminating.

Different processes can share mutexes, events, and semaphores (but not critical sections). Processes can also optionally inherit handles from the process that created them (see online help for CreateProcess).

You can obtain information about the current process by calling GetCurrentProcess (returns a pseudohandle to its own process), and GetCurrentProcessId (returns the process identifier). The value returned by these functions can be used in calls to communicate with other processes. GetExitCodeProcess returns the exit code of a process, or an indication that it is still running.

The OpenProcess function opens a handle to a process specified by its process identifier. OpenProcess allows you to specify the handle's access rights and inheritability.

A process terminates whenever one of the following occurs:

▶ Any thread of the process calls ExitProcess

▶ The primary thread of the process returns

▶ The last thread of the process terminates

▶ TerminateProcess is called with a handle to the process

ExitProcess is the preferred way to terminate a process because it notifies all attached DLLs of the termination, and ensures that all threads of the process terminate. DLLs are not notified after a call to TerminateProcess.

19.2.9   Table of Multithread Routines

Table 19-1 lists routines available for multithread programs. For information about the calling syntax of these routines, see the *Platform SDK* Reference section in HTMLHelp Viewer.

Table 19–1   *Routines for Multithread Programs*

Routine	Description
CloseHandle	Closes an open object handle.
CreateEvent	Creates a named or unnamed event object.
CreateMutex	Creates a named or unnamed mutex object.
CreateProcess	Creates a new process and its primary thread.
CreateSemaphore	Creates a named or unnamed semaphore object.
CreateThread	Creates a thread to execute within the address space of the calling process.
DeleteCriticalSection	Releases all resources used by an unowned critical section object.

Table 19–1   *Routines for Multithread Programs (Continued)*

Routine	Description
DuplicateHandle	Duplicates an object handle.
EnterCriticalSection	Waits for ownership of the specified critical section object.
ExitProcess	Ends a process and all its threads.
ExitThread	Ends a thread.
GetCurrentProcess	Returns a pseudohandle for the current process.
GetCurrentProcessId	Returns the process identifier of the calling process.
GetCurrentThread	Returns a pseudohandle for the current thread.
GetCurrentThreadId	Returns the thread identifier of the calling thread.
GetExitCodeProcess	Retrieves the termination status of the specified process.
GetExitCodeThread	Retrieves the termination status of the specified thread.
GetLastError	Returns the calling thread's last-error code value.
GetPriorityClass	Returns the priority class for the specified process.
GetThreadPriority	Returns the priority value for the specified thread.
InitializeCriticalSection	Initializes a critical section object.
LeaveCriticalSection	Releases ownership of the specified critical section object.
OpenEvent	Returns a handle of an existing named event object.
OpenMutex	Returns a handle of an existing named mutex object.
OpenProcess	Returns a handle of an existing process object.
OpenSemaphore	Returns a handle of an existing named semaphore object.
PulseEvent	As a single operation, sets (to signaled) and then resets the state of the specified event object after releasing the appropriate number of waiting threads.
ReleaseMutex	Releases ownership of the specified mutex object.
ReleaseSemaphore	Increases the count of the specified semaphore object by a specified amount.
ResetEvent	Sets the state of the specified event object to nonsignaled.
ResumeThread	Decrements a thread's suspend count. When the suspend count is zero, execution of the thread resumes.
SetEvent	Sets the state of the specified event object to signaled.
SetLastError	Sets the last-error code for the calling thread.

Table 19–1   *Routines for Multithread Programs (Continued)*

Routine	Description
SetPriorityClass	Sets the priority class for the specified process.
SetThreadPriority	Sets the priority value for the specified thread.
SuspendThread	Suspends the specified thread.
TerminateProcess	Terminates the specified process and all of its threads.
TerminateThread	Terminates a thread.
TlsAlloc	Allocates a thread local storage (TLS) index.
TlsFree	Releases a thread local storage (TLS) index, making it available for reuse.
TlsGetValue	Retrieves the value in the calling thread's thread local storage (TLS) slot for a specified TLS index.
TlsSetValue	Stores a value in the calling thread's thread local storage (TLS) slot for a specified TLS index.
WaitForMultipleObjects	Returns either any one or all of the specified objects are in the signaled state or when the time-out interval elapses.
WaitForSingleObject	Returns when the specified object is in the signaled state or the time-out interval elapses.

If a function mentioned in this section is not listed in the preceding table, it is only available through the **USE DFWIN** statement.

19.3   Compiling and Linking Multithread Programs

The support library DFORMT.LIB is a re-entrant library for creating statically linked multithread programs. The DFORMD.LIB library, which calls code in the shared DFORMD.DLL, is also re-entrant. Programs built with DFORMT.LIB do not share Fortran run-time library code or data with any dynamic-link libraries they call. You must link with DFORMD.LIB if you plan to call a DLL.

To build a multithread application that uses the Fortran run-time libraries, you must tell the linker to use a special version of the libraries. You can specify the /threads compiler option from the command line, or in the Microsoft visual development environment in the Project Settings dialog box, as described in the following paragraph.

A sample multithread project THREADS is included in the . . . \DF98\SAMPLES\ADVANCED\WIN32\THREADS folder. To build this sample, open the project workspace file and choose Build All from the Build menu. The following list are the steps for compiling and linking your own multithread program using the visual development environment.

To compile and link your multithread program:

1. Create a new project. Choose the Project tab, then specify the Project type. (The sample THREADS.F90 is a QuickWin project.)

2. Add the file containing the source code to the project.

3. From the Project menu, select Settings.

   The Project Settings dialog box appears.

4. Choose the Fortran tab, Fortran Libraries category, and set the Use Multi-Threaded Library check box and set the Use Runtime Libraries to Static (DFORMT.LIB) or DLL (DFORMD.LIB).

5. Create the executable file by choosing Build All from the Build menu.

To compile and link the sample multithread program from the command line:

1. Make sure the library files directory is specified in your LIB environment variable.

2. Compile and link the program with the DF command-line option /threads.

   For example:

```
DF /threads MYTHREAD.F90
```

The /threads compiler option (automatically set when you specify a multithread application in the visual development environment) tells the linker to use DFORMT.LIB as a default library.

To compile and link the THREADS.F90 sample, the command is:

```
DF /libs=qwin THREADS.F90
```

The /threads compiler option causes the linker to search the multithread library; the /libs=qwin requests a Quickwin multiple window application.

Select the compiler options /libs=dll and /threads if you are using both multithread code and DLLs. You can use the /libs=dll and /threads options only with console projects, not QuickWin applications.

19.4 Other Sources of Information

For a thorough discussion of threads. processes, and multithreading, see Helen Custer's book *Inside Windows NT,* available from Microsoft Press. Articles on how to accomplish multithreading have also been published in the Microsoft Developer Network (MSDN) CD-ROM and the *Microsoft Systems Journal.*

▶ The Microsoft Developer Network CD-ROM contains several articles on multithreading:

- "Multiple Threads in the User Interface," by Nancy Winnick Cluts, discusses the ramifications of adding multiple threads to the user interface. This article not only offers alternatives to multiple threads, but also covers window management and message loops for multithreading.

- "Multithreading for Rookies," by Ruediger R. Asche, focuses on practical applications of multithreading.

- "Detecting Deadlocks in Multithreaded Win32 Applications," by Ruediger R. Asche, presents deadlock detection techniques. A deadlock is a condition in which the application hangs because two or more threads are waiting for each other to release a shared resource before resuming execution.

- "Moving UNIX Applications to Windows NT," provides an overview of Windows multithreading calls, contrasting them with UNIX fork( ) calls.

▶ The Microsoft Systems Journal is also a source of information on multithreading:

- "Coordinate Win32 threads using manual-reset and auto-reset events," by Jeffrey Richter. October 1993, v8 n10.

- "Synchronizing Win32 threads using critical sections, semaphores, and mutexes," by Jeffrey Richter. August 1993, v8 n8.

20

Data Representation

Digital Fortran expects numeric data to be in native little endian order, in which the least-significant, right-most zero bit (bit 0) or byte has a lower address than the most-significant, left-most bit (or byte). For information on using nonnative big endian and Digital VAX floating-point formats, see Chapter 23 Converting Unformatted Numeric Data.

The symbol :A in any figure specifies the address of the byte containing bit 0, which is the starting address of the represented data element.

Table 20-1 lists the intrinsic data types used by Visual Fortran, the storage required, and valid ranges.

Table 20–1 *Digital Fortran Data Types and Storage*

Data Type	Storage	Description
BYTE (INTEGER (KIND=1))	1 byte (8 bits)	A BYTE declaration is a signed integer data type equivalent to INTEGER(KIND=1).
INTEGER	See INTEGER (KIND=2), INTEGER (KIND=4), and INTEGER (KIND=8).	Signed integer, either INTEGER(KIND=2) or INTEGER (KIND=4) on x86 systems, or INTEGER(KIND=2), INTEGER(KIND=4), or INTEGER(KIND=8) on Alpha systems. The size is controlled by the /integer_size:nn compiler option. The default is /integer_size:32 (INTEGER(KIND=4)).
INTEGER (KIND=1)	1 byte (8 bits)	Signed integer value from -128 to 127.
INTEGER (KIND=2)	2 bytes (16 bits)	Signed integer value from -32,768 to 32,767.
INTEGER (KIND=4)	4 bytes (32 bits)	Signed integer value from -2,147,483,648 to 2,147,483,647.

Table 20–1 *Digital Fortran Data Types and Storage (Continued)*

Data Type	Storage	Description
INTEGER (KIND=8)	8 bytes (64 bits)	Signed integer value from -9,223,372,036,854,775,808 to 9,223,372,036,854,775,807.
REAL(KIND=4) (REAL)	4 bytes (32 bits)	Single-precision real floating-point values in IEEE S_floating format ranging from 1.17549435E-38 to 3.40282347E-38. Values between 1.17549429E-38 and 1.40129846E-45 are denormalized (subnormal).
REAL(KIND=8) DOUBLE PRECISION	8 bytes (64 bits)	Double-precision real floating-point values in IEEE T_floating format ranging from 2.2250738585072013D-308 to 1.7976931348623158D-308. Values between 2.2250738585072008D-308 and 4.94065645841246544D-324 are denormalized (subnormal).
COMPLEX (KIND=4) (COMPLEX)	8 bytes (64 bits)	Single-precision complex floating-point values in a pair of IEEE S_floating format parts: real and imaginary. The real and imaginary parts range from 1.17549435E-38 to 3.40282347E-38. Values between 1.17549429E-38 and 1.40129846E-45 are denormalized (subnormal).
COMPLEX (KIND=8) DOUBLE COMPLEX	16 bytes (128 bits)	Double-precision complex floating-point values in a pair of IEEE T_floating format parts: real and imaginary. The real and imaginary parts each range from 2.2250738585072013D-308 to 1.7976931348623158D-308. Values between 2.2250738585072008D-308 and 4.94065645841246544D-324 are denormalized (subnormal).
LOGICAL	See LOGICAL (KIND=2), LOGICAL (KIND=4), and LOGICAL (KIND=8).	Logical value, either LOGICAL(KIND=2) or LOGICAL (KIND=4) on *x*86 systems, or LOGICAL(KIND=2), LOGICAL(KIND=4), or LOGICAL(KIND=8) on Alpha systems. The size is controlled by the /integer_size:*nn* compiler option. The default is /integer_size:32 (LOGICAL(KIND=4)).
LOGICAL (KIND=1)	1 byte (8 bits)	Logical values .TRUE. or .FALSE.
LOGICAL (KIND=2)	2 bytes (16 bits)	Logical values .TRUE. or .FALSE.
LOGICAL (KIND=4)	4 bytes (32 bits)	Logical values .TRUE. or .FALSE.
LOGICAL (KIND=8)	8 bytes (64 bits)	Logical values .TRUE. or .FALSE.
CHARACTER	1 byte (8 bits) per character	Character data represented by character code convention. Character declarations can be in the form CHARACTER*n, where n is the number of bytes or n is (*) to indicate passed-length format.
HOLLERITH	1 byte (8 bits) per Hollerith character	Hollerith constants.

In addition, you can define binary (bit) constants as explained in "Binary Constants" in the *Language Reference* in Visual Fortran online Help.

The following sections discuss the intrinsic data types in more detail:

▶ Section 20.1 Integer Data Representations

▶ Section 20.2 Logical Data Representations

▶ Section 20.3 Native IEEE Floating-Point Representations

▶ Section 20.4 Character Representation

▶ Section 20.5 Hollerith Representation

20.1   Integer Data Representations

On *x*86 systems, integer data lengths can be 1-, 2-, or 4-bytes in length.

On Alpha systems, integer data lengths can be 1-, 2- 4-, or 8-bytes in length.

The default data size used for an **INTEGER** data declaration is **INTEGER**(KIND=4), unless the /integer_size:16 or (on Alpha systems) the /integer_size:64 option was specified.

Integer data is signed with the sign bit being 0 (zero) for positive numbers and 1 for negative numbers.

On Alpha systems, to improve performance use **INTEGER**(KIND=4) (or **INTEGER**(KIND=8)) rather than **INTEGER**(KIND=2) or **INTEGER**(KIND=1).

The following sections discuss integer data:

▶ Section 20.1.1 **INTEGER**(KIND=1) Representation

▶ Section 20.1.2 **INTEGER**(KIND=2) Representation

▶ Section 20.1.3 **INTEGER**(KIND=4) Representation

▶ Section 20.1.4 **INTEGER**(KIND=8) Representation (Alpha Only)

20.1.1   **INTEGER(KIND=1) Representation**

INTEGER(KIND=1) values range from -128 to 127 and are stored in 1 byte, as shown in Figure 20- 1.

Integers are stored in a two's complement representation. For example:

```
+22  = 16(hex)
-7   = F9(hex)
```

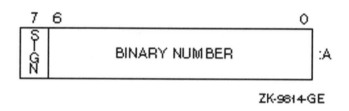

ZK-9814-GE

Figure 20–1 *INTEGER(KIND=1) Data Representation*

20.1.2 INTEGER(KIND=2) Representation

INTEGER(KIND=2) values range from -32,768 to 32,767 and are stored in 2 contiguous bytes, as shown in Figure 20-2.

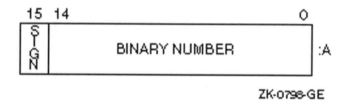

ZK-0798-GE

Figure 20–2 *INTEGER(KIND=2) Data Representation*

Integers are stored in a two's complement representation. For example:

```
+22  =  0016(hex)
-7   =  FFF9(hex)
```

20.1.3 INTEGER(KIND=4) Representation

INTEGER(KIND=4) values range from -2,147,483,648 to 2,147,483,647 and are stored in 4 contiguous bytes, as shown in Figure 20-3.

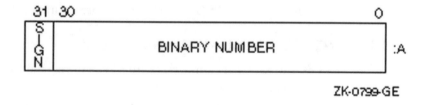

ZK-0799-GE

Figure 20–3 *INTEGER(KIND=4) Data Representation*

Integers are stored in a two's complement representation.

20.1.4 INTEGER(KIND=8) Representation (Alpha Only)

INTEGER(KIND=8) values range from -9,223,372,036,854,775,808 to 9,223,372,036,854,775,807 and are stored in 8 contiguous bytes, as shown in Figure 20-4. **INTEGER**(KIND=8) is only available on Alpha systems.

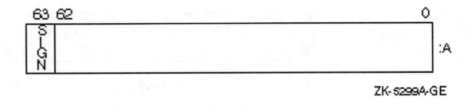

ZK-S2994-GE

Figure 20–4   *INTEGER(KIND=8) Data Representation*

Integers are stored in a two's complement representation.

20.2 Logical Data Representations

On *x*86 systems, logical data lengths can be 1-, 2-, or 4-bytes in length.

On Alpha systems, logical data lengths can be 1-, 2-, 4-, or 8-bytes in length.

The default data size used for a **LOGICAL** data declaration is **LOGICAL**(KIND=4), unless the /integer_size:16 or /integer_size:64 (Alpha systems) option was specified.

To improve performance on Alpha systems, use **LOGICAL**(KIND=4) (or **LOGICAL**(KIND=8)) rather than **LOGICAL**(KIND=2) or **LOGICAL**(KIND=1).

LOGICAL(KIND=1) values are stored in 1 byte. In addition to having logical values .TRUE. and .FALSE., **LOGICAL**(KIND=1) data can also have values in the range -128 to 127. Logical variables can also be interpreted as integer data.

In addition to **LOGICAL**(KIND=1), logical values can also be stored in 2 (**LOGICAL**(KIND=2)), 4 (**LOGICAL**(KIND=4)), or 8 (**LOGICAL** (KIND=8)) contiguous bytes, starting on an arbitrary byte boundary. **LOGICAL**(KIND=8) data is available on Alpha systems only.

If the /fpscomp:nological option is set (the default), the low-order bit determines whether the logical value is true or false. Specify /fpscomp:logical for Microsoft Fortran PowerStation logical values, where 0 (zero) is false and non-zero values are true.

The data representation (when /fpscomp:nological option is set) for the **LOGICAL** data types appears in Figure 20-5.

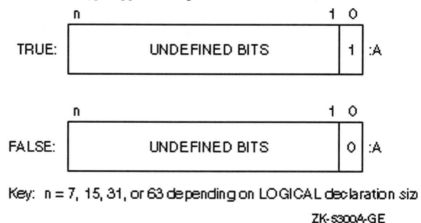

Figure 20–5 *LOGICAL(KIND=1), LOGICAL(KIND=2), LOGICAL(KIND=4), and LOGICAL (KIND=8) Data Representation*

20.3   Native IEEE Floating-Point Representations

The **REAL**(KIND=4) (S_floating) and **REAL**(KIND=8) (T_floating) formats are stored in standard little endian IEEE binary floating-point notation. (See IEEE Standard 754 for additional information about IEEE binary floating point notation.) **COMPLEX**(KIND=4) and **COMPLEX**(KIND=8) formats use a pair of **REAL**(KIND=4) or **REAL**(KIND=8) values to denote the real and imaginary parts of the data.

For IEEE S_floating and T_floating formats, fractions are represented in sign-magnitude notation,with the binary radix point to the right of the most-significant bit. Fractions are assumed to be normalized, and therefore the most-significant bit is not stored (this is called "hidden bit normalization"). This bit is assumed to be 1 unless the exponent is 0. If the exponent equals 0, then the value represented is denormalized (subnormal) or plus or minus zero.

The following sections discuss floating-point data:

▶ Section 20.3.1 **REAL**(KIND=4) (**REAL**) Representation

▶ Section 20.3.2 **REAL**(KIND=8) (**DOUBLE PRECISION**) Representation

▶ Section 20.3.3 **COMPLEX**(KIND=4) (**COMPLEX**) Representation

▶ Section 20.3.4 **COMPLEX**(KIND=8) (**DOUBLE COMPLEX**) Representation

For more information, see:

▶ Using the Bitviewer tool, see Section 22.1.1.3 Viewing Floating-Point Representations with BitViewer.

▶ Reading or writing floating-point data other than native IEEE little endian data, see Chapter 23 Converting Unformatted Numeric Data.

▶ Using floating-point numbers, see Chapter 22 The Floating-Point Environment.

20.3.1 REAL(KIND=4) (REAL) Representation

REAL(KIND=4) data occupies 4 contiguous bytes stored in IEEE S_floating format. Bits are labeled from the right, 0 through 31, as shown in Figure 20-6.

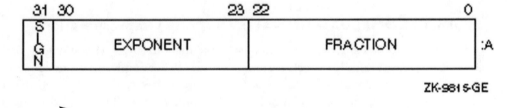

ZK-9815-GE

Figure 20–6 *REAL(KIND=4) Floating-Point Data Representation*

The form of **REAL**(KIND=4) data is sign magnitude, with bit 31 the sign bit (0 for positive numbers, 1 for negative numbers), bits 30:23 a binary exponent in excess 127 notation, and bits 22:0 a normalized 24-bit fraction including the redundant most-significant fraction bit not represented.

The value of data is in the approximate range: 1.17549435E-38 (normalized) to 3.40282347E-38. The IEEE denormalized (subnormal) limit is 1.40129846E-45. The precision is approximately one part in 2**23; typically 7 decimal digits.

20.3.2 REAL(KIND=8) (DOUBLE PRECISION) Representation

REAL(KIND=8) data occupies 8 contiguous bytes stored in IEEE T_floating format. Bits are labeled from the right, 0 through 63, as shown in Figure 20-7.

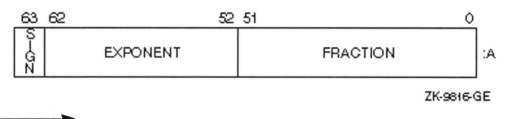

ZK-9816-GE

Figure 20–7   *REAL(KIND=8) Floating-Point Data Representation*

The form of **REAL**(KIND=8) data is sign magnitude, with bit 63 the sign bit (0 for positive numbers, 1 for negative numbers), bits 62:52 a binary exponent in excess 1023 notation, and bits 51:0 a normalized 53-bit fraction including the redundant most-significant fraction bit not represented.

The value of data is in the approximate range: 2.2250738585072013D-308 (normalized) to 1.7976931348623158D-308. The IEEE denormalized (subnormal) limit is 4.9406564584124654D-324. The precision is approximately one part in 2**52; typically 15 decimal digits.

20.3.3   **COMPLEX(KIND=4) (COMPLEX) Representation**

COMPLEX(KIND=4) data is 8 contiguous bytes containing a pair of **REAL**(KIND=4) values stored in IEEE S_floating format. The low-order 4 bytes contain **REAL**(KIND=4) data that represents the real part of the complex number. The high-order 4 bytes contain **REAL**(KIND=4) data that represents the imaginary part of the complex number, as shown in Figure 20-8.

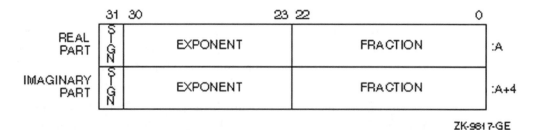

ZK-9817-GE

Figure 20–8   *COMPLEX(KIND=4) Floating-Point Data Representation*

The limits and underflow characteristics for **REAL**(KIND=4) apply to the two separate real and imaginary parts of a **COMPLEX**(KIND=4) number.

Like **REAL**(KIND=4) numbers, the sign bit representation is 0 (zero) for positive numbers and 1 for negative numbers.

20.3.4 COMPLEX(KIND=8) (DOUBLE COMPLEX) Representation

COMPLEX(KIND=8) (same as **COMPLEX*16**) data is 16 contiguous bytes containing a pair of **REAL**(KIND=8) values stored in IEEE T_floating format. The low-order 8 bytes contain **REAL** (KIND=8) data that represents the real part of the complex data. The high-order 8 bytes contain **REAL**(KIND=8) data that represents the imaginary part of the complex data, as shown in Figure 20- 9.

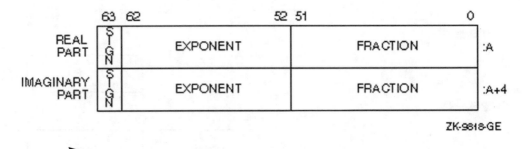

Figure 20–9   *COMPLEX(KIND=8) Floating-Point Data Representation*

The limits and underflow characteristics for **REAL**(KIND=8) apply to the two separate real and imaginary parts of a **COMPLEX**(KIND=8) number. Like **REAL**(KIND=8) numbers, the sign bit representation is 0 (zero) for positive numbers and 1 for negative numbers.

20.4   Character Representation

A character string is a contiguous sequence of bytes in memory, as shown in Figure 20-10.

A character string is specified by two attributes: the address A of the first byte of the string, and the length L of the string in bytes. The length L of a string is in the range 1 through 65,535.

20.5   Hollerith Representation

Hollerith constants are stored internally, one character per byte, as shown in Figure 20-11. Hollerith constants are Digital Fortran language extensions.

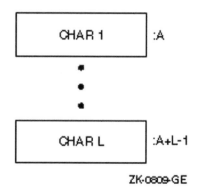

ZK-0809-GE

Figure 20–10   *CHARACTER Data Representation*

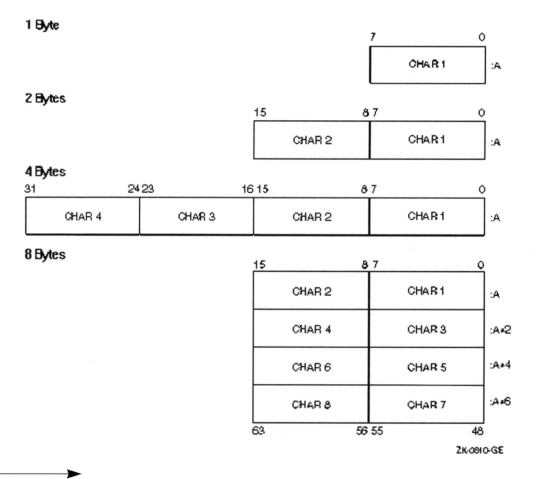

ZK-0810-GE

Figure 20–11   *Hollerith Data Representation*

21

Handling Run-Time Errors

This chapter contains information on the following topics:

▶ Section 21.1 Default Run-Time Error Processing

Describes the message format and values returned at program termination.

▶ Section 21.2 Methods of Handling Errors within your program

Describes using the END, EOR, and ERR I/O statement branch specifiers and the IOSTAT specifier.

▶ Section 21.3 Locating Run-Time Errors

Describes suggested compiler options and information about debugging exceptions.

▶ Section 21.4 Using Traceback Information

Describes techniques to help you locate the cause of severe run-time errors.

▶ Section 21.5 Run-Time Environment Variables

Describes environment variables that allow program continuation under certain conditions, disable the display of certain dialog boxes under certain conditions, and allow "just-in-time" debugging.

During execution, your program may encounter errors or exception conditions. These conditions can result from any of the following:

▶ Errors that occur during I/O operations

▶ Invalid input data

▶ Argument errors in calls to the mathematical library

▶ Arithmetic errors

▶ Other system-detected errors

The Digital Visual Fortran Run-Time Library (RTL) generates appropriate messages and takes action to recover from errors whenever possible.

For a description of each Visual Fortran run-time error message, see "Visual Fortran Run-Time Errors" in *Error Messages* in Visual Fortran online Help.

21.1 Default Run-Time Error Processing

The Visual Fortran run-time system processes a number of errors that can occur during program execution. A default action is defined for each error recognized by the Visual Fortran run-time system. The default actions described throughout this chapter occur unless overridden by explicit error-processing methods.

The way in which the Visual Fortran run-time system actually processes errors depends upon the following factors:

▶ The severity of the error. For instance, the program usually continues executing when an error message with a severity level of warning or info (informational) is detected.

▶ For certain errors associated with I/O statements, whether or not an I/O error-handling specifier was specified.

▶ For certain errors, whether or not the default action of an associated signal was changed.

▶ For certain errors related to arithmetic operations (including floating-point exceptions), compilation options can determine whether the error is reported and the severity of the reported error.

How arithmetic exception conditions are reported and handled depends on the cause of the exception and how the program was compiled. Unless the program was compiled to handle exceptions, the exception might not be reported until *after* the instruction that caused the exception condition.

For more information, see:

▶ On where Visual Fortran run-time message are displayed and their format, see Section 21.1.1 Run-Time Message Display and Format.

▶ On the Visual Fortran return values at program termination, see Section 21.1.2 Values Returned at Program Termination.

> ▶ On locating errors and the compiler options related to handling errors and exceptions, see Section 21.3 Locating Run-Time Errors and Section 21.4 Using Traceback Information.

> ▶ On DF command options and their categories in the visual development environment (Project Settings, Fortran tab), see Section 4.1.1 Categories of Compiler Options.

> ▶ On Digital Fortran intrinsic data types and their ranges, see Chapter 20 Data Representation.

> ▶ On the floating-point environment, see Chapter 22 The Floating-Point Environment.

21.1.1 Run-Time Message Display and Format

When errors occur during program execution (run time) of a program, the Visual Fortran RTL issues diagnostic messages. Where Fortran run-time messages are displayed depends upon the Fortran project type, as shown in Table 21-1.

Table 21–1 *Where Fortran Run-Time Messages Are Displayed*

Project Type	*Where Fortran Run-Time Messages Appear*
Fortran Console applications	Run-time error messages are displayed on the standard error device (unless redirected).
Fortran QuickWin and Fortran Standard Graphics applications	Run-time error messages are displayed in a separate QuickWin message box.
Fortran Windows applications	Run-time error messages are displayed in a separate message box.

Fortran run-time messages have the following format:

forrtl: *severity* (*number*): *message-text*

forrtl

Identifies the source as the Visual Fortran RTL.

severity

The severity levels are: severe, error, warning, or info (see Table 21-2).

number

This is the message number, also the IOSTAT value for I/O statements.

message-text

Explains the event that caused the message.

Table 21-2 explains the severity levels of run-time messages, in the order of greatest to least severity.

Table 21–2   *Severity Levels of Run-Time Messages*

Severity	Description
severe	Must be corrected. The program's execution is terminated when the error is encountered unless the program's I/O statements use the END, EOR, or ERR branch specifiers to transfer control, perhaps to a routine that uses the IOSTAT specifier (see Section 21.2.1 Using the END, EOR, and ERR Branch Specifiers and Section 21.2.2 Using the IOSTAT Specifier and Fortran Exit Codes). For severe errors, a hexadecimal dump of the call stack (program counter trace) is displayed after the error message. If the /traceback option was specified, the displayed call stack program counter trace includes the source file name, routine name, and source line number of your Fortran source code.
error	Should be corrected. The program might continue execution, but the output from this execution may be incorrect.
warning	Should be investigated. The program continues execution, but output from this execution may be incorrect.
info	For informational purposes only; the program continues.

For a description of each Visual Fortran run-time error message, see "Visual Fortran Run-Time Errors" in *Error Messages* in Visual Fortran online Help.

21.1.2   Values Returned at Program Termination

A Visual Fortran program can terminate in one of several ways:

▶ The program runs to normal completion. A value of zero is returned to the shell.

▶ The program stops with a **STOP** statement. A value of zero is returned to the shell.

▶ The program stops because of a signal that is caught but does not allow the program to continue. A value of 1 is returned to the shell.

▶ The program stops because of a severe run-time error. The error number for that run-time error is returned to the shell. Error numbers are listed in "Visual Fortran Run-Time Errors" in *Error Messages* in Visual Fortran online Help.

▶ The program stops with a **CALL EXIT** statement. The value passed to **EXIT** is returned to the shell.

21.2   Methods of Handling Errors

Whenever possible, the Visual Fortran RTL does certain error handling, such as generating appropriate messages and taking necessary action to recover from errors. You can explicitly supplement or override default actions by using the following methods:

▶ To transfer control to error-handling code within the program, use the END, EOR, and ERR branch specifiers in I/O statements, see Section 21.2.1 Using the END, EOR, and ERR Branch Specifiers.

▶ To identify Fortran-specific I/O errors based on the value of Visual Fortran RTL error codes, use the I/O status specifier (IOSTAT) in I/O statements (or call the **ERRSNS** subroutine), see Section 21.2.2 Using the IOSTAT Specifier and Fortran Exit Codes.

These error-processing methods are complementary; you can use any or all of them within the same program to obtain Visual Fortran run-time error codes.

On Alpha systems, if your program generates an exception, unless you are using the /fpe:0 option, consider using the /synchronous_exceptions option and recompile and relink your application.

21.2.1   Using the END, EOR, and ERR Branch Specifiers

When a severe error occurs during Visual Fortran program execution, the default action is to display an error message and terminate the program. To override this default action, there are three branch specifiers you can use in I/O statements to transfer control to a specified point in the program:

▶ The END branch specifier handles an end-of-file condition.

▶ The EOR branch specifier handles an end-of-record condition for non-advancing reads.

▶ The ERR branch specifier handles all error conditions.

If you use the END, EOR, or ERR branch specifiers, no error message is displayed and execution continues at the designated statement, usually an error-handling routine.

You might encounter an unexpected error that the error-handling routine cannot handle. In this case, do one of the following:

▶ Modify the error-handling routine to display the error message number

▶ Remove the END, EOR, or ERR branch specifiers from the I/O statement that causes the error

After you modify the source code, compile, link, and run the program to display the error message. For example:

```
READ (8,50,ERR=400)
```

If any severe error occurs during execution of this statement, the Visual Fortran RTL transfers control to the statement at label 400. Similarly, you can use the END specifier to handle an end-of-file condition that might otherwise be treated as an error. For example:

```
READ (12,70,END=550)
```

When using nonadvancing I/O, use the EOR specifier to handle the end-of-record condition. For example:

```
150 FORMAT (F10.2, F10.2, I6)
    READ (UNIT=20, FMT=150, SIZE=X, ADVANCE='NO', EOR=700) &
& A, F, I
```

You can also use ERR as a specifier in an **OPEN**, **CLOSE**, or **INQUIRE** statement. For example:

```
OPEN (UNIT=10, FILE='FILNAM', STATUS='OLD', ERR=999)
```

If an error is detected during execution of this **OPEN** statement, control transfers to the statement at label 999.

21.2.2   Using the IOSTAT Specifier and Fortran Exit Codes

You can use the IOSTAT specifier to continue program execution after an I/O error and to return information about I/O operations. As described in "Visual Fortran Run-Time Errors" in the *Language Reference* in Visual Fortran online Help, certain errors are not returned in IOSTAT.

Although the IOSTAT specifier transfers control, it can only return information returned by the Visual Fortran RTL. For additional error handling capabilities, see the **GERROR** and **PERROR** routines in the "A-Z Summary" in the *Language Reference* in Visual Fortran online Help.

The IOSTAT specifier can supplement or replace the END, EOR, and ERR branch transfers.

Execution of an I/O statement containing the IOSTAT specifier suppresses the display of an error message and defines the specified integer variable, array element, or scalar field reference as one of the following, which is returned as an exit code if the program terminates:

▶ A value of -2 if an end-of-record condition occurs with nonadvancing reads.

▶ A value of -1 if an end-of-file condition occurs.

▶ A value of 0 for normal completion (not an error condition, end-of-file, or end-of-record condition).

▶ A positive integer value if an error condition occurs. (This value is one of the Fortran-specific IOSTAT numbers listed in "Visual Fortran Run-Time Errors" in the *Language Reference* in Visual Fortran online Help.)

Following the execution of the I/O statement and assignment of an IOSTAT value, control transfers to the END, EOR, or ERR statement label, if any. If there is no control transfer, normal execution continues. For more information on transfer of control, see "Branch Statements" in the *Language Reference* in Visual Fortran online Help.

You can include the iosdef.for file in your program to obtain symbolic definitions for the values of IOSTAT.

The following example uses the IOSTAT specifier and the iosdef.for file to handle an **OPEN** statement error (in the FILE specifier):

```
      CHARACTER(LEN=40) :: FILNM
      INCLUDE 'iosdef.for'

      DO I=1,4
        FILNM = ''
        WRITE (6,*) 'Type file name '
        READ (5,*) FILNM
        OPEN (UNIT=1, FILE=FILNM, STATUS='OLD', IOSTAT=IERR, ERR=100)
        WRITE (6,*) 'Opening file: ', FILNM
!     (process the input file)
        CLOSE (UNIT=1)
        STOP

100     IF (IERR .EQ. FOR$IOS_FILNOTFOU) THEN
            WRITE (6,*) 'File: ', FILNM, ' does not exist '
        ELSE IF (IERR .EQ. FOR$IOS_FILNAMSPE) THEN
            WRITE (6,*) 'File: ', FILNM, ' was bad, enter new file name'
        ELSE
           PRINT *, 'Unrecoverable error, code =', IERR
           STOP
        END IF
      END DO
      WRITE (6,*) 'File not found. Locate correct file with Explorer and run
                again'
      END PROGRAM
```

21.3 Locating Run-Time Errors

This section provides some guidelines for locating the cause of exceptions and run-time errors. Visual Fortran run-time error messages do not usually indicate the exact source location causing the error.

To locate the cause of errors use the various compiler options to isolate programming errors at compile-time and run-time or use the debugger to locate the cause of exceptions:

▶ The /[no]warn options control compile-time diagnostic messages, which in some circumstances can help determine the cause of a run-time error. In the Microsoft visual development environment, specify the Warning Level in the General Compiler Option Category or specify individual Warning Options in the Compiler Diagnostics Compiler Option Category.

▶ The /check:*keyword* options generate extra code to catch certain conditions at run-time (see /check or in the visual development environment, specify the Runtime Error Checking items in the Run time Compiler Option Category). For example:

  • The /check:bounds option generates extra code to catch access to data beyond the array or string boundaries.

  • The /check:overflow option generates extra code to catch integer overflow conditions.

  • The /check:noformat, /check:nooutput_conversion, and /check:nopower options reduce the severity level of the associated run-time error to allow program continuation (see Section 4.1.11 /[no]check).

  • The /check:underflow option controls the reporting of floating-point underflow exceptions at run-time.

▶ The /traceback option allows program counter to source file line correlation, which simplifies the task of locating the cause of severe run-time errors. Without /traceback, a link map file and source listing are usually needed to locate the cause of the error. Certain traceback-related information accompanies severe run-time errors, as described in Section 21.4 Using Traceback Information.

▶ The /fpe option controls the handling of floating-point arithmetic exceptions (IEEE arithmetic) at run-time. In the visual development environment, specify the Floating-Point Exception Handling in the Floating Point Compiler Option Category.

For example, if you specified /fpe:3, exceptions related to exceptional IEEE values are not reported and your application may generate exceptional IEEE values, which later in your application may generate an exception or unexpected values. By recompiling the application at /fpe:0, any exceptional IEEE values generated will cause the program to terminate and report an error message earlier.

The **FOR_GET_FPE** and **FOR_SET_FPE** routines are also available to examine and set the run-time handling of certain arithmetic exceptions.

▶ On Alpha systems, the /synchronous_exceptions option (and certain /fpe:n options) influence the reporting of floating-point arithmetic exceptions at run-time. In the visual development environment, specify Enable Synchronous Floating-Point Exceptions in the Floating Point Compiler Option Category.

▶ You can use the debugger to help you locate exceptions, as described in Section 5.5 Locating Run-Time Errors in the Debugger.

21.4   Using Traceback Information

When a Fortran program terminates due to a severe error condition, the Fortran run-time system displays additional diagnostic information after the run-time message.

The Fortran run-time system attempts to walk back up the call chain and produce a report of the calling sequence leading to the error as part of the default diagnostic message report. The minimum information displayed includes:

▶ The standard Fortran run-time error message text that explains the error condition.

▶ A tabular report that contains one line per call stack frame. This information includes at least the image name and a hexadecimal PC in that image.

The information displayed under the Routine, Line, and Source columns depends upon whether your program was compiled with the /traceback option. In the visual development environment, the default is /traceback in the debug configuration, but must be requested for the release configuration (Run Time category of Project settings).

For example, if /traceback were specified, the displayed information might resemble the following:

```
forrtl: severe (24): end-of-file during read, unit 10, file
E:\USERS\xxx.dat
Image          PC          Routine     Line        Source
DFORRT.dll     1000A3B2    Unknown     Unknown     Unknown
DFORRT.dll     1000A184    Unknown     Unknown     Unknown
DFORRT.dll     10009324    Unknown     Unknown     Unknown
DFORRT.dll     10009596    Unknown     Unknown     Unknown
DFORRT.dll     10024193    Unknown     Unknown     Unknown
teof.exe       004011A9    AGAIN            21     teof.for
teof.exe       004010DD    GO               15     teof.for
teof.exe       004010A7    WE               11     teof.for
teof.exe       00401071    HERE              7     teof.for
teof.exe       00401035    TEOF              3     teof.for
teof.exe       004013D9    Unknown     Unknown     Unknown
teof.exe       004012DF    Unknown     Unknown     Unknown
KERNEL32.dll   77F1B304    Unknown     Unknown     Unknown
```

If the same program was not compiled with the /traceback option (/notraceback):

▶ The Routine name, Line number, and Source file columns would be reported as "Unknown."

▶ A link map file and source listing are usually needed to locate the cause of the error.

The /traceback option provides program counter to source file line correlation information to appear in the displayed error message information, which simplifies the task of locating the cause of severe run-time errors. For Fortran objects generated with /traceback, the compiler generates additional information used by the Fortran run-time system to automatically correlate PC (program counter) values to the routine name in which they occur, Fortran source file, and line number in the source file. This information is displayed in the run-time error diagnostic report.

Automatic PC correlation is only supported for Fortran code. For non-Fortran code, only the hexadecimal PC locations are reported.

The following sections describe traceback-related tools, lists traceback-related environment variables, discuss tradeoffs and restrictions, and provide examples:

▶ Section 21.4.1 Tools to Help You Understand Traceback Output

▶ Section 21.4.2 Relevant Fortran Run-Time Environment Variables

▶ Section 21.4.3 Tradeoffs and Restrictions

▶ Section 21.4.4 Example Programs and Traceback Information

21.4.1 Tools to Help You Understand Traceback Output

When an application fails and you need to diagnose the error, there are a few tools and aids that are helpful. Compiler-generated machine code listings and linker-generated map files can help you understand the affects of compiler optimizations and to see how your application is laid out in memory. They may help you interpret the information provided in a stack trace at the time of the error:

To generate a complete listing (.lst) file:

▶ When using the Microsoft visual development environment:

1.   Choose Settings from the Project menu

2.   Click the Fortran tab

3.   Select the Listing Files category

4.   Click (check) "Source Listing"

5.   Click "Machine Code"

6.   Click "Include Files"

7.   Make any other changes needed to the Project Settings, then click OK.

▶ When compiling from the command line, specify /show:all and /list:

```
DF file.f90 /list /show:all
```

To generate a link map (.map) file:

▶ When using the visual development environment:

1.   Choose Settings from the Project menu

2.   Click the Link tab

3.   Select the General or Debug category

4.   Select Generate mapfile

5.   Make any other changes needed to the Project Settings, then click OK.

▶ When compiling from the command line, specify /map:

```
DF file.f90 /map
```

To see what sections are defined in an executable image (.exe) file:

▶ Specify the /traceback compile option. This requests that the compiler generate PC correlation information to be used at run-time in the event of an error.

▶ This information is gathered up by the linker in the executable image in a section named ".trace". To see what sections are in an image, use the command:

```
link -dump -summary your_app_name.exe
```

To see more detailed information, use the command:

```
link -dump -headers your_app_name.exe
```

21.4.2   Relevant Fortran Run-Time Environment Variables

The Fortran Run-Time library checks certain environment variables that you can use to customize run-time diagnostic error reporting:

▶ FOR_DIAGNOSTIC_LOG_FILE

If set to the name of a file, writes diagnostic output to the specified file. The Fortran run-time system attempts to open that file (append output) and write the error information (ASCII text) to the file. The setting of FOR_DIAGNOSTIC_LOG_FILE is independent of FOR_DISABLE_DIAGNOSTIC_DISPLAY, so you can disable the screen display of information but still capture the error information in a file. The text string you assign for the file name is used literally so you must specify the full name. If the file open fails, no error is reported and the run-time system continues diagnostic processing.

▶ FOR_DISABLE_DIAGNOSTIC_DISPLAY

If set to true, disables the display of all error information. This might be helpful if you just want to test the error status of your program and do not want the Fortran run-time system to display any information about an abnormal program termination.

▶ FOR_DISABLE_STACK_TRACE

If set to true, disables the display of call stack information that follows the displayed severe error message text. The Fortran run-time error message is displayed whether or not FOR_DISABLE_STACK_TRACE is set to true.

▶ FOR_ENABLE_VERBOSE_STACK_TRACE

If set to true, more detailed call stack information is displayed in the event of an error.

The default brief output is usually sufficient to determine where an error occurred. Brief output includes up to twenty stack frames, reported one line per stack frame. For each frame, the image name containing the PC, the PC, routine name, line number, and source file are given.

The verbose output, if selected, will provide in addition to the information in brief output, the exception context record if the error was a machine exception (machine register dump), and for each frame, the return address, frame pointer and stack pointer and possible parameters to the routine. This output can be quite long (but limited to 16K bytes) and use of the environment variable FOR_DIAGNOSTIC_LOG_FILE is recommended if you want to capture the output accurately. Most situations should not require the use of verbose output.

► FOR_FULL_SRC_FILE_SPEC

By default, the traceback output displays only the file name and extension in the source file field. To display complete file name information including the path, set the environment variable FOR_FULL_SRC_FILE_SPEC to true.

21.4.3 Tradeoffs and Restrictions

The following tradeoffs and restrictions apply to using traceback:

► Effect on image size using /traceback

Using the /traceback option to get automatic PC correlation does increase the size of an image. For any application, the developer must decide if the increase in image size is worth the benefit of automatic PC correlation or if manually correlating PC's with a map file is acceptable.

The approach of providing automatic correlation information in the image was used so that no run-time penalty is incurred by building the information "on the fly" as your application executes. No run-time diagnostic code is invoked unless your application is terminating due to a severe error.

► The C Compiler Frame Pointer Omission Option (/Oy) on *x*86 Systems

At the heart of the stack walking code is the Win32 routine StackWalk found in imagehlp.dll. In the *x*86 systems environment, there are no firm software calling standards documented. Compiler developers are under no constraints to use machine registers in any particular way or to hook up procedures in any particular way. The StackWalk( ) routine therefore, bases its decisions on how to walk the call stack on a set of heuristics. That is, it makes a "best guess" to determine how a program reached a particular point in the call chain. With C code that has been compiled with Visual C++ with the Frame Pointer Omission Option (/Oy) enabled, this "best guess" is not usually the correct one.

If you are mixing Fortran and C code and you are concerned about stack tracing, consider disabling this option (/Oy-) in your C compiles. Otherwise traceback will most likely not work for you.

▶ Linker /incremental:no option

When incremental linking is enabled, automatic PC correlation does not work. Use of incremental linking always disables automatic PC correlation even if you specify /traceback during compilation.

When you use incremental linking, the default hexadecimal (hex) PC values will still appear in the output. To correlate from the hexadecimal PC values to routine containing the PC addresses requires use of a linker map file. However, if you request a map file during linking, incremental linking becomes disabled. Thus, to allow any PC values generated for a run-time problem to be helpful, incremental linking must be disabled.

In the visual development environment, you can use the Call stack display, so incremental linking is not a problem.

▶ When the Stack Trace Fails For Some Reason

Programs can fail for a multitude of reasons with unpredictable consequences. Memory corruption by erroneously executing code is always a possibility. Stack memory may be corrupted in such a way that the attempt to trace the call stack will result in access violations or other undesireable consequences. The stack tracing run-time code is guarded with a local exception filter. Should the traceback attempt fail due to a hard detectable condition, the run-time will report this in its diagnostic output message as:

```
Stack trace terminated abnormally
```

Be forewarned, however, it is also possible for memory to be corrupted in such a way that a stack trace can seem to complete successfully with no hint of a problem. The bit patterns it finds in corrupted memory where the stack used to be, and then uses to access memory, may constitute perfectly valid memory addresses for the program to be accessing. They just do not happen to have any connection to what the stack used to look like. So, if it appears that the stack walk completed normally, but the reported PC's make no sense to you, then consider ignoring the stack trace output in diagnosing your problem.

You may also see the stack trace fail if the run-time system cannot dynamically load imagehlp.dll or cannot find the routines from that library it needs to do the stack walk. In this case, you would still get the basic run-time diagnostic message. You just will not get any call stack information.

Another condition that will disable the stack trace process is your program exiting because it has exhausted virtual memory resources.

21.4.4 Example Programs and Traceback Information

The following sections provide example programs that show the use of traceback to locate the cause of the error.

Example: End-of-File Condition, Program teof

In the following example, a **READ** statement creates an End-Of-File error which the application has not handled:

```
program teof
integer*4 i,res
i=here( )
end

integer*4 function here( )
here = we( )
end

integer*4 function we( )
we = go( )
end

integer*4 function go( )
go = again( )
end

integer*4 function again( )
integer*4 a
open(10,file='xxx.dat',form='unformatted',status='unknown')
read(10) a
again=a
end
```

The diagnostic output that results when this program is built with traceback enabled and linked against the dynamic Fortran run-time library on the x86 platform:

```
forrtl: severe (24): end-of-file during read, unit 10, file
E:\USERS\xxx.dat
Image           PC          Routine       Line      Source
DFORRT.dll      1000A3B2    Unknown       Unknown   Unknown
DFORRT.dll      1000A184    Unknown       Unknown   Unknown
DFORRT.dll      10009324    Unknown       Unknown   Unknown
DFORRT.dll      10009596    Unknown       Unknown   Unknown
DFORRT.dll      10024193    Unknown       Unknown   Unknown
teof.exe        004011A9    AGAIN             21    teof.for
teof.exe        004010DD    GO                15    teof.for
teof.exe        004010A7    WE                11    teof.for
teof.exe        00401071    HERE               7    teof.for
teof.exe        00401035    TEOF               3    teof.for
teof.exe        004013D9    Unknown       Unknown   Unknown
teof.exe        004012DF    Unknown       Unknown   Unknown
KERNEL32.dll    77F1B304    Unknown       Unknown   Unknown
```

The first line of the output is the standard Fortran run-time error message. What follows is the result of walking the call stack in reverse to determine where the error originated. Each line of output represents a call frame on the stack. Since the application was compiled with /traceback, the PC's that fall in Fortran code are correlated to their matching routine name, line number and source module. PC's which are not in Fortran code are not correlated and are reported as "Unknown."

The first five frames show calls to routines in the Fortran run-time library. Since the application was linked against the single threaded DLL version of the library, the image name reported is DFORRT.dll. These are the run-time routines that were called to do the **READ** and upon detection of the EOF condition, were invoked to report the error. In the case of an unhandled I/O programming error, there will always be a few frames on the call stack down in run-time code like this.

The stack frame of real interest to the Fortran developer is the first frame in image teof.exe which shows that the error originated in the routine named AGAIN in source module teof.for at line 21. Looking in the source code at line 21, we see the Fortran **READ** statement that incurred the end-of-file condition.

The next four frames complete the trail of calls in the Fortran code that led to the routine that got the error (TEOF->HERE->WE->GO->AGAIN).

Finally, the bottom three frames are routines which handled the startup and initialization of the program.

If this program had been linked against the static Fortran run-time library. The output would then look like:

```
forrtl: severe (24): end-of-file during read, unit 10, file
E:\USERS\xxx.dat
Image           PC          Routine     Line        Source
teof.exe        004067D2    Unknown     Unknown     Unknown
teof.exe        0040659F    Unknown     Unknown     Unknown
teof.exe        00405754    Unknown     Unknown     Unknown
teof.exe        004059C5    Unknown     Unknown     Unknown
teof.exe        00403543    Unknown     Unknown     Unknown
teof.exe        004011A9    AGAIN             21    teof.for
teof.exe        004010DD    GO                15    teof.for
teof.exe        004010A7    WE                11    teof.for
teof.exe        00401071    HERE               7    teof.for
teof.exe        00401035    TEOF               3    teof.for
teof.exe        004202F9    Unknown     Unknown     Unknown
teof.exe        00416063    Unknown     Unknown     Unknown
KERNEL32.dll    77F1B304    Unknown     Unknown     Unknown
```

Notice that the initial five stack frames now show routines in image teof.exe, not DFORRT.DLL. The routines are the same five run-time routines as previously reported for the DLL case but since the application was linked against the static Fortran run-time library (dfor.lib), the object modules containing these routines were linked into the application image (teof.exe). Using the map file, you can determine that the PC reported in the top stack frame, 004067D2, is from routine _for_stack_trace, in module for_diags.obj of library dfor.lib (004067a0 < PC=004067D2 < 004079f0):

```
...
0001:000057a0  _for_stack_trace              004067a0  f
dfor:for_diags.obj
0001:000069f0  _for__find_trace_info_file 004079f0  f
dfor:for_diags.obj
...
```

Now suppose the application was compiled *without* traceback enabled and once again, linked against the static Fortran library. The diagnostic output would then appear as follows:

```
forrtl: severe (24): end-of-file during read, unit 10, file
E:\USERS\xxx.dat
Image           PC          Routine     Line        Source
teof.exe        00406792    Unknown     Unknown     Unknown
teof.exe        0040655F    Unknown     Unknown     Unknown
teof.exe        00405714    Unknown     Unknown     Unknown
teof.exe        00405985    Unknown     Unknown     Unknown
teof.exe        00403503    Unknown     Unknown     Unknown
teof.exe        00401169    Unknown     Unknown     Unknown
teof.exe        004010A8    Unknown     Unknown     Unknown
teof.exe        00401078    Unknown     Unknown     Unknown
```

```
teof.exe      00401048   Unknown    Unknown    Unknown
teof.exe      0040102F   Unknown    Unknown    Unknown
teof.exe      004202B9   Unknown    Unknown    Unknown
teof.exe      00416023   Unknown    Unknown    Unknown
KERNEL32.dll  77F1B304   Unknown    Unknown    Unknown
```

Without the correlation information in the image that /traceback previously supplied, the Fortran run-time system cannot correlate PC's to routine name, line number, and source file. You can still use the map file to at least determine the routine names and what modules they are in. Look at the beginning of the entry point list in the map file for this image:

```
Address            Publics by Value    Rva+Base      Lib:Object
0001:00000000      _TEOF               00401000  f   teof.obj
0001:00000000      _TEOF@0             00401000  f   teof.obj
0001:00000000      _MAIN__             00401000  f   teof.obj
0001:0000003d      _HERE               0040103d  f   teof.obj
0001:0000003d      _HERE@0             0040103d  f   teof.obj
0001:0000006d      _WE@0               0040106d  f   teof.obj
0001:0000006d      _WE                 0040106d  f   teof.obj
0001:0000009d      _GO                 0040109d  f   teof.obj
0001:0000009d      _GO@0               0040109d  f   teof.obj
0001:000000cd      _AGAIN              004010cd  f   teof.obj
0001:000000cd      _AGAIN@0            004010cd  f   teof.obj
0001:00000180      _for_rtl_init_      00401180  f   dfor:for_init.obj
   ...
```

After determining that the first five stack frames fall in run-time code (using portions of the map file not shown here), the sixth frame shows a PC of 00401169. Using the fragment of the map file shown above, it can be seen that this PC is greater than 004010cd but less than 00401180 and is therefore in routine _AGAIN, the first Fortran routine on the call stack. The remaining PC's can be manually correlated in a similar fashion to reconstruct the calling sequence.

Remember that compiling with /traceback increases the size of your application's image because of the extra PC correlation information included in the image. You can see if the extra traceback information is included in an image (checking for the presence of a .trace section) by typing:

```
link -dump -summary your_app.exe
```

For the teof.exe example, the following is displayed:

```
Microsoft (R) COFF Binary File Dumper Version x.xx.xxxx
Copyright (C) Microsoft Corp 1992-1998. All rights reserved.
```

```
Dump of file teof.exe

File Type: EXECUTABLE IMAGE

  Summary

    1000 .data
    1000 .idata
    1000 .rdata
    1000 .text
    1000 .trace
```

Check the file size with a simple directory command. Here's the teof.exe example linked against the dynamic Fortran library with traceback:

```
03/03/98 01:45p            5,120 teof.exe
        1 File(s)           5,120 bytes
```

Without traceback, the following appears:

```
03/03/98 01:46p            4,608 teof.exe
  1 File(s)                 4,608 bytes
```

For this simple example, the traceback correlation information added 512 bytes to the image size. In a real application, this would probably be much larger. For any application, the developer must decide if the increase in image size is worth the benefit of automatic PC correlation or if manually correlating PC's with a map file is acceptable.

For command-line use and in the release configuration in the visual development environment, traceback information is not included by default in Fortran compiles (default is /notraceback). In the visual development environment, the default is /traceback in the debug configuration. For the release configuration, request traceback in the Run Time category of the Project Settings dialog box.

If an error occurs when traceback was requested during compilation, the run-time library will produce the correlated call stack display.

If an error occurs when traceback was disabled during compilation, the run-time library will produce the uncorrelated call stack display.

Suppose you don't want to see the call stack information displayed. You can set the environment variable FOR_DISABLE_STACK_TRACE to true so it is not displayed. You will still get the Fortran run-time error message:

```
forrtl: severe (24): end-of-file during read, unit 10, file
E:\USERS\xxx.dat
```

Example: Machine Exception Condition, Program ovf

The following program generates a floating-point overflow exception when compiled with /fpe:0:

```
program ovf
real*4 a
a=1e37
do i=1,10
    a=hey(a)
end do
end

real*4 function hey(b)
real*4 b
hey = watch(b)
end

real*4 function watch(b)
real*4 b
watch = out(b)
end

real*4 function out(b)
real*4 b
out = below(b)
end

real*4 function below(b)
real*4 b
below = b*10.0e0
end
```

When this program is compiled with /traceback and /optimization:0 on an Alpha system, the traceback output appears as follows:

```
forrtl: error (72): floating overflow
Image           PC          Routine     Line        Source
ovf.exe         0040210C    BELOW           26      ovf.for
ovf.exe         004020DC    OUT             21      ovf.for
ovf.exe         004020B4    WATCH           16      ovf.for
ovf.exe         0040208C    HEY             11      ovf.for
ovf.exe         00402040    OVF              5      ovf.for
ovf.exe         00402428    Unknown     Unknown     Unknown
ovf.exe         0040226C    Unknown     Unknown     Unknown
KERNEL32.dll    77E8F2AC    Unknown     Unknown     Unknown
```

Notice that unlike the previous example of an unhandled I/O programming error, the stack walk can begin right at the point of the exception. There are no run-time routines on the call stack to dig through. The overflow occurs in routine BELOW at PC 0040210C which is correlated to line 26 of the source file ovf.for.

When the program is compiled at a higher optimization level, /optimization:4 and /traceback, the traceback output appears as follows:

```
forrtl: error (72): floating overflow
Image          PC         Routine    Line       Source
ovf.exe        00402034   OVF              26    ovf.for
ovf.exe        004023E8   Unknown    Unknown    Unknown
ovf.exe        0040222C   Unknown    Unknown    Unknown
KERNEL32.dll   77E8F2AC   Unknown    Unknown    Unknown
```

With /optimize:4, the entire program has been inlined. We can see this with a quick look in the listing file:

```
...
                          .text CNT_CODE MEM_EXECUTE
                          .globl MAIN__
                          .ent   MAIN__
                          .eflag 1
                0000    OVF:
261F0000        0000              ldah    a0, h^.literal(zero)
23DEFFF0        0004              lda     sp, -16(sp)
B75E0000        0008              stq     ra, (sp)
                          .fmask 0x00000000,-16
                          .frame $sp, 16, $26
                          .prologue 0
22100008        000C              lda     a0, l^.literal+8(a0)
D3400000        0010              bsr     ra, j^for_set_reentrancy
279F0000        0014              ldah    at, h^.literal(zero)
47E15400        0018              mov     10, .T2_
881C0004        001C              lds     A, l^.literal+4(at)
279F0000        0020              ldah    at, h^.literal(zero)
883C0000        0024              lds     f1, l^.literal(at)
                0028    L$1:
58011040        0028              muls    A, f1, f0
2000FFFB        002C              lda     .T2_, -5(v0)
58011040        0030              muls    f0, f1, f0
58011040        0034              muls    f0, f1, f0
58011040        0038              muls    f0, f1, f0
58011040        003C              muls    f0, f1, A
FC1FFFF9        0040              bgt     .T2_, L$1
A75E0000        0044              ldq     ra, (sp)
47E03400        0048              mov     1, v0
23DE0010        004C              lda     sp, 16(sp)
6BFA8001        0050              ret     (ra)
```

```
2FFE0000     0054           unop
2FFE0000     0058           unop
2FFE0000     005C           unop
                            .end MAIN__
...
```

The main program, OVF, no longer calls routine HEY. While the output is not quite what one might have expected intuitively, it is still entirely correct. You need to keep in mind the effects of compiler optimization when you interpret the diagnostic information reported for a failure in a release image.

If the same image were executed again but with environment variable FOR_ENABLE_VERBOSE_STACK_TRACE set to true, you would also see a dump of the exception context record at the time of the error. Here is an excerpt of how that would appear. Remember, the example traceback output above is from an Alpha system. You would get the same kind of information on an x86 system, but the report would be x86 architecture specific:

```
forrtl: error (72): floating overflow

Hex Dump Of Exception Record Context Information:

Exception Context: Fault Instruction PC and Processor Status
Register.

Fir: 000000000040210C Psr: 00000003

Exception Context: Processor Integer Registers.

IntV0:   000000000040602C    IntT0:   0000000000000002
IntT1:   0000000000400000    IntT2:   0000000000000010
IntT3:   0000000000000000    IntT4:   0000000000000000
IntT5:   0000000000000000    IntT6:   0000000000000000
IntT7:   0000000000000001    IntS0:   0000000000000009
IntS1:   0000000000000000    IntS2:   0000000000000000
IntS3:   0000000000000000    IntS4:   0000000000000000
IntS5:   0000000000000000    IntFp:   0000000000000000
IntA0:   000000000040602C    IntA1:   0000000000000000
IntA2:   0000000000000002    IntA3:   0000000000000000
IntA4:   0000000000000000    IntA5:   0000000000000000
IntT8:   0000000000000004    IntT9:   0000000000000000
IntT10:  0000000000000000    IntT11:  0000000000000000
IntRa:   0000000004020E0     IntT12:  000000001006BCE0
IntAt:   0000000000400000    IntGp:   0000000000000000
IntSp:   000000000012FE60    IntZero: 0000000000000000

Exception Context: Floating Point Registers.
```

```
Fpcr:        0000000000000000   SoftFpcr:   000000000000001E
FltF0:       0000000020000000   FltF1:      00000000E0000000
FltF2:       0000000000000000   FltF3:      0000000000000000
FltF4:       0000000000000000   FltF5:      0000000000000000
FltF6:       0000000000000000   FltF7:      0000000000000000
FltF8:       0000000000000000   FltF9:      0000000000000000
FltF10:      0000000000000000   FltF11:     0000000000000000
FltF12:      0000000000000000   FltF13:     0000000000000000
FltF14:      0000000000000000   FltF15:     0000000000000000
FltF16:      0000000000000000   FltF17:     0000000000000000
FltF18:      0000000000000000   FltF19:     0000000000000000
FltF20:      0000000000000000   FltF21:     0000000000000000
FltF22:      0000000000000000   FltF23:     0000000000000000
FltF24:      0000000000000000   FltF25:     0000000000000000
FltF26:      0000000000000000   FltF27:     0000000000000000
FltF28:      0000000000000000   FltF29:     0000000000000000
FltF30:      0000000000000000   FltF31:     0000000000000000
...
```

Example: Math Intrinsic Error, Program intrin_expl

The following simple program attempts to find the log of a negative number. This will cause the math library to generate a floating-point invalid operation exception:

```
program intrin_expl
real*8 a
a = abe( )
end

real*8 function abe( )
abe = lincoln( )
end

real*8 function lincoln( )
lincoln = rail( )
end

real*8 function rail( )
rail = splitter( )
end

real*8 function splitter( )
splitter = log(-1000.0d0)
end
```

If the program were compiled on an Alpha system with /traceback enabled and linked against the dynamic Fortran run-time library, the traceback output would appear as follows:

```
forrtl: error (65): floating invalid
Image              PC            Routine          Line        Source
ntdll.dll          77F4E90C      Unknown          Unknown     Unknown
KERNEL32.dll       77E920C0      Unknown          Unknown     Unknown
DFORRT.dll         10090658      Unknown          Unknown     Unknown
DFORRT.dll         1008FAD0      Unknown          Unknown     Unknown
DFORRT.dll         1007FDBC      Unknown          Unknown     Unknown
intrin_expl.exe    004020B0      SPLITTER              18     intrin_expl.for
intrin_expl.exe    00402088      RAIL                  14     intrin_expl.for
intrin_expl.exe    00402068      LINCOLN               10     intrin_expl.for
intrin_expl.exe    00402038      ABE                    6     intrin_expl.for
intrin_expl.exe    00402014      INTRIN_EXPL            1     intrin_expl.for
intrin_expl.exe    004023D8      Unknown          Unknown     Unknown
intrin_expl.exe    0040221C      Unknown          Unknown     Unknown
KERNEL32.dll       77E8F2AC      Unknown          Unknown     Unknown
```

The first line of output is the standard Fortran run-time message telling you that a floating invalid exception occurred. The following lines describe the call stack.

On Alpha, the math library is bundled in as part of the Fortran run-time library so math library routines, in this example, will be reported as part of image DFORRT.DLL. Whenever the math library needs to report an exceptional condition, it calls the WIN32 routine RaiseException( ) to do so. RaiseException( ) is in KERNEL32.DLL but actually uses code in NTDLL.DLL to execute the call. So the first two frames we see on the call stack represent the call to RaiseException( ) by the math library. The next three frames represent the code in the math library for the log( ) intrinsic and exception reporting routines. Notice that they are part of the Fortran run-time library image.

The next frame shows us where in the Fortran code the error was generated. We see that in image intrin_expl.exe, at PC 004020B0, in routine SPLITTER, at line 18 of source module intrin_expl.for, a call to log( ) occurred and generated the floating invalid error.

The rest of the call stack shows how the image was activated, initialized, and reached routine SPLITTER (INTRIN_EXPL->ABE->LINCOLN->RAIL->SPLITTER).

Example: Using Traceback in Mixed Fortran/C Applications, Program FPING and CPONG

Consider the following example that shows how the traceback output might appear in a mixed Fortran/C application. The main program is a Fortran program named FPING. Program FPING triggers a chain of function calls which are alternately Fortran and C code. Eventually, the C routine named Unlucky is called which produces a floating divide by zero error.

Source module FPING.FOR contains the Fortran function definitions, each of which calls a C routine from source module CPONG.C. FPING.FOR is compiled with the /fpe:0 /optimize:0 /traceback options enabled, on the *x*86 platform. Here's the program traceback output:

```
forrtl: error (73): floating divide by zero
Image          PC              Routine    Line        Source
fping.exe      00401161        Unknown    Unknown     Unknown
fping.exe      004010DC        DOWN4      58          fping.for
fping.exe      0040118F        Unknown    Unknown     Unknown
fping.exe      004010B6        DOWN3      44          fping.for
fping.exe      00401181        Unknown    Unknown     Unknown
fping.exe      00401094        DOWN2      31          fping.for
fping.exe      00401173        Unknown    Unknown     Unknown
fping.exe      00401072        DOWN1      18          fping.for
fping.exe      0040104B        FPING      5           fping.for
fping.exe      004013B9        Unknown    Unknown     Unknown
fping.exe      004012AF        Unknown    Unknown     Unknown
KERNEL32.dll   77F1B304        Unknown    Unknown     Unknown
```

Notice that the stack frames contributed by Fortran routines can be correlated to a routine name, line number, and source module but those frames contributed by C routines cannot be correlated. Remember, even though the stack can be walked in reverse, and PC's reported, the information necessary to correlate the PC to a routine name, line number, and so on, is contributed to the image from the objects generated by the Fortran compiler. The C compiler does not have this capability. Also remember that you only get the correlation information if you specify the /traceback option for your Fortran compiles.

The top stack frame cannot be correlated to a routine name because it is in C code. By examining the map file for the application, we can see that the reported PC, 00401161, is greater than the start of routine _Unlucky, but less than the start of routine _down1_C, so we at least know the error occurred in routine _Unlucky. Here is the pertinent section of the map file:

```
Address              Publics by Value   Rva+Base              Lib:Object
0001:00000000        _FPING             00401000          f  fping.obj
0001:00000000        _FPING@0           00401000          f  fping.obj
0001:00000000        _MAIN__            00401000          f  fping.obj
0001:0000005f        _DOWN1             0040105f          f  fping.obj
0001:0000005f        _DOWN1@4           0040105f          f  fping.obj
0001:00000083        _DOWN2@4           00401083          f  fping.obj
0001:00000083        _DOWN2             00401083          f  fping.obj
0001:000000a5        _DOWN3             004010a5          f  fping.obj
0001:000000a5        _DOWN3@4           004010a5          f  fping.obj
0001:000000c7        _DOWN4@4           004010c7          f  fping.obj
0001:000000c7        _DOWN4             004010c7          f  fping.obj
0001:00000100        _Fact              00401100          f  cpong.obj
0001:00000127        _Pythagoras        00401127          f  cpong.obj


***************************************************
The reported PC lies between the start of _Unlucky and
the start of _down1_C...
***************************************************

0001:0000014d        _Unlucky           0040114d          f  cpong.obj
0001:00000167        _down1_C           00401167          f  cpong.obj

0001:00000175        _down2_C           00401175          f  cpong.obj
0001:00000183        _down3_C           00401183          f  cpong.obj
0001:00000192        _for_check_flawed_pentium@0 00401192 f  dfordll:DFORRT.dll
0001:00000198        _for_set_fpe_@4       00401198       f  dfordll:DFORRT.dll
0001:0000019e        _for_set_reentrancy@4 0040119e       f  dfordll:DFORRT.dll
etc...
```

In a similar manner, the other PC's reported as "Unknown" can be correlated to a routine name using the map file.

When examining traceback output (or any type of diagnostic output for that matter), it is always important to keep in mind the affects of compiler optimization. The Fortran source module in the above example was built with optimization turned off, /optimize:0. Look at the output when optimizations are enabled, /optimize:4:

```
forrtl: error (73): floating divide by zero
Image           PC            Routine      Line       Source
fping.exe       00401111      Unknown      Unknown    Unknown
fping.exe       0040109D      DOWN4             58    fping.for
fping.exe       0040113F      Unknown      Unknown    Unknown
fping.exe       00401082      DOWN3             44    fping.for
fping.exe       00401131      Unknown      Unknown    Unknown
fping.exe       0040106B      DOWN2             31    fping.for
fping.exe       00401123      Unknown      Unknown    Unknown
```

```
               fping.exe        00401032     FPING           18   fping.for
               fping.exe        00401369     Unknown    Unknown   Unknown
               fping.exe        0040125F     Unknown    Unknown   Unknown
               KERNEL32.dll     77F1B304     Unknown    Unknown   Unknown
```

From the traceback output, it would appear that routine DOWN1 was never called. In fact, it has not been called. At the higher optimization level, the compiler has inlined function DOWN1 so that the call to routine down1_C is now made from FPING. The correlated line number still points to the correct line in the source code. You can see that DOWN1 was inlined by looking in the listing file, FPING.LST:

```
                                          .CODE
                                  PUBLIC  _MAIN__
                  0000    _MAIN__   PROC
55                0000              push    ebp
EC8B              0001              mov     ebp, esp
04EC83            0003              sub     esp, 4
53                0006              push    ebx
000000E8          0007              call  _for_check_flawed_pentium@0
00
04EC83            000C              sub     esp, 4
0008058D          000F              lea     eax, dword ptr .literal$+8
0002
50                0015              push    eax
000000E8          0016              call _for_set_fpe_@4
00
0004058D          001B              lea     eax, dword ptr .literal$+4
0002
50                0021              push    eax
000000E8          0022              call    _for_set_reentrancy@4
00
000035FF          0027              push    dword ptr .literal$ ; 000018
0000
000035FF          0027              push    dword ptr .literal$ ; 000018
0000


*****************************************************************
Call _down1_C from MAIN__ here, no call to DOWN1 Fortran routine...
*****************************************************************

000000E8          002D                      call    _down1_C
00
```

```
C0DD            0032            ffree   st(0)
F7D9            0034            fincstp
08C483          0036            add     esp, 8
000001B8        0039            mov     eax, 1 ; 000006
A0
5B              003E            pop     ebx
E58B            003F            mov     esp, ebp
5D              0041            pop     ebp
C3              0042            ret
_MAIN__                         ENDP
```

Finally, suppose the example Fortran code is redesigned with each of the Fortran routines split into separate source modules. Here is what the traceback output would look like with the redesigned code:

```
forrtl: error (73): floating divide by zero
Image             PC          Routine     Line        Source
fpingmain.exe     00401171    Unknown     Unknown     Unknown
fpingmain.exe     004010ED    DOWN4            12     fping4.for
fpingmain.exe     0040119F    Unknown     Unknown     Unknown
fpingmain.exe     004010C1    DOWN3            11     fping3.for
fpingmain.exe     00401191    Unknown     Unknown     Unknown
fpingmain.exe     00401099    DOWN2            11     fping2.for
fpingmain.exe     00401183    Unknown     Unknown     Unknown
fpingmain.exe     00401073    DOWN1            11     fping1.for
fpingmain.exe     0040104B    FPING             5     fpingmain.for
fpingmain.exe     004013C9    Unknown     Unknown     Unknown
fpingmain.exe     004012BF    Unknown     Unknown     Unknown
KERNEL32.dll      77F1B304    Unknown     Unknown     Unknown
```

Notice that the line number and source file correlation information has changed to reflect the new design of the code.

Here are the sources used in the above examples:

```
************************************
FPING.FOR
************************************
        program fping
        real*4 a,b
        a=-10.0
        b=down1(a)
        end

        real*4 function down1(b)
        real*4 b
!DEC$   IF DEFINED(_X86_)
        INTERFACE TO REAL*4 FUNCTION down1_C [C,ALIAS:'_down1_C'] (n)
!DEC$   ELSE
```

```
           INTERFACE TO REAL*4 FUNCTION down1_C [C,ALIAS:'down1_C'] (n)
!DEC$      ENDIF
           REAL*4 n [VALUE]
              END
           real*4 down1_C
           down1 = down1_C(b)
              end


           real*4 function down2(b)
           real*4 b [VALUE]
!DEC$      IF DEFINED(_X86_)
           INTERFACE TO REAL*4 FUNCTION down2_C [C,ALIAS:'_down2_C'] (n)
!DEC$       ELSE
           INTERFACE TO REAL*4 FUNCTION down2_C [C,ALIAS:'down2_C'] (n)
!DEC$      ENDIF
           REAL*4 n [VALUE]
              END
           real*4 down2_C
           down2 = down2_C(b)
              end


           real*4 function down3(b)
           real*4 b [VALUE]
!DEC$      IF DEFINED(_X86_)
           INTERFACE TO REAL*4 FUNCTION down3_C [C,ALIAS:'_down3_C'] (n)
!DEC$       ELSE
           INTERFACE TO REAL*4 FUNCTION down3_C [C,ALIAS:'down3_C'] (n)
!DEC$      ENDIF
           REAL*4 n [VALUE]
              END
           real*4 down3_C
           down3 = down3_C(b)
              end


           real*4 function down4(b)
           real*4 b [VALUE]
!DEC$      IF DEFINED(_X86_)
           INTERFACE TO SUBROUTINE Unlucky [C,ALIAS:'_Unlucky'] (a,c)
!DEC$       ELSE
           INTERFACE TO SUBROUTINE Unlucky [C,ALIAS:'Unlucky'] (a,c)
!DEC$      ENDIF
           REAL*4 a [VALUE]
```

```
        REAL*4 c [REFERENCE]
          END
        real*4 a
        call Unlucky(b,a)
        down4 = a
          end
```

```
***********************************
CPONG.C
***********************************
#include <math.h>
extern float __stdcall DOWN2 (float n);
extern float __stdcall DOWN3 (float n);
extern float __stdcall DOWN4 (float n);

int Fact( int n )
{
if (n > 1)
    return( n * Fact( n - 1 ));
return 1;
}

void Pythagoras( float a, float b, float *c)
{
*c = sqrt( a * a + b * b );
}

void Unlucky( float a, float *c)
{
float b=0.0;
*c = a/b;
}

float down1_C( float a )
{
return( DOWN2( a ));
}

float down2_C( float a )
{
return( DOWN3( a ));
}

float down3_C( float a )
{
return( DOWN4( a ));
}
```

```
***********************************
FPINGMAIN.FOR
***********************************
        program fping

        real*4 a,b
        a=-10.0
        b=down1(a)
          end


***********************************
FPING1.FOR
***********************************
        real*4 function down1(b)
        real*4 b
!DEC$   IF DEFINED(_X86_)
        INTERFACE TO REAL*4 FUNCTION down1_C [C,ALIAS:'_down1_C'] (n)
!DEC$    ELSE
        INTERFACE TO REAL*4 FUNCTION down1_C [C,ALIAS:'down1_C'] (n)
!DEC$    ENDIF
        REAL*4 n [VALUE]
          END
        real*4 down1_C
        down1 = down1_C(b)
          end


***********************************
FPING2.FOR
***********************************
        real*4 function down2(b)
        real*4 b [VALUE]
!DEC$   IF DEFINED(_X86_)
        INTERFACE TO REAL*4 FUNCTION down2_C [C,ALIAS:'_down2_C'] (n)
!DEC$    ELSE
        INTERFACE TO REAL*4 FUNCTION down2_C [C,ALIAS:'down2_C'] (n)
!DEC$    ENDIF
        REAL*4 n [VALUE]
          END
        real*4 down2_C
        down2 = down2_C(b)
          end
```

```
************************************
FPING3.FOR
************************************
        real*4 function down3(b)
        real*4 b [VALUE]
!DEC$   IF DEFINED(_X86_)
        INTERFACE TO REAL*4 FUNCTION down3_C [C,ALIAS:'_down3_C'] (n)
!DEC$   ELSE
        INTERFACE TO REAL*4 FUNCTION down3_C [C,ALIAS:'down3_C'] (n)
!DEC$   ENDIF
        REAL*4 n [VALUE]
        END
        real*4 down3_C
        down3 = down3_C(b)
        end


************************************
FPING4.FOR
************************************
        real*4 function down4(b)
        real*4 b [VALUE]
!DEC$   IF DEFINED(_X86_)
        INTERFACE TO SUBROUTINE Unlucky [C,ALIAS:'_Unlucky'] (a,c)
!DEC$   ELSE
        INTERFACE TO SUBROUTINE Unlucky [C,ALIAS:'Unlucky'] (a,c)
!DEC$   ENDIF
        REAL*4 a [VALUE]
        REAL*4 c [REFERENCE]
        END
        real*4 a
        call Unlucky(b,a)
        down4 = a
        end
```

21.5   Run-Time Environment Variables

The Visual Fortran run-time system recognizes the environment variables listed in Table 21-3.

Table 21–3 *Visual Fortran Environment Variables*

Environment Variable	Description
FOR_ACCEPT	The **ACCEPT** statement does not include an explicit logical unit number. Instead, it uses an implicit internal logical unit number and the FOR_ACCEPT environment variable. If FOR_ACCEPT is *not* defined, the code `ACCEPT f,iolist` reads from CONIN$ (standard input). If FOR_ACCEPT is defined (as a filename optionally containing a path), the specified file would be read.
FOR_DEFAULT_PRINT_DEVICE	Lets you specify the print device other than the default print device PRN (LPT1) for files closed (**CLOSE** statement) with the DISPOSE='PRINT' specifier. To specify a different print device for the file associated with the **CLOSE** statement DISPOSE='PRINT' specifier, set the environment variable FOR_DEFAULT_PRINT_DEVICE to any legal DOS print device before executing the program.
FOR_DIAGNOSTIC_LOG_FILE	If set to the name of a file, writes diagnostic output to the specified file. For information on using stack trace information, see Section 21.3 Locating Run-Time Errors and Section 21.4 Using Traceback Information.
FOR_DISABLE_DIAGNOSTIC_DISPLAY	If set to true, disables the display of all error information. This might be helpful if you just want to test the error status of your program and do not want the Fortran run-time system to display any information about an abnormal program termination. For information on using stack trace information, see Section 21.4 Using Traceback Information.
FOR_DISABLE_STACK_TRACE	If set to true, disables the call stack trace information that follows the displayed severe error message text. For information on locating the cause of run-time errors using stack trace information, see Section 21.3 Locating Run-Time Errors and Section 21.4 Using Traceback Information.
FOR_ENABLE_VERBOSE_STACK_TRACE	If set to true, displays more detailed call stack information in the event of an error. For information on using stack trace information, see Section 21.4 Using Traceback Information.
FOR_FULL_SRC_FILE_SPEC	By default, the traceback output displays only the file name and extension in the source file field. To display complete file name information including the path, set the environment variable FOR_FULL_SRC_FILE_SPEC to true. For more information, see Section 21.4 Using Traceback Information.

Table 21–3 *Visual Fortran Environment Variables (Continued)*

Environment Variable	Description
FOR_GENERATE_DEBUG_EXCEPTION	In Visual Fortran Version 6, you no longer need to set this environment variable for the program to stop in the debugger when a severe error occurs. Regardless of whether this environment variable is set, you can view the Call Stack display. For more information, see Section 5.5 Locating Run-Time Errors in the Debugger.
FOR_IGNORE_EXCEPTIONS	If set to true, disables the default run-time exception handling, for example, to allow just-in-time debugging. The run-time system exception handler returns EXCEPTION_CONTINUE_SEARCH to the operating system, which looks for other handlers to service the exception. For information on just-in- time debugging, see Section 2.6 Running Fortran Applications and the *Visual C++ Development Environment User's Guide.*
FOR_NOERROR_DIALOGS	If set to true, disables the display of dialog boxes when certain exceptions or errors occur. This is useful when running many test programs in batch mode to prevent a failure from stopping execution of the entire test stream.
FOR_PRINT	Neither the **PRINT** statement nor a **WRITE** statement with an asterisk (*) in place of a unit number includes an explicit logical unit number. Instead, both use an implicit internal logical unit number and the FOR_PRINT environment variable. If FOR_PRINT is *not* defined, the code `PRINT f,iolist` or `WRITE (*,f) iolist` writes to CONOUT$ (standard output). If FOR_PRINT is defined (as a filename optionally containing a path), the specified file would be written to.
FOR_READ	A **READ** statement that uses an asterisk (*) in place of a unit number does not include an explicit logical unit number. Instead, it uses an implicit internal logical unit number and the FOR_READ environment variable. If FOR_READ is *not* defined, the code `READ (*,f) iolist` or `READ f,iolist` reads from CONIN$ (standard input). If FOR_READ is defined (as a filename optionally containing a path), the specified file would be read.
FOR_RUN_FLAWED_PENTIUM	If set to true, allows the continuation of the executing program when /check:flawed_pentium (default) is in effect and a flawed Pentium chip is detected. For more information, see Section 22.5 Intel Pentium Floating-Point Flaw.

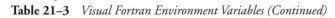

Table 21–3 *Visual Fortran Environment Variables (Continued)*

Environment Variable	Description
FOR_TYPE	The **TYPE** statement does not include an explicit logical unit number. Instead, it uses an implicit internal logical unit number and the FOR_TYPE environment variable. If FOR_TYPE is *not* defined, the code `TYPE f,iolist` writes to CONOUT$ (standard output). If FOR_TYPE is defined (as a filename optionally containing a path), the specified file would be written to.
FORTn	Lets you specify the file name for a particular unit number (*n*), when a file name is not specified in the **OPEN** statement or an implicit **OPEN** is used, and the compiler option /fpscomp:files-fromcmd was *not* specified. Preconnected files attached to units 0, 5, and 6 are by default associated with system standard I/O files.
FORT_CONVERTn	Lets you specify the data format for an unformatted file associated with a particular unit number (*n*), as described in Section 23.3 Methods of Specifying the Data Format.

On the command line, the SET command lets you:

▶ Set an *environment variable* to a *value*:

```
SET environment-variable=value
```

For example:

```
SET FOR_GENERATE_DEBUG_EXCEPTION=TRUE
```

▶ To view the current value of an environment variable, use the SET command with only the environment variable name:

```
SET FOR_GENERATE_DEBUG_EXCEPTION
FOR_GENERATE_DEBUG_EXCEPTION=TRUE
```

From within your program, you can set the appropriate environment variable by calling the **SETENVQQ** routine:

```
program ENVVAR
use dflib
integer*4 res
! Add other data declarations here
! call SETENVQQ as a function
res=SETENVQQ("FOR_GENERATE_DEBUG_EXCEPTION=T")
...
```

For a list of environment variables used with the DF command, see Section 3.4 Environment Variables Used with the DF Command.

22

The Floating-Point Environment

This chapter describes the Visual Fortran numeric environment using IEEE® arithmetic for *x*86 and Alpha systems. The following topics are covered:

▶ Section 22.1 Representing Numbers

▶ Section 22.2 Loss of Precision Errors: Rounding, Special Values, Underflow, and Overflow

▶ Section 22.3 Setting and Retrieving Floating-Point Status and Control Words (*x*86 Only)

▶ Section 22.4 Handling Arithmetic Exceptions

▶ Section 22.5 Intel Pentium Floating-Point Flaw (*x*86 Only)

When the term floating-point unit (FPU) appears, it refers to your math processor, which could be a math coprocessor for a 486 SX CPU, an integrated floating-point unit in an Intel® 486, Pentium®, or Pentium Pro processor, or software that emulates a coprocessor. The reference manual for your FPU describes its registers and features. The descriptions in this section minimize hardware-specific terminology.

Visual Fortran supplies a single library for floating-point operations. Earlier versions of Visual Fortran had several versions that you could specify, depending on your hardware configuration and your software development goals. You do not have to specify a library; the operating system selects the appropriate routines to execute at run-time. If the system on which your program executes contains an FPU, the hardware routines execute; if not, software routines emulate an FPU.

22.1   Representing Numbers

Fortran's numeric environment is flexible, which helps make Fortran a strong language for intensive numerical calculations. The Fortran standard purposely leaves the precision of numeric quantities and the method of rounding numeric results unspecified. This allows Fortran to operate efficiently for diverse applications on diverse systems.

The effect of math computations on integers is straightforward. Integers of KIND=4 consist of a maximum positive integer (2,147,483,647), a minimum negative integer (-2,147,483,648), and all integers between them including zero. Operations on integers result in other integers within this range. The only arithmetic rule to remember is that integer division results in truncation (for example, 8/3 evaluates to 2).

Computations on real numbers, however, may not yield what you expect. This happens because the hardware must represent numbers in a finite number of bits.

There are several effects of using finite floating-point numbers. The hardware is not able to represent every real number exactly, but must approximate exact representations by rounding or truncating to finite length. In addition, some numbers lie outside the range of representation of the maximum and minimum exponents and can result in calculations that underflow and overflow. As an example of one consequence, finite precision produces many numbers that, although non-zero, behave in addition as zero.

You can minimize the effects of finite representation with programming techniques; for example, by not using floating-point numbers in **LOGICAL** comparisons or by giving them a tolerance (for example, IF (x <= 10.001)), and by not attempting to combine or compare numbers that differ by more than the number of significant bits. (For more information on programming methods to reduce the effects of imprecision, see Section 22.2.1 Rounding Errors.)

For further discussion of how floating-point numbers are represented, see:

▶ Section 22.1.1 Floating-Point Numbers

▶ Section 22.1.2 Retrieving Parameters of Numeric Representations

22.1.1   Floating-Point Numbers

This version of Visual Fortran uses a close approximation to the IEEE floating-point standard (ANSI/IEEE Std 754-1985, *IEEE Standard for Binary Floating-Point Arithmetic*, 1985). This standard is common to many microcomputer-based systems due to the availability of fast math coprocessors that implement the required characteristics. Software emulation of the standard is also possible if a hardware system does not include a coprocessor.

You should choose the appropriate setting of the /fpe compiler option to select the type of default floating-point exception handling provided by the Visual Fortran run-time system.

This section outlines the characteristics of the standard and its implementation for Visual Fortran. Except as noted, the description includes both the IEEE standard and the Visual Fortran implementation. The following topics are discussed:

▶ Section 22.1.1.1 Floating-Point Formats

▶ Section 22.1.1.2 Floating-Point Representation

▶ Section 22.1.1.3 Viewing Floating-Point Representations with Bit-Viewer

▶ Section 22.1.1.4 Special Values (Signed Zero, NaN, Signed Infinity)

22.1.1.1 *Floating-Point Formats*

The IEEE® Standard 754 specifies values and requirements for floating-point representation (such as base 2). The standard outlines requirements for two formats: basic and extended, and for two word-lengths within each format: single and double.

Visual Fortran supports single-precision format (**REAL**(4)) and double-precision format (**REAL**(8)) floating-point numbers. Visual Fortran sets the process control word by default to use double-precision run-time intermediate calculations. At some levels of optimization, some single-precision numbers are stored on the floating-point stack (which defaults to double precision) rather than being stored back into memory where they would be truncated to single precision. The compiler option /fltconsistency (*x*86 only) can control floating-point consistency and request that results be stored in memory rather than on the floating-point stack.

22.1.1.2 *Floating-Point Representation*

Floating-point numbers approximate real numbers with a finite number of bits. You can see the bits representing a floating-point number with the Bit-Viewer tool. The bits are calculated as shown in the following formula. The representation is binary, so the base is 2. The bits bn represent binary digits (0 or 1). The precision P is the number of bits in the nonexponential part of the number (the significand), and E is the exponent. With these parameters, binary floating-point numbers approximate real numbers with the values:

$(-1)s\ b_0 . b_1\ b_2\ ...\ b_{P-1}\ \text{x}\ 2_E$

where s is 0 or 1 (+ or -), and $E_{min} <= E <= E_{max}$

Table 22-1 gives the standard values for these parameters for single, double, and extended-double formats and the resulting bit widths for the sign, the exponent, and the full number.

Table 22–1   *Parameters for IEEE Floating-Point Formats*

Parameter	*Single*	*Double*	*Extended Double*
Sign width in bits	1	1	1
P	24	53	64
E_{max}	+127	+1023	+16383
E_{min}	- 126	- 1022	- 16382
Exponent *bias*	+127	+1023	+16383
Exponent width in bits	8	11	15
Format width in bits	32	64	80

The standard requires that the single and double formats be normalized, so b_0 is always 1. The actual number of bits needed to represent the precisions 24 and 53 is therefore 23 and 52, respectively, because b_0 is chosen to be 1 implicitly.

Extended-double format need not be normalized, so it uses the full 64 bits for precision. A *bias* is added to all exponents so that only positive integer exponents occur. This expedites comparisons of exponent values. The stored exponent is actually:

$e = E + bias$

For more information, see:

▶ On floating-point representation, see Section 20.3 Native IEEE Floating-Point Representations.

▶ On using the Bitviewer tool, see Section 22.1.1.3 Viewing Floating-Point Representations with BitViewer.

▶ On reading or writing floating-point data other than native IEEE little endian data, see Chapter 23 Converting Unformatted Numeric Data.

22.1.1.3 *Viewing Floating-Point Representations with BitViewer*

You can view the binary representation of real numbers in single and double format with the BitViewer utility. This tool is accessed from the command line with the command BITVIEW. By default Visual Fortran installs the Bit-Viewer utility in the folder . . . \DF98\BIN.

Figure 22-1 shows the logical layout of the single and double formats. The figure shows the contents of each field, its width, and the location of the most significant bit (MSB) and the least significant bit (LSB).

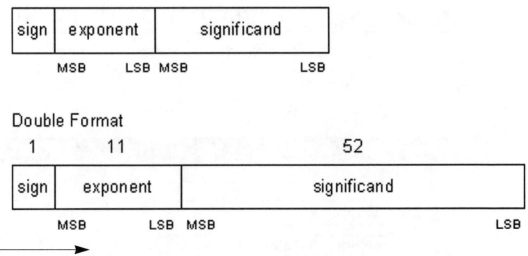

Figure 22–1 *Logical Structure of the IEEE Single and Double Formats*

To view floating-point numbers in BitViewer, open the Data Type menu, then choose Floating-Point Real (or use the F9 shortcut key). Set the precision by selecting one of the choices in the Bytes box. Four bytes, **REAL**(4), displays the number in single format (23-bit precision). Eight bytes, **REAL**(8), displays the number in double format (52-bit precision).

Figures 22-2 and Figure 22-3 show the BitViewer display of the memory storage for a 4-byte real number and an 8-byte real number, both equal to 12.6. In the double format display, the most significant part is on the bottom and the least significant 32 bits above.

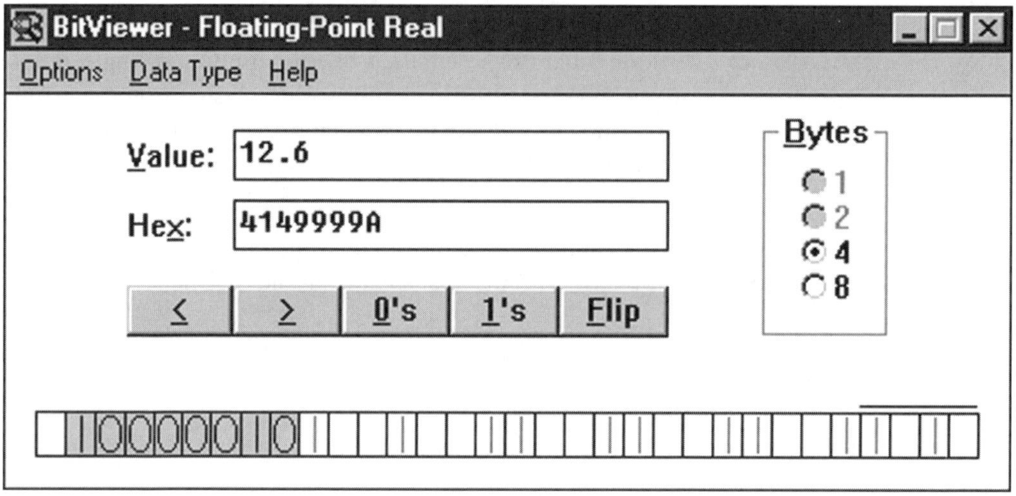

Figure 22–2   *Single Format in BitViewer*

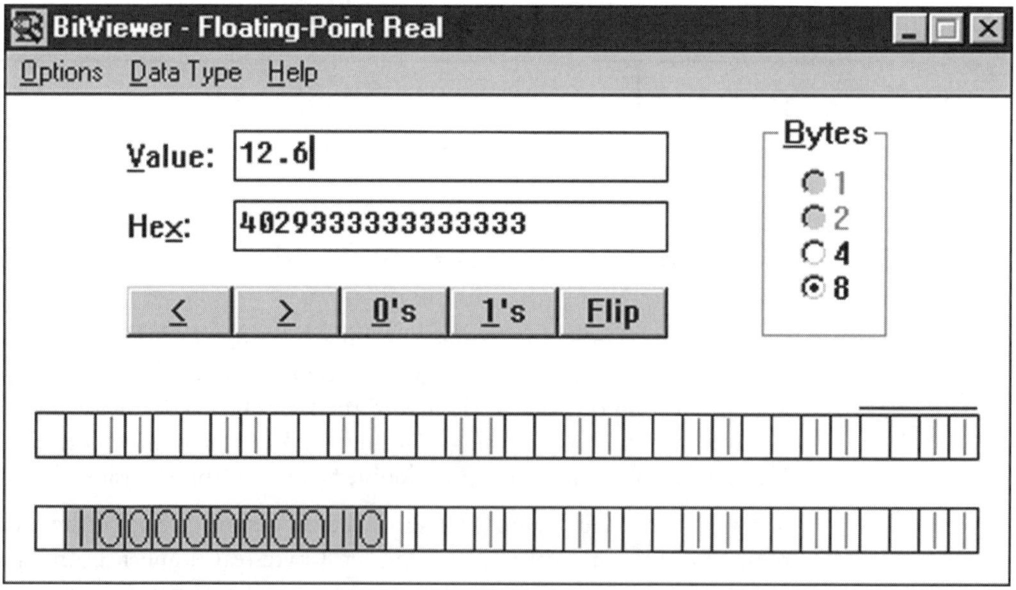

Figure 22–3   *Double Format in BitViewer*

Note: BitViewer lets you view and manipulate integer and character data as well as floating-point, and to translate between different data types. Refer to the BitViewer Help file for more information.

22.1.1.4 *Special Values*

Special cases of the exponent-significand combination represent four types of special values in addition to the normalized numbers. Table 22-2 shows all five types of values.

Table 22–2 *IEEE Floating-Point Values*

Name	Quantity	Exponent	Significand
Signed zero	$\pm\, 0$	$E = E_{min} - 1$	$sig = 0$
Denormalized number	$\pm\, 0 \cdot sig \times 2^{E_{min}}$	$E = E_{min} - 1$	sig not equal 0
Normalized number	$\pm\, 1 \cdot sig \times 2^{E}$	$E_{min} <= E <= E_{max}$	sig
Signed infinity	$\pm$ infinity	$E = E_{max} + 1$	$sig = 0$
Not a Number	NaN	$E = E_{max} + 1$	sig not equal 0

These special values are interpreted as follows:

▶ Signed zero

Visual Fortran treats zero as signed by default. The sign of zero is the same as the sign of a nonzero number. If you use the intrinsic function **SIGN** with zero as the second argument, the sign of the zero will be transferred. Comparisons, however, consider +0 to be equal to -0. A signed zero is useful in certain numerical analysis algorithms, but in most applications the sign of zero is invisible.

▶ Denormalized numbers

Denormalized numbers (denormals) fill the gap between the smallest positive number and the smallest negative number. Otherwise only (±) 0 occurs in that interval. Denormalized numbers permit gradual underflow for intermediate results calculated internally in extended-double format. A status flag (on *x86* systems, the precision bit in the FPU Status Word exception field) is set when a number loses precision due to denormalization.

▶ Signed infinity

Infinities are the result of arithmetic in the limiting case of operands with arbitrarily large magnitude. They provide a way to continue when an overflow occurs. The sign of an infinity is simply the sign you obtain for a finite number in the same operation as the finite number approaches an infinite value. By retrieving the status flags described in Section 22.3 Setting and Retrieving Floating-Point Status and Control Words (*x*86 Only), you can differentiate between an infinity that results from an overflow and one that results from division by zero. Visual Fortran treats infinity as signed by default. The output value of infinity is Infinity or -Infinity.

▶ Not a Number

Not a Number (NaN) results from an operation involving one or more invalid operands. For instance 0/0 and **SQRT**(-1) result in NaN. In general, an operation involving a NaN produces another NaN. Because the fraction of a NaN is unspecified, there are many possible NaNs. Visual Fortran treats all NaNs identically, but provide two different types:

• Signaling NAN, which has an initial fraction bit of 0 (zero).

• Quiet NaN, which has an initial fraction bit of 1.

The output value of NaN is NaN.

22.1.2 Retrieving Parameters of Numeric Representations

Visual Fortran includes several intrinsic functions that return details about the numeric representation. These are listed in Table 22-3 and described fully in the "A-Z Summary" in the *Language Reference* in Visual Fortran online Help.

Table 22–3 *Functions that Return Numeric Parameters*

Name	Description	Argument/Function Type
DIGITS	DIGITS(x). Returns number of significant digits for data of the same type as x.	x: Integer or Real result: INTEGER(4)
EPSILON	EPSILON(x). Returns the smallest positive number that when added to one produces a number greater than one for data of the same type as x.	x: Real result: same type as x
EXPONENT	EXPONENT(x). Returns the exponent part of the representation of x.	x: Real result: INTEGER(4)

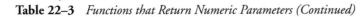

Table 22–3   *Functions that Return Numeric Parameters (Continued)*

Name	Description	Argument/Function Type
FRACTION	FRACTION(x). Returns the fractional part (significand) of the representation of x.	x: Real result: same type as x
HUGE	HUGE(x). Returns largest number that can be represented by data of type x.	x: Integer or Real result: same type as x
MAXEXPONENT	MAXEXPONENT(x). Returns the largest positive decimal exponent for data of the same type as x.	x: Real result: INTEGER(4)
MINEXPONENT	MINEXPONENT(x). Returns the largest negative decimal exponent for data of the same type as x.	x: Real result: INTEGER(4)
NEAREST	NEAREST(x, s). Returns the nearest different machine representable number to x in the direction of the sign of s.	x: Real s: Real and not zero result: same type as x
PRECISION	PRECISION(x). Returns the number of significant digits for data of the same type as x.	x: Real or Complex result: INTEGER(4)
RADIX	RADIX(x). Returns the base for data of the same type as x.	x: Integer or Real result: INTEGER(4)
RANGE	RANGE(x). Returns the decimal exponent range for data of the same type as x.	x: Integer, Real or Complex result: INTEGER(4)
RRSPACING	RRSPACING(x). Returns the reciprocal of the relative spacing of numbers near x.	x: Real result: same type as x
SCALE	SCALE(x, i). Multiplies x by 2 raised to the power of i.	x: Real i: Integer result: same type as x
SET_EXPONENT	SET_EXPONENT(x, i). Returns a number whose fractional part is x and whose exponential part is i.	x: Real i: Integer result: same type as x
SPACING	SPACING(x). Returns the absolute spacing of numbers near x.	x: Real result: same type as x
TINY	TINY(x). Returns smallest positive number that can be represented by data of type x.	x: Real result: same type as x

22.2   Loss of Precision Errors: Rounding, Special Values, Underflow, and Overflow

If a real number is not exactly one of the representable floating-point numbers, then the nearest floating-point number must represent it. The rounding error is the difference between the exact real number and its nearest floating-point representation. The floating-point number representing a rounded real number is called *inexact*.

Normally, calculations proceed when an inexact value results. Almost any floating-point operation can produce an inexact result. The rounding mode (round up, round down, round nearest, truncate) is determined by the floating-point control word.

If an arithmetic operation does not result in an exact, valid floating-point number, which includes numbers that have been rounded to an exactly representable floating-point number, it results in a special value: signed zero, signed infinity, NaN, or a denormal. Special-value results are a limiting case of the arithmetic operation involved. Special values can propagate through your arithmetic operations without causing your program to fail, and often providing usable results.

If an arithmetic operation results in an exact value, but the value is invalid, the operation causes underflow or overflow:

▶ Underflow occurs when an arithmetic result is too small for the math processor to handle. Depending on the setting of the /fpe compiler option, underflows are set to zero (they are usually harmless) or they are left as is (denormalized).

▶ Overflow occurs when an arithmetic result is too large for the math processor to handle. Overflows are more serious than underflows, and may indicate an error in the formulation of a problem (for example, unintended exponentiation of a large number by a large number). Overflows produce an appropriately signed infinity value.

Inexact numbers, special values, underflows, and overflows are floating-point exceptions. You can select how rounding is done and how exceptions are handled by setting the floating-point control word. Setting the control word is described in Section 22.3 Setting and Retrieving Floating-Point Status and Control Words (x86 Only) and exception handling in Section 22.4.1 Handling Floating-Point Exceptions.

For a further discussion of rounding errors, see Section 22.1.2 Rounding Errors.

22.2.1 Rounding Errors

Although the rounding error for one real number might be acceptably small in your calculations, at least two problems arise because of it. If you test for exact equality between what you consider to be two exact numbers, the rounding error of either or both floating-point representations of those numbers may prevent a successful comparison and produce spurious results. Also, when you calculate with floating-point numbers the rounding errors may accumulate to a meaningful loss of numerical significance.

Carefully consider the numerics of your solution to minimize rounding errors or their effects. You might benefit from using double-precision arithmetic or restructuring your algorithm, or both. For instance, if your calculations involve arrays of linear data items, you might reduce the loss of numerical significance by subtracting the mean value of each array from each array element and by normalizing each element of such an array to the standard deviation of the array elements.

The following code segment can execute differently on different systems and produce different results for n, x, and s. It also produces different results if you use the /fltconsistency or /nofltconsistency compiler options on *x*86 systems. Rounding error accumulates in x because the floating-point representation of 0.2 is inexact, then accumulates in s, and affects the final value for n:

```
      INTEGER n
      REAL s, x
      n = 0
      s = 0.
      x = 0.
1     n = n + 1
      x = x + 0.2
      s = s + x
      IF ( x .LE. 10. ) GOTO 1 ! Will you get 51 cycles?
      WRITE(*,*) 'n = ', n, '; x = ', x, '; s = ', s
```

This example illustrates a common coding problem: carrying a floating-point variable through many successive cycles and then using it to perform an **IF** test. This process is common in numerical integration. There are several remedies. You can compute x and s as multiples of an integer index, for example, replacing the statement that increments x with x = n * 0.2 to avoid round-off accumulation. You might test for completion on the integer index, such as IF (n <= 50) GOTO 1, or use a **DO** loop, such as DO n= 1,51. If you must test on the real variable that is being cycled, use a realistic tolerance, such as IF (x <= 10.001).

Floating-point arithmetic does not always obey the standard rules of algebra exactly. Addition is not precisely associative when round-off errors are considered. You can use parentheses to express the exact evaluation you require to compute a correct, accurate answer. This is recommended when you specify optimization for your generated code, since associativity may otherwise be unpredictable.

The expressions $(x + y) + z$ and $x + (y + z)$ can give unexpected results in some cases, as the Visual Fortran Sample ASSOCN.F90 in the . . .

`\DF98\SAMPLES\TUTORIAL` folder shows. This example demonstrates the danger of combining two numbers whose values differ by more than the number of significant digits.

The Sample INTERVAL.F90 in the . . . `\DF98\SAMPLES\TUTORIAL` folder shows how changing the rounding precision and rounding mode in the floating-point control word between calculations affects the calculated result of the following simple expression:

```
(q*r + s*t) / (u + v)
```

The Visual Fortran Sample EPSILON.F90 in the . . . `\DF98\SAM-PLES\TUTORIAL` folder illustrates difficulties that rounding errors can cause in expressions like 1.0 + eps, where eps is just significant compared to 1.0.

The compiler uses the default rounding mode (round-to-nearest) during compilation. The compiler performs more compile-time operations that eliminate run-time operations as the optimization level increases. If you set rounding mode to a different setting (other than round-to-nearest), that rounding mode is used only if that computation is performed at run-time. For example, the Sample INTERVAL.F90 is compiled at /optimize:0, which disables certain compile-time optimizations, including constant propagation and inlining.

For more information, see:

▶ Section 22.2.1.1 ULPs, Relative Error, and Machine Epsilon

▶ Section 4.1.64 /rounding_mode (Alpha Only)

22.2.1.1 ULPs, Relative Error, and Machine Epsilon

Several terms describe the magnitude of rounding error. A floating-point approximation to a real constant or to a computed result may err by as much as 1/2 unit in the last place (the bP-1 bit). The abbreviation *ULP* represents the measure "unit in the last place." Another measure of the rounding error uses the relative error, which is the difference between the exact number and its approximation divided by the exact number. The relative error that corresponds to 1/2 *ULP* is bounded by:

$$1/2 \ 2^{-P} <= 1/2 \ ULP <= 2^{-P}$$

The upper bound $EPS = 2^{-P}$, the machine epsilon, is commonly used in discussions of rounding errors because it expresses the smallest floating-point number that you can add to 1.0 with a result that does not round to 1.0.

Additional guard bits are included in floating-point hardware to allow rounding on the order of EPS . The result of any one floating-point operation is therefore tolerably imprecise, but the total error that results from many such operations on propagated numbers accumulates unavoidably.

22.3 Setting and Retrieving Floating-Point Status and Control Words (x86 Only)

The FPU (floating-point unit) on *x*86 systems contains eight floating-point registers the system uses for numeric calculations, for status and control words, and for error pointers. You normally need to consider only the status and control words, and then only when customizing your floating-point environment.

The FPU status and control words correspond to 16-bit registers whose bits hold the value of a state of the FPU or control its operation. Visual Fortran defines a set of symbolic constants to set and reset the proper bits in the status and control words. For example:

```
USE DFLIB
CALL SETCONTROLFPQQ(FPCW$OVERFLOW .AND. FPCW$CHOP)
! set the floating-point control word to allow overflows
! and to round by truncation
```

The status and control symbolic constants (such as FPCW$OVERFLOW and FPCW$CHOP in the preceding example) are defined as **INTEGER**(2) parameters in the module DFLIB.F90 in the . . . \DF98\INCLUDE folder. The status and control words are made of logical combinations (such as with .AND.) of different parameters for different FPU options.

The name of a symbolic constant takes the general form *name$option*. Table 22-4 lists the prefix *names*.

Table 22–4   *Prefixes for Parameter Flags*

name	Meaning
FPSW	Floating-point status word
FPCW	Floating-point control word
SIG	Signal
FPE	Floating-point exception
MTH	Math function

The suffix *option* is one of the options available for that *name*. The parameter *name$option* corresponds either to a status or control option (for example, FPSW$ZERODIVIDE, a status word parameter that shows whether a zero-divide exception has occured or not) or *name$option* corresponds to a mask, which sets all symbolic constants to 1 for all the options of *name*. You can use the masks in logical functions (such as **IAND**, **IOR**, and **NOT**) to set or to clear all options for the specified *name*. The following sections define the *option*s and illustrate their use with examples.

You can control the floating-point processor options (on *x86* systems) and find out its status with the run-time library routines **GETSTATUSFPQQ** (*x86* only), **GETCONTROLFPQQ** (*x86* only), **SETCONTROLFPQQ** (*x86* only), and **MATHERRQQ** (*x86* only). Examples of using these routines also appear in the following sections.

For more information, see:

▶ Section 22.3.1 Floating-Point Status Word (*x86* Only)

▶ Section 22.3.2 Floating-Point Control Word (*x86* Only)

22.3.1 Floating-Point Status Word (x86 Only)

On *x86* systems, the FPU status word includes bits that show the floating-point exception state of the processor. The status word parameters describe six exceptions: invalid result, denormalized result, zero divide, overflow, underflow and inexact precision. These are described in Section 22.2 Loss of Precision Errors: Rounding, Special Values, Underflow, and Overflow.

When one of the bits is set to 1, it means a past floating-point operation produced that exception type. (Visual Fortran initially clears all status bits. It does not reset the status bits before performing additional floating-point operations after an exception occurs. The status bits accumulate.)

Table 22-5 shows the floating-point exception status parameters:

Table 22–5   *Floating-Point Exception Status Parameters*

Parameter Name	Value in Hex	Description
FPSW$MSW_EM	#003F	Status Mask (set all bits to 1)
FPSW$INVALID	#0001	An invalid result occurred
FPSW$DENORMAL	#0002	A denormal (very small number) occurred
FPSW$ZERODIVIDE	#0004	A divide by zero occurred

Table 22–5   *Floating-Point Exception Status Parameters (Continued)*

Parameter Name	Value in Hex	Description
FPSW$OVERFLOW	#0008	An overflow occurred
FPSW$UNDERFLOW	#0010	An underflow occurred
FPSW$INEXACT	#0020	Inexact precision occurred

You can find out which exceptions have occurred by retrieving the status word and comparing it to the exception parameters. For example:

```
USE DFLIB
INTEGER(2) status
CALL GETSTATUSFPQQ(status)
IF ((status .AND. FPSW$INEXACT) > 0) THEN
    WRITE (*, *) "Inexact precision has occurred"
ELSE IF ((status .AND. FPSW$DENORMAL) > 0) THEN
    WRITE (*, *) "Denormal occurred"
END IF
```

22.3.2 Floating-Point Control Word (x86 Only)

On *x*86 systems, the FPU control word includes bits that control the FPU's precision, rounding mode, and whether exceptions generate signals if they occur. You can read the control word value with **GETCONTROLFPQQ** (*x*86 only) to find out the current control settings, and you can change the control word with **SETCONTROLFPQQ** (*x*86 only).

Each bit in the floating-point control word corresponds to a mode of the floating-point math processor. The DFLIB.F90 module file in the . . . \DF98\INCLUDE folder contains the **INTEGER**(2) parameters defined for the control word, as shown in Table 22-6.

Table 22–6   *Floating-Point Exception Status Parameters*

Parameter Name	Value in Hex	Description
FPCW$MCW_IC	#1000	Infinity control mask
FPCW$AFFINE	#1000	Affine infinity
FPCW$PROJECTIVE	#0000	Projective infinity
FPCW$MCW_PC	#0300	Precision control mask
FPCW$64	#0300	64-bit precision

Table 22–6 *Floating-Point Exception Status Parameters (Continued)*

Parameter Name	Value in Hex	Description
FPCW$53	#0200	53-bit precision
FPCW$24	#0000	24-bit precision
FPCW$MCW_RC	#0C00	Rounding control mask
FPCW$CHOP	#0C00	Truncate
FPCW$UP	#0800	Round up
FPCW$DOWN	#0400	Round down
FPCW$NEAR	#0000	Round to nearest
FPCW$MCW_EM	#003F	Exception mask
FPCW$INVALID	#0001	Allow invalid numbers
FPCW$DENORMAL	#0002	Allow denormals (very small numbers)
FPCW$ZERODIVIDE	#0004	Allow divide by zero
FPCW$OVERFLOW	#0008	Allow overflow
FPCW$UNDERFLOW	#0010	Allow underflow
FPCW$INEXACT	#0020	Allow inexact precision

The control word defaults are:

▶ 53-bit precision

▶ Round to nearest (rounding mode)

▶ The denormal, underflow, overflow, invalid, and inexact precision exceptions are disabled (do not generate an exception). To change exception handling, you can use the /fpe compiler option or the **FOR_SET_FPE** routine.

For more information (*x*86 only), see:

▶ Section 22.3.2.1 Exception Parameters

▶ Section 22.3.2.2 Precision Parameters

▶ Section 22.3.2.3 Rounding Parameters

22.3.2.1 *Exception Parameters*

An exception is disabled if its bit is set to 1 and enabled if its bit is cleared to 0. If an exception is disabled (exceptions can be disabled by setting the flags to

1 with **SETCONTROLFPQQ** (*x*86 only)), it will not generate an interrupt signal if it occurs. The floating-point process will return an appropriate special value (for example, NaN or signed infinity), but the program continues. You can find out which exceptions (if any) occurred by calling **GETSTATUS-FPQQ** (*x*86 only).

If errors on floating-point exceptions are enabled (by clearing the flags to 0 with **SETCONTROLFPQQ** (*x*86 only)), the operating system generates an interrupt when the exception occurs. By default these interrupts cause run-time errors, but you can capture the interrupts with **SIGNALQQ** and branch to your own error-handling routines.

You should remember not to clear all existing settings when changing one. The values you want to change should be combined with the existing control word in an inclusive-**OR** operation (**OR**, **IOR**, .OR.) if you don't want to reset all options. For example:

```
USE DFLIB
INTEGER(2) control, newcontrol
CALL GETCONTROLFPQQ(control)
newcontrol = (control .OR. FPCW$INVALID)
! Invalid exception set (disabled).
CALL SETCONTROLFPQQ(newcontrol)
```

22.3.2.2 Precision Parameters

On *x*86 systems, the precision bits control the precision to which the FPU rounds floating-point numbers. For example:

```
USE DFLIB
INTEGER(2) control, holdcontrol, newcontrol
CALL GETCONTROLFPQQ(control)
! Clear any existing precision flags.
holdcontrol = (control .AND. (.NOT. FPCW$MCW_PC))
newcontrol = holdcontrol .OR. FPCW$64
! Set precision to 64 bits.
CALL SETCONTROLFPQQ(newcontrol)
```

The precision options are mutually exclusive. If you set more than one, you may get an invalid mode or a mode other than the one you want. Therefore, you should clear the precision bits before setting a new precision mode.

22.3.2.3 Rounding Parameters

On *x*86 systems, the rounding flags control the method of rounding that the FPU uses. For example:

```
USE DFLIB
INTEGER(2) control, clearcontrol, newcontrol
```

```
CALL GETCONTROLFPQQ(control)
! Clear any existing rounding flags.
clearcontrol = (control .AND. (.NOT. FPCW$MCW_RC))
newcontrol = clearcontrol .OR. FPCW$UP
! Set rounding mode to round up.
CALL SETCONTROLFPQQ(newcontrol)
```

The rounding options are mutually exclusive. If you set more than one, you may get an invalid mode or a mode other than the one you want. Therefore, you should clear the rounding bits before setting a new rounding mode.

On Alpha systems, you can use the /rounding_mode (Alpha only) compiler option to control the rounding mode.

22.4   Handling Arithmetic Exceptions

Two levels of arithmetic exceptions occur in Visual Fortran. Low-level exceptions result from floating-point exceptions. High-level exceptions result from arithmetic errors that occur during execution of the mathematical functions. You have some flexibility in handling each type of exception.

The following sections describe:

▶ Section 22.4.1 Floating-Point Exceptions

▶ Section 22.4.2 Handling Run-Time Math Exceptions (*x86* only)

22.4.1   Handling Floating-Point Exceptions

If a floating-point exception is disabled (set to 1), it will not generate an interrupt signal if it occurs. The floating-point process will return an appropriate special value (for example, NaN or signed infinity), and the program will continue. If a floating-point exception is enabled (set to 0), it will generate an interrupt signal (software interrupt) if it occurs. Table 22-7 lists the floating-point exception signals.

Table 22–7   *Floating-Point Exception Signal Parameters*

Parameter Name	Value in Hex	Description
FPE$INVALID	#81	Invalid result
FPE$DENORMAL	#82	Denormal operand
FPE$ZERODIVIDE	#83	Divide by zero
FPE$OVERFLOW	#84	Overflow

Table 22–7   *Floating-Point Exception Signal Parameters (Continued)*

Parameter Name	Value in Hex	Description
FPE$UNDERFLOW	#85	Underflow
FPE$INEXACT	#86	Inexact precision

If a floating-point exception interrupt occurs and you do not have an exception handling routine, the run-time system will respond to the interrupt according to the behavior selected by the compiler options /fpe and /math_library. Remember, interrupts only occur if an exception is enabled (set to 0).

If you do not want the default system exception handling, you need to write your own interrupt handling routine:

▶ Write a function that performs whatever special behavior you require on the interrupt.

▶ Register that function as the procedure to be called on that interrupt with **SIGNALQQ**.

Note that your interrupt handling routine must use the **ATTRIBUTES** C directive.

The drawback of writing your own routine is that your exception-handling routine cannot return to the process that caused the exception. This is because when your exception-handling routine is called, the floating-point processor is in an error condition, and if your routine returns, the processor is in the same state, which will cause a system termination. Your exception-handling routine can therefore either branch to another separate program unit or exit (after saving your program state and printing an appropriate message). You cannot return to a different statement in the program unit that caused the exception-handling routine, because a global **GOTO** does not exist, and you cannot reset the status word in the floating-point processor.

If you need to know when exceptions occur and also must continue if they do, you must disable exceptions so they do not cause an interrupt, then poll the floating-point status word at intervals with **GETSTATUSFPQQ** (*x*86 only) to see if any exceptions occurred. Obviously, this creates processing overhead for your program. In general, you will want to allow the program to terminate if there is an exception. An example of an exception-handling routine follows. The exception-handling routine hand_fpe and the program that invokes it are both contained in SIGTEST.F90 in the Visual Fortran Samples folder . . . \DF98\SAMPLES\TUTORIAL. The comments at the beginning of the SIGTEST.F90 file describe how to compile this example.

```
! SIGTEST.F90
!Establish the name of the exception handler as the
! function to be invoked if an exception happens.
! The exception handler hand_fpe is attached below.
  USE DFLIB
    INTERFACE
      FUNCTION hand_fpe (sigid, except)
        !DEC$ ATTRIBUTES C :: hand_fpe
        INTEGER(4) hand_fpe
        INTEGER(2) sigid, except
      END FUNCTION
    END INTERFACE

INTEGER(4) iret
REAL(4) r1, r2
r1 = 0.0
iret = SIGNALQQ(SIG$FPE, hand_fpe)
WRITE(*,*) 'Set exception handler. Return = ', iret
! Cause divide by zero exception
r1 = 0.0
r2 = 3/r1
END

! Exception handler routine hand_fpe
  FUNCTION hand_fpe (signum, excnum)
    !DEC$ ATTRIBUTES C :: hand_fpe
    USE DFLIB
    INTEGER(2) signum, excnum
    WRITE(*,*) 'In signal handler for SIG$FPE'
    WRITE(*,*) 'signum = ', signum
    WRITE(*,*) 'exception = ', excnum
    SELECT CASE(excnum)
      CASE( FPE$INVALID )
        STOP ' Floating point exception: Invalid number'
      CASE( FPE$DENORMAL )
        STOP ' Floating point exception: Denormalized number'
      CASE( FPE$ZERODIVIDE )
        STOP ' Floating point exception: Zero divide'
      CASE( FPE$OVERFLOW )
        STOP ' Floating point exception: Overflow'
      CASE( FPE$UNDERFLOW )
        STOP ' Floating point exception: Underflow'
      CASE( FPE$INEXACT )
        STOP ' Floating point exception: Inexact precision'
      CASE DEFAULT
        STOP ' Floating point exception: Non-IEEE type'
    END SELECT
    hand_fpe = 1
    END
```

22.4.2   Handling Run-Time Math Exceptions (x86 Only)

On *x*86 systems, the run-time subroutine **MATHERRQQ** (*x*86 Only) handles floating-point exceptions that occur in the math functions, such as **SIN** and **LOG10**.

If you use the default version of **MATHERRQQ**, which the linker automatically includes in your executable program, then math exceptions result in a standard run-time error (such as `forrtl : severe (nnnn) : sqrt : domain error`). If you want to alter the behavior of one or more math exceptions, you need to provide your own version of **MATHERRQQ**. You have more flexibility in the way you handle run-time math exceptions than floating-point exceptions, because your error handling routine can return to the program unit that caused the exception.

The module DFLIB.F90 in the `. . . \DF98\INCLUDE` folder contains the definitions of the run-time math exceptions. These are listed in Table 22-8.

Table 22–8   *Run-Time Math Exceptions*

Parameter Name	Value	Description
MTH$E_DOMAIN	1	Argument domain error
MTH$E_SINGULARITY	2	Argument singularity
MTH$E_OVERFLOW	3	Overflow range error
MTH$E_UNDERFLOW	4	Underflow range error
MTH$E_TLOSS	5	Total loss of precision
MTH$E_PLOSS	6	Partial loss of precision

A domain error means that an argument is outside the math function's domain, for example, **SQRT** (-1). A singularity error means that an argument is a singularity value for the math function, and the result is not defined for that value, for example, **LOG10**(0.0). Overflow and underflow errors are the same as floating-point counterparts, and precision loss the same as floating-point inexact results.

You can write a **MATHERRQQ** subroutine that resolves errors generated by math functions. Your **MATHERRQQ** can issue a warning, assign a default value if an error occurs, or take other action. If you do not provide your own **MATHERRQQ** subroutine, a default **MATHERRQQ** provided with the floating-point library will terminate the program. The following gives an example of an alternative **MATHERRQQ** subroutine (in MATHERR.F90 in the . . . /DF98/SAMPLES/TUTORIAL folder):

```fortran
SUBROUTINE MATHERRQQ( name, length, info, retcode)
  USE DFLIB
  INTEGER(2) length, retcode
  CHARACTER(length) name
  RECORD /MTH$E_INFO/ info
  PRINT *, "Entered MATHERRQQ"
  PRINT *, "Failing function is: ", name
  PRINT *, "Error type is: ", info.errcode
  IF ((info.ftype == TY$REAL4 ).OR.(info.ftype == TY$REAL8)) THEN
      PRINT *, "Type: REAL"
      PRINT *, "Enter the desired function result: "
      READ(*,*) info.r8res
      retcode = 1
  ELSE IF ((info.ftype == TY$CMPLX8 ).OR.(info.ftype == TY$CMPLX16)) THEN
      PRINT *, "Type: COMPLEX"
      PRINT *, "Enter the desired function result: "
      READ(*,*) info.c16res
      retcode = 1
  END IF
END
```

The following is a Visual Fortran Sample program (MATHTEST.F90 in the . . . /DF98/SAMPLES/TUTORIAL folder) that causes **MATHERQQ** to be called:

```fortran
REAL(4) r1, r2 /-1.0/
REAL(8) r3, r4 /-1.0/
COMPLEX(4) c1, c2 /(0.0, 0.0)/
r1 = LOG(r2)
r3 = SQRT(r4)
c1 = CLOG(c2)

WRITE(*, *) r1
WRITE(*, *) r3
WRITE(*, *) c1
END
```

22.5   Intel Pentium Floating-Point Flaw (x86 Only)

Certain versions of the Intel® Pentium® processor have a flaw in rare floating-point division operations, which can also manifest itself in floating-point **TAN**, **ATAN**, and **MOD** operations. Since the number of input cases that cause this problem is very small and the associated error in the results is also very small, it is unlikely that you will ever see a problem due to this flaw. It has been estimated that only 1 out of 9 billion operations will produce even the slightest inaccuracy.

To request a check for a flawed Pentium chip, you can use the default compiler option /check:flawed_pentium option on code you suspect demonstrates the Pentium flaw, such as the code shown below. This compiler option generates run-time calls to the run-time routine **FOR_CHECK_FLAWED_PENTIUM**. The default, /check:flawed_pentium, *does* issue a run-time error message for this condition and stops program execution. To allow program execution to continue when this condition occurs, set the environment variable FOR_RUN_FLAWED_PENTIUM to true and rerun the program (see Section 21.5 Run-Time Environment Variables).

Visual Fortran does not include a software workaround for the flawed Pentium problems, and these operations could produce incorrect results on a flawed Pentium processor.

To determine if you have a flawed Pentium, you can run the following program with the /check:flawed_pentium compiler option:

```
PROGRAM go
REAL(8) op1, op2
COMMON /divide_check/ op1, op2
DATA op1 /3145727.0/, op2 /4195835.0/
IF( op2/op1 > 1.3338 ) THEN
  PRINT *,'This computer always divides correctly.'
ELSE
  PRINT *,'This computer can have divide problems.'
ENDIF
END
```

If you compile and run this program without any compiler options (the default is /check:flawed_pentium), a run-time error occurs when it is run on a flawed Pentium system.

Your operating system can also work around flawed Pentium processors by using software emulation for floating-point operations. Refer to your operating system documentation for more information. If the operating system has been configured for software emulation, then all floating-point operations in Visual Fortran will always operate correctly, including the above program. Note that the performance cost of an operating system fix can be very high, and if your program is run on another machine without the same operating system fix, it will execute incorrectly.

If you distribute software that is susceptible to the floating-point problems of a flawed Pentium, and want your program to halt if it is run on a system with such a processor, you can check the processor when your application starts. To do this, convert the program above into a simple subroutine, call the subroutine at the start of your application, and use the **STOP** statement to stop the application before it begins if a flawed Pentium processor is detected. If you distribute your software, you should compile it with the /check:flawed_pentium compiler option.

All the run-time libraries that come with Visual Fortran have been compiled to be safe with respect to the Pentium divide and **MOD** problems.

For more information on the Intel Pentium flaw, or to request a replacement Pentium processor, you can contact Intel in the US at 1-800-628-8686.

23

Converting Unformatted Numeric Data

This chapter describes how you can use Digital Visual Fortran to read and write nonnative unformatted numeric data, including Digital Fortran for OpenVMS systems numeric data.

The following topics are discussed:

▶ Section 23.1 Supported Native and Nonnative Numeric Formats

▶ Section 23.2 Limitations of Numeric Conversion

▶ Section 23.3 Methods of Specifying the Data Format

▶ Section 23.4 Additional Notes on Nonnative Data

23.1 Supported Native and Nonnative Numeric Formats

Digital Visual Fortran supports the little endian floating-point formats shown in Table 23-1.

Table 23–1 *Little Endian Floating-Point Formats*

Floating-Point Size	Format in Memory
REAL(KIND=4), COMPLEX(KIND=4)	IEEE S_floating
REAL(KIND=8), COMPLEX(KIND=8)	IEEE T_floating

If your program needs to read or write unformatted data files containing a floating-point format that differs from the format in memory for that data size, you can request that the unformatted data be converted.

Data storage in different computers uses a convention of either little endian or big endian storage. The storage convention generally applies to numeric values that span multiple bytes, as follows:

▶ Little endian storage occurs when:

- The least significant bit (LSB) value is in the byte with the lowest address.

- The most significant bit (MSB) value is in the byte with the highest address.

- The address of the numeric value is the byte containing the LSB. Subsequent bytes with higher addresses contain more significant bits.

▶ Big endian storage occurs when:

- The least significant bit (LSB) value is in the byte with the highest address.

- The most significant bit (MSB) value is in the byte with the lowest address.

- The address of the numeric value is the byte containing the MSB. Subsequent bytes with higher addresses contain less significant bits.

Figure 23-1 shows the difference between the two byte-ordering schemes.

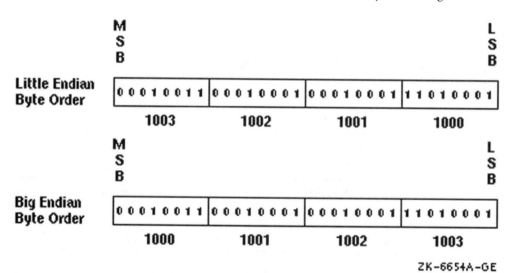

Figure 23–1 *Little and Big Endian Storage of an INTEGER Value*

Moving unformatted data files between big endian and little endian computers requires that the data be converted.

Visual Fortran provides the capability for programs to read and write unformatted data (originally written using unformatted I/O statements) in several nonnative floating-point formats and in big endian **INTEGER** or floating-point format. Supported nonnative floating-point formats include Digital VAX™ little endian floating-point formats supported by VAX FORTRAN™, standard IEEE® big endian floating-point format found on most Sun Microsystems® systems and IBM® RISC System/6000 systems, IBM floating-point formats (associated with the IBM's System/370 and similar systems), and CRAY® floating-point formats.

Converting unformatted data instead of formatted data is generally faster and is less likely to lose precision of floating-point numbers.

The native memory format includes little endian integers and little endian IEEE floating-point formats, S_float for **REAL**(KIND=4) and **COMPLEX**(KIND=4) declarations and T_float for **REAL** (KIND=8) and **COMPLEX**(KIND=8) declarations.

The keywords for supported nonnative unformatted file formats and their data types are listed in Table 23-2.

Table 23–2 *Nonnative Numeric Formats, Keywords, and Supported Data Types*

Keyword	Description
BIG_ENDIAN	Big endian integer data of the appropriate size (one, two, or four bytes) and big endian IEEE floating-point (REAL(KIND=4), REAL(KIND=8), COMPLEX(KIND=4), COMPLEX(KIND=8)) formats of the appropriate size for either real or complex numbers. INTEGER(KIND=1) data is the same for little endian and big endian.
CRAY	Big endian integer data of the appropriate size (one, two, four, or on Alpha systems, eight bytes) and big endian CRAY proprietary floating-point format of size REAL(KIND=8) or COMPLEX(KIND=8).
FDX	Little endian integer data of the appropriate size (one, two, four, or on Alpha systems, eight bytes) and Digital VAX floating-point data of format F_floating for REAL(KIND=4) or COMPLEX(KIND=4), and D_Floating for REAL(KIND=8) or COMPLEX(KIND=8).
FGX	Little endian integer data of the appropriate size (one, two, four, or on Alpha systems, eight bytes) and Digital VAX floating-point data of format F_floating for REAL(KIND=4) or COMPLEX(KIND=4), and G_Floating for REAL(KIND=8) or COMPLEX(KIND=8).

Table 23–2 *Nonnative Numeric Formats, Keywords, and Supported Data Types (Continued)*

Keyword	Description
IBM	Big endian integer data of the appropriate size (one, two, or four bytes) and big endian IBM proprietary floating-point format of size REAL(KIND=4) or COMPLEX(KIND=4) or size REAL(KIND=8) or COMPLEX(KIND=8).
LITTLE_ENDIAN	Native little endian integers of the appropriate size (one, two, four, or on Alpha systems, eight bytes) and native little endian IEEE floating-point data of the appropriate size and type (REAL(KIND=4), REAL(KIND=8), COMPLEX(KIND=4), COMPLEX(KIND=8)). These are the same formats as stored in memory. For additional information on supported ranges for these data types, see Section 20.3 Native IEEE Floating-Point Representations.
NATIVE	No conversion occurs between memory and disk. This is the default for unformatted files.
VAXD	Little endian integers of the appropriate size (one, two, four, or on Alpha systems, eight bytes) and Digital VAX floating-point format F_floating for size REAL(KIND=4) or COMPLEX(KIND=4), and D_floating for size REAL(KIND=8) or COMPLEX(KIND=8).
VAXG	Little endian integers of the appropriate size (one, two, four, or on Alpha systems, eight bytes) and Digital VAX floating-point format F_floating for size REAL(KIND=4) or COMPLEX(KIND=4), and G_floating for size REAL(KIND=8) or COMPLEX(KIND=8).

When reading a nonnative format, the nonnative format on disk is converted to native format in memory. If a converted nonnative value is outside the range of the native data type, a run-time message is displayed.

23.2 Limitations of Numeric Conversion

The Digital Visual Fortran floating-point conversion solution is not expected to fulfill all floating-point conversion needs.

For instance, data in record structure variables (specified in a **STRUCTURE** statement; a Digital Fortran language extension) are not converted. When they are later examined as separate fields by the program, they will remain in the binary format they were stored in on disk, unless the program is modified. With **EQUIVALENCE** statements, the data type of the variable named in the I/O statement is used.

If a program reads an I/O record containing multiple format floating-point fields into a single variable (such as an array) instead of their respective variables, the fields will not be converted. When they are later examined as separate fields by the program, they will remain in the binary format they were stored in on disk, unless the program is modified.

The conversion of the following file structure types are *not* supported:

▶ Binary data (FORM='BINARY')

▶ Formatted data (FORM='FORMATTED')

▶ Unformatted data (FORM='UNFORMATTED') written by Microsoft Fortran PowerStation or by Visual Fortran with the /fpscomp:ioformat compiler option in effect.

23.3   Methods of Specifying the Data Format

There are four methods of specifying a nonnative numeric format for unformatted data. If none of these methods are specified, the native LITTLE_ENDIAN format is assumed (no conversion occurs between disk and memory).

Any keyword listed in Section 23.1 Supported Native and Nonnative Numeric Formats can be used with any of these methods.

The four methods you can use to specify the type of nonnative (or native) format are:

▶ Setting an environment variable for a specific unit number before the file is opened. The environment variable is named FORT_CONVERT*n*, where *n* is the unit number.

▶ Compiling the program with an **OPTIONS** statement that specifies the /CONVERT=*keyword* qualifier. This method affects all unit numbers using unformatted data specified by the program.

▶ Specifying the CONVERT keyword in the **OPEN** statement for a specific unit number.

▶ Compiling the program with the appropriate compiler option (DF command /convert: *keyword* or visual development environment equivalent), which affects all unit numbers that use unformatted data specified by the program.

If you specify more than one method, the order of precedence when you open a file with unformatted data is to:

1. Check for an environment variable

2. Check the **OPEN** statement CONVERT specifier

3. Check whether an **OPTIONS** statement with a /CONVERT=*keyword* qualifier was present when the program was compiled

4. Check whether the compiler option /convert:*keyword* was present when the program was compiled

The following sections describe each method:

▶ Section 23.3.1 Environment Variable FORT_CONVERT*n* Method

▶ Section 23.3.2 OPEN Statement CONVERT Method

▶ Section 23.3.3 OPTIONS Statement Method

▶ Section 23.3.4 Compiler Option/convert Method

23.3.1 Environment Variable FORT_CONVERT*n* Method

You can use this method to specify multiple formats in a single program, usually one format for each specified unit number. You specify the numeric format at run time by setting the appropriate environment variable before an implicit or explicit **OPEN** to that unit number.

When the appropriate environment variable is set when you open the file, the environment variable is always used because this method takes precedence over the other methods. For instance, you might use this method to specify that a unit number will use a particular format instead of the format specified in the program (perhaps for a one-time file conversion).

For example, assume you have a previously compiled program that reads numeric data from unit 28 and writes it to unit 29 using unformatted I/O statements. You want the program to read nonnative big endian (IEEE floating-point) format from unit 28 and write that data in native little endian format to unit 29. In this case, the data is converted from big endian IEEE format to native little endian IEEE memory format (S_float and T_float) when read from unit 28, and then written without conversion in native little endian IEEE format to unit 29.

Without requiring source code modification or recompilation of this program, the following command sequence sets the appropriate environment variables before running the program (c: \users\leslie\convieee.exe):

```
set FORT_CONVERT28=BIG_ENDIAN
set FORT_CONVERT29=NATIVE
c:\users\leslie\convieee.exe
```

Figure 23-2 shows the data formats used on disk and in memory when the example file c: \users\leslie\convieee.exe is run after the environment variables are set.

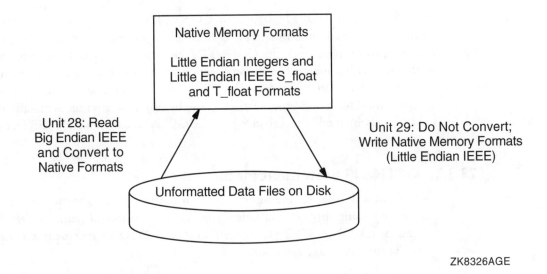

ZK8326AGE

Figure 23–2 *Sample Unformatted File Conversion*

23.3.2 OPEN Statement CONVERT Method

You can use this method to specify multiple formats in a single program, usually one format for each specified unit number. This method requires an explicit file **OPEN** statement to specify the numeric format of the file for that unit number. The CONVERT keyword for **OPEN** is a Digital Fortran language extension.

This method takes precedence over the **OPTIONS** statement and the compiler option /convert:*keyword* method, but has a lower precedence than the environment variable method.

For example, the following source code shows how the **OPEN** statement would be coded to read unformatted VAXD numeric data from unit 15, which might be processed and possibly written in native little endian format to unit 20 (the absence of the CONVERT keyword or environment variable FORT_CONVERT20 indicates native little endian data for unit 20):

```
OPEN (CONVERT='VAXD', FILE='graph3.dat', FORM='UNFORMATTED',
UNIT=15)
  .
  .
  .
OPEN (FILE='graph3_t.dat', FORM='UNFORMATTED', UNIT=20)
```

A hard-coded **OPEN** statement CONVERT keyword value cannot be changed after compile time. However, to allow selection of a particular format at run time, equate the CONVERT keyword to a variable and provide the user with a menu that allows selection of the appropriate format (menu choice sets the variable) before the **OPEN** occurs. You can also select a particular format for a unit number at run time by using the environment variable method, which takes precedence over the **OPEN** statement CONVERT keyword method.

23.3.3 OPTIONS Statement Method

You can only specify one numeric file format for all unformatted file unit numbers using this method unless you also use the logical name or **OPEN** statement CONVERT keyword method. The **OPTIONS** statement is a Digital Fortran language extension.

You specify the numeric format at compile time and must compile all routines under the same **OPTIONS** statement /CONVERT=*keyword* qualifier. You can use one source program and compile it using different DF commands to create multiple executable programs that each read a certain format.

The environment variable or **OPEN** statement CONVERT keyword methods take precedence over this method. For instance, you might use the logical name or **OPEN** CONVERT keyword method to specify each unit number that will use a format other than that specified using the DF option method. This method takes precedence over the DF /convert:*keyword* compiler option method.

You can use **OPTIONS** statements to specify the appropriate floating-point formats (in memory and in unformatted files) instead of using the corresponding DF command qualifiers. For example, to use VAX F_floating and G_floating as the unformatted file format, specify the following **OPTIONS** statement:

```
OPTIONS /CONVERT=VAXG
```

Because this method affects all unit numbers, you cannot read data in one format and write it in another format unless you use it in combination with the logical name method or the **OPEN** statement CONVERT keyword method to specify a different format for a particular unit number.

For more information, see the **OPTIONS** statement in the "A-Z Summary" in the *Language Reference* in Visual Fortran online Help.

23.3.4 Compiler Option /convert Method

You can only specify one numeric format for all unformatted file unit numbers using the compiler option /convert method unless you also use one (or both) of the previous methods. You specify the numeric format at compile time and must compile all routines under the same /convert:*keyword* compiler option, which is listed under the Compatibility category in the visual development environment, Fortran tab. You could use the same source program and compile it using different DF commands (or the equivalent in the visual development environment) to create multiple executable programs that each read a certain format.

If you specify other methods, they take precedence over this method. For instance, you might use the environment variable or **OPEN** statement CONVERT keyword method to specify each unit number that will use a format different than that specified using the DF /convert:*keyword* compiler option method for all other unit numbers.

For example, the following command compiles program file.for to use VAX D_floating (and F_floating) floating-point data for all unit numbers (unless superseded by one of the other methods). Data is converted between the file format and the little endian memory format (little endian integers, S_float and T_float little endian IEEE floating-point format). The created file, vconvert.exe, can then be run:

```
DF file.for /convert:vaxd /link /out:vconvert.exe
```

Because this method affects all unformatted file unit numbers, you cannot read data in one format and write it in another file format using the /convert:*keyword* compiler option method alone. You can if you use it in combination with the environment variable method or the **OPEN** statement CONVERT keyword method to specify a different format for a particular unit number.

For more information, see Section 4.1.14 /convert.

23.4 Additional Notes on Nonnative Data

The following notes apply to porting nonnative data:

▶ When porting source code along with the unformatted data, vendors might use different units for specifying the record length (RECL specifier) of unformatted files. While formatted files are specified in units of characters (bytes), unformatted files are specified in longword units for Digital Fortran (default) and some other vendors.

To allow you to specify the RECL units (bytes or longwords) for unformatted files without source file modification, use the /assume:byterecl compiler option (in the visual development environment, this is available in the Project menu Settings item, Fortran tab, Fortran Data category).

The Fortran 90 standard (American National Standard Fortran 90, ANSI X3.198-1991, and International Standards Organization standard ISO/IEC 1539:1991), in Section 9.3.4.5, states: "If the file is being connected for unformatted input/output, the length is measured in processor-dependent units."

▶ Certain vendors apply different **OPEN** statement defaults to determine the record type. The default record type (RECORDTYPE) with Digital Fortran depends on the values for the ACCESS and FORM specifiers for the **OPEN** statement (described in the "A-Z Summary" in the *Language Reference* in Visual Fortran online Help).

▶ Certain vendors use a different identifier for the logical data types, such as hex FF instead of 01 to denote "true."

▶ Source code being ported may be coded specifically for big endian use.

24

Using the IMSL Mathematical and Statistical Libraries

The Professional Edition of Visual Fortran includes the IMSL™ libraries, a collection of nearly 1000 mathematical and statistical functions easily accessible from the Microsoft visual development environment.

The IMSL libraries are installed with the Visual Fortran Professional Edition, as described in Using Setup to Install Visual Fortran and Related Software in *Getting Started*.

When you install IMSL, you should also install the IMSL online documentation, which lets you quickly find details on the purpose and use of any IMSL Library routine. You should view the IMSL readme file and online help provided in the Visual Fortran program folder (Professional Edition only). You can access the following topics through the IMSL Help file, available in the Visual Fortran program folder, or the Adobe® Acrobat® IMSL Routines Reference (PDF version):

▶ IMSL MATH/LIBRARY Subroutines, Volumes 1 and 2

▶ IMSL MATH/LIBRARY Special Functions

▶ IMSL STAT/LIBRARY Subroutines, Volumes 1 and 2

▶ IMSL Fortran 90 MP Subroutines

Click on any of the libraries to see a submenu of items grouped by subject. Within each category (for example, Linear Systems, Eigensystem Analysis, and so on), click on a routine for more information.

IMSL libraries are *not* included with the Standard Edition of Visual Fortran.

This chapter provides information on the following topics:

▶ Section 24.1 Using the Libraries from Visual Fortran

▶ Section 24.2 Library Naming Conventions

▶ Section 24.3 Using IMSL Libraries in a Mixed-Language Environment

24.1   Using the Libraries from Visual Fortran

To use the IMSL libraries, you need to:

1. Set the necessary IMSL environment variables for your development environment by executing the DFVARS.BAT file (installed by default in the folder `. . .  \DF98\BIN`). This sets the INCLUDE path and library (linker) search paths.

Within the Fortran command-line window in the Visual Fortran program folder, the DFVARS.BAT file is already executed. Within the Microsoft visual development environment, the equivalent of DFVARS.BAT file (as installed by Visual Fortran) is executed. You can view these directory paths within the visual development environment by:

a. In the Tools menu, click Options.

b. Click the Directory tab.

c. In the drop-down list for Show Directories, select Library files and view the library paths.

d. In the drop-down list for Show Directories, select Include files and view the include file paths.

e. Click OK if you have changed any information.

2. You may need to explicitly pass IMSL libraries to the Linker. In most cases, these are passed automatically by using the **OBJCOMMENT LIB** directive. To view the list of library names to be passed to the linker in the visual development environment:

a. If not already open, open your Project Workspace (File menu, Open Workspace).

b. In the Project menu, click on Settings.

c. Click on the Link tab to view the list of Object/Library modules (General category). The IMSL libraries are listed in Section 24.2 Library Naming Conventions and include the following library names:

```
sstatd.lib sstats.lib smathd.lib smaths.lib sf90mp.lib
```

d. Click OK if you have changed any information.

3. Make IMSL routines and their interfaces available to your program:

- When calling MATH and STAT library routines from a Fortran 90 program, you should use the numerical_libraries module to provide interface blocks and parameter definitions for the routines. Including the following **USE** statement in your calling program will verify the correct usage of the IMSL routines at compile time:

```
USE numerical_libraries
```

When calling MATH and STAT library routines from a FORTRAN 77 style program, you can use the corresponding **INCLUDE** statement to perform the equivalent of the prior **USE** statement:

```
INCLUDE IMSLF90.FI
```

For more details, see the IMSL readme file in the Visual Fortran program folder.

When calling MATH and STAT library routines, you do not need to declare the functions or subroutines separately.

- When also calling Fortran 90 MP library routines, you should instead use the imslf90 module to provide interface blocks and parameter definitions for all the Fortran 90 MP routines and the MATH and STAT library routines. Including the following **USE** statement in your calling program will verify the correct usage of the IMSL routines at compile time:

```
USE IMSLF90
```

For more information about calling the Fortran 90 MP routines, see the IMSL Libraries online Help file.

The free-form Fortran 90 example program below invokes the function AMACH and the subroutine UMACH from the IMSL Libraries. The AMACH function retrieves real machine constants that define the computer's real arithmetic. A value for positive machine infinity is returned (Infinity). The subprogram UMACH retrieves the output unit number.

```
!   This free-form example demonstrates how to call
!   IMSL routines from Visual Fortran.
!
!   The module numerical_libraries includes the Math and
!   Stat libraries; these contain the type declarations
!   and interface statements for the library routines.

PROGRAM SHOWIMSL
```

```
        USE NUMERICAL_LIBRARIES
        INTEGER NOUT
        REAL RINFP

!       The AMACH function and UMACH subroutine are
!       declared in the numerical_libraries module

        CALL UMACH(2,NOUT)
        RINFP = AMACH(7)
        WRITE(NOUT,*) 'REAL POSITIVE MACHINE INFINITY = ',RINFP
        END PROGRAM
```

For information on compiling and linking with the visual development environment, see Chapter 2 Building Programs and Libraries.

Note: IMSL routines are in general not multithread safe. In a multithread environment, you should take care that no two IMSL routines are active at the same time. To insure this, use multithread control techniques. For further information, see Chapter 19 Creating Multithread Applications.

24.2   Library Naming Conventions

The IMSL FORTRAN 77 MATH and STAT Numerical Libraries are provided in separate single- and double-precision versions. The IMSL libraries use the library names shown in Table 24-1.

Table 24–1   *IMSL Library Names*

File Name	Library Description
SMATHS	Single-precision MATH library, one of the IMSL FORTRAN 77 Numerical Libraries.
SMATHD	Double-precision MATH library, one of the IMSL FORTRAN 77 Numerical Libraries.
SSTATS	Single-precision STAT library, one of the IMSL FORTRAN 77 Numerical Libraries.
SSTATD	Double-precision STAT library, one of the IMSL FORTRAN 77 Numerical Libraries.
SF90MP	Fortran 90 MP library, a new generation of Fortran 90-based algorithms, optimized for multiprocessor and other high-performance systems.

The IMSL FORTRAN 77 Numerical Libraries are for applications in general applied mathematics and for analyzing and presenting statistical data in scientific and business applications.

For command-line window development, excuting the DFVARS.BAT file (see Chapter 3 Using the Compiler and Linker from the Command Line) sets Visual Fortran environment variables as well as IMSL (Professional Edition) environment variables (see Section 3.4 Environment Variables Used with the DF Command).

For more information on the IMSL libraries, see:

▶ The IMSL readme file provided in the Visual Fortran program folder.

▶ The IMSL online Help provided in the Visual Fortran program folder or the IMSL Routines Reference.

▶ Product information about IMSL at URL http://www.vni.com.

24.3   Using IMSL Libraries in a Mixed-Language Environment

This section explains how to use the IMSL Libraries in a mixed-language development environment with Visual Fortran and Microsoft Visual C++®.

Messages that IMSL routines write to standard output or to error output in a mixed-language application or an application for Windows can be awkward if they are written to the screen. You can avoid this by calling UMACH from a Fortran routine to remap the output and error units to a file instead of to the screen. For example, the following free-form program writes the standard output from VHSTP to the file STD.TXT, and the error message from AMACH to the file ERR.TXT:

```
PROGRAM fileout
!    This program demonstrates how to use the UMACH routine to
!    redirect the standard output and error output from IMSL
!    routines to files instead of to the screen. The routines
!    AMACH and UMACH are declared in the numerical_libraries
!    module
!
   USE numerical_libraries
   INTEGER STDU, ERRU
   REAL x, frq(10)/3.0,1.0,4.0,1.0,5.0,9.0,2.0,6.0,5.0,3.0/
!
!    Redirect IMSL standard output to STD.TXT at unit 8
!
   CALL umach(-2, STDU)
   OPEN (unit=STDU, file='std.txt')
   CALL vhstp(10,frq,1,'Histogram Plot')
   CLOSE(8)
!
!    Redirect IMSL error output to ERR.TXT at unit 9
!
```

```
CALL umach(-3, ERRU)
OPEN (unit=ERRU, file='err.txt')
x = amach(0)              ! Illegal parameter error
CLOSE(9)
END
```

The standard output from IMSL routine VHSTP written to STD.TXT is:

```
1
             Histogram Plot
Frequency-------------------------
  9  *              I              *
  8  *              I              *
  7  *              I              *
  6  *              I   I          *
  5  *         I  I   I  I         *
  4  *      I  I  I   I  I         *
  3  * I    I  I  I   I  I  I      *
  2  * I    I  I  I  I  I  I  I    *
  1  * I  I  I  I  I  I  I  I  I   *
----------------------------------
Class            5              10
```

The error output from IMSL routine AMACH written to ERR.TXT is:

```
*** TERMINAL ERROR 5 from AMACH. The argument must be between 1 and 8
***                     inclusive. N = 0
```

Consider the following simple Fortran example that uses the IMSL library:

```
USE numerical_libraries
real rinfp
rinfp = AMACH(7)
write(*,*) 'Real positive machine infinity = ',rinfp
end
```

The output is:

```
Real positive machine infinity = Infinity
```

The corresponding C example is:

```
/* FILE CSAMP0.C */
#include <stdio.h>
#include <stdlib.h>

extern float _stdcall AMACH(long *);

main( )
{
  long n;
  float rinfp;
```

```
        n = 7;
        rinfp = AMACH(&n);
        printf("Real positive machine infinity = %16E\n
          ", rinfp);

        fflush(stdout);
        _exit(0);
}
```

This C language example demonstrates the use of:

▶ The _stdcall modifier in the function prototype needed when calling the IMSL libraries.

▶ The & address operator passes the address of the variable to the subprogram (IMSL libraries expect arguments passed by reference).

The C example can be compiled by the cl command to create an object file that can be linked using the DF command.

For more information on mixed-language programming, see Chapter 18 Programming with Mixed Languages.

25

Using Visual Fortran Tools

This chapter summarizes the available Visual Fortran tools and describes how to use tools from the Console command line:

25.1   Overview of Visual Fortran Tools

Table 25-1 lists the tools are available in Visual Fortran.

Table 25–1   *Tools Available in Visual Fortran*

Tool	Description
Integrated Tools in the Visual Development Environment	
Editor	Provides general editing functionality. It recognizes Fortran syntax and can be customized. For more information, see "Text Editor" in the *Visual C++ User's Guide*.
Debugger	Provides general debug functionality. For more information, see Chapter 5 Debugging Fortran Programs
Format Editor (FRMTEDIT)	Presents format code with resulting data layout. For more information, see Section 25.11 Editing Format Descriptors with the Format Editor.
Module Wizard (MODWIZ)	Simplifies the use of Component Object Model (COM) and Automation (OLE Automation) objects with Fortran. For more information, see Chapter 17 Using COM and Automation Objects.
Profiler (PROFILE, PLIST, and PREP)	Determines unexecuted code or indicates where an application is spending most of its time. For more information, see Section 25.12 Profiling Code from the Command Line.
Resource Editors	Develops user-interface components for projects; for example, to build a dialog box. For more information, see Chapter 11 Using Dialogs and see "Resource Editors" in the *Visual C++ User's Guide*.
Source Browser (BSCMAKE)	Creates an information file with details about the symbols in your program. The browse window displays this information and lets you move among instances of the symbols in your source code. For more information, see Section 2.3.3.3 Source Browser Information for a Configuration.
Additional Tools	
Linker (LINK)	Lets you link object files and libraries, creating 32-bit executable images or DLLs. For more information, see Chapter 3 Using the Compiler and Linker from the Command Line and Chapter 4 Compiler and Linker Options.
Librarian (LIB)	Lets you manage object libraries, create import libraries to reference exported symbol definitions used when you build Dynamic Link Libraries (DLLs), and extract library members. For more information, see Section 25.8 Managing Libraries with LIB.
Microsoft Binary File Dumper (DUMPBIN)	Displays various information from .obj, .exe, and .libs files. For more information, see Section 25.10 Examining Files with DUMPBIN.

Table 25–1 *Tools Available in Visual Fortran (Continued)*

Tool	Description
Microsoft Binary File Editor (EDITBIN)	Lets you modify execution characteristics of a program. For more information, see Section 25.9 Editing Files with EDITBIN.
BitViewer (BITVIEW)	Lets you view the binary representation of real numbers in single and double format. For more information, see Section 22.1.1.3 Viewing Floating-Point Representations with BitViewer.
CVTRES	Lets you convert binary resource files (.res) to linkable object (.obj) files. For more information, see "CVTRES" below.
DDESpy (DDESPY)	Lets you monitor Dynamic Data Exchange (DDE) activity between processes. For more information, see "Windows Utilities" in the *Visual C++ User's Guide.*
FPP	Lets you preprocess Fortran files; similar to the C preprocessor (CPP). For more information, see Section 4.1.33 /fpp.
FPR	Lets you transform files formatted according to Fortran's carriage control conventions into files formatted according to line printer conventions. For more information, see Section 25.13 Fortran Tools: FSPLIT and FPR.
FSPLIT and FSPLIT90	Lets you split a multi-routine Fortran file into individual files. FSPLIT works on FORTRAN 77 files, while FSPLIT90 works on Fortran 90 files. For more information, see Section 25.13 Fortran Tools: FSPLIT and FPR.
Microsoft Program Maintenance Utility (NMAKE)	Lets you build projects based on commands contained in a description (makefile) file. For more information, see Section 25.6 Building Projects with NMAKE.
OLE Object Viewer (OLEVIEW)	Lets you browse, configure, test, and activate any COM class on your system; also called the OLEViewer. For more information, see "OLE Object Viewer" below.
PView (PVIEW)	Lets you examine and modify processes and threads running on your system. For more information, see "Windows Utilities" in the *Visual C++ User's Guide.*
Resource Compiler (RC)	Compiles various resources so they can be included in an image. For more information, see Section 25.7.3 Resource Compiler Command Line.
Running Object Table Viewer (IROTVIEW)	Lets you view the contents of the OLE Running Object Table. For more information, see "Running Object Table Viewer" below.
Spy++ (SPYXX)	Lets you monitor windows messages. For more information, see "Windows Utilities" in the *Visual C++ User's Guide.*
WinDiff (WINDIFF)	Lets you graphically compare the contents of two files or two directories. For more information, see "Windows Utilities" in the *Visual C++ User's Guide.*
ZoomIn (ZOOMIN)	Lets you capture and enlarge an area of the Windows desktop. For more information, see "Windows Utilities" in the *Visual C++ User's Guide.*

To access the "Additional Tools" listed in Table 25-1 from a command window, the Digital Visual Fortran environment must be initialized, as described in "Using the Command-Line Interface" in *Getting Started* in the Visual Fortran online Help.

Miscellaneous Tool Information

This section briefly describes tools that are not described in detail elsewhere in the documentation.

CVTRES

Binary resource files (.res) cannot be linked. CVTRES lets you convert a binary resource file into a linkable object file (.obj). For example:

```
cvtres /out:test.obj test.res
```

Running Object Table Viewer (IROTVIEW)

The Running Object Table Viewer lets you view the contents of the OLE Running Object Table (ROT). This table contains information about ActiveX™ and OLE objects currently existing in memory.

OLE Object Viewer (OLEVIEW)

The OLE/COM Object Viewer (OLEViewer) lets you do the following:

▶ Browse, in a structured way, all of the Component Object Model (COM) classes installed on your machine.

▶ See the registry entries for each class in an easy-to-read format.

▶ Configure any COM class (including Java™-based classes) on your system. This includes Distributed COM activation and security settings.

▶ Configure system-wide COM settings, including enabling or disabling Distributed COM.

▶ Test any COM class by double-clicking its name. The list of interfaces that class supports will be displayed. Double-clicking an interface entry allows you to invoke a viewer that will "exercise" that interface.

▶ Activate COM classes locally or remotely. Use this to test Distributed COM setups.

▶ View type library contents. Use this to figure out what methods, properties, and events an ActiveX Control supports.

▶ Copy a properly formatted OBJECT tag to the clipboard for inserting into an HTML document.

The OLEViewer supports plug-in interface viewers. The code for the interface viewers is included in OLEView (in IVIEWERS.DLL).

25.2   Using Tools from the Command Line

Although Visual Fortran comes with an integrated Windows-based development environment called Microsoft visual development environment, you can still use many software tools directly from the command line.

If you prefer to use a text-based environment, you can build your programs or libraries in the console (such as the Fortran Command Prompt in the Visual Fortran program folder), a command-line operating environment similar to MS-DOS provided by Windows 95 and Windows NT. However, to get the benefit of components that you cannot use from the command line, you may want to do some of your work from the console, and some of it in the visual development environment.

When you run an application for Windows (such as the Format Statement Editor) from the command line, Windows recognizes that the program does not execute within the command window and acts accordingly.

You can tell Windows to run a program with its own resources by using the START command. For example, to run the Library Manager as a separate task, the command is:

```
START LIB.EXE
```

Visual Fortran contains an extensive electronic reference you view with the HTML Help Viewer. This includes the Visual Fortran online documentation and a search engine.

To access HTML Help Viewer books from outside the visual development environment, click on the Online Documentation item in the Visual Fortran program folder. If you want to use Visual Fortran from the command line, you can still use the visual development environment to display HTML Help Viewer, and task switch between it and the console.

The following related sections discuss command-line tools:

► Section 25.3 Setting Up the Command Console

► Section 25.4 Fortran Compiler and Linker

► Section 25.5 MS-DOS Editor

► Section 25.6 Building Projects with NMAKE

► Section 25.7 Resource Compiler Options

▶ Section 25.8 Managing Libraries with LIB

▶ Section 25.9 Editing Files with EDITBIN

▶ Section 25.10 Examining Files with DUMPBIN

▶ Section 25.11 Editing Format Descriptors with the Format Editor

▶ Section 25.12 Profiling Code from the Command Line

▶ Section 25.13 Fortran Tools: FSPLIT and FPR

For a summary of all Visual Fortran tools, see Section 25.1 Overview of Visual Fortran Tools.

25.3   Setting Up the Command Console

Visual Fortran provides a command window with the appropriate environment variables already set. To start the Visual Fortran command window, open the Start menu and select Visual Fortran from the Programs submenu. Select the Fortran Command Prompt icon.

The console window provides a similar working environment to that provided by running a version of MS-DOS® instead of Windows NT, Windows 98, or Windows 95. You can use any command recognized by MS-DOS in the Windows NT console, plus some additional commands.

Because the command console runs within the context of Windows, you get the additional benefit that you can easily switch between the command console and other applications for Windows. If you want, you can even have multiple instances of the command console open at once.

When you are finished working in a command console window, use the EXIT command to close the window and end the session.

To start the command console window provided by your operating system, open the Start menu and select MS-DOS Prompt from the Programs submenu.

For more information, see:

▶ Section 25.3.1 Configuring the Command Console Window

▶ Section 25.3.2 Setting Search Paths in the Console

25.3.1   Configuring the Command Console Window

When you start a session in the command console, a window containing the command interpreter opens. The resources available, as well as the size and behavior of the window, are initially set by the operating system, but you can change these properties, including:

▶ Whether the command console takes over the entire screen or is presented in a window.

▶ The typeface and type size used to display text in the command console.

▶ The size of the command console text buffer and the position of the command console window if it is presented in a window.

▶ The colors used to display text in the command console.

▶ The size of the command history buffer used to store commands that scroll out of view.

▶ The amount of each type of memory that is available to programs running in the command console.

▶ Special configuration files to be run when the console session begins.

The controls that you use to make these adjustments depend upon which version of Windows you are using. The operating system provides a way to specify configuration settings for all subsequent sessions with the command console.

In Windows NT, use the control panel.

In Windows 95, use the Properties dialog box to set all of the initial and operating conditions for the command console. With the command window open, click the right mouse button at the top of the window. A drop-down list appears. Choose Properties. From the Properties dialog, set up the console display as you like.

25.3.2 Setting Search Paths in the Console

When the command console session begins, the search paths for libraries, module files, and so forth are those set for your user account on the PC. In Windows 98 and Windows 95, these paths are initially specified in the AUTOEXEC.BAT file that is read when the computer is booted. By default, Windows NT uses a file called AUTOEXEC.NT to perform initialization of console sessions, but you can specify your own initialization file for the command console with the PIF Editor. (See your Windows NT manual for more details about the PIF Editor.)

You can use the SET command to change these search paths manually within the console session, but your changes will only be in effect during that session. If you need to specify certain path changes each time you begin a console session, you can put the SET commands into a batch file and run it when you begin a session. The Setup program provides a batch file called DFVARS.BAT for this purpose. You can add your SET commands to this file and run it at the start of each session.

You can run DFVARS.BAT:

▶ Each time you begin a session on Windows 98 or Windows 95 systems, by specifying it in the Program tab of the Properties dialog box for the console icon.

▶ On Windows NT systems, you can specify it as the initialization file with the PIF Editor.

The instructions specify the PATH, INCLUDE, and LIB environment variables. For example, the lines in the batch file that sets the INCLUDE environment variable include:

```
set LIB=%DFcdrom%\DF98\LIB;%DFcdrom%\VC98\LIB;%LIB%
```

The batch file inserts the directories used by Visual Fortran at the beginning of the existing paths. Because these directories appear first, they are searched before any directories in the path lists provided by Windows. This is especially important if the existing path includes directories with files having the same names as those needed by Visual Fortran.

As described in "Using the Command-Line Interface" in *Getting Started* in the Visual Fortran online Help, the Visual Fortran Fortran command window sets these variables for you automatically. To activate this command window, select the Fortran Command Prompt icon in the Visual Fortran program folder.

25.4   Fortran Compiler and Linker

The DF (or FL32) command is the driver for running the compiler and linker. You can either compile and link your projects in one step with DF, or compile them with DF and then link them with LINK. You can also use LINK to build libraries of object modules. Each of these commands provides syntax instructions at the command line if you request it with the /? or /help option.

For more information about the DF and LINK commands, see:

▶ Chapter 3 Using the Compiler and Linker from the Command Line

▶ Chapter 4 Compiler and Linker Options

25.5 MS-DOS Editor

You can use the MS-DOS Editor (EDIT.EXE) or any text editor to create your source programs, but you will not be able to perform the specialized functions built into the visual development environment such as multi-file searches, and your source code will not be displayed with syntax coloring.

You invoke the MS-DOS Editor by typing EDIT followed by the name of the file you want to edit; for example, EDIT test.f90.

25.6 Building Projects with NMAKE

Some projects require an extensive set of build instructions to ensure that each component is built with the appropriate options. With the Microsoft visual development environment, you can specify build instructions by source file, and you can have separate sets of instructions for the debug and release builds of a project. In the visual development environment, you select these options in a set of dialog boxes. For information on creating (exporting) a makefile from the visual development environment, see "The Project Make-file" in Section 2.3.1 Files in a Project.

When you build projects from the command line, you can put your build instructions into a special build file, and run the build process with NMAKE, the Microsoft Program Maintenance Utility. Other command-line building methods include using indirect command files (see Section 3.8 DF Indirect Command File Use) and .BAT files.

The Microsoft Program Maintenance Utility (NMAKE.EXE) is a 32-bit tool that builds projects based on commands contained in a description file. This section discusses the following:

▶ Section 25.6.1 Running NMAKE

▶ Section 25.6.2 Contents of a Makefile

▶ Section 25.6.3 Description Blocks

▶ Section 25.6.4 Commands in a Makefile

▶ Section 25.6.5 Inline Files in a Makefile

▶ Section 25.6.6 Macros and NMAKE

▶ Section 25.6.7 NMAKE Inference Rules

▶ Section 25.6.8 Dot Directives in Makefiles

▶ Section 25.6.9 Makefile Preprocessing

25.6.1 Running **NMAKE**

The syntax for NMAKE is:

NMAKE [*option...*] [*macros...*] [*targets...*] [*@commandfile...*]

NMAKE builds only specified *targets* or, if none is specified, the first target in the makefile is used. The first makefile target can be a pseudotarget (a label used in place of a filename in a dependency line) that builds other targets. NMAKE uses makefiles specified with the /F option. If /F is not specified, it uses the MAKEFILE file in the current directory. If no makefile is specified, it uses inference rules to build command-line *targets*.

The *commandfile* text file contains command-line input. Other input can precede or follow *@commandfile*. A path is permitted. In *commandfile*, line breaks are treated as spaces. Enclose macro definitions in quotation marks if they contain spaces.

For more information, see:

▶ On targets, see Section 25.6.3 Description Blocks

▶ On macros, see Section 25.6.6 Macros and NMAKE

▶ On options, see Section 25.6.1.1 NMAKE Options

25.6.1.1 *NMAKE Options*

NMAKE options are described in the following sections. Options are preceded by either a slash (/) or a dash (-) and are not case sensitive. Use !CMD-SWITCHES (described in Section 25.6.9.1 Makefile Preprocessing Directives) to change option settings in a makefile or in TOOLS.INI.

This section describes the following topics:

▶ Section 25.6.1.2 NMAKE Option Descriptions

▶ Section 25.6.1.3 TOOLS.INI and NMAKE

▶ Section 25.6.1.4 Exit Codes from NMAKE

25.6.1.2 *NMAKE Option Descriptions*

NMAKE options are described in Table 25-2.

For more information, see:

▶ 25.6.8 Dot Directives in Makefiles (such as .SUFFIXES)

▶ 25.6.9.1 Makefile Preprocessing Directives (such as !CMD-SWITCHES)

Table 25–2 *NMAKE Options*

Tool	Description
/A	Forces build of all evaluated targets, even if not out-of-date with respect to dependents. Does not force build of unrelated targets.
/B	Forces build even if timestamps are equal. Recommended only for very fast systems (resolution of two seconds or less).
/C	Suppresses default output, including nonfatal NMAKE errors or warnings, timestamps, and NMAKE copyright message. Suppresses warnings issued by /K.
/D	Displays timestamps of each evaluated target and dependent and a message when a target does not exist. Useful with /P for debugging a makefile. Use !CMDSWITCHES to set or clear /D for part of a makefile.
/E	Causes environment variables to override makefile macro definitions.
/F *filename*	Specifies *filename* as a makefile. Spaces or tabs can precede *filename*. Specify /F once for each makefile. To supply a makefile from standard input, specify a dash (-) for *filename*, and end keyboard input with either **F6** or **Ctrl+Z**.
/HELP, /?	Displays a brief summary of NMAKE command-line syntax.
/I	Ignores exit codes from all commands. To set or clear /I for part of a makefile, use !CMDSWITCHES. To ignore exit codes for part of a makefile, use a dash (-) command modifier or .IGNORE. Overrides /K if both are specified.
/K	Continues building unrelated dependencies, if a command returns an error. Also issues a warning and returns an exit code of 1. By default, NMAKE halts if any command returns a nonzero exit code. Warnings from /K are suppressed by /C; /I overrides /K if both are specified.
/N	Displays but does not execute commands; preprocessing commands are executed. Does not display commands in recursive NMAKE calls. Useful for debugging makefiles and checking timestamps. To set or clear /N for part of a makefile, use !CMDSWITCHES.
/NOLOGO	Suppresses the NMAKE copyright message.
/P	Displays information (macro definitions, inference rules, targets, .SUFFIXES list) to standard output, and then runs the build. If no makefile or command-line target exists, it displays information only. Use with /D to debug a makefile.
/Q	Checks timestamps of targets; does not run the build. Returns a zero exit code if all targets are up-to-date and a nonzero exit code if any target is not. Preprocessing commands are executed. Useful when running NMAKE from a batch file.
/R	Clears the .SUFFIXES list and ignores inference rules and macros that are defined in the Tools.ini file or that are predefined.
/S	Suppresses display of executed commands. To suppress display in part of a makefile, use the @ command modifier or .SILENT. To set or clear /S for part of a makefile, use !CMDSWITCHES.

Table 25–2 *NMAKE Options (Continued)*

Tool	Description
/T	Updates timestamps of command-line targets (or first makefile target) and executes preprocessing commands but does not run the build.
/U	Must be used in conjunction with /N. Dumps inline NMAKE files so that the /N output can be used as a batch file.
/X *filename*	Sends NMAKE error output to *filename* instead of standard error. Spaces or tabs can precede *filename*. To send error output to standard output, specify a dash (-) for *filename*. Does not affect output from commands to standard error.
/Y	Disables batch-mode inference rules. When this option is selected, all batch-mode inference rules are treated as regular inference rules.

25.6.1.3 TOOLS.INI and NMAKE

NMAKE reads TOOLS.INI before it reads makefiles, unless the /R option is used. It looks for TOOLS.INI first in the current directory and then in the directory specified by the INIT environment variable. The section for NMAKE settings in the initialization file begins with [NMAKE] and can contain any makefile information. Specify a comment on a separate line beginning with a semicolon (;) or a number sign (#).

25.6.1.4 Exit Codes from NMAKE

By default, NMAKE halts if any command returns a nonzero exit code. The /I option causes NMAKE to ignore exit codes. Warnings from the /K option are suppressed by the /C option; the /I option overrides the /K option if both are specified.

Table 25-3 lists the exit codes.

Table 25–3 *Exit Codes from NMAKE*

Code	Meaning
0	No error (possibly a warning)
1	Incomplete build (issued only when the /K option is used)
2	Program error, possibly due to one of the following: • A syntax error in the makefile • An error or exit code from a command • An interruption by the user
4	System error—out of memory
255	Target is not up-to-date (issued only when the /Q option is used)

25.6.2 Contents of a Makefile

A makefile contains:

- ▶ Description blocks (see Section 25.6.3)
- ▶ Commands (see Section 25.6.4)
- ▶ Macros (see Section 25.6.6)
- ▶ Inference Rules (see Section 25.6.7)
- ▶ Dot Directives (see Section 25.6.8)
- ▶ Preprocessing Directives (see Section 25.6.9)

The following sections discuss other features of a makefile:

- ▶ Wildcards (see Section 25.6.2.1)
- ▶ Long filenames (see Section 25.6.2.2)
- ▶ Comments (see Section 25.6.2.3)
- ▶ Special characters (see Section 25.6.2.4)

25.6.2.1 Wildcards and NMAKE

NMAKE expands filename wildcards (* and ?) in dependency lines. A wildcard specified in a command is passed to the command; NMAKE does not expand it.

25.6.2.2 Long Filenames in a Makefile

Enclose long filenames in double quotation marks, as follows:

```
all : "VeryLongFileName.exe"
```

25.6.2.3 Comments in a Makefile

Precede a comment with a number sign (#). NMAKE ignores text from the number sign to the next newline character. The following shows examples:

```
# Comment on line by itself
OPTIONS = /MAP # Comment on macro definition line

all.exe : one.obj two.obj # Comment on dependency line
    link one.obj two.obj
# Comment in commands block
#   copy *.obj \objects # Command turned into comment
    copy one.exe \release

.obj.exe: # Comment on inference rule line
    link $<
```

```
my.exe : my.obj ; link my.obj # Error: cannot comment this
  # Error: # must be the first character
.obj.exe: ; link $< # Error: cannot comment this
```

To specify a literal number sign, precede it with a caret (^), as follows:

```
DEF = ^#define #Macro representing a Fortran compiler
directive
```

25.6.2.4 *Special Characters in a Makefile*

To use an NMAKE special character as a literal character, place a caret (^) in front of it. NMAKE ignores carets that precede other characters. The special characters are:

> : ; # ( ) $ ^ \ { } ! @ -

A caret within a quoted string is treated as a literal caret character. A caret at the end of a line inserts a literal newline character in a string or macro.

In macros, a backslash followed by a newline character is replaced by a space.

In commands, a percent symbol (%) is a file specifier. To represent a percent symbol (%) literally in a command, specify a double percent sign (%%) in place of a single one. In other situations, NMAKE interprets a single % literally, but it always interprets a double %% as a single %. Therefore, to represent a literal %%, specify either three percent signs, %%%, or four percent signs, %%%%.

To use the dollar sign ($) as a literal character in a command, specify two dollar signs ($$); this method can also be used in other situations where ^$ also works.

25.6.3 **Description Blocks**

A description block is a dependency line optionally followed by a commands block:

```
targets... : dependents...
       commands...
```

A dependency line specifies one or more *targets* and zero or more *dependents*. A target must be at the start of the line. Separate targets from dependents by a colon (:); spaces or tabs are allowed. To split the line, use a backslash (\) after a target or dependent. If a target does not exist, has an earlier timestamp than a dependent, or is a pseudotarget, NMAKE executes the commands. If a dependent is a target elsewhere and does not exist or is out-of-date with respect to its own dependents, NMAKE updates the dependent before updating the current dependency.

For more information, see:

▶ Section 25.6.3.1 Targets

▶ Section 25.6.3.2 Pseudotargets

▶ Section 25.6.3.3 Multiple Targets

▶ Section 25.6.3.4 Cumulative Dependencies

▶ Section 25.6.3.5 Targets in Multiple Description Blocks

▶ Section 25.6.3.6 Dependents

25.6.3.1 Targets

In a dependency line, specify one or more targets, using any valid filename or pseudotarget. Separate multiple targets with one or more spaces or tabs. Targets are not case sensitive. Paths are permitted with filenames. A target cannot exceed 256 characters. If the target preceding the colon is a single character, use a separating space; otherwise, NMAKE interprets the letter-colon combination as a drive specifier.

25.6.3.2 Pseudotargets

A pseudotarget is a label used in place of a filename in a dependency line. It is interpreted as a file that does not exist and so is out-of-date. NMAKE assumes a pseudotarget's timestamp is the most recent of all its dependents; if it has no dependents, the current time is assumed. If a pseudotarget is used as a target, its commands are always executed.

A pseudotarget used as a dependent must also appear as a target in another dependency; however, that dependency does not need to have a commands block.

Pseudotarget names follow the filename syntax rules for targets. However, if the name does not have an extension (that is, does not contain a period), it can exceed the 8-character limit for filenames and can be up to 256 characters long.

25.6.3.3 Multiple Targets

NMAKE evaluates multiple targets in a single dependency as if each were specified in a separate description block as follows:

```
This...                         Is evaluated as this...
bounce.exe leap.exe :           bounce.exe : jump.obj
```

```
jump.obj                      echo Building...
    echo Building...          leap.exe : jump.obj
                              echo Building...
```

25.6.3.4 Cumulative Dependencies

Dependencies are cumulative in a description block if a target is repeated as
follows:

```
This...                    Is evaluated as this...
bounce.exe : jump.obj      bounce.exe : jump.obj
bounce.exe : up.obj        up.obj
    echo Building              echo Building
bounce.exe...              bounce.exe...
```

Multiple targets in multiple dependency lines in a single description block
are evaluated as if each were specified in a separate description block, but targets that are not in the last dependency line do not use the commands block
as follows:

```
This...                    Is evaluated as this...
bounce.exe leap.exe :      bounce.exe : jump.obj
jump.obj                   up.obj
bounce.exe climb.exe :         echo Building
up.obj                     bounce.exe...
    echo Building...       climb.exe : up.obj
                               echo Building
                           climb.exe...
                           leap.exe : jump.obj
                           # invokes an inference rule
```

25.6.3.5 Targets in Multiple Description Blocks

To update a target in more than one description block using different commands, specify two consecutive colons (::) between targets and dependents.
For example:

```
target.lib :: one.f90 two.f90 three.f90
  df one.f90 two.f90 three.f90
  lib target one.obj two.obj three.obj
target.lib :: four.c five.c
  df /c four.for five.for
  lib target four.obj five.obj
```

Dependency Side Effects

If a target is specified with a colon (:) in two dependency lines in different
locations, and if commands appear after only one of the lines, NMAKE interprets the dependencies as if adjacent or combined. It does not invoke an

inference rule for the dependency that has no commands, but instead assumes that the dependencies belong to one description block and executes the commands specified with the other dependency as follows:

```
This...                          Is evaluated as this...
bounce.exe : jump.obj            bounce.exe : jump.obj
    echo Building                up.obj
bounce.exe...                        echo Building
                                 bounce.exe...
bounce.exe : up.obj
```

This effect does not occur if **::** is used as follows:

```
This...                          Is evaluated as this...
bounce.exe :: jump.obj           bounce.exe : jump.obj
    echo Building                    echo Building
bounce.exe...                    bounce.exe...

bounce.exe :: up.obj             bounce.exe : up.obj
                                 # invokes an inference rule
```

25.6.3.6 Dependents

In a dependency line, specify zero or more dependents after the colon (**:**) or double colon (**::**), using any valid filename or pseudotarget. Separate multiple dependents with one or more spaces or tabs. Dependents are not case sensitive. Paths are permitted with filenames.

Inferred Dependents

An inferred dependent is derived from an inference rule and is evaluated before explicit dependents. If an inferred dependent is out-of-date with respect to its target, NMAKE invokes the commands block for the dependency. If an inferred dependent does not exist or is out-of-date with respect to its own dependents, NMAKE first updates the inferred dependent. For more information, see Section 25.6.7 NMAKE Inference Rules.

Search Paths for Dependents

Each dependent has an optional search path, specified as follows:

directory[**;**directory...]**}** *dependent*

NMAKE looks for a dependent first in the current directory, and then in directories in the order specified. A macro can specify part or all of a search path. Enclose directory names in braces ({ }); separate multiple directories with a semicolon (**;**). No spaces or tabs are allowed.

25.6.4 Commands in a Makefile

A description block or inference rule specifies a block of commands to run if the dependency is out-of-date. NMAKE displays each command before running it, unless the /S option, .SILENT, !CMDSWITCHES, or @ is used. NMAKE looks for a matching inference rule if a description block is not followed by a commands block.

A commands block contains one or more commands, each on its own line. No blank line can appear between the dependency or rule and the commands block. However, a line containing only spaces or tabs can appear; this line is interpreted as a null command and no error occurs. Blank lines are permitted between command lines.

A command line begins with one or more spaces or tabs. A backslash (\) followed by a newline character is interpreted as a space in the command; use a backslash at the end of a line to continue a command onto the next line. NMAKE interprets the backslash literally if any other character, including a space or tab, follows the backslash.

A command preceded by a semicolon (;) can appear on a dependency line or inference rule, whether or not a commands block follows:

```
project.obj : project.f90 ; df /c project.f90
```

For more information, see:

▶ Section 25.6.4.1 Command Modifiers in NMAKE

▶ Section 25.6.4.2 Filename-Parts Syntax in NMAKE

25.6.4.1 Command Modifiers in NMAKE

You can specify one or more command modifiers preceding a command, optionally separated by spaces or tabs. As with commands, modifiers must be indented. Table 25-4 lists the command modifiers.

Table 25–4 *NMAKE Command Modifiers*

Modifier	Action
@*command*	Prevents display of the command. Display by commands is not suppressed. By default, NMAKE echoes all executed commands. Use the /S option to suppress display for the entire makefile; use .SILENT to suppress display for part of the makefile.

Table 25–4 *NMAKE Command Modifiers (Continued)*

Modifier	Action
-[*number*] *command*	Turns off error checking for *command.* By default, NMAKE halts when a command returns a nonzero exit code. If -*number* is used, NMAKE stops if the exit code exceeds *number.* Spaces or tabs cannot appear between the dash and *number;* at least one space or tab must appear between *number* and *command.* Use the /I option to turn off error checking for the entire makefile; use .IGNORE to turn off error checking for part of the makefile.
!*command*	Executes *command* for each dependent file if *command* uses $** (all dependent files in the dependency) or $? (all dependent files in the dependency with a later timestamp than the target).

25.6.4.2 *Filename-Parts Syntax in NMAKE*

Filename-parts syntax in commands represents components of the first dependent filename (which may be an implied dependent). Filename components are the file's drive, path, base name, and extension as specified, not as it exists on disk.

Use %s to represent the complete filename. Use %l[*parts*]F (note the vertical bar character following the percent symbol) to represent parts of the filename, where *parts* can be zero or more of the letters in Table 25-5, in any order.

Table 25–5 *Filename-Parts Syntax in NMAKE Commands*

Letter	Description
No letter	Complete name (same as %s)
d	Drive
p	Path
f	File base name
e	File extension

25.6.5 Inline Files in a Makefile

An inline file contains text you specify in the makefile. Its name can be used in commands as input (for example, a LINK command file), or it can pass commands to the operating system. The file is created on disk when a command that creates the file is run.

For more information, see:

▶ Section 25.6.5.1 Specifying an Inline File in Makefiles

▶ Section 25.6.5.2 Creating Inline File Text in Makefiles

▶ Section 25.6.5.3 Reusing Inline Files in Makefiles

▶ Section 25.6.5.4 Multiple Inline Files

25.6.5.1 Specifying an Inline File in Makefiles

The syntax for specifying an inline file in a command is:

<<[*filename*]

Specify two angle brackets (<<) in the command where the filename is to appear. The angle brackets cannot be a macro expansion. When the command is run, the angle brackets are replaced by *filename*, if specified, or by a unique NMAKE-generated name. If specified, *filename* must follow the angle brackets without a space or tab. A path is permitted. No extension is required or assumed.

If *filename* is specified, the file is created in the current or specified directory, overwriting any existing file by that name; otherwise, it is created in the TMP directory (or the current directory, if the TMP environment variable is not defined). If a previous *filename* is reused, NMAKE overwrites the previous file.

25.6.5.2 Creating Inline File Text in Makefiles

The syntax to create the content of an inline file is:

inlinetext
.
.
.
<<[KEEP | NOKEEP]

Specify *inlinetext* on the first line after the command. Mark the end with double brackets at the beginning of a separate line. The file contains all *inlinetext* before the delimiting brackets. The *inlinetext* can have macro expansions and substitutions, but not directives or makefile comments. Spaces, tabs, and newline characters are treated literally.

Inline files are temporary or permanent. A temporary file exists for the duration of the session and can be reused by other commands. Specify KEEP after the closing angle brackets to retain the file after the NMAKE session; an unnamed file is preserved on disk with the generated filename. Specify NOKEEP or nothing for a temporary file. KEEP and NOKEEP are not case sensitive.

25.6.5.3 Reusing Inline Files in Makefiles

To reuse an inline file, specify <<*filename* where the file is defined and first used, then reuse filename without the angle brackets (<<) later in the same or another command. The command to create the inline file must run before all commands that use the file.

25.6.5.4 Multiple Inline Files

A command can create more than one inline file. The syntax to do this is:

command << <<
inlinetext
<<[KEEP | NOKEEP]
inlinetext
<<[KEEP | NOKEEP]

For each file, specify one or more lines of inline text followed by a closing line containing the delimiter. Begin the second file's text on the line following the delimiting line for the first file.

25.6.6 Macros and NMAKE

Macros replace a particular string in the makefile with another string. Using macros, you can:

▶ Create a makefile that can build different projects

▶ Specify options for commands

▶ Set environment variables

You can define your own macros or use NMAKE's predefined macros.

For more information, see:

▶ Section 25.6.6.1 Defining an NMAKE Macro

▶ Section 25.6.6.2 Special Characters in NMAKE Macros

▶ Section 25.6.6.3 Null and Undefined NMAKE Macros

▶ Section 25.6.6.4 Where to Define Macros

▶ Section 25.6.6.5 Precedence in Macro Definitions

▶ Section 25.6.6.6 Using an NMAKE Macro

▶ Section 25.6.6.7 Macro Substitution

▶ Section 25.6.6.8 Special NMAKE Macros

25.6.6.1 Defining an NMAKE Macro

Use the following syntax to define a macro:

macroname=string

The *macroname* is a combination of letters, digits, and underscores (_) up to 1024 characters, and is case sensitive. The *macroname* can contain an invoked macro. If *macroname* consists entirely of an invoked macro, the macro being invoked cannot be null or undefined.

The *string* can be any sequence of zero or more characters. A null string contains zero characters or only spaces or tabs. The *string* can contain a macro invocation.

25.6.6.2 Special Characters in NMAKE Macros

A number sign (#) after a definition specifies a comment. To specify a literal number sign in a macro, use a caret (^), as in ^#.

A dollar sign ($) specifies a macro invocation. To specify a literal $, use $$.

To extend a definition to a new line, end the line with a backslash (\). When the macro is invoked, the backslash plus newline character is replaced with a space. To specify a literal backslash at the end of the line, precede it with a caret (^), or follow it with a comment specifier (#).

To specify a literal newline character, end the line with a caret (^), as in:

```
CMDS = cls^
dir
```

25.6.6.3 Null and Undefined NMAKE Macros

Both null and undefined macros expand to null strings, but a macro defined as a null string is considered defined in preprocessing expressions. To define a macro as a null string, specify no characters except spaces or tabs after the equal sign (=) in a command line or command file, enclose the null string or definition in double quotation marks (" "). To undefine a macro, use !UNDEF.

25.6.6.4 Where to Define Macros

You can define macros in a makefile command line, or command file.

In a makefile, each macro definition must appear on a separate line and cannot start with a space or tab. Spaces or tabs around the equal sign (=) are ignored. All *string* characters are literal, including surrounding quotation marks and embedded spaces.

In a command line or command file, spaces and tabs delimit arguments and cannot surround the equal sign. If *string* has embedded spaces or tabs, enclose either the string itself or the entire macro in double quotation marks (" ").

25.6.6.5 Precedence in Macro Definitions

If a macro is multiply defined, NMAKE uses the highest-precedence definition. The following list shows the order of precedence, from highest to lowest:

1. A macro defined on the command line

2. A macro defined in a makefile or include file

3. An inherited environment-variable macro

4. A predefined macro, such as FOR and RC

Use the /E option to cause macros inherited from environment variables to override makefile macros with the same name. Use !UNDEF to override a command line.

25.6.6.6 Using an NMAKE Macro

To use a macro, enclose its name in parentheses preceded by a dollar sign ($):

$(*macroname*)

No spaces are allowed. The parentheses are optional if *macroname* is a single character. The definition string replaces $(*macroname*); an undefined macro is replaced by a null string.

25.6.6.7 Macro Substitution

To substitute text within a macro, use the following syntax:

$(*macroname:string1=string2*)

When *macroname* is invoked, each occurrence of *string1* in its definition string is replaced by *string2*. Macro substitution is case sensitive and is literal; *string1* and *string2* cannot invoke macros. Substitution does not modify the original definition. You can substitute text in any predefined macro except $$@.

No spaces or tabs precede the colon; any after the colon are interpreted as literal. If *string2* is null, all occurrences of *string1* are deleted from the macro's definition string.

25.6.6.8 Special NMAKE Macros

NMAKE provides several special macros to represent various filenames and commands. One use for some of these macros is in the predefined inference rules. Like all macros, the macros provided by NMAKE are case sensitive.

Filename Macros

Filename macros are predefined as filenames specified in the dependency (not full filename specifications on disk). These macros do not need to be enclosed in parentheses when invoked; specify only a $ as shown in Table 25-6.

Table 25–6 *NMAKE Filename Macros*

Macro	Meaning
$@	Current target's full name (path, base name, extension), as currently specified.
$$@	Current target's full name (path, base name, extension), as currently specified. Valid only as a dependent in a dependency.
$*	Current target's path and base name minus file extension.
$**	All dependents of the current target.
$?	All dependents with a later timestamp than the current target.
$<	Dependent file with a later timestamp than the current target. Valid only in commands in inference rules.

To specify part of a predefined filename macro, append a macro modifier (listed in Table 25-7) and enclose the modified macro in parentheses.

Table 25–7 *NMAKE Macro Modifiers*

Modifier	Resulting filename Part
D	Drive plus directory
B	Base name
F	Base name plus extension
R	Drive plus directory plus base name

Recursion Macros

Use recursion macros to call NMAKE recursively. Recursive sessions inherit command-line and environment-variable macros. They do not inherit make-file-defined inference rules or .SUFFIXES and .PRECIOUS specifications. To pass macros to a recursive NMAKE session, either set an environment variable with the SET command before the recursive call or define a macro in the command for the recursive call. Table 25-8 lists the recursion macros.

Table 25–8 *NMAKE Recursion Macros*

Macro	Definition
MAKE	Command used originally to invoke NMAKE.
MAKEDIR	Current directory when NMAKE was invoked.
MAKEFLAGS	Options currently in effect. Use as /$(MAKEFLAGS).

Command Macros, Options Macros

Command macros are predefined for Microsoft products. Options macros represent options to these products and are undefined by default. Both are used in predefined inference rules and can be used in description blocks or user-defined inference rules. Command macros can be redefined to represent part or all of a command line, including options. Options macros generate a null string if left undefined. Table 25-9 lists the command and option macros.

Table 25–9 *NMAKE Command and Option Macros*

Microsoft Product	Command Macro	Defined As	Options Macro
Macro Assembler	AS	ml	AFLAGS
Basic Compiler	BC	bc	BFLAGS
C Compiler	CC	cl	CFLAGS
COBOL Compiler	COBOL	cobol	COBFLAGS
C++ Compiler	CPP	cl	CPPFLAGS
C++ Compiler	CXX	cl	CXXFLAGS
Visual Fortran Compiler	FOR	df	FFLAGS
Pascal Compiler	PASCAL	pl	PFLAGS
Resource Compiler	RC	rc	RFLAGS

Environment-Variable Macros

NMAKE inherits macro definitions for environment variables that exist before the start of the session. If a variable was set in the operating-system environment, it is available as an NMAKE macro. Use the /E option to cause macros inherited from environment variables to override any macros with the same name in the makefile.

Environment-variable macros can be redefined in the session, and this changes the corresponding environment variable. You can also change environment variables with the SET command. Using the SET command to change an environment variable in a session does not change the corresponding macro, however.

For example:

```
PATH=$(PATH); \nonesuch

all:
    echo %PATH%
```

In this example, changing PATH changes the corresponding environment variable PATH; it appends \nonesuch to your path.

If an environment variable is defined as a string that would be syntactically incorrect in a makefile, no macro is created and no warning is generated. If a variable's value contains a dollar sign ($), NMAKE interprets it as the beginning of a macro invocation. Using the macro can cause unexpected behavior.

25.6.7 NMAKE Inference Rules

Inference rules supply commands to update targets and to infer dependents for targets. Extensions in an inference rule match a single target and dependent that have the same base name. Inference rules are user-defined or predefined; predefined rules can be redefined.

If an out-of-date dependency has no commands and if .SUFFIXES contains the dependent's extension, NMAKE uses a rule whose extensions match the target and an existing file in the current or specified directory. If more than one rule matches existing files, the .SUFFIXES list determines which to use; list priority descends from left to right.

If a dependent file doesn't exist and is not listed as a target in another description block, an inference rule can create the missing dependent from another file with the same base name. If a description block's target has no dependents or commands, an inference rule can update the target. Inference rules can build a command-line target even if no description block exists. NMAKE may invoke a rule for an inferred dependent even if an explicit dependent is specified.

For more information, see:

▶ Section 25.6.7.1 Defining an Inference Rule in NMAKE

▶ Section 25.6.7.2 Search Paths in Inference Rules

▶ Section 25.6.7.3 Batch-Mode Rules

▶ Section 25.6.7.4 Predefined Inference Rules

▶ Section 25.6.7.5 Inferred Dependents and Rules

▶ Section 25.6.7.6 Precedence in NMAKE Inference Rules

25.6.7.1 Defining an Inference Rule in NMAKE

To define an inference rule, use the following syntax:

.fromext.toext :
commands

The *fromext* represents the extension of a dependent file, and *toext* represents the extension of a target file. Extensions are not case sensitive. Macros can be invoked to represent *fromext* and *toext*; the macros are expanded during preprocessing.

The period (**.**) preceding *fromext* must appear at the beginning of the line. The colon (**:**) is preceded by zero or more spaces or tabs; it can be followed only by spaces or tabs, a semicolon (**;**) to specify a command, a number sign (**#**) to specify a comment, or a newline character. No other spaces are allowed. Commands are specified as in description blocks.

25.6.7.2 Search Paths in Inference Rules

An inference rule that specifies paths has the following syntax:

{*frompath*}**.***fromext*{*topath*}**.***toext*:
commands

An inference rule applies to a dependency only if paths specified in the dependency exactly match the inference-rule paths. Specify the dependent's directory in *frompath* and the target's directory in *topath*; no spaces are allowed. Specify only one path for each extension. A path on one extension requires a path on the other. To specify the current directory, use either a period (**.**) or empty braces ({ }). Macros can represent *frompath* and *topath*; they are invoked during preprocessing.

25.6.7.3 Batch-Mode Rules

Batch-mode inference rules provide only one invocation of the inference rule when N commands go through this inference rule. Without batch-mode inference rules, it would require N commands to be invoked. N is the number of dependents that trigger the inference rule.

Makefiles that contain batch-mode inference rules must use NMAKE version 1.62 or higher. To check the NMAKE version, run the _NMAKE_VER macro available with NMAKE version 1.62 or higher. This macro returns an integer representing the NMAKE version. For example, the macro returns 162 for NMAKE version 1.62.

A batch-mode inference rule has the following syntax:

{*frompath*}.*fromext*{*topath*}.*toext*::
commands

The only syntactical difference from the standard inference rule is that the batch-mode inference rule is terminated with a double colon (::).

Note: The tool being invoked must be able to handle multiple files. The batch-mode inference rule must use $< as the macro to access dependent files.

The batch-mode inference rules can speed up the build process. It is faster to supply files to the compiler in batch, because the compiler driver is invoked only once.

25.6.7.4 *Predefined Inference Rules*

Table 25-10 lists the predefined inference rules. These rules use NMAKE-supplied command and option macros.

Table 25–10   *NMAKE Predefined Rules*

Rule	Command	Default Action
.asm.exe	$(AS) $(AFLAGS) $*.asm	ml $*.asm
.asm.obj	$(AS) $(AFLAGS) /c $*.asm	ml /c $*.asm
.c.exe	$(CC) $(CFLAGS) $*.c	cl $*.c
.c.obj	$(CC) $(CFLAGS) /c $*.c	cl /c $*.c
.cpp.exe	$(CPP) $(CPPFLAGS) $*.cpp	cl $*.cpp
.cpp.obj	$(CPP) $(CPPFLAGS) /c $*.cpp	cl /c $*.cpp
.cxx.exe	$(CXX) $(CXXFLAGS) $*.cxx	cl $*.cxx
.cxx.obj	$(CXX) $(CXXFLAGS) /c $*.cxx	cl /c $*.cxx
.bas.obj	$(BC) $(BFLAGS) $*.bas;	bc $*.bas;
.cbl.exe	$(COBOL) $(COBFLAGS) $*.cbl, $*.exe;	cobol $*.cbl, $*.exe;
.cbl.obj	$(COBOL) $(COBFLAGS) $*.cbl;	cobol $*.cbl;
.f.exe	$(FOR) $(FFLAGS) $*.f	fl32 $*.f

Table 25–10 *NMAKE Predefined Rules (Continued)*

Rule	Command	Default Action
.f.obj	$(FOR) /c $(FFLAGS) $*.f	fl32 $*.f /c
.f90.exe	$(FOR) $(FFLAGS) $*.f90	fl32 $*.f90
.f90.obj	$(FOR) /c $(FFLAGS) $*.f90	fl32 $*.f90 /c
.for.exe	$(FOR) $(FFLAGS) $*.for	fl32 $*.for
.for.obj	$(FOR) /c $(FFLAGS) $*.for	fl32 $*.for /c
.pas.exe	$(PASCAL) $(PFLAGS) $*.pas	pl $*.pas
.pas.obj	$(PASCAL) /c $(PFLAGS) $*.pas	pl /c $*.pas
.rc.res	$(RC) $(RFLAGS) /r $*	rc /r $*

25.6.7.5 Inferred Dependents and Rules

NMAKE assumes an inferred dependent for a target if an applicable inference rule exists. A rule applies if:

▶ *toext* matches the target's extension.

▶ *fromext* matches the extension of a file that has the target's base name and that exists in the current or specified directory.

▶ *fromext* is in .SUFFIXES; no other *fromext* in a matching rule has a higher .SUFFIXES priority.

▶ No explicit dependent has a higher .SUFFIXES priority.

Inferred dependents can cause unexpected side effects. If the target's description block contains commands, NMAKE executes those commands and not the commands in the rule.

25.6.7.6 Precedence in NMAKE Inference Rules

If an inference rule is multiply defined, the highest-precedence definition. The following list shows the order of precedence from highest to lowest:

1. An inference rule defined in a makefile; later definitions have precedence.

2. An inference rule defined in Tools.ini; later definitions have precedence.

3. A predefined inference rule.

25.6.8 Dot Directives in Makefiles

Specify dot directives outside a description block, at the start of a line. Dot directives begin with a period (.) and are followed by a colon (:). Spaces and tabs are allowed. Dot directive names are case sensitive and are uppercase. Table 25-11 lists the dot directives.

Table 25–11 *NMAKE Dot Directives*

Directive	Action
.IGNORE :	Ignores nonzero exit codes returned by commands, from the place it is specified to the end of the makefile. By default, NMAKE halts if a command returns a nonzero exit code. To restore error checking, use !CMDSWITCHES (described in Section 25.6.9.1 Makefile Pre-processing Directives). To ignore the exit code for a single command, use the dash modifier. To ignore exit codes for an entire file, use the /I option.
.PRECIOUS : *targets*	Preserves *targets* on disk if the commands to update them are halted; has no effect if a command handles an interrupt by deleting the file. Separate the target names with one or more spaces or tabs. By default, NMAKE deletes a target if a build is interrupted by Ctrl+C or Ctrl+BREAK. Each use of **.PRECIOUS** applies to the entire makefile; multiple specifications are cumulative.
.SILENT :	Suppresses display of executed commands, from the place it is specified to the end of the makefile. By default, NMAKE displays the commands it invokes. To restore echoing, use !CMDSWITCHES. To suppress echoing of a single command, use the @ modifier. To suppress echoing for an entire file, use the /S option.
.SUFFIXES : *list*	Lists extensions for inference-rule matching; predefined as: .exe .obj .asm .c .cpp .cxx .bas .cbl .for .pas .res .rc

To change the **.SUFFIXES** list order or to specify a new list, clear the list and specify a new setting. To clear the list, specify no extensions after the colon:

```
.SUFFIXES :
```

To add additional suffixes to the end of the list, specify:

```
.SUFFIXES : suffixlist
```

where *suffixlist* is a list of the additional suffixes, separated by one or more spaces or tabs. To see the current setting of **.SUFFIXES**, run NMAKE with the /P option.

25.6.9 Makefile Preprocessing

You can control the NMAKE session by using preprocessing directives and expressions. Preprocessing instructions can be placed in the makefile. Using directives, you can conditionally process your makefile, display error messages, include other makefiles, undefine a macro, and turn certain options on or off.

For more information, see:

▶ Section 25.6.9.1 Makefile Preprocessing Directives

▶ Section 25.6.9.2 Expressions in Makefile Preprocessing

▶ Section 25.6.9.3 Makefile Preprocessing Operators

▶ Section 25.6.9.4 Executing a Program in Preprocessing

25.6.9.1 *Makefile Preprocessing Directives*

Preprocessing directives are not case sensitive. The initial exclamation point (!) must appear at the beginning of the line. Zero or more spaces or tabs can appear after the exclamation point, for indentation. The following are preprocessing directives:

▶ !CMDSWITCHES {+ | -}*option...*

Turns each *option* listed on or off. Spaces or tabs must appear before the + or - operator; none can appear between the operator and the option letters. Letters are not case sensitive and are specified without a slash (/). To turn some options on and others off, use separate specifications of !CMDSWITCHES.

Only /D, /I, /N, and /S can be used in a makefile. In Tools.ini, all options are allowed except /F, /HELP, /NOLOGO, /X, and /?. Changes specified in a description block do not take effect until the next description block. This directive updates the MAKEFLAGS recursion macro; changes are inherited during recursion if MAKEFLAGS is specified.

▶ !ERROR *text*

Displays text in error U1050, then halts NMAKE, even if /K, /I, .IGNORE, !CMDSWITCHES, or the dash (-) command modifier is used. Spaces or tabs before text are ignored.

▶ !MESSAGE *text*

Displays text to standard output. Spaces or tabs before text are ignored.

▶ !INCLUDE [<]*filename*[>]

Reads *filename* as a makefile, then continues with the current makefile. NMAKE searches for *filename* first in the specified or current directory, then recursively through directories of any parent makefiles, then, if *filename* is enclosed by angle brackets (< >), in directories specified by the INCLUDE macro, which is initially set to the INCLUDE environment variable. Useful to pass .SUFFIXES settings, .PRECIOUS, and inference rules to recursive makefiles.

▶ !IF *constantexpression*

Processes statements between !IF and the next !ELSE or !ENDIF if *constantexpression* evaluates to a nonzero value.

▶ !IFDEF *macroname*

processes statements between !IFDEF and the next !ELSE or !ENDIF if *macroname* is defined. A null macro is considered to be defined.

▶ !IFNDEF *macroname*

Processes statements between !IFNDEF and the next !ELSE or !ENDIF if *macroname* is not defined.

▶ !ELSE [IF *constantexpression* | IFDEF *macroname* | IFNDEF *macroname*]

Processes statements between !ELSE and the next !ENDIF if the prior !IF, !IFDEF, or !IFNDEF statement evaluated to zero. The optional keywords give further control of preprocessing.

▶ !ELSEIF

Synonym for !ELSE IF.

▶ !ELSEIFDEF

Synonym for !ELSE IFDEF.

▶ !ELSEIFNDEF

Synonym for !ELSE IFNDEF.

▶ !ENDIF

Marks the end of an !IF, !IFDEF, or !IFNDEF block. Any text after !ENDIF on the same line is ignored.

▶ !UNDEF *macroname*

Undefines *macroname*.

25.6.9.2 Expressions in Makefile Preprocessing

The !IF or !ELSE IF *constantexpression* consists of integer constants (in decimal or C-language notation), string constants, or commands. Use parentheses to group expressions. Expressions use C-style signed long integer arithmetic; numbers are in 32-bit two's-complement form in the range -2147483648 to 2147483647.

Expressions can use operators that act on constant values, exit codes from commands, strings, macros, and file-system paths.

25.6.9.3 Makefile Preprocessing Operators

The DEFINED operator is a logical operator that acts on a macro name. The expression DEFINED (*macroname*) is true if *macroname* is defined. DEFINED in combination with !IF or !ELSE IF is equivalent to !IFDEF or !ELSE IFDEF. However, unlike these directives, DEFINED can be used in complex expressions using binary logical operators.

The EXIST operator is a logical operator that acts on a file-system path. EXIST (*path*) is true if *path* exists. The result from EXIST can be used in binary expressions. If *path* contains spaces, enclose it in double quotation marks.

Integer constants can use the unary operators for numerical negation (-), one's complement (~), and logical negation (!).

Constant expressions can use the binary operators shown in Table 25-12.

Table 25–12 *Binary Operators for Makefiles*

Operator	Description	Operator	Description
+	Addition	||	Logical OR
-	Subtraction	<<	Left shift
*	Multiplication	>>	Right shift
/	Division	= =	Equality
%	Modulus	!=	Inequality
&	Bitwise AND	<	Less than
|	Bitwise OR	>	Greater than
^	Bitwise XOR	<=	Less than or equal to
&&	Logical AND	>=	Greater than or equal to

To compare two strings, use the equality (= =) operator and the inequality (!=) operator. Enclose strings in double quotation marks.

25.6.9.4 Executing a Program in Preprocessing

To use a command's exit code during preprocessing, specify the command, with any arguments, within brackets ([ ]). Any macros are expanded before the command is executed. NMAKE replaces the command specification with the command's exit code, which can be used in an expression to control pre-processing.

25.7   Resource Compiler Options

With Visual Fortran, you can create dialog boxes for an interactive user interface at run-time. For example, you can provide selection lists and scroll bars and the user will not have to type in text strings or numerical control parameters. You can also create custom icons for your Fortran QuickWin and Fortran Windows applications.

The Microsoft visual development environment includes a special dialog editor for creating dialogs and placing the controls within them, and a graphic editor for drawing or importing icons. You must use the dialog editor and graphic editor in the visual development environment to design dialogs and icons. Once you have created a dialog or icon, you can compile it from the command line using the Resource Compiler (RC).

In the visual development environment, you can view the resources in your project in the ResourceView pane (a tab next to the FileView pane). The resource editor in the Microsoft visual development environment offers easy, time-saving alternatives to the traditional hand-coded scripts used to create resources. Resources are built when you build your project.

These visual tools create and manage your project's script—you don't need to hand-code scripts. For more information on the working with resources in the visual development environment, see the "Resource Editors" section in the *Visual C++ User's Guide*.

For information on creating resource-definition script files and using the RC command from the command line, see:

▶ Section 25.7.1 Including Resources in an Application

▶ Section 25.7.2 Creating a Resource Definition File

▶ Section 25.7.3 Resource Compiler Command Line

▶ The online *Platform SDK* sections under "Windows Programming Guidelines," "Platform SDK Tools," such as "Compiling" and "Using the Resource Compiler."

25.7.1   Including Resources in an Application

To include resources in your Win32-based application with RC from the command line, do the following:

1. Use the visual development environment dialog editor or graphic editor to create a resource for each dialog or icon in your application. (For more information, see "Resource Editors" in the *Visual C++ User's Guide.*)

2. Create a resource-definition file (also called a script) that describes the resources used by your application.

3. Compile the script into a resource (.RES) file with RC.EXE (RC).

4. Link the compiled resource files into the application's executable file.

   You do not use RC to include compiled resources into the executable file or to mark the file as an application. The linker recognizes the compiled resource files and links them to the executable file.

25.7.2   Creating a Resource-Definition File

After creating individual resource files for your application's dialog box and icon resources, you create a resource-definition file, or *script*. A script is a text file with the extension .RC.

The script lists every resource in your application and describes some types of resources in great detail. For a resource that exists in a separate file, such as an icon or cursor, the script names the resource and the file that contains it. For some resources, such as a menu, the entire definition of the resource exists within the script.

A script file can contain the following information:

▶ Comments (single-line comments or block line comments)

▶ Predefined macros

▶ Preprocessing directives, which instruct RC to perform actions on the script before compiling.

▶ Preprocessor operators

▶ Resource definition statements, which name and describe resources. Statements can be single-line or multiline statements.

▶ Pragmas for changing the code page

The following example shows a script file that defines the resources for an application named Shapes:

```
#include "SHAPES.H"

ShapesCursor CURSOR SHAPES.CUR
ShapesIcon ICON SHAPES.ICO

  BEGIN
    POPUP "&Shape"
      BEGIN
        MENUITEM "&Clear", ID_CLEAR
        MENUITEM "&Rectangle", ID_RECT
        MENUITEM "&Triangle", ID_TRIANGLE
        MENUITEM "&Star", ID_STAR
        MENUITEM "&Ellipse", ID_ELLIPSE
      END
  END
```

The CURSOR statement names the application's cursor resource Shapes-Cursor and specifies the cursor file SHAPES.CUR, which contains the image for that cursor. Custom cursors are not available in Visual Fortran.

The ICON statement names the application's icon resource ShapesIcon and specifies the icon file SHAPES.ICO, which contains the image for that icon.

The MENU statement defines an application menu named ShapesMenu, a pop-up menu with five menu items.

The menu definition, enclosed by the BEGIN and END keywords, specifies each menu item and the menu identifier that is returned when the user selects that item. For example, the first item on the menu, Clear, returns the menu identifier ID_CLEAR when the user selects it. The menu identifiers are defined in the application header file, SHAPES.H.

Once you create the resource-definition script (RC) file, use the Resource Compiler Command Line (see Section 25.7.3) to create the RES file.

For details about script files, see the online *Platform SDK* sections under "Windows Programming Guidelines" and "Platform SDK Tools" such as "Using the Resource Compiler."

25.7.3 Resource Compiler Command Line

To start RC, use the following command-line syntax:

RC [*options*] *script-file*

options

Is one or more of the options shown in Table 25-13.

Table 25–13 *RC Command-Line Options*

Option	Description
/?	Displays a list of RC command-line options.
/d	Defines a symbol for the preprocessor that you can test with the #ifdef directive.
/fo *resname*	Uses *resname* for the name of the .RES file.
/h	Displays a list of RC command-line options.
/i *directory*	Causes RC to search the specified *directory* before searching the directories specified by the INCLUDE environment variable.
/lcodepage	Specifies default language for compilation. For example, -l409 is equivalent to including the following statement at the top of the resource script file: `LANGUAGE LANG_ENGLISH,SUBLANG_ENGLISH_US` Alternatively, you can use #pragma code_page(409) in the .RC file.
/n	Null terminates all strings in the string table.
/r	Ignored. Provided for compatibility with existing makefiles.
/u	Undefines a symbol.
/v	Causes a display of messages that report on the progress of the compiler.
/x	Prevents RC from checking the INCLUDE environment variable when searching for header files or resource files.

Options are not case sensitive and a dash (-) can be used in place of a forward slash (/). You can combine single-letter options if they do not require additional arguments. For example, the following commands are equivalent:

```
RC /V /X SAMPLE.RC
rc -vx sample.rc
```

script-file

Specifies the name of the resource-definition script that contains the names, types, filenames, and descriptions of the resources to be compiled.

For more information on these options and the resource compiler, see the online *Platform SDK* sections under "Windows Programming Guidelines" and "Platform SDK Tools," such as "Using the Resource Compiler."

25.8   Managing Libraries with LIB

You may find it useful to create libraries of Common Object File Format (COFF) object files to organize shared components of multiple projects. In the Microsoft visual development environment, you create and manage object libraries with a variety of dialogs. From the command line, you can use the Microsoft 32-Bit Library Manager (LIB.EXE) to manage COFF object libraries, create export files and import libraries to reference exported symbol definitions when you build Dynamic Link Libraries (DLLs), and extract library members.

You use the standard libraries, import libraries, and export files LIB creates with LINK when building a 32-bit program. (LINK is described in Chapter 3 Using the Compiler and Linker from the Command Line and Chapter 4 Compiler and Linker Options.) The three LIB modes—creating standard (COFF) libraries, creating import libraries and export files, and extracting library members—are mutually exclusive. You can use LIB in only one mode at a time.

You can use LIB to perform the following library-management tasks:

▶ Add objects to a library

   Specify the filename for the existing library and the filenames for the new objects.

▶ Combine libraries

   Specify the library filenames. You can add objects and combine libraries in a single LIB command.

▶ Replace a library member with a new object

   Specify the library containing the member object to be replaced and the filename for the new object (or the library that contains it). When an object that has the same name exists in more than one input file, LIB puts the last object specified in the LIB command into the output library. When you replace a library member, be sure to specify the new object or library after the library that contains the old object.

▶ Delete a member from a library

   Use the /REMOVE option. LIB processes any specifications of /REMOVE after combining all input objects, regardless of command-line order.

Note: You cannot both delete a member and extract it to a file in the same step. You must first extract the member object using /EXTRACT, then run LIB again using /REMOVE.

This section describes the Microsoft 32-Bit Library Manager (LIB.EXE). The following topics are covered:

▶ Section 25.8.1 LIB Input/Output

▶ Section 25.8.2 Running LIB

▶ Section 25.8.3 LIB Options

▶ Section 25.8.4 Extracting a Library Member

▶ Section 25.8.5 Import Libraries and Export Files

25.8.1 LIB Input/Output

LIB expects types of input files and generates types of output files depending on the mode in which it is used. You can also get information about the resulting library with the /LIST option, and you can examine the contents of the library by using DUMPBIN with the /LINKERMEMBER option.

For more information, see:

▶ Section 25.8.1.1 LIB Input Files

▶ Section 25.8.1.2 LIB Output Files

▶ Section 25.8.1.3 Other LIB Output

▶ Section 25.8.1.4 Viewing Contents of a Library

25.8.1.1 LIB Input Files

The input files expected by LIB depend on the mode in which it is used, as shown in Table 25-15.

Table 25–14 *LIB Input Files*

Mode	Input
Default (building or modifying a library)	COFF object (.OBJ) files, COFF libraries (.LIB), 32-bit OMF object (.OBJ) files
Extracting a member with /EXTRACT	COFF library (.LIB)
Building an export file and import library with /DEF	Module-definition (.DEF) file, COFF object (.OBJ) files, COFF libraries (.LIB), 32-bit OMF object (.OBJ) files

Note: Object Model Format (OMF) libraries created by the 16-bit version of LIB cannot be used as input to the 32-bit LIB.

25.8.1.2 LIB Output Files

The output files produced by LIB depend on the usage mode as shown in Table 25-15.

Table 25–15 *LIB Output Files*

Mode	Output
Default (building or modifying a library)	COFF library (.LIB)
Extracting a member with /EXTRACT	Object (.OBJ) file
Building an export file and import library with /DEF	Import library (.LIB) and export (.EXP) file

25.8.1.3 Other LIB Output

In the default mode, you can use the /LIST option to display information about the resulting library. You can redirect this output to a file.

LIB displays a copyright and version message and echoes command files unless the /NOLOGO option is used.

When you type LIB with no other input, LIB displays a usage statement that summarizes its options.

Error and warning messages issued by LIB have the form LNK*nnnn*. The LINK, DUMPBIN, and EDITBIN tools also use this range of errors.

25.8.1.4 Viewing Contents of a Library

A library contains COFF objects. Objects in a library contain functions and data that can be referenced externally by other objects in a program. An object in a library is sometimes referred to as a library member.

You can get additional information about the contents of a library by running the DUMPBIN tool with the /LINKERMEMBER option. For more information, see Section 25.10 Examining Files with DUMPBIN.

25.8.2 Running LIB

This section presents information on running LIB in any mode. It describes the LIB command line, discusses the use of command files, and gives general rules for using options.

For more information, see:

▶ Section 25.8.2.1 LIB Command Line

▶ Section 25.8.2.2 LIB Command Files

▶ Section 25.8.2.3 Using LIB Options

25.8.2.1 *LIB Command Line*

To run LIB, type the command LIB followed by the options and filenames for the task you are using LIB to perform. LIB also accepts command-line input in command files. LIB does not use an environment variable.

Note: If you are accustomed to the LINK32.EXE and LIB32.EXE tools provided with the Microsoft Win32 Software Development Kit for Windows NT, you may have been using either the command LINK32 -LIB or the command LIB32 for managing libraries and creating import libraries. Be sure to change your makefiles and batch files to use the LIB command instead.

25.8.2.2 *LIB Command Files*

You can pass command-line arguments to LIB in a command file by using the following syntax:

LIB @*commandfile*

The *commandfile* is the name of a text file. No space or tab is allowed between the at sign (@) and the filename. There is no default extension; you must specify the full filename, including any extension. Wildcards cannot be used. You can specify an absolute or relative path with the filename.

In the command file, arguments can be separated by spaces or tabs as they can on the command line, and they can also be separated by newline characters. Use a semicolon (;) to mark a comment. LIB ignores all text from the semicolon to the end of the line.

You can specify either all or part of the command line in a command file, and you can use more than one command file in a LIB command. LIB accepts the command-file input as if it were specified in that location on the command line. Command files cannot be nested. LIB echoes the contents of command files unless the /NOLOGO option is used.

25.8.2.3 *Using LIB Options*

An option consists of an option specifier, which is either a dash (-) or a forward slash (/), followed by the name of the option. Option names cannot be abbreviated. Some options take an argument, specified after a colon (:). No spaces or tabs are allowed within an option specification. Use one or more spaces or tabs to separate option specifications on the command line.

Option names and their keyword or filename arguments are not case sensitive, but identifiers used as arguments are case sensitive. LIB processes options in the order specified on the command line and in command files. If an option is repeated with different arguments, the last one to be processed takes precedence.

The following LIB options apply to all modes of LIB:

▶ /MACHINE

Specifies the architecture of the library.

▶ /NOLOGO

Suppresses display of the LIB copyright message and version number and prevents echoing of command files.

▶ /VERBOSE

Displays details about the progress of the session. The information is sent to standard output and can be redirected to a file.

Other options apply only to specific modes of LIB. These options are discussed in the sections describing each mode.

25.8.3 LIB Options

The default mode for LIB is to build or modify a library of COFF objects. LIB runs in this mode when you do not specify /EXTRACT (to copy an object to a file) or /DEF (to build an import library).

To build a library from objects and/or libraries, use the following syntax:

LIB [*options...*] *files...*

Table 25-16 lists the *options* that apply to building and modifying a library.

Table 25–16 *LIB Options that Build and Modify Libraries*

Option	Description
/CONVERT	Converts an import library to the previous (Visual C++ version 5.0) format.
/LIBPATH:*dir*	Overrides the environment library path. For more information, see Section 4.2.26 /LIBPATH (linker option).

Table 25–16 *LIB Options that Build and Modify Libraries (Continued)*

Option	Description
/LIST	Displays information about the output library to standard output. The output can be redirected to a file. You can use /LIST to determine the contents of an existing library without modifying it.
/LINK50COMPAT	Generates an import library in the previous (Visual C++ version 5.0) format for backwards compatibility.
/OUT:*filename*	Overrides the default output filename. By default, the output library has the base name of the first library or object on the command line and the extension .LIB.
/REMOVE:*object*	Omits the specified *object* from the output library. LIB creates an output library by first combining all objects (whether in object files or libraries), then deleting any objects specified with /REMOVE.
/SUBSYSTEM	Tells the operating system how to run a program created by linking to the output library. For more information, see the description of the LINK /SUBSYSTEM option in Section 4.2.45.

Other LIB options are described in:

▶ Section 25.8.2.3 Using LIB Options

▶ Section 25.8.4 Extracting a Library Member

▶ Section 25.8.5.1 Building an Import Library and Export File

The *files* can be COFF object files, 32-bit OMF object files, and existing COFF libraries. LIB creates one library that contains all objects in the specified files. If an input file is a 32-bit OMF object file, LIB converts it to COFF before building the library. LIB cannot accept a 32-bit OMF object that is in a library created by the 16-bit version of LIB. You must first use the 16-bit LIB to extract the object, then you can use the extracted object file as input to the 32-bit LIB. The 16-bit version of LIB is not provided with Visual Fortran.

By default, LIB names the output file using the base name of the first object or library file and the extension .LIB. If a file already exists with the same name, the output file overwrites the existing file. To preserve an existing library, use the /OUT option to specify a name for the output file.

You can use LIB to perform the following library-management tasks:

▶ Add objects to a library

Specify the filename for the existing library and the filenames for the new objects.

▶ Combine libraries

Specify the library filenames. You can add objects and combine libraries in a single LIB command.

▶ Replace a library member with a new object

Specify the library containing the member object to be replaced and the filename for the new object (or the library that contains it). When an object that has the same name exists in more than one input file, LIB puts the last object specified in the LIB command into the output library. When you replace a library member, be sure to specify the new object or library after the library that contains the old object.

▶ Delete a member from a library

Use the /REMOVE option. LIB processes any specifications of /REMOVE after combining all input objects, regardless of command-line order.

Note: You cannot both delete a member and extract it to a file in the same step. You must first extract the member object using /EXTRACT, then run LIB again using /REMOVE. This behavior differs from that of the 16-bit LIB (for OMF libraries) provided in some Microsoft products.

25.8.4   Extracting a Library Member

You can use LIB to create an object (.OBJ) file that contains a copy of a member of an existing library. To extract a copy of a member, use the following syntax:

LIB *library* /EXTRACT:*member* /OUT:*objectfile*

This command creates an .OBJ file called *objectfile* that contains a copy of a *member* of a *library*. The *member* name is case sensitive. You can extract only one member in a single command. The /OUT option is required; there is no default output name. If a file called *objectfile* already exists in the specified directory (or current directory, if no directory is specified with *objectfile*), the extracted *objectfile* overwrites the existing file.

25.8.5   Import Libraries and Export Files

You can use LIB with the /DEF option to create an import library and an export file. LINK uses the export file to build a program that contains exports (usually a DLL), and it uses the import library to resolve references to those exports in other programs.

In most situations, you do not need to use LIB to create your import library. When you link a program (either an executable file or a DLL) that contains exports, LINK automatically creates an import library that describes the exports. Later, when you link a program that references those exports, you specify the import library.

However, when a DLL exports to a program that it also imports from, whether directly or indirectly, you must use LIB to create one of the import libraries. When LIB creates an import library, it also creates an export file. You must use the exports file when linking one of the DLLs.

For more information, see:

▶ Section 25.8.5.1 Building an Import Library and Export File

▶ Section 25.8.5.2 Using an Import Library and Export File

25.8.5.1 *Building an Import Library and Export File*

To build an import library and export file, use the following syntax:

LIB /DEF[:*deffile*] [*options*] [*objfiles*] [*libraries*]

When /DEF is specified, LIB creates the output files from export specifications that are passed in the LIB command. There are three methods for specifying exports, listed in recommended order of use:

▶ *c***DEC\$ ATTRIBUTES** DLLEXPORT in one of the *objfiles* or *libraries*

▶ A specification of /EXPORT:*name* on the LIB command line

▶ A definition in an EXPORTS statement in a *deffile*

These are the same methods you use to specify exports when linking an exporting program. A program can use more than one method. You can specify parts of the LIB command (such as multiple *objfiles* or /EXPORT specifications) in a command file in the LIB command, just as you can in a LINK command.

The following options apply to building an import library and exports file:

▶ /DEBUGTYPE:{CV|COFF|BOTH}

This sets the format of debugging information. Specify CV for new-style Microsoft Symbolic Debugging Information, required by Visual C++ and Visual Fortran. Specify COFF for Common Object File Format (COFF) debugging information. Specify BOTH for both COFF debugging information and old-style Microsoft debugging information.

▶ /OUT:*import*

This option overrides the default output filename for the *import* library being created. When /OUT is not specified, the default name is the base name of the first object file or library in the LIB command and the extension .LIB. The exports file is given the same base name as the import library and the extension .EXP.

▶ /EXPORT:*entryname*[=*internalname*] [,@*ordinal*[,NONAME]][,DATA]

This option exports a function from your program to allow other programs to call the function. You can also export data. Exports are usually defined in a DLL.

The *entryname* is the name of the function or data item as it is to be used by the calling program. You can optionally specify the *internalname* as the function known in the defining program; by default, *internalname* is the same as *entryname*. The ordinal specifies an index into the exports table in the range 1 to 65535; if you do not specify *ordinal*, LIB assigns one. The NONAME keyword exports the function only as an ordinal, without an *entryname*.

▶ /INCLUDE:*symbol*

This option adds the specified symbol to the symbol table. This is useful for forcing the use of a library object that otherwise would not be included.

25.8.5.2 Using an Import Library and Export File

When a program (either an executable file or a DLL) exports to another program that it also imports from, or if more than two programs both export to and import from each other, the commands to link these programs must accommodate the circular exports.

In a situation without circular exports, when you link a program that uses exports from another program, you must specify the import library for the exporting program. The import library for the exporting program is created when you link that exporting program. This requires that you link the exporting program before the importing program. For example, if TWO.DLL imports from ONE.DLL, you must first link ONE.DLL and get the import library ONE.LIB. You then specify ONE.LIB when you link TWO.DLL. When the linker creates TWO.DLL, it also creates its import library, TWO.LIB. You use TWO.LIB when linking programs that import from TWO.DLL.

However, in a circular export situation, it is not possible to link all of the interdependent programs using import libraries from the other programs. In the example discussed earlier, if TWO.DLL also exports to ONE.DLL, the import library for TWO.DLL won't exist yet when ONE.DLL is linked. When circular exports exist, you must use LIB to create an import library and exports file for one of the programs.

To begin, choose one of the programs on which to run LIB. In the LIB command, list all objects and libraries for the program and specify the /DEF option. If the program uses a .DEF file or /EXPORT specifications, specify these as well.

After you create the import library (.LIB) and the export file (.EXP) for the program, you then use the import library when linking the other program or programs. LINK creates an import library for each exporting program it builds. For example, if you ran LIB on the objects and exports for ONE.DLL, you created ONE.LIB and ONE.EXP. You can now use ONE.LIB when linking TWO.DLL; this step also creates the import library TWO.LIB.

Finally, link the program you began with. In the LINK command, specify the objects and libraries for the program, the .EXP file that LIB created for the program, and the import library or libraries for the exports used by the program. In the continuing example, the LINK command for ONE.DLL contains ONE.EXP and TWO.LIB, as well as the objects and libraries that go into ONE.DLL. Do not specify the .DEF file and /EXPORT specifications in the LINK command; these are not needed because the exports definitions are contained in the .EXP file. When you link using an .EXP file, LINK does not create an import library because it assumes that one was created when the .EXP file was created.

25.9   Editing Files with EDITBIN

You can specify execution characteristics of a program or library by selecting options in the visual development environment. For example, you might need to specify the base address at which a program is loaded by the operating system. If you work from the command line, you can use the Microsoft Binary File Editor (EDITBIN) to set these types of controls.

This section describes the Microsoft COFF Binary File Editor (EDITBIN.EXE). EDITBIN modifies 32-bit Common Object File Format (COFF) binary files. You can use EDITBIN to modify object files, executable files, and dynamic-link libraries (DLLs).

EDITBIN converts the format of an Object Module Format (OMF) input file to COFF before making other changes to the file. You can use EDITBIN to convert the format of a file to COFF by running EDITBIN with no options.

The following topics are covered in this section:

▶ Section 25.9.1 EDITBIN Command Line

▶ Section 25.9.2 EDITBIN Options

25.9.1 EDITBIN Command Line

To run EDITBIN, use the following syntax:

EDITBIN [*options*] *files*...

Specify one or more *files* for the objects or images to be changed, and one or more *options* for changing the files.

When you type the command EDITBIN without any other command-line input, EDITBIN displays a usage statement that summarizes its options.

25.9.2 EDITBIN Options

An option consists of an option specifier, which is either a dash (-) or a forward slash (/), followed by the name of the option. Option names cannot be abbreviated. Some options take arguments, specified after a colon (:). No spaces or tabs are allowed within an option specification. Use one or more spaces or tabs to separate option specifications on the command line. Option names and their keyword or filename arguments are not case sensitive.

This following sections discuss EDITBIN options:

▶ Section 29.9.2.1 /BIND

▶ Section 29.9.2.2 /HEAP

▶ Section 29.9.2.3 /LARGEADDRESSAWARE

▶ Section 29.9.2.4 /NOLOGO

▶ Section 29.9.2.5 /REBASE

▶ Section 29.9.2.6 /RELEASE

▶ Section 29.9.2.7 /SECTION

▶ Section 29.9.2.8 /STACK

▶ Section 29.9.2.9 /SUBSYSTEM

▶ Section 29.9.2.10 /SWAPRUN

▶ Section 29.9.2.11 /VERSION

▶ Section 29.9.2.12 /WS

25.9.2.1 EDITBIN Option /BIND

The /BIND option sets the addresses of the entry points in the import address table for an executable file or DLL. Use this option to reduce load time of a program.

The /BIND option has the following form:

/BIND[:PATH=*path*]

Specify the program's executable file and DLLs in the *files* argument on the EDITBIN command line. The optional *path* argument to the /BIND option specifies the location of the DLLs used by the specified files. Separate multiple directories with semicolons (;). If *path* is not specified, EDITBIN searches the directories specified in the PATH environment variable. If *path* is specified, EDITBIN ignores the PATH variable.

By default, the Windows program loader sets the addresses of entry points when it loads a program. The amount of time this takes varies depending on the number of DLLs and the number of entry points referenced in the program.

If a program has been modified with the /BIND option, and if the base addresses for the executable file and its DLLs do not conflict with DLLs that are already loaded, the operating system does not need to set these addresses. In a situation where the files are incorrectly based, the operating system will relocate the program's DLLs and recalculate the entry-point addresses; this adds to the program's load time.

25.9.2.2 EDITBIN Option /HEAP

The /HEAP option sets the size of the heap in bytes. It has the following form:

/HEAP:*reserve*[,*commit*]

The *reserve* argument specifies the total heap allocation in virtual memory. The default heap size is 1MB. The linker rounds up the specified value to the nearest 4 bytes.

The optional *commit* argument is subject to interpretation by the operating system. It specifies the amount of physical memory to allocate at a time. Committed virtual memory causes space to be reserved in the paging file. A higher *commit* value saves time when the application needs more heap space but increases the memory requirements and possibly startup time.

Specify the *reserve* and *commit* values in decimal or C-language notation.

25.9.2.3 EDITBIN Option /LARGEADDRESSAWARE

This option edits the image to indicate that the application can handle addresses larger than 2 gigabytes.

25.9.2.4 EDITBIN Option /NOLOGO

This option suppresses display of the EDITBIN copyright message and version number.

25.9.2.5 EDITBIN Option /REBASE

The /REBASE option sets the base addresses for the specified files. EDITBIN assigns new base addresses in a contiguous address space according to the size of each file rounded up to the nearest 64K. This option takes the following form:

/REBASE[:*modifiers*]

You can optionally specify one or more of the following *modifiers*, each separated by a comma (,):

▶ BASE=*address*

Provides a beginning address for reassigning base addresses to the files. Specify *address* in decimal or C-language notation. If BASE is not specified, the default starting base address is 0x400000. If DOWN is used, BASE must be specified, and *address* sets the end of the range of base addresses.

▶ BASEFILE

Creates a file named COFFBASE.TXT, which is a text file in the format expected by LINK's /BASE option.

▶ DOWN

Tells EDITBIN to reassign base addresses downward from an ending address. The files are reassigned in the order specified, with the first file located in the highest possible address below the end of the address range. BASE must be used with DOWN to ensure sufficient address space for basing the files. To determine the address space needed by the specified files, run EDITBIN with the /REBASE option on the files and add 64K to the displayed total size.

Specify the program's executable files and DLLs in the *files* argument on the EDITBIN command line in the order in which they are to be based.

25.9.2.6 *EDITBIN Option /RELEASE*

This option sets the checksum in the header of an executable file. The operating system requires the checksum for certain files such as device drivers. It is recommended that you set the checksum for release versions of your programs to ensure compatibility with future operating systems.

25.9.2.7 *EDITBIN Option /SECTION*

This option changes the properties of a section, overriding the properties that were set when the object file for the section was compiled or linked. It has the following form:

/SECTION:name[=*newname*][, *properties*][, *alignment*]

After the colon (:), specify the name of the section. To change the section name, follow name with an equal sign (=) and a *newname* for the section.

To set or change the section's properties, specify a comma (,) followed by one or more property characters. To negate a property, precede its character with an exclamation point (!). Table 25-17 lists the characters that specify memory properties.

Table 25–17   *Memory Properties for the EDITBIN /SECTION Option*

Property	Setting
c	code
d	discardable
e	executable
i	initialized data
k	cached virtual memory
m	link remove
o	link info
p	paged virtual memory
r	read
s	shared
u	uninitialized data
w	write

To control *alignment*, specify the character "a" followed by a character to set the size of alignment in bytes, as shown in Table 25-18.

Table 25–18 *Alignment Characters for the EDITBIN /SECTION Option*

Character	Alignment Size in Bytes
1	1
2	2
4	4
8	8
p	16
t	32
s	64
x	no alignment

Specify the *properties* and *alignment* characters as a string with no white space. The characters are not case sensitive.

25.9.2.8 EDITBIN Option /STACK

This option sets the size of the stack in bytes and takes arguments in decimal or C-language notation. The /STACK option applies only to an executable file. This option takes the following form:

/STACK:*reserve*[,*commit*]

The *reserve* argument specifies the total stack allocation in virtual memory. EDITBIN rounds up the specified value to the nearest 4 bytes. The optional *commit* argument is subject to interpretation by the operating system. In Windows NT, *commit* specifies the amount of physical memory to allocate at a time. Committed virtual memory causes space to be reserved in the paging file. A higher *commit* value saves time when the application needs more stack space but increases the memory requirements and possibly startup time.

25.9.2.9 EDITBIN Option /SUBSYSTEM

This option edits the image to indicate which subsystem the operating system must invoke for execution.

For more information, see the description of the LINK /SUBSYSTEM option in Section 4.2.45.

25.9.2.10   EDITBIN Option /SWAPRUN

This option edits the image to tell the operating system to copy the image to a swap file and run it from there. Use this option for images that reside on networks or removable media. It has the following form:

/SWAPRUN:{[!]NET|[!]CD}

You can add or remove the NET or CD qualifiers:

▶ NET indicates that the image resides on a network.

▶ CD indicates that the image resides on a CD-ROM or similar removable medium.

Use !NET and !CD to reverse the effects of NET and CD.

25.9.2.11   EDITBIN Option /VERSION

This option places a version number into the header of the image. It has the following form:

/VERSION:*left*[, *right*]

The whole number part of the version number (the portion to the left of the decimal point) is represented by *left*. The fractional part of the version number (the portion to the right of the decimal point) is represented by *right*.

25.9.2.12   EDITBIN Option /WS

This option adds the WS_AGGRESSIVE property to your application's image. It has the following form:

/WS:AGGRESSIVE

In Windows NT 4.0 and later, the loader recognizes this property and aggressively trims the working set of the process when the process is inactive. This has the same effect as using the following call throughout your application:

```
SetProcessWorkingSetSize(hThisProcess, -1, -1)
```

Use /WS:AGGRESSIVE for applications such as services and screen savers that must have a low impact on the system's memory pool. If the speed of your application matters, do not use /WS:AGGRESSIVE without testing the resulting performance.

25.10 Examining Files with DUMPBIN

There are times when you must examine or change OBJ, EXE, and DLL files. In the visual development environment, you can open any file as a Binary rather than as an ASCII text file and work with both hexadecimal and ASCII versions of the contents. From the command line, you can use the Microsoft Binary File Dumper (DUMPBIN) to edit these types of files.

This section describes the Microsoft COFF Binary File Dumper (DUMP-BIN.EXE). DUMPBIN displays information about 32-bit Common Object File Format (COFF) binary files. You can use DUMPBIN to examine COFF object files, standard libraries of COFF objects, executable files, and dynamic-link libraries (DLLs).

The following topics are covered in this section:

▶ Section 25.10.1 DUMPBIN Command Line

▶ Section 25.10.2 DUMPBIN Options

25.10.1 DUMPBIN Command Line

The syntax for DUMPBIN is:

DUMPBIN [*options*] *files...*

Specify one or more binary files, along with any options required to control the information. DUMPBIN displays the information to standard output. You can either redirect it to a file or use the /OUT option to specify a filename for the output.

When you run DUMPBIN on a file without specifying an option, DUMPBIN displays the /SUMMARY output.

When you type the command DUMPBIN without any other command-line input, DUMPBIN displays a usage statement that summarizes its options.

25.10.2 DUMPBIN Options

An option consists of an option specifier, which is either a dash (-) or a forward slash (/), followed by the name of the option. Option names cannot be abbreviated. Some options take arguments, specified after a colon (:). No spaces or tabs are allowed within an option specification. Use one or more spaces or tabs to separate option specifications on the command line. Option names and their keyword or filename arguments are not case sensitive. Most options apply to all binary files; a few apply only to certain types of files.

Table 25-19 lists the DUMPBIN options.

Table 25–19 *DUMPBIN Options*

Option	Description
/ALL	Displays all available information except code disassembly. Use the /DISASM option to display disassembly. You can use /RAWDATA:NONE with the /ALL option to omit the raw binary details of the file.
/ARCHIVEMEMBERS	Displays minimal information about member objects in a library.
/ARCH	Dumps the .arch section of an image.
/DEPENDENTS	Dumps the names of the DLLs from which the image imports functions. Does not dump the names of the imported functions.
/DIRECTIVES	Dumps the compiler-generated .drective section of an image.
/DISASM	Displays disassembly of code sections, using symbols if present in the file.
/EXPORTS	Displays all definitions exported from an executable file or DLL.
/FPO	DisplaysFrame Pointer Optimization (FPO) records.
/HEADERS	Displays coff header information.
/IMPORTS	Displays all definitions imported to an executable file or DLL. Output resembles the /EXPORTS option.
/LINENUMBERS	Displays COFF line numbers. Line numbers exist in an object file if it was compiled with Program Database (/Zi) or Line Numbers Only (/Zd). An executable file or DLL contains COFF line numbers if it was linked with Generate Debug Info (/DEBUG) and COFF Format (/DEBUGTYPE:COFF).
/LINKERMEMBER	The option /LINKERMEMBER[:{1|2}] displays public symbols defined in a library. Specify the 1 argument to display symbols in object order, along with their offsets. Specify the 2 argument to display offsets and index numbers of objects, then list the symbols in alphabetical order along with the object index for each. To get both outputs, specify /LINKERMEMBER without the number argument.
/OUT	The option /OUT:*filename* specifies a *filename* for the output. By default, DUMPBIN displays the information to standard output.
/PDATA	Dumps the exception tables (.pdata) from an image or object.

Table 25–19 *DUMPBIN Options (Continued)*

Option	Description
/RAWDATA	The option /RAWDATA[:{ *BYTES* | *SHORTS* | *LONGS* | *NONE* }][, *number*]] displays the raw contents of each section in the file. The arguments control the format of the display, as follows: **Argument** **Result** *BYTES* The default. Contents are displayed in hexadecimal bytes, and also as ASCII if they have a printed representation. *SHORTS* Contents are displayed in hexadecimal words. *LONGS* Contents are displayed in hexadecimal longwords. *NONE* Raw data is suppressed. This is useful to control the output of the /ALL option. *number* Displayed lines are set to a width that holds number values per line.
/RELOCATIONS	Displays any relocations in the object or image.
/SECTION	The option /SECTION:*section* restricts the output to information on the specified *section*.
/SUMMARY	Displays minimal information about sections, including total size. This option is the default if no other option is specified.
/SYMBOLS	Displays the COFF symbol table. Symbol tables exist in all object files. A COFF symbol table appears in an image file only if it is linked with the Generate Debug Info and COFF Format options under Debug Info on the Debug category for the linker (or the /DEBUG and /DEBUGTYPE:COFF options on the command line).

25.11 Editing Format Descriptors with the Format Editor

The Format Editor is an application for Windows that shows you what data formatted to match your edit descriptors will look like, and lets you edit either the descriptor list or the data. You can interactively create and edit Fortran 90 **FORMAT** statements and embedded formatting directives.

You can run the Format Editor either from the Edit menu in the visual development environment or from the command line. The Format Editor program is located in the . . . \Common\MSDev98\Bin directory, and is called FRMTEDIT.EXE. To use it from the command line, you specify the source code file name, line number and column position in the argument list, and the Format Editor operates on the formatting at the indicated location. For example:

```
FRMTEDIT test.f90 5 18
```

If the line specified by the second parameter is empty, a new format statement is created with the words *label FORMAT.*

To use the Format Editor on a multi-line format statement, the argument list must specify the first line of the format statement. In-line comments in a multi-line Format statement are lost when the Format Editor writes the updated format statement and generates new continuation marks. Similarly, the part of a formatted I/O statement that follows the formatting directives is lost when the Format Editor writes the updated directive string back to the file.

When you are finished editing the format statement, the Format Editor rewrites the source file with code for the format you have developed. If the file has the extension .F90, the revised code is written with Fortran 90 free-form syntax rules; otherwise, it is written with Fortran 90 fixed-form syntax rules.

The Format Editor is installed on the Edit menu during Visual Fortran installation. If you have removed it for any reason, and need to reinstall it, you can do so by choosing Customize from the Tools menu. The argument list, which passes the current file name, line number and column position to the Format Editor, is $File $Line $Column. For more information about adding programs to the Tools menu, select the Help button in the Customize dialog.

For more information, see Section 25.11.1 Starting the Format Editor from the Microsoft Visual Development Environment.

25.11.1 Starting the Format Editor from the Microsoft Visual Development Environment

The Format Editor presents the format code and a sample of the resulting data layout in a window that works like a dialog box. You can edit either the source code or the data layout, and the Format Editor changes the other to match.

To open the Format Editor:

1. Load a Fortran source file that contains a **FORMAT** statement or an I/O edit descriptor.

2. Place the cursor on the first line of the **FORMAT** statement or on the line containing the edit descriptor.

3. From the Edit menu, choose Format Editor. The Format Editor dialog box opens.

The Format Editor dialog box consists of the following text boxes and buttons:

▶ The edit descriptors in the upper-left text box

▶ The sample data display in the lower-left text box

▶ The New Field, Remove Field, Change Value, OK, Cancel, and Help buttons along the bottom

When you open the Format editor in a line with an edit descriptor, the editor attempts to parse the first opening quote that precedes the cursor position. When you open the editor in a line containing a **FORMAT** statement, the editor attempts to parse the edit descriptors in the statement. If the editor is successful, it displays the edit descriptors in the upper-left box and a sample data display in the lower text box. If the editor cannot parse the descriptor string or **FORMAT** statement, you will get a parse error message.

To insert new I/O edit descriptors into existing formatted I/O statements or **FORMAT** statements in the Microsoft visual development environment:

1. Place the cursor in the existing descriptor or **FORMAT** statement.

2. From the Edit menu, choose Format Editor.

3. Choose New Field from the Format Editor dialog box.

4. Choose the descriptor type (Character, Integer, and so on) and choose whether to insert the descriptor before or after the current descriptor.

5. A default value is used for the descriptor you choose (for example, I5). To change the descriptor value, select the value and type in the new value. (For example, select 5 from I5 and type 8 to get an I8 format.)

To insert a new format statement:

1. Place the cursor on a blank line.

2. From the Edit menu, choose Format Editor.

The Format Editor inserts the words *label FORMAT* into the file at the cursor. You can define the new edit descriptor with the Format Editor.

For a discussion of the features of the Format Editor in Microsoft visual development environment, choose Format Editor from the Edit menu, and click on Help in the Format Editor dialog box.

25.12 Profiling Code from the Command Line

The profiler is an analysis tool you can use to examine the run-time behavior of your programs. By profiling, you can find out which sections of your code are working efficiently and which need to be tuned. The profiler can also show areas of code that are not being executed.

Because profiling is a tuning process, you should use the profiler to make your programs run better, not to find bugs. Once your program is fairly stable, you should start profiling to find out where to optimize your code. Use the profiler to determine whether an algorithm is effective, a function is being called frequently (if at all), or if a piece of code is being covered by software testing procedures.

In the Microsoft visual development environment, you can use the Profiler to generate reports that characterize how your program executes. If you work from the command line, you can create a batch command file to run PREP, PROFILE, and PLIST, the programs that generate execution profile reports.

For information on using the Profiler from the Microsoft visual development environment and timing your application, see Section 6.2 Analyze Program Performance.

This section describes how to use the components of the profiler from the command line. The following topics are covered:

▶ Section 25.12.1 Profiler Batch Processing

▶ Section 25.12.2 Profiler Batch Files

▶ Section 25.12.3 Profiler Command-Line Options

▶ Section 25.12.4 Exporting Data from the Profiler

25.12.1 Profiler Batch Processing

Profiling requires three separate programs: PREP, PROFILE, and PLIST. The visual development environment executes all three of these programs for you automatically. To execute them efficiently from the command line, and to customize the output format or specify function and line count profiling, you must write batch files to invoke PREP, PROFILE, and PLIST. You can redirect the output of the batch file to a designated file by using the redirection character (>).

A typical profiler batch file might look like this:

```
PREP /OM /FT /EXC nafxcwd.lib %1
if errorlevel == 1 goto done
PROFILE %1 %2 %3 %4 %5 %6 %7 %8 %9
if errorlevel == 1 goto done
PREP /M %1
if errorlevel == 1 goto done
PLIST /SC %1 >%1.lst
  :done
```

Note that the PREP program is called twice—once before the actual profiling and again afterward. The command-line arguments govern PREP's behavior. Intermediate files with extensions .PBI, .PBO, and .PBT are used to transfer information between profiling steps. The first call to PREP generates a .PBI file which is passed to PROFILER. PROFILER generates a .PBO file which is passed in the second call to PREP. The second call to PREP generates a .PBT file which is passed to PLIST. The profiler data flow is shown in Figure 25-1.

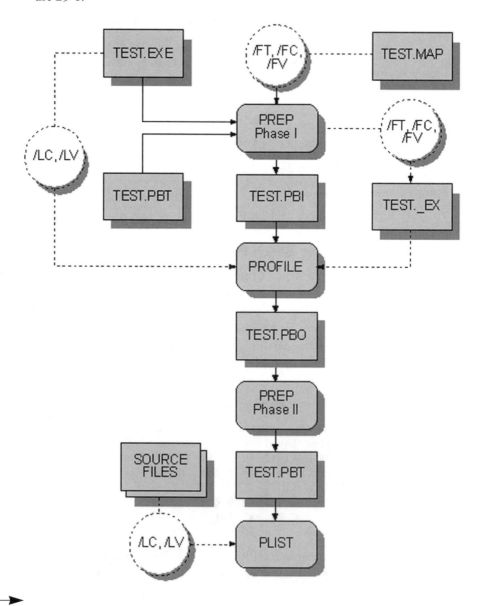

Figure 25–1 *Profiler Data Flow*

If the preceding batch file was named FTIME.BAT, and you wanted to profile the program TEST from the command prompt, you would type:

```
FTIME C:\Program Files\DF98\MYDIR\TEST.EXE
```

25.12.2 Profiler Batch Files

Like the linker, all three profiler programs accept response files. The command line:

```
PREP /OM /FT /EXC nafxcwd.lib %1
```

can be replaced by the line:

```
PREP @opts.rsp %1
```

if you create a file OPTS.RSP that contains this text:

```
/OM /FT /EXC nafxcwd.lib # this is a comment
```

The # character in a response file defines a comment that runs through the end of the line.

Table 25-20 lists the standard batch files that ship with the profiler.

Table 25–20   *Profiler Batch Files*

Filename	Description
FTIME.BAT	Function timing
FCOUNT.BAT	Function counting
FCOVER.BAT	Function coverage
LCOUNT.BAT	Line counting
LCOVER.BAT	Line coverage

These batch files contain only the minimum parameters for the initial call to PREP. Use them as prototypes for your own batch files, which should contain selection parameters. If you ran an unmodified LCOVER batch file for a complex Fortran 90 application with a large number of functions, subroutines and modules, the output report could be thousands of lines long.

25.12.3 Profiler Command-Line Options

The following sections describe the command-line options for the three components of the profiler:

▶ Section 25.12.3.1 PREP

▶ Section 25.12.3.2 PROFILE

▶ Section 25.12.3.3 PLIST

25.12.3.1 PREP

The PREP program runs twice during a normal profiling operation. In Phase I, it reads an .EXE file and then creates .PBI and .PBT files. In Phase II, it reads .PBT and .PBO files and then writes a new .PBT file for PLIST. An 'X' in the following Options table indicates that a PREP command-line option applies to a particular phase.

The syntax for PREP follows:

PREP [*options*] [*programname1*] [*programname2...programname8*]

options

Control the kind of profiling, the inclusion and exclusion of code to be profiled, whether to merge profiles, and other profiling features. Table 25-21 lists the PREP options.

PREP reads the command line from left to right, so the rightmost options override contradictory options to the left. None of the options are case sensitive. You must prefix options with a forward slash (/) or a dash (-), and options must be separated by spaces.

Table 25–21 *PREP Options*

Option	Phase I	II	Description
/AT	X		Collects attribution data for function timing and function counting. Function attribution reports which function called another function. See /STACK in this table.
/CB	X		Used with function timing, allows you to set the calibrated overhead of profiler calls in the event that your function timing calls have varied because of varied calibrated overhead values. The calibrated overhead is displayed in default (non-tab-delimited) PLIST output.
/EXC	X		Excludes a specified module from the profile (see the Remarks section below).
/EXCALL	X		Excludes all modules from the profile (see the Remarks section below).
/FC	X		Selects function count profiling.
/FT	X		Selects function timing profiling. This option causes the profiler to generate count information as well.
/FV	X		Selects function coverage profiling.

Table 25–21 *PREP Options (Continued)*

Option	Phase I	II	Description
/INC	X		Includes in profile (see the Remarks section below).
/H[ELP]	X	X	Provides a short summary of PREP options.
/IO *filename*		X	Merges an existing .PBO file (the file generated by PROFILER to be passed in the second call to PREP). Up to eight .PBO files can be merged at a time. The default extension is .PBO.
/IT *filename*		X	Merges an existing .PBT file (the file generated by the second call to PREP to be passed to PLIST). Up to eight .PBT files can be merged at a time. You cannot merge .PBT files from different profiling methods. The default extension is .PBT.
/LC	X		Selects line count profiling.
/LV	X		Selects line coverage profiling.
/M *filename*		X	Substitutes for /IT, /IO, and /OT options.
/NOLOGO	X	X	Suppresses the PREP copyright message.
/OI *filename*	X		Creates a .PBI file (the file generated by the first call to PREP). The default extension is .PBI. If /OI is not specified, the output .PBI file is *programname1*.PBI.
/OM	X		Creates a self-profiling file with _XE or _LL extension for function timing, function counting, and function coverage. Without this option, the executable code is stored in the .PBI file. This option speeds up profiling.
/OT *filename*	X	X	Specifies the output .PBT file. The default extension is .PBT. If /OT is not specified, the output .PBT file is *programname1*.PBT.
/SF *function*	X		Starts profiling with *function*. The function name must correspond to an entry in the .MAP file.
/STACK *dpt*	X		When using the /AT switch, you can also set the stack depth (*dpt*) to which functions will have their attribution data recorded.
/?	X	X	Provides a short summary of PREP options.

programname1

Filename of primary program to profile (.DBG, .EXE, or .DLL). PRO-FILE adds the .EXE extension if no extension is given. This parameter must be specified in the first call to PREP and not the second call.

programname2...programname8

Additional programs to profile. These parameters can be specified for the first call to PREP only.

Environment Variable

The PREP environment variable specifies the default PREP command-line options. If a value for the PREP environment variable is not specified, the default options for PREP are:

```
/FT /OI filename /OT filename
```

where *filename* is set to the *programname1* parameter value.

Remarks

The /INC and /EXC options specify individual .LIB, .OBJ, .FOR and .F90 files. For line counting and line coverage, you can specify line numbers with source files as in:

```
/EXCALL /INC TEST.F90(3-41,50-67)
```

In this example, the /EXCALL option excludes all modules from the profile, and the /INC option supercedes that to include only lines 3-41 and lines 50-67 from the source file TEST.F90. Note the absence of spaces in the source specification.

To specify all source lines in a particular module, specify the .OBJ file like this:

```
/EXCALL /INC TEST.OBJ
```

or by using the source filename with zero line numbers like this:

```
/EXCALL /INC TEST.F90(0-0)
```

The following statement profiles from line 50 to the end of the file:

```
/EXCALL /INC TEST.F90(50-0)
```

25.12.3.2   PROFILE

PROFILE profiles an application and generates a .PBO file of the results. Use PROFILE after creating a .PBI file with PREP.

The syntax for PROFILE follows:

PROFILE [*options*] *programname* [*programargs*]

options

Control the kind of profiling, the inclusion and exclusion of code to be profiled, whether to merge profiles, and other profiling features. Table 25-22 lists the PROFILE options.

PROFILE reads the command line from left to right, so the rightmost options override contradictory options to the left. None of the options are case sensitive. You must prefix options with a forward slash (/) or a dash (-), and options must be separated by spaces.

Table 25–22 *PROFILE Options*

Option	Description
/A	Appends any redirected error messages to an existing file. If the /E command-line option is used without the /A option, the file is over-written. This option is valid only with the /E option.
/E *filename*	Sends profiler-generated error messages to *filename*.
/H[ELP]	Provides a short summary of PROFILE options.
/ I*filename*	Specifies a .PBI file to be read. This file is generated by PREP.
/NOLOGO	Suppresses the PROFILE copyright message.
/O *filename*	Specifies a .PBO file to be generated. Use the PREP utility to merge with other .PBO files or to create a .PBT file for use with PLIST.
/X	Returns the exit code of the program being profiled.
/?	Provides a short summary of PROFILE options.

programname

Filename of program to profile. PROFILE adds the .EXE extension if no extension is given. (See the Remarks section below.)

programargs

Optional command-line arguments for *programname*. (See the Remarks section below.)

If you do not specify a .PBO filename on the command line, PROFILE uses the base name of the .PBI file with a .PBO extension. If you do not specify a .PBI or a .PBO file, PROFILE uses the base name of *programname* with the .PBI and .PBO extensions.

Environment Variable

The PROFILE environment variable specifies the default command-line options for PROFILE. If the PROFILE environment variable is not specified, there are no defaults.

Remarks

You must specify the filename of the program to profile on the PROFILE command line. PROFILE assumes the .EXE extension, if no extension is given.

You can follow the program name with command-line arguments; these arguments are passed to the profiled program unchanged.

If you are profiling code in a .DLL file, give the name of an executable file that calls it. For example, if you want to profile SAMPLE.DLL, which is called by CALLER.EXE, you can type:

```
PROFILE CALLER.EXE
```

This assumes that CALLER.PBI has SAMPLE.DLL selected for profiling.

25.12.3.3 PLIST

PLIST converts results from the .PBT file generated by the second call to PREP into a formatted text file.

The syntax for PLIST follows:

PLIST [*options*] *inputfile*

options

Control the format and organization of profiler output data. Table 25-23 lists the PROFILE options.

PLIST reads the command line from left to right, so the rightmost options override contradictory options to the left. None of the options are case sensitive. You must prefix options with a forward slash (/) or a dash (-), and options must be separated by spaces.

Table 25–23 *PLIST Options*

Option	Description
/C *count*	Specifies the minimum hit count to appear in the listing.
/D *directory*	Specifies an additional directory for PLIST to search for source files. Use multiple /D command-line options to specify multiple directories. Use this option when PLIST cannot find a source file.
/F	Lists full paths in tab-delimited report.
/FLAT	When using function attribution (see Section 25.12.3.1 PREP), displays function attribution with no indentation.

Table 25–23 *PLIST Options (Continued)*

Option	Description
/H[ELP]	Provides a short summary of PLIST options.
/INDENT	When using function attribution (see Section 25.12.3.1 PREP), displays function attribution information in indented format. This is the default display for function attribution if neither /FLAT nor /TAB is selected.
/NOLOGO	Suppresses the PLIST copyright message.
/PL *length*	Sets page length (in lines) of output. The length must be 0 or 15-255. A length of 0 suppresses page breaks. The default length is 0.
/PW *width*	Sets page width (in characters) of output. The width must be 1-511. The default width is 511.
/SC	Sorts output by counts, highest first.
/SL	Sorts output in the order that the lines appear in the file. This is the default. This option is available only when profiling by line.
/SLS	Forces line count profile output to be printed in coverage format.
/SN	Sorts output in alphabetical order by function name. This option is available only when profiling by function.
/SNS	Displays function timing or function counting information in function coverage format. Sorts output in alphabetical order by function name.
/ST	Sorts output by time, highest first.
/T	Tab-separated output. Generates a tab-delimited database from the .PBT file for export to other applications. All other options, including sort specifications, are ignored when using this option. For more information, see Section 25.12.4 Exporting Data from the Profiler.
/TAB *indent*	When using function attribution (see Section 25.12.3.1 PREP), sets tab width for indentation of function information.
/?	Provides a summary of PLIST options.

inputfile

The .PBT file to be converted by PLIST.

PLIST results are sent to STDOUT by default. Use the greater-than (>) redirection.

PLIST must be run from the directory in which the profiled program was compiled.

Environment Variable

The PLIST environment variable specifies the default command-line options for PLIST. If the PLIST environment variable is not specified, the default options for PLIST depend on the profile type, as shown in Table 25-24.

Table 25–24   *PLIST Default Options*

Profile Type	Sort Option	Hit Count Option
Function timing	/ST	/C 1
Function counting	/SC	/C 1
Function coverage	/SN	/C 0
Line counting	/SL	/C 0
Line coverage	/SLS	/C 0

25.12.4 Exporting Data from the Profiler

In addition to formatted reports, the PLIST report-generation utility can produce a tab-delimited report of profiler output. The following sections describe the data format of the report, steps for analyzing statistics in the report, and a Microsoft Excel macro that uses this report format:

▶ Section 25.12.4.1 Tab-Delimited Record Format

▶ Section 25.12.4.2 Global Information Records

▶ Section 25.12.4.3 Local Information Records

▶ Section 25.12.4.4 Steps to Analyze Profiler Statistics

▶ Section 25.12.4.5 Processing Profiler Output with Microsoft Excel

▶ Section 25.12.4.6 Generating the Tab-Delimite Report

▶ Section 25.12.4.7 Using the PROFILER.XLM Macro

▶ Section 25.12.4.8 Changing the PROFILER.XLM Selection Criteria

The PLIST /T command-line option causes PLIST to dump the contents of a .PBT file into a tab-delimited format suitable for import into a spreadsheet or database. This format can also be used by user-written programs.

For example, to create a tab-delimited file called MYPROG.TXT from MYPROG.PBT, enter:

```
PLIST /T MYPROG > MYPROG.TXT
```

The ASCII tab-delimited format was designed to be read by other programs; it was not intended for general reporting.

25.12.4.1 Tab-Delimited Record Format

Every piece of data stored by the Profiler is available through the tab-delimited report. Because not all aspects of the database are recorded by every profiling method, unused fields within a record may be zero. For example, the total time of the program will be zero if the program was profiled for counts only. Also, all included functions will be listed for function counting and timing profiles, even if those functions were not executed.

The tab-delimited format is arranged with one record per line and two to eight fields per record. Figure 25-2 shows how a database looks when loaded into Microsoft Excel. The database was produced using the PLIST /T command-line option.

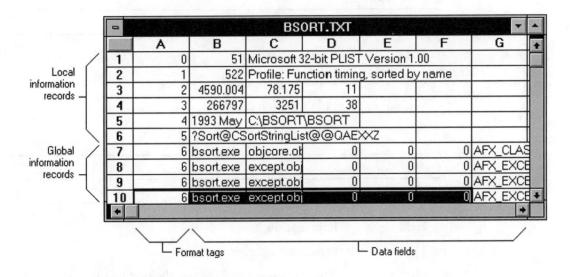

Figure 25–2 *Tab-Delimited File in Microsoft Excel*

The first item in each record is a format tag number. These tags range from 0–7 and indicate the kind of data given in the other fields of the record. The fields in each record are described in:

▶ Section 25.12.4.2 Global Information Records

▶ Section 25.12.4.3 Local Information Records

Tab-delimited reports are generated with global information records first, organized in numerical order by format tag. The local information records, containing information about specific lines or functions, are generated last. Local information records are organized by line number.

If the .PBT file contains information from more than one .EXE or .DLL file, the global information will cover them all. Local information records include the EXE field, which specifies the name of the executable file that each record pertains to.

25.12.4.2 Global Information Records

The global information records contain information about the entire executable file. The format tag numbers for global information records are 0 through 5. The record formats are as follows:

Profiling Banner

| 0 | Version | Banner |

Field	**Explanation**
0	Format tag number
Version	PLIST version number
Banner	PLIST banner

Profiling Method

| 1 | Method | Description |

Field	**Explanation**
1	Format tag number
Method	Numeric value that indicates the profiling type (see Table 25-25)
Description	ASCII description of the profiling type given by the method field

Table 25–25 *Profiling Types*

Method	Description
321	Profile: Line counting, sorted by line
324	Profile: Line coverage, sorted by line
521	Profile: Function counting, sorted by function name
522	Profile: Function timing, sorted by function name
524	Profile: Function coverage, sorted by function name

Profiling Time and Depth			
2	Total Time	Outside Time	Call Depth

Field	Explanation
2	Format tag number
Total Time	Total amount of time used by the program being profiled. This field is zero for counting and coverage profiles.
Outside Time	Amount of time spent before the first profiled function (with function profiling) or line (with line profiling) was executed. This field is zero for counting and coverage profiles.
Call Depth	Maximum number of nested functions found while profiling. Only profiled functions are counted. This field is zero for line-level profiling.

Profiling Hit Counts			
3	Total Hits	Lines/Funcs	Lines/Funcs Hit

Field	Explanation
3	Format tag number
Total Hits	Total number of times the profiler detected a profiled line or function being executed
Lines/Funcs	Total number of lines or functions marked for profiling
Lines/Funcs Hit	Number of marked lines or functions executed at least once while profiling

Profiling Date/Command Line		
4	Date	Command Line

Field	Explanation
4	Format tag number
Date	The date/time the profile was run (ASCII format)
Command Line	The PLIST command-line arguments

Profiling Starting Function Name	
5	Starting Function Name

Field	Explanation
5	Format tag number
Starting Function Name	The decorated name of the starting function identified by the PREP /SF parameter

25.12.4.3 *Local Information Records*

The local information records contain information about specific lines or functions that were profiled. The format tag numbers for local information records are 6 and 7. A report can have only one kind of local information record. The record formats are as follows:

Profiling Function Information					
6	Exe	Source	Count	Time	Child	Func

Field Explanation

6	Format tag number
Exe	ASCII name of the executable file that contains this function
Source	ASCII name of the object module (including the .OBJ extension) that contains this function
Count	Number of times this function has been executed
Time	Amount of time spent executing this function in milliseconds. This field is zero with profiling by counting or coverage

Child	Amount of time spent executing the function and any child functions it calls. This field is zero with profiling by counting or coverage.
Func	ASCII name of the function

Profiling Line Information

7		Exe		Source	Line		Count

Field	**Explanation**
7	Format tag number
Exe	ASCII name of the executable file that contains this function
Source	ASCII name of the source that contains the first line of this function
Line	Line number of this line
Count	Number of times this line has been executed. With coverage, this field is 1 if the line has been executed and 0 otherwise.

Profiling Function-Attribution Stacks

8	Number of stacks

Field	**Explanation**
8	Format tag number
Number of stacks	Number of stacks for each function call

Profiling Stack Hits and Timing

9	Stack size	Hit count	Stack time	Child time

Field	**Explanation**
9	Format tag number
Stack size	Stack size for each function call
Hit count	Hit count for this stack
Stack time	This stack's self-time
Child time	This stack's child-time

Profiling Stack Function Name	
10	Function name

Field	Explanation
10	Format tag number
Function name	Each function's name on the stack. The number of names that appear here will be equal to the stack size field in Profiling Stack Hits and Timing (above).

25.12.4.4   *Steps to Analyze Profiler Statistics*

The profiler tab-delimited report format can contain a great deal of information. You can process this data in a spreadsheet, database, or user-written program.

To process the data in the tab-delimited report:

1. Collect the cumulative data from the global information records. These lines begin with the numbers 0 through 5. Each of these lines appears only once, and always in ascending order.

2. Determine the type of database by finding the value of the "Method" field. This field is the second field of record type 1.

3. If the value in the "Method" field is greater than 400, the report comes from function profiling. If it is less than 400, the report comes from line profiling. The type of information in the local information records given later is directly related to this value.

4. In any one report, the local information records are always of the same type, either line information or function information.

5. Process data from the local information records. For example, to calculate the percentage of hits on a given function, divide the value of the "Count" field in record type 6 by the total number of hits from the "Total Hits" field of record type 3.

6. Remember that there can be only one type of local information record (either line or function information) in a report.

7. Send the results to a file or STDOUT.

25.12.4.5   *Processing Profiler Output with Microsoft Excel*

PROFILER.XLM is an example Microsoft Excel™ macro that processes a tab-delimited profiler report (generated by PLIST) and creates a graph based on the results. You will find this macro in the . . . \vc\bin directory.

The PROFILER.XLM macro is composed of four sub-macros. The first two macros, in columns A and B, are helper macros that copy and preprocess the data for use by the second pair of macros in columns C and D. The macro in column C, labeled CreateColumnChart, creates a graph showing the number of times that each function or line was executed The final macro in column D is CreateColumnTimeChart; it works like CreateColumnChart, but operates on timing information.

25.12.4.6 *Generating the Tab-Delimited Report*

To generate the tab-delimited report, use the PLIST /T option. This can be done after the normal profile run has been completed; PLIST will read the profile data from the last profiler execution. The output of PLIST /T should be redirected to a file, preferably with the .XLS extension for easy loading into Excel (Excel will interpret the tab-delimited file correctly as a text file even with the .XLS extension).

25.12.4.7 *Using the PROFILER.XLM Macro*

To run the macro, follow these steps from within Microsoft Excel:

1. Open PROFILER.XLM by choosing Open from the File menu.

2. Open the tab-delimited report that was created by PLIST by choosing Open from the File menu.

3. If you have several open worksheets, activate the one containing the profiler data by selecting it with the mouse or by choosing its title from the Windows menu.

4. Run the macro:

  ▶ Press Ctrl+C for a chart based on hit counts.

  ▶ Press Ctrl+T for a chart based on timing.

You cannot get a timing chart if the report contains only counting or coverage information.

The macro typically takes only a few seconds to execute. When it is complete, Microsoft Excel displays a 3-D bar chart based on the results in the report. You can change the chart type by using the Gallery menu.

This macro copies the data in the report to another worksheet before processing it. The original tab-delimited report is left untouched.

25.12.4.8 *Changing the PROFILER.XLM Selection Criteria*

The standard PROFILER.XLM macro displays hit counts greater than 0 (for Ctrl+C) and times greater than .01 millisecond (for Ctrl+T). If you need to narrow the selections without analyzing the macro, edit the formulas in cells C10 and D10.

25.13 Fortran Tools: FSPLIT and FPR

This section describes the Fortran command-line tools FSPLIT (includes F90SPLIT) and FPR.

FSPLIT and F90SPLIT

The FSPLIT and F90SPLIT tools split a multi-routine Fortran file into individual files. These tools are useful if you have a large Fortran program.

Use F90SPLIT when your program uses free-form source or Fortran 90/95 constructs. Use FSPLIT for FORTRAN 77 code. The FSPLIT and F90SPLIT commands have the same form:

FSPLIT [*options*] [*input-file...*]

F90SPLIT [*options*] [*input-file...*]

options

Is one of the keywords listed in Table 25-26. If more than one option is specified, separate each with a space.

Table 25–26 *FSPLIT and F90SPLIT Command Options*

-e:*name*	Processes only the program unit name. You can specify more than one -e *name* on a command line.
-extend_ source	Treats the statement field of each source line as ending in column 132, instead of column 72.
-help, ?	Displays information about the FSPLIT command.
-nologo	Suppresses the copyright notice that is displayed when FSPLIT or F90SPLIT is run.
-silent	Suppresses display of the name of each file opened (input and output files).

input-file

A Fortran source file to be split. You can specify more than one file by using a list of files. If *input-file* is omitted the FSPLIT or F90SPLIT Utility reads from standard input.

FSPLIT or F90SPLIT splits multi-routine Fortran files into separate routine files of the form filename.for, where *filename* is the name of the program unit (for example: a function, subroutine, block data, or program). The name for unnamed block data subprograms has the form blkdta*nnn*.for, where *nnn* is a 3-digit code. For unnamed main programs, the name has the form main*nnn*.for.

If there is an error in classifying a program unit, or if filename.for already exists, the program unit is put in a file named zzz*nnn*.for, where *nnn* is a 3-digit code.

Normally each subprogram unit is split into a separate file.

Avoid using the -e option for unnamed main programs and block data subprograms since you must predict the created file name.

If FSPLIT or F90SPLIT cannot find the names specified by the -e option, an error message is written to standard error device.

The following command example splits the subprogram units readit and doit into separate files:

```
FSPLIT -e readit -e doit prog.for
```

FPR

The FPR tool transforms files formatted according to Fortran's carriage control conventions into files formatted according to line printer conventions. The FPR command has the following form:

FPR [-f *record-size*] [*filename*]

record-size

Specifies a fixed-length record as input. The *record-size* must be a decimal integer.

filename

Specifies the data file to be transformed.

FPR copies the input *filename* onto itself, replacing the carriage-control characters with characters that will produce the intended effects when printed using the PRINT command. The first character of each line determines the vertical spacing, as shown in Table 25-27.

Table 25–27 *FPR Interpretation of Carriage-Control Characters*

Character	Vertical Space Before Printing
Blank	One line
0	Two lines
1	To first line of next page
+	No advance
$ or ASCII NUL	One line; no return after printing

FPR interprets the first character of every line of input, even if that character is not a recognizable control character. Control characters that are not recognized are treated as blanks and result in a single line advance.

FPR handles stream and fixed-length files. Input to FPR is assumed to be a stream (Stream_LF) file, unless you specify the -f option.

No diagnostic message is issued when FPR encounters an unrecognized control character.

Hexadecimal-Binary-Octal-Decimal Conversions

Table A-1 lists hexadecimal, binary, octal, and decimal conversion.

Table A–1 *Hexadecimal, Binary, Octal, and Decimal Conversion*

Hex Number	Binary Number	Octal Number	Decimal Number
0	0000	00	0
1	0001	01	1
2	0010	02	2
3	0011	03	3
4	0100	04	4
5	0101	05	5
6	0110	06	6
7	0111	07	7
8	1000	10	8
9	1001	11	9
A	1010	12	10
B	1011	13	11

Table A–1 *Hexadecimal, Binary, Octal, and Decimal Conversion (Continued)*

Hex Number	Binary Number	Octal Number	Decimal Number
C	1100	14	12
D	1101	15	13
E	1110	16	14
F	1111	17	15

B

Compatibility Information

Visual Fortran uses the same Digital Fortran compiler available on Digital UNIX and OpenVMS Alpha systems. Digital Visual Fortran supports extensions to the ISO and ANSI standards, including a number of extensions defined by:

▶ Microsoft Fortran PowerStation 4.0

▶ Digital Fortran for the various Digital Fortran platforms

Many language extensions associated with Microsoft Fortran PowerStation Version 4 have been added to Visual Fortran; most of these extensions have been or will be added to different releases of Digital Fortran on Alpha platforms.

The following sections describe Visual Fortran compatibility information:

▶ Section B.1 Compatibility with Microsoft Fortran PowerStation

▶ Section B.2 Compatibility with Digital Fortran on Other Platforms

B.1   Compatibility with Microsoft Fortran PowerStation

Visual Fortran recognizes the FL32 command and many of the command-line options provided by the Microsoft Fortran PowerStation Version 4 compiler. For more information on command-line compatibility, see Section 4.3 Microsoft Fortran PowerStation Command-Line Compatibility.

Visual Fortran supports many of the language extensions to the Fortran 90 Standard supported by Microsoft Fortran PowerStation Version 4. Certain extensions may require the /fpscomp compiler option (also see Section 4.1.1 Categories of Compiler Options). These extensions to the Fortran 90 Standard (and Fortran 95 Standard) include the following:

► .f, .for, .f90 source file types

► # Constants - constants using other than base 10

► C strings - NULL terminated strings

► MBCS characters in comments

► MBCS characters in string literals

► Conditional compilation and metacommand (directive) expressions ($DEFINE, $UNDEFINE, $IF, $ELSEIF, $ELSE, $ENDIF)

► !MS$ directive form (see "Compiler Directives: table" in the "A-Z Summary" in the *Language Reference* in Visual Fortran online Help)

► $FREEFORM, $NOFREEFORM, $FIXEDFORM - source file format

► $OBJCOMMENT - place library-search record in object file

► $INTEGER, $REAL - selects size

► $FIXEDFORMLINESIZE - line length for fixed form source

► $STRICT, $NOSTRICT - F90 conformance

► $ATTRIBUTES, identifier attributes (C, STDCALL, REFERENCE, VALUE, DLLIMPORT, DLLEXPORT, EXTERN, ALIAS, VARYING)

► $PACK - structure packing

► Kind numbers match bytes - kind parameters

► AUTOMATIC attribute - automatic storage class

► Integer Pointers (Cray pointers)

► VAX Structures = F90 sequence derived types

► Mixing logicals and numerics - logicals used with arithmetic operators and variables

► Argument matching for procedure calls

► Mixing integer kinds to intrinsics

► Byte data type = **INTEGER***1

► $ATTRIBUTES [ ] Form

- ▶ $ATTRIBUTES ALIAS - external name for a subprogram
- ▶ $ATTRIBUTES C, STDCALL - calling and naming conventions
- ▶ $ATTRIBUTES VALUE, REFERENCE - argument passing calling conventions
- ▶ $ATTRIBUTES DLLIMPORT, DLLEXPORT - import from/export to DLL
- ▶ Character and non-character equivalence
- ▶ Double complex data type
- ▶ .XOR. - exclusive disjunction
- ▶ Integer arguments in logical expressions
- ▶ **OPEN** statement specifier options:
  - BLOCKSIZE internal buffer size used in I/O
  - CARRIAGECONTROL controls the output of formatted files
  - MODE controls access to file on networked systems
  - TITLE affects and IOFOCUS controls QuickWin child windows
  - SHARE controls simultaneous access to file on networked systems
- ▶ Default carriage control
- ▶ Implicit open - prompt user for filenames
- ▶ Special device names for FILE in **OPEN** statements
- ▶ FORM=BINARY in **INQUIRE/OPEN** statements
- ▶ Unformatted sequential file form
- ▶ Q edit descriptor - number of characters remaining in the input record
- ▶ \ descriptor - prevents writing an end-of-record mark
- ▶ $ edit descriptor - suppresses the carriage return at the end of a record
- ▶ X edit descriptor default -1
- ▶ Ew.dDe and Gw.dDe edit descriptors - similar to Ew.dEe and Gw.dEe
- ▶ Variable Format Expressions (VFEs) - integer expression in **FORMAT** statement
- ▶ Expanded missing ,'s in **FORMAT** statements - optional commas
- ▶ Expanded namelist start/end sequences

- ▶ All path names: including driver, compiler, and **INCLUDE** statement MBCS enabled [not W95]

- ▶ UNC pathnames

- ▶ Long filenames

- ▶ 7200 character statement length

- ▶ Free form infinite line length

- ▶ $DECLARE and $NODECLARE (like **IMPLICIT NONE**)

- ▶ Logical truth: 0 = false, non-zero = true

- ▶ $ATTRIBUTES EXTERN - variable allocated in another source file

- ▶ $ATTRIBUTES VARYING - variable number of arguments

- ▶ Alternate **PARAMETER** syntax - no parenthesis

- ▶ $ in identifiers

- ▶ INTERFACE TO - subroutine/function prototype, however global scoping is *not* supported

- ▶ Argument passing modifiers - **%VAL, %REF**

- ▶ Argument passing modifiers - **%DESCR** (treated as **%REF**)

- ▶ CRAY pointer support for procedure names (for COM/OLE support)

- ▶ $ATTRIBUTES ALLOCATABLE - allocatable array

- ▶ Mixing subroutines/functions in generic interfaces

- ▶ $MESSAGE - output message during compilation

- ▶ Listing directives - $TITLE, $SUBTITLE

- ▶ STATIC attribute-static storage class

- ▶ **EOF** checks for end of file

- ▶ **LOC** equivalent to **%LOC**

- ▶ **HFIX** converts to short integer

- ▶ **INT1** converts to one byte integer by truncating

- ▶ **INT2** converts to two byte integer by truncating

- ▶ **INT4** converts to four byte integer by truncating

- ▶ **JFIX** same as **INT4**

- ▶ **MALLOC** allocates a memory block of size bytes and returns an integer pointer to the block

- **FREE** frees the memory block specified by the integer pointer

- **COTAN** returns cotangent

- **DCOTAN** returns double precision cotangent

- **IMAG** returns the imaginary part of complex number

- **IBCHNG** reverses value of bit

- **ISHA** shifts arithmetically left or right

- **ISHC** performs a circular shift

- **ISHL** shifts logically left or right

The following known source incompatibilities exist between Microsoft Fortran PowerStation Version 4 and Visual Fortran:

- **DATA** statement style initialization in attribute style declaration (not supported)

- Debug lines (other than D) (not supported)

- $OPTIMIZE - change optimization options (not supported)

- Integer array can contain format (not supported)

- Listing directives - $PAGE, $PAGESIZE, $LINESIZE, $[NO]LIST, $INCLUDE (not supported)

- $DEBUG, $NODEBUG - additional run-time checking (not supported)

- $LINE = C's #line (not supported)

- Internal files can be any type (not supported)

- Negative I/O unit numbers (not supported)

- Interface blocks using INTERFACE [TO] at the beginning of a source file to provide global scoping for subsequent program units (not supported). Visual Fortran uses standard Fortran 90 semantic rules about interface block placement and use.

- Tab continuation lines that start with characters other than digits 1 through 9 (not supported)

B.2   Compatibility with Digital Fortran on Other Platforms

Digital Visual Fortran supports extensions to the ISO and ANSI standards, including a number of extensions defined by Microsoft Fortran PowerStation 4.0 (see Section B.1 Compatibility with Microsoft Fortran PowerStation) and Digital Fortran for the various Digital Fortran platforms (operating system/ architecture pairs).

In addition to Digital Visual Fortran systems, Digital Fortran platforms include:

▶ Digital Fortran 90 and Digital Fortran 77 on Digital UNIX (formerly DEC OSF/1®) Alpha systems

▶ Digital Fortran 90 and Digital Fortran 77 on OpenVMS Alpha systems

▶ Digital Fortran 77 on OpenVMS VAX™ systems

Major additions to the FORTRAN 77 standard introduced by the Fortran 90 standard include:

▶ Array operations

▶ Improved facilities for numeric computation

▶ Parameterized intrinsic data types

▶ User-defined data types

▶ Facilities for modular data and procedure definitions

▶ Pointers (Fortran 90 pointers)

▶ The concept of language evolution

In addition, the Fortran 90 standard includes the following industry-accepted extensions to the FORTRAN 77 standard:

▶ Support for recursive subprograms

▶ **IMPLICIT NONE** statements

▶ **INCLUDE** statement

▶ **NAMELIST**-directed I/O

▶ **DO WHILE** and **ENDDO** statements

▶ Use of exclamation point (!) for end of line comments

▶ Support for automatic arrays

▶ Support for the following **SELECT CASE - CASE - CASE DEFAULT - END SELECT** statements.

▶ Support for the **EXIT** and **CYCLE** statements and for construct names on **DO - END DO** statements

Digital Visual Fortran includes the following features and enhancements also found on other Digital Fortran platforms:

▶ Support for linking against static libraries

▶ Support for linking against dynamically linked libraries (DLL)

▶ Support for creating code to be put into a dynamically linked library (DLL)

▶ Support for stack-based storage

▶ Support for dynamic memory allocation

▶ Support for reading and writing binary data files in nonnative formats, including IEEE® (little-endian and big-endian), VAX, IBM® System\360, and CRAY® integer and floating point formats

▶ User control over IEEE floating point exception handling, reporting, and resulting values.

▶ Control for memory boundary alignment of items in **COMMON** and fields in structures and warnings for misaligned data

▶ Directives to control listing page titles and subtitles, object file identification field, **COMMON** and record field alignment, and some attributes of **COMMON** blocks

▶ Composite data declarations using **STRUCTURE**, **END STRUCTURE**, and **RECORD** statements, and access to record components through field references

▶ Explicit specification of storage allocation units for data types such as:

   • **INTEGER***4

   • **LOGICAL***4

   • **REAL***4

   • **REAL***8

   • **COMPLEX***8

▶ Support for 64-bit signed integers using **INTEGER***8 and **LOGICAL***8 (on Alpha platforms only)

- ▶ A set of data types:
  - **BYTE**
  - **LOGICAL***1, **LOGICAL***2, **LOGICAL***4
  - **INTEGER***1, **INTEGER***2, **INTEGER***4
  - **LOGICAL***8 and **INTEGER***8 on Alpha platforms only
  - **REAL***4, **REAL***8
  - **COMPLEX***8, **COMPLEX***16, **DOUBLE COMPLEX**
  - Digital Fortran **POINTER** statement (CRAY style)
- ▶ Data statement style initialization in type declaration statements
- ▶ **AUTOMATIC** and **STATIC** statements
- ▶ Bit constants to initialize **LOGICAL**, **REAL**, and **INTEGER** values and participate in arithmetic and logical expressions
- ▶ Built-in functions **%LOC**, **%REF**, and **%VAL**
- ▶ **VOLATILE** statement
- ▶ Bit manipulation functions
- ▶ Binary, hexadecimal, and octal constants and Z and O format edit descriptors applicable to all data types
- ▶ I/O unit numbers that can be any nonnegative **INTEGER***4 value
- ▶ Variable amounts of data can be read from and written to "STREAM" files, which contain no record delimiters
- ▶ **ENCODE** and **DECODE** statements
- ▶ **ACCEPT**, **TYPE**, and **REWRITE** input/output statements
- ▶ **DEFINE FILE**, **UNLOCK**, and **DELETE** statements
- ▶ USEROPEN subroutine invocation at file **OPEN**
- ▶ Debug statements in source
- ▶ Generation of a source listing file with optional machine code representation of the executable source
- ▶ Variable format expressions in a **FORMAT** statement
- ▶ Optional run-time bounds checking of array subscripts and character substrings

▶ 31-character identifiers that can include dollar sign ($) and underscore (_)

▶ Language elements that support the various extended range and extended precision floating point architectural features:

- 32-bit IEEE S_floating data type, with an 8-bit exponent and 24-bit mantissa and a precision of typically 7 decimal digits

- 64-bit IEEE T_floating data type, with an 11-bit exponent and 53-bit mantissa and a precision of typically 15 decimal digits

▶ Command line control for:

- The size of default **INTEGER**, **REAL**, and **DOUBLE PRECISION** data items

- The levels and types of optimization to be applied to the program

- The directories to search for **INCLUDE** and module files

- Inclusion or suppression of various compile-time warnings

- Inclusion or suppression of run-time checking for various I/O and computational errors

- Control over whether compilation terminates after a specific number of errors have been found

- Choosing whether executing code will be thread-reentrant

▶ Kind types for all of the hardware-supported data types:

- For 1-, 2-, and 4-byte **LOGICAL** data: **LOGICAL**(KIND=1), **LOGICAL**(KIND=2), **LOGICAL**(KIND=4)

- For 1-, 2-, and 4-byte **INTEGER** data: **INTEGER**(KIND=1), **INTEGER**(KIND=2), **INTEGER**(KIND=4)

- For 8-byte **LOGICAL** and **INTEGER** data on Alpha platforms only: **LOGICAL** (KIND=8), **INTEGER**(KIND=8)

- For 4- and 8-byte **REAL** data: **REAL**(KIND=4), **REAL**(KIND=8)

- For single precision and double precision **COMPLEX** data: **COMPLEX**(KIND=4), **COMPLEX**(KIND=8)

Index

Other Books from Digital Press

Alpha Architecture Reference Manual, Third Edition by The Alpha Architecture Committee

1998   1000pp   pb   1-55558-202-8

Digital UNIX System Administrator's Guide by Matthew Cheek

1998   400pp   pb   1-55558-199-4

Object-Oriented Programming for Windows 95 and NT by Stephen Morris

1998   375pp   pb   1-55558-193-5

OpenVMS Operating System Concepts, Second Edition by David Miller

1997   550pp   pb   1-55558-157-9

OpenVMS User's Guide by Patrick J. Holmay

1998   300pp   pb   1-55558-203-6

UNIX for OpenVMS Users, Second Edition by Philip Bourne, Richard Holstein and Joseph McMullen

1998   425pp   pb   1-55558-155-2

Windows NT Infrastructure Design by Mike Collins

1998   450pp   pb   1-55558-170-6

Feel free to visit our web site at: www.bh.com/digitalpress

These books are available from all good bookstores or in case of difficulty call:
1-800-366-2665 in the U.S. or +44-1865-310366 in Europe.

JOIN THE DIGITAL PRESS E-MAIL LIST!!!

An e-mail mailing list giving information on latest releases, special promotions, offers and other news relating to Digital Press titles is available. To subscribe, send an e-mail message to majordomo@world.std.com. Include in message body (not in subject line): subscribe digital-press